THE COMPLETE MEDITERRANEAN
THE BEAUTIFUL COOKBOOK

AUTHENTIC RECIPES FROM ITALY, FRANCE, SPAIN, GREECE AND MORE

Winter Squash with Sharp Ricotta (recipe page 205)

AUTHENTIC RECIPES FROM ITALY, FRANCE, SPAIN, GREECE AND MORE

THE COMPLETE MEDITERRANEAN

THE BEAUTIFUL COOKBOOK

RECIPES AND FOOD TEXT BY
JOYCE GOLDSTEIN
LORENZA DE'MEDICI

REGIONAL TEXT BY
AYLA ALGAR

FOOD PHOTOGRAPHY BY
PETER JOHNSON

STYLED BY
JANICE BAKER

SCENIC PHOTOGRAPHY (TUSCANY)
MICHAEL FREEMAN

HarperCollins*Publishers*

The Complete Mediterranean The Beautiful Cookbook

First Edition

0-06-058031-3

For information address HarperCollins Publishers, Inc.,
10 East 53rd Street, New York, NY 10022.

Library of Congress Cataloging-in-Publication Data:

Goldstein, Joyce, Esersky.
Mediterranean, the beautiful cookbook : authentic recipes from the Mediterranean regions / recipes by Joyce Goldstein ; text by Ayla Algar ; food photography by Peter Johnson ; styled by Janice Baker.
p. cm.
ISBN 0-00-255370-8
1. Cookery, Mediterranean.
2. Mediterranean Region—Description and travel.
I. Algar, Ayla Esen. II. Title.
TX725.M35G65 1994
641.59182'2—dc20 93-42641
CIP

ISBN 0-06-757590-0 (pbk.)

Printed by Toppan in China

For information address HarperCollins Publishers, Inc.,
10 East 53rd Street, New York, NY 10022.

Library of Congress Cataloging-in-Publication Data:

De'Medici, Strucchi, Lorenza.
Tuscany, the beautiful cookbook : authentic recipes from the provinces of Tuscany / recipes and text by Lorenza de'Medici ; food photography by Peter Johnson ; scenic photography by Michael Freeman.
Includes Index.
p. cm.
ISBN 0-00-255032-6
1. Cookery, Italian—Tuscan style. 2. Tuscany (Italy)—Description and travel—1981. I. Title.
TX713.2.T86D4 1992
641.5945'5—dc20 91—42832

ISBN 0-06-757600-1 (pbk.)

99 00 01 02 03 TOP 6 5 4 3 2 1

Printed by Toppan in China

Top to bottom: Tomato Soup (recipe page 107), Vegetable Soup with Basil and Garlic (recipe page 107)

Contents

Through the ages, volcanic activity has continually altered the rugged island of Santorini, Greece.

INTRODUCTION

Assertions that a given place is the center of the world have more to do with theological self-perception than with geographical or historical reality. The spread of the globe is too vast and the history of humankind too complex for anywhere to have been the nub for all things. Within the Old World, however, a certain centrality may be claimed for the Mediterranean. Its waters wash the shores of three continents, Europe, Asia and Africa, and since antiquity most of the principal currents of world history have flowed across its surface. Little in either European or Middle Eastern history and culture can be comprehended without reference to the civilizations that arose or grew to maturity in the Mediterranean basin.

Despite these manifold connections, the Mediterranean constitutes a coherent, almost self-contained world of its own, being in essence an inland sea. Were it not for the separation of Africa from Europe at the Strait of Gibraltar, opening a chink onto the oceanic vastness of the Atlantic, the Mediterranean would be entirely landlocked. One of its two other outlets, the Suez Canal, is recent and human-made; and the other, the Dardanelles, with its continuation, the Bosporus, is little more than a channel leading to the Black Sea, which can legitimately be regarded as an annex of the Mediterranean. Other seas lying within the Mediterranean realm—the Tyrrhenian, the Adriatic, the Aegean—are mere inlets or subdivisions of the mother sea; they are cartographical conventions rather than independent geographical realities. This coherence of the Mediterranean world has meant that the peoples inhabiting its shores have often had more in common with one another, despite differences of language and religion, than with their conationals living in their respective hinterlands. Exposure to comparable climatic and geographic environments preconditioned them for the culinary interchanges that came about as the result of migration, conquest and trade. It is here that the ultimate origin of the ensemble of traditions we call Mediterranean cuisine is to be sought.

The Mediterranean world is defined, self-evidently, by the sea that lies at its heart, with the predictable consequence for cuisine that full use has always been made of its abundant fish and shellfish. This prominence of the fruits of the sea has been reinforced by another factor of geography, the relative paucity of pastureland, which tends to make beef a rarity on Mediterranean menus. Sheep farming, by contrast, is not so dependent on lush pastures, and lamb and mutton therefore enjoy some prominence in the diet. This is often limited by economic circumstance; it is not for nothing that the slaughter of a lamb has always counted as a lavish gesture of hospitality. For all the sun-drenched ease we associate with the Mediterranean—in reality little more than a vacationer's fantasy—there is an undertone of harshness to the region's beauty. The lands that ring the sea—both the mountainous peninsulas that line its northern shores and the relatively narrow coastal plains that run along its eastern and southern shores—are for the most part arid, lacking all but a fraction of the rainfall that is lavished on northern Europe; they do not yield a livelihood readily and unsparingly to their inhabitants. It is indeed remarkable that agriculture has flourished in

Ghardaia is the Algerian center for carpets; markets like these abound in North African cities.

FRANCE
PYRENEES
ANDORRA
NICE
MONACO
MARSEILLE
Ligurian Sea
Corsica
ROME
ITAL
Adriat
BARCELONA
MADRID
SPAIN
VALENCIA
Balearic Islands
Menorca
Mallorca
Ibiza
Sardinia
NAPLES
Tyrrhenian Sea
MÁLAGA
TANGER
Straight of Gibraltar
Mediterr
PALERMO
Sicily
RABAT
FÈS
ALGIERS
SKIKDA
TUNIS
CONSTANTINE
MALTA
MOROCCO
ATLAS MOUNTAINS
ALGERIA
TUNISIA
SFAX
TRIPOLI
GRAND ERG OCCIDENTAL
GRAND ERG ORIENTAL
L I
BACKHAUS

Black Sea
BELGRADE
TERRITORIES OF THE FORMER YUGOSLAVIA
SPLIT
DUBROVNIK
ALBANIA
TIRANË
ISTANBUL
ANKARA
TURKEY
Aegean Sea
GREECE
IZMIR
ATHENS
TAURUS MOUNTAINS
ANTALYA
Ionian Islands
Ionian Sea
Rhodes
SYRIA
NICOSIA
CYPRUS
LEBANON
BEIRUT
DAMASCUS
Crete
JERUSALEM
ISRAEL
ALEXANDRIA
CAIRO
Suez Canal
BANGHAZI
EGYPT
Gulf of Suez
Nile
LIBYAN DESERT
Red Sea

Situated on the inlet of a wooded promontory, the picturesque fishing village of Portofino typifies the ports of northern Italy.

the Mediterranean, the result not only of skillful cultivation but also of the peasant tenacity and hardiness of its peoples. Discernible beneath the surface of virtually all Mediterranean cuisines is this same peasant character, which has bestowed on the cooking of the area some of its best qualities: boldness of taste, purity of ingredients and simplicity of conception.

As Fernand Braudel, magisterial authority on all things Mediterranean, has remarked, "In the Mediterranean, to live is to exchange"; ports and peoples, contemplating each other across its waters, could live in no other way. The process of exchange has generally followed two principal axes, running between east and west and north and south. Moving along the first of these axes, Phoenicians, Greeks and Arabs—in order both of chronology and of significance—thus disseminated both crops and culinary techniques in the western reaches of the Mediterranean. As for the ports of the northern Mediterranean—Montpellier, Marseilles, Venice, Genoa—they all built their prosperity on trading in foodstuffs with the eastern and southern shores.

Trade is, of course, the primary form of interchange, and for many centuries the principal commodity in the trade of the Mediterranean consisted of spices. Spices in the ancient, classical and medieval worlds were not thought of simply as seasonings, but as a much broader category embracing all "particularly luxurious and fine substances used in food," especially imported ones. Few Mediterranean cuisines could be described today as pungent, but the historical importance of spices, in the capacious sense of the word, was great throughout the Mediterranean world. They impinged even on its political and military destiny. One of the several worldly motives that underlay the Crusades was gaining control of the eastern Mediterranean ports that served as termini for caravans laden with Asian spices, and it was the hope of gaining direct access to those same spices that helped impel a badly disoriented Columbus across the Atlantic.

It is not our intention to sing the praises of empires, ancient or modern, but there can be no denying their role in promoting the interchange of people and materials that is crucial in the emergence of any worthwhile cuisine, a role second only to that of trade. Bringing diverse territories under unified political control, empires have brought the products of each to the attention of the other, and the well-stocked markets that grew up in the great imperial cities—Rome, Baghdad, Constantinople—constituted a standing invitation to culinary experimentation and indulgence. Courts and palaces not only bestowed the imprint of imperial prestige on culinary styles; they sometimes participated actively in their elaboration. Nero, for example, is said to have invented aioli, certainly a greater achievement than fiddling while Rome burned, and it is to the initiative of another highly arbitrary ruler, the Ottoman Sultan Murad IV, that the invention of *hünkâr beğendi* ("the sovereign approved")—lamb on a bed of smoked eggplant cream—is attributed. Both anecdotes may be apocryphal, but they serve to exemplify the general principle of personal contributions to gastronomy by emperors. (We must of course exclude coprophagous monsters like the Roman emperor Commodus.)

For all their extensive voyaging around the Mediterranean, with culinary consequences on which we occasionally remark, the Phoenicians and Greeks were primarily traders and colonists, not empire builders. It was instead the Romans who first built an empire that knit together all the shores of the Mediterranean. They certainly developed the wheat fields of Spain, Sicily and North Africa; appreciated fine olive oil; used spices with what seems to have been a reckless, self-defeating abandon; and were, in general, adventurous eaters, ready to try almost anything. It is difficult, however, to be enthusiastic about a cuisine that regarded dormice cooked in honey as a delicacy; that thought of "hares and sow's udders, boars and antelopes, fowls and flamingoes and gazelles" as fit material for "a magnificent feast" (Juvenal); and that showed a general dislike for natural and unadulterated flavors. The use of complex sauces to disguise such flavors, considered the height of skill in certain cuisines, is relatively rare on the Mediterranean table; where it is to be found, it can be considered an echo of Roman taste. Somewhat more common, at least on the northern shores of the Mediterranean, is the mixing of different meats in the same dish, which may also point to the existence of a Roman substratum.

The Byzantines—lords of Constantinople, the "Second Rome"—sought in many ways to perpetuate or revive Roman tradition; to the kitchen, however, they brought their own skills and tastes, discussed later in our section on Greece.

The imperial concept of rule was, strictly speaking, unknown to the Arabs, and the political fragmentation of the Islamic world began quite early. The lands conquered by the Arabs were, however, truly imperial in their extent and diversity, rivaling Rome in this respect, and the Arab contribution to the cuisine of the Mediterranean world was certainly greater than that of the Roman Empire. The first emergence in the West of "sophisticated cuisine, typical of all advanced civilizations," came, according to Braudel, in the fifteenth century, the result, in large part, of several hundred years of gradual impregnation by Arab influences. There is a general reluctance to go beyond Judeo-Christian tradition and Greco-Roman civilization as sources for the intellectual and material culture of the West, and it is in keeping with this reluctance that food historian Reay Tannahill describes the fifth to the tenth centuries as "the silent centuries" of European cuisine. But silence prevailed only in northern Europe; in Arab-ruled Spain and Sicily veritable symphonies of gastronomy were being composed. The Arabs are often thought of as essentially nomadic, and the general poverty of nomad cuisine is well-known. But the fact is that the early Arabs, energized by Islam, excelled as traders, agriculturists and city builders, three essential attributes for any people wishing to excel in cuisine. The nature of their contribution is detailed in several sections that follow; here, let us evoke only rice, described by historian, Lucien Lefebvre as "the blessing brought by the Arabs."

Lying just over the horizon of the Mediterranean world, Persia (or Iran, as we are now accustomed to calling it) deserves a special mention. In its days of imperial glory, it often encroached directly on the Mediterranean world: Persian armies advanced all the way to the Asiatic shores of the Bosporus, and Egypt came intermittently under Persian rule. Integration into the Islamic world, from the seventh century onward, deprived Persia of an independent military or political role, but the dissemination of its culture actually increased and its culinary impact on the Mediterranean was manifold. Persia was the homeland of many of the fruits and vegetables the Arabs introduced to Syria, North Africa, Spain and Sicily. It had itself acquired many of these from

Because much of Algeria contains vast uninhabitable stretches of desert, most of the population lives near the life-giving Mediterranean Sea.

India or China, so that it functioned as a kind of waystation for the produce of Asia on its journey to the Mediterranean. Many of the irrigation techniques used to such good effect by the Arabs, notably the digging of subterranean channels, had been learned from the Persians. The classical cuisine of the Arabs, in both its eastern (Syro-Iraqi) and western (North African) styles, was of largely Persian inspiration, something that could still be verified today by placing a Moroccan *tagine* next to a traditional Persian *khoresh.* Nor is there any reason to suppose that the Persian influence was always indirect, mediated by the Arabs. Persian scholars and musicians are known to have made it all the way to Spain, so why not a few Persian cooks as well?

The tricontinental Ottoman Empire was the last and in many ways the greatest of the Mediterranean empires. Heir not only to the entire civilization of classical Islam but also to many Byzantine traditions (excluding, of course, the specifically religious), the Ottomans produced a powerful and rich synthesis of culinary styles that penetrated deep into Europe and triumphed throughout much of the Arab world.

In the Mediterranean world of exchanges, Jews often played a special role as traders, migrants and refugees. They lived on the sea's eastern, southern and northern shores, and were present in both the Muslim and Christian worlds, often acting as intermediaries between the two, although they were infinitely better integrated in the former than the latter. After the fall of Rome, Jews ensured the continued cultivation of the citron throughout the Mediterranean basin, needing it as they did for the ritual purposes spelled out in the Talmud, thus preparing the way for the large-scale cultivation of citrus fruits by the Arabs. Much of the trans-Pyrenean trade that conveyed to Europe the agricultural wealth of Arab Spain was conducted by Jews, and down to the early eleventh century it was also Jews who predominated in the spice trade with the eastern Mediterranean. When the Jews were expelled from Spain, they are said to have avenged themselves on their tormentors by introducing chocolate to France and thus breaking the Spanish monopoly on this commodity (although the same achievement has been attributed to a Hapsburg princess, Anne of Austria).

The Erechtheum, built in Athens in the 5th century B.C.*, marks the height of the Golden Age of Greece.*

A more palpable legacy of the Jewish departure from Spain is the cuisine of those Jews who took refuge in Ottoman Turkey; its constituent dishes, designated even today in Istanbul by their ancient Ladino names, echo the culinary traditions of Arab Spain while bearing a distinctively Jewish imprint. It has been hypothesized that the Jews of Sicily, permitted to remain on the island for almost two centuries after the end of Arab rule, played a similar role in the preservation of Sicilian Arab cuisine, and even transmitted it to northern Italy by means of the merchants with whom they traded. If this hypothesis is true, the Jews would have served as the penultimate link in a chain of transmission that began in Baghdad and ended in Venice. In general terms, Jews enriched the repertoire of Mediterranean cuisine by creating variations on many regional dishes in accordance with the requirements of dietary law.

Together with empires and trade—from neither of which can it be fully dissociated—religion has played a cardinal role in the shaping of Mediterranean cuisine. A similar statement might be made about virtually any part of the globe. There is a certain mystery about the sustenance of life just as there is about its origin, and it would be possible to write a sacred ethnology of food. But the interconnections of food and religion in the Mediterranean world are particularly dense and numerous. They begin, perhaps, with the legends of the Egyptian and Greek gods, but are equally prominent in the three Abrahamic religions. The sacred connotations of bread provide a connecting thread among most Mediterranean traditions (with the possibly significant exception of Roman religion). Egypt and Greece made ritual offerings of bread to their gods, and Judaism bakes special breads for Passover and other high days. Bread is of course central to the Christian Eucharist (together with wine, the second element in the Greek trinity of bread, wine and olive oil), and Christmas, Easter and the saints' days are still celebrated around the Mediterranean with the consumption of special breads and pastries. Islam inculcates respect for bread, to the degree that it is a religious duty to pick up a crust that has fallen by the wayside, but special types of bread for religiously significant days are baked only in Turkey, perhaps in unconscious imitation of Greek Orthodox practice. Particular breads and pastries often migrate across religious borders. Many of the rich, flaky pastries bequeathed by the Arabs to the cuisines of Spain and Sicily became, after their expulsion from those lands, the special preserve of Christian monastic communities. A common item in Turkish bakeries is the sweet braided bread known as

Mediterranean ports such as Mallorca's Porto Colom have served to export the region's products throughout the world for a millennium.

paskalya çöreği, or "Easter bread," which happens to be almost identical to the Jewish challah.

Judaism brought to cuisine its own set of dietary rules, which not only banished the pig from the menu but also forbade certain combinations of foodstuffs. The prohibition of cooking on the Sabbath gave rise to what might be called the Jewish hotpot, buried in warm ashes before the onset of the Sabbath to cook overnight and known accordingly to the Sephardic Jews of the Mediterranean by the Hispano-Arabic term *adafina,* "the buried." Christendom, heir to the omnivorous traditions of the Greeks and Romans, made little distinction between permitted and forbidden foods, but the regular abstention from meat it demanded of the faithful favored the consumption of fish. Islam contents itself with prohibiting the pig, among animals conventionally consumed in the West, although it has reservations concerning the rabbit and shellfish. The fast of Ramadan is the most rigorous exercise in abstention prescribed by any of the Abrahamic religions, but the deprivation of the day is frequently offset by feasting at night, even in the least affluent Muslim communities.

The practice of serving tea and coffee has developed into a fine art in many Mediterranean countries; here, Moroccans partake at a festival in Fès.

In a very fundamental sense, the Atlantic has for long been vivifying the Mediterranean. Every second, about one million cubic meters of Atlantic water flow into the Mediterranean past Gibraltar, while beneath the surface a slightly inferior quantity of Mediterranean water flows out into the Atlantic; it is this interchange that permits the Mediterranean to remain more or less stable. There has also been a culinary interchange between the Mediterranean and the Atlantic, or rather with the New World lying beyond the Atlantic, and it is this process that has enabled the Mediterranean world to complete its complement of necessary ingredients. Which Mediterranean cuisine could, for example, dispense with the tomato? Despite the ubiquity of the tomato, the process of its acceptance was by no means swift, nor was the route of transmission direct. Seville witnessed the European landfall of the tomato, but it was in northern Italy that it first entered the cooking pot. It was also by way of Italy that haricot beans traveled to Provence, and the bell pepper is said to have made a lengthy detour via the Persian Gulf and Ottoman Turkey before being welcomed in Europe.

Europe in return made its own donations to the diet of the Americas, in addition to which the voyages of discovery profoundly affected the cuisines of both Africa and Asia. It can be said, indeed, that the "discovery" of the New World resulted in a new world order of food, which permits us to insert the Mediterranean in a truly global pattern of change.

The tracing of cultural influences is a delicate and imprecise task. National pride is often at stake, and definitive, explicit documentation is rarely available. This is true even of literature and the arts, where a concrete body of data may be analyzed. The case of cuisine is still more difficult, for cooks do not leave permanent monuments of their art. The etymology of the names of foodstuffs and dishes is perhaps our best and most reliable guide. If an item in a given national cuisine is identified by a name borrowed or derived from a foreign language, it is reasonable to suppose that the item itself is also a borrowing, particularly if the donor language is that of a triumphant empire or civilization. Examples of this are the Arabic loanwords found in Spanish, Italian and to a lesser degree French (not to mention English), and the Turkish names embedded in the menus of Greece and the Balkans. But the etymological evidence is not infallible. The precise sense of food names may change even within the same language, a possibility that is heightened by the process of being absorbed into another language. Some names are, moreover, etymological mysteries, present in many languages and cuisines, but not indisputably indigenous to any of them. No one can pretend to be sure whence came *moussaka,* the name or the dish, and no satisfactory conclusion can be seen for the wranglings of philhellenes and Turcophiles over the genesis of *baklava*.

The task of the culinary historian is, in any event, not in the last resort to demonstrate in mechanical fashion who took what from whom. Cuisines, like other cultural enterprises, are the result of cumulative and collaborative efforts, expended by varying peoples in varying ways and to varying degrees at varying times. Preeminence indeed goes to certain societies and cultures, but there is no cuisine that has been exclusively a donor or exclusively a recipient. To doubt this would be to misread the whole history of Mediterranean cuisine.

Beyond differences of language and religion, and beneath the whole pattern of interchange, there are certain perennial features of life in the Mediterranean that have helped to maintain its cuisine as a living tradition. First comes an unconscious aesthetic of everyday life and the enjoyment of simple, accessible pleasures, foremost among them being the taking of food, especially in outdoor settings of natural beauty. Then comes the importance of family and religion—twin foci of loyalty—one narrow, the other broad. Loyalty to the nation-state, even in countries such as France and Spain where it took root relatively early, has never ranked very high in the value system of the Mediterranean peoples; the attachment has been rather to something more immediate and familiar, and to something more elevated and universal. Especially in the Mediterranean world, the family is above all the unit that prepares and eats food together (preferably in the company of guests); it is the cornerstone of all culinary tradition. Fast food, by contrast, is the culinary accompaniment to the breakup of families. The Mediterranean emphasis on religion, while not without its drawbacks, complements the succession of seasons with its own measurement of time, feasts and fasts that both support and give meaning to the sustenance of life.

There are numerous developments that threaten this pan-Mediterranean ethos. The frenetic pace of modern life and economic need draw women increasingly outside the home, and it is only through great feats of self-sacrifice that they can perpetuate the culinary traditions of their mothers and grandmothers. Tradition is also threatened by the tourist-fueled onslaught of international fast food; the Golden Arches of McDonald's are rearing up around the Mediterranean like the triumphal arches of a globally uniform consumerism. The ingredients of Mediterranean cuisine are no longer, in many places, what they used to be: battery poultry yields the same unsatisfactory results as elsewhere; the use of chemical fertilizers is introducing the Mediterranean to the joys of the anaemic and tasteless tomato; and the precious stock of its fish and seafood is being depleted by pollution so severe that its glistening and historic waters are now being compared to an open sewer.

There is a sense in which the future of Mediterranean cuisine does not depend entirely upon the region itself. Much talk is heard today in the United States of the healthful properties of the Mediterranean diet. It is lauded for spurning the use of red meat in large quantities; showing great favor to fish and seafood; using olive oil instead of animal fat; and emphasizing the importance of legumes and fresh vegetables. (This hygienic listing excludes, of course, another common feature of Mediterranean cuisines—indulgence in rich and sugary pastries!) Concern for the consequences of diet on health is itself an originally Mediterranean phenomenon. It was the Greeks who first sought to discover the essentials of a healthful regimen; their findings were confirmed, extended or modified by the Arab physicians who, either in person or through their writings, were responsible for the foundation of European dietetics in Cordoba, Salerno, Montpellier and elsewhere. If the diet of late twentieth-century *Homo americanus* is indeed to be modified by drawing on Mediterranean models, it will not only be because of the intrinsic appeal of those models, but also because of the lasting cultural influence of the Mediterranean world, long after the centers of world power have drawn far distant from its shores.

The introductory lecture is now over. Let us now embark on our voyage through the culinary history of the Mediterranean, with its seven ports of call.

The vibrant open markets of Old Nice are perfectly suited to the sun-drenched climate of the Mediterranean.

SPAIN

SPAIN

Andalusia and Catalonia

Spain, it is said, owes the origin of its name to an animal, the rabbit. According to Pliny, it made its initial appearance in Spain and then hopped across the Pyrenees into France, from where it proliferated throughout Europe. The rabbit was but the earliest culinary gift of Spain, and arguably the least significant. The greater contributions came first during the brilliant centuries of Arab rule, and then during the colonization of Hispanic America. It can even be said that the entire geopolitical history of Spain, and especially its Mediterranean shores, could be written in terms of the movement of foodstuffs and dishes.

A few basic elements of Spanish cuisine were already in place before the beginning of Roman rule in the early second century B.C. The olive had been brought from the eastern Mediterranean one or two centuries earlier; grafted onto the primitive oleaster, it was quick to flourish. The Phoenicians similarly brought the chick-pea (garbanzo) from the east. The fish off the Andalusian coast were already being harvested, and some of the techniques still used today for salting fish may go back to pre-Roman times.

The Romans, as true imperialists, developed Spanish agriculture primarily to serve the needs of the metropolis.

Previous pages: Cape Formentor, the northernmost tip of Mallorca, boasts rugged countryside and breath-taking views of the sea. Left: Labyrinthine archways and columns in Córdoba's Mezquite are the legacy of early Moorish occupation; the Mosque was begun in 785 and completed two centuries later.

Along with other colonies around the Mediterranean shores, Spain served the Romans primarily as a granary, from which large quantities went forth to the bakeries of Rome. That the consumption of bread was also fixed as a permanent part of the Spanish diet was accidental; the manifold uses of bread in cooking came much later. The Romans promoted the intensive cultivation of the olive, and Spain became the empire's principal supplier of olive oil, as well as an avid consumer. The wine and salted fish of Spain also graced the tables of Rome.

The Romans were succeeded as Spain's masters by the Visigoths, whose period of rule from the early fifth to the early eighth century was of little gastronomic significance. Fully conforming to the image of Nordic conquerors as great carnivores, the Visigoths paid much attention to livestock farming and appear to have been delighted by the qualities of the Iberian pig, said to be tastier than its northern European cousin, thanks to a steady diet of acorns. Radishes and some legumes complete the meager nutritional legacy of the era.

All the preceding influences fade into insignificance when compared to the imprint left on Spain and its cuisine by the seven centuries of Muslim rule that began with the defeat of the last Visigoth in 711. Arriving in Spain on successive waves of conquest that carried them from the far borders of Arabia to the shores of the Atlantic, the Arabs, joined by Berbers and Spanish converts to Islam, constructed a delicate, refined and tolerant civilization that was for long the most advanced in Europe. The whole of the Iberian peninsula with the exception of Galicia was brought under Arab-Muslim rule, and such was the appeal of the Islamic culture that grew up there that even Christians succumbed to it, much to the consternation of their bishops. The cuisine that developed under Arab auspices was, then, a truly "national" one that transcended confessional differences. Jews also played an important part in the life of Muslim-ruled Spain and, after the Reconquista, helped to preserve its culinary traditions in their various places of exile, principally Turkey.

The alleyways of Granada are distinguished by simple whitewashed houses and balconies adorned with potted flowers and painted pottery.

The most tangible reminders of Hispano-Arab culture are no doubt the architectural monuments that still adorn such cities as Córdoba, Seville, and Granada. But the Arabs were as gifted in agriculture as they were in the planning and embellishment of cities. They introduced to Spain superior techniques of irrigation that transformed much of the landscape: subterranean irrigation canals, aqueducts, waterwheels using buckets to scoop up the water; all these were used to bring new areas under cultivation. Windmills, too, were an Arab innovation, with an ultimate origin in Khorasan in eastern Persia; had it not been for the coming of the Arabs, Don Quixote would have had no windmills against which to tilt.

Equally important was the great range of new foodstuffs the Arabs brought with them. The list includes a good portion of what we commonly regard as worth eating: eggplants, artichokes, asparagus and spinach; quinces, pomegranates, figs, apricots and dates; almonds and pistachios; sugar and rice; and spices and seasonings such as nutmeg, cumin, cinnamon, turmeric, cloves, saffron and vanilla. In Spain, as elsewhere, the Arabs took a strong interest in the cultivation of various citrus fruits, with particular emphasis on the orange; the fame of Valencia oranges goes back to the vast market gardens established there by the Arabs. (It is curious to note that while the English word orange is derived from Arabic via Spanish—ignoring earlier links in the etymological chain—the orange is known today in Arabic, Persian and Turkish as *portaghal,* testimony to the excellence of the oranges the Arabs first planted in Portugal.) The Arabs were in general excellent horticulturists, planting for knowledge as well as profit; the botanical garden they established in Seville in 1085 was the first of its kind in Europe.

Not content with importing this cornucopia to Spain, the Arabs also gave a boost to poultry farming, abhorring as they did the chosen meat of their Roman and Visigoth predecessors, and introduced effective methods of tuna fishing—the same that they bequeathed to Sicily—that today are still known by the Arabic name *almadraba.*

The dishes that resulted from all this activity belong to almost every section of the menu. Important in particular was the combination of vegetables with meat in a single dish, with the former predominating. Apart from some Byzantine forebears, this was unprecedented in Spanish and indeed the whole of European cuisine. The use of seasonings was hardly unprecedented, but many of the seasonings were definitely new, and they were used more thoughtfully than before. Rice was cultivated and consumed primarily in coastal areas and it was therefore logical to eat it primarily in combination with fish and shellfish. This habit may lie at the origin of *paella;* one cannot be sure, for the pan in which it is customarily cooked was already known in Roman times, and pork (a meat forbidden to Muslims) and rabbit (one they generally disdain) are commonly included with the fish and seafood. The fact, however, that *paella* was classically eaten straight from the pan, with the diners seated around it in a circle, Arab-style, may point to an Arab genesis of this celebrated national dish. The Spanish habit of beginning meals with a salad (unique before it became customary in America) definitely goes back to the abundance of vegetables cultivated by the Arabs; the Syro-Lebanese *tabbouleh,* a salad made with cereals, vegetables and aromatic herbs dressed in olive oil and citrus juices, has its Andalusian counterpart. The Arabs also introduced Spain to the pleasures of pastry and sweets, prepared with a liberal use of syrup (a word of significantly Arabic derivation) and honey, and incorporating the crystallized ginger and candied fruits that were previously unknown in Europe. Marzipan, too, was an Arab invention, made possible by the abundant availability of almonds. Even certain drinks such as *aloja,* a spicy and refreshing mixture of water and honey, and a whole range of fruity concoctions are owed to the Arabs.

In 1492, the last bastion of Arab power in Andalusia fell to the forces of the Reconquista, and not much time was lost in banishing the Muslim population or forcibly converting it to Christianity. A final expulsion of the Moriscos—those Muslims who had tenaciously clung to their customs despite the adherence to Christianity that the Inquisition dictated—took place between 1609 and 1614, with deleterious consequences for Spanish agriculture, for the Moriscos had always been the best cultivators and gardeners. A vigorous effort at inducing national amnesia succeeded in disguising much of the Arab legacy, including its culinary component, and Spain assumed a new geopolitical role, for 1492 had also been the year in which Columbus "discovered" America.

The two cardinal events of 1492 were in many ways interconnected. Rivalry with Islam and a desire to secure direct access to the riches of Asia, bypassing the Muslim lands of the Middle East, were among the motives underlying Columbus's voyage. In keeping with the crusading spirit of the age, he promised his royal patrons that part of the profits he hoped to realize would be devoted to wresting Palestine from the hands of the Muslims. What happened, of course, was something different, but in terms of culinary history just as momentous. The Spanish conquests in America brought about the introduction to Europe of a whole series of new foodstuffs. Whereas, before, Spain had been the gateway to Europe for the gastronomic riches of the Middle East, it now became the port of entry for the exotic fare of the New World.

The potato was first encountered in Peru and it arrived in Seville about three decades later, but both in Spain and the rest of Europe it was for long disdained as unfit for human consumption. The tomato is a different matter. The Spaniards first made its acquaintance in Mexico in the sixteenth century, and the Moriscos, who had infiltrated the ranks of the conquistadores, showed considerable interest in it. As early as 1544, tomatoes were being eaten in Venice, but the Spaniards were slower, feeling that the tomato might even be poisonous. Then, however, they took to it with a vengeance, making it the basis of the vegetable stew known as *pisto* and the defining element of Andalusian *gazpacho.* This celebrated

Gaudí's masterpieces, including the Sagrada Familia *in Barcelona, are stunning examples of Spanish Art Nouveau architecture.*

cold soup has been attributed to the Arabs, but its name is neither Arabic nor Arabic-derived, and the only Arab antecedent it might have is the cold broth known as *tharid.* Cortés found the Aztecs imbibing vast quantities of spiced chocolate as an aphrodisiac. Spanish nuns in Mexico tamed the drink by adding milk to it, in which form it was for long favored in Spain as a daily energizer, the forerunner of coffee. The incorporation of chocolate into meat and vegetable dishes, fairly common in Mexican cuisine, found little imitation in Spain or elsewhere in the Mediterranean.

Many of the foodstuffs we have discussed passed from Spain into France (although some reached the same destination via Italy), but a partial reversal of culinary traffic accompanied the establishment of the Bourbons on the Spanish throne in 1759. French culinary styles then became popular in the capital and among the well-to-do elsewhere in the country. The eclipse of distinctively Spanish cuisine was, however, partial and temporary, and the rise of an increasingly popular element in that cuisine, tapas, is said to have come as late as the nineteenth century. Tapas are varied tidbits of meat, fish and savory pastries, eaten either as snacks in their own right or as an accompaniment to heavy wines such as sherry. The word *tapa* means "lid," and the scraps of dried meat used to cover wine vats are said to have furnished the first tapas, but this sounds very much like a folk etymology. So closely akin are tapas in conception and purpose to the *mezes* of the eastern Mediterranean, that it is difficult to conceive of them originating as late as the nineteenth century. Since the genesis of the tapa was in Andalusia, we may be correct in thinking of it as a much delayed response to the Near Eastern influences so deeply rooted in the soil of Andalusia. Alternatively, it may have been a late demonstration of the subtle culinary unity that binds the Mediterranean.

Appetizers

Garlic is among the most ancient cultivated plants in the Mediterranean.

APPETIZERS

Whether they are called *mezes,* antipasti, tapas or hors d'oeuvres, these appetizers are some of the most interesting and delicious dishes of Mediterranean cuisine—an enticing beginning for any repast. In the Mediterranean, meals are to be shared and enjoyed and hosts pride themselves on how many delectable little dishes they can offer to their guests. A table laden with an array of appetizers is symbolic of abundance and hospitality.

Commonly, these dishes are brought to the table a few at a time, or they are set out as part of a large assortment to which guests help themselves. Some of them can be expanded into main courses and, in fact, a selection of these plates can be a satisfying meal on their own.

The first category of appetizer is the purée, or what some might call a spread or dip. The Near East and Greece are home to some of the best: *hummus* made with chick-peas (garbanzos), tahini and garlic; Syrian *muhammarah,* a mixture of pomegranate and walnuts; smoky *baba ghannouj* made with roasted eggplant; Greek fava (broad) bean purée with olive oil and slivers of red onion; *skordalia* of potato or bread crumbs and a generous measure of garlic; creamy *taramasalata* made from prized fish roe. All are meant for serving with pita bread. The French *tapénade,* a spunky olive spread, is ideal on grilled country bread or it can be used as a sauce for grilled fish or vegetables.

North African vegetable salads make a particularly tasty and colorful appetizer assortment: spicy slivers of carrot; olive-strewn cauliflower; a plate of glistening grilled peppers, eggplant and tomatoes; bowls of olives; lemon wedges with an aromatic dressing. Served with Tunisian semolina bread (recipe on page 84), and followed by *b'stilla* (recipe on page 87), a North African feast is at hand.

An Italian antipasto table might include the Sicilian sweet-and-sour eggplant dish known as *caponata* or an Apulian grilled eggplant salad, sautéed slices of golden pumpkin squash with mint and garlic, marinated sardines or anchovies, crispy rice croquettes, slices of fresh mozzarella or pecorino cheese drizzled with olive oil, paper-thin sheets of house-cured prosciutto, and a slice of *scacciata* (recipe on page 74), the double-crusted pizza of Calabria and Sicily.

It is in Spain, with its tapas bars outfitted with long counters on which are laid seemingly countless platters brimming with foods, that the appetizer assortment has been elevated to an institution. Each bar is known for a specialty. People go from place to place, sipping glasses of well-chilled *fino* sherry and tasting and sampling tapas. These might include *pa amb tomaquet,* grilled bread rubbed with garlic, olive oil and tomato; wedges of *tortilla,* an omelet ribboned with golden brown potato and onion slices, marinated sardines or cooked vegetables dressed *"à la grecque"* with a Greek-style marinade that has been adopted by the French and the Spaniards as well. Salt-cod *buñuelos* and shrimp fritters, pine nut–dotted meatballs, a rice salad, some *manchego* cheese, a few slices of sausage, a mound of fried almonds, and a bowl of olives might complete the tableau.

Previous pages: Marinated Octopus Salad (recipe page 52)

Olive trees have thrived in the Peloponnese since the Greeks began exporting olive oil in the 11th century B.C.

The *meze* table, depending upon the country, would have an assortment of purées—*hummus, fava,* a rich *baba ghannouj*—crunchy *falafel* with a lemony tahini dressing, cheese-filled fried eggplant sandwiches, deep-fried mussels with walnut *tarator* sauce or rice-stuffed mussels in the shell, stuffed grapeleaves, marinated octopus, shrimp and beets with garlicky almond *skordalia,* just to mention a few. Maybe even hard-cooked eggs dipped in toasted coriander and cumin seeds.

The combinations and variations are countless. You can pair room-temperature salads—the traditional Greek mix of ripe tomatoes, cucumbers, romaine, Kalamata olives and tart feta cheese or the equally venerable Provençal *salade niçoise* of beans, potatoes, tomatoes, tuna and olives—with such hot dishes as fried mussels; croquettes of salt cod, rice, or potato; little meatballs or fried cheese. Or, at the height of tomato season, make *tabbouleh* or *fattoush,* similar in that they both bring together tomatoes, cucumbers, onions, mint, parsley and lemon, but different in that one uses bulgur (cracked wheat) and the other toasted pita bread. And don't overlook the savory pastries in the next chapter for a wealth of delicious small foods enclosed in dough.

At one time Europe depended so heavily on spices, they became common currency; here, an Egyptian merchant offers a variety of the once-traded seasonings.

For a more substantial plate, prepare Circassian chicken, the Turkish classic that combines chicken in a fragrant nut sauce, or add shellfish or tuna to an Andalusian rice salad. For rice in yet another form, set out a plate of rice-filled *dolmas* and bowls of yogurt and lemon wedges or meat-and-rice *dolmas* served warm with *avgolemono* sauce and pita bread.

In the Mediterranean eggs are not for breakfast. They appear on the menu as an appetizer or main dish, customarily served at room temperature. Street vendors sell them hard-cooked for dipping into spice mixtures. *Tortillas* in Spain, *frittate* in Italy and all manner of savory *omelettes* in France and North Africa can be substantial enough for dinner or lunch, or they can appear cut into appetizer portions on the buffet table.

This chapter is about temptation, about stimulating the palate and the appetite. Start here and move on to other courses, or stay here and eat from a bountiful table.

TUNISIA

Chalda Brouklou Sfaxinya

Cauliflower Salad from Sfax

Sfax, the second largest city in Tunisia, is an agricultural center noted especially for the cultivation of olives. This salad plays the mildness of potatoes and cauliflower off against the heat of harissa.

1 cauliflower, broken into florets
8 small red potatoes or new potatoes, unpeeled
salt to taste, plus 1 teaspoon salt
1 teaspoon *harissa* mixed with 3 tablespoons water (see glossary)
1 teaspoon ground caraway
1 teaspoon ground coriander
¼ cup (2 fl oz/60 ml) olive oil
2–3 tablespoons fresh lemon juice
grated zest of 1 lemon
sharply flavored black olives for garnish (optional)

Bring 2 saucepans three-fourths full of water to a boil. Add the cauliflower to one pan and the potatoes to the other, and salt to taste to each. Bring to a boil and cook until they are just tender; the cauliflower will take 10–15 minutes and the potatoes about 30 minutes. Do not overcook; drain well.

Cut the potatoes into bite-sized chunks about the same size as the florets. Place the vegetables in a serving bowl. In a small bowl stir together the diluted *harissa,* caraway, coriander, the 1 teaspoon salt, oil, and lemon juice and zest. Pour the mixture over the vegetables and toss well to combine. Let stand for 1 hour, then readjust the seasoning as the potatoes will absorb most of the salt.

Just before serving, garnish with olives, if desired. Serve at room temperature.

SERVES 6–8

Clockwise from left: Cauliflower Salad from Sfax, Olive Salad, Lemon Salad, Tomato and Sweet Pepper Salad

MOROCCO

SALATIT MISCHWIA

Tomato and Sweet Pepper Salad

This North African salad can be served as a starter or as an accompaniment to meat and fish dishes.

6 ripe tomatoes, peeled, seeded and diced
3 sweet green peppers (capsicums), roasted, peeled, seeded and diced (see glossary)
2 tablespoons fresh lemon juice
1 teaspoon salt
½ teaspoon freshly ground pepper
3 tablespoons olive oil
2 tablespoons chopped fresh flat-leaf (Italian) parsley
1 small hot chili pepper, seeded and finely minced (optional)
peel from ¼ preserved lemon, rinsed and finely diced (optional; see glossary)
½ teaspoon ground cumin (optional)
1 clove garlic, very finely minced (optional)

Place the tomatoes, green peppers, lemon juice, salt, ground pepper, oil and parsley in a salad bowl. Toss to mix.

If you like, add the chili pepper, preserved lemon, cumin and/or garlic to the mixture. Toss once again and serve at room temperature.

SERVES 6

MOROCCO

SALATIT LIMOUN

Lemon Salad

A specialty of the colorful city of Fès, this salad is quite tart. It can also act as a sauce for simple baked or broiled fish.

4 lemons
1 onion, finely chopped
4 tablespoons chopped fresh flat-leaf (Italian) parsley
1 teaspoon paprika
¼ teaspoon cayenne pepper
2 teaspoons ground cumin
12 black olives, pitted and chopped
salt
olive oil

Peel the lemons and remove all of the white pith. Separate into segments by cutting through and removing the membrane. Dice the segments and place in a salad bowl.

Add the onion, parsley, paprika, cayenne, cumin and olives to the lemons and toss to mix. If you think the salad needs salt, add a little. Then drizzle on just a bit of olive oil, toss lightly to coat and serve slightly chilled or at room temperature.

SERVES 4

MOROCCO

MESLALLA

Olive Salad

Although considered a salad in Morocco, this lively mixture may seem more like a condiment. Think of it as a North African tapénade *and serve it as you like. In a similar Cypriot dish that is served as a spread with bread, the olives are chopped and mixed with ¼ cup (2 fl oz/60 ml) each olive oil and vinegar; 2 cloves garlic, finely minced; and 2 teaspoons ground coriander. Be sure to use an assortment of olives—black, green, purple—for a colorful salad.*

2 cups (10 oz/315 g) mixed olives
juice of 2 large lemons (about ½ cup/4 fl oz/125 ml)
1 teaspoon paprika
½ teaspoon cayenne pepper
1 clove garlic, finely minced
1 teaspoon salt
3 tablespoons olive oil
3 tablespoons chopped fresh flat-leaf (Italian) parsley

Rinse the olives briefly under running water, then pit and place in a salad bowl. Add all the remaining ingredients and toss to mix well. Cover and chill well before serving.

SERVES 6

TUNISIA

MZOURA

Carrot Salad

A dash of fiery harissa *perks up this carrot salad.*

1 lb (500 g) carrots, peeled and thinly sliced or julienned
5 tablespoons (3 fl oz/80 ml) olive oil
2 cloves garlic, finely minced
1 teaspoon *harissa* mixed with 6 tablespoons (3 fl oz/90 ml) water (see glossary)
1 teaspoon ground caraway
1 teaspoon salt
1 teaspoon ground cumin
¼ cup (2 fl oz/60 ml) wine vinegar
chopped fresh flat-leaf (Italian) parsley or fresh cilantro (fresh coriander)

Bring a saucepan three-fourths full of salted water to a boil. Add the carrots and boil until tender, 5–8 minutes. Drain well.

In a sauté pan over low heat, warm the olive oil. Add the garlic, diluted *harissa,* caraway, salt, cumin and vinegar; stir for 2 minutes. Add the drained carrots and cook, stirring occasionally, until most of the liquid is absorbed, 5–8 minutes. Transfer to a serving dish and garnish with parsley or cilantro. Serve at room temperature.

SERVES 4–6

Carrot Salad

Eggs with Peppers, Tomatoes and Eggplant

ALGERIA

CHAKCHOUKA

Eggs with Peppers, Tomatoes and Eggplant

A chakchouka *is a North African ragout of vegetables, and sometimes* merguez *(a spicy sausage), topped with eggs. It is an ideal dish for entertaining, as the base can be prepared ahead of time and the eggs dropped in and cooked just before serving. The eggs can be cooked on top of the stove or, once added, finished in the oven. This recipe uses the Mediterranean vegetable triumverate of eggplant, peppers and tomatoes, but you can add cauliflower, potatoes, zucchini (courgettes) or artichokes as you like.*

6 tablespoons (3 fl oz/90 ml) olive oil
2 eggplants (aubergines), peeled and cut into 1-in (2.5-cm) pieces
2 red or green sweet peppers (capsicums), seeded, deribbed and cut into long, narrow strips
½ lb (250 g) *merguez,* cut into 1-in (2.5-cm) pieces (recipe on page 182)
3 tomatoes, peeled, seeded and chopped
2 cloves garlic, minced
2–3 tablespoons chopped fresh flat-leaf (Italian) parsley
6 eggs
salt and freshly ground pepper

In a large sauté pan over medium-high heat, warm 4 tablespoons (2 fl oz/6 ml) of the oil. Add the eggplant and fry, tossing and stirring occasionally, until tender, about 10 minutes.

Meanwhile, in another sauté pan, warm the remaining 2 tablespoons oil over medium heat. Add the peppers and sauté for 5 minutes. As soon as they are ready, add the peppers to the eggplant. When the eggplant is tender add the tomatoes, garlic and parsley, stir well, cover and simmer over low heat, until all the vegetables are soft, about 15 minutes longer.

In another sauté pan over medium heat, sauté the *merguez* until browned and add it to the eggplant mixture.

Remove the lid. Using the back of a spoon, make 6 hollows in the vegetable mixture. Break 1 egg into each hollow. Some recipes advise breaking the yolks, but it is not necessary. Cover and cook until the eggs are set, 4–5 minutes. Sprinkle with salt and pepper to taste and serve at once.

SERVES 3–6

TURKEY

PANCAR SALATASI
Beet Salad

In many countries along the Mediterranean, beets are dressed simply with olive oil and vinegar. Sometimes yogurt is mixed with the vinaigrette, which turns a vibrant pink once it is tossed with the beets. The beet greens can be cooked and served along with the beets, and the salad dressed with either olive oil and vinegar or with olive oil and lemon juice. Other versions toss the beets with thinly sliced oranges and red (Spanish) onions. Here, a simple Turkish beet salad is dressed with olive oil, vinegar and garlic. In France, the beets might be dressed with walnut oil and vinegar and topped with chopped toasted walnuts. In Greece, 1 teaspoon ground allspice or cinnamon would be added to the dressing, or the beets would be dressed with skordalia *made with bread and almonds (see page 58). In Spain 1 teaspoon aniseeds would flavor the dressing, while Tunisian cooks add 1 teaspoon caraway seeds.*

1 large or 2 small bunches beets (beetroots), about 1½ lb (750 g)
¼ cup (2 fl oz/60 ml) olive oil
2 tablespoons red wine vinegar
2 cloves garlic, minced
salt and freshly ground pepper

There are two methods for cooking beets, boiling and baking, with some cooks believing that baking them results in a more earthy flavor.

To boil the beets, scrub them but do not peel. Cut off the leaves but leave 1 in (2.5 cm) of the stem and root attached so the beet doesn't bleed its color into the water. Reserve the greens for another use (see greens with lemon–olive oil dressing on page 49). Put the beets into a saucepan and add water to cover. Bring to a boil, reduce the heat to medium, cover partially and simmer until tender, 20–30 minutes. Drain off the cooking water and add a little cold water to the pot to cool the beets. When they can be handled, peel the beets, then slice or quarter, depending upon the size.

To bake the beets, preheat an oven to 350°F (180°C). Prepare the beets as for boiling and place in a baking pan. Add water to a depth of 1 in (2.5 cm). Cover with foil and bake until tender, about 1 hour. Remove from the oven and, when cool enough to handle, peel and slice or quarter, depending upon the size.

Place the cut beets in a serving bowl. In a small bowl whisk together the oil, vinegar, garlic and salt and pepper to taste. Pour over the beets and toss to coat. Serve at room temperature.

SERVES 4–6

TURKEY

ADAS SALATASI
Lentil Salad

Lentil salads are served in every country of the Mediterranean with only slight variations. Green lentils take longer to cook but they hold their shape better than brown ones. Be careful not to overcook them or they will disintegrate into a purée. Dried haricot, fava (broad) or white beans can be used in place of the lentils. These beans will need to be soaked overnight in water to cover in the refrigerator before cooking. They will also require longer cooking times.

2 cups (14 oz/440 g) dried lentils
6 tablespoons (3 fl oz/90 ml) olive oil
3 tablespoons fresh lemon juice
salt and freshly ground pepper
1 onion, finely chopped
1 or 2 cloves garlic, minced
2 teaspoons ground cumin
4 tablespoons chopped fresh mint and/or fresh flat-leaf (Italian) parsley
quartered or sliced tomatoes (optional)
sliced or quartered hard-cooked eggs (optional)
black olives (optional)
crumbled feta or fresh goat cheese (optional)

Rinse the lentils and place in a saucepan. Add cold water to cover and bring to a boil. Reduce the heat to low and simmer gently, uncovered, until the lentils are tender but not falling apart. The timing will depend upon the age of the lentils; begin testing after 15–20 minutes. Some can take as long as 1 hour; others may be tender in 25 minutes. Drain the lentils well and transfer to a bowl.

While the lentils are still warm, dress with 4 tablespoons (2 fl oz/60 ml) of the olive oil and the lemon juice. Season to taste with salt and pepper.

Warm the remaining 2 tablespoons olive oil in a sauté pan over medium heat. Add the onion and cook for 3–4 minutes. Add the garlic and cumin and cook for 2 minutes.

Fold the onion mixture into the lentils, then fold in the parsley or mint. Let stand for 1 hour, then adjust the seasoning. The lentils will have absorbed some of the salt and the dressing.

Garnish with tomatoes, eggs, olives, or crumbled cheese, if desired. Serve at room temperature.

SERVES 6–8

TURKEY

ÇERKEZ TAVUĞU
Circassian Chicken

This chicken salad in walnut sauce is one of the glories of the Turkish table. The recipe was carried there by slaves brought to Turkey from Georgia. It is usually served as a meze, but you can increase the portions and serve it as a main course luncheon or supper. Some versions are quite spicy with hot pepper. Some cooks add almonds along with the walnuts. If you wish to do this, reduce the walnuts to 2 cups (8 oz/250 g) and add ¾ cup (4½ oz/140 g) almonds. The top is usually dusted with paprika and drizzled with olive oil. You can make this with a whole chicken instead of the chicken breasts; increase the cooking time accordingly.

FOR COOKING THE CHICKEN:
3 lb (1.5 kg) chicken breasts
4 cups (32 fl oz/1 l) water
1 onion, chopped
1 carrot, peeled and cut into chunks
1 bay leaf (optional)
1 fresh thyme sprig (optional)
a few whole cloves (optional)

FOR THE SAUCE:
¼ cup (2 oz/60 g) unsalted butter
1 onion, chopped
4 teaspoons finely minced garlic
2 tablespoons sweet paprika
1 teaspoon cayenne pepper
2 slices bread, crusts discarded
3 cups (12 oz/375 g) walnuts
2 cups (16 fl oz/500 ml) reduced chicken stock from cooking chicken
salt and freshly ground black pepper

FOR THE GARNISH:
3 tablespoons walnut oil
2 teaspoons paprika
chopped fresh flat-leaf (Italian) parsley

Top to bottom: Beet Salad, Lentil Salad, Circassian Chicken

To cook the chicken, place it in a saucepan with the water, onion and carrot. Add the bay leaf, thyme, and cloves, if you like. Bring to a boil and reduce the heat to medium. Simmer, uncovered, until the chicken is tender, about 25 minutes.

Remove the chicken from the stock and set aside to cool. Strain the stock and return it to the saucepan. When the chicken is cool enough to handle, bone and skin the pieces and shred the meat. Place the meat in a bowl, cover and set aside. Add the chicken bones and skin to the stock and simmer until the stock is reduced to 2 cups (16 fl oz/500 ml). Remove from heat.

To make the sauce, melt the butter in a sauté pan over medium heat. Add the onion and sauté until tender and translucent, 8–10 minutes. Add the garlic, paprika and cayenne pepper and sauté for 3 minutes. Remove from the heat.

In a bowl soak the bread in water to cover briefly, then squeeze dry and crumble into a food processor fitted with the metal blade or in a blender. Add the walnuts and grind together until fine. Add the onion mixture and pulse to combine. Add the reduced chicken stock and purée to form a smooth sauce. Season to taste with salt and pepper.

Toss half of the sauce with the chicken and then transfer to a serving plate. Top with the remaining sauce.

To make the garnish, warm together the walnut oil and paprika in a small pan. Drizzle this mixture over the walnut sauce. Sprinkle with parsley and serve at room temperature.

SERVES 6–8

Top to bottom: Puréed Yellow Split Peas, Fish Roe Dip

GREECE

Fava

Puréed Yellow Split Peas

In Turkey, Egypt and North Africa, as well as in Greece, a bean purée is often part of the meze table. Although in Greece this purée is made with yellow split peas, broad beans are generally used elsewhere. The addition of the dill is common in Turkey. If you do not drizzle lemon juice on the purée, garnish the plate with lemon wedges. Pita bread (recipe on page 82) is the usual accompaniment and, occasionally, feta cheese.

1⅛ cups (½ lb/250 g) dried yellow split peas or dried fava (broad) beans
1 small onion, chopped
3 tablespoons olive oil
3½ cups (28 fl oz/875 ml) water
1 teaspoon salt, plus salt to taste
2 tablespoons chopped fresh dill, optional
freshly ground pepper

FOR THE TOPPING:

2–4 tablespoons olive oil
2 tablespoons fresh lemon juice, optional

chopped or thinly sliced red (Spanish) onion or green (spring) onion
freshly ground pepper

- If using yellow split peas, rinse well under running water. If using fava beans, place in a bowl with water to cover generously. Refrigerate overnight. Drain and rinse well under running water.
- In a 2-qt (2-l) saucepan, combine the peas or beans, onion, oil, the water and the 1 teaspoon salt. Bring to a boil over medium heat. Reduce the heat to low, cover and simmer until the peas or beans are so soft they have disintegrated, about 1 hour.
- Transfer to a food processor fitted with the metal blade and purée. Alternatively, pass the beans and their liquid through a coarse sieve. Mix in the dill, if using, and salt and pepper to taste. Transfer the purée to a serving dish, cover with plastic wrap and allow to cool and thicken.
- To serve, drizzle with the olive oil and the lemon juice, if using. Top with the onion and a grinding of pepper.

SERVES 4–6

GREECE

TARAMASALATA

Fish Roe Dip

The basis of this dish is tarama, *or mullet roe. It is available in bulk or in jars in stores specializing in foods from the Middle East. Carp or cod can be substituted. Serve with warm crusty bread and trimmed green (spring) onions, radishes, cucumbers and celery.*

5 slices white bread, crusts discarded
5 oz (155 g) *tarama*
1 onion, coarsely chopped
1 cup (8 fl oz/250 ml) olive oil
juice of 2 large lemons (about ½ cup/4 fl oz/125 ml)
2 tablespoons chopped fresh flat-leaf (Italian) parsley or a small handful of sharply flavored black olives

- In a shallow bowl combine the bread with just enough water to cover and let soak briefly. Remove the bread, squeeze dry and place in a food processor fitted with the metal blade or in a blender.
- Add the *tarama* and onion and process to mix. With the motor running, slowly add the oil and lemon juice, processing until a smooth paste forms.
- Transfer to a shallow serving bowl. Cover and chill.
- Serve chilled, garnished with parsley or black olives.

SERVES 6

MEDITERRANEAN

SPICED OLIVES

What could be a simpler or more elegant appetizer than a bowl of marinated olives?

FOR GREEK OLIVES:

1 lb (500 g) Kalamata olives
4 tablespoons dried oregano
1 tablespoon dried rosemary
1 tablespoon dried thyme
2 strips orange zest, each about 2 in (5 cm) long and ¼ in (6 mm) wide
olive oil

FOR SICILIAN OLIVES:

1 lb (500 g) green olives
3–4 cloves garlic, cut into slivers
2 tablespoons dried oregano
1 teaspoon red pepper flakes
olive oil

FOR MOROCCAN OLIVES:

1 lb (500 g) black or green olives
6 tablespoons chopped fresh flat-leaf (Italian) parsley
6 tablespoons chopped fresh cilantro (fresh coriander)
3 cloves garlic, chopped
1 teaspoon red pepper flakes or 2 fresh chili peppers, slivered
½ teaspoon ground cumin
½ cup (4 fl oz/125 ml) olive oil
2 teaspoons fresh lemon juice, a few strips lemon or orange zest or peel and some juice from ½ preserved lemon (see glossary)

- Whether preparing Greek, Sicilian or Moroccan olives, drain the brine off the olives and rinse them well.
- To make the Greek olives, dry the rinsed olives thoroughly and combine with all the remaining ingredients, including olive oil to cover or coat.
- To make the Sicilian olives, dry the rinsed olives thoroughly and then crack or pit them. Combine with all the remaining ingredients, including olive oil to cover or coat.
- To make the Moroccan olives, crack the rinsed olives and place in cold water to cover overnight. Drain well and combine with all the remaining ingredients.
- Place the olives in a sterilized jar, cover tightly and refrigerate for at least 2 days.

EACH RECIPE YIELDS 1 LB (500 G) OLIVES

Spiced Olives

PROVENCE

TAPÉNADE

Olive Spread

This savory spread will keep in a covered container for about a week in the refrigerator. It is excellent on warm bread, as an addition to chopped hard-cooked egg yolks for stuffed eggs, or spread under the skin of a chicken before roasting or grilling. It can also be diluted with a little olive oil and used as a dressing for grilled peppers (capsicums) or eggplants (aubergines). Some versions include grated lemon or orange zest; others are flavored with chopped fresh basil.

1 cup (5 oz/155 g) Niçoise or oil-cured black olives, pitted
6 anchovy fillets in olive oil, drained and chopped (about 1 tablespoon)
2 tablespoons capers, rinsed and coarsely chopped
2 cloves garlic, finely chopped
juice of 1 lemon
4–6 tablespoons (2–3 fl oz/60–90 ml) virgin olive oil
2 tablespoons Cognac (optional)

In a food processor fitted with the metal blade or in a blender, combine the olives, anchovies, capers, garlic and lemon juice. Process to form a paste. With the motor running, slowly add enough of the oil to form a spoonable mixture. Stir in the Cognac, if using.

Transfer to a small bowl and serve at room temperature.

SERVES 6

PROVENCE

SALADE NIÇOISE

Niçoise Salad

This salad has evolved over time. At first it was a vegetable salad, but gradually anchovies and tuna worked their way onto the plate. It can be an ample first course or be expanded to be a complete meal, depending upon the portion size and the amount of tuna. The tuna is usually canned white meat tuna packed in good olive oil. Purists insist on anchovy or *tuna, and on artichokes* or *fava beans, but with such wonderful ingredients, who needs to be pure! (In Provence, cooks use young artichokes and favas for this salad and add them raw; because such tender vegetables are more difficult to find outside of France, here they have been cooked.) While cooked potatoes and green beans are not part of an authentic* salade niçoise, *they are excellent additions as well.*

If there is salad left over, you can make a sandwich called pan bagnat, *literally, "wet bread." First, cut a round loaf or baguette in half and scoop out some of the white crumb. Rub the inside of the loaf with a cut garlic clove, then sprinkle with a little vinegar and olive oil and some salt and pepper. Put a serving of the salad between the bread halves and press them together firmly. Wrap well and refrigerate for at least an hour or for up to several hours before serving.*

salt
6 tomatoes, quartered
1 cucumber, peeled and sliced
2 green sweet peppers (capsicums), seeded, deribbed and sliced crosswise
2 small bulbs fennel, cored and sliced crosswise (optional)
6 green (spring) onions, trimmed but left whole, or 1 small onion, thinly sliced (optional)
6 small artichokes, trimmed, cooked, and quartered, or 12 tiny artichokes, trimmed and cooked
½ lb (250 g) shelled young, tender fresh fava (broad) or lima beans, cooked briefly
3 hard-cooked eggs, quartered lengthwise
12 anchovy fillets in olive oil, drained and cut into thin strips, or 2 cans (6 oz/185 g each) canned tuna, broken into large flakes
2 cloves garlic, finely minced
¼ cup (2 fl oz/60 ml) red wine vinegar
½ cup (4 fl oz/125 ml) olive oil
12 fresh basil leaves, chopped
freshly ground pepper
¼ cup (1½ oz/45 g) black olives

Salt the tomato quarters. Divide the tomatoes, cucumber, sweet peppers, the fennel and onions (if using), artichokes, beans and eggs evenly among 6 individual plates, arranging them attractively. Distribute the anchovies or tuna among the vegetables. Alternatively, assemble all the ingredients on a large platter or in a large shallow bowl.

In a small bowl crush the garlic with a little salt, then whisk in the vinegar, oil, basil, and ground pepper to taste. Pour the dressing evenly over the salads.

Garnish with the olives and serve.

SERVES 6

PROVENCE

BRANDADE DE MORUE

Salt Cod Mousse

The word brandade *is Provençal dialect for "something that is stirred." Purists would sneer at the use of the food processor to assemble this purée, which is traditionally prepared in a mortar and pestle. But there is no reason to balk at progress when time is valuable and flavor is not sacrificed. Mashed potatoes can be beaten into the purée. You will need 1 pound (500 g) potatoes, peeled, boiled and mashed by hand (do not use a processor for this step or the potatoes will be gluey). If you use the potatoes, you will need to increase the olive oil by about 1 cup (8 fl oz/250 ml) and add it, warmed, to the potatoes as you mash them. The cod is then beaten into the potatoes with a fork. In Valencia, a similar mixture of salt cod and potatoes is prepared. It includes only olive oil, no milk, and a few pine nuts are mashed in with the potatoes. The dish is garnished with toasted walnuts and chopped hard-cooked eggs.*

1½ lb (750 g) boneless salt cod (see glossary)
1½ cups (12 fl oz/375 ml) olive oil
1¼ cups (10 fl oz/310 ml) milk
2 cloves garlic, puréed
juice of 1 lemon
freshly grated nutmeg
freshly ground pepper
grilled or toasted bread slices

In a bowl combine the salt cod and water to cover. Refrigerate for 24–48 hours, changing the water at least 4 times. The amount of soaking necessary will depend upon the saltiness of the cod; thicker pieces may take longer than thinner pieces.

Drain the cod and place in a large pan with water to cover. Bring to a boil, cover, reduce the heat to low and poach gently until just tender, 8–10 minutes. Drain and cool slightly.

Remove all traces of skin and any small bones and flake the cod with your fingers or a fork.

In a small saucepan heat the oil. In another pan, heat the milk. Put the flaked cod into a food processor fitted with the metal blade. Add the garlic and pulse once to combine. Add half of the warm oil, a bit at a time, processing to combine. Then slowly mix in half of the warm milk. Now slowly beat in first the remaining warm oil and then the remaining warm milk. Add only as much of the remaining oil, bit by bit, as is needed to achieve a very pale, thick and smooth mixture. Add the lemon juice and some nutmeg and season to taste with pepper.

Spoon onto a serving dish and serve warm with grilled or toasted bread.

SERVES 6–8

Top to bottom: Niçoise Salad, Salt Cod Mousse, Olive Spread

Clockwise from top: Eggplant Purée with Tahini, Bulgur Salad, Chick-pea Purée with Sesame, Toasted Bread Salad

LEBANON

TABBOULEH

Bulgur Salad

This salad is best in the summer, as it is dependent upon good tomatoes. In Turkey there is a similar salad to which chopped green sweet peppers (capsicums) are added. For an interesting variation, omit the green onions and toss ½ cup (2½ oz/75 g) chopped white onion with ½ teaspoon ground allspice, then add with the parsley.

1 cup (6 oz/185 g) fine bulgur (cracked wheat)
3 cups (4½ oz/140 g) finely chopped fresh flat-leaf (Italian) parsley
½ cup (1½ oz/45 g) chopped green (spring) onions
1½ cups (2½ oz/75 g) chopped fresh mint
2 cups (12 oz/375 g) chopped ripe tomatoes (about 4)
½ cup (4 fl oz/125 ml) fresh lemon juice
½ cup (4 fl oz/125 ml) olive oil
salt and freshly ground pepper
romaine (cos) lettuce leaves

❀ In a bowl soak the bulgur in water to cover for about 20 minutes, then drain well. Transfer to a serving bowl. Add the parsley, green onions, mint and tomatoes and toss to combine.
❀ In a small bowl whisk together the lemon juice and olive oil. Pour over the bulgur mixture and toss well. Season to taste with salt and pepper.
❀ Serve with romaine leaves for scooping up the salad.

SERVES 4–6

LEBANON

FATTOUSH
Toasted Bread Salad

This Lebanese salad replaces the bulgur wheat of the classic tabbouleh with toasted pita bread.

2 large pita bread rounds (recipe on page 82)
1½ cups (9 oz/280 g) chopped ripe tomatoes
1 cup (5 oz/155 g) peeled, seeded and diced cucumber
1 cup (3 oz/90 g) finely chopped green (spring) onions
1 cup (1½ oz/40 g) finely chopped fresh flat-leaf (Italian) parsley
½ cup (¾ oz/20 g) chopped fresh mint, or more to taste
½ cup (¾ oz/20 g) chopped fresh purslane (optional; see glossary)
seeds of 1 large pomegranate (optional; see glossary)
½ cup (4 fl oz/125 ml) olive oil
½ cup (4 fl oz/125 ml) lemon juice
salt and freshly ground pepper
1 teaspoon ground sumac (optional; see glossary)
1 or 2 cloves garlic, finely minced (optional)
6 romaine (cos) leaves, cut into long strips (optional)

❀ Preheat an oven to 350°F (180°C).
❀ Place the pita bread on a baking sheet and bake, turning once until dry, about 5 minutes. Remove from the oven and, when cool enough to handle, break into bite-size pieces. Set aside.
❀ In a salad bowl combine the tomatoes, cucumber, onions, parsley, mint, and the purslane and pomegranate seeds, if using. Toss well.
❀ In a small bowl whisk together the oil, lemon juice, salt and pepper to taste, and, if using, the sumac or the garlic. Pour half of the dressing over the tomato mixture and marinate for about 30 minutes. Fold in the toasted bread and the romaine, if using. Add the remaining dressing and toss well. Serve at once.

SERVES 4

LEBANON

BABA GHANNOUJ
Eggplant Purée with Tahini

Called mutabbal *in Syria, this dip is also popular in Israel and Jordan. Pita bread (recipe on page 82) and raw vegetables are ideal accompaniments.*

2 globe eggplants (aubergines), about 1½ lb (750 g) total weight
2 cloves garlic, very finely minced
¼ cup (2½ oz/75 g) tahini (see glossary)
⅓–½ cup (3–4 fl oz/80–125 ml) fresh lemon juice, or to taste
salt and freshly ground pepper
3 tablespoons pine nuts, toasted
3 tablespoons chopped fresh flat-leaf (Italian) parsley
1 teaspoon ground cumin (optional)
2 tablespoons pomegranate seeds (optional; see glossary)

❀ Preheat a broiler (griller).
❀ Place the eggplants on a baking sheet and slip under the broiler. Broil (grill), turning often, until charred on all sides and quite tender, 20–30 minutes. Remove from the broiler and let cool.
❀ Cut the eggplants in half and scoop the pulp from the skins into a bowl or into a food processor fitted with the metal blade. Mash with a fork or pulse to purée.
❀ Add the garlic, tahini and lemon juice to the eggplant and beat with a fork or process to purée. Add salt and pepper to taste.
❀ Transfer to a plate or shallow bowl. Sprinkle with the pine nuts, parsley, and with the cumin and pomegranate seeds, if using.

SERVES 6–8

LEBANON

HUMMUS BI TAHINI
Chick-pea Purée with Sesame

A classic dip popular in Syria and Israel as well as its native Lebanon. Serve with pita bread (recipe on page 82) or with cucumbers, radishes, carrots, and/or green (spring) onions for dipping.

1 cup (7 oz/220 g) dried chick-peas (garbanzo beans)
4 cups (32 fl oz/1 l) water
¼ cup (2½ oz/75 g) tahini (see glossary)
2 cloves garlic, finely minced
¼ cup (2 fl oz/60 ml) fresh lemon juice, or to taste
salt
pinch of cayenne pepper

FOR THE TOPPING:

2 tablespoons olive oil
3 tablespoons chopped fresh flat-leaf (Italian) parsley
1 teaspoon ground cumin (optional)
½ teaspoon cayenne pepper (optional)
3 tablespoons pomegranate seeds (optional; see glossary)

❀ Place the chick-peas in a bowl with water to cover generously. Refrigerate overnight.
❀ Drain the chick-peas and rinse well under running water. Place in a 2-qt (2-l) saucepan, add the water and bring to a boil. Reduce the heat to low, cover and simmer until very soft, 1 hour or longer.
❀ Drain the chick-peas, reserving any liquid, and transfer to a food processor fitted with the metal blade. Pulse to purée. Add the tahini, garlic, and lemon juice and purée. Add just reserved cooking liquid or enough cold water to achieve a spreadable consistency. Season with salt to taste and the cayenne.
❀ If serving immediately, spoon the purée onto a shallow plate and smooth the top with a spoon or spatula. Drizzle with the olive oil and strew with the parsley. Sprinkle on the cumin, cayenne or pomegranate seeds in a star pattern. Or you can transfer the purée to a bowl, cover and keep at room temperature for up to 6 hours or in the refrigerator for 1–2 days. Bring back to room temperature before serving. The mixture will thicken upon standing; thin with water or reserved cooking liquid.

SERVES 6–8

Clockwise from bottom: Rice Croquettes, Sweet-and-Sour Eggplant, Pumpkin Salad with Mint

SICILY

ARANCINI DI RISO

Rice Croquettes

The name means "little oranges," which these robust, golden rice croquettes resemble. They come with a variety of fillings; the simplest is cheese and prosciutto, but my favorite is meat and little peas in a tomato sauce. The arancini can be formed up to a day or two ahead of time and refrigerated. Bring to room temperature before deep-frying.

6 cups (48 fl oz/1.5 l) water
3 cups (21 oz/660 g) Arborio rice
2 eggs
½ cup (2 oz/60 g) freshly grated Parmesan cheese
salt and freshly ground pepper
2 tablespoons olive oil

1 onion, chopped
½ lb (250 g) ground (minced) veal or beef
2 tablespoons tomato paste
½ cup (4 fl oz/125 ml) dry red wine or stock (see glossary)
1 cup (8 fl oz/250 ml) tomato sauce (see glossary)
1 cup (5 oz/155 g) shelled peas, blanched for 30 seconds and drained
freshly grated nutmeg (optional)
1 cup (5 oz/155 g) all-purpose (plain) flour
3 eggs
2 cups (8 oz/250 g) fine dried bread crumbs
vegetable oil for deep-frying

In a saucepan bring the water to a boil. Add the rice, cover, reduce the heat to low and cook until the water has been absorbed, 15–20 minutes. The rice should be al dente but cooked through and still a little sticky. Mix in the eggs, one at a time, and the cheese. Season to taste with salt and pepper. Spread out on a baking sheet, cover and refrigerate to cool.

Meanwhile, in a sauté pan over medium heat, warm the olive oil. Add the onion and sauté until tender and translucent, 8–10 minutes. Add the meat and stir, breaking it up, until it browns, just a few minutes. Add the tomato paste and wine or stock and simmer for 5 minutes. Then add the tomato sauce and simmer until thickened, about 15 minutes. Remove from the heat and stir in the blanched peas. Season to taste with salt, pepper and with a little nutmeg, if you like. Let cool to room temperature.

To make the rice balls, put the flour in a shallow bowl. Break the eggs into another shallow bowl and beat lightly with a little water. Place the bread crumbs in a third shallow bowl.

You can make the rice balls small or make them the size of 3-in (7.5-cm) oranges. Put a few spoonfuls of rice in the palm of your hand and make an indentation in the center with your finger, to form a pocket. Slip a spoonful of filling into the pocket and then "fold" the rice over the filling. Roll the rice into a nicely shaped ball. Then roll the ball in the flour, dip it in the beaten egg, and then roll it in the bread crumbs. Set on a wire rack. Repeat until you have used up all of the rice and filling.

Pour oil into a deep sauté pan to a depth of 3 in (7.5 cm) and heat to 375°F (190°C), or until a rice ball dropped into the oil begins to color within moments. When the oil is ready, deep-fry the rice balls, a few at a time, until they are golden, 4–5 minutes. Using a slotted spoon remove to paper towels to drain briefly, and repeat until all of the rice balls are cooked.

Arrange on a warmed platter and serve at once.

SERVES 6–8

SICILY

CAPONATA

Sweet-and-Sour Eggplant

The variations on caponata *are almost as numerous as Sicilian families. This eggplant compote is served at room temperature as part of an antipasto assortment, or by itself with toasted bread. It is best made a day ahead of time so the flavors can marry. Adjust vinegar and salt at serving time.*

2 eggplants (aubergines)
salt
2 tablespoons plus 1½ cups (12 fl oz/375 ml) olive oil
1 cup (5 oz/155 g) diced celery
3 onions, chopped or sliced ¼ in (6 mm) thick
1 cup (8 fl oz/250 ml) tomato purée
3 tablespoons capers, rinsed and drained
12 black and/or green olives, pitted and coarsely chopped
¼ cup (1½ oz/45 g) pine nuts or slivered almonds, toasted
½ cup (4 fl oz/125 ml) red wine vinegar
2 tablespoons sugar
chopped fresh basil or fresh flat-leaf (Italian) parsley (optional)
3 tablespoons raisins, plumped in hot water and drained (optional)
freshly ground pepper

The eggplants can be peeled or left unpeeled. Cut into 1-in (2.5-cm) dice. Sprinkle with salt and place in a colander for about 1 hour to drain. Rinse and pat dry.

In a small sauté pan over medium heat, warm the 2 tablespoons oil. Add the celery and sauté briefly; it should still be crisp. Set aside.

In a wide sauté pan over medium-high heat, warm 1 cup (8 fl oz/250 ml) of the oil. Add the eggplant and sauté, turning often, until golden and cooked through, 15–20 minutes. Do not undercook. Using a slotted spoon, remove to paper towels to drain.

In the same sauté pan, warm the remaining ½ cup (4 fl oz/125 ml) olive oil over medium-high heat. Add the onions and sauté until tender and translucent, about 8–10 minutes. Add the reserved celery and the tomato purée and simmer, stirring occasionally, for 10 minutes. Add the cooked eggplant, capers, olives, nuts, vinegar, sugar and the basil or parsley and/or raisins, if using. Stir well and simmer, uncovered, over low heat for 20 minutes. Season to taste with salt and pepper.

Transfer to a serving bowl and serve at room temperature.

SERVES 6–8

SICILY

FEGATO AI SETTE CANNOLI

Pumpkin Salad with Mint

Years ago, few people in Sicily could afford to eat meat. Since pumpkin is so meaty, they called this dish fegato*—"liver."* Sette Cannoli *is the name of a fountain with seven spouts, situated in a poor neighborhood in Palermo. Use pumpkin, Hubbard, butternut or any other large yellow winter squash for this salad. Some recipes direct cooks to sauté the garlic in the oil and then discard it before adding the squash to the oil. Others omit the vinegar and cinnamon.*

⅓ cup (3 fl oz/80 ml) olive oil
1 piece pumpkin or squash, about 2 lb (1 kg), peeled and cut into slices ½ in (12 mm) thick
½ cup (¾ oz/20 g) coarsely chopped fresh mint
3 garlic cloves, sliced paper-thin
½ cup (4 fl oz/125 ml) vinegar
½ cup (4 oz/125 g) sugar
pinch of ground cinnamon
salt and freshly ground pepper

In a large sauté pan over medium heat, warm the olive oil. Add the squash slices and cook, turning once, until tender and browned on both sides, about 8 minutes, total cooking time. Remove with a slotted spoon to a serving platter. Strew the mint and garlic slivers over the top.

To the oil remaining in the pan, add the vinegar, sugar and cinnamon and cook, stirring, over high heat until the sugar dissolves and the sauce thickens, 5–7 minutes. Season to taste with salt and pepper. Pour over the squash.

Serve the salad at room temperature.

SERVES 6–8

Clockwise from left: Fried Cheese, Savory Meatballs

GREECE/CATALONIA

KEFTEDAKIA/ALBÓNDIGAS

Savory Meatballs

No one can resist small, tasty meatballs as a tapa, meze *or snack. Here are two versions.*

FOR GREEK MEATBALLS:

3 slices bread, soaked in water to cover and then squeezed dry
1 lb (500 g) lean ground (minced) lamb or beef
1 cup (5 oz/155 g) finely minced onion
1 clove garlic, finely minced
3 eggs
4 tablespoons finely minced fresh flat-leaf (Italian) parsley
1 teaspoon dried oregano
½ teaspoon ground cinnamon
salt and freshly ground pepper

FOR CATALONIAN MEATBALLS:

½ lb (250 g) ground (minced) veal or beef
½ lb (250 g) ground (minced) pork
2 cloves garlic, finely minced
3 tablespoons finely minced fresh flat-leaf (Italian) parsley
1 egg
1 slice bread, soaked in water to cover, then squeezed dry
½ teaspoon freshly grated nutmeg
1 teaspoon paprika
salt and freshly ground pepper

FOR COOKING THE MEATBALLS:

1½ cups (7½ oz/235 g) all-purpose (plain) flour for coating
vegetable oil or olive oil for panfrying

To make either one of the meatball mixtures, in a bowl combine all the ingredients, including salt and pepper to taste, and mix well, kneading the mixture with your hands until it is smooth. Cover and chill.

Place the flour in a shallow bowl. Shape the meat mixture into 1-in (2.5-cm) balls and coat evenly with the flour. In a deep sauté pan over medium-high heat, warm a little oil. When the oil is hot, add the meatballs and panfry, turning often, until golden on all sides, 8–10 minutes.

Transfer to a warmed platter and serve at once.

EACH MEATBALL RECIPE SERVES 6–8

GREECE

SAGANAKI

Fried Cheese

This dish takes its name from the two-handled pan in which the cheese is fried. In Sicily, the dish is called formaggio all'argentiera; argentiera *means "silver" and its use is a comment on cheeses being fried in the place of meat, which is expensive. Sicilian cooks use* caciocavallo, *flavor the oil with a smashed garlic clove, and sprinkle the fried cheese with a little vinegar and oregano.*

½ lb (250 g) *haloumi, kefalotiri* or *kasseri* cheese (see glossary)
all-purpose (plain) flour for dredging
olive oil
salt and freshly ground pepper
2 tablespoons chopped fresh flat-leaf (Italian) parsley
lemon wedges

Cut the cheese into slices about ½ in (12 mm) thick, 1½–2 in (4–5 cm) wide and 2–3 in (5–7.5 cm) long. Dredge in flour.

Pour oil into a frying pan to a depth of ¼ in (6 mm) and place over medium heat. When the oil is sizzling hot, slip in the cheese slices, a few at a time, and fry, turning once, until golden, 2–3 minutes on each side. Using a slotted spoon remove to paper towels to drain briefly.

Arrange on a warmed platter. Season to taste with salt and pepper, sprinkle with the parsley and garnish with lemon wedges. Serve at once.

SERVES 4–6

GREECE

HORTA LADOLEMONO

Greens with Lemon–Olive Oil Dressing

Greeks often cook greens, dress them with a classic lemon and olive oil dressing called ladolemono *and then serve them as a salad. Although they commonly gather wild greens in the countryside, cultivated greens are equally delicious prepared this way. This same sauce is good on cooked beets, fennel, fava (broad) beans, white beans and artichokes. As the greens cook down considerably, be sure to allow at least ½ pound (250 g) uncooked greens per person. Some people believe that drinking the cooking juices contributes to long life and good health.*

2 lb (1 kg) mixed young, tender greens such as arugula (rocket), sorrel, dandelion greens, beet (beetroot) greens, escarole, kale, collard greens, curly endive and frisée, in any combination

FOR THE *LADOLEMONO* DRESSING:

½ cup (4 fl oz/125 ml) olive oil
¼ cup (2 fl oz/60 ml) fresh lemon juice
salt and freshly ground pepper

Wash the greens in many changes of water, to rid them of all sand.

Bring a large pot three-fourths full of water to a boil. Add the greens and boil, uncovered, over high heat until tender, just a few minutes. Drain well. (Reserve the cooking juices if you'd like to try drinking them. You might want to add a little salt and fresh lemon juice.) Arrange the greens on a serving dish.

In a small bowl, make the dressing by whisking together the oil, lemon juice, and salt and pepper to taste.

Serve the greens warm or at room temperature. Toss with the *ladolemono* dressing at serving time.

SERVES 4

Greens with Lemon–Olive Oil Dressing

EGYPT

BEID MASLUQ

Hard-Cooked Eggs with Cumin and Coriander

The people of the Middle East love hard-cooked eggs. Here, the eggs are dipped in seasoned salt. Sometimes they are deep-fried and then dipped whole in a mixture of 2 teaspoons ground cinnamon, 2 tablespoons crushed, toasted cumin seeds, 1 teaspoon ground turmeric, 1 tablespoon coarse salt and freshly ground pepper to taste.

1 tablespoon coriander seeds
2 teaspoons cumin seeds
1 tablespoon coarse salt
6 hard-cooked eggs, cut into halves or quarters

In a small, dry pan over medium heat, combine the coriander and cumin seeds and toast, stirring or shaking the pan, until fragrant, just a few minutes. Transfer to a mortar and crush with a pestle, or grind in a spice mill.

Place in a shallow bowl and stir in the salt. Each diner dips the egg pieces into the spiced mixture.

SERVES 6

EGYPT

BEID HAMINE

Long-Cooked Eggs with Onion Skins

Hamin *means "oven," and these eggs can be cooked in a slow oven or on top of the stove. They have a creamy texture following long hours of cooking, and are a rich beige from the onion skins and coffee. In Egypt they are eaten with* ful mudammas *(recipe on page 214). But you might like to try them with a salad.*

6 eggs
skins from 6–10 yellow onions
2 cups (14 oz/440 g) coffee grounds
2 tablespoons olive oil

Place the eggs in a saucepan. Tuck the onion skins around them so that all the surfaces are covered. Add the coffee grounds and then water to cover by 2 in (5 cm) and the oil (the oil prevents the water from evaporating). Cover and simmer over very low heat for 6–8 hours.

SERVES 6

EGYPT

FALAFEL

Chick-pea Croquettes

Street food at its best. Although these crunchy croquettes are Egyptian in origin, they are now equally popular in Syria, Lebanon and Israel. For directions on cooking chick-peas, see hummus bi tahini *(recipe on page 45); use ¾ cup (5 oz/155 g) dried chick-peas for this recipe. The croquettes are delicious tucked into warm pita bread with tomato, cucumber, lettuce and tahini dressing.*

FOR THE CROQUETTES:

2 cups (12 oz/370 g) drained, cooked chick-peas (garbanzo beans)
⅓ cup (3 fl oz/80 ml) water
1 slice firm white bread, crust discarded, torn into pieces
2 tablespoons all-purpose (plain) flour, plus all-purpose flour for cooking
½ teaspoon baking soda (bicarbonate of soda)
3 cloves garlic, finely minced
1 egg, lightly beaten
2 tablespoons chopped fresh flat-leaf (Italian) parsley
½ teaspoon freshly ground black pepper
½ teaspoon cayenne pepper
½ teaspoon ground cumin
½ teaspoon ground turmeric
½ teaspoon ground coriander
1 tablespoon tahini (see glossary)
salt

FOR THE TAHINI DRESSING:

½ cup tahini (see glossary)
½ cup (4 fl oz/125 ml) fresh lemon juice
1 cup (8 fl oz/250 ml) water

Clockwise from top left: Chick-pea Croquettes, Long-Cooked Eggs with Onion Skins, Hard-Cooked Eggs with Cumin and Coriander

2 cloves garlic, finely minced
salt
freshly ground black pepper or cayenne pepper
all-purpose (plain) flour for coating
vegetable oil for deep frying
8 pita bread rounds (recipe on page 82)
chopped tomato, cucumber and lettuce

❀ To make the croquettes, pass the chick-peas through the coarse blade of a meat grinder into a bowl. Alternatively, place in a food processor fitted with the metal blade and pulse briefly to grind coarsely; transfer to a bowl. Add the water, bread, the 2 tablespoons flour, baking soda, garlic, egg, parsley, black and cayenne peppers, cumin, turmeric, coriander, tahini and salt to taste. Mix well and set aside.

❀ To make the dressing, combine all the ingredients, including salt and pepper to taste, in a food processor fitted with the metal blade or in a blender and purée until smooth. Add water as needed to thin to dressing consistency. (This same mixture can be used as a dip, in which case it should be thinned only until a spreadable consistency.)

❀ Form the chick-pea mixture into 1-in (2.5-cm) balls and flatten them slightly between the palms of your hands. You should have 16 balls. Place the flour for coating in a shallow bowl.

❀ Pour oil into a deep sauté pan to a depth of 3 in (7.5 cm) and heat to 375°F (190°C), or until a dab of the chick-pea mixture dropped into the oil begins to color within moments. When the oil is ready, coat the balls with the flour and slip them into the oil; do not crowd the pan. Deep-fry until golden, 3–4 minutes. Using a slotted spoon remove to paper towels to drain briefly, and repeat with the remaining balls.

❀ Tuck the *falafel* into the pita with tomatoes, cucumbers, lettuce and the dressing. Serve at once.

SERVES 8

GREECE

Otapodi Toursi

Marinated Octopus Salad

To guard against the octopus being tough, pound it against a hard surface a few times before cooking. Small octopus may be used in place of a single large one; the cooking time will be reduced. If you like, the sliced fennel or celery can be sautéed in a little olive oil rather than added to the octopus raw. The cooked octopus can also be cut up, threaded onto skewers, drizzled with some of the dressing and grilled or broiled. Serve the skewers with more dressing drizzled over the top and lemon wedges on the side. In Spain the cooked octopus is cut up and sautéed briefly with lots of minced garlic, paprika and red pepper flakes for a dynamic warm tapa. Be sure to bring this octopus salad to room temperature before serving.

1 octopus, about 2 lb (1 kg)
⅓ cup (3 fl oz/80 ml) red wine vinegar
⅔ cup (5 fl oz/160 ml) olive oil
2 tablespoons dried oregano
1 tablespoon finely minced garlic
grated zest of 1 lemon or orange (optional)
salt and freshly ground pepper
4 fennel or celery stalks, thinly sliced
green olives (optional)
chopped fennel fronds (optional)
chopped fresh flat-leaf (Italian) parsley

Octopus is often sold already dressed. If it has not been cleaned, invert it and cut away the mouth, pulling out the viscera along with it. Remove the ink sac as well, then rinse the octopus thoroughly.

Put the octopus in a large, heavy pot without any water; the octopus will give off liquid as it cooks. Cover and cook over low heat, making sure there is always a little liquid in the pot. The octopus will turn bright pink and will give off quite a bit of liquid. Test to see if it is tender after about 1 hour; if not, continue cooking over medium heat until tender when pierced. When ready, remove from the pot and let cool.

Cut the octopus into bite-size pieces. Transfer to a bowl or container. In a small bowl whisk together the vinegar, oil, oregano, garlic, citrus zest (if using), and salt and pepper to taste. Pour this dressing over the octopus. Cover and refrigerate for at least 4 hours or for up to 1 week.

Transfer the octopus and its marinade to a serving dish and bring to room temperature. Serve with the fennel or celery. Garnish with green olives and chopped fennel fronds or parsley, if desired.

SERVES 6

Photograph pages 30–31

ANDALUSIA

Tortillitas de Camarones

Shrimp Fritters

These small, crisp pancakes are a specialty of the city of Cadiz.

1 cup (5 oz/155 g) finely chopped onion
4 tablespoons finely chopped fresh flat-leaf (Italian) parsley
2 tablespoons minced fresh chives
½ lb (250 g) small shrimp (prawns), peeled, deveined and coarsely chopped
grated zest of 1 lemon (optional)
1 cup (5 oz/155 g) all-purpose (plain) flour
⅓ cup (2 oz/60 g) chick-pea (garbanzo bean) flour or additional all-purpose flour
salt and freshly ground pepper
vegetable oil or olive oil for deep-frying
lemon wedges

In a bowl combine the onion, parsley, chives, shrimp, lemon zest (if used), flour(s) and salt and pepper to taste. Stir in just enough water to make a mixture that has the consistency of a thick pancake batter (about 2 cups/16 fl oz/500 ml). Cover and refrigerate for 3 hours.

Pour oil into a deep sauté pan to a depth of ¼–½ in (6–12 mm) and heat to 325°–350°F (165°–180°C), or until a dab of the shrimp mixture sizzles almost immediately upon being dropped into it. When the oil is ready, drop the shrimp mixture by tablespoonfuls into the oil and flatten with a spatula; do not crowd the pan. Fry until golden on the first side, then turn and fry until golden and crisp on the second side, about 3–4 minutes total cooking time. Using a slotted spoon remove to paper towels to drain briefly.

Arrange on a warmed platter and serve at once with lemon wedges.

SERVES 4

ANDALUSIA

Ensalada de Arroz

Rice Salad

Rice salads are served in Spain, Italy and France and are usually embellished with tuna or shellfish. In northern Spain, the Spanish prefer a mayonnaise dressing, but in the south and in southern Italy and France cooks dress the rice with a vinaigrette, which results in a lighter salad. This same salad can be made with ½ pound (250 g) cooked squid, shrimp (prawns) or mussels in place of the tuna. The cooked rice will absorb maximum flavor if tossed with the vinaigrette while still warm.

1 cup (7 oz/220 g) short-grain white rice
1½ cups (12 fl oz/375 ml) water
1 teaspoon salt, plus salt to taste
1 cup (8 fl oz/250 ml) olive oil
½ cup (4 fl oz/125 ml) lemon juice or ⅓ cup (3 fl oz/80 ml) red wine vinegar
2 teaspoons finely minced garlic (optional)
½ cup (2½ oz/75 g) finely minced red (Spanish) onion
¼ cup (1½ oz/45 g) diced pimiento or other red sweet pepper (capsicum)
4 tablespoons chopped fresh flat-leaf (Italian) parsley
1 teaspoon chopped fresh tarragon (optional)
2 teaspoons dried oregano (optional)
freshly ground pepper
1 can (6–7 oz/185–220 g) oil-packed tuna, drained

In a saucepan combine the rice, the water and the 1 teaspoon salt. Bring to a boil, reduce the heat to low, cover and simmer until the rice absorbs the water and is tender, 15–20 minutes. Remove from the heat and transfer to a bowl.

In a small bowl whisk together the oil, lemon juice or vinegar and the garlic, if using. Pour two thirds of the oil mixture over the warm rice and toss to dress evenly. Add the onion, sweet pepper, parsley and the tarragon or oregano, if using. Mix well and season to taste with salt and pepper.

In a bowl combine the tuna and the remaining oil mixture. Toss well and arrange atop the salad. Serve at room temperature.

SERVES 4–6

Top to bottom: Shrimp Fritters, Rice Salad

CATALONIA

Buñuelos de Bacalao

Salt Cod Fritters

The mixture for these tasty fritters can be prepared and refrigerated 4–6 hours in advance. Deep-fry just before serving.

1¼ lb (625 g) boneless salt cod (see glossary)
1 lb (500 g) potatoes, peeled and cut into chunks
1 bay leaf
2 cloves garlic, finely minced
1 cup (8 fl oz/250 ml) water
5 tablespoons (2½ oz/75 g) unsalted butter
1 cup (5 oz/155 g) all-purpose (plain) flour
4 eggs
2 tablespoons chopped fresh flat-leaf (Italian) parsley
salt and freshly ground pepper
vegetable oil or olive oil for deep-frying

In a bowl combine the salt cod and water to cover. Refrigerate for 24–48 hours, changing the water at least 4 times. The amount of soaking necessary will depend upon the saltiness of the cod; thicker pieces may take longer than thinner pieces.

Drain the cod and place in a saucepan with water to cover. Bring to a boil, cover and remove from the heat. Let stand for about 20 minutes, then remove the cod from the water (save the water in the pan) and let cool slightly. Remove all traces of skin and any small bones and shred the cod by hand or with a fork. Set aside.

Add the potatoes and bay leaf to the salt-cod cooking water and bring to a boil. Cook until the potatoes are soft, about 15 minutes. Drain and pass through a ricer or food mill placed over a bowl. Add the salt cod and garlic to the bowl and mix well. Set aside.

In a small saucepan over medium heat, bring the water and butter to a boil. Add the flour all at once and stir well until the mixture forms a ball and pulls away from the sides of the pan, 4–5 minutes.

Transfer the flour mixture to a bowl or to a food processor fitted with the metal blade. Beat in the eggs, one at a time.

Add the egg-flour mixture and parsley to the cod mixture and mix well. Season to taste with salt and pepper.

Clockwise from top: Potato and Onion Omelet, Salt Cod Fritters, Grilled Bread with Tomato

Pour oil into a deep sauté pan to a depth of 3 in (7.5 cm) and heat to 375°F (190°C), or until a dab of the cod mixture sizzles and begins to color immediately upon being dropped into the oil. When the oil is ready, drop the cod mixture by tablespoonfuls into the oil; do not crowd the pan. Deep-fry until golden, 3–4 minutes. Using a slotted spoon remove to paper towels to drain briefly, and repeat until all of the fritters are cooked. Arrange on a warmed platter and serve piping hot.

SERVES 8–10

CATALONIA

Pa amb Tomaquet

Grilled Bread with Tomato

Bruschetta *is the Italian cousin of this Catalan appetizer. Whatever the country, this dish always starts with good-quality bread that is just grilled and then rubbed with garlic and drizzled with fruity olive oil. In summer a fresh ripe tomato is rubbed into the top, or is very finely chopped almost to a purée and then smeared on the bread. Each slice may also be embellished with chopped anchovy or a paper-thin slice of cured ham.*

6 slices country-style bread, about ⅓ in (9 mm) thick
virgin olive oil
2 cloves garlic
2 very ripe tomatoes, halved or very finely chopped
salt and freshly ground pepper

Preheat the broiler (griller) or make a fire in a charcoal grill. Brush one side of bread slice lightly with a little oil and place on a broiler pan or grill rack, oiled side up. Broil or grill, turning to toast both sides, until golden.

While the bread is still hot, rub oiled side with the garlic cloves and tomato halves or chopped tomato. Drizzle with more oil and season to taste with salt and pepper. Serve at once.

SERVES 6

CATALONIA

Tortilla Española

Potato and Onion Omelet

Tortillas *are Spanish omelets. They are thick and firm like an Italian frittata and are served at room temperature, cut into wedges, as part of every tapas selection. This is the classic* tortilla; *you could, if you like, embellish it by mixing 2–4 ounce (60–125 g) diced cured ham into the beaten eggs.*

about ¾ cup (6 fl oz/180 ml) olive oil
4 large baking potatoes, peeled and cut into slices ⅛ in (3 mm) thick
salt and freshly ground pepper
2 onions, thinly sliced
6 eggs

In a large sauté pan over medium heat, warm about 6 tablespoons (3 fl oz/90 ml) of the oil. Add half of the potatoes and cook, turning often, until tender and golden, about 15 minutes. Season to taste with salt and pepper. Using a slotted spatula remove the potatoes to a large bowl. Fry the remaining potatoes in the same manner, season with salt and pepper and remove to the bowl with the first batch.

Add enough oil to any oil remaining in pan to measure about ¼ cup (2 fl oz/60 ml). Add the onions and sauté until they are soft and tender, about 15 minutes. Sprinkle to taste with salt and pepper. Remove with the slotted spatula to the bowl holding the potatoes. Pour off the oil and reserve. Wipe out the pan well. Toss together the onions and potatoes.

Break the eggs into a bowl and beat until blended. Add the eggs to the potatoes. In the same sauté pan over medium heat, warm the reserved oil, adding as much additional oil as needed to measure 3 tablespoons. Pour in the eggs and potatoes. Reduce the heat to low and cook until golden on the bottom, 8–10 minutes. Invert a plate over the pan and, holding the pan and plate together firmly, invert the pan and lift it off. Add 1 or 2 tablespoons oil to the pan and slide the omelet back into the pan, browned side up. Cook until golden brown on the bottom, about 8 minutes.

Slide the omelet out onto a serving platter. Let cool a bit, then cut into wedges to serve.

SERVES 6–8

Marinated Sardines

APULIA

Melanzane in Insalata

Grilled Eggplant Salad

In Calabria, in addition to the mint, the eggplant is sprinkled with minced raw garlic after grilling (do not add any garlic to the oil). If you like, fry the eggplant slices in olive oil rather than grill them.

2 cloves garlic, minced
½ cup (4 fl oz/125 ml) olive oil, or as needed

2 eggplants (aubergines), peeled and cut lengthwise into slices ½–¾ in (12 mm–2 cm) thick
salt and freshly ground pepper
¼ cup (2 fl oz/60 ml) red wine vinegar
chopped fresh mint or fresh flat-leaf (Italian) parsley

Ready a fire in a charcoal grill.

In a small bowl stir the garlic into the oil and brush the eggplant slices on both sides with the oil. Sprinkle on both sides with salt and pepper and then place on the grill rack over medium-hot coals. Grill, turning once, until tender, about 3–5 minutes.

Transfer to a serving platter and sprinkle with the vinegar and the mint or parsley. Serve at room temperature.

SERVES 4

SICILY

Cazzilli

Potato Croquettes

While these potato balls could be served as an accompaniment to a simple dish of grilled meat, they are more often served as a snack. You can use baked potatoes in place of the boiled potatoes; discard the skins before you put them through the ricer. The croquettes can be formed up to 8 hours in advance and refrigerated, and then fried just before serving. Similar croquettes are made in Greece, mizithra *or* kefalotiri *cheese (see glossary) is used in place of the pecorino or Parmesan. In Turkey no herbs or cheese are used in the croquettes, but allspice is added to the potato mixture and a stuffing of lamb, onion and tomato is sometimes tucked in the center.*

2 lb (1 kg) boiling potatoes, peeled and cut into halves or quarters
2 eggs, separated
3 tablespoons chopped fresh flat-leaf (Italian) parsley
⅓ cup (1⅓ oz/45 g) freshly grated pecorino or Parmesan cheese
3–4 tablespoons chopped fresh mint or dill (optional)
¼ cup (¾ oz/20 g) finely minced green (spring) onions (optional)
1 clove garlic, minced (optional)
¼ cup (1¼ oz/40 g) pine nuts (optional)
2 oz (60 g) prosciutto, finely chopped (optional)
salt and freshly ground black pepper
all-purpose (plain) flour for coating
fine dried bread crumbs for coating
vegetable oil for deep-frying

In a saucepan combine the potatoes with water to cover. Bring to a boil, cover, reduce the heat to medium and simmer until tender, 15–20 minutes. Drain well and pass through a ricer or food mill into a bowl. Add the egg yolks, parsley, cheese, the mint or dill, onions, garlic, pine nuts and prosciutto, if using. Mix well. Season to taste with salt and pepper.

Form the potato mixture into 1-in (2.5-cm) balls. Place the flour and bread crumbs in separate shallow bowls. Place the egg whites in a separate shallow bowl and beat lightly. Dip the balls into the flour, then into the egg whites and finally into the crumbs. Place on a rack until ready to fry.

Pour oil into a deep sauté pan to a depth of 3 in (7.5 cm) and heat to 375°F (190°C), or until a dab of the potatoes dropped into the oil begins to color within moments. When the oil is ready, slip the balls into the oil, a few at a time, and fry until golden, about 3–4 minutes. Using a slotted spoon remove to paper towels to drain briefly, and repeat with the remaining balls.

Arrange on a warmed platter and serve at once.

SERVES 6–8

SICILY

Sarde Marinati

Marinated Sardines

Sardines are also served for the appetizer course in Spain and France. This same method can be used for marinating anchovies. Sliced tomatoes and cucumbers, crusty bread and chilled white wine are good accompaniments.

1 lb (500 g) fresh sardines or anchovies
1 teaspoon salt
½–⅔ cup (4–5 fl oz/125–160 ml) white wine vinegar
¼ white onion, thinly sliced or chopped
2 cloves garlic, finely minced
¼ cup (2 fl oz/60 ml) olive oil
2 tablespoons fresh lemon juice
freshly ground pepper
chopped fresh flat-leaf (Italian) parsley

Cut the heads off the fish and discard. Gut the fish, cutting the stomach cavity from the top to tail to free the viscera. Now you must fillet the fish and leave them flattened and opened like a book. To do this, first lay each fish on its stomach and press firmly on its middle. Turn the fish over and lift up and pull out the backbone from the head end, cutting it free at the tail end. Place the fish skin side down in a shallow dish or container. Repeat with the remaining fish.

Sprinkle the fish with the salt, then pour on the vinegar and scatter on the onion and garlic. Cover and refrigerate for about 24 hours.

Remove the fish from the marinade, reserving the onion and garlic. Pat the fish dry with paper towels. Arrange the fish on a shallow serving platter. In a small bowl whisk together the olive oil, lemon juice and pepper to taste. Pour the dressing evenly over the fish. Sprinkle with parsley and top with the reserved onion and garlic. Cover and refrigerate a few hours longer before serving. These will keep for a day or so.

SERVES 6–8

Left to right: Potato Croquettes, Grilled Eggplant Salad

GREECE

SKORDALIA

Garlic Sauce

Skordalia, *a pleasantly pungent garlic sauce, is a staple of the Greek table. Here are two versions. The first combines the garlic with bread crumbs, ground almonds, and olive oil; the second version is made with potatoes. Both sauces can be used as a dressing on cooked beets, cauliflower, green beans, seafood or other popular* meze *offerings. A third garlic sauce, the Sicilian* scurdalia, *is also made with potatoes; it is seasoned with a little hot chili pepper and some poppy seeds.*

FOR *SKORDALIA* MADE WITH BREAD:

3 slices white bread, crusts discarded and bread crumbled (about ½ cup/1 oz/30 g)
1 cup (5½ oz/170 g) almonds, ground
4–6 cloves garlic, minced
salt
¼ cup (2 fl oz/60 ml) red wine vinegar or 3 tablespoons fresh lemon juice
¾–1 cup (6–8 fl oz/180–250 ml) olive oil

In a food processor fitted with the metal blade or in a mortar with a pestle, grind together the bread, almonds, garlic and a little salt until a paste forms. Mix in the vinegar or lemon juice. Then add the oil, a few drops at a time, and process or work by hand until the mixture is thick and creamy and holds its shape when dropped from a spoon. Add only as much oil as is needed to achieve this consistency.

MAKES ABOUT 2½ CUPS (20 FL OZ/625 ML)

FOR *SKORDALIA* MADE WITH POTATOES:

1 lb (500 g) boiling or baking potatoes
4–6 cloves garlic, minced
salt
1 egg yolk (optional)
¼ cup (2 fl oz/60 ml) red wine vinegar
¾–1 cup (6–8 fl oz/180–250 ml) olive oil

If using boiling potatoes, peel them and then boil in water to cover generously until tender; cooking time will depend upon size of potatoes. Drain well. If using baking potatoes, prick the surface with fork tines and then bake in a 400°F (200°C) oven until tender, about 45 minutes. Let cool slightly, then remove the skins. Put the potatoes through a ricer or food mill held over a bowl.

Place the garlic and salt to taste in a mortar and grind with a pestle until a smooth purée forms. Add the garlic paste, the egg yolk, if using, and the vinegar to the potatoes, mixing them thoroughly. Then gradually add the olive oil, a few drops at a time, and beat until thick and creamy. Add only as much oil as is needed to achieve the proper consistency.

MAKES ABOUT 2½ CUPS (20 FL OZ/625 ML)

GREECE

HORIATIKI SALATA

Tomato, Cucumber and Feta Salad

If you've been to Greece, you know this is the one salad that appears on nearly every table. It is simplicity itself and its success is dependent upon sweet, vine-ripened tomatoes, flavorful cucumbers and tangy feta cheese. If you find raw onion too strong for your taste, marinate it in a bit of the dressing for 15 minutes to soften it and temper its bite.

FOR THE DRESSING:

¼ cup (2 fl oz/60 ml) red wine vinegar
½ cup (4 fl oz/125 ml) olive oil
1–2 tablespoons dried oregano
1 clove garlic, finely minced (optional)
salt and freshly ground pepper

FOR THE SALAD:

4 tomatoes, cut into 8 wedges
1 cucumber, peeled and sliced ¼ in (6 mm) thick
2 green sweet peppers (capsicums), seeded, deribbed and thinly sliced crosswise
1 red (Spanish) onion, sliced paper-thin
20 Kalamata olives
½ lb (250 g) feta cheese, coarsely crumbled

About 1 hour before serving the salad, make the dressing. In a small bowl whisk together the vinegar, olive oil, oregano and the garlic, if using. Season to taste with salt and pepper.

Combine all the salad ingredients in a large salad bowl or on individual plates. Drizzle the dressing evenly over the top. Let stand for about 1 hour and then serve.

SERVES 4

Clockwise from top: Tomato, Cucumber and Feta Salad; Garlic Sauce; Pickled Vegetables

GREECE

VEGETABLES À LA GRECQUE

Pickled Vegetables

Why the French title à la grecque *and not the Greek* khoriatiko, *which means "country style"? This cooking term is now known by cooks and diners alike in many countries to mean vegetables—artichokes, carrots, pearl onions, celery, cauliflower, mushrooms—cooked in a fragrant, herb-laced bath of olive oil, wine and water. (If you are cooking trimmed baby artichokes or pared hearts in this fashion, simmer them until the point of a knife pierces them easily, then drain and taste the marinade. If it is bitter, discard it and cover the artichokes with olive oil and lemon juice.) These lightly pickled vegetables are served at room temperature as part of a meze assortment or they are served as a side dish.*

¼ cup (2 fl oz/60 ml) olive oil
2 cups (16 fl oz/500 ml) dry white wine or 1 cup (8 fl oz/250 ml) each dry white wine and water
1 heaping tablespoon cracked coriander seeds
3 bay leaves
1 tablespoon peppercorns, bruised
2 fresh thyme sprigs
4 thin lemon slices
1 clove garlic, smashed
salt

ONE OF THE FOLLOWING VEGETABLES:

1 lb (500 g) pearl onions
1 lb (500 g) carrots, peeled, cut in half lengthwise if thick and cut into 2-in (5-cm) lengths
1 large bunch celery, trimmed and cut into 2-in (5-cm) lengths
4–5 cups (about 1 lb/500 g) cauliflower florets
1 lb (500 g) fresh cultivated button mushrooms, stem ends trimmed
chopped fresh flat-leaf (Italian) parsley

In a saucepan combine the oil, wine (or wine and water), coriander seeds, bay leaves, peppercorns, thyme, lemon slices, garlic and salt to taste. Bring to a boil. Reduce the heat to a simmer. Select one of the vegetables, add it to the pan and cook until just tender. Onions and carrots will take about 20 minutes. Celery and cauliflower will take 4–6 minutes. Mushrooms will take about 3 minutes.

Using a slotted spoon remove the vegetables to a serving bowl. Reduce the marinade by half over high heat; if desired, strain and pour over the vegetables. Sprinkle with the parsley.

Let cool to room temperature, then serve.

SERVES 8

TURKEY

MİDYE TAVASI

Fried Mussels with Tarator Sauce

Tarator *is a general name for nut sauces that are thickened with bread crumbs, usually flavored with garlic and thinned with vinegar or lemon juice. The sauces are popular in Syria and Lebanon as well as Turkey, and while walnut sauces are the most common, almonds, hazelnuts (filberts), pine nuts or pistachios can also be used. In general, walnut and hazelnut sauces are thinned with vinegar, and almond and pine nut sauces are thinned with lemon juice.* Teradot *is a* tarator *made with tahini (see glossary) used in place of the bread crumbs (use 3–4 tablespoons tahini in place of the crumbs in the following recipe and increase the lemon juice to taste).* Tarator *is best made a few hours ahead of serving, to allow the flavors to blend. It thickens upon sitting, however; thin to desired consistency with water.* Tarator *is also delicious on cooked vegetables and fried fish.*

FOR THE *TARATOR* SAUCE:

1 cup (4 oz/125 g) walnuts, toasted and then finely ground
1 tablespoon finely minced garlic
1 cup (2 oz/60 g) fresh bread crumbs
½ cup (4 fl oz/125 ml) olive oil
¼ cup (2 fl oz/60 ml) wine vinegar
salt

FOR THE MUSSELS:

36–40 mussels, scrubbed and debearded
2 cups (16 fl oz/500 ml) water
about 2 cups (10 oz/315 g) all-purpose (plain) flour
salt and freshly ground pepper
2 eggs
1½ cups (12 fl oz/375 ml) water
vegetable oil for deep-frying

To make the sauce, combine all the ingredients except the salt in a food processor fitted with the metal blade or in a blender and process until smooth. (Do not be alarmed if the walnuts tint the sauce a pale purple.) The sauce should be the consistency of thick mayonnaise. If it is too thick, thin with a little water. Season to taste with salt. Cover and set aside for a few hours, if possible, to allow the flavors to blend.

To prepare the mussels, soak 12 bamboo skewers in water for 30 minutes, then drain.

Discard any open mussels that do not close when touched, as they are dead. Combine the mussels and water in a large sauté pan. Cover, place over high heat and steam just until the mussels open. Remove the mussels from the steaming liquid and pull off any beards that may have remained. Discard any mussels that did not open.

Thread about 3 or 4 mussels on each skewer. Spread the flour on a shallow plate or baking pan and season to taste with salt and pepper. Beat the eggs and water together in a shallow bowl.

Left to right: Fried Mussels with Tarator Sauce, Stuffed Grapeleaves, Deep-Fried Eggplant Sandwiches

❀ In a deep sauté pan, pour in oil to a depth of 3 in (7.5 cm) and heat to 375°F (190°C), or until a dab of the egg-water mixture sizzles almost immediately upon being dropped in the oil. When the oil is ready, dip each skewer into the seasoned flour, then into the egg mixture, and then again into the flour. Working in batches, slip the skewers into the hot oil and deep-fry until brown and crisp, about 3 minutes. Using tongs, remove to paper towels to drain briefly, and repeat until all of the mussels are fried.
❀ Serve hot with the *tarator* sauce.

SERVES 4–6

TURKEY

DOLMAS

Stuffed Grapeleaves

The Turkish word dolma *means "to stuff," and* dolmas, *or stuffed grapeleaves, come with two types of filling: rice or meat and rice. The meatless* dolmas *are called* yalanci, *or "liar"* dolmas *because they look like the meat-filled grapeleaves. Rice-stuffed grapeleaves are usually served cold as a first course or as part of a* meze *assortment. They can be accompanied with lemon wedges or dollops of yogurt. The same rice mixture can be used to stuff mussels and vegetables such as peppers (capsicums), eggplants (aubergines), tomatoes and zucchini (courgettes). In Greece, grapeleaves or vegetables with a meat-and-rice filling are served cold as an appetizer or hot as a main course; the latter are often accompanied by* avgolemono *sauce (see glossary). To turn this Turkish rice filling into a meat filling to serve for a first or main course, reduce the rice to ½ cup (3½ oz/110 g), omit the tomatoes and mint or dill, and add ½ pound (250 g) ground (minced) lamb. Turkish cooks often serve these* dolmas *with a seasoned yogurt sauce.*

FOR THE RICE FILLING:

1 cup (7 oz/220 g) long-grain rice
3 tablespoons butter or olive oil
2 onions, chopped
3 cloves garlic, finely minced
½ teaspoon ground cinnamon
½ teaspoon ground allspice
⅔ cup (4 oz/125 g) peeled, seeded and diced tomatoes
½ cup (2½ oz/75 g) pine nuts, toasted
½ cup (3 oz/90 g) dried currants, plumped in hot water to cover and drained
2 tablespoons chopped fresh flat-leaf (Italian) parsley
2 tablespoons chopped fresh mint or dill
salt and freshly ground pepper

FOR PREPARING THE *DOLMAS:*

36 bottled grapeleaves, rinsed of brine, well drained and stemmed
1 cup (8 fl oz/250 ml) olive oil
2–3 tablespoons fresh lemon juice

❀ To make the rice filling, in a bowl combine the rice and water to cover. Let stand for 30 minutes. Drain.
❀ In a sauté pan over medium heat, melt the butter or warm the oil. Add the onions and sauté, stirring occasionally, until tender and translucent, about 10 minutes. Add the garlic, cinnamon and allspice and sauté for 3 minutes. Transfer to a bowl.
❀ Add the drained rice, tomatoes, pine nuts, currants, parsley, mint or dill, salt to taste and a nice amount of pepper. Mix well.
❀ To assemble the *dolmas,* place the grapeleaves on a work surface, smooth sides down. Place a teaspoon or so of the filling near the stem end of the leaf. Fold the stem end over the filling, fold in the sides over the filling and then roll up the leaf into a cylinder. Do not roll too tightly, as the rice will expand in cooking.
❀ Arrange the *dolmas,* seam sides down, in a large, wide sauté pan. Pour the olive oil and the lemon juice over the *dolmas.* Add enough hot water to cover by 1 in (2.5 cm). Weight down with 1 or more plates. Bring to a boil, cover, reduce the heat to very low and cook until the filling is cooked, 45–50 minutes.
❀ Alternatively, to bake in an oven, preheat the oven to 300°F (150°C). Prepare the *dolmas* as directed up to the point where they are covered, then place in the oven and bake until the filling is cooked, 45–60 minutes.
❀ Uncover the pan immediately so the *dolmas* cool quickly, then transfer to platters as soon as possible. Cover and refrigerate for up to 3 days before serving. Bring to room temperature at serving time.

MAKES 36 *DOLMAS*

TURKEY

PATLICAN BÖREGI

Deep-Fried Eggplant Sandwiches

Although traditionally served as appetizers, these cheese-filled sandwiches can also be offered as a vegetable accompaniment to a main course. The Italian version of this dish omits the oven step. The slices, which are cut thinner, are salted, drained and filled with slices of prosciutto and provolone before frying. Parmesan cheese is added to the bread-crumb coating.

3 small eggplants (aubergines), about ½ lb (250 g) total weight, peeled and cut crosswise into slices ½ in (12 mm) thick
olive oil
salt and freshly ground pepper
6 oz (185 g) *kasseri* (see glossary) or Monterey jack cheese, grated
6 oz (185 g) feta cheese, crumbled
3 eggs
2 tablespoons chopped fresh flat-leaf (Italian) parsley
1 tablespoon chopped fresh dill
1 cup (5 oz/155 g) all-purpose (plain) flour
1½ cups (6 oz/185 g) fine dried bread crumbs
vegetable oil for deep-frying

❀ Preheat an oven to 400°F (200°C). Place the eggplant slices on oiled baking sheets and brush them with oil. Sprinkle to taste with salt and pepper and bake until almost cooked through, about 15 minutes. Let cool.
❀ In a bowl combine the cheeses, 1 of the eggs, parsley and dill. Place a heaping spoonful of filling on half the eggplant slices. Top with a second slice about the same size, then press together. Place the flour and bread crumbs in separate shallow bowls. Break the remaining 2 eggs into another shallow bowl and beat lightly. Dip the eggplant sandwiches first in the flour, then in the egg, and finally in the bread crumbs, coating evenly. Place on a rack or a baking sheet lined with parchment paper. Let stand for 1 hour. (Or refrigerate for as long as overnight; bring the eggplant sandwiches to room temperature before frying.)
❀ Pour oil into a deep sauté pan to a depth of 3 in (7.5 cm) and heat to 375°F (190°C), or until a bit of bread dropped into the oil begins to color within moments. When the oil is ready, slip in the sandwiches, a few at a time for about 2 minutes. Using a slotted spoon lift out the sandwiches and let them rest for 1 minute to melt the cheese, then return them to the oil, top side down, to fry until golden, about 2 minutes longer. Using a slotted spoon remove to paper towels to drain briefly, and repeat with the remaining sandwiches.
❀ Arrange on a warmed serving platter. Cut in half and serve at once.

SERVES 8

T U R K E Y

MİDYE DOLMASI

Stuffed Mussels

Essentially, this popular meze *is a type of* dolma, *but instead of stuffing the rice mixture into a vegetable or vine leaf, the filling is put into mussel shells. This same filling can be used for stuffing hollowed-out tomatoes, eggplants (aubergines) and sweet peppers (capsicums); use water or stock in place of the mussel liquid. Most recipes call for prying open raw mussels. It is easier to steam the mussels just until they open and then spoon the rice filling over the barely steamed mussel. Allow about 5 mussels per person as these are rather rich.*

30–40 mussels, scrubbed and debearded
3 or 4 cups (24 or 32 fl oz/750 ml or 1 l) water
1 teaspoon salt

FOR THE FILLING:
¾ cup (6 fl oz/180 ml) olive oil
4 onions, chopped
¼ cup (1¼ oz/40 g) pine nuts, toasted
1 cup (7 oz/220 g) long-grain white rice
2 or 3 small tomatoes, peeled, seeded and diced
¼ cup (1½ oz/45 g) dried currants, plumped in hot water and drained
1 tablespoon sugar (optional)
½ teaspoon ground cinnamon
¼ teaspoon ground allspice
1 cup (8 fl oz/250 ml) liquid from steaming mussels
salt and freshly ground pepper

❁ Discard any open mussels that do not close when touched, as they are dead.
❁ Combine the mussels, 2 cups (16 fl oz/500 ml) of the water and the salt in a large sauté pan. Cover, place over high heat

Clockwise from left: Orange, Onion and Olive Salad, Stuffed Mussels, Pomegranate and Walnut Paste

and steam just until the mussels open. Remove the mussels from the steaming liquid, reserving the liquid. Pull off any beards that may have remained. Discard any mussels that did not open. Strain the steaming liquid through a sieve with cheesecloth (muslin). Set the mussels and liquid aside.

❀ To make the filling, in a large sauté pan over medium heat, warm the oil. Add the onions and sauté until soft, 10–15 minutes. Add the pine nuts and rice and cook for 10 minutes, stirring occasionally. Add the currants, sugar (if using), cinnamon, allspice, the reserved mussel liquid, and salt and pepper to taste. Cover and simmer over low heat for 10 minutes or so, then remove from the heat. Let the mixture stand, covered, for 15 minutes. Mix well, then adjust the seasoning.

❀ Place a spoonful of the filling in each mussel, separating the shells just enough to slip in a small spoon. Do not overstuff the shell as the filling will continue to cook. Place the mussels back in the sauté pan, or in 2 pans, as these mussels cook best in a single layer. If using 1 pan, pour the remaining 1 cup (8 fl oz/250 ml) water into it; if using 2 pans, pour 1 cup (8 fl oz/250 ml) into each pan. Weight the mussels down with a plate or lid, cover and cook over gentle heat until the rice is tender and the flavors have blended, 20–30 minutes.

❀ Remove from the heat and transfer to a serving platter. Serve at room temperature.

SERVES 6–8

TURKEY

MUHAMMARAH

Pomegranate and Walnut Paste

A common dish on the Turkish meze *table, this purée is also a delicious, spicy dip for cooked meats and fish. Syrian cooks prepare a similar dish. If pomegranate syrup is unavailable, substitute lemon juice. Serve with pita bread (recipe on page 82).*

1 tablespoon coarsely ground dried red chili pepper
1 teaspoon ground cumin
1½ cups (6 oz/185 g) walnuts, toasted
½ cup (2 oz/60 g) fine dried bread crumbs
¼ cup (2 fl oz/60 ml) olive oil
2 tablespoons pomegranate syrup (see glossary)
pinch of sugar
salt
¼ cup (2 fl oz/60 ml) tomato purée (optional)
½ teaspoon ground allspice (optional)
2 red sweet peppers (capsicums), roasted, peeled, seeded, and puréed (optional; see glossary)
chopped fresh flat-leaf (Italian) parsley

❀ In a food processor or blender, combine the chili pepper, cumin, nuts, bread crumbs, olive oil, pomegranate syrup, sugar, salt to taste, and the tomato purée, allspice, and sweet peppers, if using. Purée until smooth. Alternatively, pound the walnuts to a paste in a mortar and pestle, then mix in the other ingredients.

❀ Spoon into a small bowl and garnish with parsley. Chill until ready to serve.

SERVES 4–6

TURKEY

PORTOKAL SALATASI

Orange, Onion and Olive Salad

This salad, with minor variations, also appears in Greece, Sicily, Spain and North Africa. Sometimes mint, lemon balm, dill and parsley are chopped and strewn on top at the last minute. A popular Moroccan salad calls for lightly brushing the orange slices with olive oil mixed with fresh lemon juice and then sprinkling them with cinnamon and orange-flower water.

2 large oranges
1 red (Spanish) onion, sliced paper-thin
1 cup (4–5 oz/125–155 g) sharply flavored black olives, pitted
olive oil
pinch of cayenne pepper (optional)

❀ Peel the oranges and remove all the white pith. Slice the oranges crosswise into slices ⅛ in (3 mm) thick. Use a knife tip to remove all seeds.

❀ On a shallow serving dish, layer the orange slices and then top with the onion. Let sit for 30 minutes. Sprinkle with the olives and drizzle on a thin stream of olive oil. If you like, dust lightly with cayenne, then serve.

SERVES 4

AU MAL ASSIS
CHANGE-EXCHANGE
SAN PIETRO

FRANCE

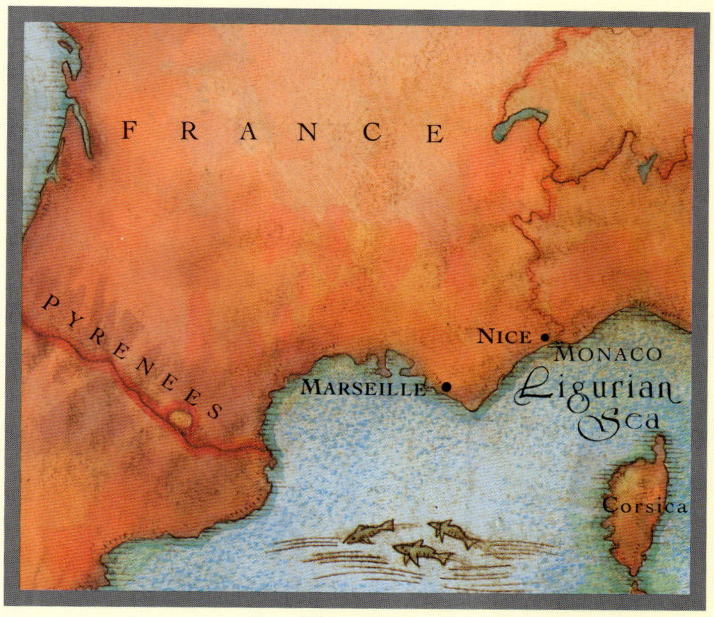

FRANCE

Roussillon,
Languedoc, Provence

If national cuisines correspond to languages, regional culinary styles may legitimately be compared to dialects. These two forms of differentiation sometimes coincide completely or overlap; the south of France is a case in point. As every aspiring Francophile is quick to learn, the Languedoc (from *langue d'oc*) is supposedly the region where *yes* is rendered as *oc,* in contrast to the realm of *langue d'oil,* the lands where *oil* signify affirmation. Even when first put forward by Dante, this classification was somewhat imprecise, for reasons that need not detain us here. It is nonetheless true that the historic provinces of Languedoc and Provence speak even today the distinct idiom that is known as Provençal. The domain of Provençal is also home to a cuisine that is more frequently eulogized than any other in the Mediterranean; in 1919, a certain Madame Daudet even suggested that the cooking of Provence is "the best of all cooking." What is certain is that it exhibits in high measure all the main characteristics of Mediterranean cuisine.

The separate identity of the south, in both linguistic and culinary terms, is particularly evident at its western

Previous pages: The picturesque Côte d'Azur, dotted with charming villages, meanders from the mouth of the Rhône to Italy.
Left: The austere simplicity of this facade in St. Cannat is characteristic of the architecture of many villages in southern France.

and eastern extremities. Languedoc was incorporated into France as early as the thirteenth century, but Roussillon, bordering on Catalonia, was acquired from Spain by Louis XIV in 1659; even today it remains resolutely Catalan in speech and cuisine. The county of Nice was joined to France as late as 1860, after five centuries of rule by the House of Savoy; it is not surprising that much Italian is still spoken there and that its version of the Provençal diet includes pasta dishes such as *cannelloni, ravioli* and *gnocchi*.

The ancient trans-Mediterranean connections of the French south have been equally important. The Greeks founded many of its most important cities: in Languedoc, Agde and Nîmes; and in Provence, Marseilles, Nice and Antibes. All except Nîmes were ports (although Agde now lies two and a half miles inland), and the maritime orientation of the south, with all that implied for trade and cuisine, was thus set two and half millennia ago. It was the Greeks, too, who endowed the region with that foremost essential of the Mediterranean diet, the olive, and who must be regarded as the progenitors of the legendary *bouillabaisse*. The Romans were so attached to the area that they regarded it as a province, not a colony—hence the name of Provence—and as a token of their attachment they drained the marshes of the Rhône Valley, making it an important center for cattle breeding

The sweeping field of lavender surrounding an old farm structure known as a mas *is a quintessential Provençal landscape.*

and dairy farming. They also added Narbonne in Languedoc to the complement of the south's ports and introduced apiculture to its hinterland.

After the silting up and gradual inland retreat of its ports, Languedoc was culturally and economically overshadowed by neighboring Provence. But in its heyday, Montpellier, now separated from the Mediterranean by several kilometers of flat land and a saltwater lagoon, was France's chief trader with the East, a role that Marseilles came to inherit. Montpellier was, indeed, purveyor of spices to the whole country, and the centrality of this trade to the city's prosperity is mirrored even in the derivation of its name, from Monspistillarius, Mount of the Spice Merchants. Highly seasoned foods remain popular in Languedoc, not only, perhaps, because of this mercantile past but also thanks to Arab influences emanating from Spain; Charles Martel notwithstanding, the Arabs occupied Narbonne for several decades and used it as a base for raids on Avignon in 734 and Lyons in 743. Significant, too, is that the preoccupation with spices and their properties led, in accordance with Greco-Arab precedent, to the study of medicine and ultimately to the establishment of the University of Montpellier. Aside from spices, there is no trace of possible Arab culinary influence on Languedoc other than its rich, flaky pastries.

Languedoc is less integrally Mediterranean than Provence. It reaches up to Lyons in the north and borders on Gascony in the east; the coastal area represents a fairly small proportion of its total surface. The counts of Toulouse, resident in a thoroughly non-Mediterranean city, seem to have had as much influence on the cuisine of Languedoc as the spice merchants of Montpellier, and it should come as no surprise that butter and animal fat take the place of olive oil throughout the province. The Provençal combination of tomato and eggplant, beloved of almost all Mediterranean cuisines, does not much appeal to the folk of Languedoc, except as an accompaniment to fish.

The pride and joy of Languedoc cuisine is, of course, *cassoulet*, a stew combining various meats—of which pork must always be one—with white beans. The essential varieties of *cassoulet* are reducible to three: that of Castelnaudry, where generous portions of ham are joined to the pork; that of Carcassonne, which favors the inclusion of hunks of mutton; and that of Toulouse, which preaches the compatibility of goose and/or duck with the pork and is also open to the use of mutton. The only historical note relevant here is that fava (broad) beans were used before haricot beans arrived from the New World by way of northern Italy.

After Paris, Provence is perhaps the region of France best known to and beloved of foreigners; for fogbound northern Europeans, the simple phrase "the south of France"—by which they mean Provence—is redolent of bright color, ease and aesthetic enjoyment. This image is not without justification, and it is for good reason that so many painters made their homes in Provence. But the picture should be modified by awareness of the annual hardship induced by the blowing of the fierce, dry northerly mistral, and of the variation of terrain among the coast, the valley of the Rhône, and the area around Aix en Provence. Even the Mediterranean littoral is not a

Annual celebrations in which the residents wear the regional costumes of Arles, in southern France, signify local pride in a long and colorful history.

uniform whole; the lack of a coastal road until comparatively recent times made each major port a world of its own, dependent on shipping for its communications with the outside. The cuisine of Provence is correspondingly more diverse than is sometimes imagined.

The factors of unity within this diversity are easily identified. First comes the combination of olive oil, garlic and tomato into the *sauce provençale,* the mere addition of which to a dish qualifies it for the description *à la provençale.* Highly typical for Provençal cuisine is also the abundant use of herbs; their profusion in the region is mythically ascribed to King Balthazar, one of the Magi, who generously scattered them on the ground as he passed through the region. Ratatouille is but the best-known example of the Provençal fondness for vegetables—tomatoes, artichokes, eggplants and bell peppers, in order of importance. Finally, Provence is noteworthy for the full exploitation of the seafood that still proliferates all along the coast, from Marseilles to Menton.

The most renowned dish of Provence is without doubt *bouillabaisse,* a fish chowder available in numerous local varieties. The comparative merits of these distinct efforts are as hotly disputed as those of the rival versions of *cassoulet* in neighboring Languedoc. The origins of *bouillabaisse* have been credibly ascribed to the Greeks, who typically enough enshrined its genesis in a tale of adultery among the gods: Venus is said to have concocted the first *bouillabaisse,* lacing it generously with supposedly soporific saffron; after her husband Volcan had drunk deeply enough of it, she sneaked off for a rendezvous with Mars. Given the Greek antecedents of the city, *bouillabaisse* supremacy might as well be awarded to Marseilles. The version produced there calls for a combination of soft- and firm-fleshed fish, onions and tomatoes, and a lengthy list of seasonings, which of course includes saffron.

Provence is more distant from Spain than is Languedoc, and Villefranche was the only settlement occupied by the Arabs, and that, quite briefly. One might nonetheless hope to discern an Arab influence on Provençal cuisine corresponding to the inspiration the troubadours derived from the poetry of Muslim Spain. Provence is certainly indebted to the agricultural enterprise of the Muslims for some of the vegetables fundamental to its cuisine, and also for the rice that is still grown in the Rhône Delta region known as the Camargue, but no particular dish seems attributable to an Arab forebear. It is nonetheless curious to note that Rabelais speaks of *coscoton à la moresque* being eaten in sixteenth-century Provence. Were, perhaps, other dishes of Arab origin also once popular? Thanks to the presence of a large community of North African immigrants, couscous is now available anew in Marseilles, but the intermingling of its aromas with the scent of *bouillabaisse* is evidence not so much of culinary continuity as of the unceasing migration of peoples and their cultures that typifies the Mediterranean.

BREADS AND SAVORY PASTRIES

The art of making leavened bread was reputedly discovered in ancient Egypt, where wheat grew in abundance.

BREADS AND SAVORY PASTRIES

In recent years a greater appreciation for rustic country breads has developed. Their rich flavor, texture and versatility have been discovered and the tasteless white, airy bread that has been the staple at many markets is being passed by. A "bread revolution" is going on and restaurants and small bakeries are feeding the hunger for good bread made with whole grains.

Muslim women make loaves of bread in front of a wall depicting the pilgrimage to Mecca.

What is new to many of us is very old indeed, however. Along with grains such as rice, pasta, bulgur (cracked wheat) and couscous, rustic breads form the basis of the daily Mediterranean diet. There is never a meal without bread. In fact, a meal might be only bread with a little cheese and tomato. Bread is baked fresh daily and because it has no preservatives, must be eaten as quickly as possible. It is made with flavorful unbleached whole-grain flours—wheat, corn, rye—and occasionally embellished with nuts, olives and herbs. Sweetened or egg-enriched breads, such as challah, and those made with refined flours are served on special occasions and are usually associated with holidays.

Butter rarely accompanies bread on the Mediterranean table. Nor is bread commonly served with a dish of olive oil for dipping, as is often the case in restaurants serving Mediterranean cuisine outside the region, unless, of course, one is trying to judge the quality of the oil and bread is the neutral vehicle. Bread is, however, ideal for sopping up oil or pan juices on a dinner plate and occasionally, in the instance of pizza, *pitta, scacciata,* and *focaccia,* it can be the plate.

The stove with oven below is a relatively new appliance in the Mediterranean home. Sometimes families built an outdoor brick beehive oven for bread baking. But more often, people delivered their bread (and casseroles) to the village baker for cooking in the wood-burning oven. In most Moroccan homes, the bread was kneaded

Previous pages: Bread of Apulia (recipe page 77)

in a large unglazed red clay pan called a *gsaa* and then sent, usually carried on the head of a child, to the community oven. The loaves of each family were identified with a wooden stamp.

In the eastern Mediterranean, bread is sacred—a gift from God. If one sees a piece of bread lying on the ground, one picks it up, kisses it and puts it in a safe place. The bakers' guilds in Ottoman Turkey had Adam as their patron saint and believed that the Archangel Gabriel taught him how to make dough after the expulsion from the Garden of Eden. To the ancient Greeks it was *artos,* from *artio,* "to flavor." In Greek the word for cook is *mageiras,* which takes its root from *maza,* "that which is kneaded." The goddess of bread was Demeter, goddess of the earth, family and property. In Italy there is the expression *Senza il pane tutta diventa orfano*—"Without bread everyone is an orphan."

Because bread is the staff of life and has sacramental associations, it is never wasted. A few crusts become the thickener for soup; the crumbs become the base for a sauce like *skordalia* or *rouille.* Leftover bread is cut into croutons for soup or salad; in *panzanella* or *fattoush,* bread is the heart of the salad and not just a garnish.

Often bread is grilled, then brushed simply with olive oil and rubbed with a clove of garlic or a cut tomato. Or it might be spread with a paste like *tapénade* or eggplant (aubergine) or bean purée. Bread chunks are threaded onto skewers between pieces of meat to absorb the juices, or small pieces are folded over and used to grasp meat or vegetables off of a plate. Some breads such as Sardinian *carta di musica* are traditionally dried for long-term storage and for carrying on journeys, and later revived, softened by a quick dampening with water.

Another crucial element of the Mediterranean diet is the vast repertoire of traditional savory pastries. These may be made with yeast dough, flaky or short pastry, or *filo* sheets, and they are an important part of the regional menu. The smaller ones like Syrian *sambusak,* Lebanese *fatayeer* and *sbanik bil ajin,* North African *briks;* Greek *tiropetes;* Turkish *böreks;* and Spanish *empanadas* are baked or deep-fried and usually are served as appetizers or snacks. Larger pastries can be meals in themselves, however. The Moroccan *b'stilla,* a sweet and savory pigeon-and-almond pie; the Greek *pitta;* vegetable pies such as *spanokopita* and *prassopita;* chicken-filled *kotopitta;* and various lamb pies are all substantial courses. Similar pies, called *peda* in Albania and *börek* in Turkish cuisine, are filled with meat, eggs, cheese and vegetables and are given the same reverent attention at table.

Along with olive oil and wine, bread is part of the quintessential Mediterranean trinity.

In a scene unaltered by centuries of farming, Turkish workers labor intensively to harvest wheat by hand.

Mastering the preparation of these pies is an art. Young women learn how to roll out paper-thin dough, *filo* (called *yufka* in Turkey, and *phyllo* in Greece) on a special round table with a thin dowel called an *oklava* in Turkey. To see them roll out a perfect round eighteen to twenty-four inches in diameter every time is a little daunting for those of us who still struggle to turn out a simple nine-inch pie crust. These large pies are baked in special heavy-duty brass pans called *tapsi* in Greece. Cooks not skilled in dough rolling may use packaged *filo* dough to produce a satisfactory interpretation of these pies.

The Greek word *pitta,* for savory pie, carried over into Italian cuisine and eventually it evolved into *pizza,* but in Calabria and Apulia these pies have retained the old name. Other double-crusted pies are made in Sicily. *Cocas* are the Catalan version of the single-crusted Italian pizza and come with a variety of toppings, while the double-crusted pies in Spain are called *empanadas* and can be large or small. They too come with an impressive repertoire of fillings. Although one may try to find a clear cultural connection to link all of these filled pastries, what they mainly have in common is peasant ingenuity and thriftiness: the use of dough to enclose small bits of leftover foods in the case of little pastries, and in the larger versions, making simple and inexpensive dishes seem more festive and special.

CALABRIA/SICILY/APULIA

SCACCIATA

Double-Crusted Pizza

Apulia, Calabria and Sicily were invaded by the Greeks, who left their culinary imprint on the food. Some of the double-crusted pies served there today are still called by the original Greek name, pitta. *Two fillings are provided here, one a classic tomato, tuna and olive mixture from Calabria and the second a simple blend of fresh and salted ricotta cheeses.*

FOR THE BASIC PIZZA DOUGH:

2½ teaspoons yeast
1¼ cups (10 fl oz/310 ml) warm water (110°F/43°C)
3½ cups (17½ oz/545 g) semolina flour
1 teaspoon salt
3 tablespoons olive oil

FOR THE TOMATO-AND-TUNA FILLING:

5 tablespoons (3 fl oz/80 ml) olive oil
2 lb (1 kg) tomatoes, peeled, seeded and chopped
3 tablespoons chopped garlic
6 anchovy fillets in oil, drained and chopped
3 tablespoons chopped fresh flat-leaf (Italian) parsley
½ cup (2½ oz/75 g) pitted sharply flavored black olives, chopped
1 tablespoon capers, rinsed and drained
5 oz (155 g) oil-packed canned white tuna

FOR THE RICOTTA FILLING:

1 rounded cup (9 oz/280 g) fresh ricotta cheese
½ cup (2 oz/60 g) grated salted ricotta cheese
¼ lb (125 g) salami, chopped
3 hard-cooked eggs, chopped

olive oil for brushing on pizza

To make the dough, in a small bowl, dissolve the yeast in ½ cup (4 fl oz/125 ml) of the warm water and let stand until bubbly, about 5 minutes.

In a large mixing bowl, stir together the flour and salt. Add the yeast mixture, the remaining ¾ cup (6 fl oz/180 ml) warm water and the oil and beat in well. Mix until the dough leaves the sides of the bowl clean. Using an electric mixer fitted with a dough hook, knead at medium speed until the dough is smooth and elastic, about 5 minutes. Alternatively, turn out the dough onto a lightly floured work surface and knead until smooth and elastic, about 10 minutes. Form the dough into a ball and place in an oiled bowl. Turn the ball to coat all surfaces with oil. Cover and let rise in a warm place until doubled in bulk, 45–60 minutes.

Preheat an oven to 450°F (230°C).

Meanwhile, make one of the fillings. To make the tomato-and-tuna filling, in a large sauté pan over medium heat, warm 3 tablespoons of the oil. Add the tomatoes and garlic and cook until thickened and most of the liquid evaporates, about 5 minutes. Set aside to cool. In a small sauté pan over medium heat, warm the remaining 2 tablespoons oil. Add the anchovies and stir for a moment or two. Then add the parsley, olives, capers and tuna fish, stir well and remove from the heat. Set aside.

To make the ricotta filling, assemble all of the ingredients.

Punch down the dough. Divide the dough in half. On a lightly floured surface, roll out half of the dough large enough to line the bottom and sides of a shallow, round 12-in (30-cm) baking pan or a shallow, rectangular 9-by-12-in (23-by-30-cm) baking pan. Carefully transfer the dough to the pan and press it in gently.

If using the tomato-and-tuna filling, spoon the reserved tomato mixture into the dough-lined pan. Top with the tuna mixture. If using the cheese filling, form a layer of the fresh ricotta in the dough-lined pan, then top with layers of the grated ricotta, salami and finally the chopped egg.

Roll out the remaining dough in the same manner and transfer to the top of the pie. Pinch the edges together to seal securely and trim away any excess dough. Brush the top lightly with oil. Bake until the crust is golden, about 15 minutes. Serve hot, cut into squares or wedges.

SERVES 6–8

LEBANON

FATAYEER SBANIKH

Spinach Pies

These savory pastries would make good luncheon "sandwiches" or picnic fare or can be made smaller and served as an hors d'oeuvre. They can be made a few hours ahead of time and reheated in a 350°F (180°C) oven for 5 minutes.

FOR THE DOUGH:

1 tablespoon active dry yeast
¾ cup (6 fl oz/180 ml) warm water (110°F/43°C)
2½ cups (12½ oz/390 g) all-purpose (plain) flour
1½ teaspoons salt
1 tablespoon olive oil

FOR THE FILLING:

1 lb (500 g) spinach
1 teaspoon salt, plus salt to taste
2 tablespoons olive oil
1 cup (5 oz/155 g) finely chopped onion
1 teaspoon ground allspice
6 tablespoons (2 oz/60 g) pine nuts, toasted
¼ cup (2 fl oz/60 ml) fresh lemon juice
3 tablespoons chopped fresh mint
½ teaspoon freshly ground pepper

olive oil for brushing on pies

To make the dough, in a small bowl, dissolve the yeast in the warm water and let stand until bubbly, about 5 minutes.

In a large bowl stir together the flour and salt. Add the yeast mixture and oil, mix well and knead briefly on a lightly floured work surface until smooth and elastic.

Shape the dough into a ball and place in an oiled bowl. Turn the ball to coat all surfaces with oil. Cover the bowl with a damp kitchen towel or plastic wrap and let rise in a warm place until almost doubled in bulk, about 1½ hours.

Meanwhile, make the filling. Stem the spinach, chop coarsely, and wash well to remove all traces of sand. Drain well, place in a colander and sprinkle with 1 teaspoon of salt. Let stand for 1 hour. Squeeze all moisture out of the spinach and then chop finely.

In a large sauté pan over medium heat, warm the oil. Add the onion and sauté until tender and translucent, 8–10 minutes. Add the allspice, stir well and cook for 1 minute longer. Stir in the chopped spinach and cook, stirring occasionally, until the spinach wilts, a few minutes. Stir in the pine nuts, lemon juice, mint, salt to taste and pepper. Remove from the heat.

Preheat an oven to 400°F (200°C). Lightly oil a baking sheet.

Punch down the dough and divide it into 12 equal portions. On a lightly floured work surface, roll out each portion into a 6-in (15-cm) round. Spoon about ⅓ cup (2½ oz/75 g) of the spinach mixture into the center of each round. Bring up the three edges of the round to meet in the center and press together to seal. The pastries will be triangular.

Place on the prepared baking sheet. Brush the pastries with oil. Bake until golden, 15–20 minutes. Remove from the oven and brush the tops with olive oil. Serve warm.

MAKES 12 PIES

Photograph pages 8–9

Double Crusted Pizza

Left to right: Corn Bread, Olive Bread

CYPRUS

ELIOPITA

Olive Bread

Olives and onions form the stuffing for this upscale Cypriot country bread. Use flavorful oil-cured olives and pit them yourself. This is easy to do: Spread out the olives on a baking sheet or work surface and smash them with a meat mallet. The dough, minus the filling, can be shaped into a long, slender loaf or into a ring, brushed with water, sprinkled with sesame seeds and baked. In Turkey, 5 tablespoons chopped fresh mint is added to the olive mixture.

3 cups (15 oz/470 g) all-purpose (plain) flour
1 tablespoon active dry yeast
1 cup (8 fl oz/250 ml) warm water (110°F/43°C)
2 teaspoons sugar
1 teaspoon salt
4 tablespoons (2 fl oz/60 ml) olive oil, plus olive oil for brushing on loaf
¾ cup (3½ oz/105 g) finely chopped onion
1¼ cups (6 oz/185 g) green or black olives, pitted and coarsely chopped

Sift the flour into a bowl. In a large mixing bowl dissolve the yeast in ¼ cup (2 fl oz/60 ml) of the warm water and let stand until bubbly, about 5 minutes. Then stir in the remaining warm water, the sugar and salt. Add about 1 cup (5 oz/155 g) of the flour and stir well. Cover with a kitchen towel or plastic wrap and let stand in a warm place until frothy, about 30 minutes.

Beat in the remaining sifted flour, then add 2 tablespoons of the oil. Using an electric mixer fitted with a dough hook, knead for about 5 minutes on medium speed. Continue to knead on medium speed until smooth and satiny, about 10 minutes longer. Alternatively, beat in the remaining flour and the 2 tablespoons oil by hand and turn out the dough onto a floured work surface. Knead until smooth and satiny, about 15 minutes.

Form the dough into a ball and place in an oiled bowl. Turn the ball to coat all surfaces with oil. Cover the bowl with a damp kitchen towel or plastic wrap and let rise in a warm place until doubled in bulk, about 1 hour.

Meanwhile, in a sauté pan over medium heat, warm the remaining 2 tablespoons oil. Add the onion and sauté until tender and translucent, 8–10 minutes. Transfer to a bowl and add the olives. Mix well and set aside.

Punch down the dough and turn it out onto a floured work surface. Press out into a rectangle about ½ in (12 mm) thick. Spread onion-and-olive mixture over the surface of the dough, leaving a 1-in (2.5-cm) border along all sides. Starting from a long side, roll up the dough, shaping it into an oblong loaf. Press ends to seal. Place on an oiled baking sheet and cut 4 shallow diagonal slashes in the top of the bread. Cover with a kitchen towel and let rise again until doubled in bulk, about 1 hour.

Meanwhile, preheat an oven to 375°–400°F (190°–200°C). Lightly brush the top of the loaf with oil. Bake until golden and the bread sounds hollow when the bottom is tapped, 35–45 minutes. Let cool on a wire rack and serve warm or at room temperature.

MAKES 1 OBLONG LOAF

GREECE

PRASSOPITTA

Leek Pie

This rich leek-and-cheese pie can also be found on tables in Greece, Albania and other Balkan countries. Some versions omit the tomatoes, use the sharper feta and kefalotiri *cheeses (but only ½ lb/250 g) and season the leeks with nutmeg and allspice. This dish can also be served in smaller portions as a first course.*

10 leeks
6 tablespoons (3 oz/90 g) unsalted butter, plus ½ cup (4 oz/125 g) unsalted butter, melted and cooled, or as needed
2 tablespoons finely chopped fresh dill
2 cloves garlic, finely minced
2 cups peeled, seeded and chopped tomatoes
4 eggs
1 lb (500 g) ricotta or *mizithra* cheese (see glossary)
1 lb (500 g) *filo* sheets (see glossary)
salt and freshly ground pepper
½ teaspoon freshly grated nutmeg (optional)

Cut the leeks in half lengthwise and wash well to remove all traces of sand. Cut crosswise into thin slices including some of the pale green, tender tops. You'll want 3–4 cups (9–12 oz/280–375 g).

In a large sauté pan over medium heat, melt the 6 tablespoons (3 oz/90 g) butter. Add the leeks and sauté until softened, about 10 minutes. Add the dill, garlic and tomatoes and simmer until all the liquid evaporates and the leeks are tender, 10–15 minutes. Remove from the heat and let cool slightly.

In a bowl beat the eggs until blended. Mix in the cheese and then the leek mixture. Season to taste with salt and pepper and add the nutmeg (if using). Butter a 9-by-13-by-3-in (23-by-33-by-7.5-cm) baking pan. Lay about 10 *filo* sheets in the pan, lightly brushing each one with melted butter before adding the next. Spoon the leek mixture atop the *filo* and spread it evenly. Lay the remaining *filo* sheets on top, brushing each one with butter before adding the next. Cover and refrigerate for a few hours.

Preheat an oven to 375°F (190°C). Using a sharp knife, score the top few sheets into 12 large or 24 small squares. Bake until golden, 30–40 minutes. Let rest for 5–10 minutes, then cut into squares and serve warm.

SERVES 8–10 *Photograph pages 78–79*

TURKEY

MISIR EKMEĞLİ

Corn Bread

Another similar Balkan corn bread uses 1 cup (8 fl oz/250 ml) sour cream in place of most of the yogurt, 1 or 2 more eggs (the eggs are separated and the whites are beaten and folded in) and adds grated sheep's milk cheese. This bread, which is from the Black Sea region, keeps well for a few days wrapped in aluminum foil.

¾ cup (4 oz/125 g) all-purpose (plain) flour
2 teaspoons sugar
2 teaspoons baking powder
1½ teaspoons salt
1 cup (5 oz/155 g) fine-grind yellow cornmeal
1 whole egg plus 1 egg yolk
1¾ cups (14 oz/440 g) yogurt
3 tablespoons olive oil

Preheat an oven to 425°F (220°C). Butter a 5-by-9-by-3-in (13-by-23-by-7.5-cm) loaf pan.

Sift together the flour, sugar, baking powder and salt into a large bowl. Stir in the cornmeal. In another bowl whisk together the whole egg, egg yolk and yogurt; stir in the olive oil. Gradually and slowly incorporate the wet ingredients into the flour mixture, stirring constantly. Beat until well blended and smooth, but do not overmix.

Pour the batter into the prepared loaf pan. Bake until the top is golden, 20–30 minutes. Remove from the oven and let rest in the pan for 5 minutes, then turn out onto a rack to cool completely.

MAKES 1 LOAF

APULIA

PANE PUGLIESE

Bread of Apulia

I owe this recipe to well-known food scholar and author Carol Field. It appears in her excellent book, The Italian Baker, *and she advises that it be made in an electric mixer because the dough is quite wet and sticky and there is a danger it will absorb too much flour if kneaded by hand. If you like, add ½ pound (250 g) pitted small black olives after the dough has been mixed.*

1¼ teaspoons active dry yeast
¼ cup (2 fl oz/60 ml) warm water (110°F/43°C)
3 cups (24 fl oz/750 ml) cold water, at room temperature
4/5 cup (6½ oz/200 g) sourdough starter (recipe on page 84)
7½ cups (2¼ lb/1.1 kg) all-purpose (plain) flour
1 tablespoon plus 1 teaspoon salt

In the bowl of an electric mixer fitted with the paddle attachment, dissolve the yeast in the warm water and let stand until bubbly, about 5 minutes. Add the cold water and sourdough starter and mix with the paddle at medium speed until incorporated. Add the flour and salt and mix until the dough comes together and pulls away from the sides of the bowl, about 2 minutes.

Attach the dough hook and knead at medium speed until the dough is soft and elastic, 3–5 minutes. It will not pull away cleanly from the sides of the bowl. Transfer the dough to a lightly floured work surface and knead for 1 or 2 minutes until it loses its stickiness.

Form the dough into a ball and place in a lightly oiled bowl. Turn the ball to coat all surfaces with oil. Cover tightly with plastic wrap and let rise until tripled in bulk, about 3 hours.

Heavily flour a work surface and heavily flour your hands. Pull the dough out of the bowl and cut it into 2 equal portions. Working with 1 portion at a time, flatten the dough into a rough oblong. Then, starting at a narrow end, roll it up tightly. Turn the dough 90 degrees, pat it flat again and again roll it up into a cylinder.

Now shape the cylinder into a tight ball by rolling it between your cupped hands. The surface of the dough should be quite taut and the ball should feel springy to the touch. Place each ball on a baking sheet that has been lined with parchment paper and dusted with flour. Cover each with a heavy towel and let rise until doubled in bulk, about 1 hour.

About 30 minutes before the bread is ready to bake, preheat an oven to 450°F (230°C). If you have a large pizza stone, place it in the oven to preheat at the same time.

Heavily flour your fingertips and dimple the tops of the loaves. Let them rest for 10 minutes. This will keep the bread from rising too high and too quickly in the oven.

Place the baking sheets in the oven or slip the loaves onto the pizza stone. Bake until the loaves are crusty and golden and sound hollow when the bottoms are tapped, about 50 minutes. Let cool on wire racks.

MAKES 2 LARGE ROUND LOAVES *Photograph pages 70–71*

GREECE

SPANOKOPITTA

Spinach and Feta Pie

Everyone knows and loves this rich pie. The same spinach mixture can be used for filling pastry triangles for serving as appetizers. Simply cut the filo sheets into long strips 3 inches (7.5 cm) wide. For each triangle, stack 2 or 3 strips, brushing each strip with oil; place a heaping tablespoonful of filling near one end, fold over the filo to form a triangle, then continue folding in the same manner, as you would a flag. Bake in a 375°F (190°C) oven until golden, about 20 minutes.

1 lb (500 g) spinach
2 tablespoons olive oil, plus olive oil for brushing on *filo*
12 green (spring) onions, chopped, including some tender green tops
¾ lb (375 g) feta cheese
4 tablespoons chopped fresh flat-leaf (Italian) parsley
4 tablespoons chopped fresh dill
pinch of freshly grated nutmeg (optional)
freshly ground pepper
12–14 *filo* sheets (see glossary)

Stem the spinach, chop it into small pieces or cut into shreds and wash well to remove all traces of sand. Drain well and dry thoroughly. In a large sauté pan over medium heat, warm the 2 tablespoons oil. Add the spinach and onions and sauté until the spinach wilts and cooks down, about 5 minutes. Transfer to a sieve and drain well, pressing out as much liquid as possible. Chop coarsely. Set aside.

In a bowl mash the feta cheese with a fork. Add the parsley, dill and the spinach mixture and mix well.

Preheat an oven to 350°F (180°C). Brush a 10½-by-16-by-2½-in (26-by-40-by-6-cm) pan with olive oil. Lay 6 *filo* sheets in the pan, lightly brushing each one with oil before adding the next. Spoon the spinach mixture atop the *filo* and spread it evenly. Lay 6–8 more *filo* sheets on top, brushing each one with oil before adding the next. Cover and chill for about 30 minutes.

Using a sharp knife, score the top four sheets into large squares. Bake until golden, about 30 minutes. Let rest for 5–10 minutes, then cut into squares and serve at once.

SERVES 8–10

GREECE

KOTOPITTA

Chicken Pie

Sometimes this chicken pie is made with just eggs and cheese to bind the filling, rather than the sauce presented here. In a similar Turkish pie, herbs are omitted and a little chopped coconut is added to the filling.

4 cups (32 fl oz/1 l) chicken stock (see glossary)
6 chicken breast halves, boned, or 1 chicken, about 4 lb (2 kg), cut into serving pieces
¼ cup (2 oz/60 g) unsalted butter, plus ½ cup (4 oz/125 g) unsalted butter, melted and cooled
1 cup (3 oz/90 g) chopped green (spring) onion
¼ cup (1½ oz/45 g) all-purpose (plain) flour
3 eggs, lightly beaten
1½ cups (7½ oz/235 g) crumbled feta cheese
1 teaspoon freshly grated nutmeg
4 tablespoons chopped fresh dill
4 tablespoons chopped fresh flat-leaf (Italian) parsley
1 tablespoon chopped fresh mint (optional)
salt and freshly ground pepper
12–14 *filo* sheets (see glossary)

Pour the chicken stock into a saucepan and bring to a boil. Add the chicken pieces and simmer gently until the chicken is tender, about 25 minutes for chicken parts with bones and 10 minutes for boneless breasts. Remove the chicken pieces from the stock and set aside to cool. Reserve the stock. When the chicken is cool enough to handle, remove the meat from the bones, if necessary, and shred into bite-sized chunks. Transfer the meat to a large bowl.

In a sauté pan over low heat, melt the ¼ cup (2 oz/60 g) butter. Add the onion and sauté until tender and translucent,

Clockwise from left: Spinach and Feta Triangles, Leek Pie (recipe on page 77), Chicken Pie

about 10 minutes. Stir in the flour and cook, stirring, for a few minutes. Gradually add 2½ cups (20 fl oz/625 ml) of the reserved stock, stirring well, and simmer, stirring occasionally, until thick, 8–10 minutes. Remove from the heat and let cool slightly.

❀ Add the sauce to the chicken. Then stir in the eggs, feta, nutmeg, dill, parsley and the mint (if using). Season to taste with salt and pepper.

❀ Preheat an oven to 350° F (180°C).

❀ Butter a 9-by-12-by-3-in (23-by-30-by-7.5-cm) square or 9-in (23-cm) baking pan. Lay 6 or 7 *filo* sheets in the pan, lightly brushing each one with melted butter before adding the next. Spoon the chicken mixture atop the *filo* and spread it evenly. Lay the remaining *filo* sheets on top, brushing each one with butter before adding the next.

❀ Using a sharp knife, score the top few sheets into large squares. Bake until golden, 40–45 minutes. Let rest for 5 minutes, then cut into squares and serve very warm.

SERVES 6–8

Clockwise from top left: Onion and Anchovy Pizza (recipe page 82), Savory Pies with Tomato and Pine Nut Topping, Turnovers with Meat or Spinach Filling

CATALONIA

EMPANADAS

Turnovers with Meat or Spinach Filling

While these little turnovers are primarily found in Galicia, they are now ubiquitous at tapas bars all over Spain. The two fillings given here are typically Catalan. In fact, the spinach filling is decidedly Arabic in flavor and resembles a Lebanese spinach pie (recipe on page 74).

FOR THE DOUGH:

1 tablespoon active dry yeast
¼ cup (2 fl oz/60 ml) warm water (110°F/43°C)
½ cup (4 fl oz/125 ml) milk
3 tablespoons lard or vegetable shortening
3½ cups (17½ oz/545 g) all-purpose (plain) flour
1½ teaspoons salt
2 eggs, lightly beaten

FOR THE SPINACH FILLING:

1 lb (500 g) spinach
3 tablespoons olive oil
2 cloves garlic, minced

6 anchovy fillets packed in olive oil, finely chopped
3 tablespoons pine nuts
6 tablespoons (2 oz/60 g) raisins, plumped in hot water to cover for 30 minutes and drained
salt and freshly ground pepper

FOR THE MEAT FILLING:

6 tablespoons (2 oz/60 g) raisins, soaked in hot water to cover for 30 minutes
3 tablespoons olive oil
2 onions, finely chopped
3 cloves garlic, finely minced
1 teaspoon dried oregano
1 teaspoon paprika
1 tablespoon ground cumin
¾ lb (375 g) ground (minced) pork
¾ lb (375 g) ground (minced) veal or beef
3 tablespoons chopped fresh flat-leaf (Italian) parsley
2 hard-cooked eggs, coarsely chopped
salt and freshly ground pepper

In a small bowl, dissolve the yeast in the warm water and let stand until bubbly, about 5 minutes. Meanwhile, in a saucepan heat the milk with the lard or shortening just until the lard or shortening melts. Cool to lukewarm.

In a large bowl stir together the flour and salt. Add the eggs, cooled milk, and yeast mixture and beat until incorporated and the dough leaves the sides of the bowls. Turn out the dough onto a lightly floured work surface and knead until smooth and elastic, 3–5 minutes.

Form the dough into a ball and place in an oiled bowl. Turn the ball to coat all surfaces with oil. Cover the bowl with a damp kitchen towel or plastic wrap and place in a warm place until doubled in bulk, about 1½ hours.

Punch down the dough and turn out onto a lightly floured work surface. Knead for a few minutes, then reshape into a ball. Cover and let rise again until doubled in bulk, about 1 hour.

While the dough is rising the second time, prepare one of the fillings. To make the spinach filling, stem the spinach and wash well to remove all traces of sand. In a large sauté pan over high heat, place the spinach with the washing water still clinging to its leaves. Cook, turning often, until wilted, just a few minutes. Transfer to a colander, drain and chop coarsely. Drain again, pressing out excess liquid. Place in a bowl.

In a small sauté pan over medium heat, warm the oil. Add the garlic, anchovies and pine nuts and warm through. Add to the spinach along with the raisins. Mix well and season to taste with salt and pepper. Set aside.

To make the meat filling, drain the raisins and reserve ¼ cup (2 fl oz/60 ml) of the soaking liquid, set aside. In a large sauté pan over medium heat, warm the oil. Add the onion and sauté until tender and translucent, 8–10 minutes. Add the garlic, oregano, paprika and cumin and sauté for a few minutes longer. Add the meats, breaking them up with a fork, and cook over high heat until they lose their red color, about 8 minutes. Add the reserved raisin liquid and cook for 5 minutes longer. Transfer to a bowl and fold in the eggs, raisins and parsley. Season to taste with salt and pepper.

Preheat an oven to 350°F (180°C).

Punch down the dough again. Divide in half. On a lightly floured board roll out half of the dough into a circle about ⅛ in (3 cm) thick. Using a cookie cutter or a glass, cut out 3-in (7.5-cm) rounds; you should have about 20 rounds in all.

Place about 2 teaspoons of filling in the center of the round and fold the round in half to form a half-moon. Using the tines of a fork, seal the edges securely. Arrange on an ungreased baking sheet.

Roll out the remaining dough and fill with the remaining filling in the same manner. Arrange on a second baking sheet.

Bake until golden, about 20 minutes. Serve very warm.

MAKES 40 SMALL TURNOVERS

CATALONIA

Cocas

Savory Pies with Tomato and Pine Nut Topping

A coca *is a Catalan version of what most people think of as a Neapolitan pizza. These pies are most often topped with tomatoes, peppers (capsicums) and sausage, with tomatoes, pine nuts and anchovies, or with cooked Swiss chard (silverbeet), diced tomatoes and chopped ham. Catalan cooks also make sweet* cocas.

FOR THE DOUGH:

1 tablespoon active dry yeast
1¼ cups (10 fl oz/310 ml) warm water (110°F/43°C)
3½ cups (17½ oz/545 g) all-purpose (plain) flour
2 teaspoons salt
2 tablespoons olive oil

FOR THE TOPPING:

olive oil
2 onions, thinly sliced
4–6 cloves garlic, finely chopped
2 green or red sweet peppers (capsicums), seeded, deribbed and thinly sliced
2 lb (1 kg) tomatoes, peeled, seeded and chopped
¼ cup (1½ oz/45 g) pine nuts, lightly toasted
salt and freshly ground pepper
½ lb (250 g) *butifarra* sausage, thinly sliced (optional; see glossary)
½ lb (250 g) bacon, cut into cubes and half-cooked (optional)
thinly sliced fresh mushrooms (optional)
chopped anchovy fillets (optional)
cornmeal for dusting baking sheet(s)

To make the dough, in a small bowl, dissolve the yeast in ¼ cup (2 fl oz/60 ml) of the warm water and let stand until bubbly, about 5 minutes.

In a large bowl, stir together the flour and salt. Add the yeast mixture, the remaining 1 cup (8 fl oz/250 ml) warm water and the oil and beat in well until the dough leaves the sides of the bowl. Using an electric mixer fitted with a dough hook, knead at medium speed until the dough is smooth and elastic, about 5 minutes. Alternatively, turn out the dough onto a floured work surface and knead until smooth and elastic, about 10 minutes.

Form the dough into a ball and place in an oiled bowl. Turn the ball to coat all surfaces with oil. Cover the bowl with a damp kitchen towel or plastic wrap and let rise in a warm place until doubled in bulk, about 1 hour.

Preheat an oven to 450°F (230°C).

Meanwhile, make the topping. In large sauté pan over medium heat, warm enough oil to form a film on the pan bottom. Add the onions and garlic and cook, stirring often, until tender and translucent, 8–10 minutes. Add the sweet peppers and tomatoes and cook until softened and most of the liquid evaporates, about 10 minutes. Transfer to a sieve and drain well. Place in a bowl and season to taste with salt and pepper.

Punch down the dough. Divide the dough in half, if you like. On a lightly floured work surface, roll or pat out into 1 or 2 rounds or ovals. They should be about ¼ in (6 mm) thick. Transfer to cornmeal-dusted baking sheet(s).

Spoon the drained tomato mixture evenly atop the dough. Scatter on the pine nuts and the sausage, bacon, mushrooms or anchovies (if using).

Bake until the crust is golden, about 15 minutes. Serve hot, cut into wedges.

SERVES 8

PROVENCE

PISSALADIÈRE

Onion and Anchovy Pizza

The name of this pie comes from pissala, *which is a salted fish paste. Recipes for this onion pie vary widely. Some call for 2 pounds (1 kg) onions and others call for as much as 6 pounds (3 kg). More important than the amount, however, is how you cook the onions. They must be cooked on low heat for a long time until almost a purée. The Italian Riviera version of this pie, called* pizza all' Andrea, *has a little tomato purée spread beneath the layer of onion. Some recipes include minced garlic and others do not. And the amount of anchovy can vary from a timid few fillets to a robust dozen.*

basic pizza dough (recipe on page 74)

For the filling:
¼ cup (2 fl oz/60 ml) olive oil, plus olive oil for mixing with anchovy fillets (optional)
3 lb (1.5 kg) onions, thinly sliced
salt
2 or 3 cloves garlic, minced (optional)
1 fresh thyme sprig (optional)
freshly ground pepper
6–10 anchovy fillets in oil
¼ cup (1½ oz/45 g) niçoise olives

Prepare the pizza dough as directed and set aside to rise.

To make the filling, in a large, heavy sauté pan over medium heat, warm the ¼ cup (2 fl oz/60 ml) oil. Add the onions, sprinkle to taste with salt, cover and simmer over low heat, stirring occasionally, until the onions have cooked down into a thick purée, 45–60 minutes. The onions should not take on any color. Add the garlic and thyme sprig halfway through cooking (if using). When the onions are ready, remove and discard the thyme sprig, if used, and season to taste with pepper.

Preheat an oven to 375°F (190°C).

Punch down the dough. On a lightly floured surface roll out the dough large enough to line a rectangular baking pan measuring 12-by-15-in (30-by-37.5-cm) or a round 15-in (37.5-cm) pizza pan.

The topping can be added in one of two ways. Chop the anchovy fillets, mix them with a little olive oil and then spread them over the dough. Top with the onions, spreading them in a thick layer. Or spread the onions on first, cut the anchovy fillets into long strips and arrange them decoratively on top. Dot with the olives.

Bake until golden, 35–40 minutes. Alternatively, begin baking the pie at 400°F (200°C); after 15–20 minutes, reduce the heat to 350°F (180°C) and continue to bake for 15–20 minutes. Serve warm, cut into squares or wedges.

SERVES 8 *Photograph page 80*

LEBANON

KHUBZ ARABI

Pita Bread

The classic pita bread, sometimes called pocket bread, is easy to make. It is known as pita *or* pitta *in Greece,* pita *in Israel, and many other Middle Eastern countries and* pide *in Turkey. You may use up to 2 cups (10 oz/315 g) fine whole-wheat (wholemeal) flour, if desired. The breads freeze well. Pack in tightly closed bags and freeze for 2–3 weeks.*

1 tablespoon active dry yeast
1 teaspoon sugar
2 cups (16 fl oz/500 ml) warm water (110°F/43°C)
about 6 cups (30 oz/940 g) unbleached all-purpose (plain) flour
2 teaspoons salt
3 tablespoons olive oil

In a small bowl dissolve the yeast and sugar in ½ cup (4 fl oz/125 ml) of the warm water and let stand until bubbly, about 5 minutes. Place 2 cups (10 oz/315 g) of the flour in a large bowl and add the yeast mixture and the remaining warm water. Beat with a wooden spoon until well blended. Cover with a kitchen towel or plastic wrap and let stand in a warm place until frothy, about 30 minutes.

Add 3 cups (15 oz/470 g) of the flour, the salt and olive oil. Using an electric mixer fitted with the dough hook, beat on low speed until mixed, about 5 minutes. Alternatively, beat by hand for 10 minutes.

Sprinkle a little of the remaining 1 cup (5 oz/155 g) flour onto a work surface. Turn the dough out onto the surface and knead, adding more of the flour as needed to reduce stickiness, until the dough is smooth and elastic, about 5 minutes.

Form the dough into a ball and place in a lightly oiled bowl. Turn the ball to coat all surfaces with oil. Cover the bowl with a damp kitchen towel or plastic wrap and let rise in a warm place until doubled in bulk, about 1½ hours.

Punch down the dough. Divide it into 12 equal balls and place them on a floured work surface. Cover with a kitchen towel and let rise again until doubled in bulk, about 30 minutes.

On a lightly floured surface roll out each ball into a 6-in (15-cm) round. Be careful not to make any breaks in the surface of the rounds or the breads may not form a pocket when baked. Place on a lightly floured work surface or baking sheets, cover with kitchen towels and let rise for 20–30 minutes.

Meanwhile, preheat an oven to 475°F (245°C). Lightly oil a heavy baking sheet.

Slide as many bread rounds as will comfortably fit onto the prepared baking sheet. Bake until puffed and golden, about 5 minutes. Turn over and return to oven to brown second side briefly. Alternatively, remove from oven and slip under a preheated broiler (griller) to brown second side. Remove to wire racks to cool. Repeat until all the breads are baked. Cover the breads with a lightly dampened towel or place in a plastic bag to keep flexible.

MAKES ABOUT 1 DOZEN ROUNDS *Photograph pages 8–9*

ISRAEL

CHALLAH

Sabbath Bread

This is the traditional Sabbath night bread. It can be formed as a single braid or as a dramatic triple-braid loaf.

2 tablespoons active dry yeast
2 tablespoons sugar
1 cup (8 fl oz/250 ml) warm water (110°F/43°C)
5 cups (25 oz/780 g) all-purpose (plain) flour
3 eggs, lightly beaten
⅓ cup (3 oz/90 g) margarine, melted, or vegetable oil
2 teaspoons salt
1 egg yolk beaten with 2 tablespoons cold water for glaze
sesame or poppy seeds

In the bowl of an electric mixer fitted with the paddle attachment, dissolve the yeast and sugar in the warm water and let stand until bubbly, about 5 minutes. Add 1 cup (5 oz/155 g) of the flour and beat at medium speed until incorporated. Add the eggs, one at a time, and then the margarine or oil. Add an additional 1 cup (5 oz/155 g) flour and beat on high speed for 3 minutes.

Sabbath Bread

❀ Attach the dough hook and add the salt and the remaining 3 cups (15 oz/470 g) flour. Knead until smooth, about 10 minutes.

❀ Alternatively, combine all the ingredients as directed, but beat them together with a wooden spoon. Once they are fully incorporated, turn the dough out onto a lightly floured work surface and knead until smooth, about 15 minutes.

❀ Form the dough into a ball and place in an oiled bowl. Turn the dough to coat all surfaces with oil. Cover with a damp kitchen towel or plastic wrap and let rise in a warm place until doubled in bulk, about 1½ hours.

❀ Punch down the dough and turn it out onto a floured surface. For a single-braid loaf, divide the dough into 3 equal portions. For 2 single-braid loaves, divide the dough in half and then divide each half into 3 equal portions. For a triple-braid loaf, divide the dough into 3 unequal portions, large, medium and small, and then divide each of those portions into 3 equal portions. In each case, using your palms, roll out each dough portion on a lightly floured surface into a rope no longer than 12 in (30 cm). The size will depend upon which loaf you are making. Braid each set of 3 ropes, pressing the ends together and tucking them under slightly. If making 1 or 2 single-braid loaves, simply place them on an oiled baking sheet once they are formed. If making a triple-braid loaf, place the largest braid on an oiled baking sheet. Lay the medium braid on top and press firmly to attach it. Then top with the littlest braid, again pressing to attach. Cover the bread(s) with a kitchen towel and let rise until doubled in bulk, about 45 minutes.

❀ Meanwhile, preheat an oven to 350°F (180°C). Just before baking brush the loaf or loaves with the egg wash and sprinkle with sesame or poppy seeds. Bake until golden, about 30 minutes for the 2 small loaves, about 40 minutes for the large single-braid loaf and as long as 50 minutes for the triple-braid loaf. Test for doneness by tapping the bottoms of the loaves; they should sound hollow. Let cool on wire racks.

MAKES 1 LARGE OR 2 SMALL LOAVES

TUNISIA

Briks á l'Oeuf

Pastries Stuffed with Tuna and Egg

For these traditional Tunisian pastries, spoonfuls of cooked meat, poultry or canned tuna are placed on sheets of ouarka *and a whole egg is nested on the filling. The pastry is then carefully sealed without breaking the egg. The meat is usually lamb seasoned with onion, cumin, paprika, cayenne, and parsley or cilantro. Other fillings include mashed potatoes seasoned with onion, garlic and parsley or chopped cooked chicken and potatoes with onion. Spring roll wrappers, or* filo, *are remarkably good substitutes for the* ouarka. *Be careful when you eat these not to dribble egg yolk down your shirt front.*

1 tablespoon peanut oil, plus oil as needed for *filo* and deep-frying
1 onion, chopped
1 can (6 oz/185 g) oil-packed tuna, drained and mashed
2 tablespoons chopped fresh flat-leaf (Italian) parsley
1–2 tablespoons fresh lemon juice
salt and freshly ground pepper
pinch of cayenne pepper or a little *harissa* (optional; see glossary)
6 Chinese spring roll wrappers or *filo* sheets (see glossary)
6 eggs
1 or 2 egg whites, lightly beaten

In a sauté pan over medium heat, warm the 1 tablespoon oil. Add the onion and sauté until tender and translucent, 8–10 minutes. Transfer the onion to a strainer to drain, then place in a bowl.

Add the tuna, parsley, lemon juice, salt and pepper to taste and cayenne or *harissa* (if using).

If you are using the spring roll wrappers, place an equal amount of the filling on each one. Using the back of a spoon, make a depression in each mound of filling. Break 1 egg into each depression. Brush the edge of each wrapper with egg white, covering a ½-in (12-mm) border. Carefully fold the wrapper in half and press firmly to form a ½-in (12-mm) rim.

If using *filo* sheets, working with 1 sheet at a time, brush the sheet lightly with peanut oil and fold in half from a narrow end. Place one sixth of the filling about 3 in (7.5 cm) in from the top of the folded sheet, leaving a 1-in (2.5-cm) border on either side. Using the back of a spoon, make a depression in the filling. Break 1 egg into the depression. Brush all the edges of the *filo* sheet with egg white. Carefully fold in the left side, then the right side, and finally fold up the bottom third to cover the filling completely. Press edges to seal securely.

Pour oil into a deep sauté pan to a depth of 5 in (7.5 cm) and heat to 375°F (190°C), or until a bit of pastry dropped in the oil begins to color within moments. When the oil is ready, add the pastries, 2 or 3 at a time, and deep-fry until golden, about 4–5 minutes. Using a slotted spoon, remove to paper towels to drain briefly, and repeat with the remaining pastries. Serve hot.

MAKES 6 PASTRIES

TUNISIA

Khubz Mbassis

Semolina Bread

Many Mediterranean breads are made with a sourdough starter. For example, the starter used here will work for Italian breads as well, such as pane pugliese *(recipe on page 77). It is difficult to make starter in small batches, but as it is just flour and water, you can afford to discard it if it becomes too sour or goes bad before you can use it. This recipe was given to me by Baroui Karoui.*

FOR THE SOURDOUGH STARTER:
1 cup (8 fl oz/250 ml) warm water (110°F/43°C)
⅛ teaspoon active dry yeast
2 cups (10 oz/315 g) all-purpose (plain) flour

FOR THE BREAD:
1 tablespoon active dry yeast
1 tablespoon sugar
2 cups (16 fl oz/500 ml) warm water (110°F/43°C)
½ cup (4 oz/125 g) sourdough starter
¼ cup (2 fl oz/60 ml) olive oil
4 tablespoons seeds of paradise (see glossary)
3 cups (15 oz/470 g) semolina flour
2 cups (10 oz/315 g) all-purpose (plain) flour
1 tablespoon salt

To make the starter, place the warm water, yeast and flour in the bowl of an electric mixer fitted with the paddle attachment and beat at medium speed until the mixture pulls away from the sides of the bowl, about 3 minutes. Alternatively, beat the ingredients together with a wooden spoon.

Place the starter in a 2-qt (2-l) plastic container or any container large enough for the starter to triple in size. Cover

Left to right: Pastries Stuffed with Tuna and Egg, Semolina Bread

and let sit at room temperature overnight. The starter may be used the next day, but if at all possible refrigerate it for a few days to develop its flavor. You will need only a small amount of the starter for this recipe; reserve the remainder in the refrigerator for up to 3 days to use in making other loaves.

❁ To make the bread, in the bowl of an electric mixer fitted with the paddle attachment, dissolve the yeast and sugar in the warm water. Add the starter and mix with the paddle until it is incorporated and the water is foamy.

❁ Attach the dough hook and add the olive oil, 2 tablespoons of the seeds of paradise, both flours and the salt. Knead on medium speed until the dough is smooth, elastic and pulls away from the sides of the bowl, about 10 minutes.

❁ Alternatively, combine all the ingredients as directed, but beat them together with a wooden spoon. Once they are fully incorporated, turn out the dough onto a floured work surface and knead until smooth and elastic, about 15 minutes.

❁ Form the dough into a ball and place in a lightly oiled bowl. Turn the ball to coat all surfaces with oil. Cover the bowl with a damp kitchen towel or plastic wrap and let rise in a warm place until doubled in bulk, 1½–2 hours. Punch down the dough, re-cover and let rise a second time until doubled in bulk, about 1 hour.

❁ Punch down the dough and divide into 2 equal portions. On a floured work surface, roll out each portion into a round 12 in (30 cm) in diameter. Working with 1 round, lightly brush the outer edge with water. At 1-in (2.5-cm) intervals, pull up the edge of the dough and press it firmly onto the moistened top, about 1 in (2.5 cm) from the edge. The dough will have a fluted appearance, much like a pie crust. Repeat with the second round.

❁ Place the breads on 1 or 2 baking sheets. Lightly sprinkle the tops with the remaining seeds of paradise. Cover them with a kitchen towel and let rise until they are half again as high, about 45 minutes.

❁ While the loaves are rising, preheat an oven to 425°F (220°C). If you have a large pizza stone, place it in the oven to preheat at the same time.

❁ Place the baking sheet(s) in the oven or slip the loaves onto the pizza stone. During the first 15 minutes of baking, lightly spray the loaves with a water mister 3 or 4 times; this will give them nice crisp crusts.

❁ Bake until the loaves are pale gold and sound hollow when the bottoms are tapped, about 45 minutes. Remove to wire racks to cool.

MAKES 2 ROUND LOAVES

Pigeon Pie

MOROCCO

B'STILLA

Pigeon Pie

This sweet-and-savory pie is traditionally made with a semolina pastry called ouarka. *The pastry is quite difficult to prepare, however, and requires considerable time and practice. Indeed, most North African cooks buy* ouarka *from those who specialize in making it rather than attempting to make it themselves. Filo sheets can be used in place of* ouarka *with good results. This pie can also be made with chicken rather than squab.*

FOR THE FILLING:

4 squab (pigeons) or poussins, about 1 lb (500 g) each, with livers and giblets
salt and freshly ground pepper
½ cup (4 oz/125 g) unsalted butter
1 cup (5 oz/155 g) chopped onion
4 tablespoons chopped fresh cilantro (fresh coriander)
2 tablespoons chopped fresh flat-leaf (Italian) parsley
1 teaspoon ground ginger
1 teaspoon ground cumin
½ teaspoon cayenne pepper
½ teaspoon ground turmeric
½ teaspoon ground cinnamon
⅛ teaspoon saffron threads, crushed
1 cup (8 fl oz/250 ml) water
2 tablespoons fresh lemon juice (optional)
8 eggs

FOR THE ALMOND LAYER:

¼ cup (2 oz/60 g) unsalted butter
1½ cup (7 oz/220 g) slivered blanched almonds
2 tablespoons sugar
½ teaspoon ground cinnamon

FOR ASSEMBLING THE PIE:

½ cup (4 oz/125 g) unsalted butter, melted and cooled
about 1 lb (500 g), 14–16 *filo* sheets, thawed in the refrigerator if frozen (see glossary)

FOR SERVING:

3 tablespoons confectioner's (icing) sugar
1 tablespoon ground cinnamon
whole blanched almonds for garnish (optional)

To make the filling, cut the birds into quarters. Rub the pieces with salt and pepper. In a large, heavy sauté pan over medium heat, melt the butter. Add the poultry pieces and brown evenly, turning often, about 10 minutes. Remove the birds to a platter.

To the butter remaining in the pan, add the onion, liver and giblets and cook over medium heat until the onion is tender and translucent, 8–10 minutes. Add the cilantro, parsley, all the spices and the water and bring to a boil. Return the birds to the pan, reduce the heat to low, cover and simmer until the birds are tender, about 40 minutes. Remove the birds, giblets and liver from the pan, reserving the juices in the pan. When cool enough to handle, remove the meat from the bones and shred it. Chop the liver and giblets.

Over high heat reduce the pan juices to about 1¾ cups (14 fl oz/430 ml). Add the lemon juice (if using).

Meanwhile, break the eggs into a bowl and beat until blended. Stir the eggs into the pan juices and cook over low heat, stirring all the while, until soft curds form. Season to taste with salt and pepper. Remove from the heat and drain the cooked egg mixture in a strainer. Set aside.

To make the almond layer, in a frying pan over medium heat, melt the butter. Add the almonds and fry, stirring occasionally, until golden brown, about 5 minutes. Using a slotted spoon remove to paper towels to drain. Chop the almonds coarsely and place in a small bowl. Add the sugar and cinnamon and toss to mix. Set aside.

To assemble the pie, preheat an oven to 350°F (180°C). Brush a round pizza pan about 14 in (35 cm) in diameter with some of the butter. Lay 8 *filo* sheets on the pan, arranging them like the spokes of a wheel and brushing each one with butter. The sheets should overlap so that all of the pan is covered and they should overhang the edges of the pan generously. Be sure to butter the overhanging portions as well. Sprinkle one third of the almond mixture in a 10-in (25-cm) circle at the center of the pan. Spoon half of the egg mixture over the almond mixture. Top this with the shredded poultry. Then spoon on the remaining egg mixture and finally the rest of the almonds. Fold the overhanging *filo* over the filling. Lay 6–8 more *filo* sheets on top, arranging them and brushing them with butter as before. This time tuck the overhang under the pie.

Bake until golden on top, about 20 minutes. Remove from the oven and carefully drain off excess butter. Invert a second, similar pan over the pie and, holding the pans together firmly, invert them. Slip the pie back into the oven to brown the top, 10–15 minutes. Turn one more time in the same manner, and then bake 5 minutes longer.

Remove from the oven and slide onto a serving platter, or serve directly from the pan. Dust with the sugar and sprinkle the cinnamon in crisscrossing lines on the top. Arrange whole almonds on top in a decorative pattern, if desired. Cut into wedges and serve warm.

SERVES 12

LEBANON

FATAYEER

Meat Pies

To make the pizzalike pastry called lahm bil ajin, *add 1 cup (8 oz/250 g) plain yogurt to the filling mixture and divide the filling equally among six 6-inch (15-cm) rounds, spreading it to within ½ inch (12 mm) of the edge of the round. Bake the rounds open-faced.*

dough for *fatayeer sbanikh* (recipe on page 74)

FOR THE FILLING:

2 tablespoons olive oil
1 onion, finely chopped (about 1 cup/5 oz/155 g)
1 lb (500 g) ground (minced) lamb shoulder
½ cup (¾ oz/20 g) chopped fresh flat-leaf (Italian) parsley
¼ cup (1½ oz/45 g) pine nuts, toasted
¼ teaspoon ground allspice
½ teaspoon ground cinnamon
1 teaspoon salt
½ teaspoon freshly ground pepper

olive oil for brushing on pies
plain yogurt for serving

Make the dough as directed. Preheat an oven to 400°F (200°C). Lightly oil a baking sheet.

To make the filling, in a sauté pan over medium heat, warm the oil. Add the onion and sauté until tender, about 5 minutes. Transfer to a bowl. Add the lamb, parsley, nuts, spices and seasonings and mix well.

Divide the dough into 24 portions and, following the basic method in *fatayeer sbanikh,* roll out into 3-in (7.5-cm) rounds. Top each round with a heaping spoonful of the filling, then enclose the filling as directed to form a triangular pastry.

Place on the prepared baking sheet. Brush the pastries with oil. Bake until golden, 15–20 minutes. Serve warm with yogurt.

MAKES 24 PIES *Photograph pages 8–9*

SYRIA

SANBUSAK

Cheese or Meat Pastries

Savory filled pastries are a staple in the Middle East. Here are two fillings that are enclosed in a rich short crust rather than a yeast dough.

FOR THE CHEESE FILLING:

1 lb (500 g) feta cheese
2 eggs
4 tablespoons chopped fresh mint or 2 tablespoons dried mint
white pepper

FOR THE MEAT FILLING:

2 tablespoons olive oil
2 onions, finely chopped
1 teaspoon ground cinnamon
½ teaspoon ground allspice
1 lb (500 g) ground (minced) lamb
¼ cup (1½ oz/45 g) pine nuts, toasted
salt and freshly ground pepper

FOR THE DOUGH:

½ cup (4 oz/125 g) unsalted butter
½ cup (4 fl oz/125 ml) olive oil
½ cup (4 fl oz/125 ml) warm water (110°F/43°C)
1 teaspoon salt
3 cups (15 oz/470 g) all-purpose (plain) flour

FOR COOKING THE PASTRIES:

1 egg, lightly beaten, if baking the pastries
6 tablespoons (2 oz/60 g) sesame seeds, for cheese-filled pastries
mild olive oil or vegetable oil, if deep-frying

Choose one of the fillings. To make the cheese filling, crumble the cheese into a bowl or mash with a fork. Add the eggs and mint and mix well. Season to taste with pepper.

To make the meat filling, in a large sauté pan over medium heat, warm the oil. Add the onion and sauté until tender and translucent, 8–10 minutes. Add the cinnamon and allspice and cook for 2 minutes longer. Add the lamb, break it up, and cook until it colors, about 5 minutes. Stir in the pine nuts and season to taste with salt and pepper. Simmer until the meat is juicy but has not released too much liquid. Remove from the heat and let cool completely before stuffing the pastries.

To make the dough, in a small saucepan over low heat, melt the butter; do not let it bubble. Remove from the heat and add the oil, warm water and salt. Transfer to a food processor and pulse once to combine. Gradually add the flour, pulsing after each addition. The dough will be very soft and should not stick to the sides of the bowl.

Alternatively, make the dough by hand, proceeding as directed but gradually beating in the flour with a wooden spoon. Do not overmix the dough; it should just come together in a rough mass.

Transfer the dough to a lightly floured surface. Divide the dough into 8 equal portions. Roll out each portion into a thin sheet and cut out 3-in (7.5-cm) rounds. You will have about 36 rounds in all.

Place a heaping teaspoonful of filling in the center of each round and fold the round in half, forming a half-moon. Using the tines of a fork, seal the edges securely.

To bake the pastries, preheat an oven to 350°F (180°C). Place the pastries on ungreased baking sheets and brush them with the beaten egg. If the pastries are stuffed with the cheese filling, sprinkle them with the sesame seeds. Bake until golden, about 30 minutes. Serve warm.

To deep-fry the pastries, pour oil into a deep sauté pan to a depth of 2–3 in (5–7.5 cm) and heat to 375°F (190°C), or until a bit of pastry dropped into the oil begins to color within moments. If the pastries are stuffed with the cheese filling, dip them into the sesame seeds and then slip them into the hot oil; do not crowd the pan. If they are filled with meat, simply slip them into the oil. Deep-fry until golden, 3–5 minutes. Using a slotted spoon remove the pastries to paper towels to drain briefly, and repeat with the remaining pastries. Serve hot.

MAKES ABOUT 3 DOZEN PASTRIES

EGYPT

SEMIT

Sesame Bread Rings

In Egypt, street vendors display these bread rings on long poles. Semit *can be eaten for breakfast or as a snack with some cheese. The savory rings are popular in Greece and Turkey as well. Seeds of paradise (see glossary) or equal parts sesame seeds and poppy seeds can be substituted for the sesame seeds.*

4 cups (1¼ lb/625 g) all-purpose (plain) flour
1 teaspoon salt
⅔ cup (5 fl oz/160 ml) milk
2 tablespoons unsalted butter
4 teaspoons active dry yeast
2 tablespoons sugar
½ cup (4 fl oz/125 ml) warm water (110°F/43°C)
1 egg
½ cup (4 oz/125 g) sesame seeds

Sift together the flour and salt into a large bowl. In a saucepan over medium heat, scald the milk. Remove from the heat, add the butter and let cool to lukewarm.

While the milk is cooling, in a small bowl dissolve the yeast and sugar in the warm water and let stand until bubbly, about 5 minutes.

Add the yeast mixture to the cooled milk. Then gradually add the milk mixture to the flour, stirring with a wooden spoon until a soft dough forms that does not stick to the sides of the bowl. Then, using an electric mixer fitted with the dough hook, knead the dough until it is smooth and elastic, about 8 minutes. Alternatively, turn out the dough onto a lightly floured work surface and knead until smooth and elastic, about 15 minutes.

Form the dough into a ball and place in an oiled bowl. Turn the ball to coat all surfaces with oil. Cover the bowl with a damp kitchen towel or plastic wrap and let rise in a warm place until doubled in bulk, 1½–2 hours.

Punch down the dough and divide it into 16 equal portions. Flour your hands. On a lightly floured work surface, use your palms to roll each portion into a long, thin rope. Then join together the ends of the rope to form a ring. Each ring should be 6–7 in (15–18 cm) in diameter. Place on oiled baking sheets or sheets lined with parchment paper, allowing 2 in (5 cm) space between the rings. In a small bowl beat the egg with a little water. Brush each ring with a little of this mixture. Sprinkle the rings with the sesame seeds. Let rise in a warm place until doubled in bulk, about 30 minutes.

Meanwhile, preheat an oven to 425°F (220°C).

Bake the bread rings for 7–10 minutes. Lower the oven temperature to 325°F (165°C) and continue to bake until golden brown, about 20 minutes longer or until the bottoms sound hollow when tapped. Let cool on wire racks.

MAKES ABOUT 16 RINGS

Left to right: Sesame Bread Rings, Cheese or Meat Pastries

Clockwise from top left: Music Paper Bread, Double-Crusted Pie with Pork Cracklings, Chick-Pea Fritters, Raisin-and-Walnut Rolls

SARDINIA

Carta di Musica

Music Paper Bread

Called pane carasau *in Sardinian, this long-keeping bread was traditionally carried by shepherds when they took their flocks to graze on distant mountains. It is a little like* lavash, *the Middle Eastern cracker bread, and* markook, *the thin Lebanese mountain bread. Some recipes call for yeast, but this yeastless version is simpler and works well.*

2 cups (10 oz/315 g) all-purpose (plain) flour
1 cup (5 oz/155 g) fine semolina flour
1 teaspoon salt
1–1¼ cups (8–10 fl oz/250–310 ml) water

In a bowl stir together the flours and salt. Gradually add the water, stirring constantly until a smooth dough somewhat like a firm pasta dough forms.

Divide the dough into 8–10 balls. Place on a floured kitchen towel or parchment paper and cover with a lightly floured towel. Let rest for 30 minutes.

Preheat an oven to 450°F (230°C). If you have them, place pizza stones or plaques (heavy metal baking pans) in the oven to preheat at the same time.

On a lightly floured surface, roll out each ball of dough as thinly as possible. Place the dough rounds on a baker's peel or on a rimless baking sheet and slide them onto the hot pizza stones or plaques. Alternatively, arrange them on heavy-gauge baking sheets and place in the oven. Bake for 2½ minutes, then turn the breads and bake about 2 minutes longer. The breads should be pale gold; do not let them get too brown. Let cool on wire racks. They can be stacked once they have cooled completely.

MAKES 8–10 BREAD ROUNDS

APULIA

Sfogliata Con Ciccioli

Double-Crusted Pie with Pork Cracklings

This double-crusted pie is a specialty of Bari.

basic pizza dough (recipe on page 74)

FOR THE FILLING:

¼ cup (2 fl oz/60 ml) olive oil
6 onions, thinly sliced
1 cup (6 oz/185 g) peeled, seeded and diced tomatoes
2 tablespoons grated salted ricotta
5 tablespoons pork cracklings
5 hard-cooked eggs, chopped
½ cup (2½ oz/75 g) pitted sharply flavored black olives, chopped
2 anchovy fillets packed in olive oil, drained and chopped
½ cup (2 oz/60 g) grated pecorino cheese

olive oil for brushing on pie

Prepare the pizza dough as directed and set aside to rise.

Preheat an oven to 350°F (180°C).

To make the filling, in a large sauté pan over medium heat, warm the oil. Add the onions and sauté until beginning to soften, about 5 minutes. Add the tomatoes and ricotta and cook, stirring, for another 5 minutes. Stir in the cracklings and sauté for 5 minutes longer. Remove from the heat and let cool. Assemble the remaining ingredients.

Punch down the dough. Divide in half. On a lightly floured surface roll out the dough large enough to line a shallow, round 12-in (30-cm) baking pan or a shallow, rectangular 9-by-12-in (23-by-30-cm) baking pan. Spoon the tomato mixture into the dough-lined pan. Top with layers of the eggs, olives, anchovies and pecorino.

Roll out the remaining dough and top the pie with it. Pinch the edges together to seal securely and trim away any excess dough. Brush the top with olive oil. Bake until golden, 30–40 minutes. Serve hot, cut into wedges.

SERVES 6–8

CORSICA

Uga Siccati

Raisin-and-Walnut Rolls

These are very like the famed Roman raisin buns called maritozzi. *The walnuts add an interesting crunch. Spread them with goat cheese or sweet butter.*

1 tablespoon active dry yeast
½ cup (4 fl oz/125 ml) warm water (110°F/43°C)
3⅓ cups (17 oz/530 g) all-purpose (plain) flour
¼ cup (2 fl oz/60 ml) unsalted butter, at room temperature
1 egg
1 teaspoon salt
½ cup (4 oz/125 g) sugar
1 teaspoon finely grated lemon zest
1 cup (6 oz/185 g) raisins, plumped in hot water to cover for 30 minutes and drained
1 cup (4 oz/125 g) chopped toasted walnuts

In a bowl dissolve the yeast in the warm water. Add ½ cup (2½ oz/75 g) flour and stir together with a wooden spoon until incorporated. Cover the bowl with a kitchen towel or plastic wrap and let stand in a warm place until frothy, about 30 minutes.

In another bowl combine the butter, egg, salt, sugar and lemon zest and mix well. Gradually beat in the remaining flour, and then the yeast mixture. If you have an electric mixer with a dough hook, knead the mixture at medium speed until smooth and elastic, about 4 minutes. Alternatively, turn out the dough onto a lightly floured work surface and knead until smooth and elastic, about 10 minutes. In both cases, add the raisins and walnuts and knead them in until they are well incorporated.

Form the dough into a ball and place in an oiled bowl. Turn the ball to coat all surfaces with oil. Cover the bowl with a damp kitchen towel or plastic wrap and let rise until doubled in bulk, about 1 hour.

Preheat an oven to 425°F (220°C).

Divide the dough into 16 portions and shape each portion into a ball about 1½ in (4 cm) in diameter. Place on lightly oiled baking sheets or on sheets lined with parchment paper. Bake until golden, about 35 minutes. Let cool on wire racks.

MAKES 16 ROLLS

SICILY

Panelle

Chick-pea Fritters

In Provence, chopped parsley is added to these fritters and they are called panisses.

1½ cups (7½ oz/230 g) chick-pea (garbanzo bean) flour (see glossary)
3 cups (24 fl oz/750 ml) water
salt and freshly ground pepper
1 tablespoon olive oil
peanut oil for deep-frying

Oil a baking sheet with sides or line the baking sheet with parchment paper and then oil it.

Put the flour in a large saucepan. Gradually whisk in the water. Then whisk in salt and pepper to taste and the olive oil. Bring to a boil over medium heat, stirring constantly to prevent lumps, and cook, stirring, until the mixture is thick and smooth, about 5 minutes.

Pour the hot mixture into the prepared baking sheet. It should form a layer no more than ½ in (12 mm) thick. Let cool completely; it will be quite firm.

Invert the pan onto a cutting surface. Cut the chick-pea sheet into strips about ½ in (12 mm) wide and 2–3 in (5–7.5 cm) long.

Pour peanut oil into a deep sauté pan to a depth of 2 in (5 cm) and heat to 325°F (190°C), or until a bit of a chick-pea strip dropped into it begins to color within moments. When the oil is ready, add the strips, a few at a time; do not crowd the pan. Fry until golden, 2–3 minutes.

Using a slotted spoon remove to paper towels to drain briefly, and repeat with the remaining strips. Arrange on a warmed platter, sprinkle with salt and pepper and serve hot.

SERVES 8

ITALY

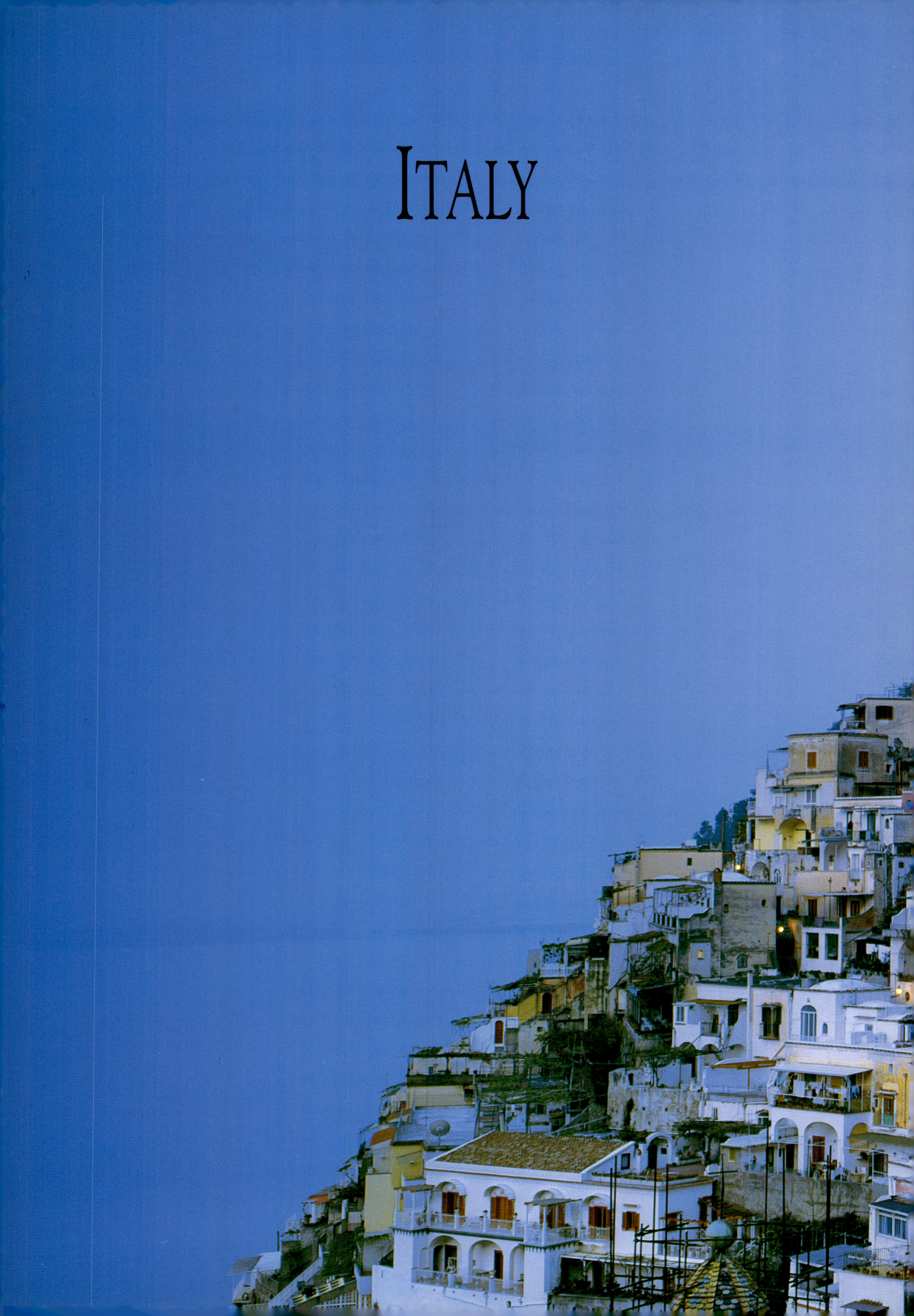

ITALY

The South, Sicily, and Sardinia

Italian unity is a relatively recent and still fragile phenomenon, not much more than a hundred years having passed since the foundation of the Italian state. This is not to deny the existence of a shared Italian ethos. Indeed, this ethos assumes what geography and history confirm: a fairly sharp dichotomy between north and south. There is, of course, no fixed line on the map precisely separating them from each other, but the south may be thought of as beginning somewhere below Tuscany, where the Apennines and their foothills swell out to fill the remainder of the Italian peninsula. In pre-Roman times, Etruscan power prevailed to the north of this invisible line, and Greek to its south.

This political division even today has its culinary reflection: Polenta, an originally Etruscan preparation, remains far more common in the north than the south. The divisive effects of geography on the cuisine are more numerous and significant, however. The terrain of the south makes it inhospitable to the cow, resulting in a general absence from its cuisine of the dairy products, especially butter, that are routine in the north. By way of compensation, the sun-baked, unpromising soil of the south is ideal for the cultivation of the olive, and olive oil is used unsparingly. The north-south dichotomy is also one of economics. The pasta of the affluent north is soft, flat and limp, made with eggs and dough, while that of the

Previous pages: The picturesque village of Positano, near Naples, was most likely founded by refugees from Paestum who were forced to flee the Saracens in the Middle Ages. Left: The Mediterranean pines of Fregene, near Rome, assume an ethereal charm as the sun begins to rise.

relatively indigent south is hard, tubular and generally eggless (macaroni and spaghetti). Here again, the south possesses a balancing advantage: The intense taste and color of its vegetables make possible the creation of pasta dishes that are unrivaled in flavor and visual appeal.

Apulia, Basilicata and Calabria constitute what might be called the deep south of Italy. This trio of regions, once known as Magna Graecia (Greater Greece), was more thoroughly impregnated with Greek influence than any other part of the Italian mainland. Some of its principal cities—Bari, Taranto, Gallipoli, Metaponto, Santa Severina—were either founded or resettled by the Greeks, and their mention is enshrined in Greek epic poetry. The Greeks also endowed the agriculture of the area with culinary essentials such as the olive and the vine.

Today Apulia is the most prosperous of the three regions; its varied produce includes wheat, olive oil, figs, melons and citrus fruits. It also boasts Bari, for centuries the most important port of the south and still thriving today with its pasta factories, olive oil refineries, and fish and vegetable canneries. In the face of considerable variation from one district to another, Apulian cuisine achieves coherence through a peasant robustness of spirit and the use of a tasty seasoning that—anomalously for the Mediterranean—eschews garlic in favor of onions. Among its noteworthy dishes are *tiella,* a souvenir of the Spanish occupation that resembles *paella,* although substituting potatoes for rice; the *caldariello* of Gravina, a supremely nonkosher dish of lamb or kid cooked in sheep's or goat's milk and said locally to be "at least three thousand years old"; and fish chowders, the *zuppa di pesce* or *brodetto* of Taranto, Brindisi and Gallipoli, which with a greater degree of precision and certainty can be assigned to the Greek legacy. It may finally be observed that the exclusive cultivation of wheat in the fertile Gargano peninsula makes bread as important a staple as pasta throughout Apulia.

Basilicata, more compact and solidly mountainous than Apulia, with narrower and shorter coastal plains, is considerably poorer than its neighbor; it is in fact the most impoverished region of the entire Italian peninsula. It is noteworthy, however, for its sausages and preserved meats, which are exported to all parts of Italy, and a general liking for hot seasonings based on ginger and chilies. This predilection for spices may be a relic of a short-lived Arab occupation in the tenth century.

Calabria is only one notch above Basilicata on the scale of Italian prosperity, but poverty has not been its companion throughout history. Among the cities founded there by the Greeks was Sybaris, which in the sixth century B.C. was a city of gastronomes where cooks were crowned for creating new dishes and thereby contributed to posterity the concept of sybaritism, pampered and decadent indulgence in all kinds of luxury. No trace remains of Sybaris, and little of any other distinctly Greek legacy, except perhaps for the technique used by the fishermen of Calabria to harpoon swordfish in the Straits of Calabria. Among later invaders and occupiers, the Arabs exerted lasting influence. They held Reggio Calabria for most of the tenth and early eleventh centuries, and the intensive cultivation of citrus fruits in that most productive part of the region goes back to their fertilizing touch. In addition, an Arabic origin—*tharid*—may be hazarded for *turiddu,* the name of a Calabrian pastry combining flour, eggs and almonds. The cuisine of contemporary Calabria is composed essentially of thick soups, pasta and vegetables, principally peppers, tomatoes and eggplants. The last-named holds pride of place in Calabria, where it is treated in original, not to say curious, ways unfamiliar to the rest of the Mediterranean. *Melanzane all'agrodolce* is, for example, a hybrid of a vegetable dish and a dessert; it consists of eggplant cooked in vinegar, cinnamon, sugar, walnuts, candied citron, raisins and chocolate.

Sicily is without any doubt the gastronomic star of the south; some would even place it at the very pinnacle of Italian cuisine, in view of the richness, variety and originality of its offerings. More than any other part of the south, it has left its imprint on the cuisine of the whole country, and contributed to European gastronomy as well.

Separate from the mainland by more than geography, Sicily can be regarded as a transitional zone between Europe and North Africa. The shores of Tunisia can sometimes be glimpsed from Trapani, in the westernmost part of Sicily, and the Pelagian islands, administered from Sicily, are in fact almost exactly equidistant between Sicily and the North African coast. The mostly barren interior of the island, with its scattered but densely populated settlements, is more reminiscent of North Africa than of the Italian mainland, even its southern regions; it is as if terrain as well as location predestined Sicily for its centuries of Arab rule.

Its destinies were, however, long tied to Greece. Sicily was even more thoroughly Hellenized than Magna Graecia, and many of its important cities were founded by the Greeks; Syracuse was a powerful city-state rivaling Athens itself. In Sicily as elsewhere the Greeks promoted the cultivation of the olive, and delighted in the abundance of wheat and vegetables they found there. All this had a mercantile aspect, for the Greeks exported much of the island's produce to the Greek mainland and to Greek settlements in North Africa. But Sicily was also

While modern life in Sicily is peaceful, there was a time when this island colony was the springboard for ambitious conquerors in the Mediterranean.

The port of Amalfi, in southern Italy, enjoyed great prominence a millennium ago when it became part of a commercial network spanning the whole of the Mediterranean.

The dramatic ruins of the 5th-century B. C. Temple of Castor and Pollux in Agrigento, Sicily, bears witness to a time when the Greeks dominated Italy.

an important center of gastronomy. Syracuse witnessed the composition of the first cookbook written in the Western world, the now lost *Art of Cooking* of Mithaecus, as well as the foundation of the first school for professional cooks, supervised by a certain Labducus. It was, however, another Sicilian city, Gela, that was home to Archestratus, the most celebrated epicure of the classical world; the surviving fragments of his work testify to a refined interest in fish, and disapproval of the gluttony that was beginning to afflict Syracuse.

Apart from the fish chowder known as *brodetto,* there is little identifiable trace of Greek influence in the Sicilian cuisine of today, and the Romans, who treated Sicily primarily as a granary for the supply of the mainland, appear to have made no lasting contribution at all. It is with the coming of the Arabs in the ninth century that Sicilian cuisine begins truly to take shape; as Waverley Root described it, whatever strikes us as "typically Sicilian" is "typically Saracen,"—that is, Arab.

According to unconfirmed gastronomic lore, the Arabs of Sicily got off to a brisk start in culinary innovation by concocting the Sicilian national dish, *pasta con le sarde*—pasta with sardines, currants and pine nuts—as soon as they landed at Mazara del Vallo on the southeast coast of the island in June 827. More verifiable and significant are the improvements the Arabs brought to Sicily, which in their totality amounted to a revolution in its agrarian economy. Irrigation was renovated throughout the island, partly through the repair of the siphon system used by the Romans and partly by digging the underground canals, of ultimately Persian inspiration, that the Arabs also introduced to Spain to such good effect. Remains of some Arab reservoirs near major Sicilian cities still survive, and it speaks for itself that most water sources on the island still bear Arabic names.

The increased availability of water made Sicily rich in horticulture: A great variety of citrus fruits, including oranges, brought to the island for the first time, were grown both for domestic consumption and export in walled gardens that were particularly numerous in its western regions. The Arabs also introduced to Sicily dates, pistachio nuts, the eggplant and buckwheat (known even today in Italian as *grano saraceno,* "Saracen grain"), as well as two items of cardinal importance for the European table, rice and sugar. The first rice plantation in Europe was established by the Arabs near Lentini, to the south of Catania in eastern Sicily; it remained under cultivation until the eighteenth century. Risotto, it is true, is largely alien to Sicilian cuisine, but its subsequent flourishing on the Italian mainland would have been unlikely to occur without this introduction of rice to Sicily. If we except Crete during the period of Arab domination, Sicily must also be counted as the first site in Europe for the cultivation of sugarcane and the industrial production of sugar. The easy abundance of the sweetener made possible the proliferation of the pastries and desserts that still constitute one of the chief glories of Sicilian cuisine.

The subtle and imaginative use of spices in various Sicilian dishes may be ascribed in general to the Arab legacy, but about certain dishes there can be no doubt. Two of them are attributed to an Emir of Catania whose name has been imperfectly preserved in Italian sources as Muhammed ibn Thummah: *tummàla,* an elaborate rice casserole containing immoderate amounts of meat, now eaten principally at Christmas (which is ironic, considering the Arab origins of the dish); and *pasticcio,* chicken baked with almonds and pistachios in a hollowed-out bread loaf. It would be unwise to be similarly categorical about an Arab contribution to the pasta of Sicily. Theories concerning the origins of Italian pasta are notoriously fragile, and the popular myth of Marco Polo carrying noodles home from China as an exotic curiosity has long since been discredited. Inspired by enthusiasm for her adopted homeland, Mary Taylor Simeti claims for Arab Sicily the origins of *pasta asciutta,* pasta covered with sauce and cheese. It is true that vermicelli was being produced in twelfth-century Sicily, under Arab auspices, and that even in present-day Sicily noodles are referred to as *tria,* a name derived from Arabic *itriya.* This word, however, is derived in turn from a Greek forebear, and it may be that the Arabs gave impetus to an existing pasta culture rather than creating one for the first time.

Arab rule of Sicily came to an end in the mid-twelfth century, and although the Norman conquerors were initially appreciative of Arab culture and cuisine, ultimately the exclusionist spirit of Europe showed itself, and by 1300 there were no Muslims left on the island. The expulsion of the Arabs, combined with the prolonged warfare that followed the collapse of Norman rule, effaced many of the agricultural achievements of the previous four centuries.

But the Arab imprint on cuisine and culture was too strong to disappear. It has remained particularly noticeable in Trapani, where couscous is still prepared, using fish—in Tunisian style—instead of mutton. The distinctively Arab technique of trapping tuna (also preserved in Spain) is even now used by the fishermen of the area, whose annual festival, *mattanza* (perhaps from the Arabic *muntazah) del tonno* is presided over by a *rais* (Arabic for "chief").

Ice cream may be a kind of delayed gift of the Arabs to Sicily, Italy, Europe and the world. After all, it was the Arabs who, in the East, first manufactured ice on a large scale; who invented, or adapted from Persian models, sherbet (itself a word of Arabic origin); and who discovered and propagated the art of candying fruit. These were the three main elements that went into Sicilian ice cream at its birth, and permit us to claim Arab spiritual ancestry for Francesco Procopio, Sicilian founder of Paris's Café Procope. More modestly, let us point out that *cassata* is derived from the Arabic *qas'ah.*

Sardinia, more distant from the Italian mainland than is Sicily, again has a distinct personality, one however that lacks the rich flamboyance of Sicily. Sardinia was visited by the usual succession of invaders and colonizers, but they settled almost exclusively on the coast and left little trace on the interior where the soil is sparse and irrigation difficult. Thus it is that this second largest island in the Mediterranean has been unflatteringly described as the "domain of the Stone Age," which means in culinary terms that game, meat and bread are the staples of its diet. Geography can hardly be blamed for the Sardinian disdain for fish, for the coasts of the island teem with all kinds of them.

In order to avoid taking leave of Italy on a discouragingly and unfairly negative note, let us suggest that the culinary function of Sardinia is to be the dour and primitive exception that proves the general Mediterranean rule of subtlety, richness and flavor.

The Mediterranean focus on family is never more apparent than at mealtime; here, an afternoon repast is enjoyed in Lípari, on the Aeolian Islands.

SOUPS

Legumes are the base of many hearty Mediterranean soups and stews.

SOUPS

The word *supper* comes from the French *souper,* literally "soup." In the Mediterranean, a robust soup is often the whole meal. Rather than serving a broth or simple purée, the thrifty Mediterranean cook adds beans, rice, pasta, bread, meat or fish to the pot, making the soup a filling and nourishing repast. Such a practice offers a more practical way to eat as well: It is more healthful to eat a large lunch that one can burn up and digest during the day and then enjoy a soup for supper. This prescription is not always possible, of course, given the increasing demands of the modern life for a quick lunch and a big dinner, but the concept is a creditable one.

Most of the soups in this chapter are hearty. Legumes are popular in the Mediterranean and many of the recipes are what are called the "bean and green" soups. The Syrian *shouraba il addis* combines lentils and greens and may be thickened with egg and lemon or served with a dollop of yogurt. Some families add rhubarb for tartness, which is an interesting use of a stalk many think of as a fruit but that is really a vegetable. (It is used in Greece and Turkey as well, in combination with tomato for a sweet-and-sour sauce for fish.) Wild fennel and bitter greens are added to the Sicilian *maccu,* a fava (broad) bean soup, which sometimes incorporates pasta as well.

White, or *borlotti,* beans are essential to *soupe au pistou* or a good minestrone. Sometimes all of the beans are puréed; other times, only a portion of them are puréed to thicken the broth and the rest are left whole for texture and contrast. An assortment of beans forms the base for *harira,* the Moroccan soup that is the traditional meal eaten to break the fast during Ramadan. In the most elaborate versions of this soup, lamb, rice, chick-peas (garbanzos) and lentils are combined, and eggs and lemon are swirled in at the end of cooking for added body. Simpler versions call for only lentils and noodles. In the Valencian *olla gitana,* or "gypsy pot," chick-peas are part of an unusual mélange of pumpkin, green beans, pears and tomatoes, and the soup is thickened with a classic *picada* of almonds, garlic and fried bread.

Egyptians still employ traditional methods in the cultivation and transportation of their crops.

Previous pages: clockwise from top left; Valencian Gypsy Soup (recipe page 108), Cádiz Fish Soup with Bitter Orange (recipe page 114), Almond Soup from Granada (recipe page 114), Cold Tomato Soup (recipe page 114)

In marketplaces throughout Morocco, everything from pottery and clothing to a surprising variety of fresh fruits and vegetables is for sale.

Those soups that are not thickened by beans are often given body by the addition of bread. *L'aïgo bouido,* the aromatic Provençal garlic soup, stirs in pasta or bread. A Sardinian fennel soup is baked in a casserole with layers of bread and cheese. The Andalusian *gazpacho* takes its name from the Arabic for "soaked bread," even though garlicky croutons sometimes replace the bread crumbs. And bread is combined with almonds in *sopa de almendras* from Granada.

Pasta is the other common soup ingredient in the Mediterranean, and not only in Italian soups. Provence is connected to the Italian Riviera both by its geography and its love of pasta. So *aïgo bouido* will often have vermicelli, as will a *soupe de poisson*. Noodles are often added to Middle Eastern soups, including noodles made from flour and fermented milk. This pasta pellet is called *trahana* in Greece, *tarhana* in Turkish and *kishk* in Arabic. In Sardinia they use another tiny pasta made from semolina called *fregula.* Not unlike couscous in texture, it enriches *minestra con le vongole,* clam soup with sun-dried tomatoes. Rice is also used for body, in *harira,* the Egyptian *melokhia,* and in some of the egg-and-lemon-based *avgolemono* soups.

Although the liquid that forms the base for many Mediterranean soups is water, when cooked with fresh vegetables it becomes a flavorful vegetable stock. Chicken and meat stocks are also used for soups, but less often. Trimmings from prosciutto and its precious bone, *pancetta* ends, lamb bones and scraps, and chicken bones and feet are treasures saved for adding to various cooking waters. Occasionally, lemon juice is used to enhance the flavor of a particularly mild stock.

When vegetables are in abundance, they are puréed for soup. Tomatoes, carrots, fennel, potatoes or pumpkins are often handled this way and then garnished simply with a splash of virgin olive oil, a dollop of yogurt or a smattering of chopped fresh herbs. Meatballs are the guest stars of vegetable soups in Sicily and Apulia, in Greek egg-and-lemon soup, in Turkish yogurt soup and in the Catalan *sopa de albóndigas.* Meat-based soups are often reserved for special occasions, where they make a festive and filling repast.

Complex fish and shellfish soups are found in the Mediterranean. As they often contain considerable seafood and are then meals in themselves, most of them can be found in the fish and shellfish chapter. Included here, however, are three simple seafood soups: the Valencian *caldo de perro gaditano* (recipe on page 114), a light broth flavored with bitter oranges and afloat with a few small pieces of fish; a clam soup from Sardinia; and the estimable Provençal *soupe de poisson* (recipe on page 108), in which fish and fish stock are puréed together.

SICILY

Maccu

Fava Bean Soup

Here is the quintessential peasant soup, a thick bean purée that can be enriched with tomatoes, wild or cultivated fennel fronds, chicory, Swiss chard, beet greens and/or mustard greens. Dried favas can usually be purchased already peeled. If you cannot find them peeled, buy about 1¼ pounds (625 g), soak as directed, drop into boiling water for 30 seconds, drain and then peel and proceed with the recipe. If you prefer, sauté only the onion and garlic and boil the greens before adding them to the soup. Cooked small pasta shapes also make a good addition.

2¼ cups (1 lb/500 g) dried fava (broad) beans
8 cups (64 fl oz/2 l) water
1 cup (1 oz/30 g) finely chopped fennel fronds
5 tablespoons (3 fl oz/80 ml) fruity olive oil, plus olive oil for garnish
1 cup (4 oz/125 g) diced onion
2 cloves garlic, finely minced
2 cups (12 oz/375 g) peeled, seeded and chopped tomatoes (optional)
8 cups (1 lb/480 g) greens such as Swiss chard (silverbeet), beet (beetroot) greens, chicory (curly endive), mustard or escarole, or a mixture, well washed and coarsely chopped
salt and freshly ground pepper
freshly grated pecorino cheese for serving (optional)

Place the beans in a bowl with water to cover generously and refrigerate overnight. Drain and rinse well. Put the beans and fennel fronds in a heavy soup pot with the water. Bring to a boil, reduce the heat to low and simmer, uncovered, until the beans are very soft and can be mashed with a spoon in the pot, 1–2 hours. Add water if the beans start to dry out before they are cooked and stir occasionally to prevent sticking and/or scorching. Stir in 3 tablespoons of the oil.

In a wide sauté pan over medium heat, warm the remaining 2 tablespoons oil. Add the onion and garlic and sauté for a few minutes. Add the tomatoes (if using) and greens. Stir to wilt the greens. The washing water clinging to the leaves should be enough moisture; if not, add about 1 cup (8 fl oz/250 ml) water to make the steam to wilt them.

Add the wilted greens mixture to the bean purée and, if necessary, thin the soup with water. (It thickens upon sitting.) Simmer for 10 minutes.

Season to taste with salt and pepper. Serve with a splash of olive oil and with a sprinkling of grated cheese, if desired.

SERVES 6

SARDINIA

Minestra con le Vongole

Clam Soup with Fregula and Sun-dried Tomatoes

Fregula *is a tiny semolina pasta not unlike couscous. As couscous is more readily available at most markets, you may use it in this soup. If you are using sun-dried tomatoes that have not been packed in oil, reconstitute them in water to cover and then add the soaking water to the saucepan with the clam liquid.*

3 lb (1.5 kg) clams in the shell, well scrubbed
4 cups (32 fl oz/1 l) water
2 tablespoons olive oil

1 large onion, chopped
1 clove garlic, crushed
6 whole sun-dried tomatoes in olive oil, drained and finely minced
½ cup (2½ oz/75 g) *fregula* or couscous
salt and freshly ground pepper

chopped fresh flat-leaf (Italian) parsley or mint

Discard any clams that do not close at the touch. In a wide saucepan bring the water to a boil. Add the clams and steam until they open, 3–5 minutes. Using a slotted spoon transfer the clams to a bowl; discard any that did not open. Pour the cooking liquid through a sieve lined with cheesecloth (muslin). Set the liquid aside. Remove the clams from their shells and discard the shells. Set the clams aside.

In a 1½-qt (1.5-l) saucepan over medium heat, warm the oil. Add the onion and garlic and sauté until tender and translucent, 8–10 minutes. Add the tomatoes and the reserved clam liquid and simmer for 10 minutes. Add the clams and *fregula* or couscous and simmer until the pasta is done, about 5–7 minutes. Season to taste with salt and pepper.

Serve hot, garnished with parsley or mint.

SERVES 4–6

Clockwise from top: Wild Fennel Soup, Clam Soup with Fregula and Sun-dried Tomatoes, Fava Bean Soup

SARDINIA

Minestra di Finocchi Selvatici

Wild Fennel Soup

It's unlikely that most people will find wild fennel where they live, but cultivated fennel, also called anise, is available at many markets. This soup is simple to prepare and can be a meal in a bowl if lots of bread and cheese are added.

2 lb (1 kg) wild or cultivated fennel bulbs
6 cups (48 fl oz/1.5 l) salted water or stock (see glossary), or as needed to cover
salt and freshly ground pepper
6 tablespoons (3 oz/90 g) unsalted butter
2 tablespoons olive oil
8–12 slices coarse country-style bread
⅓ lb (5 oz/155 g) fresh white cheese such as ricotta

Cut the fronds and stems from the fennel bulbs. Reserve the fronds for garnish, if desired. Cut fennel bulbs in half lengthwise, remove the tough core and peel off any discolored outer leaves. Slice the fennel coarsely crosswise. In a large saucepan bring the salted water or stock to a boil. Add the fennel, reduce the heat to low and simmer, uncovered, until tender, 15–20 minutes. Remove from the heat. Season to taste with salt and pepper. Set the fennel aside in the broth.

In a large sauté pan over medium heat, melt 2 tablespoons of the butter with 1 tablespoon of the oil. Add half of the bread slices and fry, turning once, until golden on both sides, about 3 minutes on each side. Drain on paper towels. Repeat with the remaining bread and oil and half of the remaining butter. Cut each slice into 2-in (5-cm) pieces.

Preheat an oven to 350°F (180°C). In a large, ovenproof earthenware casserole or individual soup ramekins, arrange a layer of bread and a layer of cheese. Using a slotted spoon remove some of the fennel from the broth and layer it on the cheese. Drizzle some of the fennel broth over the top. Repeat the layers until all the bread, cheese, fennel and broth are used.

Arrange the remaining 2 tablespoons butter in thin slivers over the top.

Place in the oven and bake until golden, about 20 minutes. Serve very hot. If you like, chop the fennel fronds and use them to garnish the soup.

SERVES 4

Garlic and Sage Soup

PROVENCE

Aïgo Bouido

Garlic and Sage Soup

As garlic and sage are considered beneficial to good health, this traditional soup is reputed to be a tonic. You may omit the vermicelli and instead whisk 6 egg yolks into a little of the soup to temper them, and then whisk the mixture into the soup. Serve the egg-enriched broth over a slice of toasted bread placed in the bottom of each bowl. Drizzle with the olive oil and sprinkle with the cheese, if desired.

6–8 cloves garlic, finely minced
3 large or 6 small fresh sage leaves
2 fresh thyme sprigs
6 cups (48 fl oz/1.5 l) water
6 oz (185 g) vermicelli
6 egg yolks, lightly beaten (optional)
salt and freshly ground pepper
3 tablespoons extra-virgin olive oil
6 tablespoons freshly grated Parmesan cheese (optional)

In a 2-qt (2-l) saucepan over high heat, combine the garlic, sage, thyme and water and bring to a boil. Reduce the heat to low and simmer, uncovered, for 20 minutes.

Add the vermicelli and cook until the noodles are tender, a few minutes longer. Season to taste with salt and pepper, stir in the oil and serve at once. Sprinkle each serving with Parmesan, if desired.

SERVES 6

PROVENCE

Soupe aux Tomates

Tomato Soup

While some recipes for this soup call for water, there is no need to add it, as the tomatoes give off quite a bit of liquid. If you like, garnish the soup with croutons, chopped fresh basil or parsley or a dollop of pistou *(recipe follows).*

3 tablespoons olive oil
2 large onions, sliced
1 clove garlic, minced
3 lb (1.5 kg) ripe tomatoes, thickly sliced or cut into chunks
3 fresh flat-leaf (Italian) parsley sprigs
5 fresh basil leaves
salt and freshly ground pepper
sugar, if needed
pinch of cayenne pepper or ground cloves (optional)

In a large, heavy-bottomed saucepan over medium heat, warm the olive oil. Add the onions and sauté until tender and translucent, 8–10 minutes. Add the garlic and sauté for 1–2 minutes longer. Then stir in the tomatoes, parsley and basil, cover and simmer over low heat, stirring occasionally to prevent scorching, until the tomatoes have given off their juices and are very tender, about 30 minutes.

Pass the soup through a food mill or, working in batches, purée in a food processor fitted with the metal blade or in a blender. Return the soup to the pan and reheat gently to serving temperature. Season to taste with salt and pepper.

If the tomatoes are tart, add a pinch of sugar for balance. A small pinch of cayenne pepper or ground cloves makes a nice, subtle addition. Serve hot.

SERVES 6

Photograph page 10

PROVENCE

Soupe au Pistou

Vegetable Soup with Basil and Garlic

There are no exact proportions for this vegetable soup. The choice of vegetables and how much of each to use is up to you. Usually soupe au pistou *contains carrots, green beans, shell beans, zucchini, potatoes, tomatoes and pasta. You can even use ½ cup (3½ oz/105 g) dried small white (navy) beans, soaked overnight in water to cover, drained and then cooked in water to cover until tender, for the fresh shell beans, adding them with the green beans. This soup sounds like minestrone—and essentially it is. And Provençal* pistou *is none other than Genoese pesto, the classic mixture of basil, garlic and Parmesan. The word* pistou *means "pounded" in Niçoise dialect, and is not too distant from* pestle, *the implement traditionally used to pound the basil and garlic to a paste.* Pistou *keeps well in the refrigerator; top it with a film of olive oil to preserve its color. Never "cook"* pistou, *as it will turn a homely brown and lose its fragrance. Simply stir it into the soup (or into pasta) once it has been removed from the heat.*

3 tablespoons olive oil
4 onions, diced (about 6 cups/1½ lb/750 g)
6 carrots, peeled and sliced (about 2 cups/8 oz/250 g)
4 celery stalks, diced (about 1 cup/5 oz/155 g)
1 lb (500 g) tomatoes, peeled, seeded and diced (about 2 cups)
8 cups (64 fl oz/2 l) water or chicken stock (see glossary), or as needed to cover
6 new potatoes, unpeeled, diced (about 3 cups/1 lb/500 g)
1 cup (5 oz/155 g) shell beans
½ lb (250 g) green beans, cut into 1-in (2.5-cm) lengths
4 zucchini (courgettes), cut in half lengthwise and then sliced ½ in (12 mm) thick
4 cups (8 oz/250 g) coarsely sliced Swiss chard (silverbeet), optional
3 oz (90 g) macaroni or small pasta shells
salt and freshly ground pepper

FOR THE *PISTOU:*

1 teaspoon finely minced garlic (about 3 cloves)
salt
⅔ cup (1 oz/30 g) tightly packed fresh basil leaves
¼ cup (1 oz/30 g) freshly grated Parmesan cheese
⅓ cup (3 fl oz/80 ml) olive oil
salt and freshly ground pepper

extra-virgin olive oil for serving (optional)
freshly grated Parmesan cheese for serving (optional)

In a large soup pot over medium heat, warm the oil. Add the onions and sauté until tender, about 10 minutes. Add the carrots and celery and sauté for a few minutes longer. Then add the tomatoes and stock and simmer, uncovered, for 10 minutes.

Add the potatoes and shell beans and simmer for 5 minutes. Then add the green beans, zucchini, Swiss chard and pasta and continue to simmer until all the vegetables and the pasta are tender, 15–20 minutes longer. Season to taste with salt and pepper.

While the soup is simmering, make the *pistou.* In a mortar with a pestle, grind the garlic to a paste with a little salt. Alternatively, chop finely. Pack the basil leaves and garlic into a blender or a food processor fitted with the metal blade. Process to combine. Add the Parmesan and process to combine. Gradually add the olive oil in a thin, steady stream and process just until a coarse emulsion forms. Do not overblend; there should still be some texture. Season to taste with salt and pepper.

Remove the soup from the heat and stir in the *pistou.* Serve at once, topped with a drizzle of fruity olive oil and a sprinkling of Parmesan, if desired.

SERVES 6–8

Photograph page 10

TURKEY / PROVENCE

Soupe de Poisson

Fish Soup

This classic soup of Nice, a purée of mild white fish, is usually eaten with toasted bread and rouille, *a garlicky sauce tinted with sweet pepper (capsicum) or tomato. Some versions of the soup add pasta and a little saffron, as does this one, although both ingredients can be omitted and the soup will still be delectable.*

4–6 tablespoons (2–3 fl oz/60–90 ml) olive oil
2 fish heads
2 fish frames
2 lb (1 kg) small mild white fish
3 onions, sliced
3 or 4 cloves garlic, chopped
¼ cup (2 fl oz/60 ml) Cognac
2 lb (1 kg) tomatoes, peeled, seeded and diced
1 fresh thyme sprig
1 bay leaf
3-in (7.5-cm) strip orange zest (optional)
7 cups (56 fl oz/1.75 l) water
½ teaspoon saffron threads, steeped in ¼ cup (2 fl oz/60 ml) dry white wine

FOR THE *ROUILLE:*

4 cloves garlic, finely minced
salt
2 slices white bread, crusts discarded, soaked in water to cover and squeezed dry
1 teaspoon cayenne pepper, or to taste
2 tablespoons tomato paste (optional)
1 sweet red pepper (capsicum), roasted, seeded, deribbed and chopped (see glossary)
6 tablespoons (3 oz/90 ml) olive oil
fresh lemon juice to taste (optional)
salt and freshly ground pepper

salt and freshly ground pepper
pinch of cayenne pepper
3 oz (90 g) dried pasta such as spaghetti or angel hair, broken
½ cup (2 oz/60 g) freshly grated Parmesan cheese

18–24 slices baguette, toasted and rubbed with garlic

In a large sauté pan over medium heat, warm 2 tablespoons of the olive oil. Add the fish heads and frames and sauté them until they start to give off some liquid, about 10 minutes. Transfer to a stockpot.

Add 2 more tablespoons of the oil to the sauté pan over medium heat and add the fish. Toss in the oil until lightly golden, about 8 minutes. Add to the stockpot.

To the oil in the pan add the onions and garlic and sauté over medium heat, adding more oil as needed to prevent sticking, until pale gold, about 15 minutes. Add the onions and garlic to the stockpot. Pour the Cognac into the sauté pan and deglaze over high heat, scraping up any browned bits. Add to the stockpot along with the tomatoes, thyme, bay, orange zest (if using) and the water. Bring to a boil, reduce the heat to low, cover and simmer until the fish is falling apart, about 30 minutes. Add the saffron and wine and simmer for 5 minutes longer.

Meanwhile, make the *rouille.* In a mortar with a pestle, grind the garlic with salt to taste to a paste. Add the bread and mix in, then add the cayenne, tomato paste (if using) and sweet pepper, mixing in well. Slowly add the olive oil, a few drops at a time, working it in steadily with the pestle. Season to taste with salt and pepper and with the lemon juice (if using). Alternatively, make this sauce in a blender, adding the olive oil gradually after the other ingredients have been puréed. Transfer to a bowl and set aside.

Remove the soup from the heat and remove the large bones, then purée it, a few ladlefuls at a time, in a blender or by passing it through a food mill. Then, in both cases, push it through a fine-mesh sieve to remove the small bones.

Put the puréed soup in a saucepan and bring to a boil. Thin with additional stock or water if desired, and season to taste with salt, pepper and cayenne. Do not be alarmed if the soup takes a lot of salt. It needs it!

Add the pasta and cook over low heat until tender, about 20 minutes.

Ladle the soup into individual bowls. Pass the *rouille,* Parmesan and toasted bread at table.

SERVES 6–8

PROVENCE

Soupe Potiron

Pumpkin Squash Soup

Pumpkin squash is the basis for many Mediterranean soups and vegetable stews. In Morocco, cooked chick-peas (garbanzo beans) or rice may be added. Cooked rice is sometimes added in France as well. In Greece, the soup is commonly thickened with semolina and garnished with sautéed thinly sliced onions, chopped fresh parsley and olive oil. In Italy, it is topped with chopped fresh sage or croutons and Parmesan or pecorino cheese. Chopped cooked greens can be added as well.

3 tablespoons olive oil
2 onions, sliced or diced
¼ teaspoon ground coriander (optional)
¼ teaspoon ground cinnamon (optional)
1 piece pumpkin squash, about 2½ lb (1.25 kg), peeled and diced
6–8 cups (48–64 fl oz/1.5–2 l) chicken stock (see glossary) or water, or as needed
1 cup (8 fl oz/250 ml) light (single) cream or milk
salt and freshly ground pepper
croutons and freshly grated Parmesan cheese for garnish

In a large saucepan over medium heat, warm the oil. Add the onion and sauté until tender and translucent, 8–10 minutes. Add the coriander and cinnamon, if using, and sauté a few minutes longer. Add the squash cubes and the stock or water and bring to a boil. Reduce the heat to low, cover and simmer until the squash is tender, 15–20 minutes.

Working in batches, transfer to a blender or a food processor fitted with the metal blade and purée until smooth. Return the soup to the pan.

Add the cream or milk and season to taste with salt and pepper. Reheat gently.

Ladle into individual bowls and garnish with croutons and Parmesan.

SERVES 6

ANDALUSIA

Olla Gitana

Valencian Gypsy Soup

Provençal cooks prepare soupe à la citrouille, *which is very similar to this soup in that it contains a combination of white beans, pumpkin squash, onion, diced ham, garlic, croutons and chopped mint. This Spanish pumpkin and bean soup, however, is made a bit more interesting with the addition of diced pears and a* picada, *a flavorful paste, of garlic, almonds and bread.*

1 cup (7 oz/220 g) dried chick-peas (garbanzo beans)
2 qt (2 l) plus 3 cups (24 fl oz/750 ml) water

Top to bottom: Pumpkin Squash Soup, Fish Soup

FOR THE *PICADA:*

½ cup (4 fl oz/125 ml) olive oil
10 blanched almonds, toasted
1 slice course country-style bread, cut into finger-sized strips
1 clove garlic
2 tablespoons wine vinegar (optional)

1 onion, diced
1 tablespoon sweet paprika
2 tomatoes, peeled, seeded and diced
pinch of saffron threads steeped in ¼ cup (2 fl oz/60 ml) hot chicken stock (see glossary)
½ lb (250 g) green beans, cut into 2-in (5-cm) lengths
1½ cups (8 oz/250 g) diced or coarsely chopped, peeled pumpkin squash
3 firm pears, peeled, cored and cut into chunks
salt and freshly ground pepper

❀ In a bowl combine the chick-peas with water to cover and let soak in the refrigerator overnight. Drain and rinse well.

❀ Place the chick-peas in a large saucepan and add the water. Bring to a boil, reduce the heat to low and simmer, partially covered, until tender, about 1 hour.

❀ While the soup is simmering, make the *picada.* In a sauté pan over medium heat, warm the oil. Add the almonds, bread and garlic and sauté until golden, about 8 minutes. Using a slotted spoon transfer to a mortar; reserve the oil in the pan. Using a pestle crush the almond mixture to a paste and then work in the vinegar (if using).

❀ To the oil in the pan, add the onion and sauté over medium heat until pale gold, about 15 minutes. Stir in the paprika and then the tomatoes and cook, stirring occasionally, for 10 minutes. Add the saffron and stock and stir well.

❀ Add the green beans, squash and pears to the chick-peas and simmer for 10 minutes.

❀ Add the *picada* and the tomato mixture to the soup and stir to combine. Simmer for 10 minutes. Season to taste with salt and pepper. Serve hot.

SERVES 6–8

Photograph on pages 100–101

Top to bottom: Lentil Soup, Lamb and Bean Soup, Melokhia Leaf Soup

SYRIA

SHOURABA IL ADDIS

Lentil Soup

Lentil soups are popular throughout the Mediterranean. Most are puréed; some include greens or rice. In Turkey lentil soup is garnished with mint and cayenne pepper warmed in butter, or with fried onions and fried bread croutons. Elsewhere, minced garlic sautéed in oil with ground coriander is strewn on the soup.

3 tablespoons unsalted butter or olive oil
1 large onion, chopped (about 1½ cups/6 oz/185 g)
1 carrot, peeled and chopped
1 celery stalk with leaves, chopped
8 cups (64 fl oz/2 l) lamb stock or water
1¾ cups (14 oz/440 g) dried red, green or brown lentils
1 cracked marrow bone (optional)
1 teaspoon ground cumin
pinch of ground allspice
2 small rhubarb stalks, trimmed and cut into 1-in (2.5-cm) pieces (optional)
1–2 tablespoons fresh lemon juice
salt and freshly ground pepper

In a heavy saucepan over medium heat, melt the butter or warm the oil. Add the onion, carrot and celery and sauté until tender and lightly golden, about 15 minutes. Add the stock, lentils and the bone, if using, and bring to a boil. Reduce the heat to low, cover and simmer until the lentils are very soft, about 45 minutes.

Remove the bone. Add the cumin, allspice and the rhubarb, if using. Simmer 15–20 minutes longer, to cook the rhubarb and blend the flavors.

Working in batches, purée the soup in a blender, then return it to the pan. Reheat gently and season to taste with lemon juice, salt and pepper. Serve hot.

SERVES 6

MOROCCO

HARIRA

Lamb and Bean Soup

Muslims serve this hearty soup to break the fast at the end of Ramadan. There are many variations on this recipe. All of them are lemony, some omit the eggs, some have only lentils, and still others add noodles or orzo (ricelike pasta).

½ cup (3½ oz/105 g) dried chick-peas (garbanzo beans)
salt
9 cups (72 fl oz/2.1 l) water
⅔ cup (5 oz/155 g) lentils
3 tablespoons white rice
3 tablespoons all-purpose (plain) flour mixed with ½ cup (4 fl oz/125 ml) water
2 tablespoons unsalted butter
1 tablespoon olive oil
½ lb (250 g) lamb, cut into ½-in (12-mm) cubes
2 onions, chopped (about 3 cups/12 oz/375 g)
2 cloves garlic, finely minced
½ teaspoon ground ginger
1 teaspoon ground cinnamon
½ teaspoon ground turmeric
2 cups (16 fl oz/500 ml) puréed canned plum (Roma) tomatoes or 1½ lb (750 g) peeled, seeded and chopped fresh plum tomatoes
½ cup (¾ oz/20 g) chopped fresh flat-leaf (Italian) parsley
¼ cup (⅓ oz/10 g) chopped fresh cilantro (fresh coriander)
2 teaspoons freshly ground pepper, or to taste
2 eggs
¼ cup (2 fl oz/60 ml) fresh lemon juice

Place the chick-peas in a bowl with water to cover generously. Refrigerate overnight. Drain and rinse well.

Transfer the chick-peas to a 1-qt (1-l) saucepan and add 3 cups (24 fl oz/750 ml) of the water. Bring to a boil, reduce the heat to low, cover and simmer until cooked through but not falling apart, about 1 hour. Remove from the heat and salt lightly. Drain the chick-peas, reserving the cooking liquid. You will have about 1½ cups (9 oz/280 g) chick-peas. Set the chick-peas and liquid aside.

Pour another 3 cups (24 fl oz/750 ml) of the water into a 3-qt (3-l) saucepan and bring to a boil. Add the lentils and rice and simmer for 20 minutes. Add the flour-water paste, stirring in well.

While the lentils are simmering, in a large sauté pan over high heat, melt the butter with the oil. Add the lamb and brown well on all sides, about 5 minutes. Add the onions, garlic, ginger, cinnamon and turmeric and sauté for a few minutes. Add the remaining 3 cups (24 fl oz/750 ml) water and simmer, uncovered, over low heat for 30 minutes.

Add the meat-onion mixture, drained chick-peas, tomatoes, parsley and cilantro to the lentils and simmer for 15 minutes. Add salt to taste and the pepper; the soup should be peppery. If it seems too thick, thin it with a little of the reserved cooking liquid. Remove the soup from the heat.

In a small bowl whisk together the eggs and lemon juice. Stir into the soup. Serve at once.

SERVES 6

EGYPT

MELOKHIA

Melokhia Leaf Soup

The melokhia *is a leaf of a species of mallow plant. The leaves resemble mint or small spinach and they form the basis of a classic and ancient Egyptian soup. They have an undistinguished taste but contribute an interesting texture to a soup. It is almost impossible to buy fresh* melokhia *outside its world of use, but you can find dried* melokhia *in stores that specialize in Middle Eastern foods. This soup is traditionally flavored with* taklia *(also called* ta'leya*), a mixture of garlic, coriander and cayenne pepper sautéed in clarified butter. Cooked rice or diced bread is also sometimes added to the soup.*

1½ cups (4 oz/125 g) dried *melokhia* leaves
6 cups (48 fl oz/1.5 l) meat or chicken stock (see glossary)

FOR THE *TAKLIA:*

2 tablespoons clarified butter (see glossary)
4 cloves garlic, finely minced
1 tablespoon ground coriander
½ teaspoon cayenne pepper
chopped onion marinated in fresh lemon juice or distilled white vinegar for garnish (optional)

In a blender or a food processor fitted with the metal blade, crush the dried *melokhia* leaves. You'll have about 1¼–1½ cups (4 oz/125 g) powder. In a bowl soak this powder in a little of the cold stock for about 20 minutes, to soften it. In a saucepan bring the remaining stock to a boil. Stir in the soaked *melokhia,* reduce the heat to low and simmer uncovered, stirring often to prevent *melokhia* from sinking to the bottom, until thickened, about 20 minutes.

While the soup is simmering, make the *taklia.* In a sauté pan over medium heat, melt the butter. Add the garlic and sauté for a few minutes. Stir in the coriander and cayenne and cook for 2–3 minutes longer.

When the soup is ready, stir in the *taklia* and simmer for 2 minutes. Ladle into individual bowls and pass the marinated onions, if desired, for diners to garnish the soup to taste.

SERVES 6

SICILY

Pallottine in Brodo

Meatball Soup

Soup is more fun to eat when such treasures as tiny meatballs are floating in the rich broth. In Spain, meatball soup includes tomatoes, a pinch of saffron and croutons. In Lebanon, cooked rice or noodles may be added, and in Greece the broth is enriched with the traditional avgolemono *mixture of egg yolks and lemon juice, a custom also found in Italian Jewish cooking. For this particular recipe, vigorously whisk together 2 egg yolks and the juice of 2 lemons and then blend in a little hot broth before whisking the mixture into the pan.*

The meatballs can be made with veal, beef or lamb. In Greece, a little garlic goes into the meatballs and they are sometimes seasoned with cumin, nutmeg, cloves, coriander and allspice. In the Arab countries, parsley, cinnamon, cumin and allspice are added. Finally, the meatballs can be sautéed first and then added to the hot broth, in which case they should be simmered only 15 minutes before continuing with the recipe.

FOR THE MEATBALLS:

½ lb (250 g) ground (minced) beef, veal or lamb
¼–½ cup (1¼–2½ oz/40–75 g) grated onion
½ cup (1 oz/30 g) bread crumbs
1 egg
3 tablespoons grated pecorino cheese
salt and freshly ground pepper

6 cups (48 fl oz/1.5 l) flavorful meat stock (see glossary)
4 cups (28 oz/875 g) cooked chopped escarole
1 cup (5 oz/155 g) cooked tiny pasta shells or other tiny macaroni shape
salt and freshly ground pepper
4 tablespoons chopped fresh flat-leaf (Italian) parsley (optional)

To make the meatballs, in a bowl combine the meat, onion, bread crumbs, egg, cheese and salt and pepper to taste. Form into tiny meatballs about ½ in (12 mm) in diameter. Set aside.

In a large saucepan combine the stock and escarole and simmer for 10 minutes. Slip in the uncooked meatballs and simmer gently over low heat until the meatballs are cooked, about 20 minutes. Add the pasta and simmer for 5 minutes.

Ladle into individual bowls and sprinkle with the chopped parsley, if desired.

SERVES 6

TURKEY

Tutmaç Corbasi

Yogurt Soup with Noodles and Small Meatballs

Tutmaç *means "do not keep us hungry." This soup will do the job. It can be made without the meatballs, in which case you can add 1 cup (6 oz/185 g) each cooked chick-peas (garbanzo beans) and (5 oz/155 g) cooked white rice and heat through. Another version of this soup calls for deep-frying the pasta before adding it to the soup.*

FOR THE MEATBALLS:

½ lb (250 g) ground (minced) lamb or beef
1 teaspoon salt
½ teaspoon freshly ground pepper
½ teaspoon paprika
2 tablespoons olive oil or unsalted butter

3 cups (1½ lb/750 g) plain yogurt
2 egg yolks
2 tablespoons all-purpose (plain) flour
2 cups (16 fl oz/500 ml) lamb stock or water
2–3 cloves garlic, crushed (optional)
5–6 oz (155–185 g) fresh or dried egg noodles, cut or broken into small pieces
1 teaspoon salt
½ teaspoon freshly ground pepper
cayenne pepper (optional)
¼ cup (2 oz/60 g) unsalted butter
1 onion, finely chopped
2 tablespoons dried mint, crumbled

To make the meatballs, in a bowl combine the meat, salt, pepper and paprika and mix well. Form into tiny meatballs about ½ in (12 mm) in diameter. In a frying pan over medium heat, warm the oil or butter. Add the meatballs and fry, turning, until lightly browned on all sides, 2–3 minutes. Set aside.

In a bowl whisk together the yogurt, egg yolks and flour until well blended. (This mixture will stabilize the soup and keep it from curdling.) Place in a heavy-bottomed saucepan and bring slowly to a simmer. Add the stock or water and the garlic, if using, and bring to a boil. Add the noodles and reduce the heat. Simmer gently, uncovered, until the noodles are cooked, 1–2 minutes for fresh and about 3 minutes for dry. Add the salt and pepper and cayenne to taste (if using).

While the soup is simmering, melt the butter in a sauté pan over medium heat. Add the onion and mint and sauté until the onion is tender and translucent, 8–10 minutes.

When the soup is ready, stir in the sautéed onion and the meatballs and warm through. Serve hot.

SERVES 6

GREECE

Tarhana

Sour Pasta Soup

The Greeks and Turks both call the sour pasta that is the basis of this soup tarhana, *which means "crispy." In Syria and Lebanon it is called* kishk. *This pelletlike pasta is made from flour, salt, eggs, sour milk and water or yogurt, and the dough is left to dry in the sun, then broken into small pieces. It keeps all winter long. While it is most often prepared in soup,* tarhana *can also be cooked like a pasta and dressed with tomatoes and butter. Look for it in stores that specialize in Middle Eastern foods. If you like, omit the lemon wedges and garnish with chopped fresh mint and fried onions, as is done in Syria and Lebanon, or with red sweet peppers (capsicums), as is done in Turkey.*

½ cup (2 oz/60 g) *tarhana*
5 cups (40 fl oz/1.1 l) meat stock (see glossary)
3 or 4 tomatoes, peeled, seeded and diced
¼ lb (125 g) *haloumi,* grated, or *kasseri* or mozzarella cheese, cut into small dice (see glossary)
lemon wedges

If the *tarhana* is in large pieces, break it into ¼-in (3-mm) pieces. In a bowl combine the *tarhana* with water to cover and let soak for 2–3 hours. Drain.

In a saucepan bring the stock to a boil. Add the soaked *tarhana,* stirring frequently. Add the tomatoes, cover, reduce the heat to low and simmer until the pasta is tender, 10–15 minutes.

Ladle into bowls and stir in the cheese. Serve hot with lemon wedges.

SERVES 6

Top to bottom: Meatball Soup, Yogurt Soup with Noodles and Small Meatballs, Sour Pasta Soup

TURKEY

CACIK

Cold Yogurt Soup

A refreshing summer soup popular in Greece and the Balkans, as well as Turkey. Without the water, this makes a delightful summer salad.

2 cups (16 oz/500 g) plain yogurt
1 clove garlic, finely minced
1 large cucumber, peeled, seeded and shredded or finely diced
3 tablespoons chopped toasted walnuts
½ cup (¾ oz/20 g) chopped fresh mint
salt and freshly ground pepper
ice water

In a bowl combine all of the ingredients except the ice water. Cover and refrigerate for 2–4 hours.

At serving time, thin with ice water to desired consistency. Taste and adjust the seasoning, then ladle into individual bowls and serve immediately.

SERVES 4

ANDALUSIA

CALDO DE PERRO GADITANO

Cádiz Fish Soup with Bitter Orange

Bitter Seville oranges are difficult to find. Here, their slightly astringent flavor is reproduced with a mixture of orange and lime juices. If you should happen upon Sevilles in the market, use ½ cup (4 fl oz/125 ml) of their juice in place of the two citrus juices. If you do not have fish stock on hand, use part chicken stock and part bottled clam juice. The mixture will not impart as sweet a flavor to the final soup, but it will still taste quite good.

1 lb (500 g) firm white fish fillet such as monkfish (anglerfish), flounder or cod
kosher salt
3 tablespoons olive oil
1 large onion, chopped
2 cloves garlic, minced
1 tablespoon finely grated orange zest (optional)
4 cups (32 fl oz/1 l) fish stock (see glossary)
⅓ cup (3 fl oz/80 ml) fresh orange juice
2 tablespoons fresh lime or lemon juice
salt and freshly ground pepper
chopped fresh mint or flat-leaf (Italian) parsley (optional)

Cut the fish into long strips ½ in (12 mm) wide and 1½ in (4 cm) long. Place in a shallow dish and sprinkle with a little kosher salt. Cover and refrigerate the fish until it is time to add it to the soup.

In a 1½-qt (1.5-l) saucepan over medium heat, warm the oil. Add the onion and sauté until tender and translucent, 8–10 minutes. Add the garlic, reduce the heat to low and sauté, stirring occasionally, for 5 minutes longer; do not allow to color.

Add the orange zest (if using; it will add extra flavor), stir well and pour in the stock. Simmer for 15 minutes. Add the fish pieces and cook until the fish is tender, 7–10 minutes.

Stir in the citrus juices and season to taste with salt and pepper. Serve immediately, garnished with mint or parsley (if using).

SERVES 4–6 *Photograph on pages 100–101*

ANDALUSIA

SOPA DE ALMENDRAS

Almond Soup from Granada

There are two famous almond soups in southern Spain. One is a chilled almond and grape gazpacho from Malaga, and the other is this hot almond soup from Granada. Both are thickened with a bread and water-base, but one is sweet and cool and the other, this one, is savory.

3 tablespoons olive oil
1 cup (5½ oz/170 g) whole blanched almonds
3 cloves garlic, minced
2 slices bread, coarsely chopped
1 teaspoon saffron threads, finely chopped
3 peppercorns, smashed
1 sweet red pepper (capsicum), seeded, deribbed and diced
2 tablespoons chopped fresh flat-leaf (Italian) parsley, plus chopped parsley for garnish (optional)
4 cups (32 fl oz/1 l) water, boiling
salt and freshly ground pepper

In a sauté pan over medium heat, warm the olive oil. Add the almonds and fry, stirring, until golden, about 8 minutes. Using a slotted spoon transfer to paper towels to drain.

To the oil remaining in the pan, add the garlic, bread, saffron, peppercorns, sweet pepper and parsley. Sauté over medium heat until the bread is golden, about 5–8 minutes. Transfer the almonds and the bread mixture to a food processor fitted with the metal blade, a blender or a mortar, and process or pound to a paste. Transfer the paste to a saucepan over low heat and gradually stir in the water. Simmer for 5 minutes. Season to taste with salt and pepper.

Serve hot, garnished with more chopped parsley, if desired.

SERVES 6 *Photograph on pages 100–101*

ANDALUSIA

GAZPACHO

Cold Tomato Soup

There are many versions of gazpacho served in Andalusia. The word is Arabic in origin and means "soaked bread." Despite the etymology, soaked bread does not appear as a thickener in every gazpacho recipe, although bread sometimes appears in the form of garlic croutons as a garnish. In some recipes, all the vegetables are puréed; in others, only half the vegetables are puréed and the remainder are finely chopped and served as a garnish. Some gazpachos include herbs; others have none. Some are served chilled; others have ice added. All the recipes have one thing in common: success is dependent upon ripe, flavorful tomatoes. This soup can be made the day before serving.

2 green sweet peppers (capsicums), seeded, deribbed and coarsely chopped
2 small cucumbers, peeled, seeded and coarsely chopped
1 onion, coarsely chopped
2 or 3 cloves garlic, coarsely chopped

2 lb (1 kg) vine-ripened tomatoes, peeled, seeded and coarsely chopped
1 cup (8 fl oz/250 ml) tomato juice, well chilled, or ice water
¼ cup (2 fl oz/60 ml) red wine vinegar
½ cup (1 oz/30 g) fresh bread crumbs, soaked in water to cover and squeezed dry (optional)
½ cup (4 fl oz/125 ml) fruity olive oil
salt and freshly ground pepper
ice cubes (optional)

Cold Yogurt Soup

FOR GARNISH:

2 cups (12 oz/375 g) diced, peeled tomatoes
1 cup (5 oz/155 g) peeled, seeded and diced cucumber
1 cup (5 oz/155 g) minced green sweet pepper (capsicum)
½ cup (2½ oz/75 g) finely minced onion
2 cups (3 oz/90 g) garlic-flavored croutons

In a blender or in a food processor fitted with a metal blade, combine the green pepper, and cucumbers and purée. Transfer to a large bowl. Add the onion and garlic to the blender or processor and again purée. Combine with the green pepper mixture. Finally, place the tomatoes in the blender or processor and purée to desired consistency; some like the purée smooth, while others prefer it chunky. Mix the tomatoes in with the other vegetables.

Stir in the tomato juice or ice water, vinegar, the bread crumbs, if using, and the oil. Season to taste with salt and pepper. Cover and chill.

Serve the soup well chilled. If you like, add an ice cube to each individual bowl. Pass the garnishes in separate bowls for each person to add to their own bowl of soup.

SERVES 6 *Photograph on pages 100–101*

GREECE AND THE BALKANS

GREECE

and the Balkans

Whether or not the present-day inhabitants of Greece are, to any degree at all, the lineal descendants of the ancient Greeks is a matter of scholarly dispute. None will deny, however, that a devotion to gastronomy and the anchoring of food in social and ritual life combine to provide an element of continuity between ancient and modern Greece.

Food, including the quintessential Mediterranean trinity of olive oil, bread and wine, figures prominently in Greek mythology, which is not surprising, considering the Greek gods had desires and appetites at least as voracious as those of mortals. The trouble seems to have started with Zeus, who, finding his father Kronos asleep after eating too much honey—obviously the primordial food—chained him and transported him to the end of the world. He then went on to disguise himself as a snake and ungallantly to seduce his sister Demeter, the earth mother. The result of this liaison was Persephone, goddess of harvests, whose annual parole from bondage in the underworld—the unfortunate consequence of ingesting a pomegranate seed at the wrong time—was appropriately fixed for harvest time. Distraught at the loss of Persephone, Demeter was consoled by a family of herdsmen, and as a token of her gratitude gave them some ears of corn she happened to be carrying. Triptolemus, the youngest son

Previous pages: Mykonos is quickly becoming the St. Tropez of the Cyclàdes Islands, where the chic descend in large numbers during the summer months. Left: Dubrovnik, founded some 1300 years ago, was considered one of the most important medieval city states on the Adriatic.

of the family, disseminated the gift among peoples who had previously been hunters and gatherers.

Demeter had an unusually turbulent life, even for a goddess; another incestuous union left her pregnant with Dionysus, god of the vine, whose devotees, not content with their privileged access to inebriation, went on to acquire a monopoly on the cultivation of figs. As for the olive, it was the gift of Pallas Athene to the city that bore her name, and the art of extracting its oil was first taught to mortals by Aristaios, son of Apollo. Little wonder, then, that every agricultural process in ancient Greece assumed a ritual aspect, and that a cook was able to remark, in a play by Menander, a poet of the third century B.C., that "our profession is somehow sacrosanct."

The diet of the ancient Greeks was at first more varied than subtle. They considered edible almost as wide a range of quadrupeds as the Chinese. In his *Regimen,* Hippocrates discusses the merits of the horse, ass, dog, fox, hedgehog and wild boar, as well as sheep, goats and pigs; the meat of the pig, including its offal, stood in particularly high esteem (after all, had not Zeus been suckled by a wild sow?). Fishing got off to a slow start, and Homer even described fish as "a wretched food, the last resource of shipwrecked sailors," but later Archestratus was able to list a wide range of fish recipes, and it is to these ancient antecedents that the present abundance of seafood dishes undeniably goes back. In the course of time, both meat and fish dishes came to be plentifully adorned with herbs and sauces; it has been credibly argued that béchamel sauce is of Greek ancestry. The Greeks realized that the aesthetic appeal of food depends on color and scent as well as on taste, as Theophrastus explains in his *Enquiry into Plants,* and the fact that the word *aroma* is of Greek origin speaks for itself. The ancient Greeks were also master bakers. They invented the brick oven for baking bread, and elaborated numerous different kinds of bread, some for ritual use; Athenaeus lists for us no fewer than seventy-two varieties. Bread was, indeed, an indispensable part of each meal, which consisted by definition of bread (maza) and the meat, fish or vegetables placed on top of it *(opson);* this combination may be regarded as the ancestor of both pizza and *pissaladière.*

A second component of Greek cuisine derives from the traditions of the Byzantine Empire and the Greek Orthodox Church, the principal legacy of the Byzantines to modern Greece. The name *Byzantine* has become a byword for intricacy and complexity, and the cuisine of the Byzantines, like that of any great empire, was certainly eclectic, drawing not only on ancient Greece but also on Syria, Persia and even India. One Byzantine empress, Lupicina, was a working cook before her elevation to imperial grandeur, and another, Theodora, first mistress and then wife of Justinian, took a personal interest in the administration of the palace kitchens. The chief contributions of the Byzantines appear to have been an enhanced use of vegetables, a marked indulgence in rich pastries, and a great emphasis on fish.

This last feature was due in large part to the adoption of Christianity. The fish was an emblem of the early Church, and Christians were often represented as fish because of their redemption by the waters of baptism.

Evzones, *Greek soldiers in traditional uniforms who stand guard outside the Presidential Palace, are familiar figures in Athens.*

More importantly, the frequent abstention from meat that was imposed on the faithful led naturally to a compensatory consumption of fish. An extensive calendar of saints' days, in addition to the principal festivals of Easter and Christmas, acquired a gastronomic accompaniment of special foods, and pilgrimage to the tombs of the saints is even now the occasion for eating as well as devotion. (This is, of course, a common feature of virtually all Mediterranean cultures, both Christian and Muslim.) One of the Three Hierarchs of the Greek Orthodox church, St. Basil of Caesarea, has a special association with food; the *vasilopita,* a bread named after him, is frequently eaten in both churches and homes, especially on New Year's Day. More generally, the sacral associations of food, inherited from ancient Greece, have been preserved by the custom of taking food and drink to the church for blessing.

Much of the substance of present-day Greek cuisine goes back to the long centuries of Ottoman dominion. This is evidenced by the large number of Turkish-derived names encountered in the Greek menu: *dolmathes,* stuffed vegetables, from *dolma; pilafi,* rice, from *pilav; keftedes,* patties of ground meat, from *köfte; tsoureki,* sweet bread, from *çörek; yuvetsi,* casserole, from *güveç; tsatziki,* cucumber and yogurt salad, from *cacik; lukoumades,* fried dough puffs, from *lokma; bourekakia,* bread pies, from *börek;* and so on. The argument that these names conceal originally Greek dishes on which the Ottoman conquerors imposed their own names is ill-advised. Like other subject peoples, the Greeks enjoyed a broad measure of cultural autonomy under Ottoman rule, and no comparable body of loanwords can be found in any other sector of Greek vocabulary. When we examine Ottoman cuisine in its own right on our next port of call, Turkey, we shall see that the traffic was in any event not all one way. The safest conclusion to draw on this contentious aspect of Greco-Turkish relations is that both peoples made their varying contributions to a culinary synthesis that came to perfection during the centuries of Ottoman rule.

Before taking leave of Greece, let us note the special case of Corfu, a Greek island in the Adriatic, which because of location and history has absorbed Venetian, French and even British influences, the last resulting not so much from the modern influx of British tourists as from a military occupation that lasted from 1810 to 1863. It must, however, be remarked with respect to Greece as a whole (as well as Spain and some parts of France) that one of the deleterious effects of mass tourism has been the increasing currency of a banal "international" cuisine and the frequent reduction of the national cuisine, at the restaurant level, to a mere parody of a handful of its best-known dishes.

If we disregard the proud Hellenic assertion that even geographically Greece is a separate world of its own, and hence not part of the Balkans, Greece can be described as the only Balkan country with a Mediterranean coastline. It is nonetheless justifiable to regard most of the territories of the former Yugoslavia, as well as Albania, together with their cuisines, as Mediterranean. The Adriatic Sea on which they front is in truth a vast inlet of the inland sea that is the Mediterranean, not a separate body of water. Moreover, the cultural and culinary characteristics of the Balkans are for the most part derived from a southward orientation toward the Mediterranean world proper.

The term "Balkanization" is firmly established in our vocabulary to mean the crumbling of a territory into unstable and mutually hostile fragments. There can indeed be no doubt that the Balkans are one of the most fractious regions on earth. It is therefore ironic that its warring populations share essentially the same cuisine, one derived from the Ottoman Turks. The coming of the Turks to the Balkans favored the growth of agriculture by greatly lessening the fiscal burden to which the peasantry was subject, and by establishing a network of routes by which the principal towns were kept well supplied. The cuisine they bestowed on the Balkans was one manifestation of a common way of life that took shape in southeastern Europe during the centuries of Ottoman rule; aesthetic tastes, attitudes to family life, domestic and urban architecture were often indistinguishable between Muslims and Christians, despite a mutuality of religious dislike. The common cuisine has also been the most tenacious aspect of the Ottoman legacy in the Balkans; even as the Serbs seek to exterminate the Muslims, whom they identify (incorrectly) as Turks, they feed on dishes bequeathed to them precisely by the Turks.

It goes without saying that the Turkish culinary imprint is deepest in those regions where widespread conversion to Islam brought about the closest identification with the Ottomans—Bosnia-Hercegovina, Macedonia and Albania. This could easily have been confirmed, before 1992, by a visit to the Ascinica, a bustling popular restaurant facing the Bascarsija, the now shattered heart of the old city of Sarajevo. The fare available there—steaming pots of invigorating soup and *pilav,* stuffed vegetables and stews, huge trays of cheese *börek*—corresponded exactly to the offerings of an average Anatolian restaurant. But common to all the central and southern territories of the former Yugoslavia were such Turkish dishes as *cevapcici,* minced lamb or beef cooked on skewers, the Turkish *şiş köfte; djuvec,* the casserole we have already encountered in Greece; *sarma,* stuffed cabbage leaves; *poğaca,* pasties or turnovers; and *kaymak,* a thick cream eaten mostly as an accompaniment to desserts but sometimes, with bread, as a food in itself.

On the other hand, certain Serbian specialties involving the use of pork are unconnected to the Ottoman legacy for obvious reasons. Examples are *plieskavica,* grilled meat patties of pork and veal; *raznjici,* pork and veal kebabs; and *bosanski lonac,* "Bosnian hotpot," a stew made with a promiscuous mixture of beef, pork, lamb, calf's feet and bacon. Vojvodina, in the north of Serbia, has a large Hungarian population, a fact reflected in the cuisine. Turkish culinary influences are also not much in evidence along the Dalmatian coast of Croatia, which facing Italy across the Adriatic has always been receptive to the Italian example, as the walled city of Dubrovnik spectacularly demonstrates. Dalmatia is accordingly fond of pasta and is famous for a kind of ham reminiscent of prosciutto. And once we enter the northward-looking heartlands of Croatia, we unmistakably exit the Mediterranean culinary zone and enter the realm of Germanic stodge.

As for Albania, it has been triply impoverished by isolation, communism and an anarchic dismantling of the collective farm system in the post-communist era. The linguistic evidence suggests, however, a general conformity to Turkish culinary models.

The entire village of Sveti Stefan, in Yugoslavia, was converted into a luxury resort hotel in the 1960s.

Fish and Shellfish

The most popular Mediterranean method for cooking fish is grilling over an open wood fire.

FISH AND SHELLFISH

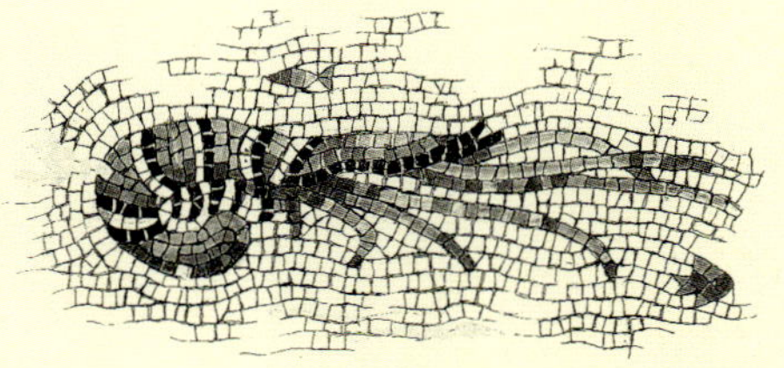

Fish is arguably the most common form of animal protein on the Mediterranean menu. Local fish markets are busy, noisy, exciting places; their numerous stalls are filled with glistening creatures from the sea. To those of us accustomed to a limited selection at our markets, much of it "fresh frozen," the variety is overwhelming.

Throughout the Mediterranean, but especially in Greece and Turkey, the red mullet is prized and is usually served pan-fried. Sea bass, called *levrek* in Turkey, *rofos* in Greece and *spigola* in Italy, can be grilled or baked. Swordfish—*kiliç* in Turkey, *pesce spada* in Italy and *xifias* in Greece—can be baked or grilled and is most popular in Turkey and Sicily. In Sicily, tuna is grilled, stewed or baked as well as added to pasta. Along with these Mediterranean favorites are John Dory, turbot, angler (monkfish), mackerel, grouper, sea bream, cod, sole, porgy, perch, sardines, anchovies, snapper, trout, pike, skate, eel, octopus, squid, scallops, a variety of shrimp and prawns, clams, mussels, lobsters, crabs and other delicacies. One never tires of the treasures of the sea or the rivers.

However plentiful and varied the fish and shellfish may be, most are prepared with a minimum of fanfare—a drop or two of fragrant olive oil, a spritz of fresh lemon or orange juice, a dash of vinegar, some slivers of garlic, a few sprigs of rosemary or marjoram, a bay leaf or two, a sprinkling of cumin, paprika or coriander. And, of course, there is always a good dusting with salt. Sometimes fish is put into a flavorful marinade for a few hours before cooking, with the Moroccan *chermoula* the pinnacle of the marinade family.

By far the most popular method for cooking fish in the Mediterranean countries is grilling over a wood fire. Sometimes herbs are thrown onto the fire to add another flavor dimension. Fish can be grilled whole, sliced into steaks or cut into cubes and threaded onto skewers. It can be wrapped in grapeleaves to prevent it from sticking to the grill and to impart a subtle flavor. When fish is cooked over a wood fire, the slightly smoky scent perfumes the delicate flesh, so only a light sauce is required. Lemon and olive oil with or without herbs is the usual marinade or sauce.

Second only to grilling is frying. Fish and shellfish can be pan-fried without a coating, as in Greek sautéed sea bass with vinegar and rosemary or the Catalan *gambas al ajillo,* shrimp with garlic and lemon. Or they are deep-fried, first cloaked in a covering that may be as simple as a quick dip in flour and then quickly immersed in hot oil, drained, and served piping hot, doused with a squeeze of fresh lemon. The fish emerge crisp on the outside, tender and succulent on the inside, and not cooked a moment longer than necessary. Tiny fish or combinations of fish and shellfish—the ubiquitous local *fritto misto* of southern Italy—are piled high on a platter and served along with a dish of cut lemons or sometimes a dipping sauce such as the Turkish walnut or hazelnut *tarator,* the Catalan *romesco,* the Provençal aioli.

Previous pages: left to right; Grilled Swordfish (recipe page 131), Stuffed Mackerel (recipe page 131)

The repertoire of baked fish and shellfish recipes has increased as the oven has appeared in more and more homes. These recipes are generally simple to prepare. Dishes such as Greek *garides youvetsi,* shrimp with feta cheese and tomato sauce; *coquilles St.-Jacques à la provençale;* Moroccan *al toune bil tomatich,* tuna with tomato sauce and preserved lemon; Sicilian *triglie in cartoccio,* red mullet in parchment; or Provençal eel with leeks, olives and wine can be assembled ahead of time and then slipped into a hot oven just before serving.

Sometimes fish is roasted as if it were meat. *Gigot de mer*—"leg of lamb of the sea"—finds monkfish (angler fish) studded with garlic and baked atop a bed of *ratatouille.* In the Sicilian *alalungo al ragu,* tuna is studded with garlic and mint, fried, and then braised either in the oven or atop the stove.

Many of the baked or braised fish dishes are served at room temperature, as in the past they were baked in the town oven and then carried home to be eaten later. In the Mediterranean, people are accustomed to room-temperature foods and find that the flavors develop as the dish rests. *Sarde a beccaficu,* Sicilian stuffed sardines, are good hot but perhaps even better cold. The Lebanese *samak bi tahini,* a whole fish coated with a rich sesame sauce, surrounded by sliced cucumbers and radishes, topped with toasted pine nuts and pomegranate seeds and served cold, is one of the most spectacular dishes of the region. Boned whole Turkish mackerel stuffed with a fragrant rice pilaf, baked and served hot or at room temperature is carefully carved at the table.

The Mediterranean is also home to what is probably the largest array of fish stews and soups. They can be simple: fish balls braised in a savory tomato sauce, mussels steamed in wine and garlic, or squid simmered in a simple tomato sauce with peas. In some stews, shellfish and fish are combined in an opulent medley to show off the day's catch. Because of the great variety offered at fish markets, an elaborate fish stew such as peppery *bourthéto* of Corfu; Sardinian *cassola,* a relative of the Spanish *zarzuela;* Provençal *bourride* or *bouillabaisse;* Tunisian fish couscous; or the pan-Italian *zuppa di pesce* can be prepared easily and without having to pray for fair weather and calm seas.

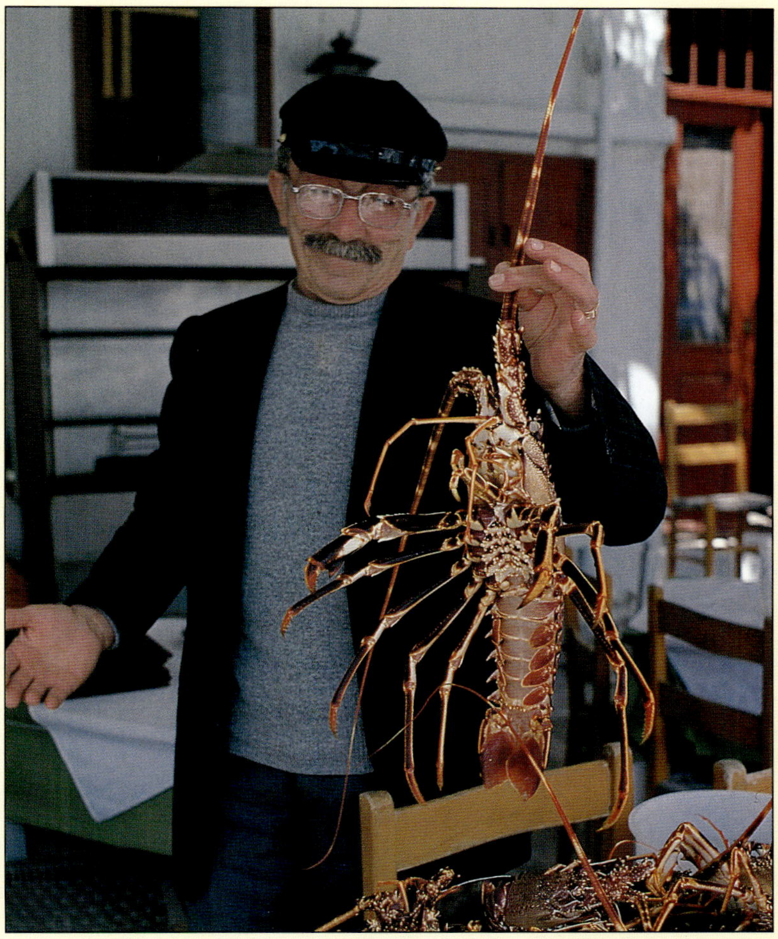

A Greek fishmonger proudly displays the morning's fresh lobster catch.

When dogfish or goby or turbot or John Dory are mentioned in a recipe but are not to be found at your local fish market, substitutes are suggested. Your fishmonger may have some excellent suggestions for you as well. Be sure the fish you buy smells sweet and is firm to the touch and glistening. Cook it the day you bring it home. Remember, unlike wine, it does not improve with age. And be careful not to overcook fish; it is best when still moist.

From ancient times, fishing has played a vital role in the economic activity of the Mediterranean basin.

Top to bottom: Shrimp with Feta Cheese, Baked Fish with Bread Crumbs and Tomatoes

GREECE

Psari Spétsiotika

Baked Fish with Bread Crumbs and Tomatoes

Named for the island of Spétsai, this dish is very easy to prepare and very tasty. The elements are simple: impeccably fresh fish, flavorful vine-ripened tomatoes and good-quality bread crumbs. You may serve it hot or cold.

2 lb (1 kg) firm white fish fillets or steaks
6 tablespoons (3 fl oz/90 ml) olive oil
1 tablespoon fresh lemon juice
salt and freshly ground pepper
2 cups (12 oz/375 g) peeled, seeded and chopped tomatoes
4 cloves garlic, finely minced
½ cup (4 fl oz/125 ml) dry white wine
1 tablespoon sugar or honey
4 tablespoons chopped fresh flat-leaf (Italian) parsley
1 teaspoon dried oregano or ground cinnamon (optional)
1 cup (4 oz/125 g) fine dried bread crumbs

❀ Arrange the fish in a baking dish in which it fits in a single layer. In a small bowl whisk together 2 tablespoons of the oil, lemon juice, salt and pepper to taste and pour over the fish. Let stand for about 30 minutes at room temperature.
❀ Meanwhile, preheat an oven to 400°F (200°C).
❀ In a saucepan over medium heat, combine the tomatoes, garlic, wine, sugar or honey, parsley and the oregano or cinnamon, if using. Bring to a simmer and cook for about 10 minutes. Season to taste with salt and pepper.
❀ Pour the tomato sauce evenly over the fish. Scatter the bread crumbs evenly over the top, then drizzle with the remaining 4 tablespoons (2 fl oz/60 ml) oil. Bake until the fish is cooked through and bread crumbs are golden brown, about 15 minutes.
❀ Serve immediately.

SERVES 4

GREECE

Garides Youvetsi

Shrimp with Feta Cheese

Although this dish is a specialty of Salonika, it is served all over Greece. It can be prepared a few hours ahead of time and then baked in ramekins just before serving.

1½ lb (750 g) shrimp (prawns), peeled and deveined
salt and freshly ground pepper to taste, plus 2 teaspoons pepper
½ cup (4 fl oz/125 ml) olive oil
1 yellow onion, chopped
1 bunch green (spring) onions, including tender green tops, minced
2 cloves garlic, finely minced
1 tablespoon dried oregano
3 tablespoons chopped fresh basil or dill (optional)
4 tomatoes, peeled, seeded and chopped
1 teaspoon honey or sugar
½ cup (4 fl oz/125 ml) dry white wine
½ lb (250 g) feta cheese, crumbled
4 tablespoons chopped fresh flat-leaf (Italian) parsley

❀ Sprinkle the shrimp with salt and pepper. In a large sauté pan over high heat, warm ¼ cup (2 fl oz/60 ml) of the oil. Add the shrimp and sear quickly on both sides. Remove from the pan and set aside. (Refrigerate if not cooking within the next 15 minutes.)
❀ In the same pan over medium heat, warm the remaining ¼ cup (2 fl oz/60 ml) oil. Add the yellow onion and sauté until tender and translucent, 8–10 minutes. Add the green onions, garlic, oregano and the basil or dill, if using, and cook for 5 minutes longer. Add the tomatoes, honey or sugar and wine and simmer briskly to thicken the mixture, 8–10 minutes. Season with the 2 teaspoons pepper; do not add too much salt as the feta will be salty.
❀ Meanwhile, preheat an oven to 400°F (200°C). Divide half of the tomato sauce among 4 ramekins. Divide the shrimp evenly among the ramekins. Spoon the remaining tomato sauce over the shrimp. Top each portion with an equal amount of the cheese. Bake until the shrimp are cooked and the cheese melts, about 10 minutes.
❀ Alternatively, cook the tomato sauce as directed. Return the seared shrimp to the tomato sauce, sprinkle the feta on top, cover and simmer until the cheese melts, about 7 minutes.
❀ Serve hot, sprinkled with the parsley.

SERVES 4

MOROCCO

Hut B'noua

Fish with Almond Paste

An exotic and unusual dish that is not too sweet. If you want to make this dish with fish fillets, place the fillets atop a bed of the saffroned onions and spread a layer of the almond paste on the fillets. Bake, basting with a little melted butter, for 10–12 minutes.

1 whole snapper, salmon or other whole mild fish, about 3½ lb (1.75 kg), cleaned
salt for rubbing on fish, plus 1 teaspoon salt
2 cups (11 oz/345 g) almonds, toasted
½ cup (4 oz/125 g) sugar
1 teaspoon ground cinnamon
1 tablespoon orange-flower water
2 tablespoons water
2 tablespoons olive oil

1 large onion, finely chopped
½ teaspoon saffron threads steeped in ¼ cup (2 fl oz/60 ml) hot water
½ teaspoon freshly ground pepper
¼ cup (2 oz/60 g) unsalted butter, melted

Rub the fish with salt, inside and out, then rinse. Cut 3 or 4 shallow diagonal slits on each side of the body. Set aside.

Put the almonds and sugar in a blender or in a processor fitted with the metal blade and grind. Add the cinnamon, orange-flower water and the water and pulse briefly to combine. Pack half of this mixture into the fish and skewer closed. Place the fish in an oiled baking pan or ovenproof baking dish. Set aside.

Preheat an oven to 400°F (200°C). In a small sauté pan over medium heat, warm the oil. Add the onion and sauté until tender and translucent, 8–10 minutes. Add the saffron and its soaking water, the 1 teaspoon salt and the pepper. Place the saffroned onions around the fish. Rub the remaining almond paste atop the fish (not on the head or tail) and evenly drizzle on the melted butter. Bake until the fish tests done when pierced with a knife, about 30 minutes.

Transfer the fish and onions to a warmed serving platter and serve at once.

SERVES 6

MOROCCO

CHERMOULA

Spicy Marinade for Fish

Chermoula *is the classic Moroccan marinade for fish. Whether you plan to bake, grill, fry or steam the fish, marinating it in* chermoula *will enhance its flavor. Allow the fish to remain in the marinade for 2–6 hours, or preferably overnight for whole fish. Once the fish is cooked, spoon a little additional* chermoula *over the fish before serving.*

There are many versions of chermoula. *Basically, the variables are whether onion, cayenne pepper or lemon are added. Here are four recipes for* chermoula; *they can also be used for preparing shellfish, chicken, squab (pigeon) and lamb.*

FOR *CHERMOULA* I:

1 onion, finely chopped
4 cloves garlic, finely minced
2 teaspoons ground cumin
1 teaspoon paprika
½ teaspoon saffron threads steeped in 2 tablespoons water
½ cup (¾ oz/20 g) chopped fresh flat-leaf (Italian) parsley
½ cup (¾ oz/20 g) chopped fresh cilantro (fresh coriander)
6 tablespoons (3 fl oz/90 ml) olive oil
¼ cup (2 fl oz/60 ml) fresh lemon juice
salt

FOR *CHERMOULA* II:

4 tablespoons chopped fresh cilantro (fresh coriander)
3 cloves garlic, finely minced
2 teaspoons paprika
2 teaspoons ground cumin
½ teaspoon cayenne pepper
½ teaspoon saffron threads steeped in 2 tablespoons water
3 tablespoons fresh lemon juice
6 tablespoons (3 fl oz/90 ml) olive oil
salt

FOR *CHERMOULA* III:

3 cloves garlic, finely minced
peel of 1 preserved lemon, rinsed and finely minced (see glossary)
½ cup (¾ oz/20 g) chopped fresh cilantro (fresh coriander)
½ cup (¾ oz/20 g) chopped fresh flat-leaf (Italian) parsley
½ teaspoon cayenne pepper
½ teaspoon saffron threads steeped in 2 tablespoons water
1 teaspoon paprika
6 tablespoons (3 fl oz/90 ml) olive oil
3 tablespoons fresh lemon juice

FOR *CHERMOULA* IV:

2 cloves garlic, finely minced
½ cup (¾ oz/20 g) chopped fresh cilantro (fresh coriander)
½ cup (¾ oz/20 g) chopped fresh flat-leaf (Italian) parsley
1 teaspoon freshly ground pepper
½ teaspoon ground cinnamon
½ teaspoon ground ginger
½ teaspoon saffron threads steeped in ¼ cup (2 fl oz/60 ml) water
2 teaspoons ground cumin
1 teaspoon paprika
1½ teaspoons salt
6 tablespoons (3 fl oz/90 ml) olive oil

To make each recipe, in a bowl whisk together all the ingredients. Then arrange the fish in a nonreactive container and pour the marinade over the top. Marinade as directed in introduction.

Each recipe yields enough marinade for about 2 lb (1 kg) whole fish or fish fillets.

Top to bottom: Spicy Marinade for Fish, Fish with Almond Paste

LEBANON

SAMAK BI TAHINI

Fish with Tahini Sauce

This is an Arab classic, served in Syria as well as Lebanon. The fish is baked, cooled to room temperature, coated with a tahini sauce and then decorated with parsley and pine nuts. Cucumber and radish slices and pomegranate seeds (see glossary) also make good garnishes. You can add 1 cup (4 oz/125 g) chopped walnuts to the sauce. Or add ½ teaspoon cayenne pepper and ½ cup (¾ oz/20 g) chopped fresh cilantro (fresh coriander) to the tahini mixture when puréeing it, spread it on the fish when it is half-cooked and return the fish to the oven for an additional 15 minutes; serve hot or at room temperature.

salt
1 whole fish such as snapper or sea bass, 2½–3 lb (1.25–1.5 kg)
3 tablespoons olive oil
2 tablespoons fresh lemon juice
freshly ground pepper

FOR THE TAHINI SAUCE:

3 or 4 cloves garlic, finely minced
1 teaspoon salt
1 cup (8 oz/250 g) tahini (see glossary)
4–6 tablespoons (2–3 fl oz/60–90 ml) fresh lemon juice
6–8 tablespoons (3–4 fl oz/90–125 ml) water, or as needed

¼ cup (1¼ oz/40 g) pine nuts, toasted
3 tablespoons chopped fresh flat-leaf (Italian) parsley

Preheat an oven to 400°F (200°C). Sprinkle salt over the fish, then rinse. Cut 3 or 4 shallow diagonal slits on each side of the body. In a small bowl whisk together the oil, lemon juice, and salt and pepper to taste and rub this mixture over the fish. Place in a baking pan.

Bake, basting occasionally with the pan juices, until the fish tests done when pierced with a knife, 25–35 minutes. Carefully lift the fish onto a serving platter and let cool.

To make the sauce, in a blender or a processor fitted with the metal blade, combine the garlic, salt, tahini and lemon juice. Purée, adding enough of the water to achieve a fluffy mixture.

Remove and discard the skin from the fish. Spread the tahini sauce on the fish. Decorate with the pine nuts and parsley, and serve.

SERVES 6

TUNISIA

KES KOW BIL HOUT

Fish with Couscous

Fish couscous is served all over North Africa, but is at its best in Tunisia. It was brought to Sicily by the Arabs, probably during the twelfth or thirteenth century, where today it is known as cuscusù trapanese. *The mystique of preparing the semolina grain more or less vanished with the advent of instant couscous. And after making the basic couscous you may wonder what all the fuss was about. Some insist that cooking the couscous by the long method is best, but if you hold the grains warm atop the stew pot in a colander lined with cheesecloth (muslin) to absorb more of the aroma and taste, and drizzle them with a little fish broth from time to time, you'll have a wonderful dish.*

This couscous can be as simple or as elaborate as you like. Sea bass, mullet and cod are good choices for the fish. Chick-peas and assorted vegetables such as carrots, potatoes, turnips and cabbage can be added. In Tunisia the harissa *is stirred into the stew and served on the side as a condiment. In Sicily* cuscusù *is made with fish, a little onion, garlic and tomatoes, and is scented with a pinch of cinnamon. Red pepper flakes are stirred into 1 cup (8 fl oz/250 ml) of the broth, which is then served as a hot sauce on the side.*

salt
2–3 lb (1–1.5 kg) mixed fish for soup, cut into thick pieces (see introduction)
couscous made with water or part fish stock and seasoned with 1 teaspoon ground cinnamon and a little olive oil or butter (recipe on page 204)
¼ cup (2 fl oz/60 ml) olive oil
2 onions, chopped
2 cloves garlic, minced
1 teaspoon *harissa* (see glossary) or ½ teaspoon cayenne pepper
1 teaspoon ground cumin
½ teaspoon freshly ground black pepper
4–5 cups (32–40 fl oz/1–1.1 l) water or fish stock (see glossary)
2 or 3 tomatoes, peeled, seeded and chopped
3 carrots, peeled and sliced 1 in (2.5 cm) thick
2 turnips, peeled and cut into 2-in (5-cm) pieces
1 cup (6 oz/185 g) cooked chick-peas (garbanzo beans), optional
8 small new potatoes, halved (optional)

Lightly salt the fish and refrigerate it while you make the soup base. Also, begin cooking the couscous.

In a large, heavy saucepan or soup pot over medium heat, warm the oil. Add the onions and garlic and sauté for 5 minutes. Stir in the *harissa* or cayenne, cumin and black pepper. Cook for about 2 minutes, then add the water or stock, tomatoes, carrots and turnips. Simmer for 15 minutes. Add the fish and chick-peas or potatoes (if using) and simmer until the fish and potatoes are done, about 20 minutes.

To serve, spoon some couscous into individual soup bowls. Ladle the fish and vegetables around the couscous and then spoon on some of the broth. Or pile the couscous on a large platter, make a well in the center and put the fish in the middle and the vegetables around the edges. Ladle some of the broth over the top and serve the remaining broth in a bowl on the side.

SERVES 6–8

EGYPT

SAMAK MAGLI KOUSBARIYEH

Fried Fish with Tomatoes and Nuts

In the Middle East fish is usually grilled or fried. Small fish are fried whole; large fish are cut into steaks or chunks. Plain fried fish can be served with tarator *sauce (recipe on page 60),* romesco *sauce (recipe on page 134) or lemon wedges. In this recipe the fish is fried and then topped with a sauce of tomatoes, onions and nuts.*

1½ cups (7½ oz/235 g) all-purpose (plain) flour
2 teaspoons salt, plus salt to taste
½ teaspoon freshly ground pepper
1 teaspoon paprika (optional)
1 teaspoon ground coriander
2 lb (1 kg) mild white fish (see note)
safflower oil, or other vegetable oil for frying

FOR THE SAUCE:

2 tablespoons olive oil
2–3 cups (7–10½ oz/210–315 g) thinly sliced onion
2 cups (12 oz/375 g) peeled, seeded and coarsely chopped tomatoes (about 3 large)

Clockwise from top left: Fish with Couscous, Fish with Tahini Sauce, Fried Fish with Tomatoes and Nuts

1 cup (5 oz/155 g) hazelnuts (filberts) or 1 cup (4 oz/125 g) walnuts, toasted and chopped
⅓ cup (1⅔ oz/50 g) pine nuts, toasted
½ cup (4 fl oz/125 ml) water
4 tablespoons chopped fresh flat-leaf (Italian) parsley
1½ teaspoons salt
½ teaspoon freshly ground pepper
½ teaspoon ground allspice

In a shallow dish stir together the flour, the 2 teaspoons salt, pepper, paprika, and coriander. Dredge the fish in the flour mixture, shaking off any excess.

In a deep sauté pan, pour in oil to a depth of about 2 in (5 cm) and heat to 375°F (190°C), or until a bit of bread dropped into it begins to color within moments. When the oil is ready, slip the fish into it and fry, turning once, until cooked through and golden brown on both sides, about 3 minutes per side. Using a slotted spoon remove to paper towels to drain. Sprinkle with salt and set aside.

To make the sauce, in a large sauté pan over medium heat, warm the oil. Add the onion and sauté until tender and translucent, 8–10 minutes. Add the tomatoes and simmer until soft, about 5 minutes. Add both kinds of nuts and cook for a few minutes longer. Finally, add the water and season with the parsley, salt, pepper and allspice. Simmer for a few minutes to blend the flavors.

Add the fried fish to the sauce. Carefully turn the fish to coat it well and then simmer for 3 minutes to heat through. Alternatively, preheat an oven to 400°F (200°C). Place the fried fish in a baking dish, pour the sauce over the top and bake for 5–8 minutes to heat through.

Arrange the fish and sauce on a warmed deep platter and serve at once.

SERVES 4–6

Clockwise from top left: Braised Albacore Tuna, Red Mullet in Parchment, Stuffed Sardines

S I C I L Y

SARDE A BECCAFICCU

Stuffed Sardines

A beccafico *is a tiny bird that gets fat from eating figs* (fichi). *This specialty of Palermo takes its name from the fact that the stuffed sardines look like very fat little birds.*

Some recipes suggest slipping bay leaves between the rolled stuffed fish, and some add cheese, capers or olives to the filling. In Catania diced caciocavallo *cheese is added to the bread-crumb mixture and the stuffed sardines are dipped in flour and fried instead of baked. The sardines can be eaten hot or cold, and would make a great addition to an antipasto assortment.*

2½ lb (1.25 kg) fresh sardines (about 24)
6 tablespoons (3 fl oz/90 ml) olive oil
1 cup (4 oz/125 g) fine dried bread crumbs
2 cloves garlic, finely minced
⅓ cup (2 oz/60 g) pine nuts, toasted and chopped
⅓ cup (2 oz/60 g) dried currants, plumped in hot water, drained and chopped
3 tablespoons chopped fresh flat-leaf (Italian) parsley
½ cup (5 oz/155 g) sharply flavored black olives, pitted and chopped (optional)
¼ cup (1 oz/30 g) grated pecorino cheese (optional)
¼ cup (1½ oz/45 g) capers, rinsed, drained and chopped (optional)
about 24 bay leaves (optional)
2–3 tablespoons fresh lemon juice
¼ cup (2 fl oz/60 ml) orange juice (optional)

Clean the sardines by cutting off the head and fins, removing any scales, splitting them open at the belly and removing the guts. Run your finger down the backbone so that the fish opens like a book. Remove the backbone, breaking it off just at the tail.

Preheat an oven to 375°–400°F (190°–200°C).

To make the filling, in a small sauté pan over medium heat, warm 2 tablespoons of the oil. Add the bread crumbs and cook, stirring constantly, for about 3 minutes. Add the garlic and sauté for 2 minutes longer. Remove from the heat and add the pine nuts, currants, parsley and, if desired, the olives, and cheese or capers. Season to taste with salt and pepper.

Open a sardine, skin side down, and place a heaping teaspoonful of the filling near the top. Starting from the head end, roll up the fish toward the tail. Place in a lightly oiled baking dish, tail end up. Stuff and roll the other sardines in the same manner and pack them tightly in the dish so they don't unroll. If you like, slip a bay leaf between the sardines as you fit them into the dish.

In a small bowl whisk together the remaining oil, the lemon juice and the orange juice (if using) and pour over the sardines. Bake until cooked through, about 10 minutes. Transfer to a platter and serve warm or at room temperature.

SERVES 6

S I C I L Y

ALALUNGO AL RAGÙ

Braised Albacore Tuna

Here is a Sicilian recipe for braised tuna that treats the fish somewhat like leg of lamb, in that slivers of garlic and mint are inserted into small incisions in the flesh. The treatment is not unlike that for gigot de mer *(recipe on page 142). Instead of roasting the tuna, however, here it is browned and braised with onions and a scented tomato sauce. Some versions add cinnamon or chili pepper to the sauce. Serve with potatoes.*

2 lb (1 kg) albacore tuna, in one piece, skinned
4 cloves garlic
12 large fresh mint leaves
salt and freshly ground black pepper
½ cup (4 fl oz/120 ml) olive oil
½ cup (4 fl oz/125 ml) dry white wine
1 large onion, chopped
2 cups (12 oz/375 g) peeled, seeded and diced tomatoes
pinch of red pepper flakes (optional)
1 cinnamon stick, about 1 in (2.5 cm) long (optional)

Make 12 incisions about ½ in (12 mm) deep all over the fish. Cut 3 of the garlic cloves into 12 slivers. Insert a garlic sliver and mint leaf into each slit. Sprinkle the fish with salt and pepper. In a heavy saucepan over medium-high heat, warm ¼ cup (2 fl oz/60 ml) of the oil. Add the fish and brown on both sides. Add the white wine and cook until it almost evaporates, just a few minutes.

Meanwhile, mince the remaining garlic clove. In another small pan warm the remaining ¼ cup (2 fl oz/60 ml) oil. Add the onion and minced garlic and sauté until tender and translucent, 8–10 minutes. Add to the tuna along with the tomatoes and, if desired, the cinnamon or pepper flakes. Cover and cook over low heat until the tuna tests done when pierced with a knife, 45–60 minutes. Season to taste with salt and pepper.

Transfer to a warmed dish and serve at once.

SERVES 6

TURKEY

KILIÇ BALIGI IZGARASI

Grilled Swordfish

Swordfish is greatly esteemed in Turkey. Usually it is marinated and grilled. For this recipe the fish is served as a steak, but it can be cut into cubes and presented as a brochette (kılıç şiş) *as well. If you skewer the swordfish, tuck bay leaves between the cubes. While more moist when eaten hot, this swordfish can be quite tasty as a room-temperature appetizer.* Tarator *sauce (recipe on page 60) can be served as a condiment.*

6 swordfish steaks, each about 6 oz (185 g) and ¾ in (2 cm) thick
1 onion, grated
2–3 tablespoons fresh lemon juice, plus lemon juice for serving (optional)
2 cloves garlic, finely minced
2 tablespoons ground coriander
pinch of cayenne pepper
1 teaspoon paprika
¼ cup (2 fl oz/60 ml) olive oil, plus oil for brushing on fish and serving (optional)
6 bay leaves
salt and freshly ground black pepper

Place the swordfish in a shallow nonreactive container. In a bowl whisk together the onion, lemon juice, garlic, coriander, cayenne, paprika and the ¼ cup (2 fl oz/60 ml) oil. Alternatively, whirl in a blender or a food processor fitted with a metal blade. Pour over the fish. Add the bay leaves. Cover and marinate in the refrigerator, turning the fish a few times in the marinade to coat well, for 5–6 hours.

Preheat a broiler (griller) or prepare a fire in a charcoal grill. Remove the fish from the marinade. Brush both sides of each steak lightly with oil and sprinkle with salt and black pepper. Place on broiler pan or on grill rack and broil or grill, turning once, until done when tested with a knife, 4–5 minutes on each side.

Transfer to a serving platter. If you like, whisk together a little oil and lemon juice to taste and spoon over the fish. Serve at once or at room temperature.

SERVES 6 *Photograph pages 122–123*

TURKEY

USKUMRU DOLMASI

Stuffed Mackerel

Here fish is treated as a dolma, *filled with a savory herb, nut and raisin stuffing, then fried, broiled (grilled), cooked over a charcoal fire or baked, and served hot or at room temperature. (If you are grilling or broiling the fish, brush it with olive oil before you begin cooking it and then cook it for about 4 minutes on each side.) Traditionally, the fish bones and meat are removed, leaving only the skin of the fish intact. Then the fish flesh is mixed with the filling ingredients and the mixture spooned back inside the skin. This delicate procedure requires practice and patience. It is far simpler to put the filling in the boned fish and sew or skewer it closed.*

2 tablespoons olive oil, plus olive oil for frying
2 onions, chopped
½ teaspoon ground allspice
1 teaspoon ground cinnamon
½ teaspoon ground cloves
3 tablespoons pine nuts, toasted
3 tablespoons chopped, toasted hazelnuts (filberts) or walnuts
¼ cup (1½ oz/45 g) raisins or dried currants, plumped in hot water and drained
4 tablespoons chopped fresh dill
4 tablespoons chopped fresh flat-leaf (Italian) parsley
1 cup (2 oz/60 g) fresh bread crumbs (optional)
salt and freshly ground pepper
4 whole mackerel, Coho salmon or salmon trout, 10–12 oz (315–375 g) each, cleaned
all-purpose (plain) flour for coating
lemon wedges

In a large sauté pan over medium heat, warm the oil. Add the onions and sauté until tender and translucent, 8–10 minutes. Add the allspice, cinnamon and cloves and sauté for 2 minutes longer. Remove from the heat and add both kinds of nuts, the raisins or currants, dill, parsley and bread crumbs (if using). Season to taste with salt and pepper. Let cool to room temperature.

Divide the filling evenly among the fish and stuff it into the cavities. Sew or skewer closed. Put flour in a large, shallow bowl and season to taste with salt and pepper. Dredge the fish in the flour and shake off the excess.

In a large sauté pan over medium heat, pour in oil to a depth of ½ in (6 mm). When the oil is hot, add the fish (do not crowd the pan) and fry until golden, turning once, about 4 minutes on each side.

Transfer to a serving platter. Serve hot or at room temperature with lemon wedges.

SERVES 4 *Photograph pages 122–123*

SICILY

TRIGLIE IN CARTOCCIO

Red Mullet in Parchment

Since not everyone can find red mullet, trout or other small whole fish will work well for this dish. And you may use aluminum foil instead of parchment paper to wrap the fish. The stuffing is more like a pesto or paste than a filling. You may grill the fish, if you like, in which case you can wrap them in aluminum foil or grapeleaves (see method on page 141).

4 tablespoons finely chopped fresh mint leaves
2 cloves garlic, finely minced
4 anchovy fillets in olive oil, drained and finely minced
¼ cup (1 oz/30 g) fine dried bread crumbs
about ¼ cup (2 fl oz/60 ml) olive oil

4 trout or large red mullet, cleaned and heads and fins removed (6–8 oz/185–250 g each after cleaning)
salt
2 teaspoons chopped fresh marjoram

Preheat an oven to 450°F (230°C). In a mortar with a pestle, pound together the mint, garlic and anchovies to form a paste. Add the bread crumbs and enough oil to form a spreadable paste.

Lay each fish on a sheet of aluminum foil or parchment paper large enough to form a loose envelope that will enclose it completely. Open the fish up and sprinkle the insides with salt. Then spread each cavity with about one-fourth of the paste. Fold the fish closed, drizzle with oil and sprinkle with ½ teaspoon of the marjoram. Fold the foil or paper over the fish and pinch edges together well to seal. Repeat with the remaining fish and filling. Bake until the fish is cooked through, 10–15 minutes. Unwrap, transfer to a platter and serve at once.

SERVES 4

SARDINIA

CASSOLA

Fish Soup

This fish soup takes its name from the cazuela, *or dish, in which it is traditionally cooked. The name seems Spanish and it is, because Sardinia was under Spanish rule for many years (1297–1714). Catalan dialect is still spoken in Cagliari, Sardinia's principal city, where this soup is a specialty. Other food terms that show Spanish influence are* impanadas *for* impanata *(a stuffed pastry),* ghisau *for* guisado *(meat braised in tomato sauce), and* lepudrida *for* l'olla podrida *(a stew of meat and vegetables). This* zuppa di pesce *is quite spicy with hot pepper, but you can temper the fire if you like. You can add crab, eel, octopus and/or squid in place of some of the fish. Or about 1½ pounds (750 g) fish fillets can replace the whole fish, and you can use already made fish stock (such as the stock for the* bourride *on page 144) instead of making the stock from the fish heads.*

2 lb (1 kg) assorted whole firm white fish, such as bass, mullet or scorpion fish
4 cups (32 fl oz/1 l) water or dry white wine
¼ cup (2 fl oz/60 ml) olive oil
2 onions, diced
2 cloves garlic, finely minced
6 fresh basil leaves
red pepper flakes or whole dried chili peppers
1 lb (500 g) tomatoes, peeled, seeded and diced
2 lb (1 kg) clams in the shell, well scrubbed
salt and freshly ground black pepper
12 slices baguette, each about ½ in (12 mm) thick, fried in olive oil

Clean the fish and remove and reserve the heads. Cut the fish into serving pieces, rinse well in salted water, drain and pat dry. Set aside. Place the heads in a saucepan, add the water or wine and bring to a gentle boil. Reduce the heat to low and simmer for 20 minutes, to create a flavorful broth. Strain and set aside.

In a large deep sauté pan over medium heat, warm the oil. Add the onions, garlic, basil and pepper flakes or whole chilies to taste and sauté until the onions are tender and translucent, 8–10 minutes. Add the tomatoes and reserved broth and bring to a boil. Then start adding the fish, slipping in the longest-cooking pieces first. Cook, uncovered, until within 5 minutes of being done, then add the clams (first discarding any that do not close at the touch), and cover to steam them open, 3–5 minutes. Discard any clams that do not open.

Taste and adjust the seasonings with salt and black pepper. Ladle into individual shallow soup plates. Serve with 2 croutons propped up along the sides of each bowl.

SERVES 6

SICILY

PESCESPADA O TONNO ALLA STEMPERATA

Swordfish or Tuna in Melted Sauce

Stemperare *means "to melt," but it also can mean "immoderate" or "excessive." There is nothing excessive about this fragrant sauce, however, except that you might eat too much of it!*

6 thick tuna or swordfish fillets, about ½ lb (250 g) each
salt and freshly ground pepper
olive oil
4 cloves garlic, finely minced
6 celery stalks, chopped
1 cup (4 oz/125 g) green olives, pitted and coarsely chopped
½ cup (3 oz/90 g) raisins, plumped in hot water and drained
¼ cup (1½ oz/45 g) capers, rinsed and drained
⅓ cup (3 fl oz/80 ml) white wine vinegar

Sprinkle the fish with salt and pepper. In 1 or 2 large sauté pans over medium-high heat, warm 2–3 tablespoons oil. Add the fish and sauté 1–2 minutes on each side until lightly colored. Using a slotted spatula, remove to a platter.

Add another 2 tablespoons oil to the pan over medium heat. Add the garlic and celery and sauté, stirring often, until golden, about 10 minutes. Add the olives, raisins and capers and simmer for 2–3 minutes longer. Pour the sauce into a bowl.

Return the fish to the pan (or pans), pour the sauce over the top and sprinkle on the vinegar. Cook for 1–2 minutes over high heat to evaporate the vinegar, then simmer until the fish is done, 3–5 minutes longer.

Transfer to a warm platter and serve immediately.

SERVES 6

SICILY

CALAMARI RIPIENI

Stuffed Squid

All of the Mediterranean countries have recipes for stuffed squid. Rice is the basis of the filling in Greece and Turkey. In France and Italy, bread crumbs bind the filling and sometimes cheese or sausage are added. Here the squid is grilled. If you have not added tomatoes to the filling, you can make a light tomato sauce for spooning over the squid when serving. Or you can stuff the squid and then braise them in a light tomato sauce (see glossary) for 30 minutes; or place them in a well-oiled baking dish, cover the dish and then bake them in a 400°F (200°C) oven for about 25 minutes, basting them occasionally with wine or olive oil. Allow 3 small or 2 medium squid per person.

8 medium or 12 small squid, cleaned with the bodies left whole and the tentacles dropped (see glossary)
1½ cups (3 oz/90 g) fresh bread crumbs
6 tablespoons (3 fl oz/90 ml) olive oil, plus additional olive oil for grilling and serving
salt and freshly ground pepper
1 large onion, chopped
2 cloves garlic, finely chopped
3 tablespoons chopped fresh flat-leaf (Italian) parsley, plus additional parsley for garnish
2 teaspoons dried oregano (optional)
1 tablespoon chopped fresh dill (optional)
2 tablespoons chopped fresh mint (optional)
1 cup (6 oz/185 g) peeled, seeded, diced and drained tomatoes (optional)
1 teaspoon fennel seeds, toasted and ground (optional)
¼ cup (1 oz/30 g) grated pecorino cheese (optional)
2 tablespoons finely minced anchovy fillet (optional)
⅓ cup (1 oz/30 g) diced prosciutto (optional)
fresh lemon juice

Preheat an oven to 400°F (200°C). Prepare the squid and set aside.

In a shallow pan toss together the bread crumbs, 4 tablespoons (2 fl oz/60 ml) of the oil and salt and pepper to taste. Bake, stirring occasionally, until crispy and golden, about 15 minutes. Remove from the oven and transfer to a mixing bowl. Set aside.

Top to bottom: Fish Soup, Swordfish or Tuna in Melted Sauce, Stuffed Squid

❀ Prepare a fire in a charcoal grill.

❀ In a sauté pan over medium heat, warm the remaining 2 tablespoons oil. Add the onion and cook until tender and translucent, 8–10 minutes. Stir in the tentacles, garlic, the 3 tablespoons parsley and one of the optional herbs (if using) and sauté for 2 minutes. Add to the bread crumbs along with tomatoes (if using). Then add any one or more of the additional optional ingredients. Mix well and season to taste with salt and pepper. (If you have added pecorino cheese or anchovy, go easy on the salt.)

❀ Stuff this mixture into the squid bodies and skewer closed with toothpicks. Thread onto skewers. Brush the squid with oil and sprinkle with salt and pepper. Place on the grill rack and grill quickly for a few minutes on each side.

❀ Transfer to a platter and serve with a drizzle of oil and lemon juice and a little chopped parsley.

SERVES 4

CATALONIA

Salsa Romesco

Sauce for Grilled Shellfish

This is Catalan "ketchup," a sauce that accompanies not only grilled shellfish, but also roast lamb, pork or chicken; salads; and grilled vegetables. There are countless variations on this recipe. Some are quite spicy, while others are mild. You can make this sauce with 2 or 3 dried ancho chilies*: Immerse them in water to cover over low heat for 10 minutes, then allow to steep for 20 minutes. Drain and remove the stems and seeds. Omit the roasted red pepper and the red pepper flakes and add cayenne, if necessary, to balance the heat. Also, although not usually made with an egg emulsion such as for aioli, you can add cayenne pepper, puréed roasted red (sweet) pepper and tomatoes, and ground toasted almonds to aioli (recipe on page 144) to create a similar sauce. Some recipes call for adding ground, peeled hazelnuts (filberts) in addition to the almonds. It is easiest to make the sauce in a blender or food processor, so the mixture will emulsify and thicken.*

¾ cup (6 fl oz/180 ml) olive oil
1 large slice white bread, about 1 oz (30 g)
½–¾ cup (3–4 oz/90–125 g) almonds, toasted
½–1 teaspoon red pepper flakes, finely ground
2–3 teaspoons finely minced garlic
1 large red sweet pepper (capsicum), roasted, seeded and deribbed (see glossary)
1 large ripe tomato, peeled, seeded and diced (about ½ cup/3 oz/90 g)
1 teaspoon paprika
salt and freshly ground black pepper
¼ cup (2 fl oz/60 ml) red wine vinegar, or as needed

In a sauté pan over medium heat, warm 3 tablespoons of the oil. Add the bread and fry, turning once, until golden on both sides, about 3 minutes on each side. Break up the bread and place in a blender or in a processor fitted with the metal blade along with the almonds, pepper flakes and garlic. Pulse briefly. Add the roasted pepper, tomato, paprika, and salt and pepper to taste and purée to form a chunky paste. Add the vinegar and pulse once. With the motor running, add the remaining oil in a very slow, thin stream and continue to process until the mixture emulsifies. Taste and adjust the seasonings.

Transfer to a bowl and serve.

MAKES 1½ CUPS (12 FL OZ/375 ML); SERVES 6

CATALONIA

Zarzuela de Mariscos

Shellfish Stew

This little "operetta" of shellfish is so festive that it calls for at least six people to dine together. Keeping the lobster in the shell and the tails on the shrimp makes for somewhat messy eating, but the shells add additional flavor to the dish and ensure a more dramatic presentation. Some versions of this recipe have crushed toasted almonds added; others call for a hint of chili pepper. Another option would be to omit both the almonds and the cayenne pepper from the stew and serve the dish with salsa romesco *(recipe above) as a condiment. Offer grilled bread at the table for sopping up the delicious juices.*

¼ cup (2 fl oz/60 ml) olive oil
1½ cups (6 oz/185 g) chopped onion
1–2 tablespoons finely minced garlic
2 red or green sweet peppers (capsicums), seeded, deribbed and finely diced
3 cups (18 oz/560 g) peeled, seeded and diced tomatoes
1 bay leaf, torn into strips
¼ teaspoon saffron threads steeped in ¼ cup (2 fl oz/60 ml) dry white wine
salt and freshly ground pepper
½ cup (3 oz/90 g) almonds, toasted and ground (optional)
pinch of cayenne pepper (optional)
1½ cups (12 fl oz/375 ml) dry white wine
2 small or medium lobsters, boiled in water to cover for 5 minutes, cleaned and cut into serving-sized chunks
12–18 mussels in the shell, well scrubbed and debearded
12–18 clams in the shell, well scrubbed
12–18 large shrimp (prawns), peeled, with tail piece intact, and deveined
½–¾ lb (500–750 g) scallops, cut in half if large
1–2 tablespoons fresh lemon juice (optional)

In a large heavy pot over medium heat, warm the oil. Add the onion and sauté for 5 minutes. Add the garlic and sweet peppers and cook until the vegetables are soft but not browned, about 5 minutes longer. Add the tomatoes, bay leaf, saffron and its soaking liquid, salt and black pepper to taste, and the almonds and cayenne pepper, if using. Bring to a boil. Reduce the heat to medium and cook, stirring occasionally, until thickened, about 10 minutes.

Add the wine and bring to a boil. Add the lobsters, mussels and clams (first discarding any that do not close at the touch), cover and cook for about 5 minutes. Reduce the heat to medium, add the shrimp and scallops and cook until the lobster, shrimp and scallops are cooked and the clams and mussels have opened, 3–5 minutes longer. Discard any clams or mussels that do not open. Taste and adjust the seasoning. Add the lemon juice, if desired, for flavor balance.

Transfer to a warmed deep serving dish. Serve immediately.

SERVES 6–8

CATALONIA

Gazpacho de Mero

Grouper Gazpacho

The similarities between this fish stew and the soup known as gazpacho are that they are both served in a bowl, include tomatoes and garlic, and are thickened with bread.

4 small dried chili peppers
9 cups (72 fl oz/2.1 l) water
½ cup (4 fl oz/125 ml) olive oil
8 cloves garlic
2 lb (1 kg) onions, thinly sliced
2 lb (1 kg) tomatoes, peeled and finely chopped
2 bay leaves
salt and freshly ground pepper
head and frame from one 2 lb (1 kg) grouper or sea bass, coarsely chopped
2 lb (1 kg) grouper or sea bass fillets, cut into 1-in (2.5-cm) chunks
1 cup (5½ oz/170 g) almonds, toasted
2 slices stale bread, finely crumbled

Remove and discard the seeds from the chili peppers. Place the pepper in a small bowl with about ½ cup (4 fl oz/125 ml) of the water.

In a stockpot or saucepan, bring the remaining water to a boil. Meanwhile, in a sauté pan over medium heat, warm ¼ cup (2 fl oz/60 ml) of the oil. Add 4 of the garlic cloves and sauté until pale gold, about 5 minutes. Add half of the onions and cook for about 5 minutes. Add the tomatoes and cook for 5 minutes longer. Transfer this mixture to the boiling water and add the bay leaves and salt and pepper to taste.

Return to the boil and simmer, uncovered, for 30 minutes. Add the fish head and frame and cook for 20 minutes longer.

Top to bottom: Sauce for Grilled Shellfish, Grouper Gazpacho, Shellfish Stew

Strain and reserve the stock. Pick off any flesh from the fish head and reserve it as well.

Drain the chili peppers. Finely mince 2 of the remaining garlic cloves. In a large saucepan over medium heat, warm the remaining ¼ cup (2 fl oz/60 ml) oil. Add the finely minced garlic and the rest of the onions and sauté for 5 minutes. Add the fish pieces and the flesh from the fish head and cook over low heat, stirring occasionally, for 5 minutes. Add the stock and bring to a boil. Reduce the heat to a simmer.

In a mortar with a pestle pound together the almonds, the remaining 2 garlic cloves and a pinch of salt until a paste forms. Add to the fish soup and simmer until the fish is tender, about 5 minutes. Add the crumbled bread and simmer for another 5 minutes.

Ladle into individual bowls and serve hot.

SERVES 4–6

CATALONIA

ROMESCO

Stewed Fish with Beans

This fish dish is not to be confused with Catalonia's spicy tomato and almond ali-oli. *It does, however, have tomatoes, almonds and hot pepper in the sauce. Cooked haricot (white) beans are added to the completed fish stew.*

1½ lb (750 g) monkfish (anglerfish) fillets, sliced about 1 in (2.5 cm) thick
1½ lb (750 g) sea bass fillets, cut into 1-in (2.5-cm) chunks
1½ lb (750 g) sole fillets, cut into wide strips (optional)
8 shrimp (prawns), peeled and deveined
1 lb (500 g) squid, cleaned and cut into wide rings (see glossary)
salt
4–5 (2–2½ fl oz/60–75 ml) tablespoons olive oil
4 cloves garlic, finely minced
2 ripe tomatoes, peeled, seeded and sliced
1 green sweet pepper (capsicum), seeded, deribbed and sliced crosswise
1 onion, thinly sliced
½ cup (2½ oz/80 g) almonds, toasted and finely chopped
pinch of saffron threads steeped in ¼ cup (2 fl oz/60 ml) dry white wine
½ teaspoon coarsely ground black pepper
1 fresh chili pepper, chopped
3 tablespoons chopped fresh flat-leaf (Italian) parsley
2 cups (12 oz/375 g) cooked white beans

Lightly sprinkle all the fish and shellfish with salt. Place in the refrigerator until needed.

In a sauté pan over medium heat, warm 4 tablespoons (2 fl oz/60 ml) oil. Add the garlic, tomatoes and sweet pepper and sauté until the pepper is tender, about 10 minutes. Using a slotted spoon, remove to a bowl. Add the onion to the oil remaining in the pan and sauté until golden, 12–15 minutes.

Return the tomato-pepper mixture to the pan and add the almonds, saffron and its soaking liquid, black pepper, chili pepper and parsley. Stir well and add water to cover the vegetables by about ½ in (12 mm). Bring to a boil, add the fish and reduce the heat to a simmer. Cover and simmer for about 10 minutes, then add the shrimp and squid and cook for 2 minutes longer. Stir in the cooked white beans and heat through. Taste and adjust the seasoning.

Transfer to a warmed serving dish and serve at once.

SERVES 6

CATALONIA

GAMBAS AL AJILLO

Shrimp with Garlic

While this is usually served as a tapa, it is too good not to eat as a main course. The same dish can be made with squid, cut into rings, or scallops. Serve with lots of bread to sop up the sauce.

¼ cup (2 fl oz/60 ml) olive oil
¼ cup (2 oz/60 g) unsalted butter
1½ lb (750 g) shrimp (prawns), peeled and deveined
4–6 cloves garlic, finely chopped or thinly sliced
¼ cup (2 fl oz/60 ml) fresh lemon juice
1 teaspoon paprika
½ teaspoon red pepper flakes
salt and freshly ground black pepper
4 tablespoons chopped fresh flat-leaf (Italian) parsley

In a wide, shallow sauté pan or casserole over high heat, warm the oil and butter. Add the shrimp and garlic and sauté quickly for about 2 minutes. Add the lemon juice, paprika, pepper flakes and salt and black pepper to taste.

Transfer to a warmed serving dish, sprinkle with the parsley and serve at once.

SERVES 4

CATALONIA

CALAMARES CON GUISANTES

Squid with Garlic and Peas

In Spain there are also versions of this pea-and-mint stew with clams or cuttlefish, but the squid variation is especially appealing. If you wish to substitute clams for the squid, steam open 4 pounds (2 kg) clams, well scrubbed, in 1 cup (8 fl oz/250 ml) white wine, then shell them. Strain the cooking liquid through a sieve lined with cheesecloth (muslin). Add the peas to the puréed and reheated sauce and then add the clams and strained sauce. Heat through and garnish as directed. A large quantity of garlic is used in this recipe, but you can add less. Romans cook a popular calamari-and-peas dish as well, but the garlic is reduced greatly and there are no tomatoes or mint.

4 lb (2 kg) peas, shelled (about 4 cups/1¼ lb/625 g shelled)
salt
½ cup (4 fl oz/125 ml) olive oil
2 heads garlic, cloves separated and peeled
2 slices coarse country-style bread, crusts discarded
1 tablespoon all-purpose (plain) flour
3 tomatoes, peeled, seeded and chopped
½ cup (4 fl oz/125 ml) dry white wine
4 tablespoons chopped fresh mint
4 tablespoons chopped fresh flat-leaf (Italian) parsley
2 lb (1 kg) squid, cleaned and cut into rings 1 in (2.5 cm) wide (see glossary)

Bring a saucepan three-fourths full of water to a boil. Add the peas and salt to taste and boil until tender, 3–5 minutes. Drain and refresh under cold running water. Drain again and set aside.

In a large sauté pan over medium heat, warm the oil. Add the garlic and sauté until golden, about 4 minutes. Using a slotted spoon, remove to paper towels to drain. Add the bread to the same oil and fry, turning once, until golden, about 3 minutes on each side. Again, remove with a slotted utensil to paper towels to drain.

In a mortar with a pestle, pound together the garlic and bread until it forms a paste. (Or purée them in a blender or a food processor fitted with the metal blade.) Set aside.

Add the flour to the oil remaining in the pan and stir over medium heat until it starts to color. Then add the tomatoes, wine, the bread-garlic mixture and 2 tablespoons each of the mint and parsley. Simmer for 15 minutes. If the sauce is too thick, add a little water. It needs to be spoonable and liquid in consistency.

Transfer the sauce to a blender or to a processor fitted with the metal blade and purée. If it is too thick, thin it with water as necessary. Return the sauce to the pan and bring to a boil. Add the squid and stir well. Cook for 1–2 minutes. Stir in the peas and heat for 1 minute longer.

Transfer to a warmed serving dish and serve at once. Top with the remaining 2 tablespoons each mint and parsley.

SERVES 6

Top to bottom: Stewed Fish with Beans, Shrimp with Garlic, Squid with Garlic and Peas

Fish Ball Tagine

TUNISIA

TAGINE KEFTA MN HOOT

Fish Ball Tagine

These lightly spicy Tunisian fish balls should be served with couscous (recipe on page 204). In Turkey, similar fish balls are seasoned with dill and green (spring) onions, dredged in flour, fried until golden and served without any sauce as an appetizer with lemon wedges. In Spain, they are seasoned with parsley and a little cheese and then fried and served with tomato sauce.

FOR THE FISH BALLS:

1½ lb (750 g) white fish fillets such as cod, sole, snapper, bass
4 tablespoons chopped fresh flat-leaf (Italian) parsley
3 cloves garlic, finely minced
2 onions, finely chopped
1½ teaspoons salt
½ teaspoon *harissa* (see glossary)
¼ lb (125 g) stale bread, sliced, crusts discarded, soaked in water to cover and squeezed dry, or 1½ cups (3 oz/90 g) fresh bread crumbs
1 egg
olive oil for frying

FOR THE SAUCE:

3 tablespoons olive oil
2 cloves garlic, minced
6 tablespoons (3 fl oz/90 ml) tomato purée
2 cups (16 fl oz/500 ml) fish stock (see glossary) or water
salt and freshly ground pepper

chopped fresh flat-leaf (Italian) parsley

To make the balls, remove any bones in the fish and chop finely. Place in a bowl. Add all the remaining ingredients except the egg and oil. Mix well. Add the egg and knead until smooth. (This mixture may instead be mixed in a food processor fitted with the metal blade.) Dip a spoon and your fingers into cold water, then remove a heaping tablespoonful of fish paste and roll it into a 1-in (2.5-cm) ball. Place on a baking sheet lined with parchment paper. Form balls from the remaining fish mixture in the same way. (If not cooking immediately, refrigerate until ready to cook.)

In a large frying pan over medium heat, pour in oil to a depth of 2 in (5 cm). When the oil is hot, add a few fish balls at a time and fry, turning, to brown lightly on all sides. Using a slotted spoon remove to paper towels to drain. To make the sauce, in a large saucepan over medium heat, warm the oil. Add all the remaining ingredients and bring to a boil, stirring to combine. Add the fish balls, reduce the heat to low and simmer, uncovered, until fish balls are cooked through and the sauce has reduced slightly, about 15 minutes.

Transfer to a warmed serving dish, sprinkle with parsley and serve.

SERVES 4

MOROCCO

Al Toune bil Tomatich

Tuna in Tomato Sauce with Preserved Lemon

Cod, snapper or another firm white fish can be used in place of the tuna here. For more flavor, add 1 teaspoon ground ginger and a pinch of saffron threads to the tomatoes while they are simmering, or add 1 teaspoon ground ginger; 1 clove garlic, finely minced; and ¼ teaspoon cayenne pepper.

A related dish is made without the tomatoes or any marinating time: Make a bed of thinly sliced preserved lemon peel in a baking dish, arrange fish slices on top, drizzle with olive oil or chermoula, *and bake as directed. Sprinkle with olives and chopped parsley just before serving.*

6 thick tuna fillets or firm fish fillets, about ½ lb (250 g) each (see introduction)
½ cup (4 fl oz/125 ml) *chermoula* marinade (recipe on page 127)
4 cups (1½ lb/750 g) peeled, seeded and diced tomatoes
4 tablespoons chopped fresh flat-leaf (Italian) parsley
peel of 1 preserved lemon, cut into thin slivers (see glossary)
18 sharply flavored black olives
2 tablespoons capers, rinsed and drained (optional)

Put the fish in a large nonreactive baking dish, pour the *chermoula* evenly over the top, cover with aluminum foil and marinate for 4 hours in the refrigerator.

Meanwhile, put the tomatoes in a saucepan over medium heat. Cook, stirring often, until they have been reduced to a thick purée, 10–15 minutes. Stir in the parsley, lemon peel, olives and capers (if using) and simmer for 5 minutes longer.

Preheat an oven to 400°F (200°C). Remove the fish from the refrigerator and pour the tomato sauce over it. Re-cover with the foil and bake until the fish is cooked, about 25 minutes.

Transfer to a serving dish or serve directly from the baking dish. Serve hot or at room temperature.

SERVES 6

Tuna in Tomato Sauce with Preserved Lemon

Clockwise from top left: Fish in Grapeleaves, Peppery Fish Stew from Corfu, Sea Bass with Vinegar and Rosemary

GREECE

PSARI SE AMBELOFILLA

Fish in Grapeleaves

This dish is not just Greek—it is pan-Mediterranean. The fish can be small like sardines or red mullet, flat like sole or meaty like shark, swordfish or tuna. They can be cooked over a charcoal fire or in a broiler (griller) rather than baked. Brush the oil-lemon mixture on both sides of each packet, sprinkle with salt and pepper and then grill or broil, turning once, 4–6 minutes on each side. The leaves keep the fish moist and add a certain fragrance and elegance of presentation. Thyme, oregano, toasted pine nuts, olives, capers, diced tomatoes or plumped currants may be added to the oil-lemon mixture for baking or spooning over the grilled fish.

2 lb (1 kg) large sardines, cleaned, or sole, swordfish or bass fillets
8 tablespoons (4 fl oz/125 ml) olive oil
4 tablespoons (2 fl oz/60 ml) fresh lemon juice
4 teaspoons chopped fresh thyme (optional)
2 tablespoons dried oregano (optional)
salt and freshly ground pepper
bottled grapeleaves, rinsed of brine and stemmed

Place the fish in a shallow nonreactive dish. In a small bowl whisk together 3 tablespoons of the oil, 2 tablespoons of the lemon juice and the thyme and oregano, if using. Pour over the fish to coat evenly, then sprinkle with salt and pepper. Marinate for about 1 hour at room temperature.

Preheat an oven to 400°F (200°C). Remove the fish from the marinade. Wrap the whole fish or fish fillets individually in grapeleaves. Oil a baking pan large enough to hold the fish in a single layer and arrange a few leaves in the bottom of the pan. Place the fish packets, seam sides down, in the pan. In a small dish whisk together 2 tablespoons of the oil and 1 tablespoon lemon juice. Drizzle over the fish packets. Bake for 10–18 minutes, depending upon the size and thickness of the fish.

Transfer to a warmed platter. Whisk together the remaining 3 tablespoons oil and 1 tablespoon lemon juice and spoon over the fish. Serve at once.

SERVES 4–6

GREECE

PSARI BOURTHETO

Peppery Fish Stew from Corfu

An assortment of meaty fish or a single variety will work for this recipe. You may marinate the fish in olive oil and lemon juice for 30 minutes before cooking if you have the time, but this step is not essential. The dish can also be baked in a 400°F (200°C) oven for 10–15 minutes. Serve this stew with roasted potatoes.

¼ cup (2 fl oz/60 ml) olive oil
2 onions, halved and thinly sliced
1 clove garlic, finely minced
1 bay leaf, torn into strips
½ teaspoon cayenne pepper, or to taste
1 teaspoon freshly ground black pepper, plus black pepper to taste
2 teaspoons chopped fresh thyme
1 teaspoon finely chopped fresh rosemary (optional)
¼ cup (2 fl oz/60 ml) red wine vinegar
½ cup (4 fl oz/125 ml) dry red or white wine
2 cups (12 oz/375 g) peeled, seeded and diced tomatoes (optional)

salt
2 lb (1 kg) firm white fish fillets, cut into 2-in (5-cm) chunks
3 tablespoons fresh lemon juice
1 teaspoon paprika
4 tablespoons chopped fresh flat-leaf (Italian) parsley

In a large, deep sauté pan or a wide saucepan over medium heat, warm the oil. Add the onions, garlic and bay leaf and sauté until the onions are tender and translucent, 8–10 minutes. Add the cayenne pepper, the 1 teaspoon black pepper, thyme and rosemary (if using) and sauté for 2 minutes. Add the vinegar, wine and tomatoes (if using) and bring to a boil. Sprinkle the fish chunks with salt and pepper and add them to the pan. Reduce the heat, cover partially and simmer until the fish is almost done, about 8 minutes.

Add the lemon juice and paprika and simmer for 2 minutes. Taste and adjust the seasoning. Transfer to a warmed serving dish, sprinkle with the parsley and serve at once.

SERVES 4

GREECE

LEVRAKIA MARINATA

Sea Bass with Vinegar and Rosemary

This dish could be prepared with any mild firm fish, whole or cut into fillets: red mullet, sardines, trout, monkfish (anglerfish) or sea bass. It can be served hot or at room temperature. Some versions add a little diced tomato to the sauce.

4 sea bass fillets, about 6 oz (185 g) each
salt and freshly ground pepper
2 tablespoons fresh lemon juice
all-purpose (plain) flour for coating
olive oil for frying

FOR THE SAUCE:

¼ cup (2 fl oz/60 ml) olive oil
2 tablespoons all-purpose (plain) flour
⅓ cup (3 fl oz/80 ml) red wine vinegar
¼ cup (2 fl oz/60 ml) water
1 or 2 cloves garlic, finely chopped
2 tablespoons chopped fresh rosemary
2 bay leaves
1 cup (6 oz/185 g) chopped, peeled tomato (optional)
salt and freshly ground pepper

additional olive oil, if serving at room temperature

Sprinkle the fish with salt and pepper to taste and the lemon juice. Place flour in a shallow dish and dredge the fish in it, shaking off the excess. In a large frying pan over medium heat, pour in oil to a depth of ¼ in (6 mm). Add the fish and fry, turning once, until cooked and golden brown, about 4 minutes on each side. Using a slotted spatula, remove the fish to paper towels to drain. Cover with aluminum foil to keep warm.

To make the sauce, drain off the oil from the frying pan and wipe it out with paper towels. Add the oil and place over medium heat. Add the flour and stir until the flour is golden, about 3–5 minutes. Add the vinegar, water, garlic, rosemary, bay leaves and tomatoes (if using). Reduce the heat to low and simmer until thickened, 3–6 minutes. Season to taste with salt and pepper.

If serving the fish hot, transfer it to a warmed platter, spoon the sauce over the top and serve immediately. If serving the fish at room temperature, arrange it on a platter, spoon the sauce over the top and let cool to room temperature. Or, if you like, cover and refrigerate overnight, then serve the next day. Bring the fish to room temperature, then drizzle a little good olive oil over the top before bringing the fish to the table.

SERVES 4

PROVENCE

MOULES À LA PROVENÇALE

Steamed Mussels

In Sardinia, toasted fine dried bread crumbs are added to this dish with the parsley. Don't forget to serve bread for sopping up the delicious juices. You can toast it, if you like.

3 tablespoons olive oil
1 onion or 3 large shallots, chopped
2 or 3 cloves garlic, finely minced
1 cup (6 oz/185 g) peeled, seeded and diced tomatoes (optional)
½ cup (4 fl oz/125 ml) dry white wine or water
4 lb (2 kg) mussels in the shell, well scrubbed and debearded (18–24 per person)
freshly ground black pepper
½ cup (¾ oz/20 g) chopped fresh flat-leaf (Italian) parsley

In a wide, heavy saucepan over medium heat, warm the oil. Add the onion or shallots and sauté until soft and turning golden, about 15 minutes. Add the garlic, tomatoes (if using) and the wine or water. Stir to mix. Add the mussels, discarding any that do not close at the touch, and bring to a boil. Cover the pan and cook over high heat until the mussels open, 3–4 minutes. Discard any that do not open.

Spoon the mussels and pan juices into soup plates, grind pepper over the top, sprinkle with the parsley and serve at once.

SERVES 4

PROVENCE

ANGUILLE À LA MARTEGALE

Baked Eel with Leeks, Olives and Wine

This dish is served in the old port of Martigues on Christmas Eve. There is no reason why you can't make this more than once a year, as it is so good. The eel must be very fresh. It should be skinned and cut into large pieces. If you like, the eel may be simmered on the stove top and then topped with toasted dried bread crumbs just before serving.

4 tablespoons (2 fl oz/60 ml) olive oil
3 leeks, including some of the tender green tops, chopped
2 cloves garlic, finely minced
4 tablespoons chopped fresh flat-leaf (Italian) parsley
salt and freshly ground pepper
1 bay leaf, torn into strips
½ cup (2½ oz/75 g) sharply flavored black olives, pitted
2 lb (1 kg) eel, skinned and cut into large pieces
¾ cup (6 fl oz/180 ml) dry white wine
½ cup (2 oz/60 g) fine dried bread crumbs

Preheat an oven to 350°F (180°C).

In a sauté pan over medium heat, warm 2 tablespoons of the oil. Add the leeks and sauté until they start to soften, about 8–10 minutes. Stir in the garlic and parsley, season to taste with salt and pepper and then fold in the bay leaf and olives. Arrange this mixture in the bottom of a shallow baking dish. Place the eel pieces on top, add the wine and then sprinkle with the bread crumbs. Drizzle with the remaining 2 tablespoons oil. Cover and bake until the eel is tender, about 1 hour.

Transfer to a warmed serving dish or serve directly from the baking dish.

SERVES 4

PROVENCE

THON EN CHARTREUSE

Tuna with Vegetables and Wine

Many people who hear about this dish for the first time assume that it is made with the liqueur from the famed monastery of the Grande Chartreuse. It actually takes its name from the vegetable mixture, however, which traditionally contains leafy greens such as cabbage or lettuce in the mix.

about 3 tablespoons fresh lemon juice
1 tuna fillet, about 1½ lb (750 g) and 2–3 in (5–7.5 cm) thick
6 anchovy fillets in oil, drained
3 tablespoons olive oil
2 onions, chopped
4–6 carrots, peeled and chopped
2 cloves garlic, minced
8 lettuce hearts such as Boston (butterhead) and romaine (cos), cut into 1-in (2.5-cm) strips
1 cup (1 oz/30 g) sorrel leaves, chopped (optional)
salt and freshly ground pepper
1 cup (8 fl oz/250 ml) dry white wine

Fill a large, wide sauté pan three-fourths full of water, add the lemon juice and bring to a boil. Add the tuna and blanch for 4–5 minutes. Drain and place on a work surface. Cut the anchovy fillets into long, thin strips. Make small slits in the tuna fillet and push the anchovy pieces into them.

In a heavy sauté pan over medium heat, warm the oil. Add the onions and carrots and sauté for a few minutes. Add the tuna, cover and cook over low heat for about 10 minutes. Add the garlic, lettuce and sorrel (if using). Season to taste with salt and pepper. Re-cover the pan and continue to cook over low heat for 10 minutes. The lettuce should give off some water, but check the pan from time to time to make sure the vegetables are not sticking.

When the lettuce water has been absorbed, add the wine. Cover and simmer over low heat, occasionally basting with the pan juices, until the fish is done, about 15 minutes longer.

Carefully remove tuna from the pan with a large spatula and place on a warmed serving platter. Surround with cooked vegetables and serve immediately.

SERVES 4

PROVENCE

GIGOT DE MER

"Leg of Lamb" of the Sea

Here's a Provençal recipe in which a meaty fish such as monkfish (anglerfish) or cod is studded with garlic cloves in the same way a leg of lamb is and baked atop a bed of ratatouille. This is best made with a whole fish, but if you can't find one, thick fish steaks can be used. The ratatouille can also be eaten alone, either warm or at room temperature. It will keep well in the refrigerator for up to 3 days.

FOR THE RATATOUILLE:

2 eggplants (aubergines), peeled
salt
6–8 tablespoons (3–4 fl oz/90–120 ml) olive oil, or as needed
2 onions, chopped
2 or 3 cloves garlic, minced
3 red or green sweet peppers (capsicums), seeded, deribbed and sliced or diced
3 zucchini (courgettes), diced or sliced ¼ in (6 mm) thick
3 or 4 tomatoes, peeled, seeded and diced

Clockwise from top right: "Leg Of Lamb" Of The Sea; Steamed Mussels; Tuna with Vegetables and Wine; Baked Eel with Leeks, Olives and Wine

salt and freshly ground pepper
4 tablespoons chopped fresh basil

---

1 whole fish, about 5 lb (2.5 kg), cleaned, or 3 lb (1.5 kg) thick fish steaks or fillets (see note)
3 cloves garlic, cut into thin slivers
salt and freshly ground pepper
a few bay leaves and fresh thyme sprigs, if using steaks or fillets
1 cup (8 fl oz/250 ml) dry white wine
2–3 tablespoons chopped fresh basil or flat-leaf (Italian) parsley

---

To make the ratatouille, slice the eggplants ½ in (12 mm) thick, then cut the slices in half or in quarters. Alternatively, cut the eggplants into 1-in (2.5-cm) cubes. Sprinkle with salt, place in a colander and let drain for about 30 minutes, to release some of the bitter juices. Rinse off the salt and pat the eggplant dry with paper towels.

In a large frying pan over medium-high heat, warm 3–4 tablespoons of the oil. Add the eggplant and sauté, turning often, until tender, 5–8 minutes. Remove from the pan to a bowl and set aside. Add 2 tablespoons oil to the same pan, add the onions and sauté until soft and pale gold, 10–15 minutes. Add the garlic and sauté 1–2 minutes longer. Using a slotted spoon remove to the bowl with the eggplant. Add enough oil to the pan to measure 2 tablespoons and warm over medium heat. Add the sweet peppers and zucchini and sauté until soft, about 10 minutes.

Return the eggplant and onions to the pan, add the tomatoes and cook over very low heat, stirring occasionally, until all the vegetables are very tender, about 15 minutes. Season to taste with salt and pepper and stir in the basil.

Meanwhile, preheat an oven to 400°F (200°C).

If using a whole fish, make slits ½ in (12 mm) deep all over the fish and insert the garlic slivers in the slits. Place the fish in an oiled baking dish. Sprinkle with salt and pepper. Pour in the wine and bake for about 15 minutes. Carefully remove the fish from the pan. Make a bed of most of the ratatouille in the baking pan. Nest the fish in this bed, mounding some along the sides of the fish. Sprinkle the remaining ratatouille over the fish and bake until it tests done when pierced with a knife, about 15 minutes longer. Carefully remove the fish from the dish, cut away and discard the skin and cut into serving pieces, discarding the bones and head. Place a bed of ratatouille on each plate and 1 or 2 slices of fish. Sprinkle with basil or parsley. Serve at once.

If using fillets or steaks, make slits ½ in (12 mm) deep all over fish and insert garlic slivers into the steaks. Sprinkle with salt and pepper, place in an oiled baking dish, tuck in the bay leaves and thyme and drizzle with the wine. Bake for 10 minutes. Carefully remove with a spatula and set aside. Place most of the ratatouille in the baking dish, return the fish to the dish and cover with remaining ratatouille. Bake until fish tests done, about 10 minutes longer. Transfer to warmed individual dishes and sprinkle with basil or parsley. Serve at once.

SERVES 6

Grilled Fish with Cumin

LEBANON

SAMAK AL KAMOUN

Grilled Fish with Cumin

Cumin is a popular seasoning for grilled fish not only in Lebanon, but also in Syria, Egypt and North Africa. The fish is either marinated in a cumin-based spice mixture and grilled, or it is baked with onions flavored with cumin. Fillets may be used for this recipe as well. Select six 6-ounce (185-g) fillets and rub them with the marinade. Reduce the grilling time to about 4 minutes on each side, or, if baking, reduce the baking time to 8–10 minutes.

1 whole fish such as striped bass or snapper, 3½–4 lb (1.75–2 kg), cleaned
salt for rubbing on fish, plus 1 teaspoon salt
6 tablespoons (3 fl oz/90 ml) fresh lemon juice
3 tablespoons cumin seeds, toasted and ground
2 tablespoons paprika
2 teaspoons finely minced garlic
½ teaspoon freshly ground pepper

½ cup (¾ oz/20 g) chopped fresh flat-leaf (Italian) parsley or fresh cilantro (fresh coriander), optional

½ cup (4 fl oz/125 ml) olive oil

Preheat a broiler (griller), prepare a fire in a charcoal grill or preheat an oven to 450°F (230°C). Rub the fish with salt, inside and out, then rinse. Cut 3 or 4 shallow diagonal slits on each side of the body. Set aside.

In a bowl stir together the lemon juice, cumin, paprika, garlic, the 1 teaspoon salt, pepper and parsley or cilantro (if using). Whisk in the oil. Rub this paste onto both sides of the fish. If baking the fish, wrap it in aluminum foil.

Place the fish on a broiler pan or on a grill rack and broil or grill, turning once, until tests done when pierced with a knife, about 10 minutes on each side. Or place the foil-wrapped fish in the oven and bake until done, 25–30 minutes.

Transfer the fish to a warmed platter (discarding foil if used) and serve at once.

SERVES 6

PROVENCE

BOURRIDE

Fish Soup with Aioli

A good fish stock and a fragrant aioli, the garlicky mayonnaise of Provence, are the basis for a rich and delicious fish stew. The fish is often served as a second course with potatoes, and the broth served as a first course with fried croutons. You could serve them all at the same time if you like.

FOR THE FISH STOCK:

2 lb (1 kg) fish frames, including heads and tails, gills removed
4 cups (32 fl oz/1 l) water
1½ cups (12 fl oz/375 ml) dry white wine
1 onion, coarsely chopped
1 celery stalk, chopped
1 strip lemon zest
2 fresh parsley sprigs
1 fresh thyme sprig
3 peppercorns
1 coriander seed
1 bay leaf
½ teaspoon fennel seed (optional)
1 orange zest strips (optional)

FOR THE AIOLI:

1 tablespoon finely chopped garlic (6–8 cloves)
1 teaspoon coarse salt, plus salt to taste
2 egg yolks
3–4 tablespoons fresh lemon juice
1½–2 cups (12–16 fl oz/375–500 ml) mild olive oil or half peanut oil and half olive oil

FOR THE SOUP:

the aioli
the strained fish stock
2½ lb (1.25 kg) firm white fish fillets, cut into 2–3 in (5–7.5 cm) pieces about 1 in (2.5 cm) thick
2 egg yolks
salt and freshly ground pepper
fresh lemon juice

12 slices coarse country-style bread, grilled or fried in olive oil, cut into bite-sized pieces

To make the stock, combine all the ingredients in a stockpot and bring to a boil. Reduce the heat to low and simmer, uncovered, for about 30 minutes, skimming the scum occasionally. Strain the stock through a sieve lined with cheesecloth (muslin). Refrigerate uncovered until cold. Then cover and refrigerate until needed. You should have 4–5 cups (32–40 fl oz/1–1.1 l).

To make the aioli, in a mortar with a pestle, pound together the garlic and the 1 teaspoon salt to a smooth purée. Place the egg yolks and half of the lemon juice in a blender or in a food processor fitted with the metal blade and blend to mix. With the motor running, gradually add the oil, a few drops at a time, until the mixture emulsifies to a thick mayonnaise. Add the garlic, the remaining lemon juice and salt to taste. If too thick, add a few drops of cold water. Transfer to a bowl and set aside. You should have about 1½ cups (12 fl oz/375 ml).

To prepare the soup, put half of the aioli in a 1½-qt (1.5-l) saucepan and set aside. In a large saucepan bring the fish stock to a boil. Add the fish and simmer, uncovered, until the fish is cooked through but still firm, about 8 minutes. Using a slotted spoon, remove the fish to a platter, drizzle a little hot stock over the top, cover loosely with foil and keep warm.

Beat the egg yolks into the aioli in the saucepan. Then gradually beat in about 1 cup (8 fl oz/250 ml) of the hot fish stock. When the aioli and yolks are warm, add the rest of the fish stock. Simmer over very low heat, stirring constantly, until the soup thickens, about 3 minutes. Do not boil! Season to taste with salt and pepper and lemon juice.

To serve, place 2 grilled or fried bread slices on the bottom of each of 6 shallow soup plates. Divide the fish and then the soup evenly among them. Serve the remaining aioli in a bowl on the side.

SERVES 6

PROVENCE

COQUILLES ST.-JACQUES À LA PROVENÇALE

Scallops with Garlic, Wine and Herbs

Scallops are surprisingly rich, so this recipe will serve four to six persons quite easily. The scallops can be sautéed à la minute *or cooked and assembled in a baking dish or ramekins and glazed under the broiler at serving time. Rice would be a nice accompaniment.*

1½ lb (750 g) scallops
¾ cup (4 oz/125 g) all-purpose (plain) flour
salt and freshly ground pepper
4 tablespoons (2 oz/60 g) unsalted butter, plus 2 tablespoons butter, if broiling
2 tablespoons shallots, finely minced
2 cloves garlic, finely minced
2 tablespoons olive oil
½ cup (4 fl oz/125 ml) dry white wine
3 tablespoons chopped fresh flat-leaf (Italian) parsley
1 teaspoon finely chopped fresh thyme
1 cup (6 oz/185 g) peeled, seeded and diced tomatoes (optional)
½ cup (2 oz/60 g) fine dried bread crumbs, if broiling

Trim the tough foot or muscle off the scallops. If the scallops are large, cut them in half horizontally. On a large plate, stir together the flour and salt and pepper to taste. Dredge the scallops in the seasoned flour, shake off the excess and place on a rack.

In a large sauté pan over medium heat, melt 2 tablespoons of the butter. Add the shallots and garlic and sauté until soft, 2–3 minutes. Remove from the pan and set aside. In the same pan melt 2 more tablespoons butter with the oil over high heat. Add the scallops and sauté quickly, turning once, until golden, just a couple minutes. (You may have to do this in batches so as not to crowd the pan.) Set the scallops aside and keep warm.

Pour the wine into the pan and deglaze over high heat, scraping up any browned-on bits. Return the shallots and garlic to the pan along with the parsley, thyme and tomatoes (if using) and cook over medium-high heat until the sauce thickens, about 8 minutes. If serving right away, spoon this sauce over scallops and serve.

Alternatively, place the scallops in buttered individual flameproof ramekins or a flameproof baking dish and spoon the sauce over the top. Cover and refrigerate until serving time (up to 6 hours). Then preheat the broiler (griller). Cut the 2 tablespoons butter into bits and use to dot the scallops. Sprinkle with the bread crumbs and slip under the broiler until hot and bubbly, about 5 minutes. Serve immediately.

SERVES 4–6

Top to bottom: Fish Soup with Aioli; Scallops with Garlic, Wine and Herbs

TURKEY

TURKEY

Some time toward the middle of the eleventh century, a Turkish army broke through to the Mediterranean coast of Anatolia and claimed the city of Antalya on behalf of their ruler, Sulayman Shah the Seljuk. The capture of Antalya, known now for its flourishing orange groves and as a center of Turkey's burgeoning tourist industry, does not conventionally rank among the turning points of Turkish history; it is certainly not on the order of the Battle of Malazgird in 1071, which sealed the fate of Byzantine rule in most of Anatolia, or the conquest of Istanbul in 1453, which consecrated the rise of the Ottomans as a leading power of the day. A mention of this event may serve to remind us, however, that the Turks have been a Mediterranean people for more than nine centuries, vigorously participating in the affairs of the region—cultural as well as military and political—throughout this period and one of the major players for a considerable part of it.

This general preeminence of the Turks was reflected in cuisine; the last of the great culinary traditions to crystallize in the Mediterranean basin, Turkish cuisine has also been among the richest and most influential. The Turks were destined to advance still farther to the west, all the way, in fact, to the walls of Vienna. Their arrival on the shores of the Mediterranean can nonetheless be regarded as the culmination of a migratory process that

Previous pages: The construction of the Blue Mosque in Istanbul was controversial because it was thought unholy to rival the six minarets of the mosque at Mecca. Left: While only one-third of Turkey's land is dedicated to agriculture, it employs well over half of the labor force.

Copperware, no longer hammered out by hand, is sold in souvenir shops, which play an important role in Istanbul's commercial life.

had begun on the borders of China, in the landlocked vastness of Central Asia. This circumstance, too, has found expression in the kitchen, for there are elements in Turkish cuisine that were acquired or developed at virtually every stage in this long progress across Asia.

Culinary traces of the earliest period in Turkish history are meager. *Mantı,* a kind of dumpling still eaten today, was no doubt acquired by the Uighurs, the earliest settled Turkish people of note, from their Chinese neighbors, for the word is of Chinese origin and the dish itself is highly reminiscent of wonton. A delight in stuffing not only pasta but also intestines and vegetables is, however, so constant and widespread in Turkish cuisine that it must be thought of as a primordial feature of the tradition, not something passively received from the Chinese.

Turkish cooking is the only Mediterranean cuisine to have such demonstrable East Asiatic antecedents. Progressive incorporation into the world of Islam, from the tenth century onward, detached the Turks quite early from the cultural sphere of East Asia, and thereby also their cuisine. Their initiation into the classical civilization of Islam came at the hands of the Persians. Persian historians of nationalist bent are, therefore, in the habit of affirming that the succession of Turkish peoples that conquered the Persian-speaking lands as they migrated westward succumbed unquestioningly to the superior cultural models they encountered. Their judgment needs to be modified, especially in the sphere of cuisine.

One of the earliest literary monuments of Turkish Islamic culture, an eleventh-century Turkish-Arabic dictionary, shows clearly that Turkish cuisine was no tabula rasa before contact was made with the Persians. It lists, for example, numerous terms relating to bread and its preparation, many of which, in an adapted form, are still used in present-day Turkish; these terms point to the existence of a rich and indigenous Turkish baking tradition that later merged quite naturally with the bread culture of the Mediterranean. The same source also shows that the early Turks were fond of milk products, including yogurt and its by-products and various types of cheese. Yogurt has been known to the Middle East since antiquity, but there can be no doubting the role played by the Turks in popularizing its consumption, both in the Mediterranean world and beyond. Francis I of France was cured of intestinal disease by a diet of yogurt prescribed by a courtier who had spent some time in Turkey; this is the first evidence of the consumption of yogurt in postmedieval Europe. And the word *yogurt,* which has passed uncontested into all European languages, is itself Turkish. Finally, we find in our dictionary mention of particular dishes, such as *tutmaç* and *börek.* The former, a kind of thick stew made with lentils and noodles, is now virtually unknown, although it was extremely popular for centuries and survived in some parts of Anatolia until the nineteenth century. As for the *börek* mentioned in the dictionary, it is difficult to be sure that it was identical with the influential and popular dish (or rather category of dishes) we now know by that name; the compiler of the dictionary was, after all, a lexicographer, not a cook.

Persian cuisine was indeed highly developed, and it had already exercised a determining influence on the genesis of Arab cuisine two centuries before the Turks joined the realm of Islam. The Turks were by no means immune to the appeal of Persian food. They appreciated the same fruit-and-meat stews the Arabs carried all the way to Morocco and Spain, and a few dishes of this type survive even today in Turkey, although only as archaic and provincial specialties. Vegetable stews known as *yakhni* were also absorbed from Persian into Turkish cuisine.

But the Turks seem to have given the Persians at least as much as they received from them. *Kebab,* the generic name for all kinds of grilled meat, is Persian, but our eleventh-century dictionary proves that the Turks had been acquainted with the art of grilling meat since very early times. Moreover, the range of kebabs developed by the Turks was—and still is—much wider than those known to the Persians. Similar remarks apply to *pilav,* cooked rice or a dish based on cooked rice. The word itself is the Turkicized version of Persian *pulau,* and rice was used, albeit on a limited scale, in Persia before the arrival of the Turks, to whom rice had been unknown in their original homeland; it was after all from Persia that the Arabs disseminated rice throughout the eastern Mediterranean. But the emergence of pilaf dishes, in all their rich variety, ran parallel to the Turkish ascent in the Islamic world, and even in Persia many rice dishes came to be known by Turkish names. Pilaf in general came everywhere to be seen as quintessentially Turkish. It was for good reason that Norman Douglas once posed the rhetorical question, "Is there anything better than a genuine Turkish pilaf?"

A number of purely Turkish dishes found great favor among the Persians as well. *Tutmaç* was eulogized by a thirteenth-century Persian poet as "the caliph of the world of appetite," and *buğra,* probably the ancestor of some varieties of present-day *börek,* held the same culinary peak in Persia that was later conquered by pilaf. A general prevalence of dishes relying on flour, dough and noodles may also be ascribed to Turkish influence.

Given all this, it seems advisable to speak of a joint Turco-Persian cuisine, in the elaboration of which a dominant role cannot be attributed to either party. It was this composite cuisine that the Turks first brought with them to Anatolia; the Seljuks who conquered and ruled much of Anatolia, had after all originated as the offshoot of a dynasty whose rule over vast areas of the Middle East was based in Persia. The content of Seljuk cuisine can be judged from the menu for a royal banquet held in 1237 in Konya: a variety of kebabs including duck and chicken broiled on spits; pepper-seasoned pilaf; a number of vegetable dishes, both fried and stewed; and as dessert *zerde,* a Persian saffron-flavored rice pudding. Information on the diet of Seljuk Anatolia is to be found also, perhaps surprisingly, in the works of the great mystical poet Rumi. A figure often sentimentalized beyond recognition, Rumi in fact took an enthusiastic interest in food, and he lovingly evokes foods that cover the whole spectrum, from vegetables, pulses, fruits and breads to pastries, milk products and even pickles.

The transformation of Anatolia into a Turkish homeland was not a swift, clear-cut process of exclusion. Numerous Greeks were progressively integrated into Turkish society through conversion to Islam. Many others who retained their Christian affiliation became neighbors of the Turks, a situation that continued in western Anatolia until the exchange of populations that took place between Turkey and Greece in 1923. There were, then, many channels and opportunities for the exchange of culinary influence. We have already suggested, while discussing Greece, that the Turks were the more influential partners in this traffic. A Greek contribution is, however, visible in at least three areas. Half a dozen Greek loanwords relating to the preparation of bread—none of them current today—point to a Greek influence in the bakery; the gradual displacement of the elongated flaps of bread still favored in Persia and Central Asia by round loaves is probably also due to Greek example. Second, although the Turks swiftly became proficient sailors and established one of the most powerful fleets in the Mediterranean, the great preponderance of Greek-derived names for all kinds of fish and seafood demonstrates that it was the Greeks who introduced the

Ölüdeniz is a popular beach along the aptly named Turquoise Coast.

The name "Turk" was given to the Mongolian tribes that migrated west in the late seventh century to conquer the Byzantine Empire.

Turks to the edible riches of the Mediterranean waters. Finally, the use of olive oil, established in Greek cuisine since antiquity, was obviously a novelty to the Turks, although some of the ways they used olive oil, such as in cold vegetable dishes seem to lack any Greek antecedent.

These particular additions to Turkish cuisine were less important in its final crystallization than the general availability of new ingredients that were garnered from the four corners of the Ottoman Empire and the great impetus the cuisine received from the elaboration of an imperial culture. The role of the Ottoman capital, Istanbul, was crucial in both respects. From the fifteenth to the nineteenth centuries, it could have been said that all roads, as well as many maritime routes, lead to Istanbul; location combined with policy to make the city a vast entrepôt for the varied produce of the Ottoman lands, extending from Wallachia in the north to Yemen in the south, plus many items imported from farther afield. As a European admirer of the city remarked, "It seems that the Dardanelles and the Bosporus exist expressly for the purpose of conveying to Istanbul treasures from all parts of the world."

The Misir Çarşisi, a spice market first built in the mid-seventeenth century, affords a glimpse at the ancient glory of Istanbul's food markets; it is still redolent today with the scents of spices, herbs, meats and cheeses mingling beneath its blackened, vaulted ceilings. Gone, however, is the lore that once surrounded the food trade in Ottoman Istanbul. Bakers and butchers, cheesemakers and yogurt merchants, pastry chefs and pickle makers—all were organized into guilds that had their special customs and rites of initiation and that stood under the symbolic patronage of one of the prophets or a companion of the Prophet Muhammad. Displaying their wares on ox-drawn floats, they participated in the municipal parades that in their own way were as impressive a tribute to the glory of Ottoman civilization as any military parade could have been.

The role of palaces in the elaboration of sophisticated cuisine is particularly well documented in the Ottoman case. Consummate bureaucrats, the Ottomans even kept records of particular meals consumed by the sultans, including one taken by Sultan Mehmed Fatih in the year he conquered Istanbul. We also have statistics for the vast supplies that went to the royal kitchens. In 1661, for example, thirty-six thousand bushels of rice were consumed, among other items, and in 1723, the court consumed sixty thousand head of mutton, along with a wealth of other kinds of meat. A kitchen staff that ran into the thousands and was arranged in a precise hierarchy of function and seniority was entrusted with the task of processing all this material. These elaborate arrangements were not made simply in order to feed the sultan and his family. Topkapi Palace, where the sultans made their home until the early nineteenth century, was also the center of the government, a miniature city where as many as ten thousand people might work and be fed in the course of one day. In addition, food would be sent regularly outside the palace walls as a mark of favor to various dignitaries, civil and religious. There were thus at least two channels whereby the culinary styles of the palace were communicated to the outside world. Although few people were in a position to duplicate them, many autobiographical memoirs make it clear that until the end of the Ottoman Empire at least the well-to-do, ensconced in their villas along the Bosporus, were eating essentially the same food as the inmates of Topkapi.

Bodrum's most prominent castle was erected in 1402 by the Knights of St. John, who came from Rhodes to establish a stronghold.

Despite the hustle and bustle of Turkey's major cities, there are quaint rural settings where old traditions endure.

For all the variety of peoples and religions that were held together by the *Pax Ottomanica,* Ottoman culture and society were profoundly Islamic; it is therefore natural that food habits should have been interwoven with the religious traditions of Islam. The connection between food and religion was most obvious—perhaps paradoxically—in the fasting month of Ramadan. Both the predawn meal taken at the beginning of each day's fast *(sahur)* and the meal that ended it *(iftar)* were rich and varied affairs, bracketing the hours of daylight abstention between gastronomic pleasures that were made more acute by the temporary experience of hunger. The essential preparation for Ramadan was, no doubt, an inward one of pious repentance for the sins of the previous year, but it was hardly less important to stock up the larder. The other chief festival of Islam, the Festival of Sacrifice, brings to an end the annual pilgrimage to Mecca. In Turkey as elsewhere, Muslims slaughter an animal (usually a sheep), the meat of which is distributed, in fixed proportions, among relatives, neighbors and the poor. Special desserts are also prepared and eaten on this occasion.

A particular place is held in the traditional Turkish practice of Islam by the *tarikats,* which are conventionally described as mystical orders but which actually had far more extensive functions than is implied by such a description. The preparation of food took on a ritual aspect in some of these orders, notably the Mevlevi (which goes back to Rumi) and the Bektaşi. Common to these two orders but widely consumed throughout Turkish society is a special kind of cold, sweet soup known as *aşure,* rich in symbolic associations.

The Ottomans had built a culture and civilization as well as an empire, and it was inevitable that with the demise of the Ottoman state in the aftermath of World War I, much should collapse or disappear. This is apparent on the culinary front as well as elsewhere. Far-reaching changes in culture and society have altered the context in which cuisine is cultivated, and the range of dishes commonly cooked has narrowed. Nonetheless, Turkish cuisine still ranks among the foremost traditions of the entire Mediterranean; the variety of tastes and textures it proffers—soups, legumes, kebabs, fishes, pilafs, vegetable dishes, pastries, milk desserts, pickles—is probably unrivaled. The culinary debt to Turkey of its neighbors is still apparent, although it is often ignored or denied. More importantly, the preparation and serving of food to family and friends remains an important expression and prop of social cohesion. This fact alone justifies our saying that cuisine is one of the principal elements of a subtle continuity that links modern Turkey with its rich and complex past.

Meat, Poultry and Game

On the Mediterranean menu of yesterday, meat and poultry were reserved for special occasions.

MEAT, POULTRY AND GAME

Although this is the chapter most people will turn to first in search of a main course, in the Mediterranean of the past these dishes would be considered festival or special-occasion fare. In the traditional Mediterranean regimen, grains, vegetables and fruits were on the table every day. Fish appeared a little less often. Finally, there would be poultry, meat and game, which were greatly appreciated and savored but eaten only on feast days, holidays and when luck caused game to cross the hunter's path. The effect was a much more healthful diet. Of course, now this is changing. Gone are the days when eating meat occurred only on the occasional celebration and was not simply the symbol of prosperity and social prestige it is today.

There are regional distinctions for each of the innumerable ways of preserving meat.

In the past when meat was special and scarce, the slaughter of an animal was a major culinary happening. A very small animal—a Moroccan lamb or a Sardinian suckling pig—might be gutted and cooked whole on a spit over a wood fire. No part of the animal was ever wasted. The head and blood were made into a kind of sausage; the brains, liver and kidneys were cooked on the grill as kebabs, quickly sautéed, or cut up, marinated and stuffed inside the intestines and grilled, in the manner of the traditional Greek Easter sausage called *kokkoretsi.* The feet, cheeks, tail and neck all concealed tasty morsels that required lengthy preparation but were worth the trouble. (Even the fat was cooked down for tallow and the skins used as coverings and the like.) Because of this peasant thriftiness and ingenuity, every Mediterranean cuisine has a vast collection of meat, poultry and game recipes.

The most popular meat in the Mediterranean diet is lamb, followed by pork, although not in the Muslim countries, of course, where the eating of pig is forbidden. Veal is next and then finally beef, which is more popular in France than in any of the other countries. European veal is usually milk-fed or free-range and because of that is more delicate in taste and texture than that raised elsewhere. Many of the recipes for tiny fried veal chops or

Previous pages: left to right; Sautéed Chicken with Tomatoes, Olives and Wine (recipe page 160); Bean Stew of Toulouse (recipe page 178).

Mediterranean preparation of fowl, such as spit-roasting, calls for little embellishment.

delicate and tender legs have been omitted here because the cuts of meat are almost impossible to find beyond the Mediterranean countries where veal is enjoyed.

Lambs and pigs are often slaughtered at between six weeks and six months, which results in meat that is sweet, rosy pink and very tender. In earlier times, there was an immediacy to the practice. The animal was slaughtered, butchered and cooked right away. The parts that could be preserved in the form of sausage or hams were processed and stored. The pigs ate chestnuts and the lamb grazed on salt marsh, so the meat tasted of the countryside. Tender cuts were grilled quickly over a wood fire or sautéed. Tougher parts were braised slowly to become meltingly tender; in the process, the meats were infused with wine, herbs, cooking liquids and fruit juices, like Moroccan lamb *tagine* with quince or the Sicilian lamb with sweet peppers. Choice lamb cuts were pounded for *kibbee,* the famed meat dish of the Levant, and the trimmings were ground and used for meatballs such as Lebanese *kefta* or for sausage like Tunisian *merguez.*

A woman carrying geese atop her head evokes the timeless image of a routine market day in Egypt.

Game—partridge, rabbit, quail—were often given festive presentations. Many traditional recipes still prepared today are in fact centuries old. Sweet-and-sour rabbit; quail with pomegranate, Sicilian style; or stuffed into eggplant, Turkish style; and Catalan partridge with cabbage and sausage are among the most celebratory of the old-time dishes.

Most of the chicken recipes presented here are simple and not time-consuming. Mediterranean cooks believe their full-flavored fowls need little embellishment. Whether roasted with only herbs and lemon, as in the Greek *kotopolo riganato;* grilled after a brief spell in an uncomplicated marinade; sautéed with tomatoes and olives *à la niçoise;* or braised Moroccan style with sweet tomato sauce, the flavor of the chicken still comes through.

When serving any of these meat and poultry dishes, set your table with breads, grains and vegetables to capture the true flavor and spirit of the Mediterranean.

Clockwise from top left: Roast Chicken with Oregano and Lemon, Roast Chicken with Rice Stuffing, Quail Stuffed Into Eggplants

TURKEY

Patlicanli Bildircin

Quail Stuffed into Eggplants

This Turkish dish is also popular on the islands of the eastern Aegean and on Cyprus, where it is known as klephtic style, named after the Klephts, guerrilla soldiers who fought in the mountains during the Greek War of Independence and often had to cook underground, to conceal their presence. Here quail are concealed in whole eggplants and baked in the oven. The use of the grated cheese and white wine reflect the Greek variation. Greek cooks also use green (spring) onions in place of the globe onion.

4 eggplants (aubergines), about 8 oz (250 g) each
salt
½ cup (4 fl oz/125 ml) olive oil, or as needed
4 quail, preferably boneless
1 onion, chopped
2 cloves garlic, minced
½ lb (250 g) tomatoes, peeled, seeded and chopped
salt and freshly ground pepper
pinch of ground allspice or cloves
½ cup (4 fl oz/125 ml) water, boiling, or dry white wine
¾ cup (3 oz/90 g) grated *kefalotiri* (see glossary) or Parmesan cheese (optional)

Peel the eggplants lengthwise in a striped pattern. Cut in half lengthwise. Carefully hollow out as much pulp as possible and reserve it for another dish. Sprinkle the eggplant cases with salt and let stand for 30 minutes. Rinse, drain well and squeeze dry.

In a large sauté pan over medium heat, warm the oil. Add the eggplant cases and fry on all sides until lightly browned, 3–5 minutes. Using a slotted spatula remove to paper towels to drain.

Preheat an oven to 375°F (190°C).

In the oil remaining in the pan, sauté the quails over high heat, turning to brown on all sides, about 8 minutes. Remove to a platter. Add the onion to the oil remaining in the pan and sauté over high heat until golden, 8–10 minutes. Then add the tomatoes, salt and pepper to taste and the allspice or cloves. Simmer for 3 minutes.

Spoon most of the tomato sauce into a baking dish large enough to hold the 4 eggplant halves, hollow sides up. If you like, sprinkle a little grated cheese into each of the halves. Place a quail in each half, then top with a dollop of the remaining tomato sauce and grated cheese. Cap with the matching eggplant halves. Pour in the boiling water or wine and cover the dish. Bake until the eggplants and quail are tender, about 40 minutes.

Transfer to a warmed platter or serve directly from the baking dish.

SERVES 4

GREECE

Kotopolo Riganato

Roast Chicken with Oregano and Lemon

You could use rosemary instead of oregano for this savory roast chicken. Potatoes can be roasted along with the chicken. Peel 2 pounds (1 kg) new potatoes, cut into quarters and place in the roasting pan along with about a dozen garlic cloves. Add 1 cup (8 fl oz/250 ml) water or chicken stock to the pan for needed moisture. Once the chicken is ready, remove it from the pan and raise the oven temperature to 450°F (230°C) for several minutes to color the potatoes. Serve the potatoes on the side with the pan juices.

1 roasting chicken, 4–5 lb (2–2.5 kg)
salt and coarsely ground pepper
1 lemon, quartered
6 cloves garlic, crushed
¼ cup (1 oz/30 g) dried oregano
½ cup (4 fl oz/125 ml) olive oil
¼ cup (2 fl oz/60 ml) lemon juice, or to taste

Preheat an oven to 375°F (190°C).

Pat the chicken dry and sprinkle inside and out with salt and pepper. Place the lemon quarters, a few garlic cloves and a little of the oregano in the cavity.

In a small saucepan over medium heat, warm the oil. Add the remaining garlic and the remaining oregano and warm through. Add the lemon juice and season to taste with salt and pepper. Remove from the heat and set aside.

Place the chicken, breast side up, on a rack in a roasting pan. Brush once with some of the oil-lemon mixture and place in the oven. Roast, basting often with more of the lemon-oil mixture, until golden brown and tender and the juices run clear when the chicken is pierced at the thigh joint, about 1½ hours.

Transfer to a warmed platter, let rest for several minutes, then carve and serve.

SERVES 4

LEBANON

Djaj al Timman

Roast Chicken with Rice Stuffing

Seasoned rice pilafs punctuated with dried fruits and nuts are typical stuffings for roast chicken in the Middle East and North Africa. You can substitute about 1½ cups (7 oz/220 g) cooked couscous for the rice and use toasted pine nuts or hazelnuts (filberts) in place of the almonds.

¼ cup (2 oz/60 g) unsalted butter, plus 6 tablespoons (3 oz/90 g) unsalted butter, melted
1 onion, finely chopped
scant ½ cup (3 oz/90 g) long-grain white rice
¼ cup (1 oz/30 g) blanched slivered almonds, toasted
3 tablespoons raisins, plumped in hot water and drained
½ teaspoon ground allspice
1 cup (8 fl oz/250 ml) water
salt and freshly ground pepper

1 roasting chicken, about 4 lb (2 kg)
honey or ground cinnamon or allspice (optional)

In a saucepan over medium heat, melt the ¼ cup (2 oz/60 g) butter. Add the onion and sauté until tender and translucent, 8–10 minutes. Add the rice and almonds and sauté for about 3 minutes. Add the raisins, allspice and the water and bring to a boil. Cover, reduce the heat to low and cook until the water is absorbed, about 15 minutes. Season to taste with salt and pepper and let cool to room temperature.

Meanwhile, preheat an oven to 375°F (190°C).

Pat the chicken dry and sprinkle inside and out with salt and pepper. Stuff the rice mixture into the cavity and sew or skewer closed. Place the chicken on a rack, breast side up, in a roasting pan. In a small bowl stir together the melted butter and salt, pepper and a little honey, cinnamon or allspice (if using) to taste.

Roast the chicken, basting occasionally with the butter mixture, until golden brown and tender and the juices run clear when the chicken is pierced at the thigh joint, about 1½ hours.

Transfer to a warmed platter and let rest for several minutes. Remove the stuffing, carve and serve.

SERVES 4

ANDALUSIA

Cordonices en Hoja de Parra

Quail in Grapeleaves

These quail, which are very simple to prepare, can be cooked in the oven, braised on top of the stove, or grilled over a charcoal fire. You can, if you like, stuff each quail with a fresh fig in place of the thyme and lemon zest. Traditionally, the quail are served with coarse country-style bread fried in lard.

8 quail, preferably boneless
salt and freshly ground pepper
8 fresh thyme sprigs
8 lemon zest strips
16 bottled grapeleaves, rinsed of brine and stemmed
8 long strips *pancetta* or bacon
½ cup (4 fl oz/125 ml) chicken stock (see glossary), if roasting or braising
½ cup (4 fl oz/125 ml) dry white wine or sherry, if roasting or braising
olive oil, if grilling

❀ Pat the quail dry with paper towels and sprinkle inside and out with salt and pepper. Stuff a thyme sprig and lemon zest strip into each cavity. Wrap each bird in 2 grapeleaves and then wrap in *pancetta* or bacon. (Some recipes reverse the order, wrapping the birds first in the meat and then the leaves.) Tie with string or skewer with toothpicks.

❀ If roasting the birds, preheat an oven to 400°F (200°C). Place the quail in a baking pan and drizzle the stock around them. Roast until they test done when pierced with a knife, about 10 minutes. Remove to a platter and snip the string or remove the toothpicks.

❀ If braising on the stove top, place the quail in a wide sauté pan, pour in the stock, cover and braise over medium heat until quail test done, 15–20 minutes. Remove the quail to a warmed platter and snip the strings or remove the toothpicks.

❀ Add the wine to the baking pan or sauté pan and reduce slightly over high heat. Pour over the quail and serve at once.

❀ If grilling the birds, prepare a fire in a charcoal grill. Brush the wrapped birds with oil, place on the grill rack and grill, turning once, until cooked 4–5 minutes on each side. Transfer to a platter and serve.

SERVES 4

SICILY

Coniglio all'Agrodolce

Sweet-and-Sour Rabbit

Rabbit braised in wine or wine vinegar is enjoyed in Calabria and Sicily. One version, alla cacciatora, *or "hunter's style," adds chopped, pitted green olives and strips of browned celery to the stew. Sage may be added as well. In this Sicilian preparation, pine nuts and raisins are mixed in and, if needed, additional vinegar and some sugar are added to give the dish an* agrodolce, *or "sweet-and-sour," accent. In some versions of the recipe, the rabbit pieces are floured before frying; others add a little tomato purée to the sauce.*

2 rabbits, 2½–3 lb (1.25–1.5 kg) each, cut into serving pieces
1 large onion, sliced
2 celery stalks, chopped
2 carrots, chopped
2 bay leaves
⅓ cup (3 fl oz/80 ml) olive oil
1 cup (8 fl oz/250 ml) red wine vinegar, plus red wine vinegar to taste
1 cup (8 fl oz/250 ml) dry red wine, or as needed
salt and freshly ground pepper
¼ cup (2 oz/60 g) lard or ¼ lb (125 g) *pancetta,* diced
2 onions, sliced
2–3 anchovy fillets in oil, drained and minced
3 or 4 fresh sage leaves (optional)
12 green olives, pitted
3 tablespoons capers, rinsed
½ cup (2½ oz/75 g) pine nuts
½ cup (3 oz/90 g) raisins, plumped in hot water to cover and drained
sugar

❀ Pat the rabbit pieces dry with paper towels. Place in a nonreactive container. Add the onion, celery, carrots, bay leaves, a few tablespoons of the oil, the 1 cup (8 fl oz/250 ml) wine vinegar and enough wine to cover. Cover and refrigerate overnight. Bring to room temperature at least 2 hours before cooking.

❀ Remove the rabbit from the marinade, reserving the marinade, and pat dry with paper towels. Sprinkle with salt and pepper. Strain the marinade and reserve. Working in batches, in a sauté pan over high heat, warm the remaining oil and fry the rabbit pieces, turning, until golden brown on all sides, about 10 minutes. Remove to a platter.

❀ Melt the lard or render the *pancetta* in the same pan over medium heat. Add the onions and sauté until tender and translucent, about 10 minutes. Add the anchovies and sage (if using) and sauté for a few minutes.

❀ Return the rabbit to the pan. Add enough of the marinade almost to cover the rabbit and simmer until tender, about 30 minutes. Add the olives, capers, pine nuts and raisins and simmer for a few minutes. If the sauce is too thin, remove the rabbit to a platter and keep warm. Reduce the sauce over high heat until thickened. Add salt and pepper to taste. Adjust the sweet-and-sour ratio by adding sugar or vinegar, as needed for balance.

❀ Transfer to a warmed serving dish. Serve immediately.

SERVES 6

PROVENCE

Poulet à la Niçoise

Sautéed Chicken with Tomatoes, Olives and Wine

A basic braise that can be made with chicken or rabbit. It can be prepared ahead of time and reheated. Greek cooks make a similar dish, called koto kapama, *but they omit the salt pork and olives and season the tomato sauce with ground cinnamon and cloves. For* pollo alla cacciatora, *add strips of sweet red or green pepper (capsicum) to the stew during the last 30 minutes. Serve with mashed potatoes,* gnocchi *or rice.*

1 chicken, 3–4 lb (1.5–2 kg), cut into serving pieces
1 lemon, halved
salt and freshly ground pepper
5–8 tablespoons (3–4 fl oz/80–125 ml) olive oil
½ cup (3 oz/90 g) chopped lean salt pork (green bacon) or *pancetta*
4 onions, cut into eighths
2–4 cloves garlic, minced
2 teaspoons chopped fresh thyme
1 teaspoon chopped fresh sage
½ cup (4 fl oz/125 ml) dry white wine
6 large ripe tomatoes, peeled, seeded and chopped
½ cup (2½ oz/75 g) sharply flavored black olives, pitted
½ cup (¾ oz/20 g) chopped fresh flat-leaf (Italian) parsley or basil, or a mixture

Clockwise from top left: Quail in Grapeleaves, Sweet-and-Sour Rabbit, Quail with Pomegranate

Rub the chicken pieces with the cut sides of the lemon. Sprinkle with salt and pepper. In a large sauté pan over high heat, warm 5 tablespoons of the oil. Add the chicken pieces and salt pork or *pancetta* and fry quickly, turning, until golden on all sides, about 10 minutes. Using a slotted spoon remove to a platter and set aside.

Add the onions to the oil in the pan and sauté over medium heat until well browned, about 15 minutes. You may need to add a bit more oil if they begin to stick. Then add the garlic, thyme, sage, wine and tomatoes and bring to a boil. Reduce the heat and simmer, uncovered, for 10 minutes. Return the chicken and salt pork or *pancetta* to the pan, cover and cook over low heat until the chicken is cooked through, about 30 minutes longer.

During the last 5 minutes of cooking, uncover, add the olives and simmer to reduce the sauce. Taste and adjust the seasonings.

Transfer to a warmed dish. Sprinkle with the parsley or basil, or a combination, and serve at once.

SERVES 4 *Photograph pages 154–155*

SICILY

QUAGLIE ALLA MELAGRANA

Quail with Pomegranate

In this very old Sicilian recipe, Arabic influence is apparent in the use of pomegranate, which adds a tartness that is balanced by the sweetness of the orange zest and juice. (In Greece, this dish would be called Byzantine, referring to the cooking style of Constantinople.) Chopped mint and Marsala add another level of sweetness, making this a complex dish. Unsalted butter or a combination of butter and olive oil can be used for browning the quail in place of the olive oil. A Catalan version of this dish omits the mint and orange juice and zest, adds onion and tomato to the chicken stock and simmers the pomegranate seeds in the sauce rather than stuffing them in the quail cavities. Serve the quail with saffron rice with almonds.

1½ cups (12 oz/375 g) pomegranate seeds (see glossary)
½ cup (4 fl oz/125 ml) pomegranate juice (see glossary)
½ cup (4 fl oz/125 ml) fresh orange juice, plus orange juice as needed for pan juices
½ cup (4 fl oz/125 ml) Marsala, plus Marsala as needed for pan juices
4 tablespoons chopped fresh mint
2 tablespoons grated orange zest
12 quail, preferably boneless
salt and freshly ground pepper
12 slices *pancetta*
¼ cup (2 fl oz/60 ml) olive oil
1 cup (8 fl oz/250 ml) chicken stock (see glossary)
orange segments from 2 oranges

In a small bowl combine the pomegranate seeds, pomegranate juice, ½ cup (4 fl oz/125 ml) of the orange juice, the ½ cup (4 fl oz/125 ml) Marsala, mint and orange zest. Marinate the quail for 2–3 hours at room temperature. Drain, reserving the liquid and seeds separately.

Preheat an oven to 400°F (200°C).

Stuff most of the pomegranate seeds into the quail, reserving some seeds for garnish. Sprinkle the quail with salt and pepper, then wrap each one in a *pancetta* slice. In a large sauté pan over high heat, warm the oil. Add the quail and turn to brown well on all sides, about 8 minutes. Using a slotted spatula, transfer to a baking dish in which they will fit in a single layer. Pour the chicken stock and reserved marinade into the sauté pan and deglaze over high heat, scraping up any browned-on bits and reducing by half. Pour over the quail. Roast until they test done when pierced with a knife, about 10 minutes.

Remove the quail to a warmed platter or individual plates and keep warm. Taste the pan juices and add more orange juice or Marsala. Add the orange segments to the pan and sauté over medium heat for a few minutes in the pan juices.

Using a slotted spoon remove the orange segments. Pour the pan juices over the quail. Garnish with the orange segments and the reserved pomegranate seeds. Serve at once.

SERVES 6

MOROCCO

MROUZIA

Lamb Tagine with Honey, Almonds and Raisins

This tagine is quite sweet, so a little goes a long way. It is usually served alongside two lighter tagines, *such as chicken with lemon and olives (recipe on page 177) and lentils and pumpkin (recipe on page 205), as part of a meal. Shoulder or neck of lamb is best for stewing, not the lean leg. For an Algerian version, substitute 2–3 cups (12–18 oz/375–560 g) pitted prunes for the raisins and sugar for the honey, or beef may be combined with the prunes and sugar and strips of lemon zest can be added. Rabbit can be used in place of the lamb as well, in which case the dish is called* arnab mrouzia.

3 lb (1.5 kg) lamb shoulder or neck, trimmed and cut into 2½-in (6-cm) cubes
1 teaspoon ground ginger
1 teaspoon freshly ground black pepper
1 tablespoon *ras el hanout* (see glossary)
¼ teaspoon saffron threads
½ cup (4 fl oz/125 ml) water
½ cup (4 oz/125 g) unsalted butter
2 onions, finely chopped
2 garlic cloves, finely minced
2 cinnamon sticks, each about 2 in (5 cm) long
1½–2 cups (9–12 oz/280–375 g) raisins
1½ cups (8 oz/250 g) blanched almonds
¾ cup (9 oz/280 g) dark honey
1–2 teaspoons ground cinnamon

Place the meat in a nonreactive container. In a small bowl combine the ginger, pepper, *ras el hanout,* saffron and water and mix well. Rub half of this paste on the meat, coating evenly. Cover the meat and the remaining paste and refrigerate overnight.

Transfer the meat to a dutch oven or other heavy pot and add the butter, onions, garlic and cinnamon sticks. Add enough water just to cover the meat, bring to a boil and skim off any scum. Reduce the heat to low, cover and simmer until tender, about 1½ hours. Stir from time to time and add more water if the pot becomes too dry.

While the lamb is cooking, place the raisins in a small bowl with hot water to cover and stir in the remaining spice paste. Let sit for 1 hour.

Add the raisins and their soaking liquid, almonds, honey and ground cinnamon to the lamb and simmer covered, stirring often to prevent scorching, until very soft and almost falling apart, 30 minutes longer. (If it is too soupy, simmer uncovered to reduce sauce to a syrupy glaze.)

Transfer to a warmed serving dish and serve immediately.

SERVES 6

MOROCCO

MOUKH M'CHARMEL

Brains with Tomato Sauce

Brains must be very fresh and cooked the day they are purchased. This dish is good hot or at room temperature. Decorate if you like with black olives and strips of preserved lemon peel (see glossary).

3 calves' brains, 6–8 oz (185–250 g) each
juice of 1 lemon, plus 1–2 tablespoons lemon juice
3 tablespoons olive oil
5 cloves garlic, minced
1 lb (500 g) tomatoes, peeled, seeded and chopped
1 tablespoon paprika
¼ teaspoon cayenne pepper
½ teaspoon ground cumin
salt
1 small bunch fresh cilantro (fresh coriander), chopped

Place the brains in a bowl and add the juice of 1 lemon and water to cover. Soak for about 1 hour, then drain, remove the membranes and rinse under cold water. Quarter the brains.

In a large sauté pan over medium heat, warm the oil. Add the garlic and sauté for a few minutes but do not allow it to color. Add the tomatoes, paprika, cayenne, cumin and salt to taste and stir well. Bring to a boil and then reduce the heat to low. Add the brains and simmer gently for 15 minutes, turning them occasionally in the sauce. Add the 1–2 tablespoons lemon juice and the cilantro and simmer until the brains are firm, about 5 minutes longer.

Transfer to a serving dish and serve hot or at room temperature.

SERVES 6

MOROCCO

TAGINE BIL SFARDJEL

Lamb and Quince Tagine

Quinces are rather difficult to find, but this tagine, *called* ayva yahnisi *in Turkey, is so fine you'll want to try it with apples or pears. You can cook the quince separately in water to cover with the cinnamon stick and honey, then add them to the completed stew and simmer together for about 20 minutes to combine the flavors. Pitted dates can be used in place of the quinces as well; garnish with fried whole blanched almonds and sesame seeds. Or use 1½–2 cups (8–12 oz/250–375 g) diced apricots and ⅔ cup (4 oz/125 g) raisins for the quinces. You may also make this with 6 lamb shanks in place of the shoulder. Some versions of this recipe brown the meat first and then combine it with onions, spices and water. In Turkey they add 1 cup (8 fl oz/250 ml) pomegranate juice (see glossary) to the cooking liquids. In Greece, pork is substituted for the lamb and the dish, called* hirino me kythonia, *is less sweet.*

3 lb (1.5 kg) lamb shoulder, cut into 2-in (5-cm) pieces
2 onions, finely chopped
2 tablespoons chopped fresh flat-leaf (Italian) parsley
3–4 tablespoons unsalted butter
1 teaspoon ground ginger
1 cinnamon stick
⅛ teaspoon saffron threads
1½ lb (750 g) quinces, quartered and cored
3–4 tablespoons honey
1 teaspoon ground cinnamon

Place the lamb, onions, parsley, butter, ginger, cinnamon stick and saffron in a dutch oven or other heavy pot. Add enough water just to cover the meat, bring to a boil and skim off any scum. Reduce the heat to low, cover and simmer until the meat is just tender, about 1 hour.

Using a slotted spoon remove the meat to a bowl and set aside. Add the quinces, honey and ground cinnamon to the pan juices. Add enough water to half-cover the quinces and stir well. Cover and simmer over low until the quinces are tender. (Some quince varieties take a very long time to soften, so don't be alarmed if this step takes longer than 1 hour; the quinces will have turned red when they are ready.)

Return the meat to the pan, cover and simmer for 15–20 minutes to blend the flavors. Taste and adjust the seasonings, then serve.

SERVES 6

Clockwise from top: Lamb Tagine with Honey, Almonds and Raisins; Lamb and Quince Tagine; Brains with Tomato Sauce

CATALONIA

Pincho Moruno

Pork Brochettes

You will find these spicy pork morsels at tapas bars all over Spain. The name of the dish, which literally means Moorish or Arabic mouthfuls, gives away its origin. Obviously, pork was not served in Arab countries and lamb was the meat used for such kebabs (this recipe is reminiscent of the Moroccan qodban *on page 172.) But in Spain pork has become the meat of choice. If you wish to serve these brochettes as tapas, cut the meat into 1-inch (2.5-cm) cubes; this amount will serve eight. The marinade can also be rubbed on a boneless pork loin, which can be roasted or grilled.*

2 lb (1 kg) pork, cut into 1½-in (4-cm) cubes
½ cup (4 fl oz/125 ml) olive oil
1 tablespoon paprika
2 tablespoons ground cumin
1 teaspoon chopped fresh thyme
2 teaspoons cayenne pepper
1 teaspoon oregano
2 teaspoons minced garlic

Place the meat in a nonreactive container.

In a small frying pan over low heat, warm together the oil and all the remaining ingredients. Let cool and rub the spice mixture on the meat to coat evenly. Cover and refrigerate overnight.

Bring the meat to room temperature. Prepare a fire in a charcoal grill, or preheat a broiler (griller).

Thread the meat onto skewers and place on the grill rack or on a broiler tray in the broiler. Grill or broil, turning once, until done to taste, about 4 minutes per side for medium-rare.

Transfer to a warmed platter and serve.

SERVES 4

CATALONIA

Habas alla Catalana

Bean and Sausage Stew with Mint

If you can find them, fresh favas may be used instead of dried beans for this savory ragout; reduce the cooking time to about 10 minutes. Flavorful sausages add richness to the beans, and chopped mint is the accent that completes the dish. The Sardinians, who were, of course, once under Spanish rule, prepare a similar stew, favata, *but they add cabbage and fennel tops and accompany the dish with fried bread and grated cheese. Although the combination can sound strange, cooked clams may be used instead of sausages. Steam them with chopped onion, tomatoes, garlic and wine and reserve the juices to add when reheating the beans. A pinch of red pepper flakes is a nice accent, as well as a little grated lemon zest. The salt pork in this case is optional.*

2 cups (14 oz/440 g) dried white beans or fava (broad) beans
2 onions, chopped
2 cloves garlic
1 bay leaf
salt and freshly ground pepper
1 lb (500 g) chorizo or *butifarra* sausages (see glossary)
olive oil, as needed
¼ lb (4 oz/125 g) salt pork (green bacon) or bacon, finely diced
3 cloves garlic, minced
1 teaspoon paprika (optional)
2 or 3 tomatoes, peeled, seeded and chopped
½ cup (4 fl oz/125 ml) water or stock (see glossary)
½ cup (4 fl oz/125 ml) dry white wine
2–3 tablespoons chopped fresh mint

Place the beans in a bowl with water to cover generously. Refrigerate overnight.

Drain the beans and transfer to a large saucepan. Add 1 of the onions, the garlic cloves, bay leaf and water to cover. Bring to a boil, cover partially, reduce the heat to low and simmer until the beans are tender, about 1 hour. Drain, discard the bay leaf and season to taste with salt and pepper; set aside.

Top to bottom: Bean and Sausage Stew with Mint, Pork Brochettes

Meanwhile, place the sausages in a frying pan and prick with a fork in a few places. Add a little water to the pan, cover and steam gently until cooked through, about 8–10 minutes. Remove from the heat and, when cool enough to handle, cut into chunks. (You can leave them whole if they are small.) Set aside.

In a large saucepan over medium heat, pour in enough oil to form a film on the pan bottom. Add the salt pork or bacon and fry until crispy, 5–8 minutes. Using a slotted spoon remove to a bowl and set aside.

To the fat remaining in the pan, add the remaining onion and sauté over medium heat until tender and translucent, about 10 minutes. Add the garlic, paprika (if using) and tomatoes and cook, stirring, for 3 minutes longer. Add the water or stock, wine, the reserved sausages and salt pork or bacon, and the mint and simmer, uncovered, for 10 minutes. Add the cooked beans, cover and simmer over low heat for 10 minutes to heat through and blend the flavors. Taste and adjust the seasoning.

Transfer to a warmed serving dish and serve hot.

SERVES 4

EGYPT

Bamia

Meat and Okra Stew

Okra must be cooked so that its slimy texture is eliminated. The Greeks have the best technique for achieving this: Trim the conical tops with a sharp knife, then soak the okra in red wine vinegar for 30 minutes, allowing ½ cup (4 fl oz/125 ml) vinegar per pound. Drain, rinse and dry the okra and proceed with the recipe. This dish is popular throughout the Middle East and can be prepared with lamb or beef. Serve with rice (recipe on page 200).

6 tablespoons (3 oz/90 g) unsalted butter or (3 fl oz/90 ml) olive oil
2 lb (1 kg) stewing lamb or beef, cut into 1-in (2.5-cm) cubes
2 onions, finely chopped
2 cloves garlic, finely minced
1 teaspoon ground cumin
1 teaspoon ground coriander
1 cup (6 oz/185 g) peeled, seeded and chopped tomatoes
3 tablespoons tomato paste
1 cup (8 fl oz/250 ml) stock (see glossary) or water, or as needed
2 tablespoons chopped fresh mint (optional)

salt and freshly ground pepper
1–1½ lb (500–750 g) okra
juice of 1 lemon

Preheat an oven to 325°F (165°C).

In a large frying pan over medium-high heat, warm 4 tablespoons of the butter or oil. Working in batches, add the meat and fry, turning, until browned on all sides, about 10 minutes. Using a slotted spoon transfer to a baking dish or stew pot.

Add the onions to the fat remaining in the frying pan and sauté over medium heat until tender and translucent, 8–10 minutes. Add the garlic, cumin, coriander, tomatoes, tomato paste, the 1 cup (8 fl oz/250 ml) stock and mint (if using). Stir well. Pour over the meat and season to taste with salt and pepper.

Cover and bake until all the liquid is absorbed, about 1½ hours. Taste and adjust the seasonings.

Meanwhile, prepare the okra as directed in the note. In a sauté pan over medium heat, warm the remaining 2 tablespoons butter or oil. Add the okra and sauté for 3 minutes, stirring gently.

Remove the stew from the oven and arrange the okra on top in a spoke pattern. Sprinkle the lemon juice evenly over the surface. Re-cover the dish and return it to the oven. Bake for 35 minutes longer. Add stock or water if the mixture seems too dry.

Serve the stew piping hot.

SERVES 4

MOROCCO

Couscous à Sept Legumes

Couscous with Lamb and Seven Vegetables

Here is a basic couscous. It can also be made with cubed lamb shanks. This version is a cross between a Tangier couscous and one from Fès.

1 cup (7 oz/220 ml) dried chick-peas (garbanzo beans)
2 lb (500 g) boneless lamb shoulder or neck, cut into 2-in (5-cm) cubes
2 large onions, chopped
2 teaspoons salt
2 teaspoons freshly ground pepper
2 teaspoons ground ginger
⅛ teaspoon saffron threads, crushed
6 tablespoons (3 oz/90 g) unsalted butter
water or lamb stock to cover
1 lb (500 g) carrots, peeled and cut into 2-in (5-cm) chunks
1 lb (500 g) turnips, peeled and quartered
1 piece pumpkin squash, about 1 lb (500 g), peeled and cut into 2-in (5-cm) chunks
1 lb (500 g) zucchini (courgettes), cut into 2-in (5-cm) lengths
3 tomatoes, peeled, seeded and chopped
½ cup (6 oz/185 g) raisins
couscous made with water or part stock and seasoned with ginger and a little olive oil or butter (recipe on page 204)
1–2 tablespoons *harissa* (see glossary)

Place the chick-peas in a bowl and add water to cover generously. Refrigerate overnight. Drain well.

Transfer the beans to a saucepan and add water to cover by about 2 in (5 cm). Bring to a boil, reduce the heat to low, cover and simmer until tender, 1 hour or longer. Drain and let cool.

In a large, heavy pot, combine the lamb, onions, salt, pepper, ginger, saffron, and butter. Turn the ingredients in the butter. Then add water or stock to cover by 1–2 in (2.5–5 cm). Bring to a boil, reduce the heat to low, cover and simmer for 1 hour. Add the cooked chick-peas and all the vegetables except the zucchini, re-cover and cook for 20–30 minutes longer. Finally, add the zucchini and raisins and cook until all the vegetables and meat are tender, about 20 minutes longer.

Pile the couscous on a warmed platter. Using a slotted spoon, lift the meat and vegetables from the pan juices and arrange them around the couscous. Alternatively, make a well in the center of the couscous and spoon the vegetables and meats into it. Adjust the seasoning of the pan juices and spoon some of the juices over the meat and vegetables. In a small bowl whisk together the *harissa* and 1 cup (8 fl oz/250 ml) of the pan juices. Serve on the side.

SERVES 6

MEDITERRANEAN

Assorted Lamb Kebabs

Everyone loves meat grilled on a skewer over a wood fire or charcoal grill. Sometimes meat is placed on skewers along with onion slices, cubed peppers, mushrooms or cherry tomatoes. Ideally they all will cook at the same time, leaving the vegetables juicy and the meat perfectly done. Peppers and onions are fairly sturdy and don't fall apart or fall off the skewer. Little tomatoes, however, can explode or fall off the skewer and into the fire or your lap, so if you want grilled tomatoes, thread them onto a separate skewer and baste them with the meat marinade.

What follows are Greek, Turkish and Tunisian marinades for lamb kebabs. For a Moroccan version, see the recipe for mechoui *on page 172. Remember to bring the meat to room temperature before grilling.*

1 boned leg of lamb, 3–4 lb (1.5–2 kg), trimmed and cut into 1½-in (4-cm) cubes

FOR GREEK MARINADE:

½ cup (4 fl oz/125 ml) olive oil
¼ cup (2 fl oz/60 ml) dry white wine
juice of 2 lemons
1 tablespoon dried oregano
4 or 5 cloves garlic, minced
3 bay leaves, broken up (optional)
freshly ground black pepper

Clockwise from left: Meat and Okra Stew, Assorted Lamb Kebabs, Couscous with Lamb and Seven Vegetables

FOR TURKISH MARINADE I:

½ cup (4 fl oz/125 ml) olive oil
1 onion, grated
1 tablespoon minced garlic
1 teaspoon ground cinnamon
2 teaspoons ground cumin
1 tablespoon thyme
pinch of cayenne pepper
salt and freshly ground black pepper to taste
½ cup (¾ oz/20 g) chopped fresh mint or flat-leaf (Italian) parsley, or a mixture (optional)

FOR TURKISH MARINADE II:

1 cup (8 oz/250 g) yogurt
1 onion, grated
salt and freshly ground black pepper, to taste
2 cloves garlic, minced
pinch of ground allspice
pinch of ground cinnamon

FOR TUNISIAN MARINADE:

¼ cup (2 fl oz/60 ml) olive oil
¼ cup (2 fl oz/60 ml) fresh lemon juice
1 tablespoon *harissa* (see glossary) mixed with ½ cup (4 fl oz/125 ml) water
2 teaspoons caraway seeds, toasted and ground
1 teaspoon ground coriander
salt and freshly ground black pepper

Place the meat in a nonreactive container. Select one of the marinades and combine the ingredients for it in a small bowl. Whisk together to combine well, then pour over the lamb. Turn the lamb to coat evenly, then cover and refrigerate for 24 hours.

Bring the meat to room temperature. Prepare a fire in a charcoal grill, or preheat a broiler (griller).

Thread the meat onto skewers and place on the grill rack or a broiler tray in the broiler. Grill or broil, turning once, until done to taste, about 4 minutes on each side for medium-rare. Serve hot.

SERVES 6–8

Clockwise from left: Stuffed Meat Roll; Lamb Ragout with Mushrooms and Sweet Peppers; Veal Rolls, Messina Style

SICILY

FARSU MAGRU

Stuffed Meat Roll

Unlike the small veal rolls that are skewered and broiled, this is a large meat roll, which is known as braciolone *in Italian and called* farsu magru *("false lean") in Sicilian dialect. It is stuffed with slices of* mortadella *and/or prosciutto, ground seasoned beef, cheese strips and hard-cooked eggs, rolled and then tied. The roll is then browned and finally it is braised in red wine and tomato sauce. The sauce that results in the braising is also superb spooned over pasta. Veal can be used in place of the round steak.*

2½ lb (1.25 kg) round steak, in one piece
½ lb (250 g) ground (minced) beef
2 slices bread, soaked in water to cover, drained and squeezed dry

1 egg
3 tablespoons chopped fresh flat-leaf (Italian) parsley
salt and freshly ground pepper
4 slices *mortadella* or prosciutto, or a mixture
4 hard-cooked eggs
¼ lb (125 g) *caciocavallo* or provolone cheese, cut into long strips
olive oil, as needed
3 cups (15 oz/465 g) diced onion
4 cups (32 fl oz/1 l) tomato sauce
2 cups (16 fl oz/500 ml) dry red wine

Butterfly the round steak and open it flat like an opened book. Place between sheets of plastic wrap and pound until about ½ in (12 mm) thick. Set aside.

In a bowl combine the ground beef, bread, egg, parsley and salt and pepper to taste. Mix well.

Place the *mortadella* slices atop the pounded beef, covering as much of the beef as possible. Top with the prosciutto, if using. Spread the ground-meat mixture in an even layer on top. Place the hard-cooked eggs in a row lengthwise down the center of the meat and then lay the cheese strips alongside the eggs. Starting from a long side, roll up the beef and tie with kitchen string in 3 or 4 places.

In a large, heavy-bottomed pot, warm a little oil over medium-high heat. Add the beef roll and cook, turning, until browned on all sides, about 10 minutes. Remove from the pot and set aside.

Pour more oil as needed into the same pot and place over medium heat. Add the onion and sauté until tender and translucent, 8–10 minutes. Add the tomato sauce and wine and bring to a boil. Return the meat roll to the pot, reduce the heat to low, cover and braise until tender, about 2 hours.

Transfer the roll to a warmed platter. Snip the strings. Cut the meat into slices ½ in (12 mm) thick. Spoon the sauce into a bowl and pass at the table.

SERVES 6

SICILY

AGNELLO AL FORNO ALLA MADONITA

Lamb Ragout with Mushrooms and Sweet Peppers

The combination of mushrooms and sweet peppers with lamb is an unusual one for Sicily. The flavors seems rather Spanish, but the perfume is pure Mediterranean. A similar Spanish dish, cordero al chilíndrón, *omits the mushrooms and adds dried tomatoes to the sweet peppers.* Capretto, *or "kid," can be used in place of the lamb in the Sicilian dish. This version is from the region of Madonie; for a Palermo-style ragout, add 1 cup (8 fl oz/250 ml) of dry red wine to the marinade.*

3 lb (1.5 kg) lamb shoulder, trimmed and cut into 2-in (5-cm) cubes
3 onions, thickly sliced
4 cloves garlic, crushed, plus 2 cloves garlic, minced
2 tablespoons fresh rosemary
¼ cup (2 fl oz/60 ml) fresh lemon juice, plus lemon juice to taste
½ cup (4 fl oz/125 ml) olive oil, plus olive oil for sautéing
½ cup (4 fl oz/125 ml) dry white wine
3 red or yellow sweet peppers (capsicums), seeded, deribbed and cut lengthwise into wide strips
1 lb (500 g) fresh large brown cultivated mushrooms or porcini, tough stems trimmed and quartered
salt and freshly ground pepper

Place the lamb in a nonreactive container. Add the onions, crushed garlic, rosemary, the ¼ cup (2 fl oz/60 ml) lemon juice and the ½ cup (4 fl oz/125 ml) oil, cover and marinate for a few hours at room temperature or overnight in the refrigerator.

Preheat an oven to 400°F (200°C).

Drain the lamb, reserving the onions, garlic and rosemary from the marinade. Place the lamb in a baking dish. In a large sauté pan over medium heat, warm a few tablespoons oil. Add the onions from the marinade and sauté briefly; scatter them over the lamb. Add the rosemary and crushed garlic from the marinade to the lamb, along with the white wine. Cover tightly and bake for 30 minutes.

While the lamb is baking, heat 2 tablespoons oil in the same sauté pan over medium heat. Add the pepper strips and sauté until soft, about 5–8 minutes. Using a slotted spoon remove to a bowl. Set aside. To the oil in the pan add a few more tablespoons oil. Add the mushrooms and minced garlic cloves and sauté until soft, about 5 minutes.

When the lamb has cooked 30 minutes, reduce the oven temperature to 325°F (165°C). Add the pepper strips and mushroom mixture to the lamb and cook until the meat is tender, about 1 hour longer. Taste and adjust the seasoning with salt, pepper and lemon juice. Transfer to a serving dish and serve at once.

SERVES 6

SICILY

INVOLTINI DI VITELLO ALLA MESSINESE

Veal Rolls, Messina Style

Messina is sometimes called the gateway to Sicily as it is only two miles from the mainland and the most common point of entry by car ferry. It was settled first by the Greeks and their influence is seen here in the use of pine nuts and currants in the filling. These veal rolls are stuffed and threaded onto skewers alternately with sliced onions and bay leaves. Cazzilli *(recipe on page 57) or mashed potatoes are a good accompaniment.*

1½ lb (750 g) veal tenderloin, cut into 18 slices each ½ in (12 mm) thick
¼ cup (2 fl oz/60 ml) olive oil, plus olive oil for brushing
1 onion, chopped
1½ cups (3 oz/90 g) fresh bread crumbs
½ cup (2 oz/60 g) grated *caciocavallo* cheese
½ cup (2½ oz/75 g) pine nuts, toasted
½ cup (3 oz/90 g) dried currants or raisins, plumped in hot water and drained
salt and freshly ground pepper
2 red (Spanish) onions, thickly sliced
bay leaves

Place the veal slices between sheets of plastic wrap and pound until they are ¼ in (6 mm) thick. Set aside.

In a sauté pan over medium heat, warm the ¼ cup (2 fl oz/60 ml) oil. Add the onion and sauté until tender and translucent, 8–10 minutes. Add the bread crumbs and cook for a few minutes longer. Remove from the heat. Add the cheese, pine nuts, currants or raisins, and salt and pepper to taste and mix well. Let cool.

Prepare a fire in a charcoal grill, or preheat a broiler (griller).

Place a heaping spoonful of stuffing on each veal slice and roll up. Thread onto skewers alternately with onion slices and bay leaves. Brush lightly with oil and sprinkle with salt and pepper.

Place the skewers on a grill rack or a broiler pan and grill or broil, turning once, until golden, 3–4 minutes on each side.

Transfer to a warmed platter and serve.

SERVES 6

GREECE

KOKKORETSI

Grilled Innards

This skewer of intestine-wrapped innards is a traditional part of the Greek Easter meal. The diced innards are marinated in herbs, spices, garlic and lemon, then wrapped or stuffed into sheep casings and grilled over a hot fire. In Sardinia, a similar dish is called cordula.

liver, heart, kidneys and sweetbreads of 1 lamb
2–3 tablespoons red wine vinegar
½ cup (4 fl oz/125 ml) olive oil
¼ cup (2 fl oz/60 ml) fresh lemon juice
1 tablespoon dried oregano
1 teaspoon dried thyme
3 cloves garlic, minced
salt and freshly ground pepper
½ lb (250 g) sausage casings, preferably sheep casings

Trim all fat, sinews, valves and membranes from organ meats and cut them into ½-in (12-mm) cubes. Combine all of the remaining ingredients except the intestines in a bowl. Add the cubed lamb innards and toss to coat evenly. Cover and refrigerate for 1 hour.

Rinse the sausage casings by running cold water through them for a few minutes. Using a slotted spoon remove the meats from the marinade; reserve the marinade. Using the sausage stuffing attachment on a grinder, a pastry bag fitted with the large plain tip or a funnel with a 1-in (2.5-mm) or larger opening, stuff the meats into the casings. Tie off the ends, and then form into a coil, if you like.

Prepare a fire in a charcoal grill, or preheat a broiler (griller). Place the sausages on the grill rack or on a broiler pan and grill or broil, turning them once and basting with the marinade, until crisp and cooked through, about 10 minutes.

Cut into thick slices, arrange on a platter and serve hot.

SERVES 8

SICILY

CAPRETTO E CARCIOFI ALL'UOVO E LIMONE

Kid and Artichokes with Egg and Lemon

While the addition of egg and lemon to the pan juices is reminiscent of the Greek avgolemono, *such sauces appear throughout Italian cuisine and are probably of Sephardic origin. This recipe is from Calabria, but* agnello brodettato *or* capretto alla guidea, *the Passover recipes of Lazio and Tuscany, are nearly identical. Instead of all olive oil, lard or prosciutto fat may be used in those recipes not of Jewish origin. The artichokes can be cooked separately and added during the last 10 minutes. Peas may also be added, as well as favas and asparagus. You can make this stew with lamb, chicken or rabbit. In the Greek kitchen, fresh dill is added in place of the marjoram or mint and fennel bulbs or quartered lettuce heads can be added.*

½ cup (4 fl oz/125 ml) olive oil, or as needed
3½ lb (1.75 kg) kid or lamb, cut into 2-in (5-cm) pieces
1 large onion, chopped
4 tablespoons chopped fresh flat-leaf (Italian) parsley
salt and freshly ground pepper
2 tablespoons all-purpose (plain) flour (optional)
1 cup (8 fl oz/250 ml) dry white wine
6 small artichokes
1 cup (5 oz/155 g) cooked shelled peas or fava (broad) beans (optional)

juice of 3 large lemons
3 egg yolks
1 tablespoon chopped fresh marjoram or mint

In a large saucepan or wide sauté pan over medium-high heat, warm the oil. Add the lamb, onion and 3 tablespoons of the parsley and sauté until the lamb is golden. Sprinkle with salt, pepper and flour (if using) and mix well. Add the wine and bring to a boil. Cook over high heat for about 5 minutes, then cover and reduce the heat to low. Simmer for about 40 minutes.

Meanwhile, remove and discard the tough outer leaves from the artichokes. Trim off the stems and prickly points of the leaves. Cut into quarters lengthwise and scoop out and remove the prickly choke. As each artichoke is cut, drop it into a large bowl of water to which has been added the juice of 1 lemon.

Drain the artichokes, pat dry and add to the lamb. Re-cover and simmer until the lamb and artichokes are tender, about 25 minutes longer. Add the cooked peas or favas and warm through. Taste and adjust the seasonings.

In a bowl whisk together the egg yolks, the remaining lemon juice, the remaining parsley and the marjoram or mint until foamy. Remove the stew from the heat and whisk in the egg-lemon mixture, stirring constantly. Re-cover the pan and allow the eggs to thicken the sauce, just a few minutes.

Transfer to a warmed bowl and serve at once.

SERVES 6

GREECE

MOUSSAKA

Eggplant and Lamb Casserole

A classic casserole found in both Greek and Turkish cuisines, moussaka *combines two of the most popular ingredients in Mediterranean cooking, lamb and eggplant. Many recipes for* moussaka *use a thicker, more floury cream sauce. Here the ricotta acts as a stabilizer, so the top custard does not need to be so rich. You can use olive oil in place of butter for sautéing the ingredients for the meat sauce. Some Turkish versions add potato slices to the dish, frying the potatoes when the eggplant is fried. The* moussaka *can be assembled a day ahead and refrigerated and then baked just before serving.*

2 or 3 eggplants (aubergines), about 2 lb (1 kg) total weight
salt and freshly ground pepper
olive oil

FOR THE MEAT SAUCE:

¼ cup (2 oz/60 g) unsalted butter
2 onions, chopped
4 cloves garlic, finely minced
2 teaspoons ground cinnamon
1–2 teaspoons dried oregano
1 lb (500 g) ground (minced) lamb
1 cup (8 fl oz/250 ml) tomato purée or 2 or 3 fresh large tomatoes, peeled, seeded and diced
2 tablespoons tomato paste
½ cup (4 fl oz/125 ml) dry red wine
4 tablespoons chopped fresh flat-leaf (Italian) parsley
salt and freshly ground pepper

FOR THE CREAM SAUCE:

2 cups (16 fl oz/500 ml) milk
¼ cup (2 oz/60 g) unsalted butter
¼ cup (1½ oz/40 g) all-purpose (plain) flour
½ teaspoon freshly grated nutmeg
salt and freshly ground pepper
4 eggs, lightly beaten
1 cup (8 oz/250 g) ricotta cheese

Clockwise from left: Kid and Artichokes with Egg and Lemon, Eggplant and Lamb Casserole, Grilled Innards

⅓ cup (1⅓ oz/45 g) grated *kasseri* (see glossary) or Parmesan cheese
⅓ cup (1⅓ oz/45 g) fine dried bread crumbs

Peel the eggplants completely, or peel them lengthwise in a striped pattern. Cut into slices ⅓ in (9 mm) thick. Sprinkle with salt and set aside in a large colander for 1 or 2 hours. Pat the slices dry with paper towels and squeeze out any excess moisture as you do.

Working in batches, in a large sauté pan over medium heat, pour in oil to a depth of ½ in (12 mm). Add the eggplant slices and fry, turning once, until lightly browned on both sides. Using a slotted spoon remove to paper towels to drain. Alternatively, brush the eggplants with oil, sprinkle with pepper and bake in a 400°F (200°C) oven until golden, 10–15 minutes.

To make the meat sauce, in a large sauté pan over medium heat, melt the butter. Add the onions and garlic and sauté until tender and translucent, about 10 minutes. Add the lamb, breaking it up, and sauté until the meat loses its red color, about 10 minutes. Add the cinnamon, oregano, tomato purée or tomatoes, tomato paste and wine; simmer until most of the liquid is absorbed, about 15 minutes. Add the parsley and season to taste with salt and pepper.

To make the cream sauce, warm the milk in a small saucepan. In a large saucepan over medium heat, melt the butter. Stir in the flour and cook, stirring constantly, for 2–3 minutes. Slowly stir in the hot milk and continue stirring until the mixture thickens and comes to a boil. Remove from the heat and stir in the nutmeg and salt and pepper to taste. Beat in the eggs and ricotta. Set aside.

Preheat an oven to 375°F (190°C). Combine the grated cheese and bread crumbs in a bowl.

Lightly oil a 4-qt (4-l) ovenproof casserole. Sprinkle the bottom with a little of the crumb-cheese mixture. Arrange one-third of the eggplant slices in a layer on top. Pour on one half of the meat sauce. Sprinkle evenly with the remaining crumbs and top with half of the remaining eggplant. Pour on the remaining meat sauce and then top with the remaining eggplant. Pour the cream sauce evenly over all.

Bake until golden and the top is set but still slightly quivery, 45–60 minutes. If the top is browning too quickly, cover with aluminum foil.

Remove from the oven and let stand for 15 minutes, then cut into squares to serve.

SERVES 8

Left to right: Roast Lamb, Lamb Kebabs with Yogurt and Tomato Sauces

TURKEY

YOĞURTLU KEBAB

Lamb Kebabs with Yogurt and Tomato Sauces

This is one of the most wonderful kebab dishes imaginable. The meat is marinated and grilled, then removed from the skewers and placed atop a bed of warmed pita bread that has been torn into large bite-sized pieces. Two sauces are then drizzled over the meat and bread, a spicy tomato sauce and a yogurt-and-garlic sauce. As if this isn't enough, a little melted butter seasoned with cayenne pepper and paprika and a few strips of hot green chilies crown the dish. The long green peppers Turkish cooks use are not easily found outside of Turkey, so poblano chilies *have been substituted here. You can omit this chili topping, if you like, and the dish will still be irresistible.*

2 lb (1 kg) lamb sirloin or leg, trimmed and cut into 1-in (2.5-cm) cubes
½ cup (4 fl oz/125 ml) plus 2 tablespoons olive oil
¼ cup (1¼ oz/40 g) grated onion
2 cloves garlic, minced, plus 2 teaspoons finely minced garlic
2 tablespoons fresh lemon juice
1 tablespoon chopped fresh thyme
4 or 5 tomatoes
pinch of red pepper flakes, crushed
dash of red wine vinegar
salt
6 tablespoons (3 oz/90 g) unsalted butter
1½ cups (12 oz/375 g) plain yogurt
freshly ground pepper
4 large pita breads (recipe on page 82)
paprika and cayenne pepper for seasoning butter
2 fresh *poblano* chilies, roasted, peeled, seeded and diced or cut into long strips (optional; see glossary)

Place the lamb in a nonreactive container. In a small bowl stir together the ½ cup (4 fl oz/125 ml) oil, onion, the 2 cloves minced garlic, lemon juice and thyme. Pour over the lamb, turn to coat well, cover and marinate in the refrigerator for several hours, or preferably overnight.

Heat a griddle or a cast-iron skillet over medium heat. Add the tomatoes and roast, turning, until blistered on all sides, about 4 minutes. Remove from the heat and, when cool enough to handle, peel, chop and put into a saucepan. Add the 2 tablespoons oil and the pepper flakes and cook over medium heat for about 5 minutes. Add the vinegar and salt to taste. Set aside and keep warm.

In a small sauté pan over medium heat, melt 2 tablespoons of the butter. Add the finely minced garlic and sauté for 1–2 minutes. Remove from the heat and let cool, then combine it with the yogurt in a small bowl. Add salt to taste and stir well. Cover and refrigerate, but bring to room temperature before serving.

Bring the lamb to room temperature. Preheat a broiler (griller), or prepare a fire in a charcoal grill.

Remove the lamb cubes from the marinade and thread onto skewers. Sprinkle with salt and pepper. Place on a broiler pan or grill rack and broil or grill, turning once, until done to taste, about 4 minutes on each side for medium-rare.

Meanwhile, warm the pita bread by wrapping it in aluminum foil and placing in a 350°F (180°C) oven for 7 minutes, or by placing it on the grill rack for a few minutes. Tear it into pieces and arrange on 4 individual plates. Melt the remaining 4 tablespoons (2 oz/60 g) butter and add paprika and cayenne to taste.

Reheat the tomato sauce. Top the bread with some of the warm tomato sauce and the yogurt sauce. Divide the lamb evenly among the plates. Top with the remaining tomato and yogurt sauces. Drizzle with the seasoned melted butter and the chilies (if using). Serve at once.

SERVES 4

MOROCCO

MECHOUI

Roast Lamb

Technically mechoui *is a whole lamb roasted on a spit over charcoal. It is unlikely that many of us will be cooking a whole lamb very often. But the flavors of the* mechoui *marinade, or* chermoula, *are so wonderful, there is no reason not to use it on leg of lamb, chops or even on kebabs, which are called* qodban. *(To be truly authentic when preparing the kebabs, skewer them alternately with cubes of lamb fat.)*

Moroccans prefer their lamb well done. You can, however, cook it to the degree of doneness you prefer. An instant-read thermometer will indicate 125°F (52°C) for rare, 135°F (57°C) for medium, 145°F (63°C) for well done. Either butter or oil can be used for the chermoula. *If you are roasting the lamb in the oven, baste it as it roasts with the pan drippings. If you are cooking on a charcoal grill or in a broiler, try to reserve a little of the* chermoula *for basting or make a little extra. Cubed liver or sweetbreads can be marinated in this same* chermoula, *then skewered and grilled.*

1 leg of lamb, about 5 lb (2.5 kg), boned and butterflied; 12 lamb chops; or 2½ lb (1.25 kg) boneless leg of lamb meat, trimmed and cut into 1½-in (4-cm) cubes

FOR THE MARINADE:

1 cup (8 oz/250 g) unsalted butter, at room temperature, or 1 cup (8 fl oz/250 ml) olive oil

1 large onion, grated
4 garlic cloves, finely minced
1 teaspoon salt
2 teaspoons ground cumin
1 teaspoon paprika
½ teaspoon cayenne pepper
½ teaspoon ground cinnamon
½ teaspoon ground ginger
1 teaspoon freshly ground black pepper
¼ cup (2 fl oz/60 ml) lemon juice
4 tablespoons chopped fresh flat-leaf (Italian) parsley
4 tablespoons chopped fresh cilantro (fresh coriander)

melted butter or olive oil seasoned with a little marinade

Trim all excess fat and sinew from the lamb. Place in a nonreactive container. In a bowl combine all the marinade ingredients, stirring to form a paste. Rub the paste on the meat to coat completely. For boneless lamb leg to be roasted in the oven, rub the inside with half of the marinade, roll the leg and tie in several places with kitchen string, then rub the rest of the marinade over the surface. Cover and marinate the meat overnight in the refrigerator.

Bring the meat to room temperature. Prepare a fire in a charcoal grill, or preheat a broiler (griller). If roasting in the oven, preheat to 350°F (180°C).

Remove the meat from the marinade. For grilled or broiled boneless lamb leg, place on the grill rack or broiler pan and grill or broil until done to taste, 10–15 minutes per side for medium-rare; baste with a little butter or oil seasoned with the marinade as it cooks. For roasted boneless lamb leg, place in a roasting pan and roast, basting with the pan drippings, until done to taste (see introduction). For chops, grill or broil, turning once, until done to taste, about 4–6 minutes per side, depending upon thickness of chops, for medium-rare. For kebabs, thread the cubes onto skewers and grill or broil, turning once, until done to taste, about 4 minutes per side for medium-rare.

Transfer to a warmed platter, carve, if necessary, and serve.

SERVES 6

MEDITERRANEAN

GRILLED CHICKEN

Grilled chicken is always welcome at the table. Whether you use whole butterflied poussins, game hens, broiler halves, chicken parts or boneless chicken cubes on skewers, you will find the following marinades intensely flavorful. The Egyptian marinade is especially good on whole butterflied squab (pigeon). Marinate the meat overnight in the refrigerator and bring to room temperature before cooking. If you like, thread blanched vegetables such as sweet pepper (capsicum) and onion chunks onto skewers and cook alongside the chicken (or thread them onto the same skewers). Serve the grilled chicken with pita bread (recipe on page 82) and lemon wedges.

2 lb (1 kg) boneless chicken breasts or part boneless thighs and part breasts or 6 small birds or broiler halves, about 1 lb (500 g) each (see note)

FOR A LEBANESE MARINADE:

4–6 cloves garlic, finely minced
½ cup (4 fl oz/125 ml) fresh lemon juice
2 teaspoons chopped fresh thyme
1 teaspoon paprika
¼–½ teaspoon cayenne pepper (optional)
1 teaspoon salt
½ teaspoon freshly ground black pepper
½ cup (4 fl oz/125 ml) olive oil

FOR A TURKISH MARINADE:

1 cup (8 oz/250 g) plain yogurt
1 tablespoon paprika
1 teaspoon ground cinnamon or 1 tablespoon ground cumin
¼ teaspoon cayenne pepper, or to taste
4 cloves garlic, minced
juice of 1 lemon
6 tablespoons (3 fl oz/90 ml) olive oil
½ teaspoon freshly ground black pepper
½ cup grated onion

FOR A MOROCCAN MARINADE:

1 tablespoon paprika
2 teaspoons ground cumin
½ teaspoon cayenne pepper
1 teaspoon ground ginger
½ cup (4 fl oz/125 ml) melted unsalted butter or olive oil
juice of 1 large lemon
salt and freshly ground black pepper, to taste

FOR AN EGYPTIAN MARINADE:

½ cup (4 fl oz/125 ml) olive oil
2 tablespoons ground cumin
1 tablespoon ground coriander
1 onion, grated
3 cloves garlic, finely minced
1 teaspoon cayenne pepper

salt and freshly ground pepper to taste

If using boneless chicken pieces, cut into 1-in (2.5-cm) cubes and place in a shallow nonreactive container. If using whole birds, butterfly them; if using broiler halves, leave whole. Select one of the marinades, then combine the ingredients for it in a bowl and pour over the chicken. Cover and marinate in the refrigerator for 6 hours or overnight.

Bring the meat to room temperature. Meanwhile, prepare a fire in a charcoal grill or preheat a broiler (griller).

Remove the meat from the marinade, reserving the marinade. If using chicken cubes, thread onto skewers. Place the skewers or butterflied or halved birds on the grill rack or a broiler pan and grill or broil until cooked through, basting with reserved marinade while cooking. Cooking time will depend upon size of poultry pieces; do not let the meat become dry.

SERVES 6

Grilled Chicken

TURKEY

Tavsan Kebabi

Grilled Rabbit

In the Mediterranean, rabbit is usually cut up and braised or sautéed quickly. It can also be left whole and slowly grilled on a spit over a wood fire. Since few of us have spits or are able to build a fire pit, in all likelihood we will be broiling the rabbit or cooking it on a charcoal grill. In both cases it is easier if you cut the rabbit in half, which will reduce the cooking time. The loin yields most of the meat, so you will need two rabbits to serve four persons. Here is a Turkish recipe for grilled rabbit adapted from spit-roasting.

2 rabbits, about 2 lb (1 kg) each, livers reserved
6 cloves garlic, cut into slivers, plus 3 cloves garlic, finely minced
12 whole cloves
1 cup (8 fl oz/250 ml) olive oil
3 tablespoons chopped fresh mint
3 tablespoons chopped fresh tarragon
6 tablespoons (½ oz/15 g) chopped fresh flat-leaf (Italian) parsley
salt and freshly ground pepper
3 tablespoons unsalted butter
1 cup (8 fl oz/250 ml) dry red wine
juice and zest of 1 lemon
1 teaspoon ground allspice

Pat the rabbit dry with paper towels. Make shallow slits all over the rabbits and insert the garlic slivers and cloves together into the slits. Place the rabbits in a nonreactive container. In a bowl combine the oil, mint, tarragon, parsley and salt and pepper to taste. Rub the mixture over the rabbits, cover and refrigerate overnight.

Prepare a fire in a charcoal grill or preheat a broiler (griller). Remove the rabbits from the marinade, reserving the marinade. If you have a spit, secure the 2 rabbits to it and position it about 2 feet (60 cm) from the heat source. Cook slowly until cooked through when pierced with a knife, about 1 hour. For grilling or broiling the rabbits, split them in half lengthwise. Place on an oiled grill rack or broiler pan and grill or broil, turning once, until tender, about 8 minutes on each side. In each case baste the rabbits as they cook with the reserved marinade.

While the rabbits are cooking, cut the livers into small pieces. In a small sauté pan over medium heat, melt the butter. Add the livers and the minced garlic and sauté for about 4 minutes. Add the wine, lemon juice and zest and allspice and sauté until the livers are done but still pink, 1–2 minutes longer.

Remove the rabbits to a warmed platter. Spoon the sauce over the rabbits and serve.

SERVES 4

MOROCCO

Djej Matisha Mesla

Chicken with Sweet Tomato Sauce

In this especially delicious dish, the tomatoes cook down to a slightly caramelized thick purée and their sweetness is heightened by the addition of honey and cinnamon. Two noted cooks and food writers, Latifa Bennani Smires and Paula Wolfert, simmer the chicken with the tomatoes, remove the chicken, thicken the sauce over high heat, and then reheat the chicken in the sauce. Another respected authority, Fattouma Benkirane, cooks the chicken and tomatoes separately, then pours the thickened sweet tomato purée over the chicken almost as if it is a condiment. For maximum richness of flavor, reheat the chicken in the sauce, whether you've cooked them together or separately. If you like, add 1 cup (5½ oz/170 g) toasted almonds to the sesame seeds before sprinkling them over the top. Also, you may omit the marinating step and simply combine all the ingredients for the marinade with the onions and water and proceed as directed.

1 teaspoon freshly ground pepper
¼ teaspoon saffron threads, crushed
½ teaspoon ground ginger
2 cloves garlic, finely minced
¼ cup (2 fl oz/60 ml) olive oil
2 chickens, about 3 lb (1.5 kg) each, quartered
2 onions, grated
2 cups (16 fl oz/500 ml) water
5–6 lb (2.5–3 kg) ripe tomatoes, peeled, seeded and diced
1 tablespoon ground cinnamon
salt
6 tablespoons (5 oz/155 g) dark honey
¼ cup (1 oz/30 g) sesame seeds, toasted

In a small bowl stir together the pepper, saffron, ginger, garlic and oil. Place the chicken quarters in a nonreactive container and rub the mixture on them to coat evenly. Cover and refrigerate overnight.

In a large, wide pan, combine the chicken and marinade, onions and the water. Bring to a boil, reduce the heat and simmer for 20 minutes. Add the tomatoes, ½ tablespoon of the cinnamon and a little salt. Simmer the chicken, turning it often in the sauce, until tender, about 30 minutes. When the chicken is cooked, remove it from the pan and set aside.

Reduce the sauce over high heat, stirring often to prevent scorching. When the sauce is thick and the oil starts to rise to the top, add the honey and remaining ½ tablespoon cinnamon and cook for a few minutes longer. Return the chicken to the sauce and reheat.

Transfer to a warmed serving dish. Sprinkle with sesame seeds and serve at once.

SERVES 8

TURKEY

Kadin Budu

Lady's Thigh

Every country's standard of beauty is different. No thin fashion models here. These round kefta *are said to resemble a woman's thighs. Beauty may be in the eye of the beholder, but we can all agree that these taste wonderful.*

2 tablespoons unsalted butter
1 large onion, finely chopped
⅓ cup (2½ oz/75 g) long-grain white rice
1 cup (8 fl oz/250 ml) water
1½ teaspoons salt
1½ lb (750 g) lamb, ground twice
3 eggs
1 teaspoon freshly ground pepper
1 teaspoon ground cinnamon, plus 1 teaspoon cinnamon for garnish (optional)
1 teaspoon ground cumin
⅓ cup (1½ oz/45 g) fresh *kasseri* cheese (see glossary)
½ cup (¾ oz/20 g) chopped fresh dill (optional)
1 cup (5 oz/155 g) all-purpose (plain) flour
vegetable oil for frying

In a saucepan over medium heat, melt the butter. Add the onion and sauté until soft, 10–15 minutes. Add the rice, the water and ½ teaspoon of the salt. Bring to a boil, cover, reduce the heat to low and cook until the water is absorbed and rice

Clockwise from left: Grilled Rabbit, Chicken with Sweet Tomato Sauce, Lady's Thigh

is cooked, 15–20 minutes. Remove from the heat and let cool. In a dry sauté pan over medium heat, sauté half of the meat, stirring often, until the meat absorbs its juices, about 10 minutes. Remove from the heat and let cool.

In a bowl combine the cooled rice and meat, the raw meat, 1 of the eggs, pepper, 1 teaspoon cinnamon, cumin, the remaining 1 teaspoon salt, cheese and the dill (if using). Knead the mixture well. Dip your hands into cold water and form the meat mixture into 18 large or 24 smaller flattened ovals. Place on baking sheets lined with parchment paper until ready to fry.

To fry, spread out the flour on a plate. In a small bowl whisk the remaining 2 eggs lightly with a fork. In a large sauté pan over medium-high heat, pour in oil to a depth of ¼ in (6 mm).

When the oil is ready, dip each oval into the flour and then into the egg. Working in batches, fry, turning once, until golden, 3–5 minutes on each side. Using a slotted spatula remove to paper towels to drain, and repeat with the remaining balls.

Arrange on a platter and sprinkle with the remaining 1 teaspoon cinnamon, if you like. Serve warm or at room temperature.

SERVES 8

Chicken with Lemon and Olives

MOROCCO

DJEJ M'CHERMEL

Chicken with Lemon and Olives

There are three classic versions of chicken with preserved lemon and olives in Moroccan cuisine. M'chermel *has an oniony sauce and ripe green-brown olives.* Djej bil zaitun *has cracked green olives in abundance, and the* djej mquali *has red-brown olives and the sauce is thickened with chicken giblets and livers. Usually the chicken is combined with onions, spices and water and simmered until tender. If you like your chicken to have color, however, brown it first in oil or butter. You can also marinate the chicken pieces overnight in a little oil with the spices and garlic. If the olives seem too bitter, soak them in cold water for an hour, or bring them to a boil with water to cover and then drain. This recipe is a middle-of-the-road interpretation of the three classics. If you wish to make a version that more closely reflects the traditional* djej bil zaitun, *add 2 cups (10 oz/315 g) cracked green olives, pitted, in place of the 1 cup (5 oz/155 g) green olives. For* djej mquali, *use ½ cup (2½ oz/75 g) Kalamata or Gaeta olives for the green olives. Serve with couscous (recipe on page 204) or rice (recipe on page 200).*

1 chicken, 3–3½ lb (1.5–1.75 kg) cut into 8 pieces, plus liver and giblets
1½ cups (7½ oz/235 g) finely chopped onion
2 cloves garlic, finely minced
2 teaspoons paprika
1 teaspoon ground ginger
½ teaspoon ground cumin
¼ teaspoon ground turmeric or saffron threads crushed
4 tablespoons chopped fresh cilantro (fresh coriander)
1 teaspoon salt
½ teaspoon freshly ground pepper
¼ cup (2 fl oz/60 ml) olive oil
4 tablespoons chopped fresh flat-leaf (Italian) parsley
1–1½ cups (8–12 fl oz/250–375 ml) water
peel from 1 preserved lemon, cut into long, narrow strips (see glossary)
1 cup (5 oz/155 g) green olives, pitted
juice of 1–2 lemons

In a large saucepan over medium-low heat, combine the chicken pieces, liver, giblets, onion, garlic, paprika, ginger, cumin, turmeric or saffron, parsley, salt, pepper and oil. Warm gradually, turning the ingredients in the oil for a few minutes, then add the water to cover. Bring to a boil, reduce the heat and simmer uncovered, occasionally turning the chicken in the sauce, until almost tender, 30–40 minutes.

Remove the chicken liver and giblets and mash them well, then return them to the sauce. Add the preserved lemon peel, olives and lemon juice and continue to cook until the chicken is very tender, about 15 minutes longer. Taste and adjust the seasonings, adding more lemon juice if you like. Transfer to a platter. If the sauce is too thin, remove only the chicken to the platter and reduce the sauce over high heat. Then spoon the sauce, olives and lemon strips over the chicken. Serve at once.

SERVES 4

PROVENCE

GIGOT D'AGNEAU À L'AIL

Leg of Lamb with Garlic

This classic Provençal leg of lamb can be served with white beans or roasted potatoes. Fenouil braisé *(recipe on page 211) or* tomates provençale *(recipe on page 210) are nice accompaniments. In a similar Provençal recipe, the lamb is cooked in wine and stock in a covered pan on the stove top or in the oven for about 3 hours until the meat is very soft, then the puréed garlic (cooked in stock or water) is added to the pan juices. In Sicily, leg of lamb was traditionally cooked on tiles in a wood-burning oven and called* cosciotto di castrato sulle tegole. *To make a version of this Sicilian dish, cut deep but short slits into the lamb leg and insert slivers of garlic, strips of* pancetta *rolled in black pepper, and needles of rosemary into them. Roast as directed, but baste with a mixture of two parts olive oil, one part fresh lemon juice, and salt and pepper to taste. For Greek* arni me yaourti, *season the leg of lamb with garlic and rosemary and roast as directed. During the last 15 minutes, coat the leg with a mixture of 1½ cups (12 oz/375 g) plain yogurt seasoned with salt, pepper, and 1 teaspoon ground cinnamon and bake until the coating sets.*

1 leg of lamb, about 5 lb (2.5 kg)
6 cloves garlic, cut into slivers, plus 24 whole cloves garlic
6 anchovy fillets in olive oil, drained and cut into slivers
3 tablespoons olive oil
salt and freshly ground pepper
1 tablespoon chopped fresh rosemary
2 teaspoons chopped fresh thyme
½ cup (4 fl oz/125 ml) dry white wine
½ cup (4 fl oz/125 ml) stock (see glossary) or water, plus stock or water as needed for thinning sauce

Preheat an oven to 350°F (180°C).

Make shallow slits all over the leg of lamb and insert a sliver of garlic and an anchovy sliver into each one. Rub the leg with the oil and sprinkle with salt and pepper to taste and the rosemary and thyme.

Place the leg of lamb in a roasting pan. Roast for about 1 hour and 20 minutes for medium-rare lamb, or until an instant-meat thermometer inserted into the thickest part registers 125°F (52°C). (The lamb will continue to cook while it rests before carving.)

While the lamb is roasting, in a saucepan combine the whole garlic cloves, and the ½ cup (4 fl oz/125 ml) each wine and stock. Bring to a boil, reduce the heat to medium-low and simmer, uncovered, until the garlic is very soft, 15–20 minutes. Transfer the garlic and cooking liquid to a blender and purée until smooth. Or mash the garlic cloves in the liquid with a fork until smooth.

When the lamb is done, remove to a platter. Add the garlic purée to the juices in the roasting pan and heat on the stove top. Add additional stock if needed to thin to proper consistency. Taste and adjust the seasonings.

Carve the lamb and serve the garlic sauce on the side.

SERVES 6

Leg of Lamb with Garlic

ALBANIA

Arnavut Ciğeri

Lamb Liver with Red Peppers

Although this spicy liver dish and accompanying wilted onion salad is usually served as a first course, it also makes a tasty luncheon or dinner menu course.

2 onions, thinly sliced into rings
1 tablespoon salt
½ cup (¾ oz/20 g) chopped fresh flat-leaf (Italian) parsley
1 teaspoon sumac (see glossary)
1 lb (500 g) lamb's liver, trimmed and cut into ½-in (12-mm) cubes
½ cup (2 oz/60 g) all-purpose (plain) flour
½ cup (4 fl oz/125 ml) olive oil
salt
2 teaspoons red pepper flakes
2 long sweet red peppers (capsicums), seeded, deribbed and cut into thin strips (optional)

Place the onions in a colander. Sprinkle with the salt and let drain for 20 minutes. Rinse under cold running water, squeeze out the excess water and pat dry. Place in a bowl with the parsley and toss well. Sprinkle with the sumac.

Place the liver cubes in a bowl, add the flour and toss well. Transfer to a large sieve and shake off the excess flour.

In a large frying pan over high heat, warm the oil. Add the liver and fry, quickly, turning often, until golden, just a few minutes. Season with salt to taste and the pepper flakes.

Transfer to a platter and arrange the onion mixture around the edges. Top with the pepper strips, if you like.

SERVES 4

TURKEY

Kilis Kuşlari

Lamb with Walnut Stuffing

A specialty of southeastern Turkey, this dish is actually Syrian in origin. The walnut-and-meat mixture is stuffed into slices of lamb and braised in the oven with a mild tomato sauce. You can brown the stuffed slices in a little olive oil over high heat before they go into the oven, but this step is unnecessary. Icli köfte, *or "mother-in-law* köfte,*" uses the same filling, but stuffs it into a mixture of lamb and bulgur (cracked wheat) similar to* kibbee *(recipe on page 182). Serve with a simple rice pilaf (recipe on page 200).*

8 slices leg of lamb, each ½ in (12 mm) thick

FOR THE FILLING:

2 tablespoons unsalted butter
1 onion, finely chopped
1 lb (500 g) ground (minced) lamb
2 ripe tomatoes, peeled, seeded and chopped
⅓ cup (1⅓ oz/45 g) chopped toasted walnuts
2 tablespoons chopped fresh flat-leaf (Italian) parsley
1 teaspoon salt
½ teaspoon ground allspice
½ teaspoon ground cinnamon
½ teaspoon ground cumin
pinch of cayenne pepper

FOR THE SAUCE:

½ cup (4 fl oz/125 ml) tomato purée
1 cup (8 fl oz/250 ml) water or lamb or chicken stock (see glossary)
2 cloves garlic, finely minced
3 bay leaves

Place the lamb slices between sheets of plastic wrap and pound until they are about ¼ in (6 mm) thick. Refrigerate until ready to stuff and roll.

Preheat an oven to 350°F (180°C). To make the filling, in a small saucepan over medium heat, melt the butter. Add the onion and sauté until tender and translucent, about 8–10 minutes. Add the lamb, breaking it up, and sauté, stirring often, until the meat loses its color, about 8 minutes. Add the tomatoes, walnuts, parsley, salt, allspice, cinnamon, cumin and cayenne and cook, stirring, for about 3 minutes to blend the flavors. Remove from the heat and let cool.

Place 2–3 tablespoons of the cooled filling on each meat slice and roll up. Skewer or tie with kitchen string. Place the rolls close together in a baking dish.

To make the sauce, combine all the ingredients in a saucepan. Bring to a simmer, stirring, and then pour over the meat rolls. Bake, basting occasionally with the sauce, until the rolls are tender, about 1 hour.

Transfer the rolls and sauce to a warmed platter and serve immediately.

SERVES 4

PROVENCE

Cassoulet de Toulouse

Bean Stew of Toulouse

In this specialty of Languedoc, white beans are simmered very slowly with sausage, lamb, pork and duck and the completed stew is topped with bread crumbs. If you like, goose or duck confit, *available in specialty-food shops, can be added as well. Also, the duck can be cut up and browned with the pork or lamb and then cooked in the ragout rather than roasted. In addition, you can layer the ingredients in the dish, putting half of the beans on the bottom, topping with the meats, then the remaining beans and finally the bread crumbs. The dish is quite rich; a green salad after such a robust main course is all that is needed. It can be prepared well ahead of time and reheated in the oven.*

FOR THE BEANS:

4½ cups (2 lb/1 kg) dried white beans
½ lb (250 g) salt pork (green bacon) or bacon, blanched 2 minutes and diced
2 onions, each stuck with 2 whole cloves
4 cloves garlic, crushed
3 fresh thyme sprigs
3 bay leaves
1 cup (6 oz/185 g) peeled and chopped fresh or canned plum (Roma) tomatoes
1 tablespoon salt
freshly ground pepper
ground cloves (optional)

FOR THE MEAT RAGOUT:

1 duck, about 5 lb (2.5 kg)
salt and freshly ground pepper
lard, bacon drippings or rendered duck or goose fat
1½ lb (750 g) lean pork, cut into 1-in (2.5-cm) cubes
1½ lb (750 g) lean lamb, cut into 1-in (2.5-cm) cubes
4 onions, chopped
4 cloves garlic, finely chopped
2 cups (16 fl oz/500 ml) dry white wine
2 cups (12 oz/375 g) peeled and chopped fresh or canned plum (Roma) tomatoes
2 cups (16 fl oz/500 ml) stock (see glossary), plus stock as needed
2 fresh thyme sprigs
2 fresh parsley sprigs
1 bay leaf

Top to bottom: Lamb Liver with Red Peppers, Lamb with Walnut Stuffing

1 lb (500 g) garlic pork sausages
1 lb (500 g) smoked pork sausages
2 cups (4 oz/125 g) fresh bread crumbs
melted unsalted butter (optional)

❀ To ready the beans, place them in a bowl and add water to cover. Let soak overnight. Drain well.

❀ Transfer the beans to a saucepan and add water to cover by about 2 in (5 cm). Add the salt pork or bacon, clove-studded onions, garlic cloves, thyme, bay and tomatoes and bring to a boil. Add the salt, reduce the heat to low, cover and simmer until the beans are tender but firm, 1–1½ hours. Remove and discard the whole cloves. Add pepper and the ground cloves (if using). Taste and adjust the seasonings.

❀ To make the meat ragout, preheat an oven to 450°F (230°C). Pat the duck dry with paper towel and then prick the duck all over with fork tines. Sprinkle with salt and pepper and place the duck, breast side up, on a rack in a roasting pan. Roast until tender, about 1 hour. As the duck fat accumulates in the pan, remove it with a bulb baster and reserve. Remove from the oven and set aside to cool.

❀ In a large, heavy frying pan over high heat, melt a little lard or other fat. Add the pork and lamb and fry, turning often, until nicely browned on all sides, about 5 minutes.

❀ Transfer to a deep stew pot or flameproof earthenware casserole. To the fat remaining in the pan, add the onions and garlic and sauté until the onions are tender and translucent, 8–10 minutes. Add to the meat, along with the wine, tomatoes and the 2 cups (16 fl oz/500 ml) stock. Gather together the thyme sprigs, parsley sprigs and bay leaf into a bouquet garni and tie securely with kitchen string. Add to the pot, cover and simmer over low heat until the meats are tender, about 1 hour. Taste and adjust the seasoning.

❀ Preheat an oven to 350°F (180°C). Cut the cooled duck into 8 or 10 pieces. Cut the sausages into large chunks. Add the duck and sausage and the cooked beans to the meat ragout. Add some stock if the mixture seems too dry. Top with the bread crumbs. Drizzle with a few spoonfuls of the reserved duck fat (warmed to liquid state, if necessary) or melted butter. Bake until the top is crusty and golden brown, about 45 minutes. Serve hot.

SERVES 8–10 *Photograph pages 154–155*

Clockwise from bottom left: Chicken Fricassee with Almonds and Eggs, Partridge with Cabbage, Duck with Figs, Chicken and Lobster

CATALONIA

Pato con Higos

Duck with Figs

Duck and figs are a classic combination. Fresh figs may be used, but they must not be soaked and should be sautéed in a little butter and cinnamon and then added at the end of cooking. Some versions of this recipe call for tomatoes. They add tartness and help to thicken the sauce. Peeled, cored pears, cut into halves or quarters, can be used instead of the figs. Poach them in the same way as you do the figs, until tender and translucent.

1 lb (500 g) dried figs
2 cups (16 fl oz/500 ml) sweet sherry
2 lemon slices
1 cinnamon stick
2 whole cloves
few peppercorns (optional)
2 ducks, about 4 lb (2 kg) each
salt and freshly ground pepper
ground cinnamon
2 tablespoons olive oil or lard
2 onions, chopped
6–8 cloves garlic, minced
2 cups (12 oz/375 g) diced, peeled tomatoes (optional)
1 cup (8 fl oz/250 ml) chicken stock (see glossary)

In a saucepan combine the figs, 1 cup (8 fl oz/250 ml) of the sherry, lemon slices, cinnamon stick, cloves, peppercorns (if using) and water to cover. Bring to a simmer and simmer until the figs are tender, 10–15 minutes. Remove from the heat and set aside.

Preheat an oven to 400°–450°F (200°–230°C).

Prick the ducks all over with fork tines, then sprinkle with salt, pepper and cinnamon. In a large, wide pan over high heat, warm the oil or lard. Add the ducks and brown on all sides, about 10 minutes. Remove the ducks, breast sides up, to a rack in a roasting pan. Pour off and reserve the fat.

Roast the ducks until they test done when pierced with a knife, about 1 hour. Transfer to a warmed platter and let rest several minutes.

Meanwhile, in a sauté pan over medium heat, warm 3 tablespoons of the duck fat. Add the onions and sauté until tender and translucent, 8–10 minutes. Add the garlic and sauté for 3 minutes longer. Add the sherry, tomatoes (if using), and stock. Drain the figs, reserving the cooking liquid. Discard the whole spices and lemon slices. Add the strained liquid to the pan and reduce over high heat until thickened, about 10 minutes. Add the figs and heat through. Taste and adjust the seasonings.

Carve the ducks and arrange on the platter. Using a slotted spoon remove the figs from the sauce. Pour the sauce over the duck. Surround with the figs and serve at once.

SERVES 4

CATALONIA

Perdiz con Coles

Partridge with Cabbage

Elegant and rustic at the same time, this dish of roasted partridges (you could use poussins or game hens) and stuffed cabbage packets is complemented by simple roasted or mashed potatoes. Another version of the recipe dices the sausage, bones the partridges and uses the partridge meat and sausage for stuffing the cabbage leaves. In that case, the sauce is thickened with a classic picada. *Yet another version uses pork but no cabbage in the stuffing and braises the cabbage packets in the sauce before returning the birds to the sauce for the final 15 minutes of cooking.*

lard or olive oil
4 partridges, about 1 lb (500 g) each
salt and freshly ground pepper
1 lb (500 g) chorizos or other spicy pork sausages
4 slices bacon, chopped
1 onion, chopped
6 cloves garlic, minced
2 carrots, peeled and sliced
1 lb (500 g) ripe tomatoes, peeled, seeded and diced
1 teaspoon chopped fresh thyme
1 teaspoon chopped fresh marjoram
grated zest of 1 orange
½ cup (4 fl oz/125 ml) dry red wine
¼ cup (2 fl oz/60 ml) brandy
1 head Savoy or regular green cabbage
½ teaspoon freshly grated nutmeg, or to taste
½ lb (250 g) ground (minced) pork (optional)
3 slices white bread, soaked in milk to cover, drained and squeezed dry
pinch of ground cinnamon or cloves
all-purpose (plain) flour
1 egg

Preheat an oven to 375°F (190°C). In a large roasting pan over medium-high heat, warm enough lard or oil to form a film on the bottom of the pan. Add the birds, sprinkle with salt and pepper and fry, turning, until golden brown on all sides, 8–10 minutes. Add the sausage and bacon and cook for a few minutes until colored. Add the onion, garlic, carrots, tomatoes, thyme, marjoram and orange zest. Reduce the heat and sauté for 10 minutes. Baste the birds with the red wine and brandy, and then place in the oven and roast until tender, about 45 minutes. While the birds are cooking, fill a large saucepan three-fourths full of water and bring to a boil. Add salt to taste and cabbage and parboil for about 10 minutes. Drain in a colander. Separate the leaves. Keep 8 perfect, large outer leaves. Remove any tough ribs and chop the rest of the cabbage.

Lay the 8 leaves out on a work surface and trim away any tough stem ends. Sprinkle with salt and pepper and a little grated nutmeg. In a bowl combine the pork (if using), soaked bread, cinnamon or cloves and some of the chopped cabbage. Mix well. Place about one-eighth of the bread mixture near the base of each cabbage leaf. Roll up each leaf, tucking in sides, to form oblong *farcellets*, or "packages."

Place the flour in a shallow dish. Beat the egg in another dish. In a deep sauté pan, pour in oil to a depth of ¼ in (6 mm) and heat over medium-high heat. Dip the packets in the flour and then in the egg and drop in the hot oil. Fry, turning once, until golden and crusty, about 8 minutes. Using a slotted spatula, remove to paper towels to drain.

When the birds and sausages are cooked, remove the birds to a large baking dish with a lid. Slice the sausage. Place the cabbage packets in between the birds and distribute the sliced sausage between the birds and the packets. Taste and adjust the seasonings for the sauce in the roasting pan and then baste the birds with the sauce. Cover the dish and return it to the oven. Bake for about 15 minutes longer, basting at the midpoint. Serve directly from the dish.

SERVES 4

CATALONIA

Mar y Muntanya

Chicken and Lobster

Whether called mar y muntanya *(sea and mountain) or* mar e terra *(sea and earth), this classic Catalan dish is delicious. It combines chicken (or rabbit) with lobster (or large shrimp) in a fragrant wine-laced tomato sauce and a* picada *of almonds, hazelnuts, garlic, fried bread and bitter chocolate. Chopped sautéed chicken livers are a good addition to the* picada *as well.*

1 chicken, about 3 lb (1.5 kg), cut into 8 serving pieces
salt, freshly ground pepper and ground cinnamon
2 lobsters, 1 lb (500 g) each, cut up, or 24 large shrimp (prawns in the shell)
olive oil and lard
2 onions, chopped
2 fresh thyme sprigs
2 fresh marjoram sprigs
2 fresh parsley sprigs
1 bay leaf
1 orange zest strip
4 tomatoes, peeled, seeded and chopped
½ cup (4 fl oz/125 ml) dry white wine
¼ cup (2 fl oz/60 ml) brandy or anisette
3 large cloves garlic, crushed
1 slice coarse country-style bread, fried in olive oil until golden on both sides and broken up
3 tablespoons almonds
¼ cup (1¼ oz/40 g) hazelnuts (filberts)
1 oz (30 g) bitter chocolate, grated
bread slices fried in olive oil for serving

Pat the chicken pieces dry and sprinkle with salt, pepper and a little cinnamon. In a large sauté pan over medium-high heat, warm enough oil and lard to form a film on the bottom of the pan. Add the chicken and fry, turning, until golden on all sides, about 10 minutes. Remove the chicken to a platter and set aside.

In the same oil sauté the lobster pieces or shrimp for a few minutes until the shells turn bright red (or pink, if using shrimp). Remove to a separate platter and set aside.

Add the onion to the same pan, adding more oil to the pan if needed. Sauté over medium heat until tender and translucent, 8–10 minutes. Gather together the thyme, marjoram and parsley sprigs, bay leaf and orange zest strip into a bouquet garni and tie securely with kitchen string. Add to the pan with the tomatoes and simmer for 5 minutes. Return the chicken to the pan and add water to reach halfway up the sides of the pieces. Simmer, uncovered, for 10 minutes. Add the wine and brandy or anisette and continue to simmer until the chicken is almost done, about 10 minutes longer. Then return the lobster or shrimp to the pan and simmer until the chicken and shellfish are done.

Meanwhile, in a mortar or a blender, combine the garlic, fried bread, both kinds of nuts and grated bitter chocolate and pound or blend until a paste forms. When cooking is complete, add this *picada* and simmer for 5 minutes.

Remove and discard the herb bouquet. Taste and adjust the seasonings. Transfer the chicken and shellfish and the sauce to a warmed dish. Serve with fried bread.

SERVES 4

CATALONIA

Pollo en Pepitoria

Chicken Fricassee with Almonds and Eggs

In Spanish, a pepita *is a "seed." In the original recipe for this dish, pine nuts were used instead of almonds and mashed hard-cooked egg yolks acted as a thickener for the sauce rather than as a garnish. This dish is probably best made with a flavorful stewing hen.*

¼ cup (2 fl oz/60 ml) olive oil
½ cup (3 oz/90 g) blanched almonds
3 cloves garlic, chopped
1 slice bread, crust discarded
1 chicken, 3–4 lb (1.5–2 kg), cut into serving pieces
salt and freshly ground pepper
¼ teaspoon saffron threads, crushed
¾ cup (6 fl oz/180 ml) chicken stock (see glossary), heated
½ cup (4 fl oz/125 ml) dry sherry
1 bay leaf
1 teaspoon chopped fresh thyme
freshly grated nutmeg
2 hard-cooked egg yolks, mashed (optional)
3 tablespoons finely minced fresh flat-leaf (Italian) parsley

In a sauté pan over medium heat, warm the oil. Add the almonds and sauté until pale gold, 4–5 minutes. Using a slotted spoon remove the almonds to a blender, a processor fitted with the metal blade or a mortar.

Add the garlic cloves to the oil remaining in the pan and sauté until lightly golden, 1–2 minutes; add to the almonds. Then fry the bread, turning once, until golden on both sides, about 1–2 minutes on each side. Add to the almonds.

Sprinkle the chicken pieces with salt and pepper. Place in the same pan and fry in the oil that remains over medium-high heat, turning, until golden on all sides, about 10 minutes. Remove from the pan to a platter.

In a small bowl steep the saffron in 2 tablespoons of the hot chicken stock. Pour the remaining stock and the sherry into the sauté pan and deglaze over high heat, scraping the pan bottom to loosen any browned-on bits. Return the chicken to the pan and add the bay and thyme. Simmer, covered, for 10 minutes.

Add the saffron and stock to the almonds, along with the egg yolks. Pound with a pestle or process until a smooth paste forms. Add the almond mixture to the chicken and simmer for a few minutes longer. Taste and adjust the seasoning with salt, pepper and nutmeg to taste.

Transfer to a warmed serving dish. Sprinkle with the parsley and serve at once.

SERVES 4

LEBANON

KEFTA

Ground Meat with Onions and Parsley

This is a versatile Lebanese ground-meat mixture that can be formed into patties and fried on a griddle (or in a heavy frying pan) or grilled as you would hamburgers. The meat mixture can be kneaded and wrapped around skewers and broiled or grilled as well. Or it can be formed into ovals, each oval stuffed with about 1½ tablespoons pine nuts or a hard-cooked egg, and then the ovals browned in butter or olive oil, placed in a baking dish, topped with tomato sauce and baked in a 350°F (180°C) oven for 30 minutes. Serve the simple kefta *tucked into warm pita bread (recipe on page 82) with tahini sauce (see* falafel *recipe on page 50) and diced tomatoes and cucumbers.*

2 lb (1 kg) finely ground (minced) beef or lamb
1 cup (5 oz/155 g) grated onion
½ cup (¾ oz/20 g) finely minced fresh flat-leaf (Italian) parsley or finely minced fresh mint
1 teaspoon salt
½ teaspoon freshly ground pepper
2 teaspoons ground cumin (optional)
1 teaspoon ground cinnamon (optional)
1 teaspoon ground allspice (optional)

olive oil, if using griddle

In a bowl combine all the ingredients. Knead well with your hands. Cover and chill for 1 hour (the chilling helps the mixture hold together better).

Preheat a griddle or prepare a fire in a charcoal grill. Form the mixture into 6–8 patties or ovals. Lightly oil the griddle, if using. Place the patties on the griddle or grill rack and cook, turning once, until done to taste. Serve at once.

SERVES 6–8

TUNISIA

MERGUEZ

Spiced Lamb Sausage

These spicy sausages are popular all over North Africa. If you have a sausage-stuffing attachment for your grinder or mixer, filling the casings will be easy. If not, you can form the mixture into patties and fry them. Serve them with pita bread (recipe on page 82) and grilled onions, if you like.

2 lb (1 kg) lean lamb or beef
6 oz (185 g) beef or lamb fat
⅓ cup (3 fl oz/80 ml) olive oil
4–6 cloves garlic, finely minced
1 teaspoon ground cinnamon
½ teaspoon cayenne pepper
2 teaspoons *harissa* (see glossary)
2 teaspoons ground coriander
1 tablespoon salt
1 teaspoon freshly ground black pepper
½ lb (250 g) sausage casings, preferably sheep casings

In a bowl combine all of the ingredients except the casings. Mix well with your hands, then cover and chill thoroughly.

Rinse the casings by running cold water through them for a few minutes. Using the sausage stuffing attachment on a grinder, a pastry bag fitted with the large plain tip or a funnel with a 1-in (2.5-cm) opening, fill the casings with the meat mixture and knot at 6-in (15-cm) intervals. Hang for 4 hours in an airy place, then refrigerate for up to 3 days. Or stuff the casings, cut into 8-in (20-cm) lengths and twist the ends. Roll into coils and refrigerate.

To cook the sausages, prepare a fire in a charcoal grill. If the sausages have been coiled, thread each coil onto a bamboo skewer that has first been soaked in water to cover.

Place the sausages on the grill rack and grill, turning to cook on all sides, until crisp and brown, about 8 minutes.

Transfer to a warmed platter and serve.

SERVES 8

LEBANON/SYRIA

KIBBEE

Ground Meat with Onion and Bulgur

Kibbee *is the national dish of both Lebanon and Syria. It is eaten raw, cooked, baked in layers, or stuffed. In the days before grinders and food processors, the meat was pounded by hand in a mortar, but today's appliances have made* kibbee *easy to prepare. The ratio of meat to grain varies from family to family. Meat for* kibbee *must be lean and it must be ground twice. The bulgur must be of a fine grind.* Kibbee nayee *is the raw mixture; it can be served as is with pita bread (recipe on page 82) and chopped parsley, chopped green (spring) onions or romaine (cos) lettuce, or it can be used to make* kibbee saneeyeh, *baked* kibbee *with pine nut stuffing (recipe follows). The raw* kibbee *can also be formed into patties and broiled (grilled) and then served with pita and yogurt.*

FOR *KIBBEE NAYEE:*

1 cup (6 oz/185 g) fine bulgur (cracked wheat)
1 lb (500 g) lean lamb or beef
1 onion, puréed in a food processor or blender (about ¾ cup/4 oz/125 g)
¼ cup (2 fl oz/60 ml) cold or ice water
1½ teaspoons salt
½ teaspoon freshly ground pepper
½ teaspoon ground allspice (optional)
½ teaspoon ground cinnamon (optional)
1 tablespoon ground cumin (optional)
melted unsalted butter or olive oil

Place the bulgur in a bowl with water to cover and let soak for 10 minutes. Drain in a sieve, squeezing to remove as much water as possible. Spread out on a baking sheet or flat platter and chill in the refrigerator for a few hours to dry it out more.

Trim all the fat and sinews from the meat. Cut the meat into small cubes. Chill for 1 hour, as it must be very cold. Put through the fine disk of a meat grinder twice. Alternatively, pulse the cubes in a food processor fitted with the metal blade until a pastelike consistency is achieved. Transfer to a bowl.

Divide into thirds the meat, onion, bulgur, salt, pepper and the allspice, cinnamon and cumin, if using. Process each batch in a food processor fitted with the metal blade until ingredients are thoroughly combined, adding ice water as needed to ease processing. Cover and chill.

To serve the *kibbee nayee,* mound the chilled *kibbee* on a platter. Spread with a fork and draw patterns on the top. Drizzle melted butter or oil over the meat and serve.

FOR *KIBBEE SANEEYEH:*

4 tablespoons (2 oz/60 g) plus ⅓ cup (3 oz/90 g) unsalted butter
½ lb (250 g) ground (minced) lamb
½ teaspoon ground cinnamon
½ teaspoon salt
¼ teaspoon freshly ground pepper
¼ cup (1¼ oz/40 g) pine nuts

Top to bottom: Ground Meat with Onion and Bulgur, Ground Meat with Onions and Parsley, Spiced Lamb Sausage

kibbee nayee (preceding recipe)
plain yogurt (optional)

❀ Preheat an oven to 350°F (180°C).
❀ In a sauté pan over medium heat, melt 2 tablespoons of the butter. Add the lamb, breaking it up with a fork. Sprinkle with the cinnamon, salt and pepper and cook, stirring, until cooked through, about 5 minutes. Meanwhile, in a separate pan, sauté the pine nuts in the remaining 2 tablespoons of butter until golden, 3–5 minutes. Add the nuts to the lamb and mix well. Let cool for a few minutes.
❀ Butter a 9-in (23-cm) baking pan. Press half of the *kibbee nayee* in the bottom. Spread half of the cooled lamb mixture over the raw *kibbee*. Top with the remaining raw *kibbee nayee*. Smooth the top well. Using a sharp knife score a diamond pattern into the top. Melt the remaining ⅓ cup (3 oz/90 g) butter and drizzle over the surface. Bake until the lamb is cooked, about 25 minutes.
❀ Meanwhile, preheat a broiler (griller). When the *kibbee* is ready, slip it under the broiler to brown the top lightly, just a few minutes.
❀ Cut into squares and serve hot with yogurt (if using).

FOR *KIBBEE* BALLS:

kibbee nayee (preceding recipe)
kibbee saneeyeh (preceding recipe)
vegetable oil for frying
plain yogurt or tahini sauce (see *falafel* recipe on page 50)

❀ Prepare the *kibbee nayee* and chill. Prepare the *kibbee saneeyeh* up to the point at which the pine nuts are mixed with the lamb; let cool.
❀ Dip your hands into cold water. Divide the *kibbee nayee* into 12–14 balls. Roll each ball into a torpedo shape about 2 in (5 cm) long. Push your wet finger into the center to make a deep, narrow pocket. Slip about 1 tablespoon of the *kibbee saneeyeh* into the pocket, then pinch the raw *kibbee* closed around the filling. Roll in wet hands to reform a football or torpedo shape. Refrigerate on a baking sheet lined with parchment paper until ready to fry.
❀ In a deep sauté pan, pour in oil to a depth of 2–3 in (5–7.5 cm) and heat to 375°F (190°C). When the oil is ready, add the balls, a few at a time, and fry, turning once, until evenly browned, about 5 minutes. Using a slotted spoon remove to paper towels to drain, and repeat with the remaining balls. Alternatively, preheat an oven to 350°F (180°C). Place the balls on an oiled baking sheet and bake until cooked through, about 25 minutes.
❀ Serve the balls hot or at room temperature. Offer yogurt or tahini sauce on the side.

EACH RECIPE SERVES 6

The Middle East

THE MIDDLE EAST

Syria, Lebanon, Israel, Egypt

The artificiality of many of the frontiers in the contemporary Middle East is betrayed, among other things, by cuisine. The lands now divided among Syria, Lebanon and Israel (including the occupied territories) were known traditionally as *Bilad al-Sham,* "the Lands of (Greater) Syria," and they formed a single cultural unit with a shared culinary tradition that varied only slightly by region. This tradition overlapped, moreover, with the cuisine of Iraq, Egypt and the Arabian Peninsula, and it is therefore more or less coterminous with the cuisine of the entire Arab East. In its heyday, lasting roughly from the eighth to the fourteenth centuries, this was one of the most brilliant and influential cuisines of the Mediterranean world.

The diet of the Arabs before their emergence from the peninsula in the seventh century was a frugal and straightforward affair, consisting for the most part of dates, bread and mutton, supplemented on festive occasions by the meat and the milk of the camel; even today, this remains the essential menu of the Bedouin throughout the Arab world. Pre-Islamic Arabia was by no means exclusively nomadic, and the cities of western Arabia where Islam came into being were important centers of international commerce. Their citizens were, however, interested in the spices from Asia that passed through their hands en route to the eastern Mediterranean only as commodities

Previous pages: The pyramids of Giza, built circa 2550–2400 B.C., are the only survivors among the Seven Wonders of the World.
Left: Colorful Egyptian tents, often hand appliquéd, are used for festivals, funerals and entertaining dignitaries.

in which to trade, not as a source of enrichment for their own food. This sparseness of diet was reinforced by the ascetic spirit of early Islam. Although the Prophet Muhammad is recorded to have had his favorite dishes, such as a mixture of dates, butter and milk, he would eat only one type of food at each meal and recommended his followers leave their stomachs one-third empty. The gastronomic future of Islam was, however, guaranteed in a sense by the verses in the Koran *(Qur'an)* that draw attention to the fruits of the earth as God's gift; encourage the pursuit of agriculture; and command the believers to eat *al-tayyibat,* "pure and wholesome food."

The lands to the north of the peninsula that the Muslims conquered with amazing speed soon after the death of the Prophet are often referred to as the Fertile Crescent, an arc of territory extending from Syria to Iraq in which climatic conditions are infinitely more favorable to agriculture than the parched wastes of Arabia. The origins of many things are attributed to this area, and agriculture is one of them. Such a categorical assertion is difficult if not impossible to prove, but it is safe to assume that the ancient civilizations of the Middle East—Assyrians, Babylonians, Phoenicians and the rest—developed their own culinary traditions, even if we know little of them today.

The date palm flourished in some regions of the Mediterranean as far back as 50,000 B.C.

Before the Muslim conquest, Syria had been under Byzantine control, and Iraq under Persian, although the frontiers of each empire fluctuated with great frequency. The first center of the caliphate outside the peninsula was Damascus, and it is to be presumed that the Umayyad caliphs who made their home there came under the influence not only of Byzantine administrative systems but also of Byzantine cuisine. The Persian influence was, however, infinitely greater in the formation of classical Arab cuisine. This was in part a function of chronology. The transfer of the caliphate to Baghdad, near the old centers of Persian imperial splendor, came at a time when the early territorial expansion had been completed and the stage was set for the elaboration of a civilization impressive in both its intellectual and material aspects. Foodstuffs from the entire Middle East and lands as far distant as France, Russia and China flowed into the markets of Baghdad, almost demanding the elaboration of a sophisticated cuisine. Perhaps most important, the Abbasid caliphs of Baghdad abandoned the frugal ways of early Islam, to which the Umayyads had still in some measure subscribed, and, ably assisted by a horde of Persian cooks, began to indulge freely in the pleasures of the table.

The importance of the Persian contribution can be gauged by glancing at the contents of a thirteenth-century manual of gastronomy written in Baghdad. Many of the dishes listed here, particularly the more intricate ones such as *bazmaward* (roast meat prepared with a multitude of spices, nuts and rose water), bear Persian names, easily distinguishable by their phonetic form. The delight commonly taken in combining nuts, fruits and vegetables with meats, often yielding a melange of sweet-and-sour tastes, is also verifiably Persian in origin.

It can in general be said that classical Arab cuisine built on Persian traditions of ingenuity and complexity to evolve a new style. One hallmark of this was the intensive but subtle use of spices, some of them now cultivated for the first time in the Middle East and others imported along a farflung network of trading routes in greater quantity than ever before. Herbs, seeds and even flowers, gathered and analyzed with scientific precision, were also put to good use. Rice had been known in the Middle East before the rise of Islam, but it was more extensively planted than before by the Arabs (who also, as we have seen, introduced it to Europe by way of Spain and Sicily); this enhanced availability of rice made it possible to begin its full incorporation into cuisine, a process completed by the Turks. Techniques for the preparation of food became more sophisticated and elaborate. The Arabs were masters of preservation by means of salt and vinegar, or lemon juice and honey; the crystallization of fruit; and numerous methods of frying, baking and grilling.

This classical cuisine of the Arab East was, in its full richness, naturally beyond the means of many people, whose sustenance was primarily dependent upon lentils and beans. But even those humble preparations were enlivened with a few vegetables and a handful of spices and herbs. The splendors of the Abbasid caliphate were, in any

The Western Wall (or Wailing Wall), remnants of the Temple Mount in Jerusalem, is considered a holy place by Jews.

event, utterly destroyed by the Mongols in the thirteenth century. The invaders also took care to destroy the intricate irrigation systems of Iraq, a blow from which the area's agriculture—and hence cuisine—never fully recovered.

As has been pointed out, the Ottoman Turks were heirs to the entire civilization of classical Islam, and this included its culinary traditions. In a sense, then, Arab cuisine continued in a new setting and guise. But the imprint and style of Ottoman cuisine were new and distinct, reflecting the great stretch of the empire and the products to which it had access. It enjoyed also the prestige of great political and military success, and soon became the favored cuisine of the affluent throughout the Arab East. The assimilation of Ottoman cuisine was particularly marked in Syria, closest of the Arab provinces in both geography and culture to the Turkish heartland of the empire. This is not to say that Turkish cuisine extinguished all traces of regional style. *Kibbee* in its numerous varieties, still popular in Syria and Lebanon, is an exoticum in Turkey, and the various religious minorities packed into Lebanon have always retained their culinary specialties, in true Mediterranean style. By and large, however, the food of Syria and Lebanon has been down to recent times a variation on that of Turkey. The principal gastronomic centers of the area have been Damascus, which surrounded by the vast leafy oasis of the Ghutah has always been well supplied with fresh produce; Aleppo, renowned for its pastries; and Beirut, which with its cosmopolitan population and devotion to pleasures of various kinds boasted the best restaurants in the Middle East before the storms of war ravaged it to near destruction. It must be admitted that the general disarray of the Arab Middle East today is mirrored in its gastronomic impoverishment. Other than a few staples like *hummus, falafel* and a handful of dishes from the Turkish kitchen, little remains of a once brilliant culinary heritage.

The various traditions of Sephardic Jews from North Africa and Turkey, Ashkenazi Jews from Eastern Europe, and other immigrants from places as diverse as Yemen

Fellucas *are a common sight along the Nile, the world's longest river and the main artery linking southern Egypt to the Mediterranean.*

The golden dome of the Mosque of Omar, built in the seventh century, is a prominent feature on the Jerusalem skyline.

and the United States, have not yet amalgamated into a distinctively Israeli cuisine, something with its own genius and amounting to more than the sum of the parts. This mirrors not only the recent origins of the state but also the continued ethnic segmentation of Israeli society. Indeed, while some cookbook writers have called *falafel,* a kind of vegetarian hamburger made from chick-peas (garbanzos), "the Israeli national dish," it is perhaps more accurately described as a perennial favorite of the eastern Arab world, particularly beloved of the Palestinians.

A description of Egypt and its cuisine as Mediterranean might appear to the uninitiated inoffensively true. Egypt has, after all, a lengthy Mediterranean coastline that includes Alexandria, the country's second largest city. In the 1940s, however, controversy raged in Egypt as to whether it was primarily a Mediterranean country, enjoying its most important affinities with, for example, France and Italy, or an Arab and Muslim country, intermediate between North Africa and the Arab East (not to mention its African identity). Like most such disputes, this one was misconceived, because Egypt has been and is all these things, although in unequal measure: both Mediterranean and Arab, both northward looking and eastward looking. These varying orientations have inevitably reflected themselves in the food, creating not so much local variations on a national cuisine as entirely separate styles and traditions. Economics have also played a great role, the affluent showing great receptivity to foreign cuisines and the poor depending upon the immemorial staples of the indigenous diet. The varied and truly Mediterranean cuisine of pre-1952 Alexandria, where Greeks, Italians, Armenians and Jews lived in great numbers, was entirely unknown to the peasant masses toiling in the narrow strip of arable land that lines the Nile Valley. Polyglot Alexandria is now but a memory, but a similar social and culinary fission currently exists between the fashionably attired students at the American University in Cairo who patronize Pizza Hut in the intervals between classes and the great majority of Cairenes who can barely afford bread.

We are fairly well informed about the cuisine of ancient Egypt. Like their Greek counterparts, the Egyptian gods seem to have taken an interest in food; Isis is said to have first taught people the use and cultivation of the olive. Poultry farming was widespread, a particular fondness being shown for geese and ducks; the latter were often force-fed to make them fatter and more delicious, a kind of ancient rehearsal for making *pâté de foie d'oie gras.* Fish were also popular, although shellfish were shunned, possibly as a result of influence by the Israelites during their Egyptian exile. The ancient Egyptians may well have been the first people to bake leavened bread, and it is certain that bread was established very early as a staple of the diet. Bread came in many forms, dates sometimes being mixed in with the dough, and the loaves might be artfully shaped like animals, a homely display of the ancient Egyptian genius for plastic representation of the animal realm. A fairly narrow range of vegetables—okra, leeks and onions—was cultivated, but they were so well appreciated that every prosperous home had a vegetable garden attached to it. Mushrooms were reserved for the pharaohs because of the magical properties they were believed to possess. Spices imported from India and points farther east were a luxury item, reserved for the privileged, as indeed they were throughout the ancient and classical Mediterranean world.

The coming of Islam in the seventh century marked a definite break with the Pharaonic past (as well as with its Coptic continuation, over which we pass in culinarily justifiable silence). It is highly remarkable, therefore, that several of the dishes most common in Egypt even today go back to ancient origins. Pride of place among these dishes goes to *ful mudammas,* the ubiquitous concoction of slowly cooked fava beans that for centuries has been the indispensable staple of the masses. The word *mudammas,* used exclusively to describe this dish, appears to mean "buried in ashes," since the pot of beans was traditionally left in the hot ashes of an oven or bathhouse to cook overnight, although now other methods are used. Beans have been a part not only of Egyptian cuisine, but also of the Egyptian psyche itself for millennia: The ancient Egyptians called the realm in which the dead await resurrection a "bean field." (Does a common devotion to beans tend to corroborate the theories of those who take one look at the pyramids of Giza and Teotihuacan and proclaim Mexico and Egypt to have been in ancient communication?)

Of comparable antiquity are *melokhia,* a kind of peasant soup made with the glutinous leaves of the plant of the same name and sometimes adding rabbit, not a meat generally favored by Muslims; and *batarekh,* the salted and dried roe of the gray mullet, a delicacy for special occasions.

Apart from these Pharaonic relics, Egypt does not seem to have made any noteworthy contribution to classical Arab cuisine. This is curious, given the high demand in which Egyptian cooks once stood throughout the eastern Arab world. Until the coming of the Ottomans in the sixteenth century, rulers and the well-to-do appear to have eaten much the same fare as their counterparts in Syria and Iraq; then it was the sophisticated cuisine of the Ottomans that took their fancy.

E. W. Lane, the great Arabic lexicographer who was also a careful observer of Egyptian life in the early nineteenth century, describes a typical Cairene meal as consisting of a *yakhni,* a meat stew containing okra or other vegetables; stuffed vine, lettuce or cabbage leaves; stuffed squash and other vegetables; kebab; and *pilav.* All this is clearly Turkish, and it argues, too, for a higher degree of prosperity than that now available. But in Lane's day there were those who could not afford such ample fare and would make a meal of bread and *dukkah,* a mixture of salt, pepper, mint or cumin seeds, and other seasonings.

Like Syria and Lebanon, Egypt is subject to multiple stresses and transformations; social, economic, cultural and political. The future of its cuisine, together with that of the Middle East as a whole, is correspondingly unpredictable.

The camel, introduced to Egypt by the Persians in the 6th century B.C., was a crucial link between the trans-Saharan trade route and the Mediterranean.

VEGETABLES, PASTA AND GRAINS

Pasta is found in varying forms in most Mediterranean cuisines.

VEGETABLES, PASTA AND GRAINS

The traditional cuisines of the Mediterranean are plant-based. They revolve around vegetables, legumes, pastas and grains, with fish and shellfish, poultry and meat served in small portions and not every day. This healthful diet is being corrupted. As people leave the village for the city, they want to dine on larger portions of meat as often as possible, as a sign of personal success. The Greeks euphemistically call this the "northern diet." As well-known fast-food emporia take over the spaces that used to be cafes, tavernas and trattorias, and as the leisurely two-hour lunch shrinks to twenty minutes of hovering at a counter, we not only regret the loss of a less stressful life-style, but also the deterioration of a healthful diet and the gradual disappearance of traditional foods. Sadly, a treasury of great recipes is threatened with being replaced by french fries, a burger and a shake.

While we can't stop "progress," we can keep in mind that healthful Mediterranean foods can be the basis of a satisfying and varied diet. At a 1992 conference at Harvard University, scientists, doctors and nutritionists discussed the relative health advantages of the traditional diet of the Mediterranean, a region recognized for its low incidence of heart disease and cancer. Their conclusion was that the ideal diet for good health should be based on recipes like those in this chapter, accompanied with fruits, small amounts of dairy products such as yogurt and cheese, some olive oil, and only occasional bites of fish and animal protein.

In the Mediterranean, vegetables are not looked upon only as an accompaniment to meat or fish. Indeed, they are often the centerpiece of the meal. An assortment of vegetable *dolmas,* a casserole of baked vegetables with tomatoes and cheese, a ragout of vegetables braised in olive oil and herbs, a pilaf studded with eggplant, or a pasta with vegetables makes a delectable meal.

The variety of Mediterranean vegetables is bountiful. At the apex is the eggplant (aubergine). It is frequently combined with the other three most popular Mediterranean vegetables, peppers, zucchini and tomatoes. (Although peppers and tomatoes were gifts from the New World, they have been firmly established in the Mediterranean repertoire for two centuries.) There are also many recipes for artichokes, pumpkins and other squashes, beets, broccoli, cauliflower, carrots, turnips, potatoes, onions, leeks, garlic, cucumbers, mushrooms, fennel, okra, green beans, fava (broad) beans, asparagus, peas and greens such as spinach, Swiss chard (silverbeet), cabbage, dandelion, radicchio, chicory (curly endive) and kale. Each time a vegetable comes into season it is eaten daily until it is no longer at its best, and it is likely to be served as a course by itself. A harvest of the first new peas or wild asparagus is cause for celebration. A platter of grilled wild mushrooms basted with garlic and olive oil, a rice-filled tomato, or *imam bayildi* (garlic-and-tomato-stuffed eggplant) is a glorious meal.

Previous pages: left to right; Fish flavored Rice (recipe page 215), Rice from Valencia (recipe page 208)

Vegetables are not viewed as merely accompaniments to meat, but are often the centerpiece of the Mediterranean meal.

Pasta is not only an Italian phenomenon, although it is clearly a driving passion and has attained its highest art form there. Flat noodles called *laganum* were part of the early Roman diet and pasta tools have been found in Etruscan tombs. Vermicelli were referred to in a twelfth-century Arab text, where they were known as *itriya,* which became shortened to *tria* in Sicilian dialect. Noodles served in ancient Persia were termed *lakhsha,* which evolved into the Arabic *rishta;* today they are still called *lakshen* in Yiddish. Ravioli appear in Sardinia as *culingiones,* and in Turkey under the name *mantı,* after the Chinese *mantou.* Dried pastas are a staple of the southern Italian diet and the number of sauce and noodle combinations are countless. Volumes on the subject of pasta will continue to be written because the body of recipes is so vast and the noodle, fresh or dried, is so highly versatile.

The ubiquitous tomato, originally a gift from the New World, has been firmly established in Mediterranean cooking for over two centuries.

Couscous, coarse semolina pellets that are a kind of mini pasta, is the premiere North African grain dish. Pre-Islamic and pre-Arabic, it is to Morocco, Tunisia and Algeria what pastas are to Italy. It has even become part of the Italian diet, having migrated to Sicily. A similar pellet, called *fregula,* appears in Sardinian cooking.

Rice of both long-grain and short-grain varieties is a staple of many Mediterranean cuisines, forming the basis for pilafs, paellas and risottos. Short-grain rice, which tends to be stickier and gives off a sort of starch that thickens sauces, is used for Spanish rice dishes and is a specialty of Valencia. The Italian Arborio rice used in risotto and in the Sicilian deep-fried rice balls called *arancini,* is its close relative. Long-grain rice is the staple grain in Greece, Turkey and most of the Middle East, and the most fragrant variety is basmati. In these cultures rice is used for a main course, a pilaf and as a filling for grapeleaves, cabbage leaves, tomatoes, peppers, eggplants (aubergines), artichokes and zucchini as well as for baked chicken and fish.

Bulgur, or cracked wheat, is the other staple grain in the Arab diet. It imparts a nutty flavor and is served hot as a pilaf or cold, as in the familiar *tabbouleh* salad. Combined with meat, fish and vegetables as in baked *kibbee,* bulgur is the signature grain of Syria and Lebanon, although rice and noodles are also found in their diets.

Clockwise from top left: "Angry" Pasta, Raviolis Filled with Cheese and Greens, "Little Ear" Pasta with Broccoli Rabe

CALABRIA

PENNE ALL'ARRABBIATA

"Angry" Pasta

Arrabbiare *means "to get angry," a simple but effective title for pasta with a fiery tomato sauce. The sauce can be prepared a little ahead of time and rewarmed before tossing it with the noodles. You can also mate this sauce with spaghetti or rigatoni.*

4 tablespoons olive oil or 2 tablespoons each olive oil and lard
2 or 3 cloves garlic, minced
2 onions, sliced
2 small dried chili peppers, cut into pieces
6 large tomatoes, peeled, seeded and chopped
salt and freshly ground black pepper
1 lb (500 g) *penne* or other dried pasta
grated pecorino cheese

In a large sauté pan over medium heat, warm the oil or the oil and lard. Add the garlic, onions and peppers and sauté until the onions are translucent and tender, 8–10 minutes. Add the tomatoes and cook, stirring occasionally, until thickened, about 8 minutes. Season to taste with salt and black pepper and keep warm until the pasta is ready.

Bring a large pot three-fourths full of water to a boil. Add the pasta and cook until al dente, about 10 minutes (it will take about 10 minutes to cook; check the package directions). Drain.

Place the pasta on a warmed platter. Spoon the sauce over the top and toss well. Sprinkle with cheese and serve immediately.

SERVES 6

SARDINIA

CULINGIONES

Raviolis Filled with Cheese and Greens

Here, cheese raviolis from Sardinia are flavored with a pinch of saffron and lightened by the addition of greens. Pecorino is available in two forms: as a fresh, soft, mildly tangy cheese and as a dry aged cheese for grating.

1½ lb (750 g) Swiss chard (silverbeet), green part only
salt
2½ cups (1¼ lb/625 g) ricotta or fresh pecorino cheese
2 eggs
pinch of saffron threads, crushed and steeped in
  2 tablespoons hot water
3–4 tablespoons all-purpose (plain) flour (optional)
salt and freshly ground pepper
dough for *manti* (recipe on page 198)
tomato sauce or meat-flavored tomato sauce
  (see glossary), heated
grated aged pecorino cheese

Bring a large pot three-fourths full of water to a boil. Add the Swiss chard and salt to taste and cook until tender, about 5 minutes. Drain well, squeeze dry and chop finely. Place in a bowl and let cool completely.

Add to the chard the ricotta or fresh pecorino, eggs, saffron and steeping liquid, and enough flour to bind the filling (if using). Season to taste with salt and pepper. Place the filling in a sieve set over a bowl and let drain in the refrigerator for a few hours or as long as overnight.

Prepare the dough as directed and let it rest for 1 hour.

Roll out the dough into long strips about 4 in (10 cm) wide and fill and cut into 2-in (5-cm) squares as directed for the *manti.* Bring 1 large pot or 2 small ones three-fourths full of water to a boil, add salt to taste and the raviolis and cook until tender, 8–10 minutes. Drain well.

Layer the raviolis in a warmed wide serving dish with the hot sauce and grated cheese. Serve immediately.

SERVES 6

APULIA

ORECCHIETTE CON BROCCOLI DI RAPA

"Little Ear" Pasta with Broccoli Rabe

These small pasta rounds resemble little ears, thus their name. The depression in the middle traps the sauce. Cooked white beans or chick-peas (garbanzo beans) may be added to the sauce. Broccoli rabe is a slightly bitter green popularly served in southern Italy. It has 6–8-inch (15–20-cm) stalks topped by small florets.

1½ lb (750 g) broccoli rabe or other bitter greens or a
  combination of broccoli, cauliflower and bitter greens
  (about 5 cups)
salt
1 lb (500 g) *orecchiette*
olive oil
1 tablespoon finely minced anchovy fillet, or to taste
3 cloves garlic, minced
freshly ground black pepper or red pepper flakes
grated pecorino cheese

Wash the greens well and trim away any tough stalks. Cut into 2-in (5-cm) lengths for the greens and into florets for the broccoli or cauliflower. Bring a large pot three-fourths full of water to a boil. Add the prepared vegetable and salt to taste and boil until tender, 5–10 minutes; timing will depend upon what vegetable you are using. Using a slotted spoon remove to a bowl and set aside.

Return the water to a boil and drop in the *orecchiette.*

While the pasta cooks, warm the oil in a wide sauté pan over medium heat. Add the anchovy and garlic and warm through. Add the cooked vegetable and heat through. Season to taste with black pepper or pepper flakes.

When the pasta is al dente (it will take about 10 minutes to cook; check the package directions), drain and place on a warmed platter. Pour the vegetables and oil over the top and toss. Sprinkle with cheese and serve immediately.

SERVES 6

CALABRIA

MELANZANE ALLA PARMIGIANA

Eggplant Parmesan

Despite the name this dish has nothing to do with either the city of Parma or Parmesan cheese. The eggplant is fried and layered with tomato sauce and sometimes with slices of mozzarella or caciocavallo *cheese and sometimes with onions or hard-cooked eggs. It is then topped with bread crumbs and grated pecorino cheese. This version is from Calabria. Greeks make a similar dish with feta cheese and tomato sauce.*

3 eggplants (aubergines), about 2½ lb (1.25 kg) total weight
salt
olive oil
1 onion, thinly sliced
2 cloves garlic, minced (optional)
2 cups (12 oz/375 g) peeled, seeded and diced tomatoes
freshly ground pepper
1 lb (500 g) mozzarella, sliced ⅛ in (3 mm) thick
2 or 3 hard-cooked eggs, sliced
½ cup (2 oz/60 g) freshly grated pecorino cheese
½ cup (2 oz/60 g) fine dried bread crumbs

Peel the eggplants and slice crosswise about ½ in (12 mm) thick. Sprinkle the slices with salt and drain in a colander for 30 minutes. Rinse and pat dry with paper towels.

Preheat an oven to 400°F (200°C).

In a large sauté pan over medium heat, pour in oil to a depth of ¼ in (6 mm). Working in batches, add the eggplant and sauté, turning once, until lightly browned, about 5 minutes. Using a slotted utensil transfer to paper towels to drain. Add oil to the pan only as needed, or the eggplant will absorb too much of it.

To the oil remaining in the pan, add the onion and garlic (if using) and sauté over medium heat for about 5 minutes. Then add the tomatoes and cook, stirring, until a saucelike consistency forms, about 10 minutes. Season to taste with salt and pepper.

Spoon about one-third of the tomato sauce into a large baking dish. Top with half of the eggplant, the mozzarella cheese (if using), then half of the remaining sauce, half of the sliced eggs, and all of the remaining eggplant. Top with the remaining eggs and then the remaining sauce. In a small bowl stir together the pecorino cheese and crumble and then sprinkle them over the top.

Bake until golden, about 20 minutes. Remove from the oven and let rest 15 minutes before serving. Cut into squares to serve.

SERVES 6 *Photograph page 203*

GREECE

PILAFI ME MELITZANES

Eggplant Pilaf

A fine accompaniment for chicken or meat dishes.

2 globe eggplants (aubergines), about 1½ lb (750 g) total weight
6 tablespoons (3 oz/90 g) unsalted butter or (3 fl oz/90 ml) olive oil
1 onion, chopped
3 large tomatoes, peeled, seeded and diced
2 oz (60 g) vermicelli, broken into 1-in (2.5-cm) lengths (about ½ cup)
1½ teaspoons salt
½ teaspoon freshly ground pepper
½ teaspoon ground cinnamon (optional)
1¼ cups (9 oz/280 g) long-grain white rice, washed and drained
3 cups (24 fl oz/750 ml) chicken or vegetable stock (see glossary), heated
⅓ cup (2 oz/60 g) currants, plumped in hot water and drained (optional)
chopped fresh mint or flat-leaf (Italian) parsley (optional)

Peel the eggplants and cut into ¾-in (2-cm) cubes. Place in a colander, sprinkle with salt and set aside for about 20 minutes to drain off the bitter juices. Dry the eggplant with paper towels.

In a large sauté pan over high heat, melt 4 tablespoons of the butter or warm 4 tablespoons of the oil. Add the eggplant and sauté, stirring often, until golden, about 10 minutes. Remove from the heat and set aside, keep warm.

In a large saucepan over medium heat, melt the remaining 2 tablespoons butter or warm the remaining 2 tablespoons oil. Add the onion and sauté until softened, 5–7 minutes. Add the tomatoes, vermicelli, salt, pepper, and cinnamon (if using). Cook, stirring often, for about 4 minutes. Add the rice and sauté, stirring often until the rice is translucent and coated with fat, about 3 minutes. Add the heated stock, bring to a boil, reduce the heat to low, cover and cook until the liquid has been absorbed and the rice is tender, about 20 minutes.

Fold into the rice the cooked eggplant and the mint or parsley and the plumped currants, if using. Turn off the heat and let the rice rest, covered, for 10 minutes. Taste and adjust the seasoning. Fluff once with a fork and transfer to a warmed platter. Serve at once.

SERVES 6

TURKEY/LEBANON

BULGUR PILAV

Bulgur Pilaf

A staple in Turkey and the Middle East, bulgur (cracked wheat) comes in a variety of grinds, from very fine for tabbouleh (recipe on page 44) and kibbee *(recipe on page 182) to coarse. Medium grind is what is found in most stores. A coarse grind will do for pilaf, however, if that is all you can find. Most bulgur recipes call for too much liquid and the resulting pilaf is often soggy. To maintain a crunchy texture, with each grain separate, a ratio of 1½ cups (12 fl oz/375 ml) liquid to 1 cup (6 oz/185 g) grain is best. If the pilaf still seems too wet, place it on a baking sheet and dry it out in a 350°F (180°C) oven for 10–15 minutes. If it seems too dry, add a bit more liquid.*

2¼–2½ cups (18–20 fl oz/560–625 ml) water or chicken stock (see glossary)
2 teaspoons salt
¼ cup (2 oz/60 g) unsalted butter
1 onion, chopped
1½ cups (9 oz/280 g) bulgur (cracked wheat)

In a saucepan combine the water or stock and salt and bring to a boil. Reduce the heat to low and keep warm. In a large sauté pan over medium heat, melt the butter. Add the onion and sauté until tender and translucent, about 10 minutes. Add the bulgur and continue to cook, stirring, for a few minutes.

Add the hot water or stock. Stir once, and reduce the heat to low, cover and cook for about 15 minutes. Turn off heat and let stand until the bulgur absorbs all the liquid, about 15 minutes longer.

Transfer to a warmed dish and serve immediately.

SERVES 6

TURKEY

MANTI

Lamb Dumplings with Yogurt Sauce

Manti *are similar to dumplings found in Cyprus, Iran and Afghanistan. Such dumplings are generally filled with lamb or cheese and the sauce is often yogurt with garlic and mint, or a combination of yogurt and tomato sauces. Some recipes place the* manti *in a low oven for about 25 minutes to color them, then ladle the hot stock over the dumplings, cover the dish and bake until the stock is absorbed and the dumplings are tender, about 25 minutes longer. The yogurt sauce and the garnish are then spooned on top. In Cyprus, melted butter forms the sauce and mint is included in the filling. Beef can replace the lamb in this recipe.*

FOR THE DOUGH:
3 cups (15 oz/470 g) all-purpose (plain) flour
1 teaspoon salt
3 eggs
3–4 tablespoons cold water

FOR THE FILLING:
¾ lb (375 g) finely ground (minced) lean lamb
¾ cup (4 oz/125 g) finely minced onion
4 tablespoons finely minced fresh flat-leaf (Italian) parsley
1 teaspoon salt
½ teaspoon freshly ground black pepper

FOR THE SAUCE:
3 cups (1½ lb/750 g) plain yogurt, drained in a sieve lined with cheesecloth (muslin) for 3 hours
6 cloves garlic, finely minced
salt and freshly ground pepper

2–2½ qt (2–2½ l) light stock (see glossary), part stock and part water, or water

FOR GARNISH:
¼ cup (2 oz/60 g) unsalted butter
1 tablespoon finely crushed dried mint
good pinch of cayenne pepper

To make the dough, sift together the flour and salt into a bowl. Make a well in the center and add the eggs and most of the water to the well. Gradually stir the dry ingredients into the wet ingredients, mixing until all the liquid is absorbed and a stiff dough forms. Add more water as needed if the dough is too dry. Turn the dough out onto a floured board and knead for 10 minutes until smooth. Cover with a towel and let rest for 1 hour.

Top to bottom: Eggplant Pilaf, Bulgur Pilaf, Lamb Dumplings with Yogurt Sauce

Alternatively, make the dough in a food processor fitted with the metal blade. Sift the flour and salt into the processor container and then, with the motor running, add the eggs and water through the feed tube and process until a stiff, workable dough forms. Knead by hand on a floured board for a few minutes until smooth, then cover and let rest for 1 hour.

To make the filling, in a bowl combine the lamb, onion, parsley, salt and pepper. Knead to mix well. Alternatively, combine in a food processor fitted with the metal blade and process to mix.

Divide the dough into 4 equal portions. Roll out each portion on a pasta machine, gradually adjusting the machine until the dough passes through the rollers adjusted to their narrowest setting. Alternatively, on a floured board roll out each portion as thinly as possible. Cut the dough into 1-in (2.5-cm) squares or into rounds 1 in (2.5 cm) in diameter. Put a scant teaspoon of the filling on the dough, moisten edges lightly with water and fold into a half-moon, if working with rounds, or bring together the points to form a triangle, if working with squares.

Alternatively, roll out the dough into long strips 2 in (5 cm) wide. Place spoonfuls of filling at regular intervals along one side of each strip, moisten the edges, fold over the uncovered side, press edges together and cut into squares with a pastry wheel. You will have 60–80 tiny dumplings.

Just before cooking the dumplings, make the sauce. In a bowl stir together the yogurt and garlic. Season to taste with salt and pepper. (If you prepare the yogurt sauce ahead of time, bring it to room temperature just before serving.)

To cook the dumplings, divide the stock and/or water between 2 pots. Bring to a boil, add the dumplings and simmer, uncovered, until tender, 10–15 minutes.

While the dumplings are cooking, make the garnish. Melt the butter in a sauté pan and add the mint, sage and cayenne pepper. Simmer for 1 minute. Using a slotted spoon, remove the dumplings from the stock and distribute evenly among 6–8 warmed plates. Spoon the yogurt-garlic sauce on top, then drizzle with the mint-cayenne mixture. Serve at once.

SERVES 6–8

Mediterranean Rice

MEDITERRANEAN

Rice and Rice Pilaf

Rice is a staple grain in the cuisines of Syria, Lebanon, Egypt, Greece and Turkey. The rice is long grain and is prepared in one of two basic ways: The water is brought to a boil and the rice is added, cooked and then buttered. Or the butter, water and salt are combined and brought to a boil and the rice is added. In both cases the ratio of water to rice is two to one. The amount of butter is usually 1 tablespoon per cup (8 fl oz/250 ml) of water. Occasionally the rice is fried in butter or oil and then the water is added, which is similar to the technique used for preparing pilaf. Once the water has been absorbed, the rice should not be stirred and it should be allowed to rest, covered, for about 10 minutes before serving. It is also important that the rice grains remain separate. Any long-grain rice will do, but the most fragrant variety and the one that stays firm the longest is basmati. Some people wash or soak the rice before cooking, especially if it has a starchy coating; some recipes call for stock or water.

Rice appears on the Italian menu, but in the form of risotto, which is more of a northern Italian dish than a southern Mediterranean one. The short-grain rice of Italy is not very different from the rice in paella and pilafs in Spain. This rice does not remain in separate fluffy kernels, but tends to be stickier and more soupy or saucy in consistency.

Three methods for preparing rice follow. If you wish to make saffron-flavored rice, crush ½ teaspoon chopped saffron threads and steep in ¼ cup (2 fl oz/60 ml) hot water or wine. Add it with the rice in the methods that call for adding the rice to the boiling water. In the method that calls for sautéing the rice, do not steep the saffron; crush the threads and sauté with the rice.

4 cups (32 fl oz/1 l) water
salt
2 cups (14 oz/440 g) long-grain white rice, washed and drained
¼ cup (2 fl oz/60 ml) melted butter or olive oil

For method one, in a saucepan bring the water to a boil. Add the salt and rice and bring back to a boil. Boil for 1–2 minutes, then reduce the heat to low, cover and cook until the water has been absorbed and the rice is cooked and small holes appear on the top, about 20 minutes. Turn off the heat and let the rice rest, covered, for 10 minutes. Spoon the butter or oil over the rice and allow the rice to absorb it for a few minutes, then transfer to a warmed dish and serve.

For method two, prepare the rice as described above, but add the butter or oil to the water with the salt.

For method three, in a heavy saucepan over medium heat, melt the butter or warm the oil. Add the rice and sauté, stirring often, until the rice is translucent and coated with fat, about 3 minutes. Add the water and salt and bring to a boil. Boil for 1 minute, then reduce the heat to low, cover and cook as described above.

SERVES 6

TURKEY

Hünkar Beğendi

Eggplant Purée with Cream and Cheese

Delicate in flavor yet quite rich on the palate, this eggplant purée is usually served as a bed for stewed lamb or small meatballs in a tomato sauce. The eggplants can be grilled over a charcoal fire instead of in a broiler or oven.

3 eggplants (aubergines), about 2½–3 lb (1.25–1.5 kg) total weight
fresh lemon juice (optional)
3 tablespoons unsalted butter
3 tablespoons all-purpose (plain) flour
1½ cups (12 fl oz/375 ml) milk or heavy (double) cream, scalded
½ cup (2 oz/60 g) freshly grated Parmesan cheese
salt and freshly ground pepper
chopped fresh flat-leaf (Italian) parsley

Preheat a broiler (griller), or preheat an oven to 450°F (230°C). Place the eggplants on a baking sheet and broil (grill) or bake, turning occasionally, until soft, 30–40 minutes. Remove from the oven and, when cool enough to handle, peel off and discard the skin. Place the pulp in a bowl and mash with a fork until smooth. Alternatively, place in a food processor fitted with the metal blade and pulse to form a smooth purée. Place in a colander for several minutes to drain off any liquid. You may want to squeeze a little lemon juice on the eggplant to keep it white while it drains.

In a large saucepan over medium heat, melt the butter. Stir in the flour and continue to stir until well blended, 2–3 minutes. Slowly add the hot milk or cream, whisking constantly. Continue to whisk until thickened, about 3–5 minutes.

Add the eggplant purée and cook, stirring, until the eggplant is heated through. Stir in the cheese and then season to taste with salt and pepper.

Transfer to a warmed serving dish, sprinkle with parsley and serve.

SERVES 6

GREECE

Anginares à la Polita

Artichokes, City Style

The city is Constantinople. But given the age-old conflict between the Greeks and the Turks, this cosmopolitan city goes unnamed here. In Greece, the leaves are usually pared away and only the hearts of the artichokes are eaten. For this recipe the artichokes are mixed with new potatoes, carrots, onions and dill. In some recipes whole pearl onions are used instead of chopped onions, but the green onions are essential to the dish. Sometimes fresh fava (broad) beans are added, making this a spring vegetable medley. To do so, remove the pods from 2 pounds (1 kg) of fresh favas, blanch the beans briefly in boiling water, drain, peel off the skins and add with the other vegetables. This springtime combination is also popular in Provence and in Italy, where it is often mixed with pasta or risotto.

2 or 3 lemons, plus about ¼ cup (2 fl oz/60 ml) lemon juice
6 large or 12 small artichokes
1 large yellow onion, chopped
6 green (spring) onions, chopped
6 medium or 12 small new potatoes, unpeeled, cut in half if they are large
6 large or 12 small carrots, peeled and cut in half if they are large
½ cup (4 fl oz/125 ml) olive oil
4 teaspoons cornstarch (corn flour) or all-purpose (plain) flour
salt and freshly ground pepper
½ cup (¾ oz/20 g) chopped fresh dill

Have ready a large bowl of water to which you have added the juice of 1 lemon and the squeezed lemon halves. To prepare the artichokes, working with one at a time, trim the stem, leaving a 1-in (2.5-cm) piece intact. Cut off the top 1 in (2.5 cm) or more of the artichoke, down to the level of the heart, and break off all the tough outer leaves. Peel the stem and pare the remaining leaf tips down to the heart. Using a sharp spoon scoop out the choke. Rub the artichoke with a cut lemon as you work, then place in the bowl of the acidulated water. If the artichokes are large, cut them lengthwise in half or in quarters.

In a large sauté pan with high sides over medium heat, warm the oil. Add the yellow onion and sauté for 8 minutes. Add the green onions and sauté for 3 minutes longer, until all the onions are tender.

Drain the artichokes and add to the pan with the potatoes and carrots. Add water to cover barely, then cover the pan and simmer until the vegetables are tender, about 25 minutes. Using a slotted spoon remove the vegetables to a hot platter and cover with aluminum foil. In a small cup stir together the cornstarch or flour and the ¼ cup (2 fl oz/60 ml) lemon juice. Stir the mixture into the juices in the pan and simmer, stirring, for a few minutes until the juices thicken. Season to taste with salt and pepper. Taste and adjust with more lemon juice, if needed. Pour the sauce over the vegetables and sprinkle with the dill. Serve hot or warm.

SERVES 6

Left to right: Eggplant Purée with Cream and Cheese; Artichokes, City Style

GREECE

DOMATES YEMISTES ME RIZI

Tomatoes Stuffed with Rice

Vegetable dolmas, *or stuffed vegetables, are an important part of Mediterranean cuisine. They can be filled with an aromatic rice or a rice-and-meat mixture. The filling for stuffed grapeleaves (recipe on page 61) can be placed in hollowed-out cooked vegetables and served garnished with yogurt, or simply dressed with lemon juice and olive oil. The stuffed tomato is the epitome of the Greek vegetable* dolma *and appears on every table during the summer. To make stuffed bell peppers (capsicums),* piperies yemistes, *cut off the tops, remove the ribs and seeds and parboil the shells 4–5 minutes before stuffing. To make stuffed small eggplants (aubergines),* melitzanes yemistes, *cut in half lengthwise, scoop out some of the pulp to make a shell, chop the pulp and sauté with the onion and rice for the filling, and then sauté the eggplant cases in olive oil for 5 minutes to soften before stuffing. To make stuffed zucchini (courgettes),* kolokythakia yemistes, *cut in half lengthwise, scoop out some of the pulp to make a shell, chop the pulp and sauté with the onion for the filling and parboil the shells for 3 minutes before stuffing. Turkish cooks would use 2 large onions, chopped fresh dill in place of the parsley and ½ teaspoon ground allspice in the filling. Toasted bread crumbs can be used to top the vegetables in place of their own caps. If you decide to do an assortment of vegetables, select those that are about the same size. This recipe makes enough filling for about 4 pounds (2 kg) of vegetables.*

12 ripe tomatoes
salt
sugar
½ cup (4 fl oz/125 ml) olive oil
1 large onion, chopped
2 cloves garlic (optional)
1½ cups (10½ oz/330 g) long-grain white rice
½ cup (3 oz/90 g) currants or raisins
1½ cups (12 fl oz/375 ml) plus ⅓ cup (3 fl oz/80 ml) hot water
4 tablespoons chopped fresh flat-leaf (Italian) parsley
3 tablespoons chopped fresh mint
freshly ground pepper
¼ cup (1¼ oz/40 g) pine nuts, toasted (optional)

Cut off the tops from the tomatoes and scoop out the pulp. Reserve the tomato pulp and all juices as well as the tops. Sprinkle the insides of the tomatoes with salt and a little sugar. Set aside. Put the tomato pulp in a blender or in a food processor fitted with the metal blade and purée. Reserve.

In a sauté pan over medium heat, warm ¼ cup (2 fl oz/60 ml) of the oil. Add the onion and sauté until tender and translucent, 8–10 minutes. Add the garlic, rice, currants or raisins, the 1½ cups (12 fl oz/375 ml) hot water, the reserved tomato juices, parsley and mint and bring to a boil. Reduce the heat to low and simmer, uncovered, until all the liquid is absorbed, 10–12 minutes. Taste and adjust the seasonings. Let cool slightly.

Preheat an oven to 350°F (180°C).

Divide the rice mixture evenly among the tomatoes; do not fill too tightly as the rice will continue to expand. Place close together in a baking dish and replace the reserved tops. Pour the ⅓ cup (3 fl oz/80 ml) hot water into the dish. Spoon the remaining ¼ cup (2 fl oz/60 ml) oil evenly over the tomatoes. Bake, basting occasionally with the pan juices, until the tomatoes are tender, about 30 minutes.

Remove to a platter and serve hot or at room temperature.

SERVES 6

Tomatoes Stuffed with Rice

SICILY

PEPERONATA

Stewed Peppers

This dish is typical of southern Italy. Red and yellow peppers are most commonly used, but use green ones if you cannot find the others. Some versions of this dish add tomato; others do not. Some add a splash of vinegar at the end of cooking; others add sugar and vinegar for an agrodolce, *or sweet-and-sour taste. Almonds and raisins can be added as well. Serve warm or at room temperature. These peppers also make a satisfying sauce for pasta.*

3 large red bell peppers (capsicums)
3 large yellow or green bell peppers (capsicums)
½ cup (4 fl oz/125 ml) olive oil
1 or 2 onions, sliced ¼ in (6 mm) thick
2 cloves garlic, finely minced
3 ripe tomatoes, peeled, seeded and diced
1 fresh chili pepper, minced (optional)
¼ cup (2 fl oz/60 ml) red wine vinegar (optional)
2 tablespoons sugar (optional)
¼ cup (1 oz/30 g) sliced almonds, toasted (optional)
¼ cup (1½ oz/45 g) raisins, plumped in hot water and drained (optional)
salt and freshly ground pepper

Cut the peppers in half lengthwise. Remove the seeds and thick ribs and then slice lengthwise into strips about ½ in (12 mm) wide. In a sauté pan over medium heat, warm the oil. Add the onions and sauté until softened, 5–8 minutes. Add the bell peppers and garlic, cover and cook over low heat until the peppers are tender, about 20 minutes.

Add the tomatoes and any of the optional ingredients and season to taste with salt and pepper. Simmer for a few minutes for the flavors to mellow.

Transfer to a dish and serve warm or at room temperature.

SERVES 6

Clockwise from top left: Eggplant Parmesan (recipe page 197); Stewed Peppers; Eggplant, Taranto Style

APULIA

MELANZANE ALLA TARANTINA

Eggplant, Taranto Style

This recipe can be prepared with large or small eggplants; only the cooking time will vary. The technique described is called scoring and it is used all over the Mediterranean. This recipe is from Apulia, but it could easily be mistaken for a Provençal or Greek dish. In fact, given the influence of Greek cuisine on this region of Italy, it may well be a Greek recipe. If you like, add 3 cloves garlic, minced and sautéed in oil for 1 minute, to the paste. The eggplants can also be cooked in a broiler (griller) rather than an oven.

3 globe eggplants (aubergines) or 12 slender (Asian) eggplants
½ cup (2½ oz/75 g) sharply flavored black olives, pitted and chopped
¼ cup (1½ oz/45 g) capers, rinsed and chopped
4 tablespoons chopped fresh basil
4 tablespoons chopped fresh mint
½ cup (2 oz/60 g) grated pecorino cheese
salt and freshly ground pepper
olive oil for drizzling

Cut the eggplants in half lengthwise and salt the cut sides. Place in a colander to drain for 30 minutes.

Preheat an oven to 375°F (190°C).

Rinse the eggplants and pat dry with paper towels. Using a sharp knife score the top of the eggplant, making the cuts about ¼ in (6 mm) deep and forming a pattern of tiny squares; be careful not to cut all the way through. In a bowl stir together the olives, capers, basil, mint, cheese, and salt and pepper to taste. Rub this paste into the scored eggplant. Place the eggplants in a baking dish, cut sides up. Drizzle oil over them. Bake until the eggplants are tender when pierced with a knife, about 30 minutes for the globe eggplants and 10–15 minutes for the small ones.

Transfer to a platter and serve hot or warm.

SERVES 6

Clockwise from top: Steamed Semolina Grain, Chick-peas in Spicy Sauce, Potatoes in Spicy Olive Oil, Lentils and Pumpkin

MOROCCO/TUNISIA

Couscous

Steamed Semolina Grain

The signature grain of North Africa, couscous is a very fine pellet made from semolina. The classic method of preparation calls for steaming the grain in a couscousière *over hot liquids. First the couscous is spread on a baking sheet and sprinkled with a little warm salted water. Then it is steamed over hot water or a stew for 20–30 minutes. The slightly swelled grains are poured back onto a baking sheet and then are raked with fingertips to break up any lumps. There is more sprinkling with warm water, steaming again for 12–15 minutes, fluffing again with a fork, steaming and so on, until the grain has puffed to the maximum and is light. If you do not have a* couscousière, *you can improvise one by placing a sieve over a pot.*

With the advent of instant couscous (available at most stores today), the method of preparation has been simplified. The hot water may be added all at once, the grain covered and left to rest, and then fluffed and held over hot water or in a warm place until serving time. It is important for the couscous to puff up completely or it will continue to puff in the stomach, causing some discomfort to the diner.

2 cups (12 oz/375 g) instant medium-grind *(moyen)* couscous
3 cups (24 fl oz/750 ml) water or stock (see glossary)
1 teaspoon salt
2 tablespoons unsalted butter or olive oil (optional)
pinch of ground cinnamon, ginger, cumin or freshly ground pepper (optional)

Place the couscous in a small baking pan that will hold 6 cups (48 fl oz/1.5 l), plus allow a little room for fluffing. In a saucepan combine the water or stock, salt and the butter or oil and spice, if using. Bring to a boil and pour over the couscous. Stir well once and cover the pan with aluminum foil. Let rest for 10 minutes.

Fluff the couscous with a fork. Re-cover and place over hot water or set in a warm place such as a turned-off gas oven until needed. Serve in a warmed dish.

SERVES 6

ALGERIA

Hmissa bil Dersa

Chick-peas in Spicy Sauce

Dersa is a spicy Algerian sauce. The heat is provided by harissa *(see glossary) or cayenne and garlic, and tomato. The spices can vary: Cumin and paprika are standard, but the addition of cinnamon, coriander and caraway is the choice of the cook. Lentils, white beans and cauliflower may be prepared this same way.*

2¼ cups (1 lb/500 g) dried chick-peas (garbanzo beans)
½ cup (4 fl oz/125 ml) olive oil
2 cloves garlic, finely minced
1 teaspoon cayenne pepper
½ teaspoon freshly ground black pepper
1 teaspoon paprika
1 teaspoon ground cumin
2–3 tablespoons tomato purée
4–5 cups (32–40 fl oz/1–1.25 l) water
1½–2 teaspoons salt
chopped fresh basil, thyme or cilantro (fresh coriander), optional

In a bowl combine the chick-peas and water to cover generously. Refrigerate overnight. Drain and set aside.

In a large saucepan over medium heat, warm the oil. Add the garlic, cayenne and black peppers, paprika and cumin and sauté for a few seconds. Add the tomato purée and the water and bring to a boil. Add the drained chick-peas, reduce the heat to low, cover and simmer until the chick-peas are tender, 45–60 minutes. Add the salt and simmer, uncovered, until most of the liquid has been absorbed or has evaporated, about 15–20 minutes. Transfer to a serving bowl and sprinkle with basil, thyme or cilantro (if using).

SERVES 6

MOROCCO

Ads be Qar wa Khli

Lentils and Pumpkin

A tagine *is a North African ceramic cooking utensil that gives its name to a variety of stews. For this* tagine *you can use pumpkin, butternut or acorn squash. Dried white beans can replace the lentils, but they will need to be soaked over night. Occasionally, ¼ pound (125 g)* khlii *(dried seasoned beef) is added to impart a meat flavor. It should be added to the pan in one piece with the onions and then removed just before the greens are added, cut into thick strips and returned to the pan. Look for* khlii *in shops specializing in North African foods.* Smen *is the Moroccan term for clarified butter (see glossary). Serve with couscous (recipe on preceding page) for a complete dinner.*

2 tablespoons *smen,* unsalted butter or olive oil
2 onions, diced
2 fresh chili peppers, thinly sliced
1 tablespoon paprika
½ teaspoon cayenne pepper
1 teaspoon ground cumin
1 cup (7 oz/220 g) dried lentils
4 tomatoes, peeled, seeded and chopped
¼ cup (2 fl oz/60 ml) tomato purée
1 piece pumpkin squash, 2 lb (1 kg), peeled and cut into 1-in (2.5-cm) cubes
1 lb (500 g) greens such as Swiss chard (silverbeet), dandelion, kale, blanched 3–5 minutes, drained well and coarsely chopped (optional)

In a saucepan over medium heat, warm the *smen,* butter or oil. Add the onions and chilies and cook until the onions begin to soften, about 10 minutes. Add the paprika, cayenne and cumin and continue to sauté until the onions are tender, a few minutes longer.

Add the lentils, tomatoes and tomato purée and water just to cover. Simmer for about 20 minutes. Add the squash and simmer until tender, about 20 minutes. Add the greens, if using, during the last 5 minutes of cooking.

Transfer to a warmed serving dish and serve immediately.

SERVES 6

MOROCCO

Batata bil Zait

Potatoes in Spicy Olive Oil

Here is a spicy potato stew, not unlike Sicilian patate al diavolicchio, *or "devilishly hot potatoes." In Italy they use hot-pepper oil and in North Africa* harissa *adds the fire. In Algeria parsley rather than mint is used, and in Tunisia caraway rather than cumin is added. Instead of cooking the potatoes fully in a sauté pan, they can be parboiled first and then sautéed in the spiced oil and garnished with the parsley or mint.*

⅓ cup (3 fl oz/80 ml) olive oil
3 cloves garlic, thinly sliced
2 tablespoons tomato purée
½–1 teaspoon *harissa* (see glossary)
1 teaspoon ground cumin (optional)
½ teaspoon salt, or to taste
2 cups (16 fl oz/500 ml) water
2 lb (1 kg) potatoes, peeled and sliced ½ in (12 mm) thick
4 tablespoons chopped fresh flat-leaf (Italian) parsley or mint

In a large sauté pan over medium heat, warm the oil. Add the garlic, tomato purée, *harissa* , cumin (if using) and salt and stir well. Add the water and the potato slices and mix well. Bring to a boil, reduce the heat to low and simmer until the potatoes are nearly cooked, 10–15 minutes. Add the parsley or mint and simmer until the potatoes are tender, about 5 minutes longer.

Transfer to a serving dish. Serve hot or at room temperature.

SERVES 6

APULIA

Zucca alla Ricotta Forte

Winter Squash with Sharp Ricotta

A specialty of Brindisi, this dish can also be made with pumpkin squash. If you cannot find ricotta salata, *a salted, hard ricotta, use a sharp or salty cheese such as pecorino or* ragusana.

5 tablespoons (3 fl oz/80 ml) olive oil
2–3 anchovy fillets in olive oil, drained and minced
1 or 2 cloves garlic, minced
1 large celery stalk, chopped
1 onion, chopped
1 butternut squash, about 1½ lb (750 g), peeled, seeded and diced
2–3 tablespoons capers, rinsed and chopped
¼ cup (1½ oz/45 g) sharply flavored black olives, pitted
2–3 tablespoons freshly grated sharp cheese
salt and freshly ground pepper
toasted bread

In a large sauté pan over medium heat, warm 2½ tablespoons of the oil. Add the anchovies, garlic, celery and onion and sauté until the vegetables begin to soften, about 5 minutes. Transfer to a bowl and set aside.

Heat the remaining 2½ tablespoons oil in the same pan over medium heat. Add the squash and brown quickly, turning to color evenly, just a few minutes. Return the onion mixture to the pan and add the capers and olives. Stir well, cover and cook until the squash is tender, about 15 minutes. Add the cheese and salt and pepper to taste and toss to mix.

Transfer to a warmed dish and serve with toasted bread.

SERVES 6

Photograph page 4

SARDINIA

Culingiones de Patate

Potato Raviolis

Potato-filled pasta sounds heavy, but in fact these raviolis are delicate and float down easily!

4 large baking potatoes, about 2 lb (1 kg) total weight
dough for *manti* (recipe on page 198)
2 tablespoons beef drippings, rendered *pancetta* fat or olive oil
2 onions, chopped
1 clove garlic, minced
1 cup (8 oz/250 g) ricotta cheese
1 cup (4 oz/125 g) grated pecorino cheese, plus grated cheese for serving
3 tablespoons chopped fresh mint
salt and freshly ground pepper
melted unsalted butter or heated tomato sauce (see glossary)

Preheat an oven to 400°F (200°C). Place the potatoes directly on the rack and bake until very tender, about 1 hour.

Meanwhile, prepare the dough as directed and let it rest for 1 hour.

Remove the potatoes from the oven and, when cool enough to handle, cut in half and scoop out the pulp. Put the pulp through a potato ricer or mash well with a fork.

In a large sauté pan over medium heat, warm the beef drippings, fat or oil. Add the onions and garlic and sauté until tender and translucent, 8–10 minutes. Add to the potatoes and let cool. Then add both cheeses and the mint and season to taste with salt and pepper.

Roll out the dough into long, narrow strips about 4 in (10 cm) wide and fill and cut into 2-in (5-cm) squares as directed for the *manti.* Alternatively, cut the dough into rounds about 3 in (7.5 cm) in diameter, top with a spoonful of filling, moisten the edges and bring up the edges to a point on top, to form a conelike shape, sealing well. Bring 1 large pot or 2 small ones three-fourths full of water to a boil. Add salt to taste and the raviolis and cook until tender, 8–10 minutes. Drain well.

Transfer the raviolis to a warmed wide serving dish and dress with butter or tomato sauce and cheese. Serve immediately.

SERVES 6

Potato Raviolis

CYPRUS

Afelia

Vegetables with Coriander

In Cyprus, both meat and vegetable dishes are called afelia, *which means cooked with cracked coriander seeds. This version can also be made with artichokes. (For directions on preparing them for cooking, see* anginares à la polita *on page 201.) They will need to cook 15–20 minutes.*

1 lb (500 g) small fresh mushrooms or 2 lb (1 kg) small new potatoes
¼ cup (2 fl oz/60 ml) olive oil
½ cup (4 fl oz/125 ml) dry red wine
salt and freshly ground pepper
2–3 teaspoons crushed coriander seeds

If using mushrooms, simply wipe with a dry paper towel. If using potatoes, dry well and crack with a mallet if small, or cut in half if larger.

In a sauté pan over medium-high heat, warm the oil. Add the mushrooms or potatoes and fry, stirring, until lightly browned, about 8–10 minutes for mushrooms or 10–12 minutes for potatoes. Reduce the heat to low and add the wine and salt and pepper to taste. Cover and simmer until tender, 20–25 minutes for potatoes or 8–10 minutes for mushrooms.

Uncover and add the coriander seeds. Cook for 3–4 minutes longer to blend the flavors.

Transfer to a warmed dish and serve.

SERVES 6

TURKEY

Kabak Mücveri

Zucchini Fritters

Fritters are very popular in the Middle East. They are eaten hot or at room temperature as a vegetable side dish or a meze.

1 lb (500 g) zucchini (courgettes)
salt
½ cup (1½ oz/45 g) chopped green (spring) onion
1 small yellow onion, grated
½ cup (¾ oz/20 g) chopped fresh dill
4 tablespoons chopped fresh flat-leaf (Italian) parsley
½ cup (2 oz/60 g) freshly grated kasseri cheese or crumbled feta cheese
4 eggs, lightly beaten
1 cup (5 oz/155 g) all-purpose (plain) flour
freshly ground pepper
olive oil for frying

Grate the zucchini and place in a colander. Sprinkle with salt and let drain for 30 minutes. Squeeze out moisture and pat with paper towels.

Place the zucchini in a bowl and add the green and yellow onions, dill, parsley, cheese, flour, and salt and pepper to taste. Mix well.

In a large sauté pan over medium-high heat, pour in oil to a depth of ¼ in (6 mm). When the oil is hot, drop the batter by tablespoonfuls into the pan, allowing space between the fritters. Fry for 2 minutes on the first side, then turn to brown on the second side for about 3 minutes. Using a slotted spatula transfer to paper towels to drain. Repeat with the remaining batter.

Arrange on a platter and serve.

SERVES 6

Top to bottom: The Imam's Delight, Zucchini Fritters, Vegetables with Coriander

TURKEY

İMAM BAYILDI

The Imam's Delight

This stuffed eggplant is the most famous of all Turkish eggplant recipes. The name has been translated as "the Imam fainted," either from the delight of eating the dish or from seeing the extravagant amount of oil used in its preparation. Turkish food authority Nevin Halici says no Turk would ever faint from surprise at seeing eggplant in lots of olive oil, however, so he must have fainted from delight. You can use 8–12 slender Asian eggplants for this dish as well. This will require less baking time; plan on about 15 minutes in the oven. The dish can be made a couple of days in advance of serving.

4 small globe eggplants (aubergine), about ½ lb (250 g) each, preferably long and thin
salt
½ cup (4 fl oz/125 ml) olive oil, plus olive oil for sprinkling
2 cups (7 oz/220 g) very thinly sliced onion
12 cloves garlic, cut into slivers or finely minced
3 or 4 tomatoes, peeled and chopped
pinch of sugar
½ cup (¾ oz/20 g) chopped fresh flat-leaf (Italian) parsley
1 cup (8 fl oz/250 ml) hot water

Peel the eggplants lengthwise in a striped pattern. Cut in half lengthwise, then rub the cut sides with salt. Let rest for 30 minutes. Rinse with water and squeeze dry.

In a large sauté pan over medium heat, warm ¼ cup (2 fl oz/60 ml) of the oil. Add the eggplant and fry, turning, until soft, about 5 minutes, adding more oil as needed. Transfer the eggplant halves to a baking dish in which they will fit in a single layer.

Preheat an oven to 350°F (180°C).

For the filling, warm the remaining ¼ cup (2 fl oz/60 ml) oil in the sauté pan over low heat. Add the onion and garlic and sauté until very soft, 12–15 minutes; do not brown. Add the tomatoes and cook for 5 minutes. Add the sugar and parsley and simmer for 5 minutes longer. Remove from the heat. Taste and adjust the seasoning.

Cut a slit in the cut side of each eggplant half but do not cut all the way through. Push the cavities open and fill each with an equal amount of the onion mixture. Sprinkle generously with oil. Add the hot water to the pan, cover with aluminum foil, and bake until eggplants are very tender, 30–50 minutes. Check the eggplant midway through baking and add a little water to the dish if it has dried out. The finished dish should have just a few tablespoons of liquid.

Transfer to a platter. Serve at room temperature or cover and refrigerate for 1–2 days; bring to room temperature before serving.

SERVES 4 AS A MAIN COURSE, 8 AS A SIDE DISH

Left to right: Stuffed Mushrooms; Spinach with Raisins and Pine Nuts; Roasted Eggplants, Peppers and Onions

ANDALUSIA

Paella Valenciana

Rice from Valencia

Paella takes its name from a two-handled shallow pan called a paellera. *Traditionally, Valencian paella is made with short-grain rice, rabbit or chicken, tomatoes, beans and often snails. In Spain, rosemary and snails rarely appear in the same recipes, since the snails feed on wild rosemary and have taken on the flavor of the herb. Here, the canned snails lack that extra flavor, so the rosemary is added. Less traditional versions include shellfish and occasionally sausage, ham or meatballs. If you want to add shrimp (prawns) to this paella, omit the snails and sauté 1 pound (500 g) shrimp in the tomato-onion mixture, remove them from the pan and then return them during the last five minutes of cooking. You can also add 36 mussels and/or clams, well scrubbed (mussels debearded), in place of the snails; tuck them into the rice once it has been stirred in, placing them with the edge that will open facing up. Chorizo (see glossary) or meatballs can be browned after the chicken and rabbit, removed from the pan and then returned to the pan with them.*

Paella is usually cooked outdoors over an open fire, but you can cook this on a stove top with great success. You will probably need two burners to accommodate a large paellera. *The rice is cooked uncovered so that it does not steam, and the cooking is stopped when the rice is still a bit underdone. It finishes cooking off the heat, where it absorbs the last of the juices. You can, if you prefer, cook the paella uncovered in a 350°F (180°C) oven for about 20 minutes once all the ingredients have been combined on the stove top. While this recipe looks like a lot of work, much of the cooking can be done in stages.*

2⅛ cups (8 oz/250 g) dried large white beans
5 tablespoons (3 fl oz/80 ml) olive oil
1½ lb (750 g) chicken parts
1–1½ lb (500–750 g) rabbit parts
salt and freshly ground pepper
1 large onion, chopped
1 clove garlic, minced (optional)
3 or 4 tomatoes, peeled, seeded and chopped
4–5 cups (32–40 fl oz/1–1.25 l) chicken stock (see glossary) or part stock and part water, heated
24 canned snails, drained
½ teaspoon saffron threads, crushed
2 fresh rosemary sprigs, chopped
2 cups (14 oz/440 g) short-grain white rice

½ lb (250 g) green beans, trimmed, cut into 3-in (7.5-cm) lengths, blanched 5 minutes and drained

Place the white beans in a bowl, add water to cover generously and let soak overnight. Drain and place in a saucepan. Add water to cover by 2 in (5 cm), bring to a boil, reduce the heat to low, cover and simmer until tender, 45–60 minutes. Drain and set aside.

In a *paellera* or very large sauté pan over medium-high heat, warm the oil. Season the chicken and rabbit pieces with salt and pepper. Add the chicken and brown on all sides, about 10 minutes. Using a slotted spoon remove from the pan and set aside. Add the rabbit pieces and brown in the same manner; set aside.

To the oil remaining in the pan, add the onion, garlic (if using) and tomatoes and sauté for about 10 minutes. Return the chicken and rabbit pieces to the pan, add the heated stock and simmer for 10 minutes.

Add the snails, white beans, saffron, rosemary and rice, stir well and cook, uncovered, over a medium heat without stirring until the liquid has been absorbed and the rice is cooked but still slightly underdone, about 20 minutes. Add the green beans during the last 5 minutes of cooking. Do not let the rice scorch and lower the heat if the rice is cooking too quickly. Cover and let stand for 5–10 minutes, until the rice is fully cooked, then serve directly from the pan.

SERVES 6–8 *Photograph pages 192–193*

CATALONIA

Champiñones Rellenos

Stuffed Mushrooms

Most baked stuffed mushrooms take a long time to cook and often do not cook evenly. The most foolproof method for preparing them is to sauté the mushroom caps quickly in olive oil or butter to brown and soften them a bit before stuffing; they can then be finished in the oven without additional liquid. In Spain, France and Italy, prosciutto, sausage or ham and onion and garlic are added to the chopped mushroom stems for the filling. The stuffed mushrooms are then topped with bread crumbs or a combination of grated cheese and crumbs. To use sausage, sauté ¼ pound (125 g) chorizo or fennel sausage meat (see glossary) until cooked and use in place of the ham or prosciutto in the recipe. The mushrooms can be assembled several hours in advance and baked just before serving.

12 large fresh mushrooms
3 tablespoons olive oil
3 tablespoons unsalted butter, plus melted butter for basting
6 tablespoons (2 oz/60 g) finely minced onion
2 cloves garlic, minced finely
¼ cup (1½ oz/45 g) minced ham or prosciutto
2 tablespoons chopped fresh flat-leaf (Italian) parsley, thyme or marjoram
¼ cup (1 oz/30 g) fine dried bread crumbs
salt and freshly ground pepper
freshly grated Parmesan cheese (optional)

Preheat an oven to 400°F (200°C).

Wipe the mushrooms clean with a damp towel or a brush. Carefully remove the stems and chop the stems finely. You'll need only 8–10 tablespoons (1½–1¾ oz/45–68 g) chopped stems.

In a large sauté pan over high heat, warm the oil. Add the mushroom caps and brown quickly. Remove from the heat and set aside, hollow side up, on a baking sheet.

In a small sauté pan over medium heat, melt the 3 tablespoons butter. Add the onion and sauté until soft, about 5 minutes. Add the garlic and mushroom stems and sauté until the stems are wilted, about 3 minutes. Add the ham or prosciutto and cook for 2–3 minutes. Stir in the parsley and bread crumbs and season to taste with salt and pepper. (Remember that prosciutto and ham will give off more salt as they heat.) Pile the sautéed mixture into the mushroom caps. Sprinkle with grated cheese (if using).

Bake, basting with a little melted butter if desired, until tender when pierced with a knife, about 15 minutes.

Transfer to a platter and serve hot or warm.

SERVES 6

CATALONIA

Escalivada

Roasted Eggplants, Peppers and Onions

Many restaurants in Spain roast vegetables in the oven, as it is easier and less time-consuming than grilling them. Grilling, however, gives the characteristic smoky taste that is essential to escalivada *(*escalivar *means "to grill"). If you do not feel like lighting a charcoal fire every time you crave this dish, you can broil the vegetables or cook them directly on the stove-top flame or on a stove-top griddle. Tomatoes can also be grilled and added to this mixture, as can garlic, which is then mashed and mixed with the oil before tossing with the vegetables.*

4 small globe eggplants (aubergines) or 8–10 slender (Asian) eggplants
3 or 4 red bell peppers (capsicums)
2 small or medium red (Spanish) onions, unpeeled
virgin olive oil, as needed
2–4 cloves garlic, minced
salt and freshly ground pepper

Prepare a fire in a charcoal grill.

Place the eggplants and peppers on the grill rack and grill, turning often, until charred on all sides and tender; the timing will depend upon the size of the vegetables and the intensity of the fire.

Place the peppers in a paper bag or a covered plastic container to steam for 15 minutes. Then peel the peppers and remove the seeds and ribs. Slice into strips about ½ in (12 mm) wide.

Place the eggplants in a colander and, when cool enough to handle, peel and discard the skin. Allow the pulp to drain in the colander to release its bitter juices, about 15 minutes. Then cut into large strips or large dice.

While the onions can be grilled, it is easiest to prepare them in a 400°F (200°C) oven unless they are very small. Rub the onions with oil and place them in a small baking pan. Bake until tender, about 45 minutes. Remove from the oven and, when cool enough to handle, peel and cut into slices about ½ in (12 mm) thick.

Combine the cooked vegetables in a serving bowl and dress with a little olive oil, minced garlic and salt and pepper to taste. Serve at room temperature.

SERVES 6–8

CATALONIA

Acelgas con Pasas y Piñónes

Spinach with Raisins and Pine Nuts

A popular dish in Spain, but also in Italy, Greece and Turkey. The Arabic influence is evident in the use of raisins and pine nuts. You can toast the pine nuts in a 350°F (180°C) oven for about 8 minutes, or you can fry them until lightly golden in the olive oil used for the dish and then remove them before you sauté the onion in the same oil.

2 lb (1 kg) spinach or Swiss chard (silverbeet)
3 tablespoons olive oil
1 small onion, finely chopped
1 clove garlic, minced
⅓ cup (2 oz/60 g) raisins, plumped in hot water and drained
¼ cup (1¼ oz/40 g) pine nuts, toasted
salt and freshly ground pepper

Chop the greens coarsely if the leaves are very large. Wash in several changes of water and drain.

In a wide sauté pan over medium heat, warm the oil. Add the onion and sauté until golden and sweet, 15–20 minutes. Add the garlic and cook for 1–2 minutes longer.

Add the greens in batches and stir well until wilted; add more as each batch shrinks. You do not need to cover the pan, as the greens will cook down in the moisture clinging to the leaves. When all the leaves are wilted, add the raisins and pine nuts and season to taste with salt and pepper.

Transfer to a serving dish and serve hot or warm.

SERVES 6

Top to bottom: Pasta with Eggplant and Tomatoes, Pasta with Sardines

SICILY

PASTA CON SARDE

Pasta with Sardines

This is one of the most famous and interesting pastas from Sicily. The Arabic influence is seen in the addition of raisins and nuts to what seems like a simple fish sauce. Do not worry if you cannot find wild fennel. Cultivated fennel will do. Use the stalks and fronds as well as the celery-textured bulb.

1½ lb (750 g) wild fennel greens
5 tablespoons (3 fl oz/80 ml) olive oil
2 onions, minced
⅓ cup (2 oz/60 g) raisins or currants, plumped in hot water and drained
⅓ cup (2 oz/60 g) pine nuts, toasted
6 anchovy fillets in oil, drained and coarsely chopped
large pinch of saffron, crushed and steeped in 2 tablespoons hot water
1 lb (500 g) fresh sardines, boned and cut into large pieces
1 lb (500 g) *bucatini, perciatelli* or other dried pasta
1 cup (4 oz/125 g) fine dried bread crumbs, toasted (optional)

Trim the fennel bulbs and remove and discard any dry or discolored leaves. Cut the bulbs in half or into quarters lengthwise. Bring a large pot three-fourths full of water to a boil. Add salt to taste and the fennel. Cook until tender, 8–10 minutes. Using a slotted spoon remove the fennel to a cutting board. Chop and set aside. Reserve the water.

In a large sauté pan over low heat, warm 2 tablespoons of the oil. Add the onions and sauté until they are pale gold, 10–15 minutes. Add the raisins or currants, pine nuts, anchovies, and saffron and steeping liquid. Simmer over low heat for 5 minutes. Remove to a bowl; keep warm.

In the large sauté pan over medium heat, warm the remaining 3 tablespoons oil. Add the sardines and sauté, turning once, until golden, 3–4 minutes on each side. Using a slotted spoon remove to a dish; keep warm. Add the chopped fennel to the sardine-flavored oil and cook over low heat to warm through. Return the sardines and the onion mixture to the pan and keep warm.

Meanwhile, return the fennel water to a boil. Add the pasta and cook until al dente, about 10 minutes (it will take about 10 minutes to cook; check the package directions). Drain.

Place the pasta on a platter. Spoon the sardine sauce over the top and toss well. Sprinkle with the bread crumbs, if using. Serve immediately or at room temperature.

SERVES 6

SICILY

PASTA ALLA NORMA

Pasta with Eggplant and Tomatoes

Vincenzo Bellini was born in Catania, where this pasta was born as well. It is named for one of his best-known operas, Norma. *If vine-ripened tomatoes are not available, canned plum (Roma) tomatoes can be substituted.*

2 globe eggplants (aubergines) or 8 slender (Asian) eggplants, about 1½ lb (750 g) total weight
salt
olive oil
2 lb (1 kg) tomatoes, peeled, seeded and coarsely chopped
2 cloves garlic, minced
12 large fresh basil leaves, chopped
freshly ground pepper
1 lb (500 g) *maccheroni* or spaghetti
grated pecorino cheese

Peel the eggplants lengthwise in a striped pattern. If the eggplants are large, cut them in half lengthwise and then thinly slice them crosswise. If they are long and thin, or if you are using long, slender eggplants, simply thinly slice them crosswise. Sprinkle the slices with salt, place in a colander and let stand for 20–30 minutes to drain off the bitter juices. Pat dry with paper towels.

In a large sauté pan over high heat, pour in oil to a depth of ¼ in (6 mm). When the oil is hot, working in batches, fry the eggplant slices, turning once, until golden brown and tender, just a few minutes. Using a slotted spoon remove to a dish.

In another sauté pan over medium heat, warm 2 tablespoons oil. Add the tomatoes and garlic and cook, stirring occasionally, until the tomatoes take on a saucelike consistency, 10–15 minutes. Add the fried eggplant and basil and warm the eggplant through. Season to taste with salt and pepper. Meanwhile, bring a large pot three-fourths full of water to a boil. Add the pasta and cook until al dente (it will take 7–10 minutes to cook; check the package directions). Drain.

Place the pasta on a warmed platter. Spoon the sauce over the top and toss well. Sprinkle with cheese and serve immediately.

SERVES 6

PROVENCE

TOMATES PROVENÇALE

Baked Tomatoes with Garlic, Parsley and Bread Crumbs

In one sense, this recipe is so simple there seems no reason to write it down. The dish, however, often suffers from flavorless tomatoes with too much liquid. Seek out vine-ripened tomatoes and be sure to rid them of excess liquid, so the tops will acquire a crusty finish.

6 large, firm but ripe tomatoes
salt
4 tablespoons (2 fl oz/60 ml) olive oil
salt and freshly ground pepper
½ cup (2 oz/60 g) fine dried bread crumbs
3 cloves garlic, minced
½ cup (¾ oz/20 g) chopped fresh flat-leaf (Italian) parsley

Preheat an oven to 375°–400°F (190°–200°C). Lightly oil a baking dish. Cut the tomatoes in half crosswise. Sprinkle with salt and drain, cut sides down, in a colander, for about 10 minutes. Dry well with paper towels.

In a large sauté pan over medium-high heat, warm 2 tablespoons of the oil. Add the tomato halves, cut side down and 4–6 at a time, and fry until golden, about 5 minutes.

Place the tomatoes, cut side up, in the prepared baking dish. Sprinkle with salt and pepper. In a small bowl stir together the bread crumbs, garlic and a little of the parsley. Spread atop the tomatoes. Drizzle with remaining 2 tablespoons oil. Bake until the tops are golden, 10–15 minutes.

Transfer to a platter and sprinkle with the remaining parsley. Serve warm or at room temperature.

SERVES 6

PROVENCE

FENOUIL BRAISÉ

Braised Fennel

Although fennel is most often eaten raw with salt and olive oil in France and Italy, it is also tasty when cooked. Precooking the fennel can be done two ways: It can be sautéed in oil or butter and then braised in stock until tender, or it can be cooked in boiling salted water. The fennel is then served as is or dressed with butter and grated Parmesan cheese and bread crumbs. Or it can be placed in a baking dish, sprinkled with cheese and crumbs and glazed under the broiler (griller). Both versions are given here.

6 large bulbs fennel, cut in half lengthwise and cored
¼ cup (2 oz/60 g) butter or (2 fl oz/60 ml) olive oil for sautéing, plus more as needed for drizzling
1 cup (8 fl oz/250 ml) chicken stock (see glossary), if braising
salt and freshly ground pepper
freshly grated nutmeg (optional)
¼ cup (1 oz/30 g) freshly grated Parmesan cheese
¼ cup (1 oz/30 g) fine dried bread crumbs, toasted

2–3 tablespoons heavy (double) cream (optional)

Preheat an oven to 400°F (200°C).

If you are sautéing the fennel, cut the fennel bulbs lengthwise into thick slices. In a large sauté pan over medium heat, warm the butter or oil. Add the fennel and sauté until golden, 8–10 minutes. Add the stock, cover and braise until tender and most of the stock is absorbed, 15–20 minutes. Season to taste with salt, pepper and nutmeg (if using). Transfer the fennel to a gratin dish, arranging it in a single layer. Cover with the cheese, crumbs and a bit of oil or butter. Bake until the top is golden, about 10 minutes. Alternatively, warm briefly in the oven and then brown under a preheated broiler (griller). Serve immediately.

Alternatively, bring a saucepan three-fourths full of water to a boil. Drop in the fennel halves and add salt to taste. Cook, uncovered, until the bulbs are tender, about 25 minutes. Drain in a colander, let cool and squeeze out excess moisture. Cut bulbs lengthwise into thick slices, keeping slices intact as much as possible. Butter or oil a baking dish and place fennel slices in it. Sprinkle with salt, pepper, and nutmeg (if using). Then top with the butter or oil, cream (if using), cheese and crumbs. Bake until the top is golden, about 10 minutes. A few tablespoons of cream may be added.

SERVES 6

Top to bottom: Baked Tomatoes with Garlic, Parsley and Bread Crumbs, Braised Fennel

Clockwise from top left: Rice Pilaf with Currants and Nuts, Pilaf Wrapped in Filo, Saffron Pilaf with Shrimp

TURKEY

YUFKALİ PİLAV

Pilaf Wrapped in Filo

Some versions of this recipe combine chicken and an almond rice pilaf in a shallow baking dish lined with overlapping sheets of filo, fold the filo over the top, bake, and then cut for serving much as one would cut baklava. You can use ½ pound (250 g) lamb in place of the chicken: Cut the lamb into ½-in (12-mm) cubes, brown in ¼ cup (2 oz/60 g) unsalted butter for a few minutes, and then simmer in 1 cup (8 fl oz/250 ml) meat stock until tender; use meat stock in place of the chicken stock for cooking the rice.

FOR THE CHICKEN:

1 small chicken, about 2½ lb (1.25 kg), or about 2 lb (1 kg) chicken pieces
1 onion, halved
1 carrot, halved
salt
6 peppercorns

¾ cup (6 oz/180 g) unsalted butter
½ cup (3 oz/90 g) almonds

1 onion, chopped
1½ cups (10½ oz/330 g) long-grain white rice, washed and drained
½ teaspoon ground cinnamon or allspice
¼ teaspoon ground cardamom
salt and freshly ground pepper
8 *filo* sheets (see glossary)

To prepare the chicken, in a saucepan combine the chicken, onion, carrot, salt to taste, peppercorns and water to cover. Bring to a boil, reduce the heat to low, cover and simmer until the chicken is tender, about 30 minutes for chicken pieces and 50 minutes for whole chicken. Remove the chicken and, when cool enough to handle, remove the bones and skin and cut the chicken meat into bite-sized pieces. Strain the stock and place in a saucepan; bring to a simmer.

In a large saucepan over medium heat, melt ¼ cup (2 oz/60 g) of the butter. Add the almonds and fry, stirring, until golden brown, a few minutes. Using a slotted spoon remove to a dish. Add the onion to the butter remaining in the pan and sauté until tender and translucent, 8–10 minutes. Add the cinnamon or allspice, cardamom and salt and pepper to taste and sauté for a few more minutes. Add the rice and sauté, stirring, until the rice is translucent and coated with fat, about 3 minutes. Add the fried almonds, chicken meat and 3 cups (24 fl oz/750 ml) of the simmering stock and bring to a boil. Reduce the heat to low, cover and cook until the liquid has been absorbed and the rice is cooked, about 20 minutes. Turn off heat and let the rice sit until cool.

Preheat an oven to 450°–500°F (230°–260°C).

In a small pan melt the remaining ½ cup (4 oz/125 g) butter. Brush a deep 2-qt (2-l) baking dish (a soufflé dish works well) generously with some of the butter. Now line the dish with the *filo* sheets, allowing each one to overhang the sides and brushing them with the butter. Make sure there is enough *filo* overhanging the sides of the dish to enclose the pilaf. Spoon the cooled pilaf evenly into the dish and bring the *filo* sheets up over the top to enclose neatly. Brush the top with the remaining butter.

Bake until golden, 15–20 minutes. Remove from the oven and let rest for 2–3 minutes. Invert onto a serving platter. Slice and serve.

SERVES 6–8

TURKEY

Iç Pİlav

Rice Pilaf with Currants and Nuts

A good accompaniment to many Turkish dishes. You can expand the dish with the addition of cooked chicken or lamb, sautéed together with the onion. Long-grain rice is essential and basmati is the best, as it holds its firmness and fragrance longer than any other varieties.

¼ cup (2 oz/60 g) unsalted butter or (2 fl oz/60 ml) olive oil
1 onion, chopped
¼ teaspoon ground allspice
½ teaspoon ground cinnamon or coriander
2 cups (14 oz/440 g) long-grain white rice, washed and drained
4 cups (32 fl oz/1 l) chicken stock (see glossary) or water, heated
1 teaspoon salt, plus salt to taste
1 cup (6 oz/185 g) currants, plumped in hot water and drained
½ cup (2½ oz/75 g) pine nuts, toasted, pistachios or almonds, toasted
freshly ground pepper (optional)
4 tablespoons chopped fresh flat-leaf (Italian) parsley or dill (optional)

In a large saucepan over medium heat, melt the butter or warm the oil. Add the onion and sauté until just translucent, about 7 minutes.

Add the allspice and cinnamon or coriander and cook, stirring, for 2 minutes. Add the rice and stir over medium heat until the grains become translucent and coated with the fat, about 3 minutes. Add the heated stock or water and the 1 teaspoon salt. Bring to a boil, reduce the heat to low, cover and simmer until the liquid has been absorbed and the rice is cooked, about 20 minutes. Turn off heat and let the rice rest, covered, for 10 minutes.

Add the currants and nuts to the rice and fluff with a fork. Season to taste with salt and with pepper, if using. Transfer to a warmed platter, sprinkle with the parsley or dill (if using) and serve.

SERVES 6

TURKEY

Karidesli Pİlav

Saffron Pilaf with Shrimp

Seafood and rice pilaf are popular in Greece as well as Turkey. While this recipe specifies shrimp, scallops, squid or cooked octopus would also be nice. Mussels are a particular favorite in Turkey. To make the pilaf with mussels, scrub and debeard about 40 mussels and then steam them open in a little white wine or water, discarding any that do not open. Shell the mussels and strain the steaming liquid. Steep the saffron in the strained liquid. Proceed with the recipe, sautéing the mussels in the butter.

¼ cup (2 oz/60 g) unsalted butter
1 lb (500 g) shrimp (prawns), peeled and deveined
1 onion, chopped
2 cloves garlic, minced
2 celery stalks or 1 small bulb fennel, trimmed and chopped (optional)
3 large tomatoes, peeled, seeded and chopped
1½ cups (10½ oz/330 g) long-grain white rice, washed and drained
¼–½ teaspoon saffron threads, crushed and steeped in ¼ cup (2 fl oz/60 ml) hot water
1 teaspoon salt
½ teaspoon freshly ground pepper
3 cups (24 fl oz/750 ml) fish or chicken stock (see glossary) or water, heated
4 tablespoons chopped fresh flat-leaf (Italian) parsley or dill

In a large saucepan over medium-high heat, melt the butter. Add the shrimp and sauté, stirring constantly, until pink, for about 2 minutes. Using a slotted spoon, remove the shrimp to a bowl.

Add the onion and garlic to the butter remaining in the pan and sauté over low heat until beginning to soften, about 7 minutes. Add the celery (if using) and tomatoes and sauté for 3 minutes longer. Add the rice and stir well. Add the saffron and its steeping liquid, salt, pepper and heated stock or water. Bring to a boil, reduce the heat to low, cover and cook until the liquid has been absorbed and the rice is cooked, about 20 minutes.

Return the shrimp to the pan, stir once, and cover the pan. Turn off the heat and let the rice rest, covered, for 10 minutes. Fluff once with a fork, transfer to a warmed platter, sprinkle with the parsley or dill and serve.

SERVES 4

Clockwise from top left: Fried Cauliflower, Green Beans with Tomatoes, Simmered Fava Beans

EGYPT

Ful Mudammas

Simmered Fava Beans

In Egypt these flavorful brown beans are served for breakfast as well as other meals. Simply put, this is the national dish of Egypt. The beans can also be puréed and served as a meze *with the same garnishes as those used for the simmered beans. If fava beans are unavailable, pinto beans can be substituted. Pita bread, of course, is an ideal accompaniment.*

2 cups (14 oz/440 g) dried fava (small broad) beans
5–6 cups (40–48 fl oz/1.25–1.5 l) water, to cover
3 or 4 cloves garlic, minced
1 teaspoon ground cumin (optional)
salt
chopped fresh flat-leaf (Italian) parsley
lemon wedges
olive oil
beid hamine (recipe on page 50)
freshly ground pepper
pita bread (recipe on page 82)

❀ In a bowl combine the fava beans and water to cover generously and let soak in the refrigerator overnight. Drain.

❀ Place the beans in a saucepan and add the water making sure the beans are covered. Bring to a boil, reduce the heat to low, cover and simmer until tender, 2–5 hours. The cooking time will depend on the age and the size of the beans. When the beans are ready, add the garlic, cumin (if using) and salt to taste.

❀ Ladle into bowls. Set out the parsley, lemon wedges, oil, *beid hamine* and pepper for diners to add as they like. Pass the pita.

SERVES 6

LEBANON

Karnabeet Maklee

Fried Cauliflower

Not quite a fritter, but very delectable indeed. You can steam the cauliflower rather than boil it; use the same timing. In Turkey, cauliflower florets are dipped in flour, then in a mixture of eggs and grated kasseri *(see glossary) or Parmesan cheese and fried. In Sicily, cauliflower florets are placed in a baking dish; topped with a mixture of minced garlic, chopped parsley, grated* caciocavallo *cheese and fine dried bread crumbs; drizzled with melted butter; and baked in a moderately hot oven until crusty and golden. In Greece, cauliflower is cooked, then layered with tomato sauce and feta cheese and baked.*

1 large head cauliflower, separated into florets
salt to taste, plus 1 teaspoon salt
4 eggs
⅓ cup (3 fl oz/80 ml) water, or as needed
¾ cup (4 oz/125 g) all-purpose (plain) flour
½ cup (3 oz/90 g) finely minced onion or (1½ oz/45 g) green (spring) onions
½ cup (¾ oz/20 g) chopped fresh flat-leaf (Italian) parsley
½ cup (¾ oz/20 g) chopped fresh mint
½ teaspoon ground cinnamon
½ teaspoon ground allspice
½ teaspoon freshly ground pepper
vegetable oil for deep-frying
lemon wedges

❀ Bring a saucepan three-fourths full of water to a boil. Add the cauliflower and salt to taste and simmer until cooked but still firm, about 4 minutes. Drain and immerse in cold water to cool. Drain again and pat dry with paper towels. Let cool completely.

❀ In a bowl combine the eggs, ⅓ cup (3 fl oz/80 ml) water and the flour and whisk until smooth. Add the onion, parsley, mint, cinnamon, allspice, the 1 teaspoon salt and the pepper.

Stir well. Alternatively, mix the ingredients in a blender or in a processor fitted with the metal blade.

In a deep sauté pan, pour in oil to a depth of 3 in (7.5 cm) and heat to 375°F (190°C), or until a bit of batter dropped into the oil begins to color within moments. When the oil is ready, dip the florets into the batter, allowing the excess to drip back into the bowl, and then slip them into the hot oil; do not crowd the pan. Fry, turning once, until golden, 3–5 minutes. Using a slotted spoon transfer to paper towels to drain, and repeat with the remaining florets.

Arrange on a platter and serve with lemon wedges.

SERVES 4–6

LEBANON

LOUBIA BZEIT

Green Beans with Tomatoes

In the Middle East, green beans are often seasoned with sautéed onion and diced tomatoes or tomato sauce. Sometimes garlic is added; oregano, dill or mint is also sometimes used. In Greece, feta cheese is crumbled atop the cooked beans. In Turkey, ½ teaspoon ground allspice is added with the tomatoes. Okra can be prepared in the same way: Cut off the hard stems and dry the okra well with paper towels. Simmer for about 1 hour and add a squeeze of lemon juice at the end of cooking. In Greece, the okra is trimmed, soaked in 1 cup (8 fl oz/250 ml) red wine vinegar for 30 minutes and then drained and rinsed before cooking. The beans are cooked for a long time until very soft. This style of cooking may seem unappealing to those accustomed to tender, crisp vegetables, but try it.

1 lb (500 g) green beans, trimmed
3 tablespoons olive oil
1 cup (4 oz/125 g) chopped onion
1 or 2 cloves garlic, minced (optional)
4 cups (1½ lb/750 g) chopped tomatoes
pinch of sugar, if needed
½ cup (4 fl oz/125 ml) canned tomato purée (optional)
salt and freshly ground pepper
chopped fresh flat-leaf (Italian) parsley, mint, dill or oregano (optional)

Ideally the green beans are young, small beans. If they are large, however, remove any strings and cut into 2-in (5-cm) lengths. Set aside.

In a large sauté pan over medium heat, warm the oil. Add the onion and sauté until lightly browned and soft, 12–15 minutes. Add the garlic, if using, and cook for 1–2 minutes. Add the green beans and sauté for a few minutes longer. Then add the tomatoes and the purée, if using, and bring to a simmer. Cover and cook over very low heat until the tomatoes form a thick sauce, 45–60 minutes.

Season to taste with salt and pepper and with one of the herbs, if using. Transfer to a serving dish and serve hot, warm or at room temperature.

SERVES 6

CATALONIA

ARROZ A BANDA

Fish-Flavored Rice

In Spain, Valencia is the home of rice cultivation and cuisine. Spanish rice is a short-grain variety, rather like the Italian Arborio. This is an unusual rice dish in that it is served in two parts. The fish is cooked in stock and set aside for a second course. The stock is strained and reduced, then the rice is browned in oil and cooked in the reduced stock. The rice is served as a course by itself, a banda, *or "apart," accompanied by a very garlicky aioli (garlic sauce). A similar dish,* fideus a banda, *is made with thin dried pasta that is browned and cooked slowly in fish stock.*

FOR THE FISH STOCK:

2 lb (1 kg) fish heads, bones, small bony fish and shellfish shells, if available
2 tablespoons olive oil
1 large onion, coarsely chopped
2 cloves garlic (optional)
1 or 2 dried chili peppers (optional)
1 leek, chopped
2 carrots, chopped
2 bay leaves
1 lemon slice
12 peppercorns
few fresh sprigs of thyme, parsley and marjoram
6–8 cups (48–64 fl oz/1.5–2 l) water
salt

FOR THE FISH COURSE:

2 lb (1 kg) halibut, monkfish (anglerfish), cod or other white fish fillets or 1½ lb (750 g) fish fillets and 1 lb (500 g) shrimp (prawns), peeled and deveined

FOR THE RICE:

6 tablespoons (3 fl oz/90 ml) olive oil
4 cloves garlic, minced
2 tomatoes, peeled, seeded and chopped, or 2 tablespoons tomato paste
2 teaspoons paprika
2 cups (14 oz/440 g) short-grain rice, washed and drained
¼ teaspoon saffron threads, crushed
salt and freshly ground pepper

aioli made with 8 cloves garlic (recipe on page 144)

To make the stock, rinse the fish parts well and set aside. In a stockpot over medium heat, warm the oil. Add the onion, garlic and chili peppers (if using) and sauté for a few minutes. Add the fish parts and sauté, stirring often, for 1–2 minutes. Add all the remaining ingredients except the salt, adding the water as needed to cover.

Bring to a boil, skimming off any scum that forms on the surface. Reduce the heat to a simmer and cook for 25 minutes, skimming often. Strain the stock and reduce further over high heat to intensify the flavor. It will be used for cooking the fish and rice; you will need a little more than 4 cups (32 fl oz/1 l). Season to taste with salt.

To prepare the fish, bring the fish stock to a simmer in a wide, shallow saucepan. Add the fish and poach gently until it is cooked through but not falling apart; timing will depend upon thickness of fillets. Using a slotted spatula remove from the stock and set aside in a dish. Cover with just a little of the stock to keep it moist. If using shrimp add them to the stock separately and poach them until they turn pink, just a few minutes. Set aside with the fish.

In a paella pan or wide sauté pan over medium heat, warm the oil. Add the garlic and when it starts to turn pale gold, add the tomatoes or tomato paste. Cook, stirring, for about 5 minutes, then add the paprika and cook for 2 minutes longer. Add the rice and cook, stirring often, until colored a bit, about 3 minutes. Stir in the saffron and salt and pepper to taste.

Add 4 cups (32 fl oz/1 l) fish stock and cook for 5 minutes over high heat. Reduce the heat to low and simmer, uncovered, until the liquid has been absorbed and the rice is tender, about 15 minutes. Alternatively, cook the rice over high heat, uncovered, for 5 minutes, then place in a 350°F (180°C) oven for 15 minutes. Turn off the heat (or remove from the oven) and let the rice rest, covered, for 10 minutes.

Taste and adjust the seasoning.

Transfer the rice to a warmed platter and serve with the aioli. Serve the poached fish as a second course.

SERVES 6

Photograph pages 192–193

NORTH AFRICA

NORTH AFRICA

Morocco, Algeria, Tunisia

We complete our circuit of the Mediterranean by advancing in the footsteps of the Muslim armies of the seventh century, from Egypt along the coast of North Africa until we face Spain, our point of departure, from across the Strait of Gibraltar. The three modern states through which we pass, Morocco, Algeria and Tunisia, form a coherent geographical whole, consisting of a fairly narrow coastal plain separated from a vast desert hinterland by the Atlas and Aurès mountains. The western and eastern extremities of the region—northern Morocco and eastern Tunisia—are almost within shouting distance of Europe. North Africa thus served both as the base from which the Arab conquests of Spain and Sicily were launched, and as a refuge for Andalusians fleeing before the Reconquista. And as we noted earlier in connection with Marseilles, traffic between the North African and northern shores of the Mediterranean still continues unabated.

North Africa also possesses a distinct identity within the Arab world, being known as *al-Maghrib,* "the West," as opposed to *al-Mashriq,* "the East," consisting of historic Syria, Iraq and the Arabian peninsula. The dialects of Arabic spoken in North Africa are barely comprehensible to the easterner, and the specificity of the region is further underlined by the presence of the Berbers, its indigenous inhabitants since time immemorial. North Africa pos-

Previous pages: Although 85 percent of Algeria lies in the vast Sahara Desert, it has fertile oases that produce the most delicately flavored dates in the world. Left: Romans were perfecting the art of pottery in Nabeul, Tunisia, as early as 2000 years ago.

sesses accordingly its own rich and distinctive cuisine, one not only different, in large part, from the cuisine of the Arab East, but also infinitely better preserved. (Not surprisingly, this is true of traditional culture in general; no country in the Arab East, with the possible exception of Yemen, can boast of a perfectly preserved medieval city like Fès.)

If we except Ulysses's visit to the lotus eaters of Djerba, an island off the Tunisian coast (who may in any event have been eating ground jujube), North Africa is largely absent from the gastronomic lore of the ancient Mediterranean world. Essential elements of the Mediterranean diet were nonetheless available there quite early; the Carthaginians planted fruit trees, olive trees and cereal crops in the fifth century B.C. They were, however, essentially traders, and it was left to the Romans to develop North African agriculture on the grand scale. They treated the whole area as they did Spain and Sicily, as a granary to supply Rome, and to this end they built the canals and barrages, of which traces still remain, and organized the fertile lands of Numidia—eastern Algeria, in terms of contemporary geography—into latifundia, vast monocultural estates for the growing of wheat. It is doubtful that the Romans had any effect on the eating habits of the Berbers; the similarity between couscous, the grain, and polenta, that Etruscan remnant in the Roman diet, is slight and probably fortuitous.

Roman rule was brought to an end in the early fifth century A.D. by the Vandals, who after their expulsion from Spain were eager to pounce on the wheat fields of Numidia. As might be expected of a people whose achievements are immortalized in the word *vandalism,* the Vandals made no contribution, culinary or otherwise, to North Africa during their century of dominion. A degree of prosperity returned with the Byzantines, who repaired irrigation systems and reorganized the latifundia in keeping with their overall ambition of restoring the traditions of Roman rule throughout the Mediterranean. Unlike the Romans, however, the Byzantines believed in the need to impose direct rule, as well as their own mores, on the Berbers; this led to constant uprisings that combined with internecine strife among the Byzantines to devastate North African agriculture anew.

Sousse, a Tunisian port town that has recently found its niche as a tourist resort, caters to visitors searching for rugs and carpets.

The Arab-Muslim conquest of North Africa in the seventh century fixed the character and destiny of the region permanently as a distinct and culturally important zone of the Islamic world, linked not only to the Arab East but also to Spain (until the end of the fifteenth century) and to the Muslim lands of West Africa. All these connections were reflected in its cuisine, a circumstance that was in part the consequence of the unified rule established over Spain, Morocco, western Algeria and parts of Senegal by the Almoravide dynasty in the twelfth century. As in the Fertile Crescent, Spain and Sicily, the coming of Islam to North Africa ushered in a great flourishing of agriculture. The Roman irrigation systems were put in order once more, and in both Tunisia and Morocco subterranean canals were dug on the Iranian model to prevent the water from evaporating. The invasion of North Africa by the Bani Hilal nomads in the eleventh century damaged many of these installations, but they remain operative down to the present. The skill of the Arabs in extracting, conserving and channeling water contributed to the gastronomic well-being of North Africa in two interconnected ways. First, it increased the land available for cultivation of the new crops that arrived from the East: all manner of citrus fruits, a wider range of vegetables than those previously available, rice and sugar. Second, as the great reservoir outside the now-deserted city of Qayruwan makes clear, it made possible the foundation of great cities that, with their abundantly stocked markets and affluent courts, developed, almost automatically, regional styles of cuisine. It is no accident that what the Moroccan tourist brochures call the Royal Cities—Fès, Marrakech, Meknes and Rabat—are even today the principal centers of traditional Moroccan cuisine.

The two chief strands in North African cuisine are the Arab and the Berber. Most of its best-known dishes contain elements that can be assigned to the one or the other, but by and large it can be said that the Berber contribution is the original conception, and that of the Arab, the use of new ingredients and more sophisticated techniques of preparation. The word *couscous,* designating both the granules of semolina that are the foundation of the dish and the complete, bipartite preparation, including both the semolina and the stew poured over it, is an etymological mystery, being neither Berber nor Arab. The names *seksu* in Morocco and *ta'am* in Algeria (the latter having, significantly enough, the literal meaning of "food") are, in any event, more common. But the dish itself began no doubt as a simple Berber preparation of grain flavored only with butter. Then, as agriculture and abundance increased after the arrival of the Arabs, first chick-peas (garbanzos), pumpkins and gourds were added for extra flavor and substance, and then the dish was perfected with vegetable and meat stews. Couscous is justifiably the most celebrated food of North Africa, coming in a wide range of styles that reflect both different degrees of prosperity and regional preferences. The brightest star in the couscous constellation is perhaps that of Fès, prepared with chicken and lamb, seven vegetables, and seven spices that are offset by the sweetness of raisins. Tunisia likes its couscous unambiguously spicy, and often substitutes fish for chicken and lamb. Most lavish of all couscous dishes and furthest removed from Berber origins are those ceremonial preparations in which stuffed pigeons are embedded in the grain. Couscous is also the most widely traveled of all North African dishes; it is found in Sicily, Senegal and even Brazil.

The standard accompaniment for couscous is *harissa,* a hot sauce of red chilies. Chili peppers being an import from the New World, *harissa* cannot be ascribed to the original repertoire brought to North Africa by the Arabs. The suggestion that its name is derived from Orissa, a chili-growing district in India, is quite baseless, but there is a remarkable similarity between *harissa* and the *sambal oelek* of Malay-Indonesian cuisine, although the latter is made of only chilies and salt while spices go into *harissa.*

Tagine, the rich and varied stew of North Africa, belongs by contrast quite clearly to the classical Arab cuisine that was so heavily influenced by Iran. The mixture of sweet-and-sour tastes and the combination of a wide range of fruits as well as vegetables with a variety of meats were after all hallmarks of that cuisine, although it is now almost exclusively in North Africa that they are honored. Noticeable, too, is the frequent use of pigeons in *tagines,* as well as in some other dishes. Elsewhere in the Arab world, with the exception of Egypt, pigeons are these days generally spared from the cooking pot, their only role being to flutter peacefully in the courtyards of mosques. Among *tagines* particularly challenging to the palate we can mention lamb *tagine* with artichokes, lemons, and olives, and pigeon *tagine* with prunes and onions.

The jewel in the crown of North African cuisine is *b'stilla,* the intricate, flaky pie of pigeon or chicken prepared in differing ways in Fès, Rabat, Tetuan, Meknes and Marrakech. Its origins are sometimes thought to be Andalusian, since the word sounds vaguely Spanish and the rich combination of tastes proffered by *b'stilla* seems somehow to mirror all the restrained opulence of Hispano-Arab culture. As Paula Wolfert points out, however, *bestila* is a Berber word meaning "chicken cooked in butter and saffron," which is the very foundation of *b'stilla;* we may therefore conclude that the creation of this magnificent dish was a joint Berber and Arab enterprise. Here, the Arab contribution appears to have been the Persian-derived concept of enclosing meat with spices and nuts in pastry; the technique of making *ouarka,* thin layers of pastry akin to the *filo* used in making Turkish and Balkan *börek* but differing from it in some important respects; and the use of cinnamon and other seasonings.

Despite its tempestuous political history, North Africa has remained largely impregnable to external culinary influences after the Arab-Muslim conquest. It is to be noted, however, that the Andalusian refugees and migrants who came to North Africa in continuous waves, from the twelfth until the seventeenth century, brought with them something of their own culinary traditions. One of them, Ibn Zarin al-Tujibi, compiled a book of recipes with the express purpose of preserving Andalusian traditions; it is useful also for the comparisons it makes with the culinary styles of the Arab East. Andalusian cuisine, marked among other things by a complete eschewal of the butter beloved of the Berbers in favor of olive oil, is still cultivated in Tetuan and some districts of Fès.

Decorative mosaic art was an Eastern technique perfected in Andalusia and imported to Morocco by the Muslims of Spain.

North Africa underlined its separate identity by resisting full absorption into the Ottoman Empire, unlike the Arab East. Morocco never came under Ottoman dominion, and Ottoman rule was generally nominal in Algeria and Tunisia. There are, nonetheless, some traces of Ottoman culinary influence, faint in Morocco and somewhat stronger in Algeria and Tunisia. They consist of *kefte,* grilled mincemeat, the Turkish *köfte;* the *briks* of Tunisia, reminiscent, perhaps, of Moroccan *b'stilla,* but more clearly indebted in both substance and name to the Turkish *börek;* and *shurba,* the rich, pungent soup of Algeria and Tunisia, which mirrors in its name the Turkish fondness for soups, while using a hotter combination of spices than most Turks would countenance.

It is curious to note that it was the English merchants of Tangier who introduced the Moroccans to tea, although the tea they now drink—poured over mint leaves—is quite different; fortunately, there is no other trace of English influence on the food of North Africa. As for the French who colonized Algeria for 130 years and established shorter-lived protectorates in Morocco and Tunisia, their influence on the North African diet appears to have been minimal; not even the Francophone ruling elite that they trained saw any reason to trade in its cuisine for that of the conquerors.

Desserts, Preserves and Beverages

While the most common dessert is fruit, Mediterranean cuisines excel in rich and sugary pastries.

DESSERTS, PRESERVES AND BEVERAGES

In the Mediterranean, the most common dessert is a piece of fruit, and sweets and pastries are reserved for special occasions or for accompanying afternoon coffee or tea. When fruits are in season they are served at both lunch and dinner, on plates or in big bowls; during the hot-weather months, they are set in vessels filled with ice water. While these fruits can be eaten out of hand, they are often pared and sliced deftly with a knife and fork.

When fruits are in great abundance and cannot be eaten instantly, they are turned into compotes, baked, dried, candied or put up into jewellike jams and preserves. The assortment of Mediterranean fruits is rich with diversity: peaches, apricots, plums, strawberries, raspberries, tart and sweet cherries, green and black figs, dates, all kinds of melons, loquats, quince, apples, pears, pomegranates, persimmons, grapes and a variety of citrus fruits. Bananas and avocados are grown in Israel, and even pineapple and mangoes appear at the market.

While many fruit preserves in the Mediterranean are eaten with bread, in the eastern countries they are more often served with rich black coffee or eaten from a spoon with a glass of ice cold water for sipping afterward. Sometimes the preserves are served with a bit of thickened cream. Rose-petal preserves are especially nice spooned on top of vanilla ice cream and add an exotic closing note to dinner. Candied fruit peels are served with little pastries as part of coffee service.

Ice creams, sherbets and *granite* are seldom made at home; they are served in cafes and special ice cream shops or sold from carts by street vendors. The variety of flavors—apricot, chocolate, coffee, vanilla, lemon, hazelnut, strawberry, pistachio—is amazing and one is tempted to sample as many as possible, followed by a cool glass of water and a long walk. In the eastern Mediterranean, ice cream is made with *sahleb* (ground dried orchid) and mastic, which give it a chewy texture that may seem out of place to those familiar only with creamy custard-based ice creams.

Along with ice creams, puddings made with dried fruit, rice, bread, semolina and milk are much enjoyed. Both honey and sugar are used for sweetening desserts and pastries. Nuts appear in profusion: walnuts, almonds, hazelnuts, pine nuts and pistachios. Dried fruits—apricots, figs, dates—and nuts are cooked in compotes flavored with rose water or orange-blossom water, or are tucked into cookies, *filo* and *konafa* pastries, and tarts. Fresh soft-curd cheese is used as a filling for tarts and small pastries. Because coffee and tea are so central to Mediterranean culture, there is a whole range of cookies, small pastries and candies that are associated with these drinks. Some are baked and others are fried.

The popularity of French and Italian bakeries and restaurants throughout the world has given many people the opportunity to experience fine examples of pastries and sweets of southern France and Italy. Most of us are more poorly informed about the pastries of the eastern Mediterranean, which, when discovered in shops outside

Previous pages: Rose Petal Preserves (recipe page 228)

the region, are too often leaden, overly sweet and soggy with syrup. The pastries presented here will assure that these same sweets can be as light and delicate as any French creation. They are usually prepared with *konafa* or *filo* dough. The former looks like wiry strands of wheat and is sometimes sold under the name *kadayifi filo.* It is made by passing a batter of flour and water through a brass sieve onto hot metal sheets. The dough sets up in moments and then the strands are pushed to the side to clear the way for making more. *Filo* leaves are the well-known thin pastry sheets of Greece. *Ouarka,* their Moroccan and Tunisian cousins, like *filo,* require considerable skill to make and thus are usually purchased from shops that specialize in turning out the fragile dough.

While wine is served with meals throughout France, Italy, Spain and Greece, in the Muslim countries alcoholic beverages are replaced by teas, yogurt drinks, and syrups and fruit juices mixed with ice, soda or water and called *sharbat,* from the Arabic *shariba,* "to drink." In France, Italy, Spain and Greece flavored liqueurs are savored after dessert and coffee. Some of these are made at home according to recipes that have been in families for years, such as the Provençal orange brandy called *ratafia.* Liqueurs are made from nuts or fruits or are scented with spices and herbs and even flower petals.

Coffee is an important part of daily life in Italy, France and the Middle East. The Arabs, Turks and Greeks prepare coffee in a special single-handled pot with very finely ground coffee powder and sweeten it according to personal taste, which is sometimes too sweet for the outside visitor. Cardamom seeds, rose water or orange-blossom water may be added. After the coffee is drunk, the cups are turned upside down and left for about ten minutes. They are then righted and the sediment is "read" by a fortune-teller.

Coffee houses emerged in Mediterranean cities in the sixteenth century.

The ritual of serving coffee and sweets is the essence of Mediterranean hospitality. Today, with so many women active in the workplace, home baking is gradually becoming only a memory. Most pastries are now purchased from shops bursting with a tempting variety of traditional sweets. (In Athens I once tasted nine versions of baklava at a single coffee-filled sitting, to discover how they differed and to find my favorite.) For special holidays, however, the old recipes are prepared at home by those who still remember. Some of these recipes appear here, culled from books and family recipe collections.

Egyptian boys shimmy up palm trees to get to the hanging clusters of delectable dates.

Left to right: Cherry Pancake, Pears in Red Wine

PROVENCE

Clafouti aux Cerises

Cherry Pancake

Some cooks make this dessert with eggs and milk, and serve it as a warm custard. Others pour the custard into a rich pie shell and serve it as a cherry custard pie. The most popular version, however, adds flour to the custard and turns it into a savory pancake. In France, they seldom pit the cherries, so diners are always on the alert for the pits. You will worry less about your guests if you pit the cherries first.

3 cups (1 lb/500 g) pitted Bing cherries
1½ cups (12 fl oz/375 ml) milk
4 eggs
½ cup (2½ oz/75 g) all-purpose (plain) flour
¼ cup (2 oz/60 g) granulated sugar
2 teaspoons vanilla extract (essence)
1 tablespoon kirsch
confectioners' (icing) sugar

Preheat an oven to 350°F (180°C). Butter a 1½-qt (1.5-l) shallow baking dish or wide gratin dish or a 10-in (25-cm) pie plate.

Pat the cherries dry with paper towels. Spread the cherries on the bottom of the prepared pan.

To make the batter, in a blender or in a food processor fitted with the metal blade, combine the milk, eggs, flour, granulated sugar, vanilla and kirsch. Process until mixed. Stop the machine and scrape down the sides of the container, then process again. Alternatively, in a bowl with an electric mixer set on medium speed, beat together the eggs and granulated sugar. Slowly add the milk, vanilla and kirsch, continuing to beat until fully incorporated. The batter should be lump-free. If it is not, strain it through a fine-mesh sieve.

Pour the batter evenly over the cherries. Bake on the middle shelf of the oven until the top is golden brown and a knife inserted in the center comes out clean, 45–60 minutes. Sprinkle with confectioners' sugar and serve while still very warm.

SERVES 6

FRANCE

Poires au Vin Rouge

Pears in Red Wine

Spain, France, Greece and Italy all claim this dessert with minor variations. While cinnamon, cloves and strips of orange or lemon zest are traditionally added to the poaching liquid, a few black peppercorns or bay leaves will also contribute a wonderful perfume to the pears. The pears become crimson in the syrup and intensify in color the longer they macerate, so you may want to make this dessert a few days ahead.

3 cups (24 fl oz/750 ml) dry red wine
1 cup (8 oz/250 g) sugar
2 cinnamon sticks, each about 2 in (5 cm) long
4 whole cloves
1 orange or lemon zest strip, about 3 in (7.5 cm) long, or both
1 teaspoon fennel seeds or aniseeds (optional)
a few peppercorns (optional)
2 small bay leaves (optional)
6 large firm pears, peeled, and cored from the bottom leaving the stem intact

In a saucepan combine the wine, sugar, cinnamon sticks, cloves, citrus zest and the fennel seeds, aniseeds, peppercorns or bay leaves, if using. Bring to a boil, stirring until the sugar dissolves. Simmer for 5 minutes, then slip the pears into the syrup, cover and simmer until the pears are tender, about 25 minutes.

Using a slotted spoon remove the pears from the syrup and place in a serving bowl. Cover and refrigerate. Remove and discard the citrus zest, cinnamon stick, cloves, peppers and seeds from the poaching syrup. If the syrup is thin, reduce it over high heat until thickened enough to coat a spoon, then remove from the heat and let cool.

When the syrup is cold, pour it over the pears. Re-cover and chill for a few hours before serving.

SERVES 6

PROVENCE

Tarte au Citron

Lemon Tart

The perfect balance of sweet and tart, encased in a rich pie shell. You may garnish the tart with whipped cream or berries, if you like.

FOR THE PASTRY:

1¼ cups (6½ oz/200 g) all-purpose (plain) flour
pinch of salt
2 tablespoons sugar
½ cup (¼ lb/125 g) unsalted butter, chilled and cut into ¼-in (6-mm) pieces
1 egg yolk
2 teaspoons fresh lemon juice
1 tablespoon grated lemon zest
1 tablespoon ice water, or as needed

FOR THE FILLING:

4 eggs, separated
¾ cup (6 oz/185 g) sugar
juice of 2 large lemons (about ½ cup/4 fl oz/125 ml)
grated zest of 2 large lemons (about 2 tablespoons)
1 teaspoon cornstarch (cornflour) dissolved in 2 tablespoons water
pinch of salt

❀ To make the pastry, in a food processor fitted with the metal blade, combine the flour, salt and sugar. Add the butter and, using on-off pulses, process until the mixture resembles cornmeal. Add the egg yolk, lemon juice and zest, and the 1 tablespoon ice water and process just until the dough holds together. Add a few drops more ice water if dough is too dry. Gather into a ball, enclose in plastic wrap and refrigerate for about 1 hour. Alternatively, to make by hand, in a bowl stir together the flour, salt and sugar. Add the butter and, using a pastry blender or 2 knives, cut in until the mixture resembles cornmeal. Using a fork, mix in the egg, lemon juice and zest, and ice water. Once the dough forms a rough mass, gather it into a ball and wrap and refrigerate as directed.

❀ Preheat an oven to 400°F (200°C).

❀ On a lightly floured surface, roll out the dough into a round large enough to fit a 9-in (23-cm) tart pan with removable bottom. Transfer the dough round to the pan and ease it into the pan. Trim off the excess dough. Prick with a fork and then line with aluminum foil and weight with pie weights, beans or rice. Bake for about 10 minutes, then remove the weights and foil. Reduce the heat to 350°F (180°C) and continue to bake the crust until set, about 10 minutes longer. Remove from the oven and let cool.

❀ To make the filling, in a bowl with an electric mixer set on high speed, beat together the yolks and half the sugar until pale and thick. Beat in the lemon juice and zest and the cornstarch mixture. Transfer to a saucepan and place over very low heat. Cook, stirring often, until the mixture thickens to the consistency of mayonnaise, about 5 minutes. Remove from the heat and rest in a bowl of ice to cool completely.

❀ Meanwhile, again preheat the oven to 400°F (200°C). In a bowl place the egg whites and the salt. Beat, gradually adding the remaining sugar, until stiff peaks form. Stir about one-fourth of the whites into the yolk mixture to lighten it, then gently fold in the remaining whites.

❀ Spoon the lemon mixture into the pastry shell. Bake until the crust is lightly browned and the filling is set, about 15 minutes.

❀ Remove from the oven to a wire rack to cool, then cut into wedges to serve.

SERVES 8

Lemon Tart

GREECE

Syka Sto Fournou

Baked Figs

Although this dessert has a Greek name, it turns up in Turkey, France, Spain and Italy as well. It doesn't matter if the figs are the green Adriatic or the black Mission variety. They just need to be ripe and heavy in the hand. You can make this dish with lemon zest and add a little lemon juice to the mixture if the orange juice is very sweet. Spanish cooks would use anisette instead of brandy. If you like, omit the almonds and top with a dollop of sweetened thickened yogurt (see glossary).

24 small or 12 large ripe figs
¼ cup (3 oz/90 g) fragrant honey
½ cup (4 fl oz/125 ml) orange juice
¼ cup (2 fl oz/60 ml) brandy
4–6 small bay leaves
a few thin orange zest strips
½ cup (2½ oz/75 g) almonds, toasted (optional)

Preheat an oven to 350°F (180°C).

Prick the figs in a few places with the tines of a fork so that they can absorb the cooking juices. Place upright in a baking dish. In a small bowl stir together the honey, orange juice and brandy and pour over the figs. Add a little water, if necessary, so that the liquid covers the bottom of the dish to a depth of about ¼ in (6 mm). Tuck in the bay leaves and the strips of zest.

Cover and bake, basting occasionally with the pan juices, until the figs are soft, 25–35 minutes. Transfer to individual dishes and sprinkle with the almonds. Serve warm or at room temperature.

SERVES 6

GREECE

Karithopitta

Walnut Cake

This walnut cake is traditionally soaked in syrup, making it quite rich. Without the syrup, however, it is very light and can be served with a fruit compote or a little sweetened yogurt (see glossary) or whipped cream.

FOR THE SYRUP:

¾ cup (6 oz/185 g) sugar
1 cup (8 fl oz/250 ml) water
½ cup (6 oz/185 g) honey
4 whole cloves
1 tablespoon fresh lemon juice
1 lemon zest strip (optional)

½ cup (4 oz/125g) unsalted butter, at room temperature
⅓ cup (3 oz/90 g) sugar
6–8 eggs, separated
¼ cup (1½ oz/45 g) all-purpose (plain) flour
2 teaspoons baking powder
2 teaspoons ground cinnamon
¼ teaspoon ground cloves
pinch of salt
2½ cups (10 oz/315 g) ground walnuts
½ cup (1½ oz/45 g) zweiback crumbs (optional)
1 tablespoon grated orange zest (optional)

To make the syrup, in a saucepan combine the sugar, the water and honey. Bring to a boil over medium heat, stirring to dissolve the sugar. Add the whole cloves and lemon juice and zest (if using), reduce the heat to low and simmer until thickened, about 10 minutes. Remove from the heat and remove and discard the cloves and zest, if used. Let cool completely.

Preheat an oven to 350°F (180°C). Lightly butter and flour a 9-by-12-by-3 in (23-by-30-by-7.5-cm) cake pan.

In a bowl with an electric mixer set on high speed, cream together the butter and sugar until fluffy. Add the egg yolks, one at a time, beating well after each addition. Beat until fully incorporated.

In another bowl sift together the flour, baking powder, cinnamon, ground cloves and salt. Fold this into the egg mixture. Fold in the nuts, the zweiback crumbs and orange zest (if using).

In yet another bowl beat the whites until stiff peaks form. Stir one-third of the whites into the batter to lighten it, then gently fold in the remaining whites. Pour into the prepared pan.

Bake until the cake is dark golden brown and springs back when touched with a finger, about 40 minutes. Remove from the oven and immediately pour the cooled syrup over the cake. Let cool completely in the pan.

To serve, cut into 12–16 squares or lozenges.

MAKES 12–16 PIECES

TURKEY

Gül Reçelİ

Rose Petal Preserves

Fragrant and exotic, this preserve is nice over vanilla ice cream or just eaten with a spoon.

½ lb (250 g) pesticide-free fresh red rose petals with a strong fragrance
juice of 2 lemons
1 cup (8 fl oz/250 ml) water
2 cups (1 lb/500 g) sugar
2 tablespoons rosewater

Wash the petals without bruising them and place in a bowl. Squeeze the juice of 1 lemon over them. Let sit for 10 minutes. Transfer to a food processor fitted with the metal blade. Pulse until finely chopped. Or finely chop by hand.

Transfer the petals to a large nonreactive saucepan with any lemon juice remaining in the bottom of the bowl. Add the water and bring to a boil. Reduce the heat to low and simmer until the petals are tender. This can take as little as 10 minutes or as long as 30 minutes, depending upon the roses. Add the sugar and the juice of the second lemon and simmer until the syrup thickens to a jam consistency, about 30 minutes longer. It should register about 220°F (104°C) on a candy thermometer when ready or until a large spoonful dropped onto a saucer chilled in the freezer sets within 2 minutes.

Remove from the heat and stir in the rosewater. Let cool, then skim. Ladle into hot, sterilized jars and seal according to manufacturer's instructions. Store in a cool, dark place.

MAKES 2–3 HALF-PINTS (16–24 FL OZ/500–750 ML)

Photograph pages 222–223

Left to right: Walnut Cake, Baked Figs

T U R K E Y

KADAYİF

Konafa Pastry

The pastry used to make this sweet resembles shredded wheat or vermicelli, is called konafa *in Arabic and is sold in 1-pound (500-g) packages. It dries out very quickly so keep it covered until you brush it with butter. This pastry can be filled with nuts, semolina cream or sweetened cheese. All three fillings are included here; select the one that appeals to you. The pastry can be prepared in large pans in the same manner as baklava, or it can be cut into 5-inch (13-cm) lengths, some filling placed at one end and rolled. It is usually covered with a cold syrup while it is still hot.*

FOR THE SYRUP:

3 cups (1½ lb/750 g) sugar
2 cups (16 fl oz/500 ml) water
1 tablespoon fresh lemon juice
1 orange zest strip (optional)

FOR THE ALMOND FILLING:

1½ cups (6 oz/185 g) ground almonds
1 cup (8 oz/250 g) sugar
1 tablespoon ground cinnamon
½ cup (4 fl oz/125 ml) fresh orange juice

FOR THE CHEESE FILLING:

1½ cups (12 oz/375 g) ricotta cheese
1 tablespoon rosewater or orange-flower water
½ cup (4 oz/125 g) sugar

FOR THE CREAM FILLING:

2 cups (16 fl oz/500 ml) milk
3 tablespoons sugar
¼ cup (1½ oz/45 g) fine semolina
1 tablespoon rosewater

½–1 cup (4–8 oz/125–250 g) unsalted butter, melted
1 package (1 lb/500 g) *konafa* pastry

To make the syrup, in a saucepan combine the sugar, the water, lemon juice and orange zest (if using). Bring to a boil over medium heat, stirring to dissolve the sugar. Reduce the heat to low and simmer until thickened, about 10 minutes. Remove from the heat and remove and discard the zest, if used. Cool the syrup completely.

Make one of the fillings: To make the almond filling, in a bowl stir together the almonds, sugar, cinnamon and orange juice, mixing well. To make the cheese filling, in a bowl stir together the ricotta, flower water and sugar, mixing well. To make the cream filling, in a small saucepan over medium heat, combine the milk and sugar and bring to a boil, stirring to dissolve the sugar. Place the semolina in a small bowl and stir a little of the warm milk into it to make a smooth paste. Stir this paste into the pan of milk and then cook over low heat, stirring, until the mixture thickens, about 5 minutes. Remove from the heat, stir in the rosewater and let cool.

Preheat an oven to 350°F (180°C). Using a wide pastry brush, spread melted butter on the bottom and sides of a 9-by-12-by-3-in (23-by-30-by-7.5-cm) baking dish. Open the pastry packet and pull apart the strands. In a bowl toss half the pastry with about half of the melted butter, or as needed to coat. Place in the prepared baking dish. Spread with the almond, cheese or cream filling. Toss the remaining pastry strands with as much melted butter as needed to coat. Distribute the pastry evenly atop the filling. Tuck in any loose strands.

Bake until the top is golden, 45–60 minutes. Remove from the oven and immediately pour the cooled syrup over the hot pastry. Let cool completely.

To serve, cut into 16–20 squares.

MAKES 16–20 SQUARES

G R E E C E

BAKLAVA

Filo Pastry with Nuts

The most famous of Middle Eastern pastries. The word baklava *is Turkish for "lozenge." The dessert, however, is found in Greek, Turkish and Arab sweets shops and the variations on the theme are countless. Not only can it be filled with nuts, but also with semolina-thickened cream, fruit, and in Athens once I even ate chocolate baklava! The most common baklava is made with walnuts or a combination of walnuts and almonds. Some syrups are made with clove and cinnamon; others include lemon juice or a fragrant flower water. Although most people have come to associate baklava with a rich, sticky honey syrup, most Greek (and Turkish) recipes do not include honey. While this is not a light dessert, it is infinitely lighter minus the honey. Some recipes call for layering half the pastry sheets on the bottom, topping with the nuts and then layering with the remaining pastry; this recipe, however, layers only 6–8 pastry sheets at a time. The story goes that, in any case, there must be 40 layers of pastry, to represent the 40 days of Lent. But who's counting?*

FOR THE SYRUP:

1¼ cups (10 oz/315 g) sugar
½ cup (4 fl oz/125 ml) water
1 tablespoon fresh lemon juice
1 lemon zest strip (optional)
1 cinnamon stick, about 2 in (5 cm) long, and 2 whole cloves (optional)
1 tablespoon orange-flower water or rosewater (optional)

½ lb (250 g) walnuts or half walnuts and half almonds, coarsely ground
3 tablespoons sugar
1 teaspoon ground cinnamon (optional)
1 cup (8 oz/250 g) unsalted butter, melted and clarified or skimmed of froth (see glossary)
28–32 *filo* sheets (see glossary)

To make the syrup, in a saucepan combine the sugar, the water, lemon juice and the lemon zest and cinnamon stick or cloves, if using. Bring to a boil, stirring to dissolve the sugar. Reduce the heat to low and simmer until thickened, about 10 minutes. Remove from the heat and, if necessary, discard the zest, cinnamon stick, and cloves. Stir in the flower water, if using, and set aside to cool and allow the flavors to mellow.

In a bowl stir together the ground nuts, sugar and ground cinnamon (if using).

Preheat an oven to 350°F (180°C). Using a wide pastry brush, spread melted butter on the bottom and sides of a 12-by-15-by-3-in (30-by-37.5-by-7.5-cm) pan or dish (or a pan that is the exact size of the *filo* sheets, if you can find one). One by one and brushing each sheet with butter, layer about 8 *filo* sheets in the pan. Top with about one-third of the nuts. Layer 6–8 more *filo* sheets, buttering each sheet, then half of the remaining nuts. Top with another 6–8 buttered *filo* sheets, then the remaining nuts. End with 8 buttered *filo* sheets on top. Butter the top layer generously. (If possible, cover and refrigerate the baklava for about 30 minutes, so the butter can set up. It will make cutting the pastry easier before baking.) Using a sharp knife, cut the baklava into 25–30 diamond shapes.

Bake for 30 minutes, then reduce the heat to 300°F (150°C) and bake until the top is golden, 15–20 minutes longer.

Remove from the oven and immediately pour the cooled syrup over the hot baklava. Let cool completely. To serve, recut the pastry with a sharp knife.

MAKES 25–30 PIECES

Left to right: Konafa Pastry, Filo Pastry with Nuts, Coffee

TURKEY

Kahve

Coffee

Turkish coffee, sometimes labeled Arab coffee, is available at stores specializing in foods of the Middle East. It is drunk throughout the region. The coffee comes finely ground and is prepared in a small brass or metal pot variously called a cezve *in Turkey and a* jazoua, ibrik, rakwi *or* tanaka, *depending upon which other country in the region you are in. This pot has a long handle and a narrow neck. In some countries there is a belief that the coffee must boil up 3–5 times for luck; the difference in number of times depends upon tradition. Some people add cardamom seeds, a pinch of cinnamon or some rosewater or orange-flower water. After the coffee boils and is poured, the grounds must not be disturbed. One can ask for his or her coffee to be brewed to a specific sweetness:* helou *or* sekerli *(sweet),* mezbout *or* orta *(medium) and* murra *or* sade *(unsweetened), but the coffee is usually sweet regardless of pronouncements.*

Some people boil the water and sugar first, then stir in the coffee, but it is easier to combine all three and then bring the mixture to a boil. If you are using the seeds, add them while the coffee is boiling. Add the flower water after the coffee has boiled.

FOR EACH SERVING:

1 heaping teaspoon sugar
1 heaping teaspoon finely ground Turkish coffee
½ cup (4 fl oz/125 ml) water
a few cardamom seeds (optional)
a few drops of rosewater (optional)

❀ In a small, narrow pan combine the sugar, coffee, water and cardamom seeds (if using) multiplying the amounts according to the number of people you are serving. Stir well to combine and then bring to a boil and let the mixture foam up to the top of the pan. Remove from the heat for 1 minute. Return the coffee to the heat and bring to a frothy boil. Pour into small cups and serve at once. Be sure that everyone gets some foam, by wiggling the pot while you pour.

SERVES 1

TURKEY

Kabagi Tatlisi

Pumpkin with Walnuts

In Turkey, there is a story that Prophet Mohammed ate pumpkin before ascending to heaven, so this dish is usually made on Mirac, his ascension day. In Sicily and Spain, the pumpkin is cooked first in water until tender for 10–15 minutes, drained and then cooked in sugar syrup for about 35 minutes until it forms a jam. It is used as a cake filling. In Sicily the pumpkin might be cooked with jasmine flowers or with a little cinnamon, orange-flower water or rosewater. In Spain this same basic mixture is known as cabello d'angel.

1 small pumpkin or piece of pumpkin, 2 lb (1 kg), peeled, seeded and cut into 1-in (2.5-cm) cubes
⅔–1 cup (5–8 oz/155–250 g) sugar
½ cup (4 fl oz/125 ml) water, or as needed
lemon zest, cinnamon stick or whole cloves (optional)
⅔ cup (2½ oz/75 g) chopped toasted walnuts or almonds
kaymak or clotted cream for serving (see glossary)

Layer the pumpkin pieces in a shallow saucepan, sprinkling the sugar between the layers. Add the water and the lemon zest, cloves or cinnamon stick, if using. Bring to a simmer, cover and cook over low heat until the pumpkin has absorbed almost all the water and is tender, about 30 minutes. Remove from the heat and let cool.

Transfer to a serving dish or individual dishes. Sprinkle with the nuts and serve with *kaymak* (cut into slices) or clotted cream on the side.

SERVES 8

TURKEY

Ayva Kompostosu

Quince Compote

The seeds of the quinces contribute to the wonderful rosy color of the cooked fruits. So even though you remove the seeds from the fruit for cooking, always add them to the cooking liquids, if you want the quince to turn red. Long simmering is also required for the color to change. If you want to speed up the coloring process, add pomegranate juice to the cooking liquids.

6 quinces, about 2 lb (1 kg) total weight
12 whole cloves
1½ cups (12 oz/375 g) sugar
3 cups (24 fl oz/750 ml) water or part pomegranate juice (see glossary)

Peel the quinces, cut them in half lengthwise and remove the cores and seeds. Tie the peels and seeds in a small piece of cheesecloth (muslin).

Arrange the quince halves hollow side up, in a wide saucepan. Insert a clove in the middle of each quince. Tuck the seed packet among the quinces, then sprinkle with sugar and add the water, or water and pomegranate juice. Bring to a boil, reduce the heat to very low, cover and simmer until the quinces are soft, about 1 hour.

To serve, transfer to individual plates and spoon the syrup over the top. Serve warm or at room temperature.

SERVES 6

Top to bottom: Quince Compote, Oranges in Fragrant Syrup, Pumpkin with Walnuts

TURKEY

Portokal Kompostosu

Oranges in Fragrant Syrup

A version of this dessert is at home in Turkey, Greece, North Africa and Provence. The oranges are covered in a syrup perfumed with orange-flower water and cinnamon. Serve garnished with just the orange zest in the syrup, or top with toasted almonds or chopped fresh mint.

6 large oranges
1½ cups (12 oz/375 g) sugar
½ cup (4 fl oz/125 ml) water
1 cinnamon stick, about 2 in (5 cm) long
¼ cup (3 oz/90 g) honey
3 tablespoons orange-flower water

Using a vegetable peeler remove the zest from the oranges. Cut away all traces of the bitter white pith. Cut the orange zest into thin, narrow strips. Separate the oranges into segments by carefully cutting between the membranes with a sharp knife. Put the segments into a bowl, cover and refrigerate.

Bring a saucepan three-fourths full of water to a boil. Add the orange zest and boil for 3–5 minutes. Drain and refresh in cold water. Drain again and set aside.

In a saucepan combine the sugar, the water, cinnamon stick and honey and bring to a boil over high heat. Cook briskly until a very thick syrup forms, about 230°F (110°C) on a candy thermometer. Remove from the heat.

Remove and discard the cinnamon stick. Stir in the reserved orange zest and the orange-flower water. Pour the syrup over the orange segments, re-cover and chill for about 4 hours.

To serve, transfer to individual plates. Spoon the syrup with the zest over the top.

SERVES 6

SICILY

Cassata alla Siciliana

Layered Ricotta Cake

The best Italian desserts are arguably found in Sicily. The classic pan di spagna *("Spanish bread"), or sponge cake, is layered with ricotta laced with candied fruits and sometimes shaved chocolate. The assembled* cassata *can be frosted with egg-white icing, a layer of marzipan or chocolate. This* cassata *is not to be confused with* cassata gelata, *a frozen dessert, or* cassata al forno, *a tart filled with the same ricotta mixture. The word* cassata *comes from the Arab* quasat, *which means "round pan" or "bowl." You may find it easier to assemble and serve the* cassata *in a loaf shape, however.*

FOR THE SPONGE CAKE:

6 large eggs
1 cup (8 oz/250 g) sugar
pinch of salt
1 cup (4 oz/125 g) cake flour
pinch of ground cinnamon
1 teaspoon grated orange zest
2 teaspoons vanilla extract (essence)

FOR THE RICOTTA FILLING:

2 cups (1 lb/500 g) ricotta cheese
¼ cup (2 fl oz/60 ml) heavy (double) cream
½ cup (4 oz/125 g) sugar
½ teaspoon ground cinnamon
½ cup (3 oz/75 g) semisweet chocolate bits or chopped chocolate
¼ cup (1 oz/30 g) diced candied fruits such as citron and orange zest

½ cup (4 fl oz/125 ml) sweet Marsala, dark rum, Cointreau or crème de cacao

FOR THE ICING:

¾ lb (375 g) semisweet chocolate, chopped
¾ cup (6 fl oz/180 ml) double-strength brewed coffee
½ cup (¼ lb/125 g) unsalted butter
¼ cup (2 fl oz/60 ml) dark rum or crème de cacao

Preheat an oven to 350°F (180°C). Butter a 10½-by-15½-in (26.5-by-39-cm) jelly roll pan, then line with parchment paper.

To make the cake, in a mixing bowl placed over (not touching) warm water, whisk together the eggs, sugar and salt. Whisk until the sugar is dissolved and the mixture feels warm. Using an electric mixer set on high speed, beat until the mixture is thick and pale and holds a 3-second ribbon when the beater is lifted. Sift together the flour and cinnamon over the batter, then add the orange zest and vanilla and fold until blended.

Pour the batter into the prepared pan. Bake until the cake shrinks away from the sides of the pan and a tester inserted in the center comes out clean, 10–15 minutes. Remove from the oven and cool in the pan.

To make the filling, by hand or with an electric mixer, beat together the ricotta, cream, sugar and cinnamon until light and fluffy. Fold in the chocolate and candied fruits.

To assemble the cassata, line the bottom and sides of a 5-by-9-by-3-in (13-by-23-by-7.5-cm) loaf pan with parchment paper.

Turn the cake out of the pan onto a work surface and peel off the parchment. Cut the cake crosswise into thirds to fit the insides of the loaf pan precisely. Place 1 strip on the bottom of the loaf pan and brush with some of the wine or liqueur. Spread half of the ricotta filling on the cake. Place another strip of cake over the filling, brush with more wine or liqueur and then spread the remaining filling on top. Cover with the third cake strip and brush with the remaining liqueur. Cover with plastic wrap and refrigerate for at least 2 hours, preferably, or for up to 1 day.

Left to right: Layered Ricotta Cake, Lemon Ice

To make the icing, combine the chocolate and coffee in the top pan of a double boiler and heat over simmering water, stirring occasionally, until melted. Remove from the heat and stir in the butter and then the rum or liqueur. Let cool completely, stirring occasionally.

Carefully invert the loaf pan onto a serving platter and lift it off of the cake. Whip the icing until it is fluffy and spread it over the top and sides of the cake. Serve immediately or cover and refrigerate for up to 1 hour, then bring to room temperature before serving.

To serve, bring the cake to room temperature and cut into slices 1 in (2.5 cm) thick.

SERVES 8

SICILY

Granita di Limone

Lemon Ice

Orange or grapefruit juice and zest can be used in place of the lemon. Adjust the sweetness to taste. Berries make a nice garnish.

1 cup (8 fl oz/250 ml) water
1 cup (8 oz/250 g) sugar
pinch of salt
2 cups (16 fl oz/500 ml) strained fresh lemon juice
2 tablespoons grated lemon zest (optional)

In a small saucepan combine the water, sugar and salt. Bring to a simmer over medium heat, stirring until the sugar dissolves. Pour into a shallow metal pan. Cover and place in the freezer until ice crystals begin to form, 2–3 hours, depending upon the freezer.

Break up the crystals with a fork, re-cover and freeze again. Repeat this process every 30 minutes until the mixture is slushy, 2–3 hours.

Spoon the *granita* into dessert bowls and eat promptly before it melts.

SERVES 4–6

TURKEY

EKMEK KADAYİF

Bread and Honey Pudding with Kaymak

If you don't have time to make kaymak *as a garnish for this pudding, use whipped or clotted cream or crème fraîche. This dessert of honey-coated bread is very sweet and rich, but delicious. It needs the cream for relief.*

1 small round loaf white French or Italian bread, unsliced
½ cup (4 fl oz/125 ml) milk
1½ cups (18 oz/560 g) fragrant honey
juice of 2 large lemons (about ½ cup/4 fl oz/125 ml)
kaymak made with 2 cups (16 fl oz/500 ml) heavy (double) cream, sliced (see glossary)

Preheat an oven to 350°F (180°C).

Cut the bread in half horizontally. Remove and discard the crusts. Cut each half into a slice 1½ in (4 cm) thick. Place the 2 bread slices on a baking sheet.

Bake until toasted, golden and almost crisp, 15–20 minutes. Remove from the oven, sprinkle the slices with the milk and then wrap them in a cloth towel until the milk is absorbed, about 5 minutes. Reduce the oven temperature to 300°F (150°C).

In a saucepan combine the honey and lemon juice and bring to a boil. Meanwhile, unwrap the bread slices and place them in a shallow baking dish just large enough to hold them. If you like, cut the bread into 2–3-in (5–7.5-cm) square pieces.

Pour the hot honey mixture evenly over the bread. Bake until the honey is absorbed and the bread is golden, about 30 minutes. Remove from the oven and let rest until warm.

Transfer the warm pudding to individual plates and garnish with the slices of *kaymak* cream. (If the kaymak is not firm enough to slice, it will still be wonderful as thickened cream atop the dessert.) Serve at once.

SERVES 6–8

LEBANON

MUHALLABIA AMARDINE

Amardine Cream

Sheets of dried apricots, or amardine, *are used to make this dessert, but individually dried apricots can be used as well. These dried apricots vary in sweetness, so adjust the sugar to suit your taste. Cornstarch is traditionally used in many Arab recipes, but it is not actually necessary in most cases, so you may omit it here if you like.*

1 lb (500 g) dried apricots or apricot leather
4 cups (32 fl oz/1 l) water, or to cover
1 cup (8 oz/250 g) plus 2 tablespoons sugar, or to taste
2 tablespoons cornstarch (cornflour) dissolved in ¼ cup (2 fl oz/60 ml) water (optional)
1 cup (8 fl oz/250 ml) heavy (double) cream
2 teaspoons orange-flower water
2 teaspoons grated orange zest (optional)
2 tablespoons chopped toasted pistachio nuts

Place the apricots in a bowl and add the water. Let stand overnight.

The next day, transfer the apricots and their soaking water to a saucepan, adding more water if necessary to cover, and bring to a boil. Reduce the heat to medium and simmer until the apricots are very soft, about 30 minutes.

Transfer the apricots and their cooking liquid to a food processor fitted with the metal blade or to a blender and purée. Alternatively, pass the apricots through a food mill or a sieve.

Return the purée to the pan and bring to a simmer. Stir in the 1 cup (8 oz/250 g) sugar and the cornstarch mixture (if using). Simmer, stirring occasionally, until thickened, 2–3 minutes. Transfer to 6 individual serving bowls. Cover and refrigerate.

At serving time, whip the cream with the 2 tablespoons sugar (or more to taste) until soft peaks form and then beat in

Clockwise from left: Bread and Honey Pudding with Kaymak, Amardine Cream, Almond Rice Pudding

the orange-flower water until the peaks are of a medium stiffness. Fold in the orange zest (if using). Place a dollop of cream on each serving. Top with chopped pistachio nuts and serve.

SERVES 6

LEBANON

MAHALLABIA

Almond Rice Pudding

The name means "made with milk." Unlike some rice puddings prepared with cooked rice, this uses ground rice or rice flour. Some recipes add a little cornstarch as a thickening agent. This pudding can be flavored with rosewater or orange-flower water and garnished with toasted coconut, chopped pistachios or almonds, or pomegranate seeds. In Turkey, a tablespoon of ground coffee dissolved in hot water is added to the mixture.

4½ cups (36 fl oz/1.1 l) milk
1 cup (4 oz/125 g) ground blanched almonds
1 cup (8 oz/250 g) sugar
¼ teaspoon freshly grated nutmeg or ground cinnamon
¼ cup (4 oz/125 g) rice flour (see glossary)
2 tablespoons cornstarch (cornflour)
2 tablespoons orange-flower water or rosewater, or to taste
chopped almonds or pistachios (optional)
toasted coconut (optional)
pomegranate seeds (optional; see glossary)

In a 2-qt (2-l) saucepan bring 4 cups (32 fl oz/1 l) of the milk to a boil. Stir in the ground almonds, sugar and nutmeg or cinnamon and remove from the heat. Steep the mixture for 30 minutes.

In a bowl stir together the rice flour and cornstarch. Gradually add the remaining ½ cup (4 fl oz/125 ml) cold milk to the flour mixture, stirring until a smooth paste forms. Bring the sweetened almond milk back to a boil. Add a little of the hot almond milk to the rice flour paste, stirring constantly. Then pour all of the rice flour paste into the saucepan and cook over low heat, stirring very often, until the mixture thickens, 10–15 minutes. Do not allow the mixture to scorch and do not scrape the bottom of the pan.

Stir in the flower water and cook, stirring, for 3–4 minutes longer. Remove from the heat and divide among 6–8 dessert bowls. Cover and refrigerate until cold.

Serve plain or garnish with nuts, coconut or pomegranate seeds.

SERVES 6–8

MOROCCO

M'HENCHA

Coiled Pastry Filled with Almond Paste

*A traditional Moroccan almond dessert. It is shaped like a coiled snake (*m'hencha *means, literally, "the snake") and makes a dramatic presentation.*

FOR THE FILLING:

1½ cups (8 oz/250 g) blanched almonds
1 teaspoon almond extract
¼ cup (2 oz/60 g) unsalted butter, melted
¾ cup (3 oz/90 g) confectioners' (icing) sugar
3–4 tablespoons orange-flower water

Coiled Pastry filled with Almond Paste

1 egg
½ teaspoon ground cinnamon (optional)

12 *filo* sheets (see glossary)
5 tablespoons (2½ oz/75 g) unsalted butter, melted
1 egg, beaten with a little water
confectioner's (icing) sugar
1 teaspoon ground cinnamon

To make the filling, in a food processor fitted with the metal blade, combine all the ingredients. Pulse well to combine. Turn out onto a work surface and knead until it holds together. Divide into 12 equal portions and form each portion into a ball. Cover and chill well.

On a work surface and using the palms of your hands, roll each chilled ball into a log about ½ in (12 mm) in diameter.

Preheat an oven to 350°F (180°C).

Place a *filo* sheet on the work surface and brush with melted butter. Cover with a second sheet and brush with butter. Place 4 logs, end to end, along a long edge of the stack, placing them about 2 in (5 cm) from the edge. Fold the 2-in (5-cm) border over the logs and roll up tightly, tucking in the ends as you do. Repeat with the remaining 10 *filo* sheets and logs, forming 6 rolls in all.

Brush a cake pan or baking sheet with melted butter. Coil one roll in the center of the pan. Continue to coil the rolls, sticking the ends of the rolls together with a little of the beaten egg, so that the rolls join to look like one long coiled snake. Brush the entire pastry with the beaten egg.

Bake until crisp and pale gold, about 30 minutes. Invert onto another pan or baking sheet, return to the oven and crisp on the other side, about 10 minutes longer.

Remove from the oven and invert onto a serving plate. Sprinkle liberally with the sugar. Sprinkle on the cinnamon in lines to form a pattern. Cut into wedges and serve warm or at room temperature.

SERVES 8

GREECE

Kythoni sto Fournou

Baked Quinces Filled with Walnuts

In the fall and winter, quinces are a popular dessert in Greece and throughout the Balkans. Some varieties turn a delightful shade of Venetian red when cooked. If the quince you have are not the variety that turn red, or if you are not cooking them long enough for them to change color, you can cook them with pomegranate juice. If you do not have access to quince, apples can be used for this recipe.

6 large quinces
3 tablespoons butter, at room temperature
½ cup (2 oz/60 g) chopped walnuts
½ cup (4 oz/125 g) sugar
1 teaspoon ground cinnamon
¼ cup (2 fl oz/60 ml) water or pomegranate juice (see glossary)
clotted cream, *kaymak* or thickened plain yogurt for serving (see glossary)

Preheat an oven to 350°F (180°C).

Rub off the fuzz from the quinces and cut them in half lengthwise. Remove the core and seeds. Place in a buttered baking dish, hollow side up.

In a small bowl combine the butter, walnuts, sugar and cinnamon and mix well. Place a spoonful in the center of each quince half. Add the water or pomegranate juice to the pan.

Bake, basting occasionally with the dish juices, until tender, about 30 minutes. Transfer to individual dishes and serve warm or at room temperature with clotted cream, *kaymak* (cut into slices), or thickened yogurt.

SERVES 6

SYRIA

Teekh Mouraba

Watermelon Preserves

Serve this melon conserve with chicken or roast meat.

1 lb (500 g) watermelon rind
8 cups (64 fl oz/2 l) water
1 tablespoon fresh lime juice or salt
boiling water, to cover
2 cups (1 lb/500 g) sugar
1 lemon, thinly sliced
1 cinnamon stick, about 2 in (5 cm) long

Pare the green from the watermelon rind and trim away the pink edge. Cut into 1-in (2.5-cm) cubes. In a bowl combine 4 cups (32 fl oz/1 l) of the water and the lime or salt. Add the rind and let stand overnight.

The next day, drain well and rinse with cold water. Place in a nonreactive saucepan and add boiling water to cover. Simmer for 15 minutes and then drain. In the same saucepan combine the remaining 4 cups (32 fl oz/1 l) water and the sugar and bring to a boil, stirring to dissolve the sugar. Boil for 5 minutes. Add the rind, lemon slices and cinnamon and boil rapidly over high heat until the rind is translucent, 15–20 minutes. Remove from the heat and let the rind stand in the syrup overnight.

The next day, return the rind and syrup to a boil and ladle into hot, sterilized jars. Seal according to the manufacturer's instructions. Store in a cool, dark place.

MAKES 3 PT (48 FL OZ/1.5 L)

Baked Quinces Filled with Walnuts

Left to right: Orange Brandy, Tomato Preserves, Watermelon Preserves

PROVENCE

Confiture de Tomates

Tomato Preserves

An unusual preserve that is good with cheese or spread on toast.

2½ lb (1.25 kg) ripe tomatoes, peeled and chopped
2 lb (1 kg) sugar
pinch of salt
zest of 2 lemons, cut into long, narrow strips
½ vanilla bean (optional)
¼ cup (1 oz/30 g) chopped walnuts (optional)

In a nonreactive saucepan combine the tomatoes, sugar and salt. Bring to a boil, stirring often to prevent scorching. Reduce the heat to low and simmer for about 30 minutes. Add the lemon zest and vanilla bean (if using). Continue to simmer until the mixture is very thick and the jell point is reached, 221°–224°F (105°–106°C) on a candy thermometer or until a large spoonful dropped onto a saucer chilled in the freezer sets within 2 minutes. This will take about 15–20 minutes.

If adding the nuts, stir them in at the end. Discard the vanilla bean, if used. Ladle into hot, sterilized jars and seal according to the manufacturer's instructions. Store in a cool, dark place.

MAKES ABOUT 4 PT (64 FL OZ/ 2 L)

PROVENCE

Ratafia

Orange Brandy

Just the tonic to cure what ails you. This mixture can be prepared months ahead of time and left in a cool, dark place to be sampled on a day when a little malaise strikes.

6 oranges
2 cups (1 lb/500 g) sugar
1 teaspoon ground coriander
¼ teaspoon ground cinnamon
4 cups (32 fl oz/1 l) brandy or Cognac

Wash and dry the oranges well. Using a vegetable peeler, remove the zest (no bitter white pith), then finely chop it. Place in a large mixing bowl. Squeeze the juice from the oranges and add it to the bowl. Add the sugar, coriander, cinnamon and brandy and stir well.

Pour into a large jar or crock and cap with a tight-fitting lid. Let rest in a cool, dark place for 2 months.

Strain through a fine-mesh sieve lined with cheesecloth (muslin) and pour into a clean bottle. Close securely and store in a cool, dark place.

MAKES 4 CUPS (32 FL OZ/1 L)

GREECE

KOURAMBIEDES

Butter Cookies

Even though these rich little shortbread morsels are Christmas cookies, they are served at weddings, birthday parties, baptisms, and other celebrations because they are too good to have only once a year. They are best eaten within a day or so of baking, but they can be made a week ahead and stored in a tightly sealed tin.

1 lb (500 g) unsalted butter
2 egg yolks
3 tablespoons confectioners' (icing) sugar, plus confectioners' sugar for coating
⅛ teaspoon baking soda (sodium bicarbonate)
3 tablespoons fresh orange juice
1½ tablespoons brandy
5 cups (1½ lb/750 g) all-purpose (plain) flour
about 36 whole cloves

Preheat an oven to 350°F (180°C). Line 2 baking sheets with parchment paper.

In a heavy saucepan over low heat, melt the butter. Let it cook for a minute, then transfer it to a bowl and let cool completely. Beat the egg yolks into the cooled butter and then beat in the 3 tablespoons confectioner's sugar. In a cup dissolve the baking soda in the orange juice and brandy and add to the butter mixture. Beat well until very light in color. Gradually add the flour, beating well until a soft dough forms.

On a lightly floured surface, knead the dough until it is soft, smooth and almost silky, about 5 minutes. Roll the dough between your palms into balls 1½ in (4 cm) in diameter. You will have about 3 dozen. Place 1 clove in the center of each ball. Place the cookies, well spaced, on the prepared baking sheets. Bake until pale brown, about 20 minutes. Remove from the baking sheets to wire racks and let the cookies cool a little. They are fragile, so handle with care.

Place a little confectioners' sugar in a shallow bowl. Very gently roll each cookie in the sugar; be generous with the topping.

MAKES ABOUT 3 DOZEN

GREECE

KOPENHAYI

Almond Custard Filo Pastry

This dessert was created to honor King George I of Greece when he began his reign in 1862. He was Danish and this almond-filled filo *pastry was named for Denmark's famed Copenhagen. Some versions of this recipe have a pie crust–type bottom pastry and* filo *only on top. Some cooks grind the almonds; others separate the eggs, beat the yolks into the almond paste mixture and then beat the whites until stiff and fold them into filling.*

FOR THE SYRUP:

2 cups (1 lb/500 g) sugar
1 cup (8 fl oz/250 ml) water
2 tablespoons fresh lemon juice
1 orange zest strip, about 3 in (7.5 cm) long
1 cinnamon stick, about 2 in (5 cm) long

1 lb (500 g) almond paste (see glossary)
½ cup (4 oz/125 g) sugar
8 eggs
2 teaspoons all-purpose (plain) flour
1½ teaspoons baking powder
½ teaspoon ground cinnamon
2 tablespoons brandy (optional)
½ cup (4 oz/125 g) unsalted butter, melted and clarified or skimmed of froth (see glossary)
16 *filo* sheets (see glossary)

To make the syrup, in a heavy saucepan combine the sugar, water, lemon juice, orange zest and cinnamon stick. Bring to a boil over high heat, stirring to dissolve the sugar. Reduce the heat to low and simmer until thickened, about 15 minutes. Remove from the heat and remove and discard the orange zest and cinnamon stick. Cool the syrup completely.

Preheat an oven to 325°F (165°C).

In a bowl with an electric mixer set on medium speed, beat together almond paste and sugar. Beat in the eggs, one at a time, beating well after each addition. Add the flour, baking powder and cinnamon and continue to beat until the mixture is creamy. Beat in the brandy, if using.

Using a wide pastry brush, spread melted butter on the bottom and sides of an 11-by-16-by-2½-in (28-by-40-by-6-cm) baking pan or dish. One by one and brushing each sheet with butter, layer 8 *filo* sheets in the pan. Pour in the almond mixture to cover evenly. Top with the remaining *filo* sheets, again buttering each one. Butter the top layer generously. Using a sharp knife, score the pastry into 16–24 diamond shapes.

Bake until the top is golden, 45–50 minutes. Remove the pastry from the oven and immediately pour the cooled syrup over the hot pastry. Return to the oven for 2–3 minutes, then remove from the oven and let stand for a few hours before serving.

To serve, recut the pastry with a sharp knife.

MAKES 16–24 PIECES

GREECE

FLAOUNES KYPRIOTIKES

Minted Cheese Tart

This interesting cheese tart also appears as a dessert in Spain and as a savory tart in Cyprus (although the Cypriots sometimes add raisins and cinnamon to the mint-scented cheese). Rather than use a soft, fresh cheese like ricotta, in Cyprus they combine haloumi, mizithra *and* kasseri *cheeses (see glossary), and add a little mastic to the crust in place of the yeast.*

FOR THE PASTRY:

2 cups (10 oz/315 g) all-purpose (plain) flour
¼ cup (2 oz/60 g) lard
1 egg
1 tablespoon sugar
1 teaspoon active dry yeast dissolved in ½ cup (4 fl oz/125 ml) milk

FOR THE FILLING:

2 cups (1 lb/500 g) fresh ricotta or cream cheese
1 cup (8 oz/250 g) sugar
4 eggs
¼ cup (2 fl oz/60 ml) Pernod or anise liqueur
12 whole fresh mint leaves
pinch of ground cinnamon (optional)

To make the pastry, combine the flour, lard, egg, sugar and yeast mixture. Turn out onto a floured work surface and knead to form a smooth dough. Cover the dough with a kitchen towel or plastic wrap and let the dough rest for 20 minutes.

Alternatively, in a food processor combine the flour, sugar and lard and pulse once or twice. With the processor on, add the egg and yeast mixture. Process until combined.

On a lightly floured surface, roll out the dough into a round large enough to fit a 10-in (25-cm) tart pan with a removable

Top to bottom: Butter Cookies, Almond Custard Filo Pastry, Minted Cheese Tart

bottom. Transfer the dough round to the pan and ease it into the pan. Trim off the excess dough.

Preheat an oven to 350°F (180°C).

To make the filling, in a bowl with an electric mixer set on medium speed, beat together the cheese, sugar and eggs until creamy. Add the liqueur and beat well. You can chop 2 of the mint leaves and stir them in, if you like, along with the cinnamon (if using).

Pour the cheese mixture into the pastry shell. Arrange the whole mint leaves on top and push them down just a bit. Bake until set at the edge but still quivery in the center, 25–30 minutes. Transfer to a wire rack to cool.

Cut into wedges to serve.

SERVES 8

CATALONIA

SANGRÍA

Wine Punch

Every family has a special recipe for this Spanish wine cooler. Some add brandy or liqueur; others vary the fruit or amount of soda.

1 bottle (3 cups/24 fl oz/750 ml) dry red wine
2 tablespoons brandy or orange-flavored liqueur
2 tablespoons sugar
juice of 1 lemon
juice of 2 oranges
1 lemon, sliced paper-thin
1 orange, sliced paper-thin and slices cut into quarters
3 cups (24 fl oz/750 ml) soda water
8–10 ice cubes

In a large pitcher or bowl, combine the wine, brandy or liqueur, sugar and citrus juices. Add the sliced fruits and steep for several hours in the refrigerator.

Add the soda water and ice and serve.

SERVES 6–8

CATALONIA

PANELLETS

Sweet Potato Cookies

A traditional treat on All Saints' Day, these cookies are most often rolled in pine nuts before baking. Less often a combination of pine nuts and chopped hazelnuts (filberts) is used. They will keep in tightly covered containers at room temperature for about 1 week.

½ lb (250 g) sweet potatoes (2 small or 1 large)
3½ cups (1¼ lb/625 g) almonds, chopped
2 cups (1 lb/500 g) sugar
2 egg yolks
1 teaspoon vanilla extract (essence)
1 tablespoon grated lemon zest
½ cup (2½ oz/75 g) all-purpose (plain) flour
1 cup (5 oz/155 g) pine nuts
1 cup (5 oz/155 g) hazelnuts (filberts), chopped
2 egg whites, beaten until medium-stiff peaks form

Peel the sweet potatoes and cut into chunks. In a saucepan combine the sweet potatoes with water to cover. Bring to a boil and cook until soft, about 15 minutes. Drain well, place in a large bowl and mash. Alternatively, boil the sweet potatoes whole in their skins until soft, about 30 minutes, then peel and mash. Let cool.

Add the almonds, sugar, egg yolks, vanilla and lemon zest to the cooled sweet potatoes and mix well with a wooden spoon to form a smooth dough that looks a bit like mashed potatoes. Knead for a few minutes in the bowl, then cover with a kitchen towel and allow the dough to rest for 30 minutes.

Preheat an oven to 350°F (180°C). Oil 3 large baking sheets.

Combine the pine nuts and hazelnuts in a shallow bowl. Pinch off pieces of dough the size of a walnut and roll each piece between your palms into a ball. Flatten each ball a bit. Brush on all sides with the egg white, then roll in the nuts. Place the cookies, well spaced, on the prepared baking sheets.

Bake until golden, 15–20 minutes. Remove to wire racks to cool.

MAKES ABOUT 4 DOZEN

CATALONIA

CREMA CATALANA

Caramelized Custard

Caramelized custard such as this silky dessert is served in practically every restaurant in Barcelona. It is sometimes called crema de San José, *as it is traditionally served on St. Joseph's Day. Although the custard is usually chilled and then caramelized, the most voluptuous version I can remember was one in which the custard was still a little warm and the topping very crunchy.*

1 tablespoon cornstarch
1 cup (8 fl oz/250 ml) milk
1 cup (8 fl oz/250 ml) half-and-half or heavy (double) cream
3 lemon zest strips, each about 2 in (5 cm) long

Clockwise from top left: Caramelized Custard, Sangría, Sweet Potato Cookies

1 cinnamon stick, about 2 in (5 cm) long
5 or 6 egg yolks
½ cup (4 oz/125 g) granulated sugar
⅓ cup (2½ oz/75 g) brown or ⅓ cup (3 oz/90 g) granulated sugar

In a small bowl dissolve the cornstarch in a few tablespoons of the milk. In a saucepan combine the remaining milk, the cream, lemon zest and cinnamon stick. Place over medium heat and just before it comes to a boil, turn off the heat. Cover and set aside.

In a bowl with an electric mixer, beat together the egg yolks and ½ cup (4 oz/125 g) granulated sugar until pale. Remove and discard the lemon zest from the warm milk. Whisk some of the warm milk into the egg yolks, then whisk the egg yolks into the milk mixture. Add the cornstarch mixture and whisk well. Place the saucepan over low heat and simmer, stirring constantly, until the mixture thickens, about 10 minutes. Strain the mixture through a fine-mesh sieve into a pitcher. Then divide the mixture evenly among six ½-cup (4-fl oz/125-ml) custard cups or shallow earthenware ramekins designed for this dish, or one 3- to 4-cup (24–32 fl oz/750 ml–1 l) ramekin. Cover and refrigerate until cool or chilled.

To caramelize the custard, preheat a broiler (griller). Sprinkle a scant 1 tablespoon brown or granulated sugar over the top of each custard or the ⅓ cup (2½ oz/75 g) over the large custard. Slip it into the broiler and broil (grill) until the sugar melts and is golden. Alternatively, light a small propane torch or heat an iron plate specially designed for caramelizing to red hot over a gas flame and place atop the custard(s) until golden. Serve immediately.

SERVES 6

SICILY

Gelato di Zabaglione

Marsala Ice Cream

What could be more Sicilian than an ice cream made with Marsala? Serve garnished with berries, if desired.

¾ cup (6 fl oz/180 ml) plus 2 tablespoons sweet Marsala
4 cups (32 fl oz/1 l) heavy (double) cream
¾ cup (6 oz/185 g) sugar
pinch of salt
8 egg yolks

Pour the ¾ cup (6 fl oz/180 ml) Marsala into a saucepan and boil until reduced to ¼ cup (2 fl oz/60 ml). Remove from the heat and let cool to room temperature.

In a saucepan over medium heat, combine the cream, sugar and salt. Heat until just hot, stirring to dissolve the sugar; do not boil.

In a bowl lightly whisk the yolks until blended. Whisk in 1 cup (8 fl oz/250 ml) of the hot cream, then whisk the egg mixture into the hot cream in the saucepan. Cook over medium heat, stirring constantly, until the mixture thickly coats a spoon, 3–5 minutes; do not boil.

Pour the cream mixture through a fine-mesh sieve into a mixing bowl. Nest the bowl in another bowl filled with ice so the mixture cools down quickly. Stir in the reduced Marsala. Cover and chill well.

Stir the remaining 2 tablespoons Marsala into the chilled cream. Pour into an ice cream maker and freeze according to the manufacturer's instructions.

MAKES 1 QT (1 L)

SICILY

Gelato di Pistacchio

Pistachio Ice Cream

Sicily is known for fabulous ice cream and this is one of the island's best. Don't be disappointed if your ice cream is not the bright green color that one associates with commercial pistachio ice cream. The color is added artificially.

2½ cups (10 oz/315 g) pistachios
3½ cups (28 fl oz/875 ml) heavy (double) cream

Left to right: Coffee Ice, Apricot Ice Cream, Pistachio Ice Cream, Marsala Ice Cream

1½ cups (12 fl oz/375 ml) milk
1 cup (8 oz/250 g) sugar
7 egg yolks

Preheat an oven to 350°F (180°C). Spread the nuts on a baking sheet and toast until fragrant, 6–8 minutes. Transfer to a food processor fitted with the metal blade and process to chop coarsely. Or chop by hand. Set aside.

In a large saucepan combine the cream and milk and heat to boiling. Add all but ½ cup (2 oz/60 g) of the nuts and let steep for 2 hours.

Line a sieve with cheesecloth (muslin) and strain the cream through it into a bowl, pressing on nuts to extract as much flavor as possible. Return the cream to the saucepan with ½ cup (4 oz/125 g) of the sugar and bring to a boil, stirring to dissolve the sugar.

In a bowl whisk together the egg yolks and the remaining ½ cup (4 oz/125 g) sugar until combined. Whisk in 1 cup (8 fl oz/250 ml) of the hot cream, then whisk the egg mixture into the hot cream in the saucepan. Cook over medium heat, stirring constantly, until the mixture thickly coats a spoon, 3–5 minutes; do not boil.

Pour the cream mixture through a fine-mesh sieve into a mixing bowl. Nest the bowl in another bowl filled with ice so the mixture cools down quickly. Then cover and refrigerate overnight.

Pour into an ice cream maker and freeze according to the manufacturer's instructions. Fold in the reserved nuts just before the ice cream is set.

MAKES 1 QT (1 L)

SYRIA

Dondurma Mish Mish

Apricot Ice Cream

Fruit-flavored ice creams are popular in the Middle East. If sahleb *is not in your pantry, use cornstarch.*

½ lb (250 g) apricots
2 teaspoons grated orange zest (optional)
1 teaspoon *sahleb* (see glossary) or 1½ tablespoons cornstarch (cornflour)
2 cups (16 fl oz/500 ml) milk
1 cup (8 fl oz/250 ml) light (single) cream
⅔ cup (5 oz/155 g) sugar
2 teaspoons rosewater or orange-flower water

Bring a saucepan three-fourths full of water to a boil. Add the apricots and blanch for about one minute. Drain and, when cool enough to handle, peel, pit and slice. Place in a food processor fitted with the metal blade or in a blender. Add the orange zest (if using) and purée until smooth.

Dissolve the *sahleb* or cornstarch in a little of the milk and set aside.

In a saucepan combine the remaining milk, the cream and sugar. Bring slowly to a boil over medium heat, stirring until the sugar dissolves. Add the apricot purée and *sahleb* or cornstarch mixture. Cook over low heat, stirring, until mixture thickens enough to coat the back of a spoon, about 3 minutes. Remove from the heat, stir in the flower water and beat with a spoon until thickened. Let cool.

Pour into an ice cream maker and freeze according to the manufacturer's instructions.

MAKES 1 QT (1 L)

SICILY

Granita di Caffè

Coffee Ice

A granita *is a refreshing alternative to ice cream during hot weather.*

½–¾ cup (4–6 oz/125–185 g) sugar
3 cups (24 fl oz/750 ml) hot, strong brewed espresso
1½ cups (12 fl oz/375 ml) heavy (double) cream
3 tablespoons sugar
2 teaspoons ground cinnamon (optional)

Stir the sugar into the hot espresso until it dissolves. Pour into a shallow metal pan. Cover and place in the freezer until ice crystals begin to form, 2–3 hours, depending upon the freezer.

Break up the crystals with a fork, re-cover and freeze again. Repeat this process every 30 minutes until the mixture is slushy, 2–3 hours.

Pour the cream into a bowl and beat until thick. Add the sugar and cinnamon (if using) and beat until soft peaks form. Place a dollop of cream on the bottom of each of 4–6 dessert glasses. Divide the *granita* evenly among the dishes. Top with the remaining cream. Eat at once before it melts!

SERVES 4–6

Left to right: Fig Conserve, Quince Preserves

TURKEY

AYVA REÇELI

Quince Preserves

Great spread on bread or as a cookie filling.

2 lb (1 kg) quinces
3 whole cloves (optional)
1 cinnamon stick, about 2 in (5 cm) long (optional)
4 cups (32 fl oz/1 l) water
4 cups (2 lb/1 kg) sugar
¼ cup (2 fl oz/60 ml) fresh lemon juice
¼ cup (2 fl oz/60 ml) rosewater (optional)

Peel and core the quinces, then grate them and place in a nonreactive saucepan. Tie the peel and seeds of the quince and the cloves and cinnamon stick, if using, in a piece of cheesecloth (muslin) and add to the pan. Add cold water to cover. Bring to a boil and boil until tender, about 30 minutes. Pour through a sieve, collecting the liquid in a pitcher or bowl; reserve the quinces and cloth bag. Measure the liquid and add hot water, if necessary, to measure 1¾ cups (14 fl oz/440 ml).

Pour the liquid into a saucepan, bring to a boil and boil for 2 minutes. Add the reserved quinces and cloth bag and boil, uncovered, for 5 minutes. Remove from the heat and let stand until the mixture turns pink, about 3 hours.

Bring to a boil again, add the lemon juice and cook until the jell point is reached, 221°–224°F (105°–106°C) on a candy thermometer or until a large spoonful dropped onto a saucer chilled in the freezer sets within 2 minutes. This will take 20–30 minutes.

Discard the cloth bag. Stir in the rosewater, if desired. Ladle into hot, sterilized jars and seal according to manufacturer's instructions. Store in a cool, dark place.

MAKES 4 PT (64 FL OZ/2 L)

PROVENCE

CONFITURE DE FIGUES

Fig Conserve

Great on walnut bread or any kind of toast. This is the taste of summer.

4 cups (2 lb/1 kg) sugar
2 cups (16 fl oz/500 ml) water
grated zest of 1 lemon
2½–3 lb (1.25–1.5 kg) figs, peeled, stemmed and quartered
½ vanilla bean (optional)
1 teaspoon aniseeds or fennel seeds (optional)
1 cinnamon stick, about 2 in (5 cm) long (optional)
2 whole cloves (optional)
¼ cup (2 fl oz/60 ml) fresh lemon juice

In a large nonreactive saucepan combine the sugar and water. Slowly bring to a boil, stirring until sugar is dissolved. Remove from the heat and add the lemon zest and figs. Tie the seeds, cinnamon sticks and/or cloves, if using, in a piece of cheesecloth (muslin) and add to the pan. Let stand at room temperature for a few hours or overnight.

Bring the fig mixture to a boil. Reduce the heat to medium and simmer until thickened to a jam consistency, or until a candy thermometer reads 221°–224°F (105°–106°C). Alternatively, drop a large spoonful onto a saucer chilled in the freezer; it should set with in 2 minutes. This simmering process should take about 2 hours. Add the lemon juice during the last 30 minutes of cooking.

Discard the cloth bag. Ladle into hot, sterilized jars and seal according to the manufacturer's instructions.

MAKES ABOUT 3½ PT (56 FL OZ/1.75 ML)

ALGERIA

Acir

Citrus Drinks

Very refreshing on a hot day. The juice infusions can be made ahead of time and the chilled mineral water added when served.

FOR THE LEMON-GRAPEFRUIT DRINK *(acir el qaress):*

juice of 6 large lemons
juice of 1 grapefruit
⅔ cup (5 oz/155 g) sugar

FOR THE ORANGE-LEMON-GRAPEFRUIT DRINK *(acir tchina):*

juice of 1 orange
juice of 1 lemon
juice of 1 grapefruit
½ cup (4 oz/125 g) sugar
1 orange, peeled and thinly sliced

ice cubes
3 cups (24 fl oz/750 ml) mineral water

Select one of the drinks to make. Both the drinks are made the same way: Combine the juices and sugar in a pitcher and stir to dissolve the sugar. For the orange-lemon-grapefruit drink, add the orange slices to the juice mixture.

Fill 3 or 4 tall glasses with ice and pour one-third or one-fourth of the infusion into each glass. Top off with mineral water and serve.

EACH DRINK SERVES 3 OR 4

Citrus Drinks

S Y R I A

MA'MOUL

Stuffed Butter Cookies

These Syrian Easter cookies are easy to prepare once you master folding the dough around the filling. They can be stuffed with a date or a nut filling. Choose the filling that appeals to you. Store in an airtight tin at room temperature for up to 1 week.

FOR THE DATE FILLING:

1 lb (500 g) pitted dates, chopped
½ cup (4 fl oz/125 ml) water
grated zest of 1 orange
½ teaspoon ground cinnamon

FOR THE NUT FILLING:

2 cups (8 oz/250 g) chopped walnuts, almonds or pistachios
1 cup (8 oz/250 g) granulated sugar, or to taste
1 tablespoon rosewater
2 teaspoons ground cinnamon

1 cup (½ lb/250 g) unsalted butter, at room temperature
2 tablespoons granulated sugar
2 cups (8 oz/250 g) sifted all-purpose (plain) flour
1 tablespoon rosewater or orange-flower water
2–4 tablespoons milk or water
sifted confectioners' (icing) sugar

Choose either the date or the nut filling. To make the date filling, in a saucepan combine the dates and the water and bring to a boil. Reduce the heat to low and simmer, uncovered, stirring occasionally, until the dates form a paste, about 5 minutes. Stir in the orange zest and cinnamon. To make the nut filling, in a bowl stir together all the ingredients.

Cookie platter: (outside ring) Stuffed Butter Cookie, (inside) Almond Cookies, Mint Tea

❀ Preheat an oven to 300°F (150°C).
❀ In a bowl and using an electric mixer, beat together the butter and granulated sugar until light and fluffy. Beat in the flour and then beat in the milk and flower water. Knead in the bowl until the dough holds together and is easy to shape.
❀ Pinch off a walnut-size piece of dough. Roll it between your palms into a ball and hollow it out with your thumb. Pinch the sides up to form a pot shape. Place a spoonful of filling into the hollow, then pinch the dough closed over the filling. Press and then score the sealed edge, if desired.
❀ Place the filled balls on an ungreased baking sheet. Bake until firm and fully set, about 20 minutes; do not brown. Carefully transfer the cookies to wire racks. Sprinkle them generously with confectioners' sugar while still warm, then cool completely.

MAKES ABOUT 2½ DOZEN

ALGERIA

MAKROUD EL LOUSE

Almond Cookies

To grind nuts without making them oily or pasty, place them, in batches, in a food processor or blender with the sugar. These cookies are sweet and chewy and can be made a week ahead of time and kept in a covered container.

1¼ lb (625 g) blanched almonds, finely ground (about 3 cups)
1¼ cups (10 oz/315 g) granulated sugar
1 tablespoon grated lemon zest
2 eggs
all-purpose (plain) flour for dusting
1 cup (8 fl oz/250 ml) water
1 tablespoon orange-flower water
2 cups (8 oz/250 g) confectioners' (icing) sugar

❀ Preheat an oven to 350°F (180°C). Line 2 large baking sheets with parchment paper or leave ungreased.
❀ In a large bowl combine the almonds, 1 cup (8 oz/250 g) of the granulated sugar and the lemon zest and stir to mix. Make a well in the center and add the eggs to the well. Gradually mix the dry ingredients into the wet ingredients. Continue to mix until a smooth dough forms.
❀ Divide the dough in half. On a heavily floured surface and using floured palms, roll each half into a log about 18 in (45 cm) long and 1½ in (4 cm) in diameter. Flatten the log into an oblong about 1½ in (4 cm) thick and 2 in (5 cm) wide. Cut on the diagonal into slices 1½ in (4 cm) thick. Dust the slices with flour and place on the prepared baking sheets about 1 in (2.5 cm) apart. Bake until pale gold, about 15 minutes. Transfer to wire racks to cool.
❀ In a saucepan combine the remaining ¼ cup (2 oz/60 g) granulated sugar and the water. Bring to a boil over high heat, stirring until the sugar dissolves. Cook over high heat, uncovered, until a thin syrup forms. Pour into a shallow bowl and let cool. Stir the flower water into the cooled syrup.
❀ Spread the confectioner's sugar in a shallow pan. Dip the cooled cookies first in the syrup and then in the sugar. Set on a rack to dry.

MAKES ABOUT 6 DOZEN

MOROCCO

CHAY

Mint Tea

The drama of tea service is most important here. The tea is poured into glasses from high in the air, to aerate the tea on its way to the vessel and thereby heighten its flavor.

2 tablespoons green tea
6 tablespoons (3 oz/90 g) sugar
1 large handful stemmed fresh mint leaves
6 cups (48 fl oz/1.5 l) water, boiling
a few orange zest strips or 1 teaspoon orange-flower water (optional)

❀ Place the tea on the bottom of a teapot. Top with the sugar, then the mint leaves and finally the orange zest strips or flower water. Holding the kettle about 1 ft (30 cm) above the teapot, pour in the boiling water. Stir well and then let steep for 10–15 minutes.
❀ Pour out 1 glass of tea, then pour it back into the pot, again to aerate it. To aerate the tea further, again pour the tea into the glasses from about 1 ft (30 cm) above them. Serve hot.

SERVES 6

GLOSSARY

ALI-OLI
Sometimes written *aioli.* Spanish version of French aioli, a garlic-infused mayonnaise.

ALMOND
White oval nut used throughout the Mediterranean as both an ingredient and a garnish. Sold whole, slivered or sliced; blanched or unblanched; or even still in its beige pitted shell.

ALMOND PASTE
Made from ground blanched almonds, sugar and a little glycerine or a similar ingredient, to keep it malleable, almond paste is sweeter and coarser than its close relative marzipan. Sometimes almond extract is added to intensify its flavor. Used mainly for pastries; in Morocco used as a stuffing for fish.

AVGOLEMONO
Egg-and-lemon mixture used in Greek cooking. In its thin form, it is added to soups and stews and served spooned over stuffed grapeleaves (recipe on page 61). In its thick form, it accompanies meat-filled zucchini or other stuffed vegetables. To make a thin *avgolemono,* beat 2 or 3 whole eggs or 3 egg yolks with 4–5 tablespoons (about 2 fl oz/60 ml) fresh lemon juice. Gradually add 1 cup (8 fl oz/250 ml) stock from the dish being cooked and whisk constantly. Heat, stirring constantly, until warmed through and thickened, or stir into the soup or stew you are flavoring and stir until thoroughly combined and heated through. Alternatively, beat 3 egg whites until stiff, and then fold the yolk-lemon juice mixture into the whites before adding the stock. To make a thick sauce, melt 2 tablespoons unsalted butter in a saucepan over medium heat. Whisk in 2 tablespoons all-purpose (plain) flour until smooth and cook, stirring, a couple minutes. Gradually add 2 cups (16 fl oz/500 ml) boiling stock and continue whisking until it comes back to a boil. Reduce the heat to low. In a small bowl, beat together 3 whole eggs or egg yolks and 4–5 tablespoons (about 2 fl oz/60 ml) fresh lemon juice. Slowly add a little of the hot sauce to the egg mixture, whisking well, then stir the mixture into the pan. Whisk constantly until heated through but do not boil.

BOUQUET GARNI
A neatly tied bundle of herbs and other seasonings that is added to soups, stews and other dishes to impart flavoring, and is easily removed after cooking. The contents of a bouquet garni varies with the dish being cooked.

BRIK
Tunisian deep-fried savory pastry. Filled with cooked meat, poultry or fish and usually a whole egg.

BRIOUAT
Moroccan pastry made from *ouarka* (q. v.), which is both savory or sweet. It is either filled with meat, poultry, seafood or nuts, baked until crisp and golden and then dipped in honey.

BULGUR
Also known as burghul. Hulled wheat that has been steamed until partially cooked, then dried and ground. Sold in fine, medium and coarse grinds. Recipes usually specify which grade should be used. For example, tabbouleh requires fine bulgur. The flavor is nutty and the texture somewhat crunchy. Available in shops specializing in Middle Eastern foods and in natural-foods stores that sell whole grains in bulk.

BUTIFARRA
A white pork sausage from Catalonia spiced with cinnamon, nutmeg and cloves. Italian sweet sausage can be used as a substitute.

CACIOCAVALLO
A southern Italian cheese that originated in Campania but is now also made in Sicily. Its name means "cheese on horseback;" it comes from the fact that the cheese is dried by hanging it in pairs astride a horizontal pole, which makes it appear as if it is hung over a saddle. It also is formed into horse shapes in Palermo and Apulia. This pale yellow cow's milk cheese can be eaten fresh or aged. It is sometimes smoked as well.

CAPERS
The buds of a Mediterranean bush, prepared by pickling in brine or packing in salt. (Sometimes the leaves are pickled as well.) Harvested in early summer, the buds are cleaned and sun-dried before preserving. They take about 1 month to cure and can be stored for about 1 year. Rinse before using to remove excess brine or salt. Buy small imported capers for the finest flavor.

CHORIZO
Spanish cured pork sausage heavily flavored with paprika and garlic. Unlike Latin American versions, Spanish chorizo is mild rather than hot. It is used as an ingredient in cooking and is eaten as a cold cut.

CLARIFIED BUTTER
Unsalted butter that has been slowly melted, thereby separating the milk solids (which sink to the bottom of the pan) and water from the butter itself. The white foam is skimmed off from the top, and the golden, clear liquid is carefully poured off into another container; the milk solids on the pan bottom are then discarded. Clarified butter has a higher smoking point than regular butter and is ideal for sautéing, as the milk solids that cause the butter to burn have been eliminated. It will keep longer in the refrigerator than regular butter because the milk solids promote rancidity. *Smen* (q.v.) and *samneh* are related.

CLOTTED CREAM
A specialty of Devonshire, England, made by gently heating rich unpasteurized milk until a semisolid layer of cream forms on the top. After cooling, the thick cream is removed. It can be stored in the refrigerator for about 4 days and is similar in texture to *crème fraîche,* but not tangy or nutty in taste. Used as a topping for desserts, especially in place of the traditional Turkish *kaymak* (q.v.).

COGNAC
A fine brandy from the region of Cognac in France that is double distilled and aged in Limousin oak for at least 3 years.

COUSCOUS
Staple starch of North African cuisine, couscous is a tiny pastalike pellet made from semolina flour and salted water. It is available prepackaged in boxes labeled by grain size (moyen, or medium, is most common) and most of it is of the instant variety. Traditionally steamed in the top perforated pan of a *couscousière,* over a lower pan holding simmering stew or water. It can also be prepared in a regular saucepan or baking dish by pouring the hot liquid over the grains, about 1½ cups (12 fl oz/375 ml) liquid to 1 cup (5 oz/155 g) couscous.

CUMIN
Tiny yellow-brown seeds with a pungent, spicy taste. Commonly available already ground, although for fullest aroma it is best to grind them just before using. They can be easily reduced to a powder in a spice mill or a blender.

CURRANTS see Raisins, currants

FETA
Originally a Greek cheese, feta is a soft, crumbly white cheese made from goat or sheep's milk. Feta is now made in many other countries, such as France, Israel, Bulgaria and Romania. Firmer fetas are made from cow's milk and can be used in salads or appetizers. To keep feta for a long time, be sure it remains covered with salted whey or the original brine, in a refrigerated container.

FAVA BEAN
Also known as broad bean. When very young, the whole beans, pods and all, are eaten. When mature, the fresh beans are shelled. The beans themselves have a tough skin that should be removed before cooking. Dried favas range in color from green to purplish brown; they are commonly available already peeled. A variety of small fava bean is used in Egyptian *ful mudammas* (recipe on page 214).

FILO
Also spelled phyllo; means "leaf" in Greek. Paper-thin dough sheets used in Greek, Turkish and Middle Eastern sweet and savory preparations such as baklava, *spanokopitta,* borek and so on. Can be used as a substitute for *ouarka* (q.v.) and *malsouqua,* respectively the Moroccan and Tunisian paper-thin dough used in such pastries as

b'stilla, brik and *briouat.* Can be purchased fresh or frozen; frozen, thaw in the refrigerator. *Filo* dries out easily, so it must be kept covered well when not using.

HALOUMI
Salty sheep's milk cheese with a stringlike consistency. Made in Cyprus, where it is flavored with mint, and in Lebanon, where black cumin is added.

HARISSA
North African hot sauce made from chili pepper and cumin. Can be purchased in tubes or jars. Tunisian *harissa* may have caraway and coriander added. To make *harissa,* combine 1½ tablespoons cayenne, ¼ cup (2 oz/60 g) ground cumin and ½ cup (4 fl oz/125 ml) olive oil in a mortar and grind with a pestle until a paste forms. Add a little salt to taste and up to 2 teaspoons ground caraway.

HAZELNUT
Also called filberts. Rich-flavored pale yellow nut covered by brown skin and a hard shell. To remove the skins, shell the nuts and then toast in a 350°F (180°C) oven for 7–10 minutes, or until the skin begins to flake, then wrap in a kitchen towel and rub vigorously while the nut is warm to remove as much of the skin as possible.

KASSERI
Hard Greek sheep's milk cheese, with a few scattered tiny holes. Popular as a table cheese, or it can be cooked in butter or olive oil and served with lemon wedges (see *saganaki* on page 48).

KAYMAK
Turkish thickened cream, also known as *eishta,* used principally for desserts. It is cooked until it is so thick that it sets up firmly enough to be rolled and sliced. To make *kaymak,* pour 2 cups (16 fl oz/500 ml) heavy (double) cream into a wide, deep saucepan and place over low heat. Bring just to a boil, then cook over low heat, stirring often, for about 1½ hours. Every now and again, lift out some of the cream with a ladle and then pour it back into the pan. The cream has thickened sufficiently when the bubbles that form are large. Pour the cream into a shallow pan, cover lightly and let stand in a warm place for 2–6 hours, then refrigerate for 6–8 hour suntil fully set. To unmold, run the point of a knife around the edges of the cream to loosen it and invert onto a large plate or flat baking sheet. At serving time, roll up the cream into a cylinder and slice crosswise into pieces about 1 in (2.5 cm) wide or simply cut as desired. If the cream does not set up completely, it can be scooped out with a spoon for serving. Clotted cream (q.v.) or French *crème fraîche* can be used in place of *kaymak.*

KEFALOTIRI
A common Greek grating cheese. Hard and yellow, it is made from unpasteurized sheep or goat's milk. The fresh (8 months old) cheese can be eaten as a table cheese.

KIBBEE
Arabic mixture of pounded lamb and bulgur (q.v.). Can be served raw, baked or fried (recipe on page 182).

MARSALA
Wine first made by John Woodhouse in 1773 for the English, who loved such fortified wines. Production centers in the town of Marsala and neighboring towns in western Sicily. Marsala can be sweet or dry and is about 18 percent alcohol.

MASTIC
This resin extracted from a small evergreen acacia tree has long been used as a chewing gum. It is powdered and added to sweet yeast breads, milk puddings and ice cream for flavoring. Available in shops specializing in Greek and Middle Eastern foods.

MELOKHIA
Edible green leaf of the hibiscus family, related to okra, it gives off a similar viscous and gluey liquid, but its taste is more like spinach or sorrel. Used to make a classic Egyptian soup (recipe on page 111) and can be purchased dried in stores that specialize in Middle Eastern foods.

MERGUEZ
A North African sausage, quite spicy, made with lamb or beef (recipe on page 182).

MIZITHRA
A Greek soft-curd "cottage" cheese made from the whey that remains from the making of a feta cheese (q.v.). Fresh ricotta is substituted as *mizithra* is not exported.

MORTADELLA
A popular Italian sausage. It has a distinctive pattern that is achieved by the mixing of finely ground (minced) pork with coarsely diced pork fat. The slowly cooked sausage, which usually measures 6 in (15 cm) in diameter, is a popular sandwich meat or stuffing for pasta and meat dishes.

MOZZARELLA
A rindless, white southern Italian cheese traditionally made from the milk of the water buffalo, but now commonly made from cow's milk.

OLIVES
Green and black cured olives are popular throughout the Mediterranean (recipe on page 41). There are many different varieties and ways to flavor them. Among the most common types are niçoise, small brownish black Provençal brine-cured olives packed in olive oil; Kalamata, brine-cured black Greek olives packed in vinegar; Gaeta, small salt-cured Italian black olives; and dark green cracked olives popular in Provence and Greece.

OLIVE OIL
Fundamental to the cooking of all the Mediterranean countries. Olive oil is labeled according to different grades, which are based on acidity. The best olive oils are called extra-virgin, first cold pressing. Other grades include superfine, fine, virgin and pure. Extra-virgin oils lose their bouquet when cooked; use them for cold dishes or add them at the end of cooking. Mild olive oils are suitable for sautéing.

ORANGE FLOWER WATER
A fragrant liquid distilled from orange blossoms used for flavoring syrups and pastries. Available at stores that specialize in Middle Eastern foods and in gourmet sections of fine food stores. Because of its intense flavor, add it judiciously.

OUARKA
Paper-thin leaves of semolina pastry used in Moroccan cuisine to make *b'stilla, briouat* and *brik.* Known as *malsouqua* in Tunisia. *Filo* (q.v.) or Chinese spring roll wrappers can be used as a substitute.

PANCETTA
Italian cured pig belly, the same cut used to make bacon. Most often rolled into a sausagelike shape, but sometimes available flat. Flavored with cloves and black pepper, it is cured for at least 20 days. Occasionally available smoked.

PECORINO CHEESE
One of Italy's best-known sheep's milk cheeses. It is served fresh (2 weeks old) as a slightly salty table cheese, aged as a grating cheese. The most popular varieties are from Rome *(pecorino romano)* and Sardinia *(pecorino sardo).*

PEPPERS
Both chili peppers and sweet peppers (capsicums) are used in Mediterranean cooking. Among the fresh chilies used is a long, dark green hot pepper that is wider at the stem end and tapers to a point, and the cayenne, a small, thin pepper that is commonly dried and ground. To roast and peel fresh peppers, place the peppers directly over a gas flame on the stove top, under a preheated broiler (griller) or atop a charcoal fire and, turning as needed, blacken evenly on all sides. Transfer to a closed paper bag and let sweat for 10–15 minutes, then peel away the blackened skin. Remove the stem, seeds and ribs and cut as directed in individual recipes.

PICADA
Unique to Catalonia, this paste or finely minced mixture of garlic, saffron, fried bread, nuts and occasionally unsweetened chocolate is used as a thickening agent and is added to soups, stews and so on, usually at the end of cooking.

PINE NUT
The long, thin nut of the stone pine tree. Used in many dishes both sweet and savory, throughout the Mediterranean. An Asian

variety of pine nut is sometimes stronger in flavor and not as desirable for use in Mediterranean dishes.

PISTACHIO NUT
Native to the Middle East, the pistachio nut is enclosed in a light brown shell that is easily opened. The nut itself is covered by a brown papery skin and it has green flesh. Used in both sweet and savory dishes.

POMEGRANATE JUICE AND SEEDS
Juice and seeds of an ancient fruit of the Middle East that is a symbol of fertility and abundance. The fruits are sold in specialty markets and keep well for months in a cool, dry place if not picked too ripe. The pomegranate is enjoyed as a fruit, and the sweet-tart juice extracted from its seeds is used for syrups, sherbets and in drinks. The juice is also available in bottles in Middle East shops. The seeds also are used as a garnish for soups, puddings and so on, and can be frozen.

POMEGRANATE SYRUP
A bottled concentrate made from pomegranate juice. To dilute the syrup to make juice, add about 1½ tablespoons syrup to 1 cup (8 fl oz/250 ml) of water.

PORCINI
Large, wild mushrooms (Boletus edulus), known as *cèpes* in France and *steinpilz* in Germany, prized for their meaty texture and woodsy flavor. They have two seasons, early spring and fall. When fresh, they are commonly grilled whole or sliced and sautéed. They are also one of the best mushrooms for drying, and are widely available in this form year-round. To use dried porcini, rinse well to remove surface dirt, cover with hot water and soak for 1 hour. Strain the soaking liquid through a cheesecloth-lined sieve to remove any dirt or sediment; reserve the liquid for cooking, as it is quite tasty.

PRESERVED LEMONS
An important condiment in Moroccan cooking. To make at home, scrub 16 lemons (about 4 lb/2 kg) with a stiff-bristled brush and place in a nonreactive container. Add cold water to cover and let stand for 3 days, changing the water at least once a day. Drain the lemons, then, using a sharp knife, slice lengthwise but leave attached at the top and bottom. Push 1 tablespoon coarse salt into the center of each lemon. Then place 1 tablespoon coarse salt in the bottom of several small sterilized jars. (Small jars are best to use because the lemons do not keep long once the jars are opened.) Pack the salted lemons tightly into the jars, add fresh lemon juice to cover and tightly seal the jars. (Some cooks add boiling water in addition to the lemon juice, but plain lemon juice is best.) Store in a cool, dry place for 3–4 weeks before using. Turn the jars occasionally during this period and do not be alarmed if a white film forms on the lemons; it will wash off and will not affect the flavor. Once the jars are opened, be careful not to get any oil in them or touch the lemon you are removing with a greasy spoon, as you will spoil the remaining lemons in the jar. Refrigerate after opening. To use the lemons, rinse well under running water. Squeeze out the juice and remove the pulp; discard the juice and pulp. Cut the peel as directed in individual recipes.

PROSCIUTTO
Raw salt-cured ham that has been aged to produce moist, lightly veined, intense pink meat with an edge of fat.

PROVOLONE
Southern Italian cheese made with cow's milk. Available in a variety of shapes and sizes—round, oval, pear shaped, cylindrical. Young provolone is sweet; strong provolone has been aged for up to 1 year. Available smoked as well.

PURSLANE
Wild green with reddish stalks used as a salad ingredient for the *fattoush* (recipe on page 45) of Syria and Lebanon and in salads in Greece and other nearby countries. Discard the stalks before using the tender, fleshy leaves.

RAISINS, CURRANTS
Dried fruits used extensively in Mediterranean cooking. They can be added directly to stews if they will have time to simmer in liquids and soften. If not, plump them in hot water to cover (or wine, if specified in the recipe) for about 30 minutes, then drain. If you like, reserve the soaking liquid for adding to the dish.

RAS EL HANOUT
Commonly used in meat and game dishes, this Moroccan spice mixture translates as "top of the shop." Usually includes ginger, peppercorns, cinnamon, allspice, cloves, cardamom, black cumin, aniseed, coriander, cayenne, ginger or galingal, lavender, mace or nutmeg and turmeric, as well as such exotics as belladonna, cantharides, rosebuds and so on. Many of these exotic spices are reputed to be aphrodisiacs. Available in shops specializing in North African foods.

RICE
Rice, both short grain and long grain, is widely used in Mediterranean cooking. In Italy four different kinds of rice are grown: *ordinario,* a very short round rice used for puddings; *semifino,* a round grain of medium length used for soups and salads; *fino,* a round longer grain rice used for risotto; and *superfino,* a fat longer grain rice that is ideal for risotto. The best varieties of superfino are Arborio and Camaroli. These are cooked uncovered and the liquids are added gradually. In Spain most of the rice is cultivated in the province of Valencia and it is a short-grain variety. It is cooked uncovered, all the liquid is added at once and the rice is usually finished off the heat. The rice is used in paella and other rice-based dishes, as well as in soups, salads and so on.
Although some short grain rice is used in the Middle East for puddings, the majority of rice is of the long-grain variety. Its grains are fluffy but firm and separate. The best and most fragrant is basmati ("queen of fragrance"), which is aged to reduce its moisture content. This thin, long rice can be found in markets that specialize in Indian and Middle Eastern foods. In the Middle East rice is usually soaked before cooking and is always cooked covered. In Syria the water is salted and brought to a boil and the drained rice is added; butter or oil is added after the rice is cooked. In Lebanon the butter or oil is added to the cooking water. In Egypt the rice is sautéed in butter or oil, and then the water and salt are added. In all cases the rice boils hard for 2 minutes, the heat is reduced to a simmer and the pan is tightly covered. The rice cooks for about 20 minutes or until small holes appear on the top. Then the heat is turned off and the rice rests for 10 minutes before serving.

RICE FLOUR
A powdery flour made from white rice used in baked goods.

RICOTTA
The name means "recooked," the cheese is made by heating the whey of another cooked cheese like mozzarella or provolone. Soft, white mildly sweet and a little grainy but creamy in texture, ricotta is used in desserts such as *cannoli* and *cassata,* and in fillings for ravioli and other filled pastas. Aged, salted ricotta is a specialty of Sicily. There are also smoked ricottas.

ROMESCO
Also spelled *romescu.* Catalan olive oil-based sauce seasoned with hot pepper, almonds, garlic and tomato. Served with shellfish, meat, grilled leeks.

ROSE WATER
Distilled from fragrant rose petals and used as a flavoring for desserts and syrups. It can be very powerful, so use with caution.

SAFFRON
Saffron, the Arab word for "yellow," is the golden yellow stamens of a purple crocus flower and the world's most high-priced spice. The use of saffron originated in Asia Minor, but most of the best saffron now comes from Spain. Do not be fooled by cheap imitations, which are often crushed marigold petals or turmeric. Available in powdered and in thread form; the latter is preferred. To use the threads, pound in a mortar and steep in warm liquid to bring out the flavor.

SAHLEB
A beige powder made from the dried tubers of a species of orchid. It has a gelatinous quality similar to cornstarch or arrowroot. In Greece and Turkey it is made into a hot drink with milk and sugar. In Lebanon and Syria it is used as the thickener for the custard base for ice cream.

SALT COD
Fresh cod that has been roughly filleted and then salted. Normally, if soaked for 24 hours in cold water to cover, salt cod is ready to use. Depending upon its origin and the length of time it has been in salt, this timing can vary from 12 to 36 hours. Check with your merchant about soaking time when buying salt cod. To soak, immerse the cod in a large bowl of cold water; refrigerate, changing the water several times over the period of soaking. It will have whitened and doubled in bulk when it is ready to be cooked.

SAUSAGE CASINGS
Can be purchased from your butcher. The casings are usually lamb intestines and come cleaned and heavily salted. Soak overnight in water to cover, then rinse thoroughly, holding them under the tap so the cold water rushes through them.

SEEDS OF PARADISE
A combination of equal parts aniseeds, fennel seeds, brown sesame seeds and black caraway seeds; used as a topping for Tunisian bread. Not to be confused with grains of paradise, a kind of peppercorn.

SEMOLINA
Also known as pasta flour. A hard-wheat flour made from durum wheat; prized for pasta-making because it produces a dough that cooks up firmly.

SMEN
North African herb-flavored cooked salted butter, slightly pungent in flavor. Related to *samneh,* Arabic clarified butter made from cow or sheep's milk.

SQUID
To clean a squid, pull the head and clinging innards free from the body pouch. Pull out and discard the transparent quill-like cartilage from the pouch. Squeeze out the small beak from the mouth at the base of the tentacles and, using scissors, cut away the eyes. Using your fingers, clean out the pouch under cold running water. Discard everything except the tentacle-head portion and the body pouch with the attached wings. Rub off the brownish violet skin. Rinse all the squid parts well, then cut as directed in individual recipes.

STOCK: BEEF, CHICKEN AND FISH
Homemade stocks are easy to make and can be frozen for future use. Canned broth may be substituted for stock in most recipes, but it should be used with discretion because most of these products are very salty.

To make beef stock: Roast 4 lb (2 kg) beef bones (with some meat on them) in a 450°F (230°C) oven in a roasting pan for 30 minutes, turning once. Place the bones in a large pot and add 2 onions, peeled and halved, 3 whole carrots, 3 whole celery stalks, 1 bay leaf, a handful of parsley sprigs, 1 teaspoon salt and ½ teaspoon cracked peppercorns. Discard the fat from the roasting pan and deglaze the pan with two cups of water. Add to the pot with 3 additional quarts (3 l) of water. Bring to a boil, then reduce the heat and simmer very gently, partially covered, for about 5 hours, skimming off any foam that rises to the surface for the first 30 minutes or so. Strain through several thicknesses of cheesecloth and let cool, uncovered. Makes about 3 quarts (3 l).

To make chicken stock: Place about 4 lb (2 kg) chicken pieces (backs, wings, necks and the remains of a roast chicken) in a large pot. Add 2 onions, peeled and halved, 2 whole carrots, 2 whole celery stalks, a handful of parsley sprigs, 1 bay leaf, 6 crushed peppercorns, 1 teaspoon dried thyme and 1 teaspoon salt. Pour in about 4 quarts (4 l) of water, or enough to cover ingredients by 1 in (2.5 cm). Bring to a boil and reduce heat and simmer gently, partially covered for about 4 hours, skimming off any foam that rises to the surface for the first 30 minutes or so. Strain through several thicknesses of cheesecloth and let cool, uncovered. Makes 3 quarts (3 l).

To make fish stock: Rinse about 4 lb (2 kg) combined white-fleshed fish heads and meaty skeletons under running water and place in a large pot. Add 2 onions, peeled and sliced, 2 carrots, peeled and thinly sliced, 2 stalks celery, sliced, 1 bay leaf, 8 crushed peppercorns and 1 teaspoon salt. Add 2 cups (16 fl oz/500 ml) dry white wine and about 3 quarts (3 l) of water, or enough to cover the ingredients by 1 in (2.5 cm). Bring to a boil, and reduce the heat and simmer, uncovered, for about 45 minutes, skimming any foam that forms on the surface. Strain through several thicknesses of cheesecloth and cool uncovered. Makes 3 quarts (3 l).

SUMAC
Crushed dried red berries of a species of nonpoisonous sumac shrub. It has a sour, somewhat lemony taste with a hint of pepper. It is sprinkled over rice in Persian cooking and on grilled meats. In Lebanon it is combined with marjoram and sesame to make a topping called *zaatar* (q.v.). The whole berries are soaked and the resulting flavored liquid is used in cooking. Whole and ground berries are available in Middle Eastern stores.

TABIL
Tunisian spice mixture of garlic, caraway, coriander, and hot pepper, in almost equal parts.

TAGINE
Name for a Moroccan terra-cotta cooking utensil and for the stew that is cooked in it.

TAHINI
Also spelled *tahina.* A thick, oily paste of ground sesame seeds used in Middle Eastern cooking in savory and sweet dishes. Tahini separates upon standing and requires stirring before use to reincorporate the oil that settles on the top. Sold in bottles and cans in Middle Eastern shops, well-stocked food stores and health-food stores. Refrigerate after opening to prevent rancidity.

TARAMA
Mullet or carp roe preserved in salt and sometimes in oil. It is imported from Greece and comes in jars. It is puréed with bread, garlic, onion, olive oil and lemon and served as a spread called *taramasalata* (recipe on page 41).

TARATOR
An Arabic sauce made with tahini (q.v.), lemon juice and garlic. In Lebanon, Syria and Egypt, this paste is spread over cooked fish (recipe on page 60). In Turkish *tarator,* the tahini is usually omitted; instead, olive oil is mixed with bread crumbs, garlic, lemon juice or vinegar and walnuts or hazelnuts, or occasionally with almonds or pine nuts. It is served with fried fish or cooked vegetables.

TOMATO SAUCE
To make a simple, light tomato sauce, place 2½ lbs (1.25 kg) canned plum (Roma) tomatoes with their juices, in a food processor fitted with the metal blade. Pulse until finely chopped but not puréed. Transfer to a large heavy nonaluminum saucepan and stir in 1 cup (8 fl oz/250 ml) canned tomato purée. Heat slowly, stirring often, until a low boil is reached, then reduce the heat to a simmer. Cook until thickened; the timing will depend upon the juiciness of the tomatoes and how thick you want the sauce to be. If desired, stir in 2–3 tablespoons olive oil or unsalted butter and then season to taste with salt and freshly ground pepper. This is a basic tomato sauce; you may add garlic, herbs or spices to taste. Store in the refrigerator for about 1 week.

YOGURT
In the Middle East yogurt is made every day. While all varieties of yogurt from whole milk to nonfat are available in stores, you also can make your own: Purchase yogurt with a live culture. In a saucepan, combine 6 cups (48 fl oz/1.5 l) milk and ¾ cup (3 oz/90 g) milk powder and heat, stirring, until it reaches 180°F (82°C), and then cool to 110°–115°F (43°–46°C). Add ¼ cup (2 oz/60 g) yogurt and mix well. Pour into a jar, cover the jar with towels and keep in a warm, draft-free place for 6–12 hours. The longer it sits, the tarter it becomes. Refrigerate when set. Chill for at least 2 hours before using, and use within a few days. Some recipes specify drained, thickened yogurt. To drain, place in a sieve lined with cheesecloth (muslin) in a cool place or in the refrigerator and let drain from 3 hours to up to 1 day. It will thicken considerably and become like a soft cheese.

ZAATAR
Can refer either to the herb thyme or to a powdered mixture of sesame, sumac (q.v.) and thyme used on oiled pita bread and as a flavoring in meat dishes. Occasionally marjoram is added to this blend as well.

ACKNOWLEDGMENTS

Joyce Goldstein would like to thank Dan Glazier and Jennifer Millar. The photographer and stylist would like to thank the following: Accoutrement, Mosman; Bay Tree, Woollahra; The Art of Food and Wine, Woollahra; David Jones, Sydney; Corso de Fiori, Chatswood; Orson, and Blake, Woollahra; In Residence, Woollahra; Sentimental Journey, Woollahra; Sandy de Beyer, Mosman; Simple Pleasures, Neutral Bay; Sewita Marble, Silverwater; Hale Imports, Villeroy & Boch and John Dufficey. The publishers and the photographers would like to thank the following people and organizations for their assistance in the preparation of this book: Sigrid Chase, Richard Van Oosterhout, Kim Green, Miriam Coupe, Dawn Low, Janique Poncelet, Tori Ritchie, Fee-ling Tan, Jonette Banzon, Patty Hill, Angela Williams, Laurie Wertz, Wendely Harvey, Bruce Bailey, Tarji Mickelson.

PHOTOGRAPHY CREDITS

The publishers would like to thank the following photographers and organizations for permission to reproduce their photographs:
(Abbreviations: b=below, t=top)

Allstock/David Barnes 23; Allstock/Ric Ergenbright 66; Allstock/Guy Marche 68; Allstock/Gary Braasch 73t; Allstock/Art Wolfe 94; Allstock/Connie Coleman 157t; Allstock/Will & Deni McIntyre 225b

Australian Picture Library/Leo Meier 121

Comstock/Georg Gurster 72b; Comstock/Bill Elizey 102b, 157b; Comstock/Hartman-DeWitt 189t; Comstock/Ed Pieratt 225t

FPG International/Yoichiro Miyazaki 26; FPG International/Travel Pix 64–65; FPG International/Ann & Myron Sutton 118; FPG International/Farrell Graham 150; FPG International/Richard Nowitz 152b; FPG International/Richard Hamilton Smith 194; FPG International/Travel Pix 195t; FPG International/Michael Goldman 195b; FPG International/Ulf Sjostedt 220

Image Bank/Grafton Marshall Smith 125b

Susan Katz 156t, 188

Odyssey-Chicago/Robert Frerck 24–25

Stock Market/David Ball 18; Stock Market/Tibor Bognár 33b; Stock Market/Luis Villota 73b; Stock Market/Dick Durrance 92–93; Stock Market/Johanna Simeone Huber 97; Stock Market/Bill Wassman 102t, 124; Stock Market/Harvey Lloyd 125t; Stock Market/Zefa-Everts 216–17

Tony Stone Worldwide/Steve Vidler 2–3, 146–47, 218; Tony Stone Worldwide/Stephen Studd 6; Tony Stone Worldwide/Robert Frerck 12–13; Tony Stone Worldwide/Warren Jacobs 14; Tony Stone Worldwide/Hugh Sitton 15, 184–85; Tony Stone Worldwide/David C. Tomlinson 21; Tony Stone Worldwide/Manfred Mehlig 28; Tony Stone Worldwide/Jon Bradley 29; Tony Stone Worldwide/Michael Busselle 32; Tony Stone Worldwide/Charlie Waite 33t; Tony Stone Worldwide/Nicholas DeVore 69, 96, 99; Tony Stone Worldwide/Richard Passmore 72t, 191; Tony Stone Worldwide/Joe Cornish 98; Tony Stone Worldwide/George Grigoriou 116–17; Tony Stone Worldwide/David Hanson 151; Tony Stone Worldwide/Linny M. Cunningham 156b; Tony Stone Worldwide/Leonard Nadel 186; Tony Stone Worldwide/Sylvain Grandadam 189b, 190, 221

Harold Sund 20, 120, 148, 152t, 153

Westlight/Jim Zuckerman cover; Westlight/Lawrence Manning endpapers; Westlight/Jon Gardey 19; Westlight/Craig Aurness 22, 103; Westlight/Brent Bear 224

ILLUSTRATION GUIDE

CONTENTS: The Copts, native Egyptian Christians who resisted conversion to Islam throughout the centuries, carved this limestone architectural relief of a dolphin in the fourth or fifth century.

INTRO: The legacy of over 700 years of Moorish occupation in Spain is evidenced by this Islamic gold dinar. While the last of the Muslims were forced out as early as 1492, Arabic coins were still being minted in Madrid in the eighteenth century.

SPAIN: A long succession of invaders in Spain has left an equally varied history of artistic influences in this country. This Roman-style architectural relief is the legacy of the early conquerors of the second century B.C.

FRANCE: European monks often Christianized pagan legends to illustrate the hazards of sin to their illiterate public. As a subject for medieval carvers hired by the Church, the mermaid was a universal favorite.

ITALY: This relief from a limestone sarcophagus (circa second century b.c.) marks the height of the Etruscan civilization. What little is known today of the Etruscan culture is gleaned from the contents of their excavated tombs.

GREECE: Mycenaean artists cultivated a highly skilled individual style. This Greek storage jar from the fourteenth century depicts the formality and restraint characterized by Mycenaean motifs.

TURKEY: Decorative Kufic and Naskhi scripts from the Ottoman period have been manipulated to represent Noah's Ark. Ornamental Kufic became an important element in Islamic art as early as the eighth century.

MIDDLE EAST: The power of ancient Phoenicia (modern-day Lebanon) was drawn from the Mediterranean Sea. Master shipbuilders and navigators, Phoenicians had established themselves as a trading empire and a diplomatic and commercial center of the ancient world by 1250 B.C.

NORTH AFRICA: This Moroccan pendant, designed to emulate a hand holding a fish, symbolizes a respect for the life-giving powers of the Mediterranean. From the earliest known civilizations, the sea has been a vital link for sustenance and commerce.

TUSCANY
THE BEAUTIFUL COOKBOOK

AUTHENTIC RECIPES FROM THE PROVINCES OF TUSCANY

Fried Noodle Nests (top, recipe page 334) and Wide Noodles with Hare Sauce (bottom, recipe page 325)

AUTHENTIC RECIPES FROM THE PROVINCES OF TUSCANY

TUSCANY
THE BEAUTIFUL COOKBOOK

TEXT AND RECIPES BY
LORENZA DE' MEDICI

FOOD PHOTOGRAPHY BY
PETER JOHNSON

STYLED BY JANICE BAKER

SCENIC PHOTOGRAPHY BY
MICHAEL FREEMAN

HarperCollins*Publishers*

First published in the USA by Collins San Francisco.

Produced by Weldon Owen Inc.
814 Montgomery Street
San Francisco, CA 49133 USA
Phone (415) 291-0100 Fax 415 291-8841

Weldon Owen Inc.:
Chairman: Kevin Weldon
President: John Owen
General Manager: Stuart Laurence
Co-Editions Director: Derek Barton
Manging Editor: Jane Fraser
Project Coordinator: Laurie Wertz
Translator: Jennifer Grillo, with Monica Smith
Editor: Sharon Silva
Proofreader: Jonathan Schwartz
Production: Stephanie Sherman, Mick Bagnate
Design: Tom Morgan, Blue Design
Design Concept: John Bull,
The Book Design Company
Map: Mike Gorman
Illustrations: Neil Shigley

For information address HarperCollins Publishers, Inc., 10 East 53rd Street, New York, NY 10022.

Library of Congress Cataloging-in-Publication Data:

De'Medici, Strucchi, Lorenza.
Tuscany, the beautiful cookbook : authentic recipes from the provinces of Tuscany / recipes and text by Lorenza de' Medici ; food photography by Peter Johnson ; scenic photography by Michael Freeman.
Includes Index.
ISBN 0-00-255032-6
1. Cookery, Italian—Tuscan style. 2. Tuscany (Italy)—Description and travel—1981. I. Title.
TX713.2.T86D4 1992
641.5945'5—dc20 91—42832

ISBN 0-06-757600-1 (pbk.)

99 00 01 02 03 TOP 6 5 4 3 2 1

Printed by Toppan in China

Pages 2–3: A solitary rower glides past the Ponte Vecchio.

Right: The crew from Ardenza trains for the Palio Marinaro race in Livorno.

Pages 8–9: Dipped Celery (recipe page 37) *and Deep-Froed Baby Artichokes* (recipe page 37).

Pages 12–13: Farmhouse and newly planted olive trees near Bibona.

Endpapers: Detail from Lorenzo Ghiberti's bronze doors, Baptistry, Florence.

AGENZIE IPPICHE
DI LIVORNO
NAUTICA

Fried Red Mullet in Tomato Sauce (recipe page 417). Photographed in Livorno.

Contents

Flag throwers dazzle the crowd during the Palio parade in Siena.

INTRODUCTION

It is no exaggeration to say that traditional Tuscan cuisine goes back three thousand years. Ample evidence of the Etruscan diet has been found at many archaeological sites, from the famous Tarquinia tombs near southern Tuscany to recently discovered house remains near Lucca in the north. These findings confirm that Tuscan eating habits have maintained a continuity through the centuries.

It is the Tuscans' attitude toward food that appears to have changed the least. The approach is based on a love of wine, freshly pressed olive oil and bread. In fact, the secret of Tuscan cookery is, and always has been, its simplicity. Sole or lamb described as *all'etrusco* on a Tuscan menu is not mere whimsy. These dishes actually forge a solid link with the past and incorporate the three basic elements of wine, oil and bread, which to the Tuscans are almost sacred.

Bread and olives were the food of slaves in Etruscan times, and today bread and olives are still found together on the shelves of most bakeries. Garlic, onions and leeks were often eaten with bread, not only for their taste but because they were considered good for the health, stimulating, and even, it was said, aphrodisiac. Bread continues to play an important role in Tuscan cuisine. The classic unsalted loaf is the perfect foil for the assertive flavors of country ham, sheep's milk cheese and salami. To a Tuscan, nothing is more satisfying than a slice of coarse country bread toasted over the fire, rubbed with garlic and sprinkled with oil.

Bread is never thrown away in Tuscany. It is the basic ingredient of several of the most popular dishes. *Ribollita* (or *frantoiana*—the name changes from place to place) is a thick, comforting soup made from bread, green vegetables, beans, black cabbage and extra virgin olive oil. Its summer equivalent is *panzanella,* a salad composed of bread, tomatoes, onion and oil.

Good olive oil is also vital to Tuscan cooking. Olives for the production of extra virgin olive oil must be picked very carefully, in the same way that they have been harvested for two thousand years. Olives for pressing should never touch the ground, so large tarpaulins are placed under the trees to catch any that fall while the others are carefully gathered by hand. It is essential that the olives be dry when they are harvested and that they be pressed immediately, so that none of their fragrance is lost. The grindstones used today for cold pressing are more or less identical to those used by the Etruscans.

There are, of course, large plants where olive oil is produced in quantity, but those operations use chemical solvents to release the oil, which changes the flavor and, even more importantly, increases the acid content. The production of olive oil is strictly controlled, and only cold-pressed oil may be described as "extra virgin olive oil." In the market there are same-sized bottles of oil that

The arches of Via Cavour, the main street in Poppi.

differ widely in price. Remember, an inexpensive bottle of oil cannot contain extra virgin oil, because the costs of producing it are far too high.

Many scholars agree that the first people known to have used olive oil for seasoning their food were the Etruscans. And now, after almost three millennia, dietitians all over the world, led by American scientists who have thoroughly investigated the original Mediterranean diet, have discovered that the oleic acid present in olive oil is the only fat that does not increase the cholesterol content of the blood.

The use of olive oil is common not only to Tuscany but to all of central and southern Italy. Interestingly enough, the famous Gothic Line that divided the part of Italy liberated by the Allied forces from the rest still held by the Germans in the last war, more or less coincides with the dividing line between the Italians who use oil and those in the north who cook with butter and lard.

One of the first physicians known to have emphasized the importance of limiting the use of lard and animal fat was Michele Savonarola, who informs readers in his sixteenth-century work *Libreto de tute le cose che se manzano communamente* ("All the things we generally eat") that it is much healthier to eat meat cooked on a spit, which, incidentally, is another Tuscan custom. He also insisted that olive oil should be used whenever possible. In Savonarola's day, however, it was not easy to find olive oil outside the areas where it was produced. In fact, in the poorer homes of northern Italy, olive oil was only used on special occasions until quite recently.

The third great element of the Tuscan kitchen is wine. Strong and light, red and white wines were drunk by the Etruscans and are still essential to the Tuscan table. The Etruscans were inclined to infuse their wines with honey and herbs, to enhance their taste and their own good spirits. Tuscany remains very much a civilization in which wine is not just a drink but a flavoring and an ingredient, a solace and a boon.

Catching up on the latest news is a favorite pastime in the Piazza del Duomo, San Gimignano.

TUSCANY
Bologna
EMILIA-ROMAGNA
CARFAGNANA
ALPI APUANE
APPENNINI
Abetone
Carrara
Massa
Barga
VERSILIA
Forte dei Marmi
Pistoia
Viareggio
Montecatini
Prato
L. di Massaciuccoli
Serchio
LUCCA
Fiesole
Sieve
CASENTINO
FIRENZE
Pisa
Arno
Greve
VALDARNO
PRATOMAGNO
San Miniato
Greve in Chianti
LIVORNO
Sansepolcro
Tiber
CHIANTI
Radda in Chianti
Badia a Coltibuono
Montevarchi
San Gimignano
AREZZO
Monterchi
Volterra
VAL DI CHIANA
SIENA
UMBRIA
Cecina
Cortona
COLLINE METALLIFERE
Arbia
Lago di Trasimeno
Perugia
Merse
Montepulciano
Montalcino
Pienza
Massa Marittima
Chiusi
Piombino
Follonica
MAREMMA
ELBA
Punta Ala
Ombrone
GROSSETO
Scansano
Sorano
Pitigliano
Lago di Bolsena
Pianosa
Formiche de Grosseto
Orbetello
LAZIO
ARGENTARIO
Montecristo
Giglio
Giannutri
TYRRHENIAN SEA
Tarquinia

Cypress trees nestle up to a chapel near San Quirico d'Orcia. Planted to mark boundaries and flank entrances to churches, cypresses are the unofficial sentinels of the Tuscan landscape.

Gastronomically speaking, Tuscany covers a large region made up of seacoast and hills, plains and mountains, cities, suburbs and villages, all populated by individualists. As Ugo Tognazzi, the very popular Italian film star and cook, said, "In Florence, if there are eighteen apartments in a building, there will be eighteen different recipes for *ribollita* soup." For simplicity's sake, Tuscany may be divided roughly into the coastal region and the interior. The former does not have a venerable history, because for so long it was a malaria-ridden marsh and therefore sparsely populated. It is true that Etruscans probably cooked *cee* (baby eels) and Livorno's famed *cacciucco* (a fish soup now prepared all along the Versilia coast), but it is not biased to say that the great Tuscan culinary traditions of roasts, stews, soups and *pappardelle* (wide noodles) originated in the inland areas.

Until a few years ago, Tuscans did not even know how to cook spaghetti. But the tradition of fresh pasta is centuries-old: *pappardelle* are said to have been unearthed in an Etruscan kitchen, together with a serrated wheel for cutting pasta dough. *Pappardelle* are still enjoyed today, along with *pici,* a type of thick, fresh spaghetti from Montalcino; *ravioli* filled with spinach and ricotta; and, in Lucchesia, meat-filled pasta called *tordelli.*

Another feature of Tuscan cookery, both ancient and modern, is the presence of certain herbs, including sage, rosemary, parsley, thyme, marjoram and bay leaves. The Etruscans made particular use of bay leaves and parsley. Herbs are now central to the Tuscan pantry. They are used to enhance the flavors of foods, which results in less fat being needed and thus a lighter final result. In fact, long before the first recipe book appeared in Tuscany, information on cooking was gleaned from herbals and medical books, indicating that there is a long tradition of attention to the medicinal and dietetic properties of the herbs used in cooking.

Not many cakes and desserts are native to Tuscany, although the excellent *panforte* a rich, flat fruitcake, comes from Siena, and there are a few fine sweet breads. *Brigidini,* large flat wafers from Lamporecchio, are sold at village fairs, and *castagnaccio* a chestnut flour cake, originally came from Lucca.

Chestnut trees have always thrived in the Garfagnana, the mountainous region in the province of Lucca, and until the last war chestnut flour was used to prepare a variety of dishes. The chestnuts were gathered and taken to a *metato,* a chestnut oasthouse, where they were spread on lattice frames and dried by the heat from a slow-burning fire on the floor below. The dried chestnuts were then ground into flour. Although there are only a few such mills left in Lucchesia, the flour is still available in grocery stores. During the chestnut season, friends gather around their fireplaces to roast chestnuts or to cook *necci,* chestnut flour pancakes baked over the embers in round iron molds. They are eaten either plain or filled with ricotta.

There is another Tuscan cuisine well worth remembering, and it is the one that was almost lost. Until a few years ago, those who knew and loved the old dishes based on variety meats and the tougher cuts complained bitterly that they had practically disappeared. Now, thanks to a few intelligent restaurant owners and keen private cooks, dishes like *cibreo* from Florence, *frittata di fegatini* (chicken liver frittata) from Prato, and *scottiglia* from Arezzo (made with various meat and chicken cuts) have been revived.

Caterina de' Medici was very fond of *cibreo*. Made of cockscombs and chicken liver and served on a bed of artichokes, she took it, and Tuscan cooking in general, with her to France. *Scottiglia* was originally a very humble dish made from the meat that stuck to the calf skins when they were taken to Arezzo to be tanned. It is believed that the Tuscans' fondness for these more unusual cuts goes back to ancient times when men and children gathered in the kitchen to keep the women company while they watched over the slowly simmering meat.

The popularity of vegetables in Tuscany has an equally long history. During the Renaissance, Florentine monks prepared great dishes of leeks and meat for the feast of San Lorenzo. Tuscans often cook fish and vegetables together; cuttlefish with Swiss chard and salt cod with chick-peas or leeks are, for example, typically Tuscan preparations. Bean dishes and molds made from spinach, fennel, carrots or all manner of other vegetables are delicious and frequent fare in Tuscan restaurants and private homes as well.

Almost everywhere in Tuscany, meat is grilled over open fires. What could appear more simple, yet at the same time be more difficult, than to match perfectly the quality and texture of meat with the temperature of burning embers? Everywhere in Italy, except in Florence, people ask for a grilled *fiorentina,* meaning a

Florence's Palazzo degli Uffizi was designed by Vasari as administrative offices for the Medici. The dramatic U-shaped building now houses one of the world's most important art collections.

T-bone steak. Although to the uninitiated a *fiorentina* is symbolic of Tuscan food, it is actually a fairly recent acquisition, born out of the custom of English noblemen ordering steaks when they stopped on the Grand Tour to winter between Fiesole and the Ponte Vecchio.

Tuscans have a preference for earthenware pots and pans; they believe cooking in them brings out the true flavor of sauces, stews and soups. Indeed, the presence of a special ceramic bean pot, in which beans can be simmered slowly and very gently, is de rigueur for the classic Tuscan kitchen.

Traditional Tuscan cheese is also much the same as it was in Etruscan times. Most of it is made from sheep's milk or goat's milk, although cow's milk is now frequently substituted for the latter. As Panunto, an early Florentine writer, explained, "Sheep's milk cheese is much healthier than cheese made from cow's milk because it smells nicer, the flavor is better balanced because it is made with milk that has a better complexion, and, furthermore, cow's milk cheese makes your blood thicker because it is more fatty than sheep's milk." *Pecorino,* a sheep's milk cheese produced around Arezzo, the Maremma, Volterra, Chianti and Pienza, is never missing from a Tuscan table. There is an old Tuscan proverb that says, "If you want good cheese and a good time, send your sheep to graze on thyme." Another old Tuscan saying declares that a dinner is not a dinner if you do not finish with cheese.

Not surprisingly, Italy's first known book on gastronomy appeared in Tuscany, where food has always played an important role. *Il libro della cocina* ("The kitchen book"), by an anonymous Tuscan author, appeared toward the end of the fourteenth century and probably refers to even earlier sources. It contains suggestions for special occasions and includes the following recipe entitled The Garden: "On important feast days, such as Easter, make a large tree, vine or trellis out of pasta. Then make pastry apples, pears, birds, bunches of grapes or whatever else you fancy and brush them with egg. Fill them with the mixture mentioned above [the recipe is provided] and color them yellow, green, white or black. Then hang them on the branches of the trees. Decorate the top of the tree with a cage filled with real birds. You may also hang seasonal fruit from the branches of your tree. When you carry the tree or vine or trellis out into the courtyard or garden, build a fire of a variety of sweet-smelling twigs nearby."

This effort certainly cannot be compared with the sumptuous banquets of the Tuscan nobility served during the Renaissance, a time when Italian cuisine led Europe, thanks mostly to Caterina de' Medici. Much of the literature on medieval banquets was written by Tuscans such as Folgore from San Gimignano, the Sienese Pietro di Viviano Corsellino, and Pucci from Florence. The first person to introduce science to the Italian kitchen was a Tuscan by adoption. In 1891, Pellegrino Artusi published *La scienza in cucina e l'arte di mangiare bene—manuale pratico per le famiglie* ("Science in the kitchen and the art of eating well—a practical family manual") in Florence, and it is still one of the most frequently consulted cookbooks in Italian households.

Many of the restaurant owners in northern Italy were originally from Tuscany. One wave of migration began in the nineteenth century, when the first grand hotels were opened on the shores of Lake Maggiore and Lake Como. Whole families moved there to work in the

Tourists flock to Pisa to see the Leaning Tower, the famous belltower that has been inching its way toward horizontal since its completion in 1372.

Fishermen cast their nets at the mouth of the Arno River in Marina di Pisa. In wintertime the catch will be tiny baby eels called cee*, a local specialty.*

hotel kitchens and they were followed by others, who stayed on in the large northern cities. Some Tuscans started as vendors of bread made out of chick-pea flour or chestnut flour; others sold tripe. Later they opened trattorias and, more recently, the better chefs started their own restaurants. This Tuscan tradition of preparing and serving food, however, began much earlier. There was, of course, the army of chefs who went to France with Caterina de' Medici's court in the sixteenth century, but even before then, in the Middle Ages, the Knights of Altopascio were known to ring a bell at night to call passing travelers to share a bowl of soup. It is no surprise that today all over the world there are literally thousands of restaurateurs who originally came from Altopascio or the neighboring towns of Montecatini and Lucca.

From the earliest times, Tuscany has been a leader of the arts. So it is not surprising that Tuscan cuisine is a leader of the culinary arts. All the basic ingredients are finer in Tuscany than in any other region of Italy. The mountains are rich in mushrooms and chestnuts. All kinds of berries, from raspberries to blackberries, grow wild, and the hills around Abetone are carpeted with blueberries. Trout are caught in the streams, and fish are taken straight from the sea to the markets. Vegetables are cultivated in abundance in the reclaimed Maremma soil. Game birds, wild boar and hare are bagged throughout the area. In the Val di Chiana the famous Chianina cattle are raised for their meat, generally considered the best in Italy. Sheep and goats graze on the hills around Siena, and pigs are raised everywhere, hence the excellent Tuscan ham, sausages and salamis.

A famous Florentine restaurateur loves to tell about the time he was invited to present a Tuscan dinner at a grand hotel in another region of Italy. He was not very keen on the idea, but he was assured that he would have no problems. All he had to do was bring his cooks with him. Wisely he sent his chef ahead to check the situation. But the chef called in despair. The oil came from Liguria, and although it was very good, it was much lighter than Tuscan oil, which is greener, thicker and sharper. The peas were canned. The asparagus were by no means Tuscan. And instead of the hearty Tuscan bread there were dainty little rolls, probably perfect for a grand international hotel, but quite unsuitable for Tuscan cooking. Thus the restaurateur—and it should be said that Tuscans are not famous for their tact—loaded a truck with local ingredients and set off, taking all the necessary supplies with him.

FIRENZE

FIRENZE

There are many splendid cities in Tuscany, all with their marvelous art and atmosphere and food. But it must be granted that Florence, the Tuscan capital, is supreme in art and cuisine. This accolade is not so much due to present-day Florentine cooking as it is to the very significant contribution made by Florence to the history of Italian gastronomy—and to the European table as well.

During the Renaissance, women played a fundamental role in this story. Curiously enough, most of the poulterers and greengrocers were women, and toward the end of the fifteenth century Florence had eight woman-run shops selling game woodcock and hare, venison and foxes, wild boar and peacocks. At the market, women presided over fruit, vegetable and flower stalls and also sold medicinal herbs, the most common of which were nettles, calamint and mallow.

It is, however, thanks to the ladies of the Medici court that Florentine cooking was developed and refined. Noblewomen from all over Italy and even from abroad joined the court. They were women who knew how to combine their native dishes with local recipes so that a real cuisine, as well as the art of entertaining, evolved and reached a peak during the Renaissance. Clarice Orsini, Lorenzo the Magnificent's wife, introduced elements of Roman cooking, while Eleonora of Toledo, wife of Cosimo I, brought the specialties of her Spanish homeland. Yet other new ideas arrived with Giovanna of Austria, the first wife of Francesco I, and Bianca Cappello

Left: Just south of the bustling streets of Florence, across the Arno, lies a serene world of grand villas and country retreats. Previous pages: The city's oldest bridge, the Ponte Vecchio, was originally home to blacksmiths and butcher shops until a Medici ruler replaced them with jewelers in 1593.

The Palazzo Vecchio has served as Florence s political center since medieval times. Today it is the town hall. Perched on the mast are a lion and a lily, the city's symbols.

from Venice, his second wife. All of these women influenced the food and style of entertaining in Florence, until the dishes and decorations at the Medici court were considered works of art. Dinners became veritable banquets, with an infinite number of ever subtler courses.

Sorbets made with oranges and lemons plucked from the citrus trees in the formal gardens were regularly served at the Florentine court, and even nowadays they are considered a refinement. Not far from the church of Santa Maria Novella, carefully collected winter ice was stored in specially dug deep trenches to prevent it from melting during the hot summer months. Sorbets generally came at the end of the meal, but if the banquet was particularly rich they were served between the main courses to stimulate the diners' digestion.

Although usually thought of as French, béchamel sauce actually came from Tuscany. One of the royal chefs apparently aroused the envy of other courtiers who would have preferred he name it for them rather than for Louis de Béchameil, Marquis de Nointel, who was majordomo to Louis XIV. No doubt the chef was right to do so, because when Caterina de' Medici introduced the sauce to France it had the rather unfortunate moniker of *colla,* which means "glue." As the fourteen-year-old bride of Henry II of France, Caterina took with her a great gift for politics, a battalion of cooks, and the dishes of her native land.

At court, good wine was always present on the table. Trebbiano and Greco, imported from the islands of Giglio and Elba where the Greeks had planted Ansonica vines, were particularly prized. From a letter written by Lorenzo the Magnificent we learn that "vermiglio" from the vineyards at Badia a Coltibuono was also enjoyed. However, it appears that white wine was preferred to red at the time.

By the Renaissance, the Tuscans' love of good wine was already well established. When Leonardo da Vinci, who was born in wine country, moved to the court of Ludovico il Moro in Milan, he asked for vines to be planted in the garden. And during those same years, many of the Florentine noble families were selling wine from their country estates.

Church prelates did not lag far behind the Medici court when it came to food. They seem to have had a weakness for *biancomangiare*—pounded chicken or veal and ground almonds cooked together to make a white meat jelly. A sweet version made with honey, almonds and sheep's milk eventually became *blancmange.* We also have to thank the ecclesiastic cooks for being the first to introduce to Italian regional cooking the novelties brought from the East by the crusaders.

The first expert to recognize the importance of Arab confectionery was Bartolomeo Scappi, whose *Opera dell'arte di cucinare* ("Work on the art of cooking") is the most important book on this subject published during the Renaissance. Scappi, for example, gave detailed and accurate instructions on how to prepare the wafers that are still made in Montecatini. Wafers have been popular in Florence for centuries, and wafermakers were considered important enough to be members of the Bakers' Guild. Many of these culinary craftsmen came from Sicily, where there had been a strong Arab influence. *Brigidini* are famous Tuscan wafers that take their name from the Convent of Santa Brigida in Pistoia.

Another very famous Renaissance cook, Bartolomeo Sacchi, was strongly influenced by Tuscany. Although he was born near Cremona in 1421, he spent many years

An explosion of poppies and daisies graces a hillside near Buggiano. The Tuscan landscape has inspired centuries of artists and writers who have come here to surround themselves with natural beauty and human genius.

Late-afternoon traffic crowds the Ponte Santa Trinita in Florence. Despite the constant roar of motorcycles and buses the city remains a walker's paradise, a treasure trove of Renaissance art, architecture and spirit.

in Florence, where he evolved a unique philosophy of food. Sacchi is just as well-known for the advice he gave about eating as he is for his recipes. Some of his suggestions are still valid today: "First eat all those things that activate the stomach and give light and measured nourishment, such as an apple or some pears . . . also lettuce or anything that can be eaten either raw or cooked, dressed with oil and vinegar. Then eggs, and confectionery sweetened with spices, honey and sugar."

There was also a middle-class kitchen, which was slightly richer than the Florentine cooking of today. This is a list from a sixteenth-century recipe book that is not far removed from a modern shopping list: "Mullet from the sea, eel from the Ombrone or from Orbetello; pike, carp and tench from Lake Bolsena; partridge, hare, larks, peacocks, pullets; lambs and half a kid; herbs and leaf vegetables; cabbages, beans, chick-peas; horseradish, lupine seeds, leeks, garlic; pasta, barley, spelt; wafers and sheep's milk cheese; anise, sage, cloves and cinnamon for biscuits."

Among the middle classes, capon was the most popular meat and was prepared in several different ways. It was stuffed and sometimes seasoned with bunches of herbs. Bay leaves, thyme, rosemary, marjoram and sage were as popular in Florence as they were in the rest of Tuscany. Capon was also roasted in the same way as duck and goose, with the cooking juices used as a pasta sauce. *Arrosto morto,* meat slowly cooked in wine and chopped vegetables, was another classic roast of the era.

The same tradition brings us mixed cuts of meat roasted on a spit, slowly turned over embers sprinkled with cloves, pine needles and juniper berries to enhance the flavor. Braised meat, which before the discovery of America and the advent of the tomato was cooked in *agresto* (the juice of unripe grapes and thyme), is still very popular. Florence is celebrated for its stews simmered in shallow earthenware casseroles and seasoned with wild fennel, garlic, lemon peel and mixed spices.

Yet another feature of Florentine cooking is the sauce called *dolceforte,* or "sweet and pungent." It is often used with wild boar and tongue and is made very simply by dissolving sugar in vinegar to which raisins, pine nuts and a little chocolate may be added.

The diet of the poorer Florentines consisted of bread, millet, fava (broad) beans and chestnuts, and many of these ingredients remain important. A variety of wild plants were and still are used to flavor bread and eggs. A soup called *panata* stems from those times and is made with stale bread, which is ground and mixed with egg, grated cheese and nutmeg. Many lower-class families had some connection with the well-to-do houses and were given leftovers, which they ate with *agliata* and *porrata,* sauces made with garlic and leeks respectively. Even today busy women who work and cook for their families prepare double portions and serve the leftovers with these same sauces.

Undoubtedly one of the most vivid descriptions of sixteenth-century Florentine food that is still relevant today was written by the Italian satirist Pietro Aretino. He describes the peaches as "lusty and greedy," the melons as "pandering to one's palate" and the oysters as "delighting the appetite." He was also an expert on salad: "It is certainly not unimportant to know just how to mitigate the sharp and bitter flavor of some leaves with the sweeter and gentler flavors of others, creating such a smooth mixture that you would keep on eating it . . . scentless lettuce and chicory, a handful of wild radicchio, sprinkled with a little calamint, lemon balm and rue. I think that the creator of such a thing could only have been a Florentine. It could not have been anyone else, because setting the table, decorating it with roses and shining glasses, putting plums in syrup, dressing up livers, creating dishes with millet, and serving fruit after a meal all came from Florence."

GLI ANTIPASTI

A selection of cured meats on display along the Via di Citta in Siena.

Gli Antipasti

During the Renaissance, antipasti were already being served in Tuscany. Although the word literally means "before the meal," in early times this course was called *primi servizi di credenza,* or "first services from the sideboard."

White meat and almond aspics, hams, salamis and small game birds were included in this opening course. Nowadays we still meet them in the antipasti, with different names but very similar flavors. For example, pig's head in gelatin is today's headcheese. At one time aspic jelly was used a great deal, but now it seldom appears except at buffets. In fact, aspic was so important on the Renaissance table that Francesco Berni, a fifteenth-century Tuscan poet, was moved to write seventy-three lines in praise of it.

A clear, flavorful stock was once considered the prince of antipasti. It was said to open the stomach and to prepare it for what was yet to come. *Crostini* and slices of cured meats followed, and they are still the mainstay of Tuscan antipasti, even though plain stock is seldom served today.

On the coast, however, *antipasto di mare* (seafood antipasto) reigns supreme. Clams, both large and small, are sautéed in their shells with oil, garlic and a pinch of chili and served hot. *Crostini* are spread with a mixture of warm seafood. Then there are stuffed mussels and clams, as well as cold shrimp in an olive oil, vinegar and parsley dressing.

Crostini have assumed the role that aspic played during the Renaissance. When Tuscans say *crostini,* by definition they mean chicken liver pâté on rounds of bread. All other *crostini*—and there are many others—are usually described by their color.

At first glance, all chicken liver *crostini* appear to be exactly alike. After all, the basic ingredient is always the same. Nevertheless, if you make a tour of Tuscan restaurants, you will never find precisely the same *crostini* served in two different places. Some cooks add onion,

The everpresent sign of good taste, olive oil is a staple in every Tuscan pantry. For the best flavor and health benefits, it must be extra virgin, which means the olives have been hand picked and cold pressed.

Previous pages, front: Zucchini Flowers Stuffed with Sausage (page 292), Marinated Shrimp (page 290), Fried Sage Leaves (page 292). Rear: Chicken Liver Toasts (page 289), Anchovies with Oil, Garlic and Chili (page 295).

others do not. Some flavor them with bay leaves, others are horrified at the mere idea. An occasional cook even breaks the golden rule of Tuscan food and uses butter instead of olive oil. Even the bread and wine vary. Some toast the bread, some fry it, some moisten it with stock, some serve it warm, some serve it cold. There are chefs who flavor the pâté with white wine and those who swear by red, and yet others who flame it with cognac. One thing is certain, however: whatever the subtle changes may be, in a Tuscan restaurant *crostini* are everpresent.

Cured meats are another essential to a plate of mixed antipasti. They range from Tuscan ham, drier and more strongly flavored than the famous Parma and San Daniele hams, to coarse-grained Tuscan salami, from *biroldo,* a blood sausage, to *finocchiona,* a large, fairly fresh salami seasoned with fennel seed. The most celebrated *finocchiona* comes from Colonnata in the Apuan Alps, where it is left to dry in the marble caves.

All over Tuscany, fried dough is served with antipasti. The sizes of the dough pieces and the names vary, but essentially bread dough is fried in good olive oil, which makes it crisp and full of flavor. In Versilia it is called *panzerotti;* in Lucca, *pane fritto;* and in Prato, *figattole.*

Another popular antipasto is *panzanella,* a very simple dish that probably originated in farmhouse kitchens when the farmers' wives moistened stale bread and mixed it with whatever salad ingredients were available from the kitchen garden. The *pan lavato* ("washed bread") mentioned by Boccaccio was very similar. In the sixteenth century, the painter Bronzino was inspired to write a poem about *panzanella:* "He who would fly over the stars should dip his bread and eat it until . . . "

Panzanella, like *crostini,* boasts a hundred different versions. Moistened bread, tomato and onion are the essential ingredients, but there are those who add cucumber and celery and others who toss in greens. The simplest version is probably the best, however.

Stuffed with sausage, zucchini blossoms make a savory antipasto. The flowers are available in Tuscan markets throughout the summer.

Crostini and cured meats are the everyday antipasti, but on special occasions there are additions. Eggs are stuffed in a variety of ways and are always delicious. Then there are the vegetables, either pickled in the local wine vinegar or preserved in the magnificent olive oil of the region. *Porcini* mushrooms in extra virgin oil are a delight to the most jaded palate, and onions and carrots in white vinegar whet the dullest appetite.

A display of the freshest cheeses and meats lures customers to this market stall at Pisa's Piazza Vettovaglie.

Grosseto

CROSTINI DI CACCIA

Game Toasts

Tuscans are keen hunters, and each province has its own game dishes. In the Maremma, the area around Grosseto, wild boars are in abundance; excellent ham and sausages are made from their meat. If you are not lucky enough to find wild boar's liver, calf's liver may be used instead.

2 slices dried *porcini* mushrooms
6 oz (200 g) wild boar's liver or calf's liver
2 tablespoons extra virgin olive oil
2 oz (60 g) *pancetta,* chopped
¼ cup (2 fl oz/60 ml) dry red wine
1 plum (egg) tomato, peeled and chopped
1 teaspoon fennel seed
1 teaspoon juniper berries
salt
1 tablespoon unsalted butter, at room temperature
12 slices coarse country bread or French baguette

❧ In a small bowl, soak the mushroom slices in warm water to cover for 30 minutes. Drain and squeeze out any excess moisture. Meanwhile, preheat an oven to 350°F (180°C). Cut the liver into 2-in (5-cm) slices about ¼ in (6 mm) thick.

❧ In a skillet over high heat, warm the olive oil. Add the liver and *pancetta* and cook, stirring, until the liver changes color, about 5 minutes.

❧ Add the wine, tomato, fennel seed, juniper berries, mushrooms and salt to taste. Reduce the heat to moderate and cook until the liquid evaporates, about 5 minutes.

❧ Remove from the heat and put the liver mixture through the fine disc of a food mill. Alternatively, place the mixture in a food processor and mix until fairly smooth; be careful not to overprocess. Add the butter and blend in with a fork just until combined.

❧ Just before serving, toast the bread slices in the oven until golden. Remove the bread and, while it is still hot, spread the liver mixture on it. Arrange the toasts on a platter and serve immediately.

SERVES 6

Firenze

CROSTINI DI TONNO

Tuna Fish Toasts

In Florence tuna fish preserved in oil, mixed with white beans and finely sliced onion, is a popular summer salad. This recipe, in which tuna is served on country bread, becomes a delicious appetizer when accompanied with a glass of cold white wine.

1 can (6 oz/180g) tuna fish in olive oil, drained
¼ cup (2 oz/60 g) unsalted butter, softened
1 tablespoon chopped flat-leaf (Italian) parsley
1 tablespoon chopped yellow onion
1 teaspoon fresh lemon juice
pinch of white pepper
12 slices coarse country bread or French baguette

❧ Preheat an oven to 350°F (180°C). Flake the tuna and place it in a bowl. Add the butter, parsley, onion and lemon juice and, using a fork, mash them into the tuna until thoroughly combined. Add the pepper and mix well.

❧ Toast the bread slices in the oven until golden. Remove the toast and, while it is still hot, spread the tuna mixture on it.

❧ Arrange the toasts on a platter and serve.

SERVES 6

Livorno

CROSTINI DI PESCE

Seafood Toasts

The secret to the success of this recipe lies in the quality of the seafood, which must be small, tender and very fresh. Scallops may be substituted for the cuttlefish if you prefer them.

1 small cuttlefish or squid or 6 sea scallops
6 mussels
6 clams
6 headless shrimp (prawns)
3 tablespoons extra virgin olive oil
2 garlic cloves, chopped
pinch of ground dried chili
¼ cup (2 fl oz/60 ml) dry white wine
1 plum (egg) tomato, peeled and chopped
salt
12 slices French baguette
1 tablespoon finely chopped fresh flat-leaf (Italian) parsley

❧ Preheat an oven to 350°F (180°C).

❧ Pull the tentacles from the cuttlefish (or squid) body. Discard the entrails, ink sac and cartilage from the body. Cut the tentacles off at the point just above the eyes and discard the head. Rinse the body and tentacles under cold running water. Set aside.

❧ Remove the mussel and clam meats from their shells. Peel and devein the shrimp.

❧ Heat the olive oil in a large skillet over moderate heat. Add the cuttlefish (or scallops), mussels, clams, shrimp, garlic and chili and cook, stirring, for 2 minutes. Add the wine and tomato and season to taste with salt. Cook until the liquid evaporates, about 3 minutes. Remove from the heat.

❧ Scoop the seafood mixture from the skillet onto a cutting surface. Chop the mixture fairly finely. Return it to the skillet off the heat.

❧ Just before serving, toast the bread slices in the oven until golden. At the same time, gently reheat the seafood mixture. Add the parsley and stir well.

❧ Remove the bread and, while it is still hot, spread the mixture on it. Arrange the toasts on a warm platter and serve immediately.

SERVES 6

Lucca

CROSTINI DI POLENTA

Deep-Fried Polenta

Leftover polenta is generally used for frying. The cold polenta is cut into thick slices, deep-fried in olive oil and served immediately. When a lighter version is required, the polenta slices are brushed on both sides with a little oil and baked in a 350°F (180°C) oven until just golden, about 20 minutes.

3½ cups (30 fl oz/900 ml) water
1¾ cups (7 oz/210 g) coarse-grained cornmeal
salt
5 cups (40 fl oz/1.2 l) extra virgin olive oil

❧ In a deep saucepan, bring the water to a boil and add a little salt. Slowly add the cornmeal in a thin, steady stream, stirring constantly. Cook for about 40 minutes over low heat, stirring constantly with a wooden spoon. The polenta should be quite thick and pull away easily from the sides of the pan.

❧ Dampen the bottom and sides of a large, shallow bowl with cold water and pour the polenta into the bowl. Smooth the surface with a wet knife and let cool completely.

Clockwise from top right: Deep-Fried Polenta, Seafood Toasts, Game Toasts and Tuna Fish Toasts

❧ Unmold the cooled polenta by inverting the bowl onto a cutting board. Cut the polenta into slices about ⅜ in (1 cm) thick. Then cut the slices into rectangles about 2 in (5 cm) by 4 in (10 cm). If you prefer rounds, cut the polenta slices with the rim of a glass measuring 2 or 2½ in (5 or 6 cm) in diameter.

❧ In a deep, heavy skillet, heat the olive oil to 350°F (180°C). A few at a time, slip the polenta pieces into the oil without crowding the pan. Fry until golden, about 10 minutes. With a slotted spoon, remove the polenta pieces to absorbent paper towels to drain briefly. Continue frying the remaining polenta pieces in the same manner.

❧ Transfer the polenta to a warm plate and serve very hot.

SERVES 6

Elder Flower Flat Bread

Arezzo

SCHIACCIATA AL SAMBUCO

Elder Flower Flat Bread

The slight sweetness of elder flowers gives this flat bread a delightful taste. It is baked in the summertime, when the blossoms are abundant. If fresh elder flowers are unavailable, fresh rosemary leaves, in the same quantity, may be substituted.

⅔ cup (5 fl oz/160 ml) lukewarm water (105° to 115°F/42° to 46°C)
1 oz (30 g) fresh cake yeast or 2 packages (1 scant tablespoon each) active dry yeast
2½ cups (10 oz/300 g) all-purpose (plain) flour
pinch of salt
½ cup (3 oz/90 g) fresh, pesticide-free stemmed elder flowers or fresh rosemary leaves
2 tablespoons extra virgin olive oil

❧ Place the lukewarm water in a bowl. Sprinkle the yeast on top of the water and let stand until dissolved and foamy, about 10 minutes.

❧ Heap the flour on a work surface and make a well in the center. Pour the dissolved yeast into the well along with the salt and elder flowers. With a fork, gradually whisk in the flour until all the liquid is absorbed and a soft dough forms. On a lightly floured surface, knead the dough until it is soft and elastic, at least 10 minutes. Shape into a ball.

❧ Transfer the dough ball to a lightly floured bowl and cover with plastic wrap. Let rise at room temperature until doubled in bulk, about 1 hour.

❧ Turn the risen dough out onto a floured work surface. Punch down the dough and knead again briefly. With the palms of your hands, flatten the dough into a round about 9 in (23 cm) in diameter and ⅜ in (1 cm) thick. Sprinkle a 9-in (23-cm) cake pan with flour. Place the dough in the pan and let rise at room temperature for 20 minutes. Meanwhile, preheat an oven to 400°F (200°C).

❧ With a fingertip make several shallow indentations in the surface of the dough. Sprinkle the dough with the olive oil. Bake until the bread begins to turn golden, about 30 minutes.

❧ Remove from the oven, let cool for a few minutes and turn out of the pan onto a wire rack to cool.

❧ Cut into wedges and serve at room temperature.

SERVES 6

Siena

Uova Sode al Dragoncello

Stuffed Eggs with Tarragon

In Siena the antipasto generally served is a plate of crostini *and cured meats, such as fennel-flavored salami and thick slices of salty Chiantigiano ham. Occasionally, extra delicacies like these eggs are added. Stuffed eggs are also served in Tuscany as a* piatto di mezzo *(see recipe for* uova sode alla maremmana, *page 359).*

6 eggs
2 tablespoons finely chopped fresh tarragon or flat-leaf (Italian) parsley
2 tablespoons extra virgin olive oil
1 tablespoon capers in wine vinegar, drained and chopped
2 tablespoons canned tuna fish in olive oil, drained
salt and freshly ground black pepper

❧ Place the eggs in a saucepan and add cold water to cover barely. Bring the water to a boil. When it reaches a boil, cook for 8 minutes from that moment. Remove the eggs from the pan and let cool to room temperature before shelling.

❧ Shell the eggs, cut them in half lengthwise and remove the yolks. Place the yolks in a mixing bowl. Cut a very thin slice off the rounded base of each egg white so that the egg half will stand upright. Set the whites aside.

❧ Add the tarragon, olive oil, capers and tuna to the egg yolks. Mash the ingredients together with a fork to form a smooth mixture. Season to taste with salt and pepper.

❧ Spoon the yolk mixture into the reserved egg white halves. Arrange on a plate and serve.

MAKES 12 STUFFED EGGS; SERVES 6

Stuffed Eggs with Tarragon

VERGINE

Arezzo

Intintino con la Salvia

Bread Dipped in Sizzling Oil and Sage

This very different version of panunto *comes from Arezzo. Sage leaves are fried in olive oil and then bread is dipped into the flavored oil while it still sizzles. The best way to serve this dish is to place the pot on a burner in the middle of the dining table so that the oil stays very hot. Provide each guest with a long-handled fork for spearing and dipping the bread.*

1 cup (8 fl oz/240 ml) extra virgin olive oil
10 large fresh sage leaves
1 garlic clove
6 slices coarse country bread, sliced into finger-sized strips
salt

❧ Pour the olive oil into a pot, preferably made of flameproof earthenware, and warm over moderate heat to 325°F (165°C). Add the sage leaves and garlic and cook until the leaves are crisp, about 1 minute, or until the temperature reaches 350°F (180°C).

❧ Spear the bread onto the prongs of a long-handled fork and immerse the bread in the hot oil until the bread is golden, about 3 minutes.

❧ Lift the bread out of the oil, allowing any excess oil to drip back into the pot. Season the bread with a little salt and eat immediately.

SERVES 6

Firenze

Crostini di Fegatini

Chicken Liver Toasts

These are the most traditional Tuscan crostini. *The pâté is often served on toasted country bread slightly moistened with stock. In the local trattorias,* crostini *are a must with the antipasti, which nearly always include a slice of* sopressata *(a cured meat made of pig's head) and a slice of* finocchiona *(a salami laced with fennel seed).*

13 oz (400 g) chicken livers
2 tablespoons extra virgin olive oil
2 garlic cloves
6 bay leaves
salt and freshly ground black pepper
¼ cup (2 fl oz/60 ml) dry white wine
1 cup (8 fl oz/240 ml) light chicken stock (recipe on page 325)
1 tablespoon capers in salt
4 canned flat anchovy fillets in olive oil, drained
2 tablespoons unsalted butter
12 slices coarse country bread or French baguette

❧ Remove and discard any fat and connective tissue from the chicken livers. Slice the livers into fairly large pieces.

❧ In a skillet over high heat, warm the olive oil. Add the garlic, bay leaves and chicken liver pieces. Season very lightly with salt and pepper. Stirring frequently, cook over high heat until the mixture starts sticking to the skillet, about 5 minutes.

❧ Add the wine, scrape the browned bits from the bottom of the skillet and cook over high heat until the wine evaporates, about 2 minutes. Add ¼ cup (2 fl oz/60 ml) of the stock, lower the heat to medium and cook for 5 minutes. Remove from the heat.

❧ Remove and discard the bay leaves. Put the liver mixture through the fine disc of a food mill, collecting the mixture in a small pan.

❧ Rinse the capers in cold water to remove the salt. Place the capers and anchovies on a cutting board and chop together finely. Add the caper-anchovy mixture to the liver mixture along with the butter.

❧ Place the pan over low heat and cook, stirring constantly, until the ingredients are well blended and smooth, just a few minutes. Do not allow the mixture to boil. Transfer the mixture to a bowl and let cool, stirring occasionally.

❧ Meanwhile, preheat an oven to 350°F (180°C). Toast the bread slices in the oven until golden. Remove the bread and, while they are still hot, dip each slice quickly into the remaining ¾ cup (6 fl oz/180 ml) stock. Spread the toasts with the liver mixture and serve.

SERVES 6 *Photograph pages 280–81*

Siena

Bocconcini di Carciofi

Deep-Fried Baby Artichokes

Small purple artichokes are ideal for this recipe. On the Chianti hills they ripen in late spring and are often eaten raw with olive oil and salt. They are so small that each one is only a mouthful.

juice of 1 lemon
18 small purple artichokes
5 cups (40 fl oz/1.2 l) extra virgin olive oil for frying
salt

❧ Fill a large bowl with water and add the lemon juice. Remove the tough outer leaves and cut away the sharp leaf points from the tops of the artichokes. Cut the stalks off. As each artichoke is trimmed, drop it into the water to prevent discoloration.

❧ In a deep, heavy skillet, heat the oil to 350°F (180°C).

❧ Drain the artichokes and dry them well with absorbent paper towels. A few at a time, slip the artichokes into the hot oil and fry until golden, about 5 minutes. With a slotted spoon, remove the artichokes to drain briefly on absorbent paper towels. Continue frying the remaining artichokes in the same manner.

❧ Transfer the artichokes to a warm plate and sprinkle with salt to taste. Serve very hot.

SERVES 6 *Photograph pages 260–61*

Firenze

Sedani in Pinzimonio

Dipped Celery

During the winter months, white celery hearts dipped in newly pressed olive oil are particularly crunchy and delicious. Every vegetable garden near Florence has rows of celery plants; each plant has been carefully wrapped and buried in the ground to keep it white and very tender. The stalks are used for cooking and the hearts are eaten raw.

1 cup (8 fl oz/240 ml) extra virgin olive oil
salt and freshly ground black pepper
6 white celery hearts

❧ Divide the olive oil among 6 little bowls. Season each portion with just a touch of salt and pepper.

❧ Trim the celery hearts as needed and arrange them on a serving plate. Provide each diner with a bowl of the seasoned oil in which to dip the celery.

SERVES 6 *Photograph pages 260–61*

Bread Dipped in Sizzling Oil and Sage

Firenze

FIGATTOLE

Anchovies Fried in Dough

Until a few years ago, Florence was full of friggitorie, *shops where food was fried and sold piping hot from the pan. Customers waited to buy little fried fish from the Arno, meatballs and a variety of vegetables, and then usually consumed them on the spot. Sadly these shops have almost all disappeared and, with them, the custom of popping in for a quick snack and a glass of wine.*

10 oz (300 g) risen bread dough (any favorite white bread recipe)
9 canned flat anchovy fillets in olive oil, drained
5 cups (40 fl oz/1.2 l) extra virgin olive oil for frying

❧ On a floured surface, roll out the dough 3/16 in (.5 cm) thick. Cut into 18 rectangles about 2 in (5 cm) by 4 in (10 cm). Cut the anchovy fillets in half crosswise. Place half an anchovy fillet lengthwise on the center of each rectangle. Fold each rectangle in half to form a square and press the edges firmly together to seal.

❧ In a deep, heavy skillet, heat the olive oil to 350°F (180°C). A few at a time, slip the squares into the hot oil without crowding the pan. Fry until puffy and golden, about 3 minutes.

❧ With a slotted spoon, remove the squares to absorbent paper towels to drain briefly. Continue frying the remaining squares in the same manner.

❧ Transfer the squares to a warm plate and serve very hot.

MAKES 18 SQUARES; SERVES 6

Livorno

GAMBERETTI ALL'AGRO

Marinated Shrimp

The best shrimp are caught close to rocks, and the tiny gray variety is a specialty of Livorno. Headless medium-sized shrimp can be used if small ones are not available. The delicate shellfish may be left to marinate in a cool place for several hours, but should not be refrigerated, as they lose their flavor at low temperatures.

4 cups (32 fl oz/1 l) water
salt
2 lb (900 g) small shrimp (prawns) in the shell
juice of 2 lemons
white pepper
2 tablespoons chopped fresh flat-leaf (Italian) parsley
¼ cup (2 fl oz/60 ml) extra virgin olive oil

❧ In a saucepan, bring the water to a boil and add a little salt. Add the shrimp and cover the saucepan immediately. When the water returns to a boil, allow the shrimp to cook for only 2 minutes. Drain the shrimp and cool under running water.

❧ Peel the shrimp, being careful not to tear the bodies. Put the peeled shrimp into a bowl, pour the lemon juice over them and season to taste with salt and pepper.

❧ Marinate in a cool place for 2–6 hours, turning gently from time to time.

❧ Drain the shrimp. Arrange them on a serving dish. Sprinkle with the parsley, drizzle with the olive oil and serve.

SERVES 6 *Photograph pages 280–81*

Anchovies Fried in Dough

Livorno

GAMBERETTI ALLA SALVIA

Fried Shrimp with Sage

Fried shrimp have always been served in Livorno on the feast of San Giuseppe in March. In early spring the shrimp are very small and are cooked whole with young sage leaves. For this recipe use the smallest shrimp you can find.

1 lb (450 g) very small shrimp (prawns) in the shell, with or without heads
½ cup (4 fl oz/120 ml) extra virgin olive oil
10 fresh sage leaves
salt and freshly ground black pepper

❧ Rinse the shrimp under cold running water and pat them dry with absorbent paper towels; set aside.
❧ In a heavy skillet over moderate heat, warm the olive oil. Add the sage leaves and cook for 2 minutes. Add the shrimp, cover the skillet and cook for 2 minutes. Remove the lid, season to taste with salt and pepper and lower the heat. Cook, uncovered, for 2 minutes.
❧ Transfer the shrimp mixture to a warm platter and serve immediately.

SERVES 6

Siena

FIORI DI ZUCCA RIPIENI DI SALSICCIA

Zucchini Flowers Stuffed with Sausage

Zucchini flowers are prepared in a slightly different way in every Tuscan town. They can be served as an antipasto or as a vegetable accompanying a meat or fish dish (see fiori di zucca *recipe, page 450). In Siena they are particularly tasty, as they are stuffed with sausages made in the Chianti region, which are famous for being lean and full of flavor. Be sure to buy flowers that are still closed.*

3 tablespoons extra virgin olive oil
30 unopened zucchini (courgette) flowers
8 oz (240 g) sweet Italian sausages
1 egg
½ cup (2 oz/60 g) freshly grated Parmesan cheese
1 garlic clove, chopped
salt and freshly ground black pepper

❧ Preheat an oven to 350°F (180°C). Brush a 20-by-12-in (50-by-30-cm) baking dish with half of the olive oil.
❧ With a small, sharp knife, make a small incision in the side of each flower and remove the pistil. Cut off the stalk.
❧ Skin the sausages and crumble the meat into a mixing bowl. Add the egg, Parmesan and garlic; mix well. Carefully open the incision in each flower and insert a little of the sausage mixture. Squeeze the opening closed.
❧ Arrange the stuffed flowers in the prepared baking dish in rows. Season to taste with salt and pepper and sprinkle with the remaining olive oil.
❧ Cover the dish with aluminum foil and bake until the flowers and their stuffing are cooked and sizzling hot, about 15 minutes.
❧ Arrange the flowers on a warm serving dish and serve very hot.

SERVES 6 *Photograph pages 280–81*

Lucca

FOGLIE DI SALVIA FRITTE

Fried Sage Leaves

Sage bushes are grown all over Tuscany, where they are valued as much for their scent and decorativeness in the garden as they are for their contributions in the kitchen. Sage is used to flavor roasts, soups and sauces. When the leaves are large, they are delicious fried in a light batter.

1 egg
¼ cup (2 fl oz/60 ml) water
pinch of salt
½ cup (2 oz/60 g) all-purpose (plain) flour
1 tablespoon extra virgin olive oil, plus 5 cups (40 fl oz/1.2 l) for frying
18 large fresh sage leaves

❧ In a small bowl, beat together the egg, water and salt until well blended. Pour the flour into a bowl.
❧ Gradually add the egg mixture and then the 1 tablespoon olive oil to the flour, whisking constantly to keep lumps from forming. Whisk until the batter is the consistency of thick cream.
❧ In a deep, heavy skillet, heat the frying oil to 350°F (180°C). Dip each sage leaf into the batter and immediately drop it into the hot oil; do not crowd the pan. Fry until lightly golden, about 3 minutes.
❧ With a slotted spoon, remove the leaves to absorbent paper towels to drain briefly. Continue coating and frying the remaining sage leaves in the same manner.
❧ Transfer the leaves to a warm plate and serve very hot.

SERVES 6 *Photograph pages 280–81*

Arezzo

FRITTURA DI MELANZANE

Fried Eggplant

Eggplants are at their best in summer and autumn. During the season local restaurants serve various eggplant preparations that are generally associated with southern Italy. The dishes are said to have been introduced by Neapolitans who came to work in the tanneries near Arezzo in the nineteenth century.

3 Asian (slender) eggplants (aubergines), about 1¼ lb (600 g) total, cut crosswise into slices ⅜ in (1 cm) thick
1½ cups (6 oz/180 g) all-purpose (plain) flour
5 cups (40 fl oz/1.2 l) extra virgin olive oil for frying
salt and freshly ground black pepper

❧ Dredge the eggplant slices in the flour and shake off any excess.
❧ In a deep, heavy skillet, heat the oil to 350°F (180°C). A few slices at a time, slip the eggplant slices into the hot oil; do not crowd the pan. Fry until golden on both sides, about 3 minutes.
❧ With a slotted spoon, remove the eggplant slices to absorbent paper towels to drain briefly. Continue frying the remaining eggplant slices in the same manner. Season to taste with salt and pepper.
❧ Arrange the eggplant slices on a warm platter and serve piping hot.

SERVES 6

Fried Eggplant (rear) and Fried Shrimp with Sage (front)

Wild Boar Sausages Wrapped in Pastry

Grosseto

SALSICCIE DI CINGHIALE IN CROSTA

Wild Boar Sausages Wrapped in Pastry

In the Maremma hunters generally stop for a lunch of wild boar sausages cooked on an open fire. They also toast bread, douse it with olive oil and wash it down with good red wine. In local trattorias these sausages, either fresh or dried, are nearly always on the menu.

1¼ cups (5 oz/150 g) all-purpose (plain) flour
⅓ cup (3 oz/90 g) unsalted butter
pinch of salt
1 tablespoon water
12 small fresh wild boar sausages or sweet Italian sausages (about 1 lb/450 g)
3 tablespoons extra virgin olive oil
1 tablespoon red wine vinegar

❧ Heap the flour on a board. Using your fingertips, work in small pieces of the butter until all the flour has been absorbed by the butter. Add the salt and water and shape the pastry dough quickly into a ball. Wrap the dough ball in plastic wrap and refrigerate it for about 1 hour.

❧ The sausages should be about 2 in (5 cm) in length and a bit narrower than that. If necessary, cut larger sausages to about that size.

❧ In a skillet over moderate heat, warm 2 tablespoons of the olive oil. Add the sausages and cook them until they begin to brown, about 5 minutes. Pour in the vinegar and continue cooking until it evaporates, about 1 minute. Remove from the heat and let the sausages cool to room temperature.

❧ Preheat an oven to 350°F (180°C). Brush a 20-by-12-in (50-by-30-cm) baking dish with the remaining 1 tablespoon oil.

❧ On a lightly floured work surface, gently roll out the pastry about 1/16 in (2 mm) thick. Cut the pastry into 12 squares, each measuring about 2⅜ in (6 cm). Place a sausage on each square. Roll the pastry around the sausage and fold in the ends to enclose the sausage completely. Seal the seams with a little water.

❧ Arrange the wrapped sausages in the prepared baking dish and bake until golden, about 20 minutes. Serve very hot.

SERVES 6

Livorno

ACCIUGHE ALL'AGLIO E PEPERONCINO

Anchovies with Oil, Garlic and Chili

Anchovies preserved in salt are much tastier than those packed in oil. Before using them, however, they must be well rinsed under cold running water and then dried thoroughly.

1¼ lb (600 g) anchovies in salt
½ cup (4 fl oz/120 ml) extra virgin olive oil
3 garlic cloves, finely chopped
2 tablespoons chopped fresh flat-leaf (Italian) parsley
pinch of ground dried chili

❧ Rinse the anchovies under cold running water and pat dry with absorbent paper towels. Slit them open lengthwise along the belly, keeping the fillets intact. Remove and discard the bones.

❧ Arrange the fillets on a slightly concave serving plate. Pour the oil over the fillets and sprinkle with the garlic, parsley and chili.

❧ Let stand at room temperature for about 2 hours before serving.

SERVES 6 *Photograph pages 280–81*

Chick-pea Flat Bread

Garlic Toasts

Lucca

Cecina

Chick-pea Flat Bread

This flat, savory bread made with chick-pea flour is slightly salty and is sometimes seasoned with rosemary. It makes an excellent antipasto with a glass of the dry Montecarlo white wine produced near Lucca. Cecina *is sometimes served instead of regular bread; when cut into small cubes and added to vegetable stock, it gives a great lift to a simple dish. Chick-pea flour is available in health food stores.*

4 tablespoons (2 fl oz/60 ml) extra virgin olive oil
2½ cups (10 oz/300 g) chick-pea (garbanzo) flour
3½ cups (30 fl oz/900 ml) water
generous pinch of salt
1 tablespoon chopped fresh rosemary

❧ Preheat an oven to 350°F (170°C). Oil a 9-in (23-cm) cake pan with 1 tablespoon of the olive oil.

❧ Pour the flour into a large bowl. Gradually add the water to the flour, whisking constantly to keep lumps from forming. Add the salt, rosemary and the remaining 3 tablespoons olive oil. Whisk until the batter is smooth. Pour the batter into the prepared pan. Bake until golden, about 40 minutes.

❧ Remove the bread from the oven and let cool for a few minutes. Remove from the pan and cut into slices. Serve hot.

MAKES 1 ROUND LOAF; SERVES 6

Lucca

Panunto

Garlic Toasts

Recently panunto, *sometimes called* fettunta, bruschetta *or* fegolotta, *has become fashionable in restaurants all over the world. In Tuscany, however, it has always been everyone's favorite snack. When I was a child and went on holiday to the seashore in Versilia, my companions and I loved to ride our bicycles into the hinterland, where the farmers' wives offered us this variation on a classic.*

6 large slices coarse country bread
2 garlic cloves
1 ripe tomato, cut in half
6 tablespoons (3 fl oz/90 ml) extra virgin olive oil
salt

❧ Prepare a fire in a charcoal grill or preheat an oven to 350°F (180°C).

❧ Toast the bread slices on the grill or in the oven until golden. Remove the bread and, while it is still hot, rub one side of each slice with the garlic and then with a cut side of the tomato. Sprinkle each slice with 1 tablespoon of the olive oil and season to taste with salt.

❧ Arrange the toasts on a platter and serve immediately.

SERVES 6

SIENA

SIENA

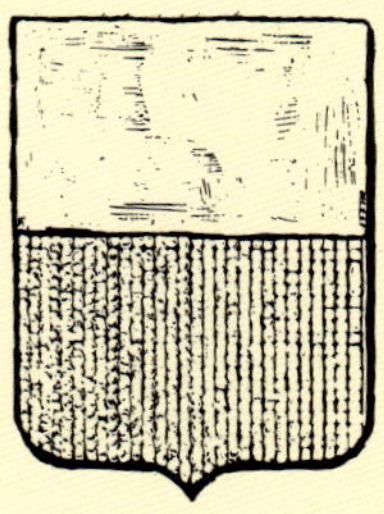

If one declares Florence the heart of Tuscany's culture, then Siena is the heart of its magic. With its narrow streets, distinctive *contrade* (neighborhoods), tall palaces and sculpted, almost Nordic air, Siena is a city of mystery and contrast. The most striking contrast is visible when the mad, colorful excitement of the Palio is set amidst these severe surroundings. Every July and August for the last several hundred years, the entire city has thrown itself with a vengeance into the oldest and most dangerous horse race in the world. To the Sienese the Palio race is only incidentally a tourist attraction. It is instead their very life, something that explodes twice a year in the Piazza del Campo, the most beautiful setting in Italy.

The city of Siena is only the beginning, though. Many of the loveliest places in all of Tuscany are set, like so many jewels in a crown, in the province of Siena. They range from Etruscan Volterra with its alabaster to San Gimignano and its towers, from the mystical Abbey of Monte Oliveto Maggiore to the mysterious Abbey of San Galgano.

The Sienese are reserved but fiery, something especially apparent on the two days of the Palio. They love life, and therefore good food. Dante described them as great eaters, and they have good reason to be, living in the oldest part of Tuscany, the former land of the Etruscans. Some of the recipes of those ancient peoples, such as fish from the lake at Chiusi cooked in an earthenware pan, are still used. When Chiusi was Etruscan and called Chamars,

Left: An abandoned farmhouse near Bagno Vignoni seems to blend into the surrounding countryside. Even in the most remote areas of Tuscany lie subtle reminders of man's presence on the land. Previous pages: Members of the Pantera contrada *(district) celebrate their horse's victory at Siena's famed Palio race, held every July 2 and August 16.*

Around every corner in Siena is a small piece of the city's tumultuous history. This statue in Piazza Salimbeni honors Sallustio Antonio Bandini (1677–1760), a famous political economist from Siena.

the entrails of these same fish were used by soothsayers to peer into the future.

The Siena countryside has long been known for its excellent produce. In a nineteenth-century book on the region, an eminent scientist wrote, "The food available in Siena makes one's stay a very happy one . . . the dishes prepared here, all authentic specialities, are envied by experts from all over the world."

The meat, for example, enjoys great fame. True Florentine T-bone steaks are cut from Chianina beef, a breed raised in the Val di Chiana, an area stretching from Arezzo to Chiusi and Montepulciano. The beef from these cattle was first enjoyed by the Etruscans and later by the Romans. In fact, for the last two thousand years these cattle have been constantly bred to improve their extraordinary meat, which, while tender, is not too fatty.

Even Sienese poultry has a particular flavor. Hens raised in confinement have never become popular in this area. Chickens still wander around pecking in large open runs, feeding on grain and leftovers from country kitchens. They are certainly much tougher than supermarket chickens, which disintegrate at a touch, but their flavor is wonderful.

Local farmers husband their animals not only for their meat but also for their milk, and the best Tuscan cheeses are made in the province of Siena. There is good grazing land in the rather wild, uncultivated areas, and a long history of cheesemaking from sheep's milk. In the 1950s, when farmers all over Italy started to leave the land, Sardinian shepherds moved in. Together with the few Tuscans who kept their flocks, these Sardinians have managed to preserve the traditions. Even today Sienese *pecorino, raveggiolo, cacciotte, marzolino* and ricotta are made in the same way as they were centuries ago.

The countryside is still home to many varieties of game. Wild boar root about in the holly forests and scrub. Pheasant are shot and stuffed with chopped meat and liver, and wild duck are very popular. Hare are cooked in a sweet and strong sauce made with local biscuits called *cavallucci.*

The whole of Tuscany is renowned for its cured meats, but the very best come from the province of Siena because of the high quality of the local meat. *Finocchiona,* a large salami flavored with fennel seed, is produced here, and so is *capocollo* (made from the upper neck meat of the pig), *soppressata* (headcheese), dried wild boar sausages and *scriccioli* (crisply fried pork fat).

Siena is the Tuscan city with the longest tradition of cake- and biscuitmaking, and honey goes into many of the recipes because it is particularly good here. Sienese sweetmeats were born in the Middle Ages and have a strong Arab influence. *Cavallucci, beriguocoli, ricciarelli* and *panforte* have been appreciated beyond the city walls for many years. Together with the Piazza del Campo, *panforte* (a flat fruitcake) is almost the city's symbol. Centuries ago it was made in the monasteries, but early in the last century *panforte* began to be produced commercially. As though to prove that despite its austere facade Siena is the sweetest city in Tuscany, there are many other desserts produced here, such as *budinone di riso* (a rice pudding), *cenci* (very lightly fried biscuits whose name means "rags"), *copata* (invented in a monastery) and the classic *castagnaccio* (a cake made with chestnut flour).

The Sienese use more herbs in their cooking than do other Tuscan cooks. There are no dishes here without a little sage, calamint, basil, rosemary, mint or thyme. Sometimes recipes that are otherwise very simple are made important by the herbs, so much so that during the last century a famous Italian statesman was moved to say, "It is a poor man's kitchen fit to be served to a king." A corner of every Sienese garden is devoted to the cultivation of herbs, and in towns they are grown in pots

A young boy in the Palio parade. To visitors the Palio may look like just a raucous horse race, but to the Sienese it is a sacred tradition. A local proverb says "He who has not seen the Palio does not know Siena."

The skyline of San Gimignano was once crowded with 72 towers, built by two warring families who tried to outdo one another by building higher and higher structures. Today only 15 towers remain.

decorating the windowsills. At the best restaurants and trattorias in the province, such as La Bottega del Trento at Castelnuovo Berardenga, the restaurant at Badia a Coltibuono, L'Antica Trattoria in Colle di Val d'Elsa, La Chiusa in Montefollonico, and Mugolone in Siena, herbs contribute to the dishes in a hundred different ways.

In addition to these local herbs, a French plant, tarragon, has been adopted by the Sienese. Legend has it that tarragon was first brought to Siena by Charlemagne's troops in the eighth century. During the Middle Ages it was considered a medicinal plant, but now tarragon, used both fresh and dried, even seasons the local salamis.

As though Siena's beautiful buildings, museums, atmosphere and cuisine were not enough, there are yet two other features that make the province of unparalleled importance. They are its wine and its olive oil. The oil is certainly not only the best and most fragrant in all Tuscany, but it also has the lowest acid content. Recent internationally recognized medical studies have confirmed that olive oil is good for the health. But even as long ago as the fourteenth century, this fragrant oil was already defined in Italy as "essential to human life."

The Sienese countryside is home to yet another nectar—wine. In this small area some of the most famous Italian wines are produced. It is not by mere chance that the Enoteca Italica Permanente, the most prestigious promotional center for the great Italian vintages, is situated at the Fortezza Medicea in Siena. Brunello di Montalcino, Vino Nobile di Montepulciano, Vin Santo and Vernaccia di San Gimignano are just a few of the famous local wines.

But, above all, there is Chianti. The area called Chianti, which lies between Florence and Siena, is an old land rich in treasures from every historical period: hilltop villages, towers, Renaissance villas, imposing monasteries, small parish churches and vineyards. The 170,000 acres that yield the famed Chianti Classico correspond more or less to those proclaimed by the Grand Duke of Tuscany in 1716. This was the first time in the long history of winemaking that a legal document defined an area in which a particular wine could be produced, and it would be another two hundred years before such an initiative would again be taken anywhere else in the world.

Wine has been made for centuries in Chianti, and documents related to winemaking dated 1037 were found in the archives at Badia a Coltibuono. Chianti Classico, depending on its age, goes perfectly with Tuscan food. When it is young and fresh it should be served with antipasti, soups and fried foods. Between two and five years old, it goes well with white meat and young cheese. A robust, well-aged wine is ideal with roast or braised meat, game and well-aged cheese.

One of the most famous dessert wines in Italy, Vin Santo, was born in Chianti and then spread through the rest of Tuscany. Its praises were sung by poets such as Cecco Angiolieri and Boccaccio, and indeed a fine Vin Santo is the pride of its producer, be he prince or peasant. Always made in the same way, it is aged in small sealed casks called *caratelli.* Vin Santo is said by some to have received its name because it is the wine that every priest would like to have on his altar. It is such a superb wine that, around 1760, Pope Clement wrote a glowing letter of thanks to a friend who had sent him a present of some bottles: "Dear Son, as long as you continue to send this Vin Santo, your Pope will always thrive."

I Primi

Bread has been a basic ingredient in Tuscan soups for centuries.

I PRIMI

While antipasti, meat and game dishes, and the brilliant use of the spit for roasting all originated in the kitchens of the Tuscan courts, church prelates and merchants, first courses have far humbler beginnings.

The various soups, *acquecotte, ribollite* and *pappe,* which, in their infinite interpretations are the most traditional first courses in Tuscany, were originally the staple diet of poor families. Their basic ingredient was, and still is, bread. In early times these bread soups were at best occasionally enriched with a little lard or wild herbs. *Zuppa di pane* (bread soup) was distributed to the poor by monks who soaked stale bread and made it into a pap. Sometimes they pounded the bread with garlic and leeks to give it more flavor and nourishment.

It could almost be said that the basis of Tuscan first courses is still bread enriched with beans, black cabbage, leafy greens and other vegetables, plus, of course, olive oil. Each area has its own bread soup, and each claims that its version is the most authentic and, naturally, the most delicious. *Acquacotta,* literally "cooked water," is a good example, although nowadays it is more than just boiled herbs and water. The actual number of varieties of this soup is still a mystery. It is made in Siena, the Maremma, Grosseto and Arezzo, but, as with so many recipes, there are no two houses where it is prepared in the same way, let alone two areas.

Another very old tradition in the mountains of Tuscany is to mix vegetables with polenta. Although called by various names, this dish is substantially the same everywhere. In the Garfagnana it is called *infarinata* and is excellent sliced and fried. In Versilia it is *intruglia,* meaning "mixture," and in Lunigiana it is *incatenata,* or "chained." In Tuscany cornmeal is made into gnocchi,

Pasta for sale at Siena's Manganelli shop. The hundred-year-old establishment sells spices, candies, wines and other groceries.

Previous pages: Meat Soup (left, page 323) and Cornmeal and Vegetable Soup (right, page 318).

Tuscans have always made the most of their fertile land, from the vast, sweeping vineyards to the tiniest kitchen garden.

which, without varying much from place to place, are called different things ranging from puffs to billiard balls. Basically, fairly thick polenta is rolled into gnocchi and smothered with meat sauce.

In the mountains there are also several first courses prepared with chestnuts, such as *tortelli* stuffed with a mixture of ricotta and chestnuts, or *manifregoli,* a polenta made with chestnut flour and cold milk. For hundreds of years these dishes, together with *incaciata,* a polenta prepared with chestnut flour and dressed with olive oil and sheep's milk cheese, were the usual fare of the marble cutters in the Apuan Alps.

In the Garfagnana spelt continued to be an essential part of the diet long after it had been abandoned in other regions. Now, after centuries, this reddish-tinged grain is becoming fashionable all over Italy, and not only with the health-conscious.

Although soups are considered the highlights of Tuscan first courses, it does not mean that there are no excellent pastas. *Pappardelle alla lepre,* wide ribbons of fresh pasta with hare sauce, is said to be Etruscan in origin. Purists still leave tomatoes out of the sauce, because it was cooked without them for several hundred years before tomatoes were brought from the New World. There are also Tuscan *maccheroni,* a word which causes a great deal of confusion even to Italians. In the rest of Italy, *maccheroni* is short with a hole in the middle, but in Lucchesia it is about three inches wide, flat and made with egg. Just to add to the confusion, the same pasta is sometimes called *tacconi.*

Some stuffed pastas are also of Tuscan origin. *Tordelli,* stuffed with meat, chard and ricotta, originated in Versilia. Then there are *tortelli* filled with a mixture of potato and chopped bacon, a very economical dish from the hills of Mugello.

Tuscan cuisine even includes a few risottos. This method of preparing rice is not originally Tuscan, but the risottos were developed to use local ingredients. Perhaps the best one of all is black rice with cuttlefish and chard from Livorno.

And finally, at the coast, there is a long list of fish soups and pasta sauces that are well worth trying.

Arezzo

MINESTRA DI CECI E BACCALÀ

Chick-pea and Salt Cod Soup

Friday is by custom fish day in Italy, so on Thursdays salt cod is already soaking in the markets of inland Tuscany. If you buy unsoaked salt cod, it should be soaked in water to cover for a day to soften it and rid it of the salt.

7 oz (210 g) salt cod
1½ cups (10 oz/300 g) dried chick-peas (garbanzos)
3 tablespoons extra virgin olive oil
1 small yellow onion, chopped
8 cups (64 fl oz/2 l) water
10 oz (300 g) plum (egg) tomatoes, peeled and diced

Soak the salt cod in water to cover in the refrigerator for 24 hours, changing the water 3 or 4 times. Drain.

Meanwhile, in a bowl, soak the chick-peas in water to cover for 12 hours. Drain and set aside.

Remove and discard the skin and bones from the salt cod. Chop the cod into bite-sized pieces. In a deep saucepan over low heat, warm the olive oil. Add the onion and salt cod and fry gently, stirring frequently, until the onion is translucent, about 5 minutes. Add the water, tomatoes and chick-peas and stir well. Bring to a boil, cover, lower the heat and simmer gently until the chick-peas are very tender, about 2 hours. Remember not to add any salt.

Pour into a tureen and serve very hot.

SERVES 6

Chick-pea and Salt Cod Soup

Lucca

MINESTRONE DI RISO E CASTAGNE

Chestnut and Rice Soup

Nearly all Tuscan soups are made with at least some beans. In autumn, however, when chestnuts are at the height of their season, they often replace beans in the soup pot.

10 oz (300 g) chestnuts
3 tablespoons extra virgin olive oil
1 small yellow onion, chopped
2 carrots, peeled and chopped
2 celery stalks, trimmed and chopped
1 potato, peeled and coarsely diced
8 cups (64 fl oz/2 l) light chicken stock (recipe on page 325)
2 bay leaves
1 cup (7 oz/210 g) Arborio rice
salt

With a small, sharp knife, make an X on the flat face of each chestnut. Bring a medium saucepan of water to a rolling boil and add the chestnuts. Boil for about 5 minutes, then drain. While the chestnuts are still hot, remove both the hard outer shell and the furry inner skin. (The chestnuts are more difficult to peel if they cool completely.) Chop the chestnuts coarsely and set aside.

In a deep saucepan over low heat, warm the olive oil. Add the onion and fry gently, stirring frequently, until translucent, about 5 minutes. Add the carrots, celery and potato and stir well. Add the chestnuts, stock and bay leaves and bring slowly to a boil. Reduce the heat to a simmer, cover and cook for 1¾ hours.

Add the rice and boil gently for exactly 15 minutes. Season to taste with salt.

Remove and discard the bay leaves and pour the soup into a tureen. Serve immediately.

SERVES 6

Lucca

INFARINATA

Polenta with Vegetables

In the Garfagnana, the mountainous region near Lucca, polenta is served with beans, sausages or small pieces of fried whole-wheat bread. One of the simplest dishes, however, is this polenta flavored with vegetables and olive oil.

5 cups (40 fl oz/1.2 l) water
salt
2½ cups (10 oz/300 g) coarse-grained cornmeal
1 lb (450 g) mixed vegetables, such as carrots, celery, yellow onions and broccoli raab, diced
⅓ cup (3 fl oz/90 ml) extra virgin olive oil

In a deep saucepan, bring the water and salt to a boil. Slowly add the cornmeal in a thin, steady stream, stirring constantly. Add the vegetables and cook over low heat for about 40 minutes, stirring constantly. The polenta is ready when it starts pulling away easily from the sides of the pan.

Dampen the inside of a deep bowl with water. Pour in the polenta and smooth the surface with a wet knife. Cover and let rest for about 10 minutes.

Invert the bowl to unmold the polenta onto a cutting surface. Cut the polenta into slices about ⅜ in (1 cm) thick and arrange on a serving plate. Sprinkle with the olive oil. Serve hot.

SERVES 6

Polenta with Vegetables (top) and Chestnut and Rice Soup (bottom)

Firenze

TAGLIERINI IN BRODO

Thin Noodles in Broth

Some Tuscan cooks scorn pasta machines, saying that it is quicker to make dough by hand, roll it out with a rolling pin and slice it with a knife, but of course pasta machines are widely used.

1¾ cups (7 oz/210 g) all-purpose (plain) flour
2 eggs
2 tablespoons extra virgin olive oil
7 oz (210 g) chicken livers, trimmed and chopped
2 bay leaves
½ cup (4 fl oz/120 ml) dry white wine
6 cups (48 fl oz/1.5 l) light chicken stock (recipe on page 325)
salt

❧ Heap the flour in a mound on a work surface. Make a well in the center and break the eggs into it. Beat the eggs lightly with a fork, then gradually work the flour into the eggs until a loose ball of dough forms. Knead the dough on a lightly floured surface until soft, smooth and elastic, about 5 minutes. Using a pasta machine, roll out the dough very thinly. Allow to stand for a few minutes, then, using the narrow cutter on the machine, cut the dough into long, thin strips about 1/16 in (2 mm) wide. Roll the noodles into nests about 2 in (5 cm) in diameter and place on a clean cloth. Sprinkle very lightly with flour.
❧ In a large skillet over moderate heat, warm the olive oil. Add the chicken livers and bay leaves and cook, stirring frequently, until the livers start to brown. Pour in the wine, stir well and simmer until the wine evaporates, about 5 minutes. Meanwhile, in a saucepan, bring the stock to a boil. Season to taste with salt. Add the noodles and boil them for exactly 2 minutes.
❧ Remove and discard the bay leaves. With a slotted spoon, transfer the chicken livers to the noodles and stock. Pour the soup into a tureen immediately.

SERVES 6

Lucca

ZUPPA DI FARRO

Spelt Soup

This farmhouse soup can be refined by making it with capon stock instead of water. Farmers' wives generally leave it to cook gently on the corner of a wood-burning stove; the fire gradually dies out during the night and by morning the soup is perfectly cooked. If you have a way of cooking very, very slowly, there is no need to soak the spelt.

2½ cups (14 oz/420 g) spelt
3 tablespoons extra virgin olive oil
½ yellow onion, chopped
2 garlic cloves, chopped
1 fresh rosemary sprig, chopped
10 oz (300 g) plum (egg) tomatoes, peeled and diced
pinch of fennel seed
8 cups (64 fl oz/2 l) light capon or chicken stock (recipe on page 325)

❧ In a bowl, soak the spelt in water to cover for 12 hours. Drain the spelt and set aside.
❧ In a large saucepan over low heat, warm the olive oil. Add the onion, garlic and rosemary and fry gently, stirring frequently, until the onion is translucent, about 5 minutes. Add the spelt, tomatoes, fennel seed and stock and bring slowly to a boil. Lower the heat, cover and simmer gently for 2 hours.
❧ Pour into a tureen and serve very hot.

SERVES 6

Spelt Soup (left) and Thin Noodles in Broth (right)

Top to bottom: Cabbage Soup, Ribollita, and Cabbage with Bread and Oil

Siena

Zuppa di Cavolo

Cabbage Soup

A kitchen garden in Tuscany always has at least one row of black cabbages. They are never eaten until after the first frosts, when they are much tastier and more tender, and they are an important ingredient in the preparation of a variety of soups. If unavailable, Savoy cabbage may be used as a substitute.

1⅛ cups (7 oz/210 g) dried *cannellini* beans
2 lb (1 kg) black cabbage or Savoy cabbage
4 tablespoons (2 fl oz/60 ml) extra virgin olive oil
1 yellow onion, chopped
2 garlic cloves, chopped, plus 2 whole garlic cloves
1 carrot, peeled and chopped
1 celery stalk, trimmed and chopped
3 plum (egg) tomatoes, peeled and chopped
8 cups (64 fl oz/2 l) light vegetable stock (recipe on page 325)
1 tablespoon fresh thyme leaves
salt
6 slices coarse country bread
freshly ground black pepper

❧ In a bowl, soak the beans in water to cover for 12 hours. Drain and set aside.

❧ Remove and discard the hard stalks from the cabbage leaves. Slice the leaves roughly; set aside.

❧ In a deep saucepan over moderate heat, warm 2 tablespoons of the olive oil. Add the onion and chopped garlic and fry gently, stirring frequently, until translucent, about 5 minutes. Add the carrot, celery, tomatoes and cabbage. Stir and then let cook until the vegetables wilt, about 10 minutes. Add 1¼ cups (10 fl oz/300 ml) of the stock; season with thyme and salt to taste.

❧ Cover and slowly bring to a boil. Boil gently for 30 minutes, stirring frequently. Add the remaining stock and the beans. Stir well and continue to cook, covered, for 1½ hours, stirring occasionally.

❧ Meanwhile, preheat an oven to 350°F (180°C). Toast the bread in the oven until golden. Rub the toast on one side with the whole garlic cloves and place it in the bottom of a soup tureen, garlic side up.

❧ Pour the soup over the toast. Adjust seasoning with salt. Sprinkle with pepper and drizzle with the remaining 2 tablespoons olive oil. Serve piping hot.

SERVES 6

Grosseto

Acquacotta Maremmana

Egg and Vegetable Soup

The vegetables vary with the seasons and an egg is broken over the bread in this richer version of the famed Sienese soup of the same name. This is a favorite of the Maremma cowherds.

⅓ cup (3 fl oz/90 ml) extra virgin olive oil
12 fresh sage leaves
1 cup (4 oz/120 g) shelled broad (fava) beans
1 carrot, peeled and diced
1 celery stalk, trimmed and diced
4 oz (120 g) Swiss chard (silverbeet), trimmed and chopped
1 yellow onion, sliced
6 cups (48 fl oz/1.5 l) water
salt and freshly ground black pepper
6 slices coarse country bread
6 eggs

In a medium saucepan over low heat, warm the olive oil. Add the sage and fry gently, stirring frequently, until the sage is golden. Add the broad beans, carrot, celery, Swiss chard and onion and stir until they wilt, about 5 minutes. Pour in the water and bring to a boil. Reduce the heat to low and simmer for 30 minutes. Season to taste with salt and pepper.

Meanwhile, preheat an oven to 350°F (180°C). Toast the bread in the oven until golden. Put a slice of toast into each of 6 individual soup bowls. Break 1 egg onto each piece of toast.

Ladle some of the piping hot soup into each bowl and serve immediately.

SERVES 6

Siena

Ribollita

Twice-Cooked Soup

Ribollita, *Tuscany's most famous bread soup, is so-called because it is always reboiled before being served the first time and is often saved for the next day and boiled yet again. Although officially a soup,* ribollita *is often thick enough to eat with a fork.*

1⅛ cups (7oz/210 g) dried *cannellini* beans
1¼ lb (600 g) black cabbage or Savoy cabbage
9 tablespoons (4½ fl oz/150 ml) extra virgin olive oil
2 yellow onions, sliced
1 tablespoon tomato paste
3 ripe plum (egg) tomatoes, peeled and chopped
3 celery stalks, diced
3 carrots, peeled and diced
8 cups (64 fl oz/2 l) water
1 tablespoon fresh thyme leaves
salt and freshly ground black pepper
6 slices coarse country bread
2 garlic cloves

In a bowl, soak the beans in water to cover for 12 hours. Drain the beans and set aside.

Remove and discard the hard stalks from the cabbage leaves. Slice the leaves roughly; set aside.

In a deep saucepan over moderately low heat, warm 3 tablespoons of the olive oil. Add three fourths of the onion and fry gently until translucent, about 5 minutes. Add the tomato paste, tomatoes, celery and carrots. Cook, stirring frequently, for 5 minutes. Add the cabbage and pour in the water. Add the beans and thyme. Season to taste with salt and pepper and bring to a boil. Reduce the heat to low, cover and simmer for about 2 hours.

Meanwhile, preheat an oven to 350°F (180°C). Toast the bread in the oven until golden. Rub the toast on one side with the garlic and place it in the bottom of a deep bowl, garlic side up. Pour the soup over the toast and let stand until completely cool.

Before serving, return the soup and the toasted bread to the cooking pot. Bring to a boil and pour into a tureen. Taste and adjust the seasoning. Sprinkle the soup with the remaining onion and the remaining 6 tablespoons olive oil. Serve immediately.

SERVES 6

Siena

Cavolo con le Fette

Cabbage with Bread and Oil

This is a simple country dish that is much in vogue in Chianti in December, when the olive oil has just been pressed and is still quite sharp. Black cabbage is widely eaten in Tuscany and, as the name suggests, the leaves are very dark, long and curly. Savoy cabbage may be used instead.

2 lb (1 kg) black cabbage or Savoy cabbage
8 cups (64 fl oz/2 l) water
6 slices coarse country bread
2 garlic cloves
salt and freshly ground black pepper
6 tablespoons (3 fl oz/90 ml) extra virgin olive oil

Remove and discard the hard stalks from the cabbage leaves. In a large saucepan, bring the water to a boil and salt lightly. Add the leaves and cook until tender, about 30 minutes.

Meanwhile, preheat an oven to 350°F (180°C). Toast the bread in the oven until golden. Rub the toast on one side with the garlic and place 1 slice on each of 6 individual serving dishes, garlic side up; keep warm.

Drain the cabbage well and arrange the leaves on the toast. Season to taste with salt and pepper and sprinkle each serving with 1 tablespoon of the olive oil. Serve immediately.

SERVES 6

Egg and Vegetable Soup

Siena

ACQUACOTTA ALLA SENESE

Bread Soup, Siena Style

Literally "cooked water," this was once a very humble soup made out of a little tomato, onion and celery boiled in water and poured over toasted bread. Nowadays cooks use their imaginations to add to it in various ways.

3 oz (90 g) fresh *porcini* mushrooms or button mushrooms
3 tablespoons extra virgin olive oil
3 oz (90 g) sweet Italian sausages, skinned and crumbled
1 large yellow onion, chopped
1 celery stalk, chopped
10 oz (300 g) plum (egg) tomatoes, peeled and chopped
6 cups (48 fl oz/1.5 l) water
salt and freshly ground black pepper
6 slices coarse country bread

♣ Clean the mushrooms by rubbing them with a dampened cloth; do not wash them. Trim the mushroom stems, then

Left to right: Siena-Style Bread Soup, Chick-pea Soup and Chianti Soup

slice the mushrooms; set aside.
❧ In a large, deep pot over low heat, warm the olive oil. Add the sausage and onion and fry gently, stirring frequently, until the onion is translucent, about 5 minutes. Add the celery, mushrooms, tomatoes and water. Bring to a boil and season to taste with salt and pepper. Allow the soup to boil for about 15 minutes.
❧ Meanwhile, preheat an oven to 350°F (180°C). Toast the bread in the oven until golden. Place in the bottom of a soup tureen. Pour the boiling soup over the toast slices and serve immediately.

SERVES 6

Siena

MINESTRA DI CECI

Chick-pea Soup

Fresh pasta plays an important role in many Tuscan soups. It is usually cut by hand into fairly wide short strips.

1½ cups (10 oz/300 g) dried chick-peas (garbanzos)
4 tablespoons (2 fl oz/60 ml) extra virgin olive oil
1 tablespoon chopped fresh rosemary
3 garlic cloves, chopped
8 cups (64 fl oz/2 l) light meat stock (recipe on page 325)
salt and freshly ground black pepper
1¾ cups (7 oz/210 g) all-purpose (plain) flour
2 eggs

❧ In a bowl, soak the chick-peas in cold water to cover for 12 hours. Drain and set aside.
❧ In a large, deep saucepan over low heat, warm 1 tablespoon of the olive oil. Add the rosemary and garlic and fry gently for 2 minutes. Add the chick-peas and stock, bring to a boil, reduce the heat to low, and simmer gently for 2 hours. Season to taste with salt and pepper.
❧ Meanwhile, heap the flour in a mound on a work surface. Make a well in the center and break the eggs into it. Beat the eggs lightly with a fork, then gradually work the flour into the eggs until a loose ball of dough forms. Knead the dough on a lightly floured surface until soft, smooth and elastic, about 5 minutes. Using a pasta machine, roll out the dough very thinly. Allow to stand for a few minutes, then, using a long, sharp knife, cut the dough into strips ¾ in (2 cm) wide by 4 in (10 cm) long. Set the noodles aside on a clean cloth.
❧ Remove half of the chick-peas from the saucepan and purée them. Return the purée to the soup. Bring the soup to a boil and add the pasta. Cook for exactly 2 minutes.
❧ Pour the soup into a soup tureen. Sprinkle with the remaining 3 tablespoons olive oil and season with a little pepper. Serve immediately.

SERVES 6

Siena

BRODO AL CHIANTI

Chianti Soup

A good piece of meat, which is used later for making croquettes or stuffings, generally goes into the pot when preparing the stock for this classic soup. If the meat is fatty, the stock must be left to cool and the fat removed from the surface before the stock can be used.

8 cups (64 fl oz/2 l) Chianti Classico or other good red wine
3 whole cloves
1 cinnamon stick
4 cups (32 fl oz/1 l) light meat stock (recipe on page 325)
salt and freshly ground black pepper
3 egg yolks

❧ Pour the wine into a saucepan, add the cloves and cinnamon and bring to a boil. Reduce the heat to low and simmer for about 15 minutes.
❧ In another saucepan, bring the stock to a boil. Season to taste with salt and pepper.
❧ Place the egg yolks in the bottom of a soup tureen and whisk until well blended. Slowly add the stock, stirring well. Pour the wine through a fine sieve into the tureen. Stir and serve very hot.

SERVES 6

Lucca

GARMUGIA

Spring Vegetable Soup

This soup is made with fresh spring vegetables. Swiss chard (silverbeet), celery and zucchini (courgettes) may be substituted for those vegetables that are listed, but the soup will not be nearly as tasty.

2 yellow onions
juice of 1 lemon
2 globe artichokes
1¼ lb (600 g) asparagus, trimmed
3 oz (90 g) sweet Italian sausages
2 tablespoons extra virgin olive oil
3 oz (90 g) ground (minced) veal
3 oz (90 g) shelled broad (fava) beans (about ¾ cup)
¾ cup (3 oz/90 g) shelled green peas
8 cups (64 fl oz/2 l) light chicken stock (recipe on page 325)
salt and freshly ground black pepper

❧ Chop half of 1 onion and thinly slice the remaining 1½ onions; set aside.
❧ Fill a large bowl with water and add the lemon juice. Cut the stalks off the artichokes. Remove the tough outer leaves and cut away any sharp leaf points from the tops. Pull the leaves apart gently and, with a spoon, scoop out and discard the prickly choke. Thinly slice the artichokes lengthwise, dropping them as you do into the water to prevent discoloration.
❧ Cut the asparagus into ½-in (1-cm) pieces. Skin the sausage and crumble the meat.
❧ In a deep saucepan over low heat, warm the olive oil. Add the chopped onion and cook gently, stirring frequently, until translucent, about 5 minutes. Add the veal and sausage and cook and stir for 2 minutes. Add the sliced onion, artichokes, broad beans, peas and asparagus. Cook, stirring, for 10 minutes. Pour in the stock and bring to a gentle boil. Cover and simmer for 2 hours.
❧ Taste and adjust seasoning with salt and pepper. Pour into a soup tureen and serve.

SERVES 6

Salt Cod and Leek Soup (bottom) and Pheasant Broth (top)

Livorno

ZUPPA DI PORRI E BACCALÀ

Salt Cod and Leek Soup

Sailors seem to prefer salt cod to fresh fish, perhaps because it is tasty and nutritious and keeps forever.

5 oz (150 g) salt cod
1 lb (450 g) leeks
2 tablespoons extra virgin olive oil
10 oz (300 g) plum (egg) tomatoes, peeled and chopped
6 cups (48 fl oz/1.5 l) water
6 slices coarse country bread

❧ Soak the salt cod in water to cover in the refrigerator for 24 hours, changing the water 3 or 4 times. Drain. Remove and discard the skin and bones from the salt cod. Cut the cod into bite-sized pieces; set aside.
❧ Cut off and discard the green tops and roots from the leeks. Wash the leeks well to rid them of all dirt and slice them finely.
❧ In a deep saucepan over low heat, warm the oil. Add the leeks and cook gently, stirring frequently. When they begin to turn golden, add the tomatoes and stir well. Pour in the water and bring to a boil over high heat. Add the fish, lower the heat, cover and simmer for 30 minutes.
❧ Meanwhile, preheat an oven to 350°F (180°C). Toast the bread in the oven until golden. Put a slice of toast in each of 6 individual soup bowls. Ladle some of the hot soup into each bowl and serve at once.

SERVES 6

Grosseto

BRODO DI FAGIANO

Pheasant Broth

Pheasant must be aged before being cooked, and traditionally this is done by hanging it in a cool, breezy place until the body detaches from the head. The pheasant must, however, be well protected from flying insects that would render it inedible.

1 pheasant
3 qt (3 l) water
1 carrot, peeled and chopped
1 celery stalk, trimmed and chopped
1 yellow onion, chopped
3 bay leaves
1 teaspoon black peppercorns
salt
½ cup (4 fl oz/120 ml) Vin Santo or white dessert wine

❧ Place the pheasant in a deep saucepan. Add the water, carrot, celery, onion, bay leaves and peppercorns and bring to a boil. Lower the heat, cover with the lid ajar and simmer for 4 hours, at which time the liquid should be reduced to about 6 cups (48 fl oz/1.5 l).
❧ Strain the liquid and return it to the saucepan. (The meat from the pheasant can be reserved for making a pâté.) Place over high heat and bring to a boil. Add salt to taste and the Vin Santo.
❧ Serve immediately.

SERVES 6

Spring Vegetable Soup

Arezzo

GNOCCHI DEL CASENTINO

Casentine Gnocchi

The Casentino mountains are among the highest in Tuscany. They are home to many monasteries, including the Camaldoli Hermitage and La Verna, where the monks are renowned not only for their liqueurs, but also for their recipes using wild greens gathered on the nearby mountainside.

2½ lb (1.2 kg) mixed wild greens (such as dandelion, chicory [curly endive] or nettles) or spinach, trimmed
1¼ cups (10 oz/300 g) ricotta
1 egg
1⅔ cups (5 oz/150 g) freshly grated Parmesan cheese
pinch of freshly grated nutmeg
salt and freshly ground black pepper
⅔ cup (3 oz/90 g) all-purpose (plain) flour
⅓ cup (3 oz/90 g) unsalted butter

❧ In a large saucepan, cook the greens in a little boiling water until tender. Drain thoroughly, wrap in a cloth and squeeze until the greens are very dry. Chop finely and place in a bowl.
❧ Add the ricotta, egg, ⅔ cup (3 oz/90 g) of the Parmesan and nutmeg to the greens. Season to taste with salt and pepper.
❧ Sprinkle your hands with some of the flour and roll the greens mixture into balls about 1¼ in (3 cm) in diameter. Dredge the balls lightly in the remaining flour.
❧ Bring at least 6 qt (6 l) salted water to a boil in a shallow saucepan. Drop the gnocchi, a few at a time, into the water. As soon as they rise to the surface, remove them with a slotted spoon, draining well. Arrange on a warm serving dish and keep warm. Continue cooking the remaining gnocchi in the same manner.
❧ Meanwhile, melt the butter in a small saucepan. Sprinkle the gnocchi with the remaining Parmesan and the melted butter. Serve hot.

SERVES 6

Livorno

BORDATINO

Cornmeal and Vegetable Soup

Bordatino *is a coarse striped cloth used for making aprons and kitchen towels. This hearty country soup was probably named after that sturdy fabric because it is thick and yellow colored.*

2 lb (1 kg) black cabbage or Savoy cabbage
⅓ cup (3 fl oz/90 ml) extra virgin olive oil
1 yellow onion, chopped
3 garlic cloves, chopped
8 cups (64 fl oz/2 l) water
salt and freshly ground black pepper
1¾ cups (7 oz/210 g) coarse-grained cornmeal

❧ Remove and discard the hard stalks from the cabbage leaves. Slice the leaves roughly; set aside.
❧ In a deep saucepan over low heat, warm the olive oil. Add the onion and garlic and fry gently, stirring frequently, until translucent, about 5 minutes. Add the cabbage and cook, stirring, until it wilts.
❧ Add the water, season to taste with salt and pepper and bring to a boil. Add the cornmeal in a thin, steady stream, stirring constantly. Lower the heat, cover and simmer for about 40 minutes, stirring from time to time.
❧ Pour the soup into a tureen and serve very hot.

SERVES 6 *Photograph pages 304–305*

Arezzo

CREMA DI POLLO

Creamed Chicken Soup

It is essential to use a chicken with very little fat, preferably free-range, for this delicate soup made from an ancient recipe. If all you can find is a fatty chicken, remove all the visible fat before cooking.

1 chicken, about 2½ lb (1.2 kg), with gizzard and liver
6 whole cloves
1 yellow onion
2 bay leaves
1 celery stalk, trimmed and chopped
8 cups (64 fl oz/2 l) light chicken stock (recipe on page 325)
salt

❧ Remove the gizzard and liver from the chicken. Stick the cloves into the onion and wrap it in a small piece of cheesecloth (muslin) together with the gizzard, bay leaves and celery. Tie the cheesecloth bag closed and place the chicken and cheesecloth bag in a deep, heavy pot. Pour the stock into the pot and bring to a boil. Lower the heat, cover and simmer gently for about 2 hours.
❧ Remove the chicken and cheesecloth bag from the pot and discard the bag. Skin the chicken and then bone it, keeping the meat from half of the chicken breast intact. Cut the reserved breast meat into julienne strips and set aside. Put all of the remaining chicken meat through the fine disc of a food mill or purée it in a food processor.
❧ Add the puréed chicken to the stock with salt to taste. Bring to a boil, stirring to combine well. Add the julienned chicken and heat through.
❧ Pour the soup into a tureen and serve.

SERVES 6

Arezzo

MINESTRA DI CASTAGNE

Chestnut Soup

There are sweet chestnut trees all over the rural areas of Arezzo, and on autumn weekends whole families drive out to the countryside to gather chestnuts, leaving behind the prickly husks. Chestnuts that are not immediately roasted over the fire are often made into this delicious soup.

2 lb (900 g) chestnuts
2 tablespoons extra virgin olive oil
3 bay leaves
6 cups (48 fl oz/1.5 l) light meat stock (recipe on page 325)
1 teaspoon dried mint
salt and freshly ground black pepper

❧ With a small, sharp knife, make an X on the flat face of each chestnut. Bring a large saucepan of water to a rolling boil and add the chestnuts. Boil for about 5 minutes, then drain. While the chestnuts are still hot, remove both the hard outer shell and the furry inner skin. (The chestnuts are more difficult to peel if they cool completely.) Chop the chestnuts coarsely and set aside.
❧ In a deep saucepan over low heat, warm the olive oil. Add the chestnuts and bay leaves and fry gently, stirring frequently, about 5 minutes. Pour in the stock, sprinkle with the mint and simmer for about 30 minutes.
❧ Remove and discard the bay leaves and season to taste with salt and pepper. Serve piping hot.

SERVES 6

Top to bottom: Chestnut Soup, Casentine Gnocchi and Creamed Chicken Soup

Arezzo

ZUPPA FRANTOIANA

Olive Press Soup

This soup is so-called because it is generally made in December, when the olives have just been pressed in the frantoio *(olive press) and the oil is still very sharp. Another important ingredient is the bread, which should not only be coarse-textured but also fairly hard.*

1½ cups (10 oz/300 g) dried cranberry (borlotti) beans
1 large yellow onion
1 lb (450 g) black cabbage or Savoy cabbage
¾ cup (6 fl oz/180 ml) extra virgin olive oil
1 carrot, peeled and diced
1 zucchini (courgette), trimmed and diced
1 celery stalk, trimmed and diced
1 large boiling potato, peeled and diced
2 plum (egg) tomatoes, peeled and chopped
8 cups (64 fl oz/2 l) water
1 tablespoon fresh thyme leaves
1 teaspoon fennel seed
salt
12 slices coarse country bread
2 whole garlic cloves

In a large bowl, soak the beans in water to cover for 12 hours. Drain the beans and put them in a deep saucepan. Add water to cover by 1 in (2.5 cm) and slowly bring to a boil. Lower the heat, cover and simmer for 1 hour.

Drain the beans and put them through the fine disc of a food mill or purée them in a food processor. Set aside.

While the beans are cooking, cut the onion in half. Chop one half of the onion and slice the other half. Remove and discard the hard stalks from the cabbage leaves. Shred the leaves and set aside.

In a deep saucepan over low heat, warm half of the olive oil. Add the chopped onion and fry gently, stirring occasionally, until translucent, about 5 minutes. Add the carrot, zucchini, celery, potato, tomatoes, cabbage and the sliced onion. Stir well and cook for 5 minutes. Add the puréed beans, the water, thyme and fennel seed. Season to taste with salt, cover and simmer over low heat for 2 hours.

Meanwhile, preheat an oven to 350°F (180°C). Toast the bread in the oven until golden. Rub the toast with the garlic cloves and place a layer of toast in the bottom of a soup tureen. Drizzle half of the remaining olive oil over the toast and then ladle in half of the vegetables and stock. Top with the remaining toast. Drizzle with the remaining olive oil and pour in the rest of the soup. Serve very hot.

SERVES 6

Olive Press Soup

Lamb Soup

Grosseto

ZUPPA D'AGNELLO

Lamb Soup

Great flocks of sheep are raised in the countryside of Grosseto, where the shepherds are famous for the excellent pecorino, *sheep's milk cheese, they make. Because the flavor is much more delicate, lamb is slaughtered when it weighs little more than 20 lb (10 kg).*

3 tablespoons extra virgin olive oil
1 small yellow onion, chopped
1 carrot, peeled and chopped
1 celery stalk, trimmed and chopped
1 tablespoon chopped fresh flat-leaf (Italian) parsley
3 garlic cloves, chopped
10 oz (300 g) ground (minced) lamb
10 oz (300 g) plum (egg) tomatoes, peeled and chopped
6 cups (48 fl oz/1.5 l) light meat stock (recipe on page 325)
salt and freshly ground black pepper
6 slices coarse country bread

In a deep saucepan over moderate heat, warm the olive oil. Add the onion, carrot, celery, parsley and garlic and fry gently, stirring frequently, for 5 minutes. Add the lamb, mix in well and cook, stirring occasionally to blend the flavors, for 5 minutes. Add the tomatoes and stir well. Pour in the stock, season to taste with salt and pepper and bring to a boil. Reduce the heat, cover with the lid ajar and simmer gently for 1 hour.

Meanwhile, preheat an oven to 350°F (180°C). Toast the bread in the oven until golden. Place in the bottom of a soup tureen. Ladle the soup into the tureen and serve very hot.

SERVES 6

Left to right: White Bean Soup, Bean and Rice Soup, and Tripe Soup

Firenze

ZUPPA DI FAGIOLI

White Bean Soup

A ham bone is traditionally used to flavor this soup. In every Tuscan kitchen there is a locally produced, pleasantly salty ham that family members slice whenever they are hungry.

1½ cups (10 oz/300 g) dried *cannellini* beans
half of a ham bone or 3 oz (90 g) *pancetta,* in one piece
3 garlic cloves, chopped, plus 2 whole garlic cloves
6 fresh sage leaves
6 tablespoons (3 fl oz/90 ml) extra virgin olive oil
2 celery stalks, chopped
4 plum (egg) tomatoes, peeled and chopped
8 cups (64 fl oz/2 l) light meat stock (recipe on page 325)
salt and freshly ground black pepper
6 slices coarse country bread

❧ In a bowl, soak the beans in water to cover for 12 hours. Drain and set aside.

❧ Combine the ham bone (or *pancetta*), chopped garlic and

sage in a deep saucepan. Add 3 tablespoons of the olive oil and cook over low heat until the garlic is golden. Add the celery, tomatoes, beans and stock and bring to a slow boil. Reduce the heat to low and simmer gently until the beans are tender, about 2 hours.

❧ Remove the ham bone (or *pancetta*) and season the soup to taste with salt and pepper. Remove half of the beans from the saucepan and purée them. Return the purée to the pot and bring the soup to a simmer.

❧ Meanwhile, preheat an oven to 350°F (180°C). Toast the bread in the oven until golden. Rub the toast on one side with the whole garlic cloves and place in the bottom of a soup tureen, garlic side up. Drizzle the remaining 3 tablespoons olive oil over the toast and then sprinkle with a little pepper.

❧ Pour the soup into the tureen and serve immediately.

SERVES 6

Firenze

Minestra di Riso e Cannellini

Bean and Rice Soup

The most popular local beans in Tuscany are cannellini, *which are small, white and very tender. They are at their best in late summer, when they are sold fresh in all the markets. Dried beans must be soaked in cold water to cover for at least 12 hours before cooking; fresh beans will cook in 1½ hours without soaking.*

1¼ cups (8 oz/240 g) dried *cannellini* beans
1 tablespoon extra virgin olive oil
2 oz (60 g) *pancetta,* chopped
1 fresh rosemary sprig, chopped
1 small yellow onion, chopped
8 cups (64 fl oz/2 l) light meat stock (recipe on page 325)
1 cup (7 oz/210 g) Arborio rice
salt and freshly ground black pepper

❧ In a bowl, soak the beans in water to cover for 12 hours. Drain and set aside.

❧ In a soup pot over low heat, warm the olive oil. Add the *pancetta,* rosemary and onion and cook, stirring occasionally, for 5 minutes. Add the beans and stock and bring to a simmer. Cover and simmer gently until the beans are just tender, about 1½ hours.

❧ Add the rice and season to taste with salt and pepper. Cook for another 17 minutes.

❧ Pour into a soup tureen and serve immediately.

SERVES 6

Firenze

Minestra di Trippa

Tripe Soup

Before being sold, tripe is skinned and boiled for three or four hours, depending on whether it is veal or beef. Ruminants have three stomachs, which means that the texture of the tripe you purchase will vary accordingly. Honeycomb tripe is the best type to use for this hearty soup.

3 tablespoons extra virgin olive oil
1 yellow onion, chopped
3 oz (90 g) *pancetta,* chopped
1 lb (480 g) honeycomb tripe, cut into narrow strips
1 celery stalk, trimmed and chopped
1 carrot, peeled and chopped
6 fresh sage leaves
1 tablespoon fresh thyme leaves
1 bay leaf
1 lb (480 g) Swiss chard (silverbeet), torn into pieces
3 plum (egg) tomatoes, peeled and chopped
2 tablespoons tomato paste
6 cups (48 fl oz/1.5 l) water
salt and freshly ground black pepper

❧ In a soup pot over low heat, warm the olive oil. Add the onion and *pancetta* and fry gently until the onion is translucent, about 5 minutes. Add the tripe and cook for 5 minutes, stirring frequently.

❧ Add the celery, carrot, sage, thyme, bay leaf, Swiss chard, tomatoes and tomato paste. Cook for 5 minutes, stirring from time to time. Pour in the water, cover and simmer over low heat until the tripe is tender, about 1 hour.

❧ Season to taste with salt and pepper. Pour into a soup tureen and serve hot.

SERVES 6

Arezzo

Zuppa di Carne

Meat Soup

The Aretines are great meat-eaters, and the cattle raised in the Chiana valley are famous all over Italy for their meat, particularly the T-bone steaks. Aretines are also very fond of bread, so much so that they often put it in soup when other Italians would use pasta or rice.

2 tablespoons extra virgin olive oil
6 oz (180 g) lean beef
6 oz (180 g) lean veal
6 oz (180 g) lean pork
2 oz (60 g) *pancetta,* chopped
1 fresh rosemary sprig, chopped
6 fresh sage leaves
1 small yellow onion, chopped
1 lb (450 g) plum (egg) tomatoes, peeled and chopped
1 celery stalk, trimmed and chopped
1 bay leaf
pinch of ground dried chili
salt
6 cups (48 fl oz/1.5 l) light meat stock (recipe on page 325)
6 slices coarse country bread

❧ In a deep saucepan over moderate heat, warm the olive oil. Add the meats, *pancetta,* rosemary and sage and cook, stirring frequently, until the meat browns, about 10 minutes. Add the onion, tomatoes, celery, bay leaf and chili. Season to taste with salt, cover and lower the heat. Simmer for 2 hours, gradually adding about half of the stock to prevent the sauce from sticking to the bottom of the pan.

❧ Remove the meat from the pan and chop fairly finely. Return the meat to the pan and, if necessary, add a little more stock to thin the sauce; it should be quite thin.

❧ Meanwhile, preheat an oven to 350°F (180°C).

❧ Heat the remaining stock in a saucepan on the stovetop until very hot. Toast the bread in the oven until golden. One by one, dip the toast slices in the stock, place in individual soup dishes and top each slice with part of the meat sauce. Pour the hot stock over the meat sauce and serve immediately.

SERVES 6 *Photograph pages 304–305*

Livorno

SBURRITA

Salt Cod and Mint Soup

Although this Livornese soup is simple and inexpensive to make, it is full of flavor and the herbs infuse it with fragrance. Traditionally it is seasoned with calamint, which grows wild around Livorno, but spearmint or fresh thyme can be substituted.

7 oz (210 g) salt cod
10 garlic cloves, chopped
1 large handful of fresh mint leaves
pinch of ground dried chili
6 cups (48 fl oz/1.5 l) water
6 slices coarse country bread

Soak the salt cod in water to cover in the refrigerator for 24 hours, changing the water 3 or 4 times. Drain. Remove and discard the skin and bones from the salt cod. Chop the cod into bite-sized pieces; set aside.

Combine the garlic, mint and chili in a medium saucepan. Add the water and bring to a boil over high heat. Cook for 10 minutes. Add the cod, reduce the heat to low and cook, uncovered, for 20 minutes.

Meanwhile, preheat an oven to 350°F (180°C). Toast the bread in the oven until golden. Place the toast in the bottom of a soup tureen. Ladle the fish pieces and the stock over the toast. Serve immediately.

SERVES 6

Lucca

ZUPPA LOMBARDA

Lombard Soup

Lombard soup is a strange name for a strictly Tuscan soup that has never been heard of in Lombardy. Legend has it that it was named after a group of workmen from Lombardy who went to Lucca in the early nineteenth century and very much appreciated the dish, but other Tuscan provinces claim the soup as well.

1½ cups (10 oz/300 g) dried *cannellini* beans
9 tablespoons (4½ fl oz/150 ml) extra virgin olive oil
12 fresh sage leaves
6 cups (48 fl oz/1.5 l) water
6 slices coarse country bread
salt and freshly ground black pepper

In a bowl, soak the beans in water to cover for 12 hours.

Preheat an oven to 325°F (160°C).

Drain the beans and place them in a heavy ovenproof pot with 3 tablespoons of the olive oil, the sage and water. Cover and bring very slowly to a gentle boil on the stovetop. Transfer the pot to the oven and cook for about 3 hours.

Just before the soup is ready, toast the bread in the oven until golden. Put a slice of toast in each of 6 individual soup bowls. Sprinkle 1 tablespoon of the remaining olive oil over each slice and then season with a little salt and pepper.

Ladle the bean soup over the toast and serve immediately.

SERVES 6

Salt Cod and Mint Soup

Lucca

BRODO LEGGERO DI CARNE O POLLO

Light Meat or Chicken Stock

Tuscan stock is very light but flavorful because the taste of the vegetables and herbs comes through. If you like, add thyme, basil, sage or any other herb you might choose, or a tomato. When light stock is called for in various recipes in this book, this is the stock required. The cooked beef can be used for making croquettes, while the chicken can be shredded for a salad. You can use this recipe to make a light vegetable stock by omitting the chicken or beef and adding slightly more vegetables.

1 beef brisket or whole chicken, about 2 lb (900 g)
2 celery stalks, sliced
1 small yellow onion, sliced
2 carrots, sliced
1 zucchini (courgette), trimmed and sliced
1 handful of flat-leaf (Italian) parsley
1 bay leaf
1 teaspoon black peppercorns
3 qt (3 l) cold water
salt and freshly ground black pepper

❧ Place the beef or chicken in a deep pot with all of the vegetables, the parsley, bay leaf and peppercorns. Add the water and bring to a boil. Lower the heat, skim off any foam that forms on the surface, cover with the lid ajar and simmer gently until the liquid has been reduced by half, about 2 hours.
❧ Strain the stock, let cool to room temperature and refrigerate to solidify the fat on the surface.
❧ Lift off the fat and reheat the stock. Season to taste with salt and pepper. Pour into soup cups and serve or use in recipes as directed. Any leftover stock should be frozen in ice-cube trays and the cubes stored in plastic bags for ease of use.

MAKES ABOUT 6 CUPS (48 FL OZ/1.5 L); SERVES 6

Light Chicken Stock (left) and Lombard Soup (right)

Firenze

PAPPARDELLE ALLA LEPRE

Wide Noodles with Hare Sauce

Pappardelle, *the most Tuscan of pastas, are sometimes cut with a serrated wheel to make them more decorative. The hare should be cooked in its own blood, but if the blood is not available, the same quantity of rich beef stock may be substituted.*

SAUCE
1¼ lb (600 g) piece of hare or rabbit
3 tablespoons extra virgin olive oil
2 oz (60 g) *prosciutto*, chopped
2 small yellow onions, chopped
2 celery stalks, trimmed and chopped
2 carrots, peeled and chopped
1 tablespoon all-purpose (plain) flour
small pinch of freshly grated nutmeg
1 whole clove
salt and freshly ground black pepper
1¼ cups (10 fl oz/300 ml) dry red wine
⅓ cup (3 fl oz/90 ml) hare's blood or rich beef stock

NOODLES
2½ cups (10 oz/300 g) all-purpose (plain) flour
3 eggs

½ cup (2 oz/60 g) freshly grated Parmesan cheese

❧ To prepare the sauce: cut the hare into medium-sized pieces. In a heavy pot over low heat, warm the olive oil. Add the *prosciutto* and onion and fry gently for 5 minutes. Add the celery, carrot and hare pieces. Fry over moderate heat, stirring from time to time, until the hare colors, about 5 minutes. Sprinkle with the flour and nutmeg. Add the clove and season to taste with salt and pepper.
❧ Pour about one third of the wine and the blood (or beef stock) into the pot. Stir well, scraping up any small browned bits stuck on the bottom of the pot. Lower the heat, cover the pot and cook slowly for about 1½ hours. Gradually add the remaining red wine throughout this cooking period.
❧ Bone the hare and chop the meat coarsely. Return the meat to the pot, adding a little water if the sauce seems too dry. Keep warm.
❧ To prepare the noodles: heap the flour in a mound on a work surface. Make a well in the center and break the eggs into it. With a fork, gradually work the flour into the eggs until a loose ball of dough forms. Knead the dough on a lightly floured surface until soft, smooth and elastic, about 5 minutes. Using a pasta machine, roll out the dough very thinly. Allow to stand for a few minutes, then, using a long, sharp knife, cut into strips 1¼ in (3 cm) wide and 4 in (10 cm) long.
❧ In a saucepan, bring at least 6 qt (6 l) salted water to a boil. Add the noodles and boil them for exactly 2 minutes. Drain and tip onto a warm serving platter.
❧ Spoon the sauce over the noodles and toss. Sprinkle with the Parmesan and serve immediately.

SERVES 6 *Photograph page 256*

Lucca

RISOTTO CON LE BIETE

Swiss Chard Risotto

In the springtime Swiss chard is very tender and the entire leaf may be used. Later in the season, the white ribs become tough and should be removed for this recipe, and the quantity of chard must be doubled.

6 slices dried *porcini* mushrooms
1 small yellow onion
2 canned flat anchovy fillets in olive oil, drained
6 cups (48 fl oz/1.5 l) light meat stock (recipe on page 325)
6 tablespoons (3 fl oz/90 ml) extra virgin olive oil
3 cups (1¼ lb/600 g) Arborio rice
1¼ lb (600 g) Swiss chard (silverbeet), trimmed and sliced
1 tablespoon chopped fresh flat-leaf (Italian) parsley
¾ cup (3 oz/90 g) freshly grated Parmesan cheese
salt and freshly ground black pepper

❧ In a small bowl, soak the mushrooms in warm water to cover for 30 minutes. Drain and squeeze out any excess moisture. Combine the mushrooms, onion and anchovy fillets on a cutting surface and chop together.

❧ In a saucepan, bring the stock to a boil, then reduce the heat to maintain a very slow simmer. Meanwhile, in a saucepan over low heat, warm 4 tablespoons of the olive oil. Add the anchovy mixture and fry gently, stirring frequently, about 5 minutes. Add the rice, stir well and allow the flavors to blend for a few minutes. Add the Swiss chard and mushroom mixture. Add a ladleful of the warm stock to the rice so that it is just covered with liquid; stir well. As the liquid is absorbed, add a little more stock, stirring after each addition. The rice should never be allowed to become dry. It should constantly be just covered with liquid. Exactly 15 minutes after you began adding the stock, remove the saucepan from the heat and stir in the remaining 2 tablespoons oil, the parsley and Parmesan. Season to taste with salt and pepper. Cover and let stand for precisely 2 minutes. The rice should be tender but firm and the risotto should flow without being runny. (You may not have needed all of the stock. Any leftover stock may be refrigerated or frozen for another use.)

❧ Pour the risotto onto a large platter and serve immediately.

SERVES 6

Grosseto

TOPINI AL CINGHIALE

Gnocchi with Wild Boar Sauce

In this recipe wild boar is used only to flavor the sauce. The meat itself is served as a separate course or together with the gnocchi for a buffet. Gnocchi are called topini, *or "little mice," in Tuscany because their shape resembles the tiny animals.*

SAUCE

2½ lb (1.2 kg) boneless wild boar, preferably cut from the leg
1½ cups (12 fl oz/400 ml) dry red wine
1 tablespoon juniper berries
2 bay leaves
6 fresh sage leaves
3 tablespoons extra virgin olive oil
1 small yellow onion, chopped
1 carrot, peeled and chopped
1 celery stalk, trimmed and chopped
1¼ lb (600 g) plum (egg) tomatoes, peeled and chopped
salt and freshly ground black pepper

GNOCCHI

2½ lb (1.2 kg) baking potatoes
1¾ cups (7 oz/210 g) all-purpose (plain) flour
2 egg yolks

❧ To prepare the sauce: in a glass or ceramic vessel, combine the wild boar, wine, juniper berries, bay leaves and sage. Marinate the boar in a cool place for 12 hours.

❧ Drain the meat and pat it dry with absorbent paper towels. Strain the marinade, reserving the liquid and seasonings separately; set aside.

❧ In a flameproof casserole over moderate heat, warm the olive oil. Add the meat and cook until browned on all sides, about 10 minutes. Add the onion, carrot and celery and cook, stirring, over low heat for 2 minutes. Add the tomatoes and the seasonings from the marinade and continue cooking over

Gnocchi with Wild Boar Sauce (left) and Swiss Chard Risotto (right)

low heat for about 50 minutes. When the liquid from the tomatoes has evaporated, add 1 cup of the marinade liquid. Cook the boar for about 3 hours, gradually adding the remaining marinade so that the sauce never sticks to the pan. When the sauce is ready, season to taste with salt and pepper. Remove the boar and keep it and the sauce warm.

❧ Meanwhile, prepare the gnocchi: steam the potatoes in their skins until tender, about 30 minutes. Remove the potatoes from the steamer and peel them. Place in a bowl and mash while still hot.

❧ Add half of the flour and the egg yolks and work them very quickly into the potatoes until the mixture forms a firm, smooth dough.

❧ Flour the palms of your hands and a work surface with some of the remaining flour. Using the palms of your hands and the surface, roll the dough into cylinders about ¾ in (2 cm) in diameter. Cut the cylinders into pieces about 1⅛ in (3 cm) long. Roll each piece over the prongs of a fork, pressing it in the center lightly with your thumb. As the gnocchi are made, place them on another lightly floured surface.

❧ Bring at least 6 qt (6 l) salted water to a boil in a shallow saucepan. Drop the gnocchi, a few at a time, into the water. As soon as they rise to the surface, remove them with a slotted spoon, draining well. Arrange on a warm serving dish. Continue cooking the remaining gnocchi in the same manner.

❧ As soon as all the gnocchi are ready, ladle the hot sauce over them. Slice the wild boar and arrange it around the edges of the dish. Serve immediately.

SERVES 6

Firenze

Risotto al Sugo di Carne

Risotto with Meat Sauce

Florentines are very fond of meat sauce, which is also served on noodles, lasagna and timbales. Their meat sauce is made with more tomato than the Bolognese version.

6 slices dried *porcini* mushrooms
3 tablespoons extra virgin olive oil
1 tablespoon chopped yellow onion
2 oz (60 g) *pancetta,* chopped
2 tablespoons chopped fresh sage
2 tablespoons chopped fresh rosemary
5 oz (150 g) ground (minced) beef
5 oz (150 g) ground (minced) veal
3 oz (90 g) chicken livers, trimmed and chopped
1¼ lb (600 g) plum (egg) tomatoes, peeled and chopped
salt and freshly ground black pepper
4 cups (32 fl oz/1 l) light meat stock (recipe on page 325)
2½ cups (1 lb/480 g) Arborio rice
1 cup (8 fl oz/240 ml) dry white wine
¾ cup (3 oz/90 g) freshly grated Parmesan cheese

❧ In a small bowl, soak the mushroom slices in warm water to cover for 30 minutes. Drain well and squeeze out any excess moisture. Chop the mushrooms and set aside.

❧ In a heavy saucepan over low heat, warm the olive oil. Add the onion, *pancetta,* sage and rosemary and fry gently until just golden, about 5 minutes. Add the mushrooms, beef, veal and livers and stir to break up the meat. Increase the heat to moderate and cook for 5 minutes, stirring from time to time. Add the tomatoes and season to taste with salt and pepper. Reduce the heat to low, cover and simmer until the liquid evaporates, about 50 minutes.

❧ In a saucepan, bring the stock to a boil, then reduce the heat to maintain a very slow simmer. Meanwhile, pour the rice into the meat sauce and stir a few minutes over moderate heat to blend the flavors. Add a ladleful of the warm stock and a little of the wine to the rice so that it is just covered with liquid; stir well. As the liquid is absorbed, add a little more stock and some of the wine, stirring after each addition. The rice should never be allowed to become dry. It should constantly be just covered with liquid. Exactly 15 minutes after you began adding the stock, remove the pan from the heat and stir in the Parmesan. Cover and let stand for precisely 2 minutes. The rice should be tender but firm and the risotto should flow without being runny. (You may not have needed to add all of the stock. Any leftover stock may be refrigerated or frozen for another use.)

❧ Pour the risotto onto a large platter and serve immediately.

SERVES 6

Risotto with Meat Sauce

Grosseto

Risotto con le Beccacce

Risotto with Woodcock Sauce

The hinterland of Grosseto is sparsely populated, still unpolluted and rich in game, so there is a great deal of hunting. If woodcocks are not available, other small birds such as partridge and pigeons (squab) may be used for this sauce. The woodcocks should be dressed with the liver and gizzard left inside.

1 oz (30 g) black truffle, finely chopped (optional)
1 tablespoon juniper berries, chopped
2 woodcocks, about 10 oz (300 g) each, with liver and gizzard inside
2 tablespoons extra virgin olive oil
2 oz (60 g) *pancetta,* chopped
1 tablespoon chopped yellow onion
salt and freshly ground black pepper
⅞ cup (7 fl oz/210 ml) good red wine
6 cups (48 fl oz/1.5 l) light meat stock (recipe on page 325)
3 cups (1¼ lb/600 g) Arborio rice

❧ Place the truffle and juniper berries inside the woodcocks but do not truss them.

❧ In a shallow saucepan over moderate heat, warm the olive oil and *pancetta.* Add the onion and fry gently until beginning to soften, about 3 minutes. Place the birds on the *pancetta* and onion and cook gently until golden. Season to taste with salt and pepper and add half of the wine. Cover and cook over low heat for about 1 hour, gradually adding the rest of the wine to keep the cooking juices moist.

❧ In a saucepan, bring the stock to a boil, then reduce the heat to maintain a very slow simmer.

❧ Meanwhile, bone the birds, retrieving the gizzard and liver. Chop the meat, gizzard and liver and place in a medium saucepan.

❧ Add the cooking juices and warm over moderate heat. Add the rice and cook, stirring, for 2 minutes. Add a ladleful of the warm stock to the rice so that it is covered with liquid; stir well. As the liquid is absorbed, add a little more stock, stirring after each addition. The rice should never be allowed to become dry. It should constantly be just covered with liquid. Exactly 15 minutes after you began adding the stock, remove the saucepan from the heat. Season to taste with salt and pepper. Stir well, cover and let stand for precisely 2 minutes. The rice should be tender but firm and the risotto should flow without being runny. (You may not have needed all of the stock. Any leftover stock may be refrigerated or frozen for another use.)

❧ Pour the risotto onto a large warm platter and serve immediately.

SERVES 6

Spaghetti with Sea Urchin Sauce (left) and Risotto with Woodcock Sauce (right)

Grosseto

SPAGHETTI AI RICCI DI MARE

Spaghetti with Sea Urchin Sauce

There are beautiful beaches and maritime pinewoods around Grosseto, and at the foot of Monte Argentario lie Porto Ercole and Porto Santo Stefano, fashionable sailing resorts where it is still possible to pick off sea urchins from the rocks. If sea urchins are too expensive, you may substitute mussels.

30 sea urchins or mussels in the shell or 6 oz (180 g) sea urchin meat
⅓ cup (3 fl oz/90 ml) extra virgin olive oil
3 garlic cloves, chopped
small piece of dried chili
1¼ lb (600 g) plum (egg) tomatoes, peeled and chopped
salt
1¼ lb (600 g) spaghetti
1 tablespoon chopped fresh flat-leaf (Italian) parsley

❧ Holding each sea urchin gently in a gloved hand, cut the urchin in half with a pair of kitchen scissors. Empty the contents into a bowl and set aside.

❧ If using mussels, scrub and debeard them. Place the mussels in a shallow saucepan, cover and place over moderate heat until the shells open, about 5 minutes. Pluck the mussels out of their shells, discarding any that did not open. Set aside.

❧ In a large skillet over low heat, warm the olive oil. Add the garlic and chili and fry gently until the garlic begins to change color, about 3 minutes.

❧ Add the tomatoes, season to taste with salt and simmer uncovered until the liquid is almost evaporated, about 50 minutes.

❧ Meanwhile, in a saucepan, bring at least 6 qt (6 l) salted water to a boil. Add the spaghetti and cook until almost *al dente,* about 5 minutes. Drain and transfer to the skillet with the tomato sauce. Add the sea urchins or mussels, stir gently and let the flavors blend over low heat for 2 minutes. Sprinkle with the parsley.

❧ Transfer the spaghetti to a warm platter and serve immediately.

SERVES 6

Risotto with Chianti (front), Naked Ravioli (right) and Bread and Tomato Salad (rear)

Firenze

Ravioli Ignudi

Naked Ravioli

These ravioli are called naked because they are not covered with the usual fresh pasta. In Florence they are generally made with Swiss chard, but spinach may be substituted. Sometimes a little finely ground roast meat or mortadella *is added to the mixture.*

10 oz (300 g) ricotta
2 lb (900 g) Swiss chard (silverbeet), leaves only
3 oz (90 g) *mortadella,* very finely chopped
1⅓ cups (5 oz/150 g) freshly grated Parmesan cheese
½ teaspoon freshly grated nutmeg
2 egg yolks, lightly beaten
⅔ cup (3 oz/90 g) all-purpose (plain) flour
⅓ cup (3 oz/90 g) unsalted butter
8 whole fresh sage leaves
salt

❧ To prevent the ricotta from lumping, press it through a sieve into a mixing bowl or whisk it well. Set aside.

❧ Bring a large saucepan filled with salted water to a boil, add the Swiss chard and boil until tender, about 5 minutes. Drain thoroughly, wrap in a cloth and squeeze until the chard is very dry. Chop very finely.

❧ Gradually combine the Swiss chard with the ricotta. Add the *mortadella,* about two thirds of the Parmesan, the nutmeg and egg yolks. Mix thoroughly. Scoop up a small quantity of the mixture with a spoon and, with well-floured hands, form it into an oval about 1¼ in (3 cm) wide. Dredge the oval lightly with some of the flour and set aside. Form ovals with the remaining ricotta mixture in the same manner.

❧ In a large saucepan, bring at least 6 qt (6 l) lightly salted water to a boil. Meanwhile, in a small pan, melt the butter with the sage leaves and keep warm.

❧ When the water reaches a rapid boil, add the ravioli, a few at a time, and cook until they rise to the surface. Remove the ravioli with a slotted spoon, draining well, and arrange them on a warm serving dish; keep warm. Continue cooking the remaining ravioli in the same manner.

❧ Dust the ravioli with the remaining Parmesan, sprinkle with the melted butter and sage and serve.

SERVES 6

Firenze

PANMOLLE

Bread and Tomato Salad

Panmolle, *or* panzanella *as it is also called, is very much a summer salad. It is essential to use coarse-textured bread, excellent extra virgin olive oil and sun-ripened tomatoes for this recipe.*

10 oz (300 g) coarse country bread
3 ripe tomatoes, diced
1 yellow onion, thinly sliced
1 cup loosely packed fresh basil leaves, torn into pieces
salt
2 tablespoons red wine vinegar
⅓ cup (3 fl oz/90 ml) extra virgin olive oil
freshly ground black pepper

❧ Slice the bread and then break the slices into 2-in (5-cm) pieces. Place the pieces in a bowl, add water to cover completely and soak for about 5 minutes.
❧ Drain the bread pieces and squeeze out all excess moisture. Crumble the bread into a salad bowl. Add the tomatoes, onion and basil. Toss all the ingredients together with the bread.
❧ In a small bowl, dissolve salt to taste in the vinegar and sprinkle it over the bread mixture. Pour in the olive oil, add pepper to taste and toss well.
❧ Serve immediately at room temperature.

SERVES 6

Siena

RISOTTO AL CHIANTI

Risotto with Chianti

This risotto should be made with a fairly old Chianti Riserva, which will give it an excellent wine flavor without being too sharp. The wine must be added in small quantities to prevent a sudden drop in temperature while the rice is cooking.

6 cups (48 fl oz/1.5 l) light meat stock (recipe on page 325)
4 tablespoons (2 oz/60 g) unsalted butter
3 tablespoons extra virgin olive oil
1 small yellow onion, finely chopped
3 cups (1¼ lb/600 g) Arborio rice
1½ cups (12 fl oz/360 ml) Chianti Riserva or other good red wine
1⅓ cups (5 oz/150 g) freshly grated Parmesan cheese
salt and freshly ground black pepper

❧ In a saucepan, bring the stock to a boil, then reduce the heat to maintain a very slow simmer.
❧ Meanwhile, in a saucepan over moderate heat, melt the butter with the olive oil. Add the onion and fry gently, stirring occasionally, until translucent, about 5 minutes. Add the rice, stir well and allow the flavors to blend for a few minutes. Add a little of the wine and enough warm stock to cover the rice; stir well. As the liquid is absorbed, add a little more stock and some of the wine every minute or so, stirring after each addition. The rice should never be allowed to become dry. It should constantly be just covered with liquid. Exactly 15 minutes after you began adding the stock, remove the saucepan from the heat, stir in the Parmesan and season to taste with salt and pepper. Cover and let stand for precisely 2 minutes. The rice should be tender but firm and the risotto should flow without being runny. (You may not have needed to add all of the stock. Any leftover stock may be refrigerated or frozen for another use.)
❧ Pour the risotto onto a large serving platter and serve immediately.

SERVES 6

Grosseto

RISOTTO COI CARCIOFI

Artichoke Risotto

The best artichokes in Tuscany are grown around Grosseto. They are at their peak in May when they are small and purple and need almost no trimming. If ordinary globe artichokes are used, keep only the heart; the leaves can be used to make a soup.

juice of 1 lemon
6 small artichokes or 6 globe artichoke hearts
6 cups (48 fl oz/1.5 l) light meat stock (recipe on page 325)
⅓ cup (3 fl oz/90 ml) extra virgin olive oil
2 oz (60 g) *pancetta,* chopped
3 cups (1¼ lb/600 g) Arborio rice
salt and freshly ground black pepper

❧ Fill a large bowl with water and add the lemon juice. Remove the tough outer leaves and cut away the sharp leaf points from the tops of the small artichokes. Cut the stalks off. Thinly slice the artichokes, dropping them as you do so into the water to prevent discoloration. When all of the artichokes have been cut, drain them and pat dry with absorbent paper towels. If you are using globe artichokes, see the above note.
❧ In a saucepan, bring the stock to a boil, then reduce the heat to maintain a very slow simmer. Meanwhile, in a saucepan over low heat, warm the olive oil and *pancetta.* Add the sliced artichokes and fry gently for about 5 minutes. Add the rice and cook, stirring, for 2 minutes. Add a ladleful of the warm stock to the rice, so that it is just covered with liquid; stir well.
❧ As the liquid is absorbed, add a little more stock, stirring after each addition. The rice should never be allowed to become dry. It should constantly be just covered with liquid. Exactly 15 minutes after you began adding the stock, remove the saucepan from the heat. Stir well, season to taste with salt and pepper, cover and let stand for precisely 2 minutes. The rice should be tender but firm and the risotto should flow without being runny. (You may not have needed all of the stock. Any leftover stock may be refrigerated or frozen for another use.) Pour the risotto onto a large warm platter and serve immediately.

SERVES 6

Artichoke Risotto

Risotto with Spring Greens

Siena

Risotto all'Erbe

Risotto with Spring Greens

In springtime the Tuscan countryside is blanketed in wildflowers and many edible plants. The farmers' wives gather dandelions, arugula (rocket) and chicory (curly endive) for salads, soups and pasta stuffings. Sometimes these plants are boiled briefly and dressed with oil and lemon, or they are used for a delicious risotto.

8 cups (64 fl oz/2 l) light meat stock (recipe on page 325)
⅓ cup (3 fl oz/90 ml) extra virgin olive oil
1 yellow onion, finely chopped
1¼ lb (600 g) spring greens (see note above), Swiss chard (silverbeet) or spinach, trimmed and chopped
3 cups (1¼ lb/600 g) Arborio rice
1⅓ cups (5 oz/150 g) freshly grated Parmesan cheese
salt and freshly ground black pepper

In a saucepan, bring the stock to a boil, then reduce the heat to maintain a very slow simmer. Meanwhile, in a heavy saucepan over low heat, warm the olive oil. Add the onion and greens and fry gently, stirring frequently, about 5 minutes. Add the rice, stir well and allow the flavors to blend for a few minutes. Add a ladleful of the warm stock to the rice so that it is just covered with liquid; stir well. As the liquid is absorbed, add a little more stock, stirring after each addition. The rice should never be allowed to become dry. It should constantly be just covered with liquid. Exactly 15 minutes after you began adding the stock, remove the saucepan from the heat, stir in the Parmesan and season to taste with salt and pepper. Cover and let stand for precisely 2 minutes. The rice should be tender but firm and the risotto should flow without being runny. (You may not have needed all of the stock. Any leftover stock may be refrigerated or frozen for another use.)

Pour the risotto onto a large platter and serve immediately.

SERVES 6

Livorno

RISOTTO ALLA LIVORNESE

Fish Risotto, Livorno Style

In Livorno this risotto is prepared with inexpensive fish such as sea robin (gurnard or grondin), scorpionfish (sculpin), mackerel, dogfish (rock salmon) and salpa. All of them are very tasty, but they also have many bones and are therefore not considered choice.

4 tablespoons (2 fl oz/60 ml) extra virgin olive oil
1 carrot, peeled and chopped
1 celery stalk, trimmed and chopped
2 lb (900 g) mixed fish (see note above), cleaned
10 oz (300 g) plum (egg) tomatoes, peeled and chopped
1 bay leaf
4 cups (32 fl oz/1 l) water
salt
2 garlic cloves, chopped
2¼ cups (1 lb/450 g) Arborio rice
1 tablespoon finely chopped fresh flat-leaf (Italian) parsley

In a heavy pot over low heat, warm 2 tablespoons of the olive oil. Add the carrot, celery and all of the fish. Cook, stirring occasionally, for 10 minutes. Add the tomatoes, bay leaf and water and bring to a boil. Season to taste with salt and cook for 10 minutes.

Pass the tomato-fish mixture carefully through a sieve to eliminate all the fish bones and other inedible parts. Return the strained sauce to the pot and bring back to a boil.

In a separate, shallow saucepan, heat the remaining 2 tablespoons olive oil over moderate heat. Add the garlic and rice and cook, stirring, for 3 minutes. Add a ladleful of the warm sauce to the rice so that it is just covered with liquid; stir well. As the liquid is absorbed, add a little more sauce, stirring after each addition. The rice should never be allowed to become dry. It should constantly be just covered with liquid. Exactly 15 minutes after you began adding the sauce, remove the saucepan from the heat, add the parsley and stir well. Cover and let stand for precisely 2 minutes. The rice should be tender but firm and the risotto should flow without being runny.

Pour the risotto onto a large platter and serve immediately.

SERVES 6

Livorno

SPAGHETTI ALLO SCOGLIO

Spaghetti with Mussel and Mushroom Sauce

This sauce is particularly delicious when it is made with date shell mussels. They embed themselves in rocks, however, making them difficult to gather and therefore quite expensive. Regular mussels may be substituted.

6 slices dried *porcini* mushrooms (optional)
4 lb (1.8 kg) mussels
6 tablespoons (3 fl oz/90 ml) extra virgin olive oil
½ yellow onion, chopped
2 garlic cloves, chopped
1 lb (480 g) spaghetti
salt and freshly ground black pepper
1 tablespoon chopped fresh flat-leaf (Italian) parsley

In a small bowl, soak the mushrooms in warm water to cover for 30 minutes.

Meanwhile, scrub and debeard the mussels. Place the mussels in a shallow saucepan, cover and place over moderate heat until the shells open, about 5 minutes. Remove from the heat and pluck the mussels out of their shells, discarding any that did not open. Strain the liquid the mussels released into the saucepan and set aside.

Drain the mushrooms and squeeze out any excess moisture. Chop coarsely and set aside.

In a wide skillet over low heat, warm 3 tablespoons of the olive oil. Add the onion and garlic and fry gently, stirring frequently, until translucent, about 5 minutes. Add the mussels, mushrooms and half of the liquid from the mussels. Cook for 2 minutes.

Meanwhile, in a saucepan, bring at least 6 qt (6 l) salted water to a boil. Add the spaghetti and cook until *al dente,* about 5 minutes. Drain the spaghetti and transfer to the skillet with the sauce. Season to taste with salt and pepper. Cook, stirring, for 2 minutes.

Sprinkle the remaining 3 tablespoons olive oil over the pasta and sauce and transfer to a warm serving bowl. Sprinkle with the parsley. Serve piping hot.

SERVES 6

Spaghetti with Mussel and Mushroom Sauce (left) and Livorno-Style Fish Risotto (right)

Livorno

SPAGHETTI ALLA FORNAIA

Baker's Spaghetti

If you use very fresh walnuts and the inner skin is still pale, it must be removed because it will be bitter. If the skin is brown, it may be left on.

1½ cups (5 oz/150 g) walnuts
3 garlic cloves
½ cup (4 fl oz/120 ml) extra virgin olive oil
3 oz (90 g) fine dry bread crumbs
salt
1 lb (450 g) spaghetti
1 tablespoon chopped fresh flat-leaf (Italian) parsley

❧ Chop the nuts and garlic finely with a knife.
❧ In a skillet over low heat, warm half of the olive oil. Add the nuts, garlic and bread crumbs and fry until the garlic is just golden, about 5 minutes. Season to taste with salt.
❧ Meanwhile, in a saucepan, bring at least 6 qt (6 l) salted water to a boil. Add the spaghetti and cook until *al dente,* about 7 minutes. Drain and tip into a warm serving bowl.
❧ Add the remaining ¼ cup (2 fl oz/60 ml) olive oil and the nut sauce to the spaghetti and toss well. Sprinkle with the parsley and serve immediately.

SERVES 6

Firenze

TAGLIERINI FRITTI

Fried Noodle Nests

Frying is an art in Florence. It is essential to use extra virgin olive oil because it reaches the smoking point at a higher temperature than seed oils and therefore produces less toxins.

2½ cups (10 oz/300 g) all-purpose (plain) flour
3 eggs
2 lb (900 g) plum (egg) tomatoes, peeled and chopped
1 garlic clove, chopped
1 tablespoon granulated sugar
pinch of ground chili
salt
2 tablespoons extra virgin olive oil, plus 4 cups (32 fl oz/1 l) for frying
6 tablespoons (1½ oz/45 g) freshly grated Parmesan cheese

❧ Heap the flour in a mound on a work surface. Make a well in the center and break the eggs into it. Beat the eggs lightly with a fork, then gradually work the flour into the eggs until a loose ball of dough forms. Knead the dough on a lightly floured surface until soft, smooth and elastic, about 5 minutes. Using a pasta machine, roll out the dough very thinly. Allow to stand for a few minutes, then, using the narrow cutter on the machine, cut the dough into long, thin strips about ¹⁄₁₆ in (2 mm) wide. Roll the noodles into nests about 2 in (5 cm) in diameter and place on a clean cloth. Sprinkle very lightly with flour.
❧ Combine the tomatoes, garlic, sugar and chili in a saucepan. Season to taste with salt and cook over low heat until the liquid evaporates, about 50 minutes. Remove from the heat, add the 2 tablespoons olive oil and stir well.
❧ In a large, deep, heavy skillet heat the oil for frying to 350°F (180°C). Add half of the noodle nests and fry, turning gently, until crisp and golden, about 5 minutes. With a slotted spoon, remove to absorbent paper towels to drain; keep warm. Continue frying the remaining nests in the same manner.
❧ Reheat the sauce gently. Arrange the fried nests on a serving platter and sprinkle with a little salt and the Parmesan cheese. Serve immediately. Pass the sauce separately.

SERVES 6 *Photograph page 256*

Baker's Spaghetti

Livorno

CACCIUCCO ALLA LIVORNESE

Fish Soup, Livorno Style

Although originally from Livorno, this rich soup has been copied all over Italy. It is generally very peppery and made with inexpensive fish, which add to the intense flavor but risk making it bony. A variety of large and small fish and a few shrimp are essential.

4 lb (1.8 kg) mixed fish and shellfish, such as sole, red mullet, sea robin (gurnard or grondin), dogfish (rock salmon) and shrimp (prawns)
3 tablespoons extra virgin olive oil
½ yellow onion, chopped
3 garlic cloves, chopped
2 lb (900 g) plum (egg) tomatoes, peeled and chopped
¾ cup (7 fl oz/210 ml) water
salt and freshly ground black pepper
6 slices coarse country bread
1 tablespoon chopped fresh flat-leaf (Italian) parsley

❧ Clean the fish and peel the shrimp. Remove the heads and tails from the larger fish and discard, then cut the fish into thick slices. Leave the small fish whole.
❧ In a shallow saucepan over low heat, warm the olive oil. Add the onion and garlic and fry gently, stirring frequently, until translucent, about 5 minutes. Add the tomatoes and water and simmer uncovered for 10 minutes. Add the fish and season to taste with salt and pepper. Cook at a gentle simmer for about 10 more minutes.
❧ Meanwhile, preheat an oven to 350°F (180°C). Toast the bread in the oven until golden. Place a slice of toast in each of 6 soup bowls and sprinkle each with a little of the parsley.
❧ Divide the hot soup and fish pieces evenly among the bowls. Serve immediately.

SERVES 6

Wide Noodles with Wild Boar Sauce

Livorno

LINGUINE CON GLI SCAMPI

Linguine with Shrimp Sauce

The markets and restaurants in Livorno offer a great variety of shrimp, the best of which are spannocchie, *or imperial prawns, which are usually about 8 in (20 cm) long. They are always sold whole, but if unavailable, headless shrimp may be used instead.*

⅓ cup (3 fl oz/90 ml) extra virgin olive oil
1 small yellow onion, chopped
4 lb (1.8 kg) whole imperial shrimp (prawns) or 10 oz (300 g) headless shrimp, peeled
10 oz (300 g) plum (egg) tomatoes, peeled, chopped and then drained for at least 30 minutes
2 tablespoons Marsala wine
salt
1 lb (450 g) linguine

❧ In a medium saucepan over low heat, warm the olive oil. Add the onion and fry gently, stirring frequently, until translucent, about 5 minutes. Add the shrimp and cook for 2 minutes for small shrimp and 7 minutes for imperial shrimp. Add the tomatoes, Marsala and a little salt. Cook over moderate heat until the liquid evaporates, about 3 minutes. Keep warm over very low heat.
❧ Meanwhile, in a saucepan, bring at least 6 qt (6 l) salted water to a boil. Add the linguine and cook until *al dente,* about 6 minutes. Drain and tip onto a warm serving platter.
❧ Pour the hot sauce directly over the linguine, toss and serve. If you were able to find imperial shrimp, arrange them on top of the linguine.

SERVES 6

Grosseto

PAPPARDELLE AL CINGHIALE

Wide Noodles with Wild Boar Sauce

The Maremma is famous for its wild boar, which appears on nearly every restaurant menu in one form or another. The meat is full of flavor but, as it tends to be tough, it should be marinated before being cooked.

SAUCE
1 lb (450 g) wild boar meat, preferably from the leg
1½ cups (12 fl oz/400 ml) good red wine
½ yellow onion, chopped
1 tablespoon juniper berries
½ teaspoon black peppercorns
2 bay leaves
1 fresh rosemary sprig
3 tablespoons extra virgin olive oil
1 tablespoon all-purpose (plain) flour
10 oz (300 g) plum (egg) tomatoes, peeled and chopped
salt

PASTA
2½ cups (10 oz/300 g) all-purpose (plain) flour
3 eggs

❧ To prepare the sauce: cut the meat into 1½-in (3-cm) cubes and place them in a deep glass or ceramic bowl. Add the wine, onion, juniper berries, peppercorns, bay leaves and rosemary. Let stand to marinate in a cool place for 12 hours.
❧ Drain off, strain and reserve the marinade. Dry the meat well with absorbent paper towels. In a shallow saucepan over moderate heat, warm the olive oil. Add the meat and brown on all sides, about 10 minutes.

Linguine with Shrimp Sauce (left) and Cacciucco (right)

❧ Sprinkle the meat with the flour and stir well. Add the tomatoes and marinade and stir well, scraping up any browned bits on the pan bottom. Bring to a boil over high heat. Reduce the heat to low, cover and simmer gently until nearly all the liquid has been absorbed, about 2 hours. Remove the meat from the pan with a slotted spoon and chop it finely. Return the chopped meat to the pan, stir well, season with salt and simmer to blend. Set the sauce aside.

❧ To make the noodles: heap the flour in a mound on a work surface. Make a well in the center and break the eggs into it. Beat the eggs lightly with a fork, then gradually work the flour into the eggs until a loose ball of dough forms. Knead the dough on a lightly floured surface until soft, smooth and elastic. Using a pasta machine, roll out the dough very thinly. Allow to stand for a few minutes, then, using a long, sharp knife, cut into long strips about 1¼ in (3 cm) wide and 4 in (10 cm) long.

❧ In a saucepan, bring at least 6 qt (6 l) salted water to a boil. Add the noodles and boil them for exactly 2 minutes. Drain and tip onto a warm serving dish.

❧ Reheat the sauce. Pour the hot sauce over the noodles, toss and serve immediately.

SERVES 6

Lucca

TAGLIERINI CON PICCIONI

Thin Noodles with Pigeon

Tuscan farmers breed pigeons for the pot, but they leave them free to fly around so that their meat will have plenty of flavor. In this recipe dry linguine are a satisfactory substitute for homemade pasta.

2 pigeons (squab), about 10 oz (300 g) each
3 tablespoons extra virgin olive oil
½ yellow onion, chopped
½ carrot, peeled and chopped
½ celery stalk, trimmed and chopped
10 oz (300 g) plum (egg) tomatoes, peeled and chopped
salt
2½ cups (10 oz/300 g) all-purpose (plain) flour
3 eggs
3 oz (90 g) *prosciutto*, chopped

❧ Cut the pigeons into quarters and set aside.

❧ In a saucepan over low heat, warm the olive oil. Add the onion, carrot and celery and fry gently, stirring frequently, for about 5 minutes. Add the pigeons and, turning occasionally, fry them for about 10 minutes. Stir in the tomatoes, season to taste with salt and cover the pan. Cook for 1 hour, adding a little water if the pan begins to dry.

❧ Meanwhile, heap the flour in a mound on a work surface. Make a well in the center and break the eggs into it. Beat the eggs lightly with a fork, then gradually work the flour into the eggs until a loose ball of dough forms. Knead the dough on a lightly floured surface until soft, smooth and elastic, about 5 minutes. Using a pasta machine, roll out the dough very thinly. Allow to stand for a few minutes, then, using the narrow cutter on the machine, cut into long, thin strips about 1/16 in (2 mm) wide. Roll the noodles into nests about 2 in (5 cm) in diameter and place on a clean cloth. Sprinkle very lightly with flour.

❧ Remove the pigeon pieces from the saucepan, bone them and chop the meat coarsely. Return the meat to the pot and reheat gently with the *prosciutto*.

❧ In a saucepan, bring at least 6 qt (6 l) salted water to a boil. Add the noodles and boil them for exactly 2 minutes. Drain the noodles and tip them onto a warm serving dish. Toss with the sauce and serve.

SERVES 6

Lucca

MINESTRONE DI CAVOLO

Cabbage Soup

This is a very thick soup that is often prepared in quantity, because farm workers take it with them to the fields to have cold for lunch.

1⅛ cups (7 oz/210 g) dried *cannellini* beans
3 oz (90 g) pork fat or *pancetta*, thinly sliced
10 oz (300 g) curly-leaf cabbage
10 oz (300 g) black cabbage or Savoy cabbage
⅓ cup (3 fl oz/90 ml) extra virgin olive oil
2 yellow onions, chopped
2 celery stalks, chopped
1 large potato, peeled and cubed
10 oz (300 g) Swiss chard (silverbeet), sliced
1 tablespoon fresh thyme leaves
salt and freshly ground black pepper
8 cups (64 fl oz/2 l) water

❧ In a bowl, soak the beans in water to cover for 12 hours. Drain the beans and put them into a deep saucepan. Add water to cover by 1 in (2.5 cm) and the pork fat. Slowly bring to a boil. Lower the heat, cover and simmer for 1½ hours.

❧ Remove and discard the hard stalks from both types of cabbage leaves. Slice roughly and set aside.

❧ In another deep saucepan over moderate heat, warm the

Cabbage Soup (left) and Thin Noodles with Pigeon (right)

olive oil. Add the onion and celery and fry gently, stirring frequently, for 5 minutes. Add both types of cabbage, the potato, Swiss chard and thyme and season to taste with salt and pepper.

Drain the beans and add their liquid and the pork fat to the saucepan with the vegetables. Cover and simmer for about 10 minutes, then add the water and bring to a boil. Cover and boil gently for 2 hours.

Meanwhile, purée half of the beans. When the vegetables have finished cooking, add the whole beans and the purée to the soup and cook for 10 minutes.

Pour the soup into a tureen and serve immediately.

SERVES 6

Gnocchi with Fake Sauce

Arezzo

Topini al Sugo Finto

Gnocchi with Fake Sauce

Tuscans love ragù *and make infinite varieties of it. To them it is the only "real" sauce, which is why they call this tomato and vegetable sauce* sugo finto, *or "fake sauce."*

SAUCE

3 tablespoons extra virgin olive oil
1 small yellow onion, chopped
1 carrot, peeled and chopped
1 celery stalk, chopped
2 lb (900 g) plum (egg) tomatoes, peeled and chopped
½ cup (4 fl oz/120 ml) dry red wine
salt and freshly ground pepper to taste
1 tablespoon chopped fresh flat-leaf (Italian) parsley

GNOCCHI

2 lb (900 g) baking potatoes
1½ cups (6 oz/180 g) all-purpose (plain) flour
2 egg yolks

❧ To prepare the sauce: in a saucepan over low heat, warm the olive oil. Add the onion, carrot and celery and fry gently for 5 minutes.
❧ Add the tomatoes and wine. Stir and season to taste with salt and pepper. Cover and cook until the sauce is thick and the liquid evaporates, about 50 minutes.
❧ To prepare the gnocchi: steam the potatoes in their skins until tender, about 30 minutes.
❧ Remove the potatoes from the steamer and peel them. Place in a bowl and mash while still hot. Add half of the flour and the egg yolks and work them very quickly into the potatoes until the mixture forms a firm, smooth dough.
❧ Flour the palms of your hands and a work surface with some of the remaining flour. Using the palms of your hands and the surface, roll the dough into cylinders about ¾ in (2 cm) in diameter. Cut the cylinders into pieces about 1⅛ in (3 cm) long. Roll each piece over the prongs of a fork, pressing it in the center lightly with your thumb. As the gnocchi are made, place them on another lightly floured surface.
❧ Bring at least 6 qt (6 l) salted water to a boil in a shallow saucepan. Drop the gnocchi, a few at a time, into the water. As soon as they rise to the surface, remove them with a slotted spoon, draining well. Arrange on a warm serving dish. Continue cooking the remaining gnocchi in the same manner.
❧ As soon as all the gnocchi are ready, pour the hot sauce over them and sprinkle with the parsley. Serve immediately.

SERVES 6

Firenze

Crespelle alla Ricotta

Crêpes with Spinach and Ricotta

In Florence these crêpes are often served instead of lasagna. They are much lighter and have a delicate flavor. On Italian menus alla fiorentina *generally means "with spinach." Crêpes are also tasty filled with cream sauce or meat sauce.*

CRÊPES

2 eggs
⅓ cup (3 fl oz/90 ml) milk
2 tablespoons extra virgin olive oil, plus extra for frying
pinch of salt
¾ cup (3 oz/90g) all-purpose (plain) flour, sifted

FILLING

1¼ lb (600 g) spinach, trimmed
1¼ cups (10 oz/300 g) ricotta

Crêpes with Spinach and Ricotta

3 tablespoons freshly grated Parmesan cheese
1 egg, lightly beaten
pinch of freshly grated nutmeg
salt

SAUCE

1 tablespoon unsalted butter
¼ cup (1 oz/30 g) all-purpose (plain) flour
2 cups (16 fl oz/480 ml) milk
3 tablespoons freshly grated Parmesan cheese
salt and freshly ground black pepper

❧ To prepare the crêpes: whisk the eggs in a bowl until well blended. Add the milk, the 2 tablespoons olive oil and salt. Gradually mix in the flour. The batter should be smooth and have the consistency of thick cream.
❧ Brush a 6-in (15-cm) nonstick skillet with oil and place over moderate heat. Pour in just enough batter to create a very thin sheet when the pan is tilted. Cook for 1 minute until the edges lift easily. Turn with a spatula and cook the other side for 30 seconds. Remove the crêpe from the pan to a flat surface to cool. Continue cooking the crêpes in the same manner until the batter is finished. There should be about 18 crêpes in all.
❧ To prepare the filling: cook the spinach in a little salted boiling water until tender, about 2 minutes. Drain well, pressing out any excess liquid. Finely chop the spinach and place in a mixing bowl. Add the ricotta, Parmesan, egg and nutmeg and mix well. Season to taste with salt.
❧ Preheat an oven to 350°F (180°C). Spoon a little filling in a line down the center of each crêpe and roll up. Set the crêpes aside, seam side down.
❧ To prepare the sauce: in a small saucepan over moderate heat, melt the butter. Add the flour, blend in well and cook, stirring constantly, until very smooth, 2–3 minutes. Gradually add the milk, stirring constantly, and cook, continuing to stir, until the sauce has thickened, about 5 minutes. Remove from the heat and stir in the Parmesan. Season to taste with salt and pepper.
❧ Pour enough sauce into a shallow 12-by-16-in (30-by-40-cm) baking dish to form a thin layer. Arrange the crêpes side by side and seam side down on top of the sauce. Spoon the remaining sauce over the crêpes. Bake until the sauce bubbles slightly and the crêpes are heated through, about 20 minutes.
❧ Remove from the oven and serve immediately.

SERVES 6

LUCCA

Pensateci stanotte.
Con Panda, Uno e Tipo le vacanze cominciano con un lieve anticipo.
E durano fino a gennaio '92.

LUCCA

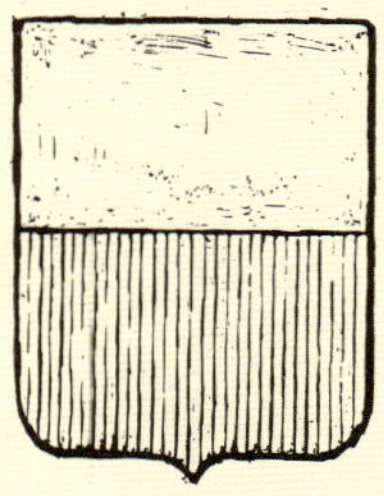

Although Byron and Shelley loved Lucca, and Heine and Montaigne visited often, until a few years ago it was unique among Tuscan cities in that it was practically unknown to tourists. Its three miles of protective walls, all beautifully intact, perhaps saved it from the great floods of tourists who have altered the character of other Tuscan towns, Florence above all.

Today Lucca is very fashionable. Milanese and Britons, Americans and Germans compete to bid small fortunes for the few country houses still for sale. But Lucca has managed to remain unchanged. It could be that the locals have always been reluctant to accept busloads of daytrippers laden with cameras and instead have welcomed visitors who are interested in learning about their city and spending some time there.

The uniqueness of Lucca may not captivate a visitor immediately, but its cuisine most certainly will. Only a few miles from the sea and with mountains behind it, the city and its surroundings enjoy a varied local table. The offerings range from dishes made with spelt (the ancient grain still cultivated on the slopes of the Garfagnana mountains) to a cornucopia of soups made from black cabbage, from succulent poultry and rabbit preparations to delicious creations based on fish fresh from the lakes, streams and sea.

Lucca has maintained its long traditions, and not even the restaurateurs in the city have succumbed to the demands of nouvelle cuisine. The great variety of local

Left: The real life of Italy takes place out on the street, whether it be a lively festa *in the village* piazza, *or a quiet morning spent reading the papers in a sidewalk café. Previous pages: A villa lies nestled in the hills near Barga. This mountainous region of Lucca province is known as the Garfagnana.*

Amidst the red roofs of Lucca lies San Pietro Somaldi, one of the many Romanesque churches built during the city's glory days of the twelfth and thirteenth centuries. This view is from the top of Guinigi Tower.

dishes all share a common denominator: their simplicity and the quality of their ingredients. The olive oil produced near Lucca is among the finest in Italy. Wild herbs are mixed with the produce from the innumerable market gardens, and these, together with farmyard animals like hens and rabbits, are the basic ingredients of most local recipes.

Special flours, such as chick-pea, corn and chestnut, have always played an important role in Lucchese kitchens. In fact, until the end of the last war, chestnut flour was the staple diet of the farmers in the Garfagnana area, where there are still great chestnut woods. Although the flour is now used much less, no self-respecting Lucchese would ever give up roasting chestnuts on the fire or cooking *necci* in iron molds on the embers. *Necci,* which are pancakes made of chestnut flour, were traditionally spread with olive oil and fresh *pecorino* (sheep's milk cheese) or with *biroldo.* Made all over Tuscany, *biroldo* is a pig's blood salami that is a specialty of Lucca, where it is seasoned with pine nuts and raisins.

Restaurant owners in Lucchesia must be given a great deal of credit for having made the real Lucchese cuisine well-known. Sauro Brunicardi, owner of La Mora in Ponte a Moriano, is one of several restaurateurs whose faith in traditional recipes has made them famous throughout the world. His *gran farro* alone merits more than one visit to Lucca.

It is worth devoting a few lines to *farro,* or, as it is called in English, spelt. Although in ancient times this grain was grown so widely that it was even found in the pharaohs' tombs, after the advent of wheat its cultivation was nearly abandoned outside Lucchesia. Recently, however, some health food stores in Europe and North America have begun stocking it. Spelt was grown by the Romans and was, in fact, the staple food of Caesar's legions during their military campaigns. In the Garfagnana there are still several mills that grind *farro* in the same way it was produced centuries ago, and the local cooks use it in soups and cakes. In this region people live very long lives, which they attribute to the fact that they eat so much spelt.

Herbs, from borage and thyme to calamint and rosemary, are also much in evidence. Cesare, a young and enterprising restaurateur whose Ristorante Vipore has one of the most beautiful views of Lucca, bases his recipes on herbs. He has an herb garden behind his restaurant and constantly experiments with new and delicious ways of using them.

As in the rest of Tuscany, very few cakes are made in Lucchesia. The only exception is *bucellato,* a ring-shaped cake that is as much a symbol of Lucca as its walls and the Guinigi Tower. This cake, with its strong aniseed accent, dates back to very early times. Even the ancient Romans had a ring-shaped bread that they called *buccelatum.* During the Middle Ages, vassals took gifts of *bucellato* to their feudal lords, and today it is the traditional present godparents give to their godchildren on confirmation day. It is at its best when eaten with strawberries.

The most popular first courses in Lucchesia are soups, such as *frantoiana,* made with black cabbage; *infarinata,* thickened with cornmeal; or *garmugia,* a delicate blend of young broad (fava) beans, peas, asparagus and tiny artichokes. Mario Tobino, a famous Italian writer who was born in Viareggio, describes the last-named soup thus: "Garmugia, the secret dish of the sixteenth century, was used by the well-to-do in Lucca when recovering from a long illness or affliction or when, to save their souls, they decided to bring comfort to the poor. The finest herbs and chopped meat were left to bubble over the burning embers." Even for one without an infirmity, a spoonful of *garmugia* is grateful to the palate.

The typical pastas from Lucchesia are *maccheroni,* which, despite their name, bear no resemblance to the usual Italian *macccheroni.* They are rather like small lasagna and are generally served with mushroom sauce. Then there are broad *tagliatelle* and *tordelli,* the classic first courses. *Tordelli* are twice the size of the typical Italian *tortellini* from Emilia-Romagna, and their filling is much tastier. *Tordelli* are to Lucca what pizza is to Naples.

Red meat has never played an important part in Lucca's cooking. The farmers were poor and lived off what they had: pork and all its derivatives; chicken and rabbit, either stewed or grilled; and, because all Tuscans are keen hunters, game. Vegetables are another vital ingredient. Not only are they used in numerous soups, but in omelets, savory cakes and molds. They are also cooked with meat and fish. Salt cod with chick-peas and cuttlefish with Swiss chard are two typical examples of Lucchese cookery. Mushrooms are very important too, because even today they spring up in great quantity in the Garfagnana.

Lucchese cuisine also means fish. By the sixteenth century, there was a port in Viareggio, just a few miles from Lucca, but it was not until the beginning of this century that the town became a fashionable bathing resort. Aristocrats and the rich middle classes from central and northern Italy spent and continue to spend their summer holidays in Viareggio and nearby Forte dei Marmi. Beautiful art nouveau houses, such as the Salone Margherita, line the seafront at Viareggio. The fishermen go out to sea at dawn, but regrettably they no longer sail down the Burlamacca canal or from the Darsena, instead using the new port. But they still return at dusk, their boats laden with fish. At restaurants like Tito del Molo, da Roma, the Patriarca, and the Buonamico in Viareggio, and at Pino or Lorenzo in Forte dei Marmi, the fish are prepared in the simple traditional way that leaves the natural flavor intact.

In Lucchesia, however, fish also means fresh-water fish. There are trout from the streams, eels from the Serchio River and fish from Lake Massaciuccoli, which lies in a nature reserve where rare species of migratory birds find shelter. Giacomo Puccini, who had a house at Torre del Lago on the side of the lake near the sea, loved the fish from Lake Massaciuccoli and also enjoyed shooting coot from a boat hidden among the reeds. His villa is now open to the public, and every summer the famous Puccini Festival is held in the adjoining gardens. It is said that Puccini, a pure-blooded Lucchese, chose to build a villa there, not so much for the beautiful lake as for the hunting. When he first went there in 1891, its few inhabitants were all said to be poachers.

At Torre del Lago, Puccini, a man who lived life to the full, founded the Club la Bohème with a group of friends. The club itself was little more than a tavern where he met his friends to play cards, drink wine, eat good food and create new recipes. In this area there are numerous dishes attributed to Puccini, and although doubt is cast on some of these attributions, everyone agrees that he truly did invent coot *alla Puccini.*

The best place from which to admire Lucchesia's breathtaking natural beauty is undoubtedly Torre del Lago. With the sea a mile or so behind it, the town looks up at the Apuan Alps. Even in midsummer the peaks appear to be covered with snow. It is not snow, however, but the famous white Carrara marble. This is the same Versilia coast loved by Michelangelo, who, on the peak of Mount Altissimo, had wished to sculpt a statue large enough to be seen from the sea. He never fulfilled his wish, but the sparkling apex of the mountain is still a monument to the great master.

Laundry day in the Garfagnana village of Gioviano. The windows of Tuscany frame the small delights of everyday life.

An afternoon of fishing at Torre del Lago, Lake Massaciuccoli. The composer Giacomo Puccini, who built a house here, described the lake as his "supreme joy, paradise, Eden."

Lucca is one of the few cities where the pleasures of the table could always be indulged, even when other cities in Tuscany, the rest of Italy and Europe were at war. The rich population invariably preferred to pay off their enemies rather than find them armed at their gates. In all their long history, the mighty walls of Lucca have never been used in battle, and only once did they defend the city. That was in 1812, when the nearby Serchio River overflowed. The gates were closed and the water that flooded the surrounding countryside did not spill into the city.

Their philosophy of avoiding conflict left the citizens of Lucca free to devote their attention to silkmaking, banking and to the creation of plaster figurines, which for many years they exported around the world. And, of course, to their excellent table.

1989
Vernaccia
di San Gimignano
APPORTA
ELEMENTI
MINERALI
UTILI

I Piatti di Mezzo

A wine shop plaque boasts a black rooster (gallo nero), *the symbol of authentic Chianti Classico.*

I PIATTI DI MEZZO

In Florence, from the Middle Ages through the Renaissance, there was a meal called *la matta cena,* or "the mad supper." It was rather more than a snack but less than a normal evening meal. From Boccaccio we learn that "mad" really meant improvised, and that a few light dishes were prepared as an excuse to gather friends. Most of the items served were those we now call *piatti di mezzo,* or "middle dishes"—frittatas, vegetable loaves and molds. Nowadays they all make excellent luncheon dishes, although at formal dinners, as the name suggests, they are served as entrées between the first and main courses.

Vendors prepare for another day of selling at Florence's indoor San Lorenzo market.

Torta di verdura (vegetable loaf) is fairly common throughout Tuscany, but perhaps the best version is prepared in Lunigiana, where it is called *scarpazza* and is made with leeks, zucchini and wild salad plants that vary with the seasons. Borage and chicory are typical ingredients. A different kind of vegetable loaf is made in Versilia and the Garfagnana, where ricotta and sheep's milk cheese are also used and occasionally lard or bacon. An excellent fourteenth-century version that has chicken livers among its ingredients is still very popular.

There is a long tradition of stuffing either whole cabbages or cabbage leaves. Evidence of this legacy can be found in a cookbook published in 1885 by Arezzo chef Giobatta Magi, who points out that her cabbage recipe is very old. In fourteenth-century Florence, *la porrata,* a leek dish, was offered to the population outside the Basilica of San Lorenzo on the feast of St. Lawrence.

Vegetables mixed with cream sauce are the basis of a grand assortment of molds in which cooks can indulge their whims. The most classic molds are made with spinach, green beans, peas or cardoons. They are baked in a ring shape and, after being turned out, the hole in the center is filled with chicken liver and sage or with the famous Florentine *cibreo,* made with cockscombs and other delicacies.

Previous pages, front to rear: Snails with Sausage and Tomato Sauce (page 354), Green Pea and Ham Frittata (page 364) and Chicken Liver Frittata (page 356).

Another interesting *piatto di mezzo* is stuffed celery. It is the great specialty of Prato, where it is prepared in the most traditional way. The celery stalks are filled with chicken liver and chopped meat, but here too there are numerous interpretations, including the addition of dried mushrooms and ham. Although the stuffed celery in Lunigiana is not as renowned as that of Prato, it is equally delicious.

It is, however, the infinite variety of the frittata that reigns supreme over the *piatti di mezzo.* Whether mixed with onions or zucchini, artichokes or herbs, cauliflower or asparagus, sausage or potato, these open-faced omelets are always a pleasure to eat. Frittatas are also a great disguise for leftovers such as boiled meat and spaghetti. In Versilia the well-known dish called *miglieccio* is actually a frittata made from leftover minestrone. Local housewives are said to make too much minestrone so that they will have enough for *miglieccio* the next day. Then there is *frittata con gli zoccoli,* which translates as "frittata with clogs." The clogs are actually pieces of fried bacon, which leads one to believe that in the past bacon was much tougher. This particular dish is sometimes folded rather than cooked on both sides in the classic Italian manner. At one time these folded omelets were called *pesce d'uova,* or "egg fish."

Tuscans maintain that making frittatas is a fine art. Until the advent of nonstick pans, they were always fried in heavy iron skillets that were never washed. For a Tuscan, a frittata cannot even be considered seriously unless it stands nobly high, is golden on both sides, and is lusciously soft at the center. Any meats and vegetables used must be absolutely cold before being stirred into the eggs, or the eggs would start cooking and spoil the entire operation.

A shopkeeper stands proudly by his produce in the medieval village of Sovana.

Zucchinis are a popular choice for the recipes known as piatti di mezzo*—frittatas, vegetable loaves and vegetable molds.*

Savory Spelt Cake (left) and Chestnut Flour Polenta (right)

Whitebait Omelet

Lucca

POLENTA DI NECCIO

Chestnut Flour Polenta

Because there are so many chestnut woods around Lucca, there are dozens of recipes calling for chestnut flour. The local cooks are particularly proud of their necci, *chestnut pancakes made in a mold and cooked over an open fire. Chestnut flour is available in health food stores and specialty food markets. This polenta is excellent served with fried* pancetta, *sausages or stewed pork.*

5 cups (40 fl oz/1.2 l) water
salt
2½ cups (10 oz/300 g) chestnut flour
3 tablespoons extra virgin olive oil
½ cup (2 oz/60 g) freshly grated *pecorino* cheese or Parmesan cheese

In a large saucepan, bring the water to a boil and add a little salt. Lower the heat to a simmer. Whisking constantly, slowly add the flour in a thin, steady stream. Return the mixture to a boil and cook, stirring from time to time, until done, about 40 minutes. The polenta is ready when it starts pulling away easily from the sides of the pan.

Pour the polenta onto a warm platter. Sprinkle the surface with the olive oil and cheese. Serve very hot.

SERVES 6

Livorno

TORTINO DI BIANCHETTI

Whitebait Omelet

Bianchetti *are tiny whitebait, actually sardines and anchovies caught when they are only ¾ in (2 cm) long. Their season is very short and they are considered a great delicacy.*

3 eggs
14 oz (420 g) small whitebait
salt and freshly ground black pepper
1 teaspoon freshly grated lemon zest
1 tablespoon extra virgin olive oil

In a mixing bowl, whisk the eggs until well blended. Add the whitebait with a touch of salt and pepper and the lemon zest. Mix carefully as the whitebait break very easily.

Warm the oil in an 8-in (20-cm) nonstick skillet over moderate heat. Pour in the egg mixture. Cook, occasionally moving the egg with a wooden spoon, until the egg sets and only the surface is runny, about 5 minutes. Turn the omelet out onto a plate, browned side up. Slide the omelet back into the skillet and cook the other side for 1 minute.

Turn the omelet out onto a serving plate. Serve immediately.

SERVES 6

Lucca

TORTA DI FARRO

Savory Spelt Cake

Spelt is very popular in Lucchesia, where it has been eaten since Etruscan times. It is excellent in soups and with meat dishes and is available in health food stores.

1¾ cups (10 oz/300 g) spelt
3 eggs
10 oz (300 g) ricotta
1 handful of fresh borage leaves, chopped
salt and fresh ground black pepper
extra virgin olive oil for brushing pan

In a bowl, soak the spelt in water to cover overnight.

Drain the spelt and transfer to a saucepan. Add water to cover and cook over low heat, stirring occasionally, until the water is absorbed, about 1 hour.

Preheat an oven to 350°F (180°C).

Place the spelt in a mixing bowl Add the eggs, ricotta, borage and salt and pepper to taste.

Brush a round 9-in (23-cm) cake pan with olive oil. Spoon the spelt mixture into the prepared pan, forming a layer about 1 in (2.5 cm) deep. Bake until the cake is just golden, about 45 minutes.

Remove the pan from the oven and let cool a few minutes. Run a thin, sharp knife blade around the edge of the pan to loosen the cake, then remove the cake to a serving dish. Serve warm but not hot.

SERVES 6

Firenze

TORTINO DI CARCIOFI

Artichoke Omelet

The difference between an artichoke omelet served in Florence and those made elsewhere is that the Florentine version is never cooked in an oven or turned, and the artichokes are fried before being mixed with the egg.

juice of 1 lemon
6 globe artichokes
¾ cup (3 oz/90 g) all-purpose (plain) flour
4 cups (32 fl oz/1 l) extra virgin olive oil for frying
6 eggs
salt and freshly ground black pepper

❧ Fill a large bowl with water and add the lemon juice. Cut the stalks off the artichokes. Remove the tough outer leaves and cut away the sharp leaf points from the tops. Cut the artichokes into quarters and remove and discard the furry chokes. Immediately drop them into the bowl of water to prevent discoloration. When all of the artichokes have been cut, drain them and pat dry with absorbent paper towels.

❧ Dredge the artichoke quarters in the flour and shake off any excess.

❧ Meanwhile, reserve 1 tablespoon of the olive oil and pour the remainder into a deep, heavy skillet. Heat the oil in the skillet to 350°F (180°C). A few at a time, slip the artichoke quarters into the hot oil without crowding the pan. Fry until golden, about 5 minutes. With a slotted spoon, remove the artichokes to absorbent paper towels to drain. Let cool completely.

❧ In a bowl, whisk the eggs until well blended and season to taste with salt and pepper.

❧ In a 9-in (23-cm) nonstick skillet, warm the 1 tablespoon olive oil over moderate heat. Pour the eggs into the skillet and arrange the artichoke quarters on top. Cook, occasionally moving the egg with a wooden spoon, until the egg thickens and sets, about 5 minutes.

❧ Slide the omelet onto a serving plate and serve hot.

SERVES 6

Lucca

TORTA DI CECI

Chick-pea Cake

Around Lucca and in the Garfagnana mountains, flat breads made of unusual flours such as chick-pea, chestnut and cornmeal are often served instead of ordinary bread.

2½ cups (10 oz/300 g) chick-pea (garbanzo) flour
3½ cups (28 fl oz/900 ml) water
salt and freshly ground black pepper
¼ cup (2 fl oz/60 ml) extra virgin olive oil

❧ Pour the flour into a large bowl. Gradually add the water to the flour, whisking constantly to keep lumps from forming. You should have a smooth, runny batter. Season to taste with salt and pepper and let stand for at least 3 hours. With a slotted spoon, skim the froth that forms on the surface.

❧ Preheat an oven to 350°F (180°C). Pour the olive oil into a shallow ovenproof pan, then pour in the batter, making a layer about ¼ in (6 mm) deep. Bake until just golden on top, about 30 minutes.

❧ Remove from the oven pan and cut into serving pieces. Serve piping hot.

SERVES 6

Arezzo

CHIOCCIOLE ALLA SALSICCIA

Snails with Sausage and Tomato Sauce

Snails are considered a great delicacy around Arezzo. They require a lot of preparation, however, because they must be cleaned thoroughly before being cooked. After a rainfall women go out to gather snails in covered baskets. They leave the snails in their new woven homes and feed them with three handfuls of flour and a few stalks of mint, which flushes out the impurities and improves their flavor. After about a week the snails are rinsed several times in cold water. They are then sprinkled with half a quart (500 ml) of vinegar and a handful of salt and moved around frequently. After half an hour they are again rinsed in cold water until they stop frothing. At this point they are ready to be cooked. But of course you can also buy good quality shelled snails in cans at specialty markets.

2 tablespoons extra virgin olive oil
1 small yellow onion, chopped
3 oz (90 g) sweet Italian sausages, skinned and crumbled
36 snails, without shells, prepared for cooking
½ cup (4 fl oz/120 ml) dry white wine
juice of 1 lemon
7 oz (210 g) plum (egg) tomatoes, peeled and chopped
salt and freshly ground black pepper

❧ In a large skillet over low heat, warm the olive oil. Add the onion and sausage and cook over low heat, stirring frequently, for about 5 minutes.

❧ Add the snails, wine, lemon juice, tomatoes and salt and pepper to taste. Cook, stirring frequently, for 20 minutes.

❧ Arrange the snails on a platter and pour the sauce over them. Serve piping hot.

SERVES 6 *Photograph pages 348–49*

Firenze

SALVIATA

Baked Omelet with Sage

In the spring when the sage is young and tender, Tuscan cooks prepare this simple omelet. In Florence, salviata is traditionally cooked in a brown earthenware dish so that the omelet forms a crust on top but stays deliciously soft at the center, but any ovenproof dish will do.

10 eggs
pinch of salt
2 tablespoons all-purpose (plain) flour
¼ cup (2 fl oz/60 ml) milk
12 fresh sage leaves
1 tablespoon extra virgin olive oil

❧ Preheat an oven to 350°F (180°C). Combine the eggs and salt in a large bowl. Whisk the eggs until well blended. Whisking constantly, gradually add the flour through a sieve to prevent lumps from forming. Whisk in the milk. Tear the sage leaves into pieces with your fingers and add them to the mixture.

❧ Brush an ovenproof earthenware dish that measures about 8 by 12 in (20 by 30 cm) with the oil. Pour in the egg mixture. Bake until the omelet has formed a golden crust but is still soft at the center, about 20 minutes. Serve hot from the dish.

SERVES 6

Top to bottom: Baked Omelet with Sage, Chick-pea Cake and Artichoke Omelet

Stuffed Turkey Neck

Arezzo

COLLO DI TACCHINO RIPIENO

Stuffed Turkey Neck

Occasionally chicken livers instead of sausage meat are used in this stuffing for turkey neck. This dish is served at room temperature with mayonnaise, pickled onions and gherkins.

8 slices dried *porcini* mushrooms
4 oz (120 g) crustless coarse country bread
1 cup (8 fl oz/240 ml) milk
1 turkey neck (about 1¼ lb/600 g)
7 oz (210 g) sweet Italian sausages, skinned and crumbled
3 oz (90 g) ground (minced) turkey breast
1 egg
1 tablespoon chopped fresh flat-leaf (Italian) parsley
salt and freshly ground black pepper

❧ In a bowl, soak the mushrooms in warm water to cover for 30 minutes. At the same time, in a separate bowl, soak the bread in the milk for 30 minutes. Drain the mushrooms and squeeze out any excess moisture. Chop the mushrooms and place in a mixing bowl.

❧ Squeeze all the milk out of the bread and add the bread to the bowl as well.

❧ Meanwhile, keeping the skin intact, remove the skin from the neck. To do this, very gently turn the skin inside out while carefully detaching it from the bone. When the skin is completely detached turn the skin right side out again.

❧ Add the sausage, turkey breast, egg and parsley to the bowl. Season to taste with salt and pepper and mix thoroughly.

❧ Stuff the turkey neck with the sausage mixture. Sew up both ends with kitchen thread. Prick the skin with a needle in several places.

❧ Bring a large saucepan filled with salted water to a gentle boil. Add the turkey neck, reduce the heat to low and simmer uncovered for 1 hour.

❧ Drain the turkey neck and let cool completely. Cut into slices about ⅜ in (1 cm) thick and serve at room temperature.

SERVES 6

Grosseto

PANE FRITTO ALLA SALSICCIA

Fried Bread Dipped in Egg with Sausage

The Maremma is a land of hunters and strong flavors. After a day out, hunters fry bread in large skillets over open fires and spread it with air-cured wild boar sausages.

3 eggs
salt and freshly ground black pepper
6 slices coarse country bread
4 cups (32 fl oz/1 l) extra virgin olive oil for frying
13 oz (390 g) air-cured wild boar sausages or other spicy sausages

❧ In a shallow bowl, whisk the eggs until well blended. Season to taste with salt and pepper. Soak the bread slices in the beaten egg.

❧ Meanwhile, in a deep skillet, heat the olive oil to 350°F (180°C).

❧ Slip the bread, 2 or 3 slices at a time, into the hot oil and fry until just golden, about 3 minutes. With a slotted spoon, remove to absorbent paper towels to drain. Continue frying the remaining bread slices in the same manner. Skin the sausages and spread the meat on the hot fried bread. Serve while the bread is still hot.

SERVES 6

Siena

FRITTATA DI FEGATINI DI POLLO

Chicken Liver Frittata

The Sienese use lamb's liver for this dish during the spring months, but the rest of the year they make it with chicken livers, which are just as delicious.

10 oz (300 g) chicken livers
3 tablespoons extra virgin olive oil
1 handful of fresh sage leaves
6 eggs
salt and freshly ground black pepper

❧ Remove and discard any fat and connective tissue from the chicken livers. Slice them into fairly large pieces.

❧ In a skillet over moderate heat, warm 2 tablespoons of the olive oil.

❧ Add the sage and chicken livers and cook until the livers are firm but still pink in the center, about 2 minutes. Remove from the heat and cool to room temperature.

❧ In a medium bowl, whisk the eggs until well blended. Season to taste with salt and pepper and mix in the chicken livers.

❧ Heat the remaining 1 tablespoon olive oil in a 9-in (23-cm) nonstick skillet over moderate heat. Pour in the egg mixture. Cook, occasionally moving the egg with a wooden spoon, until the egg sets and only the surface is slightly runny, about 5 minutes.

❧ Turn the frittata out onto a plate, browned side up. Slide the frittata back into the skillet and cook the other side for 1 minute.

❧ Turn the frittata out onto a serving plate. Serve hot.

SERVES 6

Photograph pages 348–49

Fried Bread Dipped in Egg with Sausage

Grosseto

Crostoni di Uova alla Cacciatora

Hunters' Eggs

These eggs are traditionally prepared for excursions to Monte Amiata, a tall mountain with an enormous cross on its summit. The area abounds in game and wild mushrooms.

12 slices dried *porcini* mushrooms
6 tablespoons (3 fl oz/90 ml) extra virgin olive oil, plus 5 cups (40 fl oz/1.2 l) for frying
1 small yellow onion, chopped
1 lb (450 g) plum (egg) tomatoes, peeled and chopped
small piece of dried chili
salt
6 slices coarse country bread
6 eggs

Soak the mushrooms in warm water to cover for 30 minutes. Drain and squeeze out any excess moisture; set aside.

In a saucepan over moderate heat, warm 3 tablespoons of the olive oil. Add the onion and fry gently, stirring frequently, until translucent, about 5 minutes. Add the tomatoes, chili, mushrooms and salt to taste. Simmer over low heat until the liquid evaporates, about 30 minutes.

In a deep skillet, pour in the olive oil for frying and heat to 350°F (180°C). Add the bread, 2 or 3 slices at a time, and fry until golden, about 3 minutes. With a slotted spoon, remove to absorbent paper towels to drain; keep warm. Continue frying the remaining bread in the same manner.

In a large nonstick skillet over moderate heat, warm the remaining 3 tablespoons olive oil. Break the eggs into the skillet and fry sunny side up (without turning).

Arrange the fried bread on a serving plate. Place an egg on each slice and cover with the tomato sauce. Serve immediately.

SERVES 6

Livorno

Panzanella con Scampi

Bread, Tomato and Seafood Salad

Panzanella, *a strictly Tuscan dish, acquires a taste of the sea in Livorno, where shrimp and cuttlefish are added to the classic recipe.*

13 oz (390 g) coarse country bread
6 oz (180 g) cuttlefish or squid
6 oz (180 g) shrimp (prawns), peeled and deveined
3 salad tomatoes, chopped
1 small yellow onion, very finely chopped
1 handful of fresh basil leaves, torn into pieces
1 tablespoon chopped fresh flat-leaf (Italian) parsley
salt
1 tablespoon white wine vinegar
¼ cup (2 fl oz/60 ml) extra virgin olive oil
1 garlic clove, chopped

Break the bread into pieces. Place in a bowl, add water to cover and soak for about 10 minutes.

Meanwhile, pull the tentacles from each cuttlefish (or squid) body. Discard the entrails, ink sac and cartilage from the bodies. Cut the tentacles off at the point just above the eyes and discard the heads. Rinse the bodies and tentacles under cold running water.

Bring a medium saucepan filled with salted water to a boil. Add the shrimp and cook until they turn pink and are opaque, about 2 minutes. Remove with a slotted spoon and set aside to cool. Add the cuttlefish to the boiling water and cook for 15 minutes. Drain and cool completely. Cut the shrimp and cuttlefish into fairly small pieces and place in a salad bowl.

Drain the bread and squeeze out any excess moisture. Crumble the bread into the salad bowl. Add the tomatoes, onion, basil and parsley. In a small bowl, dissolve salt to taste in the vinegar. Add the olive oil and garlic; mix well. Sprinkle the dressing over the salad. Toss well. Serve at room temperature.

SERVES 6

Hunters' Eggs

Maremma-Style Stuffed Eggs (left) and Bread, Tomato and Seafood Salad (right)

Grosseto

UOVA SODE ALLA MAREMMANA

Stuffed Eggs, Maremma Style

Wild boar sausages are very strong, so if they are not available, another spicy sausage should be substituted.

6 eggs
7 oz (210 g) air-cured wild boar sausages or other spicy sausages, skinned

❧ Place the eggs in a saucepan and add cold water to cover barely. Bring the water to a boil. When it reaches a boil, cook for 8 minutes from that moment. Remove the eggs from the pan and let cool to room temperature.

❧ Shell the eggs, cut them in half lengthwise and remove the yolks. Place the yolks in the bowl of a food processor fitted with a metal blade. Cut a very thin slice off the rounded base of each egg white so that the egg half will stand upright. Set the whites aside.

❧ Add the sausages to the food processor. Process until a creamy mixture forms.

❧ Spoon the yolk mixture into the reserved egg white halves. Arrange on a plate and serve.

SERVES 6

Arezzo

CROSTONI DI PANE FRITTO

Fried Country Bread

This fried bread is generally eaten plain, but sometimes eggs scrambled with a little tomato and mushroom are served on it.

6 slices coarse country bread, about ⅜ in (1 cm) thick
5 cups (40 fl oz/1.2 l) extra virgin olive oil for frying
salt and freshly ground black pepper

❧ In a deep, heavy skillet, heat the oil to 350°F (180°C). Slip the bread, 2 or 3 pieces at a time, into the hot oil and fry until just golden on both sides, turning once if necessary, about 3 minutes.

❧ With a slotted utensil, remove to absorbent paper towels to drain. Continue frying the remaining bread in the same manner.

❧ Sprinkle the fried bread lightly with salt and pepper. Arrange on a warm platter and serve immediately.

SERVES 6

Grosseto

FRITTATA DI RICOTTA

Ricotta Frittata

The hilly area between Grosseto and Siena is referred to as the Upper Maremma. Flocks of sheep are sent to graze on the hills, and the shepherds' wives produce very good pecorino *cheese and* ricotta.

1¼ cups (10 oz/300 g) ricotta
4 eggs
1 teaspoon fennel seed
salt and freshly ground black pepper
1 tablespoon extra virgin olive oil

❧ Place the ricotta in a mixing bowl. One at a time, add the eggs, stirring well after each addition to prevent lumps from forming. Add the fennel seed and season to taste with salt and pepper.

❧ Heat the oil in an 8½-in (22-cm) nonstick skillet over moderate heat. Pour in the egg mixture and cook, occasionally moving the egg with a wooden spoon, until the egg sets and only the surface is runny, about 5 minutes. Turn the frittata out onto a plate, browned side up. Slide the frittata back into the skillet and cook on the other side for 1 minute.

❧ Turn the frittata out onto a platter. Serve immediately.

SERVES 6

Grosseto

MELANZANE ALLA MAREMMANA

Fried Eggplant Frittata

Along the Maremma coast toward Rome, there were once only eucalyptus trees. Now the land is covered with vast market gardens where tomatoes, peppers and eggplants are grown.

3 Asian (slender) eggplants (aubergines), about 1 lb (450 g) total weight
4 cups (32 fl oz/1 l) extra virgin olive oil for frying
1 cup (4 oz/120 g) all-purpose (plain) flour
3 eggs
3 plum (egg) tomatoes, peeled and chopped
salt and freshly ground pepper

❧ Cut the eggplants crosswise into slices about ⅛ in (3 mm) thick. Reserve 1 tablespoon of the olive oil and pour the remainder into a deep, heavy skillet. Heat the oil in the skillet to 350°F (180°C).

❧ Lightly dredge the eggplant slices in the flour. A few at a

Left to right: Ricotta Frittata, Fried Country Bread and Fried Eggplant Frittata

time, slip the eggplant slices into the hot oil and fry until golden, about 2 minutes. With a slotted spoon, remove to absorbent paper towels to drain. Continue frying the remaining eggplant slices in the same manner. Let cool completely.

❧ In a mixing bowl, whisk the eggs until well blended. Add the tomatoes and fried eggplant. Season to taste with salt and pepper.

❧ In a nonstick skillet over moderate heat, warm the 1 tablespoon olive oil. Pour in the egg mixture and cook, occasionally moving the egg with a wooden spoon, until the egg sets and only the surface is runny, about 5 minutes. Turn the frittata out onto a plate, browned side up. Slide the frittata back into the skillet and cook the other side for 1 minute.

❧ Turn the frittata out onto a platter. Serve immediately.

SERVES 6

Stuffed Mussels on the Half Shell

Arezzo

Torta di Erbe

Green Vegetable Tart

This tart is generally made with such wild leaf vegetables as chicory (curly endive), dandelion, St. Peter's grass, nettles and the like, but spinach or Swiss chard may be used instead.

2 lb (900 g) spinach or Swiss chard (silverbeet), trimmed
6 tablespoons (3 fl oz/90 ml) extra virgin olive oil, plus extra for tart pan
2 garlic cloves, chopped
salt and freshly ground black pepper
3 eggs
1¾ cups (7 oz/240 g) all-purpose (plain) flour
½ cup (4 fl oz/120 ml) water

Bring a large saucepan of salted water to a boil. Add the spinach (or Swiss chard) and cook for just a few minutes. Drain well and squeeze out any excess water. Chop and set aside.

In a large skillet over low heat, warm 3 tablespoons of the olive oil. Add the garlic and spinach and season to taste with salt and pepper. Cook, stirring occasionally, for 10 minutes. Remove from the heat and let cool to room temperature. Stir in the eggs.

In a large bowl, combine the flour, the remaining 3 tablespoons olive oil and the water. Mix well until the ingredients come together in a ball. Transfer the ball to a lightly floured surface and knead until it forms a smooth, elastic dough, about 5 minutes.

Preheat the oven to 350°F (180°C). Brush an 8½-in (22-cm) tart pan with a removable bottom with olive oil. On a lightly floured board, roll out the dough with a rolling pin into a round about 10 in (25 cm) in diameter. Carefully transfer it to the prepared pan and press it gently against the bottom and sides of the pan. Trim the dough even with the rim of the tart pan. Spoon the vegetable mixture into the pastry shell and smooth the surface.

Bake the tart until the crust is browned and the center is set, about 40 minutes.

Remove from the oven and let cool slightly. Remove the pan rim and transfer the tart to a serving plate. Serve hot or at room temperature.

SERVES 6

Livorno

Cozze Ripiene

Stuffed Mussels on the Half Shell

In Livorno the stuffed mussels differ from those of other regions because of the addition of a little sausage meat to the classic mixture of herbs and bread crumbs.

7 oz (210 g) sweet Italian sausages, skinned and crumbled
3 tablespoons fine dry bread crumbs
2 tablespoons chopped fresh flat-leaf (Italian) parsley
2 garlic cloves, chopped
2 plum (egg) tomatoes, peeled and chopped
1 egg
salt
5 lb (2.4 kg) large mussels
2 tablespoons extra virgin olive oil

❧ In a mixing bowl, combine the sausage, 2 tablespoons of the bread crumbs, the parsley, garlic, tomatoes and egg. Season to taste with salt, mix well and set aside.

❧ Scrub and debeard the mussels. Place the mussels in a shallow saucepan, cover and place over moderate heat until the shells open, about 5 minutes. Remove from the heat and discard any mussels that did not open. Open the mussels and discard the top shells. With a small, sharp knife, loosen the mussel meats from the bottom shells and leave them nestled in the shells.

❧ Preheat an oven to 350°F (180°C). Divide the sausage mixture among the mussels, mounding it on top. Sprinkle with the remaining 1 tablespoon bread crumbs and the olive oil.

❧ Arrange the mussels on a flat ovenproof pan. Bake for 15 minutes.

❧ Serve very hot.

SERVES 6

Arezzo

Frittata Affogata

Drowned Frittata

Because porcini *grow so abundantly in the Casentino mountains, local cooks often add them to the simple tomato sauce in which they "drown" this frittata. They dry the mushrooms for winter by slicing them and threading them onto strings, which are either hung in front of the fire or, on sunny days, stuck on the branches of thorn trees outdoors.*

3 tablespoons extra virgin olive oil
1 small carrot, peeled and chopped
1 yellow onion, chopped
½ celery stalk, trimmed and chopped
2 lb (900 g) plum (egg) tomatoes, peeled and chopped
1 tablespoon chopped fresh flat-leaf (Italian) parsley
salt and freshly ground black pepper
8 eggs

❧ In a large skillet over low heat, warm 2 tablespoons of the olive oil. Add the carrot, onion and celery and fry gently, stirring frequently, until the onion is translucent, about 5 minutes. Stir in the tomatoes and parsley. Season to taste with salt and pepper and simmer until the liquid evaporates, about 50 minutes.

❧ In a bowl, whisk the eggs until well blended. Season lightly to taste with salt and pepper. Heat the remaining 1 tablespoon olive oil in an 8-in (20-cm) nonstick skillet over moderate heat. Pour in the egg and cook, occasionally moving the egg with a wooden spoon, until the egg sets and only the surface is runny, about 5 minutes. Turn the frittata out onto a plate, browned side up. Slide the frittata back into the skillet and cook the other side for 1 minute.

❧ Turn the frittata out onto a serving plate. Cover with the tomato sauce and let stand for 2 minutes to allow the flavors to blend. Serve hot.

SERVES 6

Green Vegetable Tart (left) and Drowned Frittata (right)

Siena

SFORMATINI DI FUNGHI

Mushroom Timbales

Mushrooms that are less expensive than prized porcini *can be used for preparing this dish. If you use fresh button mushrooms, however, it is a good idea to add a few soaked dried* porcini *to intensify the flavor.*

1¼ lb (600 g) fresh *porcini* mushrooms
3 tablespoons extra virgin olive oil
1 tablespoon fresh thyme leaves
3 eggs
2 tablespoons all-purpose (plain) flour
¼ cup (2 fl oz/60 ml) milk
2 tablespoons unsalted butter
¾ cup (3 oz/90 g) fine dry bread crumbs

❧ Preheat an oven to 350°F (180°C). Clean the mushrooms by wiping them with a dampened cloth; do not wash them in water. Trim off the ends of the mushroom stems. Thinly slice the mushrooms.
❧ In a medium skillet over moderate heat, warm the olive oil. Add the mushrooms and sauté until tender, about 5 minutes. Add the thyme, stir to combine and set aside to cool completely.
❧ In a bowl, whisk the eggs until well blended. Whisking constantly, gradually add the flour through a sieve to prevent lumps from forming. Whisk in the milk and then stir in the cooled mushrooms.
❧ Butter 6 ramekins each about 4 in (10 cm) in diameter and then coat them evenly with the bread crumbs. Divide the egg mixture evenly among the prepared ramekins. Place the ramekins in a baking dish and pour water into the dish to a depth of 1 in (2.5 cm). Bake in the center of the oven until the custard sets and the tops are golden, about 30 minutes.
❧ Remove the ramekins from the oven. Run a thin, sharp knife blade around the edge of each ramekin and then invert the timbales onto individual serving plates. Serve hot.

SERVES 6

Siena

UOVA TRIPPATE

Omelet Strips with Tomato Sauce

Egg dishes are particularly popular all over Tuscany because new-laid eggs are still available from the farmers. This recipe is so named because it looks like tripe.

3 tablespoons extra virgin olive oil
1 tablespoon chopped yellow onion
4 oz (120 g) *prosciutto,* chopped
1¼ lb (600 g) plum (egg) tomatoes, peeled and chopped
10 eggs
2 tablespoons all-purpose (plain) flour
¼ cup (2 fl oz/60 ml) milk
salt

❧ In a saucepan over moderate heat, warm 2 tablespoons of the olive oil. Add the onion and *prosciutto* and fry gently until the onion is translucent, about 5 minutes. Add the tomatoes and simmer over low heat until the liquid evaporates, about 50 minutes.
❧ In a bowl, whisk the eggs until well blended. Whisking constantly, gradually add the flour through a sieve to prevent lumps from forming. Whisk in the milk and season to taste with salt.
❧ To make the omelets, heat a little of the remaining olive oil in a 7-in (18-cm) nonstick skillet. Add just enough of the egg mixture to the skillet to make a thin sheet, tilting the skillet to spread it evenly. Cook until the egg thickens, about 2 minutes. Turn the omelet over and cook the other side, about 30 seconds. Slide the omelet from the skillet and set aside on a flat surface. Continue making the omelets in the same manner until all the egg mixture is used.
❧ Roll up each omelet in a cylinder and slice into strips about ⅜ in (1 cm) wide. Toss the omelet strips in the tomato sauce and heat for 1 minute. Serve immediately.

SERVES 6

Firenze

MIGLIACCIO

Polenta with Pancetta and Rosemary

This dish is sometimes prepared with chestnut flour and occasionally with millet. At one time a little corn was grown on every Tuscan farm, but now most of it comes from northern Italy.

2 tablespoons extra virgin olive oil
6 oz (180 g) *pancetta,* thinly sliced
5 cups (40 fl oz/1.2 l) water
salt
2⅓ cups (10 oz/300 g) coarse-grained cornmeal
2 tablespoons chopped fresh rosemary

❧ In a skillet over moderate heat, combine the olive oil and *pancetta.* Fry gently until the *pancetta* is crisp, about 5 minutes. Set aside.
❧ In a deep saucepan, bring the water to a boil and add a little salt. Slowly add the cornmeal in a thin, steady stream, stirring constantly. Cook for about 20 minutes over low heat, stirring constantly with a wooden spoon, until the polenta thickens.
❧ Meanwhile, preheat the oven to 350°F (180°C). Line the bottom of an 8-by-12-in (20-by-30-cm) baking dish with half of the *pancetta.*
❧ Cover the *pancetta* with the polenta, smoothing the surface with a wet knife. The polenta should be about 1⅛ in (3 cm) thick. Arrange the remaining *pancetta* on top and sprinkle with the rosemary.
❧ Bake until the top is just golden, about 20 minutes. Serve hot.

SERVES 6

Firenze

FRITTATA DI PISELLI E PROSCIUTTO

Green Pea and Ham Frittata

Despite the fact that Tuscans pick peas when they are very young, they cook them for quite a long time to bring out their flavor.

3 tablespoons extra virgin olive oil
3 oz (90 g) *prosciutto,* chopped
1 small yellow onion, chopped
3 lb (1.3 kg) fresh green peas, shelled
6 eggs
salt and freshly ground black pepper

❧ In a skillet over low heat, warm 2 tablespoons of the olive oil. Add the *prosciutto* and onion and fry gently, stirring fre-

Polenta with Pancetta and Rosemary (left), Mushroom Timbales (right) and Omelet Strips with Tomato Sauce (rear)

quently, until the onion is translucent, about 5 minutes.

❧ Add the peas and then add water just to cover. Simmer over low heat until the water has been absorbed, about 20 minutes. Remove from the heat and let cool to room temperature.

❧ In a bowl, whisk the eggs until well blended, then mix in the cooled peas. Season to taste with salt and pepper.

❧ Heat the remaining 1 tablespoon olive oil in a 9-in (23-cm) nonstick skillet over moderate heat. Pour in the egg mixture. Cook, occasionally moving the egg with a wooden spoon, until the egg sets and only the surface is runny, about 5 minutes. Turn the frittata out onto a plate, browned side up. Slide the frittata back into the skillet and cook the other side for 1 minute.

❧ Turn the frittata out onto a serving plate. Serve hot.

SERVES 6 *Photograph pages 348–49*

Siena

SFORMATO DI FORMAGGIO

Cheese Mold

The house of my friend Signora Titti Nepi has one of the most beautiful views in Siena. This recipe, a favorite of hers, calls for sheep's milk cheese, but Parmesan or Swiss (Gruyère) may be used quite successfully.

¼ cup (2 fl oz/60 ml) extra virgin olive oil
½ cup (2 oz/60 g) all-purpose (plain) flour
2⅓ cups (20 fl oz/600 ml) milk, at room temperature
3 eggs
pinch of freshly grated nutmeg
½ lb (240 g) sheep's milk, Parmesan or Swiss cheese, grated
salt and freshly ground black pepper
2 tablespoons unsalted butter

❧ Preheat an oven to 350°F (180°C). In a medium saucepan over moderate heat, warm the olive oil. Add the flour and cook, stirring continuously, until the flour has absorbed all of the oil, about 2 minutes. Continuing to stir, gradually add the milk and cook until you have a smooth, thick sauce, about 5 minutes. Remove from the heat and let cool to room temperature.

❧ Add the eggs, one at a time, to the sauce, mixing well after each addition. Then mix in the nutmeg and all but 2 tablespoons of the cheese. Season to taste with salt and pepper.

❧ Grease a 5-cup (40-fl oz/1.2-l) mold with the butter and then coat it evenly with the reserved 2 tablespoons cheese. Pour in the cheese mixture.

❧ Place the mold in a baking dish and pour water into the dish to a depth of 1 in (2.5 cm). Bake in the center of the oven until set and the top is golden, about 1 hour.

❧ Remove the mold from the oven. Run a thin, sharp knife blade around the edge of the mold and then invert it onto a serving platter. Serve hot.

SERVES 6

Lucca

NIDI DI ERBUCCE

Green Nests

In Lucchesia wild leaf vegetables are used often, either combined with other greens or on their own. They are also delicious eaten at room temperature with an oil and lemon dressing or tossed in a pan with oil and garlic and served hot.

2¼ lb (1.2 kg) mixed wild leaf vegetables (such as borage, dandelion or chicory [curly endive]) or spinach, trimmed
4 tablespoons (2 fl oz/60 ml) extra virgin olive oil
salt and freshly ground pepper
6 eggs

❧ Bring a large saucepan filled with salted water to a boil. Add the vegetables and cook for a few minutes. Drain well and let cool. Squeeze out any excess water.

❧ In a large skillet over moderate heat, warm 2 tablespoons of the olive oil. Add the vegetables and fry gently, stirring frequently, until tender, about 5 minutes. Season to taste with salt and pepper. Remove from the heat and let cool to room temperature.

❧ Preheat an oven to 350°F (180°C). Divide the vegetables into 6 equal portions and roll each portion into a firm ball. With a fingertip, make a hollow in the center of each ball to form a nestlike indentation.

❧ Brush an 8-by-12-in (20-by-30-cm) baking dish with the remaining 2 tablespoons olive oil and arrange the balls in it, hollow side up. Break 1 egg and drop the white of the egg into one of the hollows; set the yolk aside. Repeat with the remaining eggs, dropping a white into each "nest" and setting the yolks aside so that they can also be added individually.

❧ Bake the nests until the egg white solidifies, about 10 minutes. Remove the dish from the oven and drop a yolk over the white in each hollow. Return the dish to the oven and bake for 2 minutes. Transfer to a platter and serve immediately.

SERVES 6

Cheese Mold

Green Nests

Front to rear: Zucchini Omelet, Omelet Cake and Stuffed Zucchini

Firenze

TORTINO DI ZUCCHINE

Zucchini Omelet

This omelet may also be served with meat sauce, sautéed sweetbreads or a simple tomato sauce.

3 tablespoons extra virgin olive oil
2 lb (900 g) small zucchini (courgettes), trimmed and thinly sliced
4 eggs
3 tablespoons milk
pinch of freshly grated nutmeg
salt and freshly ground pepper
¼ cup (1 oz/30 g) all-purpose (plain) flour
½ cup (2 oz/60 g) freshly grated Parmesan cheese
12 fresh basil leaves, torn into pieces
⅔ cup (3 oz/90 g) fine dry bread crumbs

❧ Preheat an oven to 350°F (180°C).
❧ In a skillet over moderate heat, warm 2 tablespoons of the olive oil. Add the zucchini and fry, stirring frequently, until all the liquid released by the zucchini evaporates and the zucchini are just golden, about 10 minutes.
❧ In a bowl, whisk together the eggs and milk until well blended. Add the nutmeg and season to taste with salt and pepper. Whisking constantly, gradually add the flour through a sieve to prevent lumps from forming. Add the zucchini and Parmesan and mix well. Stir in the basil.
❧ Oil an 8-in (20-cm) ring mold with the remaining 1 tablespoon olive oil. Coat the mold with the bread crumbs. Pour in the egg mixture.
❧ Bake until slightly golden, about 1 hour. Remove the mold from the oven. Run a thin, sharp knife blade around the edge of the mold to loosen it, then invert onto a warm serving dish. Serve hot.

SERVES 6

Firenze

TORTINO DI FRITTATE

Omelet Cake

This very popular dish makes an excellent lunch when served with sautéed vegetables or a salad. The omelet may be flavored with ham, cheese or mushrooms instead of pancetta.

5 oz (150 g) *pancetta,* finely chopped
3 eggs
¾ cup (3 oz/90 g) all-purpose (plain) flour
2 cups (16 fl oz/480 ml) milk
4 tablespoons (2 fl oz/60 ml) extra virgin olive oil
2 garlic cloves, chopped
1¼ lb (600 g) plum (egg) tomatoes, peeled and chopped
2 tablespoons unsalted butter
½ cup (2 oz/60 g) freshly grated Parmesan cheese
salt and freshly ground black pepper

❧ In a nonstick skillet over low heat, gently fry the *pancetta* until crisp. With a slotted spoon, remove to absorbent paper towels to drain and cool completely.
❧ In a bowl, whisk the eggs until well blended. Whisking constantly, gradually add ½ cup (2 oz/60 g) of the flour and ⅔ cup (5 fl oz/150 ml) of the milk. Stir in 2 tablespoons of the olive oil and the *pancetta.* Let the batter stand for about 30 minutes.
❧ In a medium saucepan over moderate heat, warm 1 tablespoon of the olive oil. Add the garlic and fry gently, stirring frequently until just golden, about 3 minutes. Add the tomatoes and simmer over low heat until most of the liquid evaporates and the sauce is thick, about 50 minutes. Keep the sauce warm.
❧ Meanwhile, in a heavy-bottomed saucepan over low heat, melt the butter. Add the remaining ¼ cup (1 oz/30 g) flour and cook, stirring constantly, for 2 minutes. Stirring constantly, gradually add the remaining 1⅓ cups (11 oz/330 ml) milk. Cook, continuing to stir, until the sauce thickens, about 5 minutes. When the sauce is ready, remove it from the heat and stir in the Parmesan. Season to taste with salt and pepper.
❧ Lightly oil a 7-in (18-cm) nonstick skillet with a little of the remaining 1 tablespoon olive oil and warm over low heat. Add just enough batter to the skillet to make a very thin omelet, tilting the pan to spread it evenly. Cook until the batter sets, about 2 minutes. Turn the omelet over and cook the other side, about 30 seconds. Slide the omelet from the pan and set aside on a flat surface.
❧ Continue making omelets until you have used all the batter, adding oil to the pan as needed. You should have about 12 omelets in all.
❧ Preheat an oven to 325°F (160°C).
❧ In the center of an ovenproof serving dish, place an omelet. Cover it with a little of the white sauce. Place an omelet on top and spoon a little more white sauce on it. Repeat until all of the omelets and white sauce have been used, ending with some sauce.
❧ Bake until heated through and bubbly, about 20 minutes.
❧ Remove from the oven and spoon the hot tomato sauce over the top. Serve immediately.

SERVES 6

Firenze

ZUCCHINE RIPIENE

Stuffed Zucchini

Stuffed zucchini are often served as a main course for family suppers. Leftover cooked meats, ham or various cheeses may be used for the stuffing.

4 tablespoons (2 fl oz/60 ml) extra virgin olive oil
1 tablespoon chopped yellow onion
1¼ lb (600 g) plum (egg) tomatoes, peeled and chopped
salt and freshly ground black pepper
6 zucchini (courgettes)
5 oz (150 g) ground (minced) veal
1 tablespoon chopped fresh flat-leaf (Italian) parsley

❧ In a large skillet over low heat, warm 2 tablespoons of the olive oil. Add the onion and fry gently until translucent, about 5 minutes. Add the tomatoes, season to taste with salt and pepper and cook until the sauce has just begun to thicken but is still runny, about 30 minutes.
❧ Trim both ends off the zucchini. Using an apple corer, scoop out the centers, leaving a shell about ¼ in (6 mm) thick. Finely chop the zucchini centers and place in a bowl. Add the meat and mix well. Season to taste with salt and pepper.
❧ In a skillet over moderate heat, warm the remaining 2 tablespoons olive oil. Add the meat-zucchini mixture and cook, stirring, for about 5 minutes. Remove from the heat.
❧ Stuff the hollowed zucchini with the meat mixture. Arrange the stuffed zucchini in the skillet with the tomato sauce. Cook until the sauce is thick and the zucchini is tender, about 20 minutes.
❧ Arrange the zucchini and sauce on a warm platter. Sprinkle with the parsley and serve.

SERVES 6

Siena

SFORMATINI DI ZUCCHINE

Zucchini Timbales

At the Mugolone Ristorante in Siena, the chef sometimes makes these timbales with peas or chopped green beans. This recipe is also excellent cooked in a ring mold.

4 tablespoons (2 fl oz/60 ml) extra virgin olive oil
1¼ lb (600 g) zucchini (courgettes), trimmed and thinly sliced
¼ cup (1 oz/30 g) all-purpose (plain) flour
1¼ cups (10 fl oz/300 ml) milk, at room temperature
½ cup (2 oz/60 g) freshly grated Parmesan cheese
3 eggs
salt and freshly ground black pepper
2 tablespoons unsalted butter
¾ cup (3 oz/90 g) fine dry bread crumbs

❧ Preheat an oven to 350°F (180°C).

❧ In a skillet over moderate heat, warm 2 tablespoons of the olive oil. Add the zucchini and fry gently, stirring frequently, until the zucchini are just golden, about 10 minutes. Remove from the heat and let cool.

❧ In a medium saucepan over moderate heat, warm the remaining 2 tablespoons olive oil. Add the flour and cook, stirring continuously, until the flour has absorbed all of the oil, about 2 minutes. Continuing to stir, gradually add the milk and cook until a smooth, thick sauce forms, about 5 minutes. Remove from the heat and let cool to room temperature.

❧ Add the zucchini and Parmesan to the sauce. Then add the eggs, one at a time, mixing well after each addition. Season to taste with salt and pepper.

❧ Butter 6 ramekins each about 4 in (10 cm) in diameter and then coat them evenly with the bread crumbs. Divide the egg mixture evenly among the prepared ramekins.

❧ Place the ramekins in a baking dish and pour water into the dish to a depth of 1 in (2.5 cm). Bake in the center of the oven until the custard sets and the tops are golden, about 30 minutes.

❧ Remove the ramekins from the oven. Run a thin, sharp knife blade around the edge of each ramekin and then invert the timbales onto individual serving plates. Serve immediately.

SERVES 6

Siena

CANESTRINI DI PATATE

Deep-Fried Potato Baskets

Although usually served on their own, these potato baskets are a perfect accompaniment to roast pork or chicken at a dinner party.

1 oz (30 g) dried *porcini* mushrooms
1 tablespoon extra virgin olive oil
4 oz (120 g) chicken livers
salt and freshly ground black pepper
4 oz (120 g) cooked ham
2½ lb (1.2 kg) boiling potatoes
2 eggs, separated
2 tablespoons all-purpose (plain) flour
1 cup (4 oz/120 g) fine dry bread crumbs
5 cups (40 fl oz/1.2 l) extra virgin olive oil for frying

❧ In a small bowl, soak the mushrooms in warm water to cover for 30 minutes. Drain and squeeze out any excess moisture.

❧ In a medium skillet over moderate heat, warm the olive oil. Add the mushrooms and chicken livers and sauté, stirring occasionally, for 5 minutes. Season to taste with salt and pepper. Remove from the heat and transfer the mushrooms and livers to a cutting surface.

❧ Add the ham to the mushrooms and livers and chop the ingredients together. Return the mixture to the skillet and keep warm without cooking.

❧ Meanwhile, in a saucepan, boil the potatoes in salted water to cover until tender, about 30 minutes. Drain the potatoes

Deep-Fried Potato Baskets (left) and ingredients for Zucchini Timbales (right)

and peel them. Place in a bowl and mash while still hot. Set aside to cool completely.

❧ When the potatoes are at room temperature, add the egg yolks and mix well. Sprinkle your hands with the flour and roll the potato mixture into 2-in (5-cm) balls. You should have 18 balls in all. Flatten the balls slightly and, with a fingertip, form a hollow in the middle. In a small bowl, beat the egg whites until slightly thick but not stiff. Put the bread crumbs in a small, shallow bowl. Coat the balls with the egg whites and then roll them in the bread crumbs to coat evenly. Set aside on a plate.

❧ In a deep skillet, heat the olive oil to 350°F (180°C). Slip the potato baskets, a few at a time, into the hot oil and fry until just golden, about 5 minutes. With a slotted spoon, remove to absorbent paper towels to drain. Continue frying all the baskets in the same manner.

❧ Fill the hollows of the hot potato baskets with the ham-liver mixture. Serve immediately.

SERVES 6

Top to bottom: Potato Croquettes, Stuffed Celery and Frittata with Pancetta

Lucca

CROCCHETTE DI PATATE

Potato Croquettes

Deep-fried vegetables, a Tuscan specialty, are particularly good in Lucchesia, where excellent extra virgin olive oil is produced. Frying oil should be used only once, because when the oil is reheated it releases toxins.

2¼ lb (1.2 kg) boiling potatoes
½ cup (2 oz/60 g) freshly grated Parmesan cheese
3 eggs, separated
pinch of freshly grated nutmeg
2 tablespoons chopped fresh flat-leaf (Italian) parsley
salt and fresh ground black pepper
1 cup (4 oz/120 g) all-purpose (plain) flour
1¾ cups (7 oz/210 g) fine dry bread crumbs
4 cups (32 fl oz/1 l) extra virgin olive oil for frying

❧ In a saucepan, boil the potatoes in their skins in salted water to cover until tender, about 30 minutes. Drain the potatoes and peel them. Place in a bowl and mash while still hot. Let cool completely.

❧ When the potatoes are at room temperature, add the Parmesan, egg yolks, nutmeg and parsley. Season to taste with salt and pepper and mix thoroughly.

❧ Sprinkle your hands with a little of the flour and form the potato mixture into ovals about 2 in (5 cm) long. You should have about 30 ovals in all.

❧ Put the remaining flour in a small, shallow bowl. Put the bread crumbs in a separate bowl. In another small bowl, lightly beat the egg whites until blended. Roll the ovals in the flour, dip them in the egg white and then roll them in the bread crumbs.

❧ In a deep skillet, heat the olive oil to 350°F (180°C). Slip the ovals, a few at a time, into the hot oil and fry until golden, about 5 minutes. With a slotted spoon, remove to absorbent paper towels to drain. Continue frying the remaining ovals in the same manner.

❧ Serve piping hot.

SERVES 6

Lucca

SEDANI RIPIENI

Stuffed Celery

Every Tuscan cook seems to have his or her own version of this old favorite. Served with meat sauce, this is a good supper dish. The celery is sometimes fried before going into the sauce. Green celery can be used in place of the white, but it is slightly bitter.

¼ cup (2 fl oz/60 ml) extra virgin olive oil
1 small yellow onion, chopped
1 garlic clove, chopped

1¼ lb (600 g) plum (egg) tomatoes, peeled and chopped
salt and freshly ground black pepper
1 oz (30 g) dried *porcini* mushrooms
4 oz (120 g) crustless coarse country bread
1 cup (8 fl oz/240 ml) milk
2 large heads white celery
4 oz (120 g) sweet Italian sausages
½ cup (2 oz/60 g) freshly grated Parmesan cheese
1 egg

In a medium saucepan, warm the olive oil over low heat. Add the onion and garlic and fry gently for 2 minutes. Add the tomatoes and season to taste with salt and pepper. Cook over low heat until the liquid evaporates, about 50 minutes.

Meanwhile, in a small bowl, soak the mushrooms in warm water to cover for 30 minutes. In a separate bowl, soak the bread in the milk for about 10 minutes.

Break off the celery stalks. With a small knife, remove the strings and cut off and discard the leaves.

In a large saucepan, blanch the celery in boiling salted water to cover for 1 minute. Drain the celery and cut into pieces about 2 in (5 cm) long. Press the hollow side of each piece lightly to open it up.

Drain the mushrooms and squeeze out any excess liquid. Chop them finely and place in a mixing bowl. Drain the bread and squeeze out the milk.

Add the bread to the bowl. Skin the sausages and crumble the meat into the bowl as well.

Add the Parmesan and egg to the bowl and mix well. Fill half of the pieces of celery with this mixture. Cover with the remaining halves, hollow side down, and press firmly together.

Add the stuffed celery to the tomato sauce. Cook over low heat until the filling is cooked and the celery is tender and has absorbed the flavor of the sauce, about 10 minutes. Serve immediately.

SERVES 6

Firenze

Cardi Trippati

Fried Cardoon in Tomato Sauce

Tuscans describe these cardoons as being trippati, *or "triped," because they are served in the same sauce used for tripe in Florence.*

juice of 1 lemon
1 large cardoon, about 3 lb (1.3 kg)
2 eggs
salt
1 tablespoon extra virgin olive oil, plus 5 cups (40 fl oz/1.2 l) for frying
2 oz (60 g) *pancetta*
1 tablespoon chopped yellow onion
2 garlic cloves, chopped
1¼ lb (600 g) plum (egg) tomatoes, peeled and chopped
⅔ cup (3 oz/90 g) all-purpose (plain) flour
¾ cup (3 oz/90 g) freshly grated Parmesan cheese

Fill a large bowl with water and add the lemon juice. Remove and discard the base from the cardoon and discard any tough stalks. Trim and discard the leaves and spurs from the tender stalks and then scrape the stalks with a small knife to remove all strings and fibers. Cut each stalk crosswise into pieces 2 in (5 cm) long and immediately drop them into the water so that they do not discolor. Drain and pat dry with absorbent paper towels.

In a deep bowl, whisk the eggs with a little salt. Add the cardoon to the bowl and set aside.

In a medium saucepan over moderate heat, warm the 1 tablespoon olive oil and the *pancetta*. Add the onion and garlic and fry gently until the onion is translucent, about 5 minutes. Add the tomatoes and simmer until the liquid evaporates and the sauce thickens, about 50 minutes.

Meanwhile, in a deep, heavy skillet, heat the olive oil for frying to 350°F (180°C). Put the flour in a small shallow bowl. Remove the cardoon pieces from the egg and roll them in the flour. Slip the pieces a few at a time into the hot oil and fry until golden, about 5 minutes. Remove with a slotted spoon to absorbent paper towels to drain. Continue cooking the remaining cardoon pieces in the same manner.

When all of the cardoon pieces have been fried, transfer them to the tomato sauce. Cook gently over low heat to allow the cardoon pieces to absorb the flavor of the sauce, about 10 minutes.

Arrange the cardoon pieces and sauce on a warm serving dish, sprinkle with the Parmesan and serve.

SERVES 6

Lucca

Frittata con gli Zoccoli

Frittata with Pancetta

In Tuscany bits of crisp pancetta *are called* zoccoli, *or "clogs." Here* pancetta *is saltier and sharper than that of other regions, and it is often eaten raw on bread.*

8 eggs
salt and freshly ground black pepper
2 tablespoons extra virgin olive oil
4 oz (120 g) thick *pancetta* slices, diced

In a medium bowl, whisk the eggs until well blended. Season to taste with salt and pepper.

In a skillet over moderate heat, warm the olive oil. Add the *pancetta* and fry until crisp and golden, about 5 minutes. With a slotted spoon, remove to absorbent paper towels to drain and cool. Reserve the drippings in the skillet.

Stir the cooled *pancetta* bits into the beaten egg.

Pour 1 tablespoon of the *pancetta* drippings into an 8-in (20-cm) nonstick skillet and warm over moderate heat. Pour in the egg mixture and cook, occasionally moving the egg with a wooden spoon, until the egg sets and only the surface is runny, about 5 minutes. Turn the frittata out onto a plate, browned side up. Slide the frittata back into the skillet and cook the other side for 1 minute. Turn the frittata out onto a serving plate. Serve hot.

SERVES 6

Fried Cardoon in Tomato Sauce

Livorno

Uova Strascicate al Pomodoro e Cipolle

Scrambled Eggs with Onion and Tomato

A very simple family dish that can be made with fresh tomatoes or the excellent canned tomatoes from Donoratico, a coastal village famous for the quality of its plum tomatoes. The flavor of the olive oil gives scrambled eggs a real lift.

3 tablespoons extra virgin olive oil
2 large yellow onions, chopped
1¼ lb (600 g) plum (egg) tomatoes, peeled and chopped
6 eggs
salt and freshly ground black pepper

❧ In a nonstick skillet over moderate heat, warm the olive oil. Add the onion and fry gently until it starts to turn golden, about 6 minutes. Add the tomatoes and cook over low heat until the liquid evaporates, about 40 minutes.

❧ Meanwhile, in a bowl, whisk the eggs until well blended. Season with a little salt and pepper. Add the eggs to the tomato and cook over moderate heat, stirring constantly and scraping the bottom of the skillet with a wooden fork. Remove from the heat as soon as the eggs begin to set but are still very moist, about 3 minutes.

❧ Turn the eggs out onto a serving plate. Serve immediately.

SERVES 6

Scrambled Eggs with Onion and Tomato

Game Terrine

Grosseto

PASTICCIO DI CACCIA

Game Terrine

This terrine is prepared with whatever the hunter has bagged, from pheasant to hare. Guinea fowl or quail, which have a lot of flavor and are now raised commercially, may be substituted for the game.

1 pheasant, about 3 lb (1.3 kg), including the liver
¼ cup (2 fl oz/60 ml) extra virgin olive oil
6 oz (180 g) mild Italian sausages, skinned and crumbled
1 yellow onion, chopped
2 garlic cloves, chopped
3 fresh bay leaves
1 tablespoon juniper berries
½ cup (4 fl oz/120 ml) Vin Santo or white dessert wine
salt and freshly ground black pepper
2 egg yolks
6 tablespoons (3 oz/90 g) unsalted butter, at room temperature, cut into small pieces, plus extra for buttering pan

Cut the pheasant into large pieces.

In a heavy pot over moderate heat, warm the olive oil. Add the pheasant, liver, sausage, onion, garlic, bay leaves and juniper berries and cook over moderate heat, stirring occasionally, until the pheasant is golden, about 10 minutes.

Add the wine and stir well, scraping the pot bottom to dislodge any browned bits. Season to taste with salt and pepper. Cover and cook over low heat for about 1 hour. Add a little water if necessary to keep the contents moist.

Remove the pot from the heat and let cool. Bone the pheasant and put the meat in a food processor fitted with a metal blade. Remove and discard the bay leaves. Add the remaining contents of the pot to the food processor. Add the egg yolks and butter and process just long enough to form a well-blended mixture that is not too loose.

Line a 3-by-8-in (8-by-20-cm) bread pan with parchment (greaseproof) paper, then butter the paper well. Pour the pheasant mixture into the pan and smooth the top. Cover and refrigerate for about 2 hours before serving.

Invert onto a serving dish, lift off the pan and peel off the paper. Serve at room temperature.

SERVES 6

Anchovies in Vinegar

Livorno

Alici in Carpione

Anchovies in Vinegar

Fresh anchovies are always available in the fish markets near Livorno. Every morning fishing boats set out and return in the evening with their catch.

1¼ lb (600 g) fresh anchovies
1 cup (4 oz/120 g) all-purpose (plain) flour
5 cups (40 fl oz/1.2 l) extra virgin olive oil for frying
salt
2 large yellow onions, sliced
⅞ cup (7 fl oz/210 ml) white wine vinegar
pinch of ground dried chili

❧ Remove and discard the heads from the anchovies. Slit the bodies lengthwise along the belly and remove and discard the bones. Rinse the anchovies and pat dry on absorbent paper towels. Dredge the anchovies in the flour.

❧ Reserve 3 tablespoons of the olive oil and pour the remainder into a deep, heavy skillet. Heat the oil in the skillet to 350°F (180°C). A few at a time, add the anchovies and fry until they begin to turn golden, about 3 minutes. With a slotted spoon, remove to absorbent paper towels to drain. Season with salt. Continue frying the remaining anchovies in the same manner.

❧ In a large skillet over low heat, warm the 3 tablespoons olive oil. Add the onions, season to taste with salt and fry gently until translucent, about 5 minutes. Add the vinegar and continue cooking until it evaporates, about 5 minutes. Remove from the heat.

Arrange the anchovies on a serving plate. Sprinkle them with the chili and then cover them with the onion.

Let stand at room temperature for about 2 hours before serving.

SERVES 6

Arezzo

FOGLIE DI CAVOLO RIPIENE DI SALSICCIA

Stuffed Cabbage Leaves

In Arezzo, cooks often use wild boar sausages, which are more strongly flavored than pork sausages. This recipe is very successful when leftover roast or stewed meat is used for the stuffing.

4 oz (120 g) crustless coarse country bread
1 cup (8 fl oz/240 ml) milk
10 oz (300 g) plum (egg) tomatoes, peeled
18 large Savoy cabbage leaves
10 oz (300 g) sweet Italian sausages, skinned and crumbled
½ cup (2 oz/60 g) freshly grated Parmesan cheese
1 egg
3 tablespoons extra virgin olive oil
salt

In a bowl, soak the bread in the milk for 10 minutes. Drain the bread and squeeze out any excess moisture; set aside.

Put the tomatoes through a food mill; set aside.

Bring a large saucepan filled with salted water to a boil. Add the cabbage leaves, a few at a time, and blanch for 30 seconds. Remove the leaves with a slotted spoon, drain well and place them side by side on a board. Continue blanching the remaining leaves in the same manner.

In a mixing bowl, combine the sausage, Parmesan, egg and bread. Blend well.

Divide the sausage mixture evenly among the cabbage leaves, placing a mound of it about one third of the way in from the stalk end of the leaf. First fold in the sides of each leaf, then roll them up to enclose the mixture completely.

Secure the rolls loosely with kitchen string and place them side by side in a heavy pot. Sprinkle the olive oil over the rolls and cook over moderate heat for 5 minutes, carefully turning the rolls occasionally.

Pour the sieved tomatoes over the rolls and cook for 15 minutes. Season to taste with salt.

Arrange the rolls with the tomato sauce on a warm platter and serve hot.

SERVES 6

Livorno

FRITTELLE DI PESCE

Fish Rissoles

These rissoles may be made with any boiled or baked fish. If you have a mix of leftovers, the rissoles will be even more interesting. The fish should be chopped very finely by hand; a food processor makes it too smooth.

1 large boiling potato
1 lb (450 g) any variety of white fish, cooked and boned
2 tablespoons chopped fresh flat-leaf (Italian) parsley
1 garlic clove, chopped
2 egg yolks, plus 2 whole eggs
salt
1 cup (4 oz/120 g) all-purpose (plain) flour
5 cups (40 fl oz/1.2 l) extra virgin olive oil for frying
lemon wedges

In a small saucepan, boil the potato in its skin in salted water to cover until tender, about 30 minutes. Drain and peel. Place in a mixing bowl and mash while still hot. Set aside to cool completely.

Chop the fish finely and add to the bowl with the potato. Add the parsley, garlic and egg yolks. Season to taste with salt and mix well.

In a small bowl, beat the whole eggs until well blended. Pour the flour into a separate small bowl. Roll the fish mixture into balls about the size of an egg. Flatten the balls slightly. Dredge the balls in the flour and then dip them in the beaten egg.

In a deep skillet, heat the oil to 350°F (180°C). A few at a time, slip the rissoles into the hot oil and fry until golden, about 5 minutes. With a slotted spoon, remove to absorbent paper towels to drain. Continue frying the remaining rissoles in the same manner.

Arrange on a warm platter. Serve hot with lemon wedges.

SERVES 6

Stuffed Cabbage Leaves (top) and Fish Rissoles (bottom)

AREZZO

Antichita

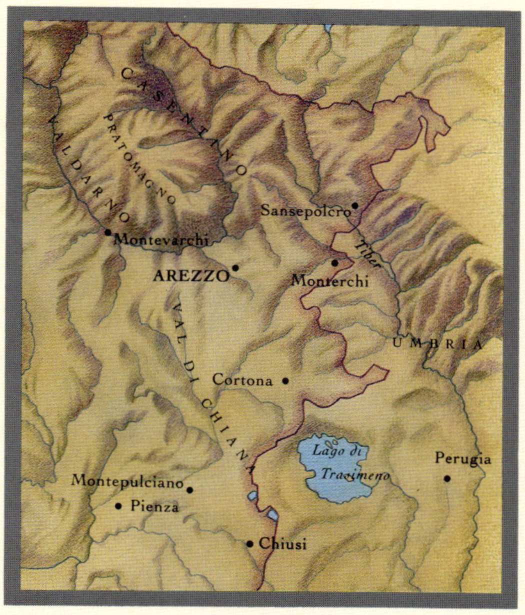

AREZZO

Va, mia canzone, ad Arezzo in Toscana," Guittone d'Arezzo sang in the thirteenth century. "Go, my song, to Arezzo in Tuscany." One of the greatest lyric poets of his time, he was the first sonneteer and he described his birthplace as "sweet Aretine land . . . of every delight."

Arezzo, known as Aretium to the Etruscans when it was their economic capital, is still a pleasant land. Its charms, however, are revealed little by little. This is upland Tuscany, the severest and the coldest area of the region. Consequently, its cuisine is often said to be less refined and inventive than in the rest of Tuscany, but that is a mistake! Aretine cooking, with its ancient flavors and mountain simplicity, is well worth discovering.

Others say that Arezzo is more like a northern city than a Tuscan one, that it is hard and never lets itself go. But this is quite fallacious too. Arezzo could be described as reserved, but when it does relax it produces the very best that Tuscany has to offer.

Over the centuries many great men of letters have come from here: Maecenas, the friend and patron of Horace and Virgil; Petrarch, who rivals Dante as the greatest Italian poet; Guido d'Arezzo, the father of the modern system of musical notation; Titian's friend, Pietro Aretino, whose satirical pen was highly feared during the Renaissance; and Giorgio Vasari, whose *Lives* has for centuries been indispensable to the study of the history of Italian art. Some of Italy's foremost painters were also

Left: The medieval hill town of Cortona is known for its steep, narrow streets. Built atop ancient Etruscan foundations, the town is one of Italy's oldest. Previous pages: An evening vignette in the village of Poppi, stronghold of the powerful Guidi family, who ruled this region until defeated by Florence in 1440.

Piazza San Francesco lies at the heart of Arezzo, a bustling city in the midst of a rich agricultural region defined by the Val di Chiana and Valdarno.

born here: Piero della Francesca, Luca Signorelli, Masaccio, Paolo Uccello and, above all, Michelangelo, who was born in Michelangelo Caprese, just a few miles from Arezzo. Michelangelo told Vasari that if there was anything good in his talent, it was most certainly due to the fine air in Arezzo.

It is also a land of mysticism. Many great Italian monasteries stand majestic on the Casentino mountains: the Abbey of Vallombrosa, the Hermitage of Camaldoli, and La Verna, where St. Francis received the stigmata in the autumn of 1224.

Arezzo and its surroundings can arouse deep emotions. This may even happen when one takes up a knife and fork in an extraordinary restaurant like Il Vicolo del Convento in Castelfranco di Sopra. The tastes and aromas can somehow remind one that this land belonged to Etruscans and Romans, to poets and writers, to painters and great noble families.

One such family were the Tarlati, whose name was given to a very famous Aretine recipe, *zuppa del Vescovo Tarlati,* or Bishop Tarlati's soup. It is said that the bishop, who was also Signore d'Arezzo in 1312, took this chicken-and-egg soup from Arezzo to Avignon when he had an audience with Pope John XXII, and that it was appropriated by the French, who named it *soupe à la reine.* But there is the usual dispute about the provenance of this recipe, some claiming that in fact the bishop brought it back with him from France.

Chicken soup is very popular in this area because the indigenous black hens from the Valdarno make an excellent stock. Furthermore, local legend maintains that chicken stock gives strength and increases virility, which is probably why a soup called *ginestrata,* "yellow broom," is still to be found. Actually there is no broom in the soup, but the color is the same as the flower. A glance at the ingredients lends support to the popular belief. It is made with strong chicken stock, an egg per person, Vin Santo, cinnamon, saffron, nutmeg, lemon and a little sugar, all beaten together. It is perhaps not surprising that this soup was traditionally served to couples when they returned from their honeymoon.

In addition to such benefits, good chicken stock in Arezzo is also the perfect foil for the delicious local *cappelletti.* These stuffed pasta "hats" originated in Emilia, but the ones made in Arezzo provide serious competition.

Brodo del parto, "childbirth soup," probably originated in these parts, too. The Madonna del Parto, one of Piero della Francesca's most famous frescoes, is on the wall of a little chapel in the cemetery at Monterchi. Pregnant women visit this chapel, light a candle before the magnificent Madonna and pray for an easy delivery. *Brodo del parto* is a meat stock seasoned with herbs to which a little strong wine is added as a tonic.

There are many other first courses in Arezzo beyond soups, the most famous being *gnocchi del Casentino.* The Guidi family, who were the lords of Poppi, are said to have eaten large quantities of them in their castle above the Arno. Gnocchi are little dumplings that are one of the earliest forms of pasta. When Boccaccio described "maccheroni rolled down a mountain of grated cheese" in the *Decameron,* he was probably referring to gnocchi, which in the Casentino are made of ricotta and spinach.

Another very early recipe that is said to be Etruscan is *bringoli,* thick spaghetti from Anghiari, a place not far from Arezzo noted for a great battle fought there between the armies of Florence and the Duke of Milan in 1440. Drawings made by Leonardo da Vinci for a fresco in Florence's Palazzo Vecchio depicting this famous battle can still be seen here. *Acquacotta,* a soup made all over Tuscany, is also considered Etruscan. It is particularly well liked in the Casentino, where, at one time, it was a favorite with the many coopers living there.

In this district, gravy from Aretine ducks is used to dress *pappardelle,* wide egg pasta. Ducks had a significant role in Etruscan culture, and frescoes portraying them were found in tombs in Tarquinia. They served as a symbol of marital fidelity, and a special duck was raised to celebrate a wedding.

Pork liver is treated in a unique way in Arezzo. In the rest of Tuscany it is seasoned with bay leaves and sage, but here only fennel seed is used. Traditionally, cooked pork liver is preserved in lard and stored in either glass jars or earthenware pots.

Many other Aretine recipes include fennel seed as well. After being crushed in a mortar with a pestle, it is sprinkled abundantly over duck and chicken, a custom dating from the thirteenth century. Fennel was also used for medicinal purposes. The leaves cooked with chickpeas were considered an efficient diuretic and effective in the treatment of snake and scorpion bites.

The most celebrated main course in Arezzo is undoubtedly *scottiglia,* which is very much like the Sienese *buglione.* Both dishes are composed of mixed meats, but while *buglione* has tomato in it and the meat is cooked to a mush, the various meats in *scottiglia* are still distinguishable. A good *scottiglia* should include pieces of beef, pork, chicken, guineafowl, duck, rabbit and lamb.

As usual, there are two tales describing the origin of this very ancient stew. Some say that it goes back to the Middle Ages, when the landowners left the remains of their banquets—chicken wings and necks, pork trotters and lamb offal—for the peasants. Others maintain that it comes from the age-old Tuscan custom of gathering to chat in front of the farmhouse fire during the long winter evenings. Everyone apparently arrived bearing his own piece of meat.

A farmhouse enjoys views of the fertile Casentino valley. These fields of the upper Arno were first cultivated by the Etruscans, who exported crops and wine to Greece.

The piazzas of Arezzo come alive during the evening passegiata. *Among the famous Aretines who once walked these streets are the poet Petrarch and the artist-historian Giorgio Vasari.*

Pietro Aretino, the Renaissance writer, praised this Tuscan country custom: "Sitting at table requires bird song, the murmur of running water, a breath of breeze and the sweet smell of fresh grass; but four dry logs are all you need to sit and chat for four or five hours with chestnuts on the fire and a bottle of wine between your knees. We love winter, the springtime for lively minds." A man who certainly did not mince his words, Aretino was also convinced that the best oil and olives came from his part of the world. In writing to Madonna Bartolina he said, "Spanish olives are so huge they are conceited . . . the olives from Puglia are so small they should be called bread crumbs. So it is your side [Tuscany] that may boast the best." Perhaps because Arezzo has fewer olives than other parts of Tuscany, the appreciation of olive oil has always been a cult. But there have been olive trees in the area for centuries. In Roman times, Minerva, the goddess of wisdom, was worshipped in Arezzo, and olive oil has always been associated with her rites.

The "sweet Aretine land" also offers several local desserts. *Berlingozzo* is a fifteenth-century Easter cake; *baldino* is a chestnut cake; and *gatò aretino* is served at country weddings. Then there is *panina gialla,* also known as *pan co' l'uve*—bread dough to which olive oil, raisins, saffron, cinnamon, cloves and coriander are added with pleasing results.

I Secondi

Ewes and their lambs graze in the Maremma.

I Secondi

Main dishes—*i secondi*—were the glory of Tuscan cuisine during the Renaissance. Although many of today's main courses were served at the Florentine court, at that time they were divided into three distinct groups. *Il primo servizio di cucina,* the first service from the kitchen, included roast turkey, chicken and duck, often stuffed and flavored with truffles. *Il secondo servizio di cucina,* the second service, offered boiled meats: choice cuts of beef, capon stuffed with chestnuts, and lamb flavored with spices, served with a variety of sauces. *Il terzo servizio di cucina,* the third service, consisted of braised meats, meat loaves, soup, and fish and shellfish.

It is, above all, in the main courses that Florentine cooking lost its supremacy over French cuisine. Many famous French dishes originated in Tuscany, the outstanding example being the renowned duck *à l'orange,* the very same Tuscan *papero alla melarancia* described by an anonymous author in a fourteenth-century book on Tuscan cooking.

During the Renaissance, however, the Italians dedicated themselves far more to painting and sculpture and left the art of cooking to the French. It is hard to say who was correct, but one thing is certain: Michelangelo, Leonardo da Vinci and Raphael are well-known all over the world, while it is a little more difficult to remember the names of famous French chefs of the same period. But enough of national pride.

The celebrated *bistecca alla fiorentina* should be mentioned at once, although it is so-called only outside Tuscany. Here it is simply called *costata.* Apparently nothing could be more simple than grilling a steak, but a great deal depends on the quality of the meat and the cook's skill. The word *bistecca,* a corruption of the English

Fresh fish is available in the large towns of Tuscany every day. Delivery trucks bring fish to the small hill towns on Thursdays and Fridays.

Previous pages: Lamb with Articholes (left, page 424) and Fried Pork Chops with Tarragon (right, page 429).

The end of summer signals the start of porcini *season, when the most enthusiastic* porcini *lovers take to the woods and begin their search. The coveted mushroom shows up in many* secondi *recipes.*

"beef steak," came into being with the advent of the first British tourists, who were actually noblemen doing the Grand Tour. For centuries before that, these steaks were called *carbonata,* because they were grilled on *carbone,* or wood charcoal. A real *fiorentina* should be hung for several days and should never be thicker or thinner than 1⅛ inches (3 centimeters).

Another typically Tuscan meat dish is *arista di maiale,* or loin of pork. There has been considerable debate over why this roast is called *arista.* No two experts seem to agree. What is certain is that the name comes from the Greek word *aristos,* meaning "the best," and the dish in its simplicity is undoubtedly exquisite.

On Sundays, roast or fried chicken or rabbit is nearly always found on the Tuscan table. Until the 1950s, the peasants lived off the land as they had for centuries, so it is understandable that farmyard animals still play an important role in the Tuscan kitchen.

There are also excellent Tuscan braised meats and stews. Many visitors to Florence have been converted to tripe after tasting it there. Some of these tripe dishes, like *cibreo fiorentino* and *cioncia* from Pescia, originated in the Middle Ages. It is well worth seeking out such specialties in the few restaurants where they are now served after years of neglect. *Cibreo,* for example, was reintroduced by Annie Feolde of the famous Enoteca Pinchiorri in Florence.

As Tuscany is a land of enthusiastic hunters, many main courses are made with venison and game birds. Wild boar and hare, pheasant and woodcock, quail and mallard are excellent reasons for visiting the numerous restaurants and trattorias where they are served during the hunting season.

Tuscany is also blessed with a long coastline. To tell the truth, however, fish is not one of the highlights of the Tuscan kitchen, except for the famous Livornese fish soup called *cacciucco,* and *cee,* baby eels from Pisa. Although there are not many Tuscan recipes for fresh fish, curiously enough there are several original dishes made with salt cod, dried cod and herring. Cooking fish *in zimino,* or with vegetables—usually spinach or Swiss chard—is another regional tradition.

Grosseto

PICCIONI IN TEGAME

Pot-Roasted Pigeons

Starting the pigeons in cold oil with raw vegetables adds to their flavor. They may also be prepared this way but first stuffed with bread, egg, Parmesan, and their sautéed and chopped giblets.

6 oz (180 g) *pancetta,* chopped
2 garlic cloves, chopped
1 small yellow onion, chopped
1 carrot, peeled and chopped
1 celery stalk, trimmed and chopped
1 tablespoon chopped fresh flat-leaf (Italian) parsley
1 tablespoon chopped fresh rosemary
3 tablespoons extra virgin olive oil
3 pigeons (squab), about 1 lb (450 g) each

Left to right: Pot-Roasted Pigeons, Braised Chicken with Mushrooms, and Fried Chicken

salt and freshly ground black pepper
1½ cups (12 fl oz/360 ml) dry red wine

❧ In a shallow pan, combine the *pancetta,* garlic, onion, carrot, celery, parsley and rosemary. Drizzle the olive oil over the vegetable mixture and place the pigeons on top. Season to taste with salt and pepper.
❧ Place the pan over moderate heat and cook, stirring the vegetables and turning the pigeons once, until the pigeons start to turn golden, about 10 minutes. Add half of the wine, lower the heat, cover and cook for 1½ hours, gradually adding the rest of the wine as the pan becomes dry.
❧ Remove the pigeons from the pan and cut each pigeon in half. Spoon the cooking juices over the pigeons and serve immediately.

SERVES 6

Livorno

Pollo Fritto

Fried Chicken

The Livornese are fond of fried food, which they are masters at cooking. It is always crisp and golden and free of oil. Fried chicken is usually served with a salad only.

1 chicken, about 4 lb (1.8 kg), cut into serving pieces
⅔ cup (3 oz/90 g) all-purpose (plain) flour
2 eggs
salt and freshly ground black pepper
5 cups (40 fl oz/1.2 l) extra virgin olive oil for frying

❧ Dredge the chicken pieces in the flour, shaking off any excess. In a bowl, whisk the eggs with a little pepper.
❧ In a deep, heavy skillet, heat the olive oil to 350°F (180°C). A few pieces at a time, dip the floured chicken pieces into the egg and then slip them into the hot oil without crowding the pan. Fry until crisp and golden on all sides, about 7 minutes. With a slotted utensil, remove to absorbent paper towels to drain. Sprinkle with salt and pepper. Continue frying the remaining chicken in the same manner.
❧ Arrange the chicken on a platter and serve very hot.

SERVES 6

Siena

Pollo ai Funghi

Braised Chicken with Mushrooms

Monte Amiata, near Siena, is famous for its autumn mushrooms. If porcini *mushrooms are not available, button mushrooms or* shiitake *may be used instead.*

6 tablespoons (3 fl oz/90 ml) extra virgin olive oil
3 garlic cloves, chopped
1 chicken, about 4 lb (1.8 kg), cut into serving pieces
1 cup (8 fl oz/240 ml) dry white wine
salt and freshly ground black pepper
1¼ lb (600 g) fresh mushrooms
1 tablespoon fresh calamint or thyme leaves

❧ In a heavy pot over low heat, warm 3 tablespoons of the olive oil. Add the garlic and fry gently until translucent, about 3 minutes. Add the chicken pieces and fry, turning occasionally, until golden, about 10 minutes. Pour in the wine and season to taste with salt and pepper. Cover and cook over very low heat until tender, about 1½ hours, adding a couple of tablespoons of water from time to time to keep the contents very moist.
❧ Clean the mushrooms by rubbing them with a dampened cloth; do not wash them. Trim the mushroom stems, then slice the mushrooms. In a skillet over moderate heat, warm the remaining 3 tablespoons olive oil. Add the mushrooms and calamint and cook, stirring occasionally, for 3 minutes. Add the mushrooms to the chicken, stir well and cook for 2 minutes.
❧ Arrange the chicken on a platter and serve immediately.

SERVES 6

Lucca

Piccioni sul Crostone

Stuffed Pigeons

Although very tasty wild pigeons are shot during the hunting season, most of the pigeons eaten in Tuscany are raised by farmers. In fact, nearly all the farmhouses have small, square towerlike constructions that serve as dovecotes.

3 oz (90 g) crustless coarse country bread
1 cup (8 fl oz/240 ml) milk
6 oz (180 g) sweet Italian sausages, skinned
1 egg
1 tablespoon chopped fresh flat-leaf (Italian) parsley
2 tablespoons chopped celery stalk
2 tablespoons chopped carrot
2 tablespoons chopped yellow onion
salt and freshly ground black pepper
3 pigeons (squab), about 1 lb (450 g) each
2 oz (60 g) *pancetta,* thinly sliced
6 tablespoons (3 fl oz/90 ml) extra virgin olive oil
1 cup (8 fl oz/240 ml) dry red wine
6 slices coarse country bread

❧ Soak the 3 oz (90 g) bread in the milk for 10 minutes. Squeeze out any excess milk from the bread and place the bread in a mixing bowl.

❧ Preheat an oven to 350°F (180°C). Skin the sausages and crumble them into the bowl with the bread. Add the egg, parsley and 1 tablespoon each of the chopped celery, carrot and onion. Mix well and season to taste with salt and pepper.

❧ Stuff the pigeons with the sausage mixture and truss them securely with kitchen string. Cover the breasts with the *pancetta.*

❧ In a roasting pan over moderate heat, warm 3 tablespoons of the olive oil. Arrange the pigeons in the pan and brown on all sides for about 10 minutes. Place in the oven and roast for 1 hour, turning frequently.

❧ Add the remaining chopped vegetables and the wine to the pan and roast for 30 minutes longer. At the same time, brush the bread slices with the remaining 3 tablespoons olive oil and toast in the oven until golden, about 10 minutes.

❧ Remove the pigeons from the pan and keep warm. Purée the cooking juices and return them to the pan. Reheat gently over low heat. If the sauce is too thin, reduce it over moderate heat.

❧ Cut the pigeons in half. Arrange the toast slices on a platter and place half a pigeon on each slice. Pour the sauce over the pigeons and serve immediately.

SERVES 6

Goose Stuffed with Sausage

Lucca

Ocio Ripieno alla Salsiccia

Goose Stuffed with Sausage

Stuffed goose with chestnuts is traditional Christmas fare in Lucca. As geese are fairly large, this recipe will serve twelve.

1 goose, about 9 lb (4.2 kg)
10 oz (300 g) sweet Italian sausages
1 teaspoon fresh thyme
1 teaspoon juniper berries
3 tablespoons extra virgin olive oil
1 cup (8 fl oz/240 ml) dry red wine
salt and freshly ground black pepper

❧ Preheat an oven to 325°F (160°C).

❧ If the liver and gizzard have come with the goose, remove them from the cavity and reserve them for another use. Skin the sausages and place the meat in a bowl. Add the thyme and juniper berries and mix well. Stuff the goose with this mixture and truss it closed with kitchen string.

❧ In a roasting pan over moderate heat, warm the olive oil. Add the goose and cook, turning the goose so that it browns on all sides, for about 10 minutes.

❧ Place the pan in the oven and roast the goose, basting occasionally, until tender, about 3 hours.

❧ Remove the goose from the pan and keep it warm. Skim most of the fat off the cooking juices. Add the wine to the pan juices and place over moderate heat. Cook, scraping the browned bits from the bottom of the pan, until the sauce reduces a little. Season to taste with salt and pepper.

❧ Scoop the stuffing from the goose cavity and place it on a large platter. Cut the goose into serving pieces and arrange them alongside the stuffing. Serve the sauce in a bowl on the side.

SERVES 12

Stuffed Pigeons

Top to bottom: Chicken in Red Wine, Braised Chicken with Mushrooms, and Deviled Chicken on the Bone

Lucca

Pollo al Vino Rosso

Chicken in Red Wine

Chicken cooked in red wine with the addition of baby onions is a popular Sunday lunch in Lucca.

1 chicken, about 4 lb (1.8 kg)
3 tablespoons extra virgin olive oil
3 oz (90 g) *pancetta*, chopped
1½ cups (12 fl oz/400 ml) dry red wine
1¼ lb (600 g) pearl onions
salt and freshly ground black pepper

❧ Preheat an oven to 400°F (200°C). Truss the chicken with kitchen string.

❧ Pour the olive oil into a roasting pan. Add the *pancetta* and place the chicken in the pan. Roast for 30 minutes, turning a couple of times so that it is golden all over.

❧ Add the wine and lower the temperature to 350°F (180°C). Cook for another 40 minutes, basting occasionally.
❧ Add the onions and season to taste with salt and pepper. Cook until the onions are tender, about 20 minutes.
❧ Transfer the chicken and onions to a serving dish and keep warm. Skim the fat off the cooking juices and then strain the juices into a small saucepan. Reduce the juices over high heat until you have a fairly thick sauce. Pour the sauce over the chicken and serve immediately.

SERVES 6

Livorno

Pollo in Cacciucco

Braised Chicken with Mushrooms

The chicken should be cut into serving pieces and cooked very slowly for this classic Livornese dish. The name comes from the similarity in preparation to the fish dish called cacciucco.

6 slices dried *porcini* mushrooms
3 tablespoons extra virgin olive oil
2 garlic cloves, chopped
1 yellow onion, chopped
1 carrot, peeled and chopped
1 celery stalk, trimmed and chopped
2 tablespoons chopped fresh flat-leaf (Italian) parsley
1 chicken, about 4 lb (1.8 kg), cut into serving pieces
2 lb (900 g) plum (egg) tomatoes, peeled and chopped
salt and freshly ground black pepper

❧ In a bowl, soak the mushrooms in warm water to cover for 30 minutes. Drain the mushrooms and set aside.
❧ In a heavy pot over low heat, warm the olive oil. Add the garlic, onion, carrot, celery and parsley and fry gently until the onion is translucent, about 5 minutes. Add the chicken and cook over moderate heat, turning the pieces, until golden on all sides, about 10 minutes.
❧ Add the mushrooms and tomatoes and season to taste with salt and pepper. Lower the heat, cover and cook for 1½ hours, adding a little water if the sauce becomes too thick.
❧ Arrange the chicken and sauce on a platter and serve.

SERVES 6

Firenze

Pollo alla Diavola

Deviled Chicken on the Bone

This dish, one of the most famous Florentine specialties, is served in nearly all the city's restaurants. It is particularly good at a very old trattoria called Oreste, in Pian dei Giullari, one of the loveliest parts of Florence. Traditionally it is grilled over an open fire, but it can be cooked under an ordinary broiler.

2 chickens, about 2 lb (900 g) each
⅓ cup (3 fl oz/90 ml) extra virgin olive oil
salt and freshly ground black pepper
1 lemon

❧ Cut the chickens along the length of the breastbone and open them up. With a meat mallet, gently flatten each chicken, being careful not to shatter the bones. In a shallow plate, stir together the olive oil and salt and pepper to taste. Brush the chicken thoroughly with this mixture and marinate for about 2 hours. Remove the chicken from the dish, reserving the olive oil.
❧ Prepare a fire in a charcoal grill or preheat a broiler (grill).
❧ Place the chickens on the grill rack over a hot fire or slip it under the broiler. Cook for about 10 minutes on each side, frequently brushing them with the reserved oil and turning them when necessary to prevent burning. The chickens should be crisp and golden when they are done.
❧ Cut the chickens into serving pieces and arrange them on a platter. Squeeze the lemon over the top and serve.

SERVES 6

Firenze

Fegatini di Pollo alla Salvia

Sautéed Chicken Livers with Sage

Sage is not only used in the preparation of several first courses, but also often serves as a seasoning for white meat as well as chicken and pork liver. The fragrant herb is at its best during the summer but, because of Florence's mild climate, it is in leaf throughout the year.

2 lb (900 g) chicken livers
¼ cup (2 fl oz/60 ml) extra virgin olive oil
1 large handful of fresh sage leaves
salt and freshly ground black pepper

❧ Remove and discard any fat and connective tissue from the chicken livers. Cut the livers in half.
❧ In a skillet over high heat, warm the olive oil and sage leaves. Add the chicken livers and cook, stirring, for about 3 minutes. Season to taste with salt and pepper.
❧ Transfer to a serving dish and serve immediately.

SERVES 6

Sautéed Chicken Livers with Sage

Siena

ANATRA ALL'ARANCIA

Roast Duck with Orange Sauce

Duck with orange sauce is said to have originated in Siena and then taken to France by Caterina de' Medici's chefs. It is usually prepared with wild duck during the hunting season, but is also very good when domestic duck is used.

2 oranges
2 ducks, about 3 lb (1.5 kg) each
3 tablespoons extra virgin olive oil
2 tablespoons granulated sugar
1 tablespoon white wine vinegar
1 cup (8 fl oz/240 ml) dry white wine
salt and freshly ground black pepper

❧ Preheat an oven to 350°F (180°C). Remove the zest from the oranges in long, thin strips; make sure that none of the pith is attached. Squeeze the juice from the oranges. Set the juice and zest aside.
❧ Truss the ducks with kitchen string. In a heavy ovenproof pot over moderate heat, warm the olive oil. Add the trussed ducks and cook them, turning, until they start to turn golden on all sides, about 10 minutes.
❧ Transfer the pot to the oven and roast the ducks until tender, about 1½ hours.
❧ Meanwhile, combine the sugar and vinegar in a small, heavy saucepan and caramelize the sugar by placing it over moderate heat until the sugar dissolves, then stir while the sugar deepens to a rich brown. Be sure that the sugar does not burn. Remove from the heat, add the orange zest, stir well and pour in the orange juice. Set the pan aside.
❧ Remove the ducks from the pot and cut them into serving pieces. Place the pieces on a platter and keep them warm.
❧ Skim the fat off the roasting juices and reheat the juices over moderate heat. Add the wine and scrape the browned bits off the bottom of the pan. Add the caramelized orange mixture and cook the juices until they reduce and thicken to a sauce. Season to taste with salt and pepper. Pour the hot sauce over the duck pieces and serve immediately.

SERVES 6

Arezzo

ANATRA IN PORCHETTA

Duck Stuffed with Pork

This duck is called in porchetta *because the herb-sausage stuffing gives it the flavor of the whole pigs cooked for country fairs. Because ducks have so much fat, they should be cooked slowly at low temperature so that the fat dissolves and the meat is tender.*

6 oz (180 g) sweet Italian sausages
1 tablespoon chopped fresh sage
1 tablespoon chopped fresh rosemary
2 garlic cloves, chopped
salt and freshly ground black pepper
1 duck, about 4 lb (1.8 kg)
2 bay leaves
3 oz (90 g) *pancetta,* thinly sliced
¼ cup (2 fl oz/60 ml) extra virgin olive oil

❧ Preheat an oven to 325°F (160°C).
❧ Skin the sausages and crumble them into a bowl. Add the sage, rosemary and garlic and mix well. Season to taste with salt and pepper. Stuff the duck with this mixture and truss it securely with kitchen string. Lay the bay leaves on the breast and cover with the *pancetta* slices. Tie in place with kitchen string.
❧ Pour the olive oil into a roasting pan and place the duck in the pan, breast side up. Roast in the oven for about 3 hours, basting occasionally. When the duck is ready, the skin should be fairly dark and very crisp.
❧ Remove the duck from the oven, draining off as much of the fat as possible. Discard the *pancetta* and bay leaves. Cut the duck into serving pieces. Arrange on a platter and serve immediately.

SERVES 6

Duck Stuffed with Pork

Roast Duck with Orange Sauce

Lucca

PETTO DI TACCHINO AI FUNGHI

Turkey Breast with Mushrooms

Tuscans consider turkey breast very much a family dish, as it is easy to prepare and inexpensive. Any leftovers are delicious served cold with mayonnaise and salad.

1 tablespoon chopped fresh sage
1 tablespoon chopped fresh rosemary
3 garlic cloves, chopped
salt and freshly ground black pepper
2 lb (900 g) turkey breast, butterflied
4 oz (120 g) *pancetta,* thinly sliced
1 piece caul fat, about 20 in (50 cm) long
3 tablespoons extra virgin olive oil
6 slices dried *porcini* mushrooms
1 cup (8 fl oz/240 ml) dry white wine

❧ Preheat an oven to 350°F (180°C).
❧ In a small bowl, combine the sage, rosemary, garlic and salt and pepper to taste. Spread the turkey breast out flat and pound it with a meat mallet until it is about ¼ in (6 mm) thick. Cover it with the *pancetta* and sprinkle it with the sage mixture. Roll up the turkey breast into a cylinder shape, wrap it in the caul fat, and tie tightly with kitchen string.
❧ In a roasting pan over moderate heat, warm the olive oil. Add the turkey and cook, turning, until golden on all sides, about 10 minutes. Place the pan in the oven and cook for about 1 hour.
❧ Meanwhile, in a small bowl, soak the mushrooms in warm water to cover for 30 minutes. Drain and squeeze out any excess water. Finely chop the mushrooms and add them and the wine to the pan. Cook for 10 more minutes.
❧ Remove the turkey breast from the pan. Reheat the pan juices on the stovetop, scraping up any browned bits on the pan bottom, and reduce slightly to form a sauce. Snip the string off the turkey breast. Slice the breast and arrange on a platter. Pour the sauce over the slices and serve immediately.

SERVES 6

Arezzo

POLLO AFFINOCCHIATO

Roast Chicken with Fennel Seed

Despite the fact that excellent beef is raised in the Val di Chiana, the people of Arezzo are very fond of chicken, rabbit and pork, prepared in a variety of ways.

2 garlic cloves, chopped
3 tablespoons fennel seed
salt and freshly ground black pepper
1 chicken, about 4 lb (1.8 kg)
¼ cup (2 fl oz/60 ml) extra virgin olive oil

❧ Preheat an oven to 350°F (180°C).
❧ In a small bowl, combine the garlic, fennel seed and salt and pepper to taste. With a fingertip and starting from the breast, gently loosen the skin from the chicken, being careful not to tear the skin. Still using a fingertip, gently spread the garlic mixture evenly between the meat and skin of the chicken breast, back and legs. Truss the chicken.
❧ Pour the olive oil into a roasting pan and place the chicken in the pan. Roast for 1½ hours, basting frequently with the pan juices. When the chicken is ready, the skin should be fairly dark and crisp.Remove the chicken from the oven. Cut into serving pieces and arrange on a platter. Serve immediately.

SERVES 6

Grosseto

POLLO CON LE OLIVE

Sautéed Chicken with Olives

In Grosseto the local olives are cured in brine with grated orange zest, fennel seed and a little garlic. Chicken cooked with these olives is quite tasty. If they are not available, the same result can l obtained by cooking the chicken with the ingredients in this recipe.

Left to right: Sautéed Chicken with Olives, Turkey Breast with Mushrooms, and Roast Chicken with Fennel Seed

3 tablespoons extra virgin olive oil
2 garlic cloves
1 chicken, about 4 lb (1.8 kg), cut into serving pieces
1 tablespoon fennel seed
chopped zest of 1 orange
salt and freshly ground black pepper
1 cup (8 fl oz/240 ml) dry white wine
6 oz (180 g) black Gaeta olives, pitted

☙ In a heavy pot over moderate heat, warm the olive oil and garlic. Add the chicken pieces and cook over moderate heat, turning the pieces occasionally, until they start to turn golden, about 10 minutes.

☙ Add the fennel seed, orange zest and salt and pepper to taste. Pour in the wine, cover the pot and lower the heat. Cook for 1 hour, occasionally adding a little water if the pan becomes too dry. Add the olives and cook for another 10 minutes.

☙ Arrange the chicken and olives on a platter and serve immediately.

SERVES 6

Left to right: Roast Rabbit, Braised Rabbit and Rabbit Cooked in Wine and Stock

Siena

CONIGLIO ARROSTO

Roast Rabbit

All around the walls outside Siena there are small private vegetable gardens where chickens and rabbits are also raised.

2 fresh rosemary sprigs
2 bunches of fresh sage
1 rabbit, about 4 lb (1.8 kg)
3 garlic cloves, chopped
salt and freshly ground black pepper
3 tablespoons extra virgin olive oil
1 cup (8 fl oz/240 ml) dry white wine

❧ Preheat an oven to 350°F (180°C).
❧ Chop half of the rosemary and sage. Rub the rabbit with the chopped rosemary, sage, garlic and salt and pepper to taste. Place the rest of the rosemary and sage in the cavity. Fold the rabbit in half by bringing the head and tail end together. Truss the rabbit securely with kitchen string.
❧ Pour the olive oil into a roasting pan and add the rabbit. Place in the oven and roast until tender, about 1½ hours. Baste the rabbit frequently with the pan juices and turn it over frequently so that it browns well on both sides.
❧ Remove the rabbit and discard the herbs. Cut the rabbit into serving pieces and place on a serving platter; keep warm.
❧ Add the wine to the pan juices and place over high heat. Cook, scraping the browned bits from the bottom of the pan, until the wine reduces a little. Pour the sauce over the rabbit and serve very hot.

SERVES 6

Grosseto

CONIGLIO STRASCICATO

Braised Rabbit

Wild rabbits thrive in the Maremma, the coastal area of Grosseto. Their meat is darker than that of domestic rabbits, and they are usually larger and taste more like hare. They also take longer to cook than ordinary rabbit and should be braised in plenty of liquid.

2 tablespoons extra virgin olive oil
2 oz (60 g) *pancetta,* chopped
1 stewing rabbit, about 4 lb (1.8 kg), cut into serving pieces
2 garlic cloves
1 small bunch of fresh sage, tied with kitchen string

1 fresh rosemary sprig
1 cup (8 fl oz/240 ml) dry white wine
1 yellow onion, chopped
1 celery stalk, trimmed and chopped
salt and freshly ground black pepper
1¼ lb (600 g) plum (egg) tomatoes, peeled and puréed

❧ In a heavy pot over moderate heat, warm the olive oil. Add the *pancetta* and fry until transparent, about 5 minutes. Add the rabbit, garlic, sage and rosemary. Cook, turning the rabbit pieces until they are golden on all sides, about 10 minutes. Pour in the wine and add the onion, celery and salt and pepper to taste. Cover, lower the heat and cook until the wine evaporates, about 10 minutes.
❧ Add the puréed tomatoes, stir well, cover and simmer for about 1½ hours, adding a little water if the pan becomes too dry.
❧ Remove and discard the sage, rosemary and garlic and arrange the rabbit on a platter. Serve immediately.

SERVES 6

Grosseto

LEPRE IN DOLCEFORTE

Hare in Sweet and Sour Sauce

This recipe may also be used for wild boar, although the cooking time would be slightly longer. As is always the case, the wine should be of high quality, because a sauce is only ever as good as the wine that went into it.

4 lb (1.8 kg) hare, cut into serving pieces
1 bottle (3 cups/24 fl oz/750 ml) good red wine
2 yellow onions, quartered
2 carrots, peeled and halved
2 celery stalks, trimmed and halved
2 bay leaves
1 tablespoon juniper berries
2 whole cloves
3 tablespoons extra virgin olive oil
salt and freshly ground black pepper
¼ cup (2 oz/60 g) granulated sugar
2 garlic cloves
1 cup (8 fl oz/240 ml) red wine vinegar

❧ Place the hare pieces in a glass or ceramic dish. Add the wine, onions, carrots, celery, bay leaves, juniper berries and cloves. Mix well, cover and marinate in the refrigerator for 24 hours.
❧ Remove the hare pieces from the marinade, reserving the marinade, and dry them with absorbent paper towels. In a heavy pot over moderate heat, warm the olive oil. Add the hare and cook, turning occasionally, until browned on all sides, about 10 minutes.
❧ Meanwhile, drain the marinade, reserving both the liquid and the vegetables. Add the vegetables to the browned hare, stir well and season to taste with salt and pepper. Pour in 1 cup of the marinade liquid. Cover and simmer over very low heat for 2 hours, gradually adding the remaining marinade as the pan becomes dry.
❧ Put the sugar in a small saucepan. Crush the garlic and add it to the sugar. Place over moderate heat until the sugar dissolves, then cook, stirring, until the sugar caramelizes and turns a golden brown. Remove from the heat and stir in the vinegar. Add the sugar mixture to the pan with the hare and stir well. Simmer for another 10 minutes.
❧ With a slotted utensil, remove the hare pieces from the sauce and arrange them on a serving dish; keep warm. Put the vegetables from the sauce through the fine disc of a food mill. Return the puréed vegetables to the sauce, stir well and reheat to serving temperature.
❧ Pour the sauce over the hare and serve immediately.

SERVES 6

Lucca

CONIGLIO ARROSTO MORTO

Rabbit Cooked in Wine and Stock

Arrosto morto, *literally "dead roast," is halfway between roasting and braising. In Lucca this method is often used for cooking chicken and veal. The meat is started in oil, with wine and stock added later.*

1 rabbit, about 4 lb (1.8 kg)
3 tablespoons extra virgin olive oil
6 fresh sage leaves
1 fresh rosemary sprig
1 cup (8 fl oz/240 ml) white wine
salt and freshly ground black pepper
1 small carrot, peeled and diced
1 celery stalk, trimmed and diced
1 small yellow onion, diced
1 cup (8 fl oz/240 ml) light meat stock (recipe on page 325)
1 bay leaf

❧ Preheat an oven to 350°F (180°C).
❧ Fold the rabbit in half by bringing the head and tail end together. Truss the rabbit securely with kitchen string.
❧ In a heavy ovenproof pot over moderate heat, warm the olive oil. Add the rabbit, sage and rosemary. Cook, turning the rabbit so that it browns lightly on all sides, for about 10 minutes. Add the wine and season to taste with salt and pepper.
❧ Cover the pot, place in the oven and cook for 1 hour. Add the carrot, celery, onion, stock and bay leaf. Re-cover and cook for 30 minutes longer, turning occasionally.
❧ Remove the rabbit from the pot and cut it into serving pieces. Place on a serving dish and keep warm. Remove and discard the bay leaf from the pot. Put the vegetables through the fine disc on a food mill and return them to the pot. Stir the puréed vegetables into the pan juices and reheat on the stovetop. If the sauce is too thin, reduce it over moderate heat.
❧ Pour the sauce over the rabbit and serve.

SERVES 6

Hare in Sweet and Sour Sauce

Arezzo

POLPETTONE ALL'ARETINA

Meat Loaf from Arezzo

The meat loaf made in Arezzo is particularly delicious because it uses fresh mushrooms when they are in season and dried ones the rest of the year. This meat loaf is excellent served cold.

7 oz (210 g) coarse country bread
1 cup (8 fl oz/240 ml) milk
1 oz (30 g) dried *porcini* mushrooms
1¼ lb (600 g) lean ground (minced) beef
2 eggs
½ cup (2 oz/60 g) freshly grated Parmesan cheese
3 oz (90 g) *prosciutto*, chopped
pinch of freshly grated nutmeg
salt and freshly ground black pepper
3 tablespoons all-purpose (plain) flour
2 tablespoons extra virgin olive oil
⅓ cup (3 fl oz/90 ml) dry white wine

In a bowl, soak the bread in the milk for 30 minutes. At the same time, in a separate bowl, soak the mushrooms in warm water to cover for 30 minutes.

Preheat an oven to 350°F (180°C). Squeeze out any excess moisture from the bread and place it in a large bowl. Drain the mushrooms and squeeze out any excess moisture. Chop them and add them to the bowl with the bread.

Add the beef, eggs, Parmesan, *prosciutto* and nutmeg. Season to taste with salt and pepper. Thoroughly mix the ingredients with your hands and then shape the mixture into an oval about 2½ in (6 cm) in diameter. Dredge the loaf lightly with the flour.

In a roasting pan over moderate heat, warm the olive oil. Add the meat loaf and brown it on all sides, turning it very gently, about 10 minutes. Pour in half of the wine and place the pan in the oven. Bake for 1 hour, gradually adding the rest of the wine as the pan becomes dry.

Remove the meat loaf from the pan and let it cool slightly. Slice and arrange on a serving dish. Serve warm or at room temperature.

SERVES 6

Arezzo

SCOTTIGLIA

Medley of Mixed Meats

Braised mixed meats, a feature of the Arezzo kitchen, sometimes appear on menus as cacciucco di carne. *The name comes from the fact that there are always at least seven different varieties of meat, cooked in the same way as the famous* cacciucco *from Livorno, which is composed of fish varieties.*

4 lb (1.8 kg) mixed meats (rabbit, chicken, veal, pork, guinea hen, pigeon or squab or lamb)
2 garlic cloves
¼ cup (2 fl oz/60 ml) extra virgin olive oil
1 small carrot, peeled and chopped
½ celery stalk, trimmed and chopped
½ yellow onion, chopped
1¼ lb (600 g) plum (egg) tomatoes, peeled and puréed
½ cup (4 fl oz/120 ml) light meat stock (recipe on page 325)
salt and freshly ground black pepper
6 slices coarse country bread
1 tablespoon chopped fresh flat-leaf (Italian) parsley
1 tablespoon chopped fresh basil

Chop all the meats into medium-sized pieces and set aside.

Chop 1 of the garlic cloves. In a heavy pot over low heat, warm the olive oil. Add the chopped garlic, carrot, celery and onion and fry gently until translucent, about 5 minutes.

Raise the heat to moderate and add the meats. Brown well on all sides. Add the tomatoes and lower the heat. Cover and cook for about 10 minutes.

Pour the stock into the pot, stir to mix and season to taste with salt and pepper. Cook, stirring occasionally, until the sauce is thick, about 1 hour. If necessary, add a little water to keep the meats moist.

Meanwhile, preheat an oven to 350°F (180°C). Toast the bread slices in the oven until golden. Rub one side of each slice of toast with the remaining garlic clove and place the slices on individual serving plates, garlic side up.

Divide the meats and sauce among the 6 slices of toast. Sprinkle with the parsley and basil and serve very hot.

SERVES 6

Scottiglia, Pork on a Spit and Meat Loaf from Arezzo (rear)

Arezzo

Porchetta allo Spiedo

Pork on a Spit

In Tuscan markets there is always a freshly roasted whole pig, which is carved on the spot and is generally still warm. Pigs weighing as much as 200 lb (100 kg) are highly seasoned with garlic, rosemary and sage and baked in enormous bread ovens. On market days there are always groups of people standing patiently waiting for their pork served on thick slices of country bread. This is the recipe for the homemade version.

1 tablespoon chopped fresh sage
1 tablespoon chopped fresh rosemary
6 garlic cloves, chopped
salt and freshly ground black pepper
2½ lb (1.2 kg) boneless tied pork loin
¼ cup (2 fl oz/60 ml) extra virgin olive oil

❧ Preheat an oven with or without a spit to 350°F (180°C).

❧ In a small bowl, combine the sage, rosemary, garlic and salt and pepper to taste. Mix well and rub this mixture onto the entire surface of the prepared roast. In a roasting pan over moderate heat, warm the olive oil. Add the pork and brown it on all sides, about 10 minutes.

❧ Thread the pork onto the oven spit and cook for 1½ hours, basting frequently with the olive oil. If your oven does not have a spit, pour the olive oil into a roasting pan. Add the pork and roast in the oven, turning frequently, for 1½ hours.

❧ Remove the pork from the spit or pan and snip off the string. Cut the pork into slices and arrange them on a platter to serve.

SERVES 6

Pan-Fried Sausage and Mushrooms (front) and Beef Croquettes (rear)

Grosseto

TEGAMATA DI SALSICCIA E FUNGHI

Pan-Fried Sausage and Mushrooms

Around Grosseto this dish is usually prepared with sharp-tasting wild boar sausages, but sweet Italian sausages are a satisfactory substitute. If porcini *mushrooms are unavailable, you may use* shiitake *or button mushrooms. If the latter are used, add a few dried* porcini *to give the dish more flavor.*

1¼ lb (600 g) fresh *porcini* mushrooms
2 lb (900 g) wild boar sausages or sweet Italian sausages
3 tablespoons extra virgin olive oil
⅓ cup (3 fl oz/90 ml) red wine vinegar
3 garlic cloves, chopped
salt
1 tablespoon chopped fresh mint or thyme

❧ Clean the mushrooms by rubbing them with a dampened cloth; do not wash them. Trim the mushroom stems, then slice the mushrooms; set aside.

❧ Prick the sausages with a fork. In a skillet over moderate heat, warm the olive oil. Add the sausages and fry until they start to turn brown, about 5 minutes. Remove some of the cooking fat and pour in the vinegar. Continue cooking until the vinegar evaporates, about 5 minutes.

❧ Add the mushrooms and garlic and cook for another 5 minutes. Season to taste with salt, sprinkle with the mint and stir well.

❧ Arrange the sausages on a platter and serve very hot.

SERVES 6

Grosseto

POLPETTE RIFATTE

Beef Croquettes

Tuscan pancetta *is cured with salt and a lot of pepper, is flat and not round, and is called* rigatino, *meaning "little line," because it is fatty with thin layers of pink meat.*

3 oz (90 g) crustless coarse country bread
1¼ lb (600 g) beef bottom round or top round, very thinly sliced
4 oz (120 g) ground (minced) beef
1 garlic clove, chopped
3 oz (90 g) *pancetta,* chopped
1 tablespoon chopped fresh flat-leaf (Italian) parsley
3 tablespoons extra virgin olive oil
1 cup (8 fl oz/240 ml) dry red wine
1¼ lb (600 g) plum (egg) tomatoes, peeled and puréed
salt and freshly ground black pepper

❧ Soak the bread in water to cover for 30 minutes. Drain, squeeze out any excess moisture and place in a bowl.

❧ With a meat mallet, gently flatten the beef slices until they are about ⅛ in (3 mm) thick.

❧ Add the ground beef, garlic, *pancetta* and parsley to the bowl with the bread and mix well. Spread a little of this mixture evenly on each slice of beef, fold in the sides, roll up and secure with a wooden toothpick.

❧ In a roasting pan over moderate heat, warm the olive oil. Add the beef rolls and brown them on all sides, about 10 minutes. Pour in the wine and cook until it evaporates, about 10 minutes.

❧ Add the tomatoes and season to taste with salt and pepper. Lower the heat, cover and cook until the sauce thickens, about 40 minutes.

❧ Arrange the rolls and sauce on a platter. Serve immediately.

SERVES 6

Firenze

ANIMELLE CON PISELLI

Sweetbreads with Peas

In Italy sweetbreads are very popular, as are all the other variety meats (offal)—brains, liver, kidney and tripe.

2 lb (900 g) calf's sweetbreads
juice of 1 lemon
3 tablespoons all-purpose (plain) flour
¼ cup (2 fl oz/60 ml) extra virgin olive oil
3 oz (90 g) *prosciutto,* diced
⅓ cup (3 fl oz/90 ml) Marsala wine
3½ cups (14 oz/420 g) shelled green peas
½ cup (4 fl oz/120 ml) water, boiling
salt and freshly ground black pepper

Soak the sweetbreads in cold water to cover for 1 hour; drain.

Bring a large saucepan of water to a boil and add the lemon juice. Add the sweetbreads and boil for about 6 minutes. Drain the sweetbreads and plunge in cold water to cool. Carefully remove the membrane covering the lobes and any tough connective tissue. Place the sweetbreads between 2 plates and top with a weight. Chill for 2 hours in the refrigerator.

Cut the sweetbreads into fairly large pieces. Dredge the pieces in the flour.

In a deep skillet over moderate heat, warm the olive oil. Add the sweetbreads and cook until they are golden on both sides, about 10 minutes total cooking time. Add the *prosciutto* and cook, stirring, for another 2 minutes. Pour in the Marsala and cook until it evaporates, about 5 minutes.

Add the peas and boiling water, lower the heat, cover and cook until the peas are tender, about 10 minutes. Season to taste with salt and pepper.

Transfer the sweetbreads to a serving dish and serve immediately.

SERVES 6

Firenze

COSTATA ALLA FIORENTINA

Florentine Steaks

Florentine steaks, which are 1¼ in (3 cm) thick and weigh a minimum of 2½ lb (1.2 kg), come from the cattle raised in the Val di Chiana and are very similar to T-bone steaks. They are the classic Sunday lunch and are generally grilled on an open wood-burning fire; they may, however, be cooked under an ordinary broiler. One costata *is the usual portion for just two people!*

2 T-bone steaks, about 2½ lb (1.2 kg) each
2 tablespoons extra virgin olive oil
salt and freshly ground black pepper

Brush the steaks with the olive oil and sprinkle with pepper to taste. Marinate at room temperature for about 30 minutes.

Meanwhile, prepare a fire in a charcoal grill or preheat a broiler (grill). Place the steaks on the grill rack over a hot fire or slip them under the broiler. Cook, turning occasionally, until done to your liking, about 15 minutes for medium-rare.

Remove the steaks to a serving dish, sprinkle them with salt and serve.

SERVES 6

Sweetbreads with Peas

Florentine Steak

Roast Lamb (left) and Ossobuco with Tomato (right)

Lucca

OSSIBUCHI AL POMODORO

Ossobuco with Tomato

The best ossibuchi *(veal shanks) are those cut from about halfway down the shank part of the leg, because that is where the proportion of meat and marrow is just right. Although this dish is a specialty of Lombardy, the people of Lucca have developed their own distinctive recipe that uses onions and tomato.*

6 slices dried *porcini* mushrooms
6 veal shanks, about 8 oz (240 g) each
3 tablespoons extra virgin olive oil
2 yellow onions, chopped
1 tablespoon finely chopped celery stalk
1 tablespoon finely chopped carrot
10 oz (300 g) plum (egg) tomatoes, peeled and puréed
salt and freshly ground black pepper
⅓ cup (3 fl oz/90 ml) dry white wine
1 tablespoon chopped fresh flat-leaf (Italian) parsley

❧ In a small bowl, soak the mushrooms in warm water to cover for 30 minutes. Drain and squeeze out any excess water. Chop the mushrooms and set aside.

❧ Tie each *ossobuco* around the edges with a piece of kitchen string. In a roasting pan over moderate heat, warm the olive oil. Add the *ossibuchi* and brown them on both sides for a few minutes. Add the onions, celery and carrot. Lower the heat, cover and cook until the vegetables are translucent, about 5 minutes.

❧ Add the mushrooms and tomatoes and season to taste with salt and pepper. Cover the pan and cook over low heat for 1½ hours, gradually adding the wine to keep the contents moist.

❧ Snip the string off the *ossibuchi* and arrange them on a platter. Cover them with the hot pan juices, sprinkle with the parsley and serve.

SERVES 6

Arezzo

AGNELLO AL FORNO

Roast Lamb

Spring lamb is considered the choicest because it is tender and has a mild flavor. Around Arezzo, farmers' wives cook lamb in their bread ovens after they have finished baking because the wood-burning ovens are at just the right temperature. Diced potatoes are often added for the last half hour.

3 garlic cloves, chopped
2 tablespoons fresh rosemary leaves
salt and freshly ground black pepper
5 lb (2.5 kg) leg of lamb
¼ cup (2 fl oz/60 ml) extra virgin olive oil
20 bay leaves

❧ Preheat an oven to 350°F (180°C).

❧ In a small bowl, mix together the garlic, rosemary and salt and pepper to taste. Rub the lamb with this mixture. Place the lamb in a large roasting pan. Sprinkle the olive oil over the lamb and add the bay leaves. Place the pan in the oven and roast for about 1½ hours, turning the lamb occasionally so that it browns on all sides.

❧ Remove the lamb from the roasting pan and carve into servings. Arrange on a platter and serve very hot.

SERVES 6

Grosseto

BISTECCHE ALLA CACCIATORA

Steak with Mushrooms and Marjoram

These steaks are cooked in a tomato sauce flavored with the marjoram that grows wild all along the Grosseto coast. They owe their name to the fact that they are suited to the robust appetites of the cacciatori, *or huntsmen.*

1 oz (30 g) dried *porcini* mushrooms
6 thin flank (rump) steaks, about 6 oz (180 g) each
2 tablespoons extra virgin olive oil
2 garlic cloves, chopped
1 cup (8 fl oz/240 ml) dry red wine
1 tablespoon tomato paste
1 tablespoon fresh marjoram leaves or 1 teaspoon dried marjoram
1 tablespoon juniper berries
salt and freshly ground black pepper

In a bowl, soak the mushrooms in warm water to cover for 30 minutes. Drain the mushrooms and reserve the soaking liquid. Strain the liquid and set aside. Squeeze out any excess moisture from the mushrooms and chop the mushrooms.

In a skillet large enough to hold the steaks in a single layer, warm the olive oil over moderate heat. Add the garlic and steaks and cook on each side for 2 minutes, when they will start to brown.

Lower the heat and add the wine, tomato paste, marjoram, juniper berries and mushrooms. Season to taste with salt and pepper and cover the skillet. Cook for 10 minutes, adding a little of the mushroom liquid if the pan becomes too dry. The sauce should not be too thick.

Arrange the steaks and sauce on a platter. Serve at once.

SERVES 6

Steak with Mushrooms and Marjoram

Firenze

POLPETTE DI LESSO

Fried Meatballs

Tuscans are very parsimonious and never waste food. Any leftovers are transformed into something quite different. These meatballs are an interesting way of using leftover boiled meat.

2 boiling potatoes
2 lb (900 g) boiled or roasted beef, chicken or veal
2 eggs
1 tablespoon chopped fresh flat-leaf (Italian) parsley
1 tablespoon chopped fresh sage
1 garlic clove, chopped
1 teaspoon freshly grated lemon zest
pinch of freshly grated nutmeg
3 tablespoons freshly grated Parmesan
salt and freshly ground black pepper
⅔ cup (3 oz/90 g) fine dry bread crumbs
5 cups (40 fl oz/1.2 l) extra virgin olive oil for frying

In a saucepan, boil the potatoes in salted water to cover until tender, about 30 minutes. Drain the potatoes and peel and mash them while still hot.

Chop the meat very finely using a knife or *mezzaluna* and place in a bowl. Add the mashed potato, eggs, parsley, sage, garlic, lemon zest, nutmeg and Parmesan. Mix thoroughly and season to taste with salt and pepper. Using your hands, form the mixture into ovals about 2½ in (6 cm) long and 1 in (2.5 cm) in diameter. Coat them evenly with the bread crumbs.

In a deep, heavy skillet, heat the olive oil to 350°F (180°C). A few at a time, slip the meatballs into the hot oil without crowding the pan. Fry until golden, about 5 minutes. With a slotted spoon, remove the meatballs to absorbent paper towels to drain briefly. Continue frying the remaining meatballs in the same manner.

Arrange the meatballs on a platter and serve piping hot.

SERVES 6

Fried Meatballs

Siena

Brasato al Chianti

Beef Braised in Chianti

Several different cuts of beef may be used to prepare good braised meat, but one of the best is chuck or rump roast. The meat is usually simmered for at least 4 hours in order for it to become very tender.

2½ lb (1.2 kg) beef chuck or rump roast (boned and rolled beef topside)
1 bottle (24 fl oz/750 ml) Chianti Riserva
1 carrot, peeled and sliced
1 yellow onion, sliced
1 celery stalk, trimmed and sliced
2 bay leaves
½ tablespoon whole black peppercorns
1 tablespoon juniper berries
6 slices dried *porcini* mushrooms
3 tablespoons extra virgin olive oil
2 plum (egg) tomatoes, peeled and chopped
salt

♣ Place the meat in a large bowl and pour the bottle of wine over it. Add the carrot, onion, celery, bay leaves, peppercorns and juniper berries. Marinate in the refrigerator for at least 24 hours, turning the meat occasionally so that it is always moist.

♣ In a small bowl, soak the mushrooms in warm water to cover for 30 minutes. Meanwhile, remove the meat from the marinade and dry it with absorbent paper towels. Strain the marinade and set the vegetables aside. Reserve the marinade liquid.

♣ In a heavy oval pot just large enough to accommodate the meat, warm the olive oil over moderate heat. Add the meat

Twice-Cooked Boiled Beef (left), Beef Braised in Chianti (right) and Meat Loaf with Mushroom-Tomato Sauce (rear)

and brown well on all sides, about 10 minutes.

❧ While the meat is browning, drain the mushrooms and reserve the liquid. Strain the liquid and set the mushrooms and liquid aside. Lower the heat under the beef and add the reserved vegetables, tomatoes, mushrooms and salt to taste. Add a little of the marinade liquid; cover and simmer very gently. As the beef cooks, gradually add the marinade liquid, alternating it with the mushroom liquid, so that the meat always remains very moist.

❧ After about 4 hours, remove the meat and place on a serving platter. Slice the meat and keep it warm.

❧ Pass the vegetables through a fine sieve and return them to the pot. Stir the puréed vegetables into the cooking juices and cook over moderate heat until thickened to a sauce.

❧ Pour the sauce over the sliced meat and serve immediately.

SERVES 6

Siena

POLPETTONE IN UMIDO

Meat Loaf with Mushroom-Tomato Sauce

In Tuscany there are various ways of making meat loaf. It is sometimes boiled, resulting in the added bonus of an excellent stock, but in Siena it is usually served with a mushroom-tomato sauce.

6 slices dried *porcini* mushrooms
6 oz (180 g) crustless coarse country bread
1 cup (8 fl oz/240 ml) milk
1¼ lb (600 g) lean ground (minced) beef
2 eggs
1 tablespoon fresh thyme leaves
3 oz (90 g) *prosciutto,* chopped
salt and freshly ground black pepper
⅓ cup (3 fl oz/90 ml) extra virgin olive oil
1 cup (8 fl oz/240 ml) dry red wine
1 lb (450 g) plum (egg) tomatoes, peeled and puréed
1 tablespoon chopped fresh flat-leaf (Italian) parsley

❧ In a small bowl, soak the mushrooms in warm water to cover for 30 minutes. In a separate bowl, soak the bread in the milk for 10 minutes.

❧ Preheat an oven to 350°F (180°C).

❧ Squeeze out any excess milk from the bread and place it in a large bowl. Add the beef, eggs, thyme, *prosciutto* and salt and pepper to taste. Thoroughly mix the ingredients with your hands, and then shape the mixture into an oval about 2½ in (6 cm) in diameter.

❧ In a heavy ovenproof pot over moderate heat, warm the olive oil. Add the meat loaf and cook, turning, until browned on all sides, about 10 minutes.

❧ Meanwhile, drain the mushrooms and reserve the liquid. Squeeze the mushrooms dry and then chop them finely. Strain the liquid and set aside.

❧ Add the wine, puréed tomatoes and mushrooms to the pot and bring slowly to a boil. As soon as the tomato mixture starts to boil, transfer the pot to the oven and cook, turning the meat a few times, until tender, about 1 hour. Should the sauce become too dry, add a little of the reserved mushroom liquid.

❧ Remove the pot from the oven and place the meat loaf on a serving platter. Slice the meat. Season the sauce to taste with salt and pepper; pour it over the meat. Sprinkle with parsley and serve.

SERVES 6

Siena

LESSO RIFATTO

Twice-Cooked Boiled Beef

Being very thrifty, the Tuscans have many different ways of disguising leftovers. This excellent dish is traditionally made with boiled meat, but roast meat can also be used.

3 tablespoons extra virgin olive oil
1 lb (450 g) yellow onions, thinly sliced
1¼ lb (600 g) plum (egg) tomatoes, peeled and chopped
pinch of freshly grated nutmeg
salt and freshly ground black pepper
2 lb (900 g) boiled beef or veal, sliced

❧ In a skillet over low heat, warm the olive oil. Add the onions and fry gently until they are translucent, about 5 minutes. Add the tomatoes and nutmeg and continue cooking until the sauce thickens slightly and the onion disintegrates, about 30 minutes. Season to taste with salt and pepper. Add the meat and cook for 10 minutes to allow the flavors to blend.

❧ Arrange the meat and sauce on a platter. Serve immediately.

SERVES 6

Firenze

TRIPPA ALLA FIORENTINA

Florentine Tripe

Tripe is very popular all over Tuscany, but particularly so in Florence. When buying tripe, always choose the honeycomb type, which has the best texture. Because tripe is tough it should be well cooked, but care should be taken not to overcook it or it loses its flavor.

2 carrots
2 yellow onions
2 celery stalks
1 bay leaf
1 teaspoon green peppercorns
2 lb (900 g) veal or beef tripe
¼ cup (2 fl oz/60 ml) extra virgin olive oil
1 lb (450 g) plum (egg) tomatoes, peeled and chopped
salt and freshly ground black pepper
½ cup (2 oz/60 g) freshly grated Parmesan cheese

Bring a large saucepan of salted water to a boil. Add 1 each of the carrots, onions and celery stalks, the bay leaf and the peppercorns. When the water returns to a boil, add the tripe, cover and simmer for 30 minutes.

Drain the tripe and discard the vegetables. Cut the tripe into narrow strips. Peel the remaining carrot and trim the remaining celery stalk. Chop the carrot, celery and onion.

In a fairly large saucepan over low heat, warm the olive oil. Add the chopped carrot, celery and onion and cook until the onion is translucent, about 5 minutes. Add the tripe and stir for a few minutes. Add the tomatoes and cook until the liquid evaporates, about 30 minutes.

Season to taste with salt and pepper. Ladle the tripe onto a platter, sprinkle with the Parmesan and serve.

SERVES 6

Braised Veal Cubes (left) and Beef Stew from Impruneta (right)

Firenze

PEPOSO DEL FORNACIARI DELL'IMPRUNETA

Beef Stew from Impruneta

Impruneta is a village outside Florence where the most beautiful handmade tiles and terra-cotta pots are produced. The wives of the furnace workmen make this robust stew for their husbands to take to their jobs.

¼ cup (2 fl oz/60 ml) extra virgin olive oil
1 white onion, chopped
1 garlic clove, chopped
2 lb (900 g) boneless beef shank (shin), cut into 1¼-in (3-cm) cubes
2 bay leaves
1 teaspoon whole black peppercorns
⅓ cup (3 fl oz/90 ml) dry red wine
1 lb (450 g) plum (egg) tomatoes, peeled and chopped
salt

Florentine Tripe

☙ In a heavy pot over moderate heat, warm the olive oil and onion. Add the garlic, meat, bay leaves and peppercorns.
☙ Cook, stirring occasionally, until the meat is browned on all sides, about 10 minutes. Pour in the red wine and cook until it evaporates, about 5 minutes.
☙ Add the tomatoes, cover and lower the heat. Simmer until the meat is tender, about 1½ hours. Should the stew become too dry, add water, a little at a time. Season to taste with salt.
☙ Ladle the stew into a serving dish and serve immediately.

SERVES 6

Firenze

SPEZZATINO IN UMIDO

Braised Veal Cubes

This stew is usually served either with a vegetable mold, potatoes stewed in a tomato sauce, or fresh green peas sautéed in oil.

¼ cup (2 fl oz/60 ml) extra virgin olive oil
1½ lb (900 g) veal rump roast (boneless veal topside), cut into 1¼-in (3-cm) cubes
1 tablespoon all-purpose (plain) flour
⅓ cup (3 fl oz/90 ml) dry white wine
½ white onion, chopped
1 carrot, peeled and chopped
1 celery stalk, trimmed and chopped
⅓ cup (3 fl oz/90 ml) light meat stock (recipe on page 325)
salt and freshly ground black pepper
juice and grated zest of 1 lemon
2 tablespoons chopped fresh flat-leaf (Italian) parsley

☙ In a heavy pot over moderate heat, warm the olive oil. Add the veal cubes and cook, stirring occasionally, until the meat is browned on all sides, about 10 minutes. Sprinkle the meat with the flour and pour in the wine. Lower the heat, cover and cook for 10 minutes over low heat.
☙ Add the onion, carrot, celery and stock and stir well. Recover and continue cooking for 1½ hours. Should the stew become too dry, add water, a little at a time.
☙ Season to taste with salt and pepper. Add the lemon juice and zest, stir well and sprinkle with the parsley. Place the veal on a platter and serve.

SERVES 6

Left to right: Baked Anchovies, Sole and Red Mullet Soup, and Salt Cod with Spinach

Livorno

ZUPPA DI SOGLIOLE E TRIGLIE

Sole and Red Mullet Soup

Livorno is famous for both its sole and its red mullet. In this recipe local cooks manage to combine them in a delicious and filling soup that is usually served as a main course.

2 sole, about 1⅓ lb (690 g) total weight
3 red mullet, about 1⅓ lb (690 g) total weight
¼ cup (2 fl oz/60 ml) extra virgin olive oil
2 garlic cloves, chopped, plus 1 whole garlic clove
1 small yellow onion, chopped
1 carrot, peeled and chopped
1 celery stalk, trimmed and chopped
2 tablespoons chopped fresh flat-leaf (Italian) parsley
1 cup (8 fl oz/240 ml) dry white wine
1¼ lb (600 g) plum (egg) tomatoes, peeled and chopped
salt and freshly ground black pepper
6 slices coarse country bread

❧ Cut the heads off the fish and save them. Fillet the bodies and discard the bones. Set the fillets and heads aside.

❧ In a heavy pot over low heat, warm the olive oil. Add the chopped garlic, onion, carrot, celery and parsley and cook until the onion is translucent, about 5 minutes. Add the fish heads and wine and cook until the wine evaporates, about 10 minutes. Add the tomatoes and cook until the sauce begins to thicken, about 40 minutes.

❧ Preheat an oven to 350°F (180°C).

❧ Remove and discard the fish heads from the pot and then put the sauce through a food mill. Return the puréed sauce to the pot and add the fish fillets. Season to taste with salt and pepper. Cook over low heat for no more than 10 minutes, gradually adding a little water to keep the sauce fairly thin.

❧ Meanwhile, toast the bread slices in the oven until golden. Rub one side of each slice with the remaining whole garlic clove. Place the slices in individual soup bowls, garlic side up.

❧ Ladle the soup and fish over the toast. Serve immediately.

SERVES 6

Firenze

SEPPIE COI FAGIOLI

Squid and Beans

Although the Florentines are not great fish-eaters, they are very fond of salt cod, eel and squid. This is a particularly delicious recipe for squid.

1½ cups (10 oz/300 g) dried *cannellini* beans
6 tablespoons (3 fl oz/90 ml) extra virgin olive oil
1 handful of fresh sage leaves
2 lb (900 g) squid
2 garlic cloves
1¼ lb (600 g) plum (egg) tomatoes, peeled and chopped
salt and freshly ground black pepper

❧ In a bowl, soak the beans in water to cover for 12 hours.
❧ Drain the beans and transfer them to a heavy saucepan. Add 2 tablespoons of the olive oil, the sage and water just to cover. Bring slowly to a boil over low heat. Simmer gently for 1½ hours, by which time the water should be absorbed and the beans will be almost the consistency of porridge.
❧ Meanwhile, clean the squid. Pull the tentacles from each body. Discard the entrails, ink sac and the cartilage from the body. Cut the tentacles off at the point just above the eyes and discard the head. Rinse the body and tentacles under cold running water. When all of the squid are cleaned, slice the squid bodies and chop the tentacles.
❧ In a large skillet over moderate heat, warm the remaining 4 tablespoons (2 fl oz/60 ml) olive oil with the garlic. Add the squid and cook, stirring occasionally, for 5 minutes. Add the tomatoes, lower the heat and cook until the liquid almost completely evaporates, about 30 minutes.
❧ Add the beans to the squid. Stir and heat together for about 5 minutes. Season to taste with salt and pepper.
❧ Transfer to a serving dish and serve immediately.

SERVES 6

Livorno

TORTA DI ACCIUGHE

Baked Anchovies

In this classic Livornese recipe, filleted anchovies or sardines are opened flat and arranged in concentric circles in a baking dish.

¾ cup (3 oz/90 g) fine dry bread crumbs
1 tablespoon dried marjoram or oregano
3 garlic cloves, chopped
salt
2½ lb (1.2 kg) fresh anchovies or sardines
¼ cup (2 fl oz/60 ml) extra virgin olive oil

❧ Preheat an oven to 350°F (180°C).
❧ In a small bowl, combine half of the bread crumbs, the marjoram, garlic and salt to taste. Mix well and set aside.
❧ Remove the heads from the fish. Slit the bodies lengthwise along the belly and open them flat. Remove and discard the bones. Rinse the fish and pat dry on absorbent paper towels.
❧ Pour half of the olive oil into a round ovenproof dish. Sprinkle with the bread crumb mixture. Arrange the fish in the dish in concentric circles, slightly overlapping them if necessary. Sprinkle the fish with the remaining crumbs and then drizzle with the remaining olive oil. Bake for 20 minutes. Serve hot.

SERVES 6

Livorno

BACCALÀ ALL'INZIMINO

Salt Cod with Spinach

All'inzimino *means "cooked with leaf vegetables," and all over Tuscany cuttlefish, tuna and salt cod are cooked in this way.*

2 lb (900 g) salt cod
2½ lb (1.2 kg) Swiss chard (silverbeet) or spinach, trimmed
⅓ cup (3 fl oz/90 ml) extra virgin olive oil
2 garlic cloves, chopped
pinch of ground dried chili
10 oz (300 g) plum (egg) tomatoes, peeled and chopped

❧ Soak the salt cod in water to cover in the refrigerator for 24 hours, changing the water 3 or 4 times.
❧ Bring a large saucepan of water to a boil. Add the Swiss chard (or spinach) and boil for 1 minute. Drain well and chop; set aside.
❧ Drain the salt cod. Remove and discard the bones and skin. Dry with absorbent paper towels. Cut the cod into large pieces.
❧ In a heavy saucepan over moderate heat, warm the olive oil. Add the garlic and salt cod. Sprinkle the chili over the top and cook, turning the cod, until it is just golden on all sides, about 5 minutes.
❧ Add the Swiss chard and tomatoes. Lower the heat, cover the pan and continue cooking over low heat until the liquid evaporates and a fairly thick sauce forms, about 20 minutes.
❧ Arrange the cod pieces and sauce on a platter and serve.

SERVES 6

Squid and Beans

Top to bottom: Baked Marinated Prawns, Stuffed Cuttlefish and Grilled Trout

Grosseto

SEPPIE RIPIENE

Stuffed Cuttlefish

The long coastline near Grosseto accounts for the numerous fish recipes in the area.

6 cuttlefish or squid, about 6 oz (180 g) each
7 oz (210 g) crustless coarse country bread
1 egg
1 tablespoon chopped fresh flat-leaf (Italian) parsley
1 tablespoon chopped fresh basil
½ cup (2 oz/60 g) freshly grated Parmesan cheese
2 garlic cloves, chopped
pinch of ground dried chili
salt and freshly ground black pepper
3 tablespoons extra virgin olive oil
1 cup (8 fl oz/240 ml) dry white wine

❧ Pull the tentacles from each cuttlefish (or squid) body. Discard the entrails, ink sac and cartilage from each body, being careful not to tear it. Cut the tentacles off at the point just above the eyes and discard each head.
❧ Rinse the bodies and tentacles under cold running water. Chop the tentacles and place in a mixing bowl. Set the bodies aside.
❧ In a bowl, soak the bread in water to cover for 10 minutes. Drain and squeeze out any excess moisture. To the bowl with the tentacles, add the bread, egg, parsley, basil, Parmesan, garlic, chili and salt and pepper. Mix thoroughly. Stuff the cuttlefish with this mixture and secure them closed with wooden toothpicks.
❧ In a large skillet over moderate heat, warm the olive oil. Add the cuttlefish and cook, turning once, until pink, about 6 minutes.
❧ Pour in the wine and season to taste with salt and pepper. Lower the heat, cover and cook for 30 minutes, adding a little water if the pan becomes too dry.
❧ Arrange the cuttlefish on a platter and serve.

SERVES 6

Arezzo

TROTE AL FRANTOIO

Grilled Trout

Fishing in the small lakes around Arezzo is a favorite Sunday pastime. The fishermen build fires beside the lake to grill their catch. They are called al frantoio *(olive oil press) because they are cooked with olive oil that has just been pressed.*

6 bay leaves
6 whole trout, about 8 oz (240 g) each
6 tablespoons (3 fl oz/90 ml) extra virgin olive oil
salt and freshly ground black pepper
½ lemon

❧ Prepare a fire in a charcoal grill or preheat a broiler (grill).
❧ Place a bay leaf in the cavity of each trout.
❧ Brush a grill rack with 3 tablespoons of the olive oil. Arrange the trout on the rack over the charcoal or slip into a broiler and cook for a few minutes on each side. Sprinkle the trout with salt and pepper to taste while they are cooking.
❧ Place the fish on a serving dish, squeeze the lemon over them, sprinkle with the remaining 3 tablespoons olive oil and serve.

SERVES 6

Livorno

TRIGLIE ALLA LIVORNESE

Fried Red Mullet in Tomato Sauce

This is one of the tastiest ways of cooking red mullet, which are particularly excellent in Livorno because they are fished near rocks. Red mullet are quite fragile, so they should be handled with great care.

6 red mullet, about ½ lb (240 g) each
⅔ cup (3 oz/90 g) all-purpose (plain) flour
5 cups (40 fl oz/1.2 l) extra virgin olive oil for frying
3 garlic cloves, chopped
1¼ lb (600 g) plum (egg) tomatoes, peeled and puréed
salt and freshly ground black pepper
2 tablespoons chopped fresh flat-leaf (Italian) parsley

❧ Gently pat the fish dry with absorbent paper towels. Dredge the fish in the flour.
❧ Reserve 3 tablespoons of the olive oil and pour the remaining olive oil into a deep, heavy skillet. Heat the oil in the skillet to 350°F (180°C). One at a time, slip the mullet into the hot oil and fry until golden, about 5 minutes. With a slotted utensil, remove to absorbent paper towels to drain. Continue frying the remaining mullet in the same manner.
❧ In a heavy saucepan over low heat, warm the 3 tablespoons olive oil. Add the garlic and fry gently until translucent, about 3 minutes. Add the tomatoes and continue cooking over low heat until the sauce is fairly thick, about 40 minutes.
❧ Gently place the mullet in the sauce and heat them for a few minutes. Season to taste with salt and pepper and sprinkle with the parsley.
❧ Arrange the mullet and sauce on a platter and serve.

SERVES 6 *Photograph page 262*

Lucca

SPANNOCCHIE ALLO SCOGLIO

Baked Marinated Shrimp

On the long coast of Lucchesia there are several holiday resorts, the most famous of which are Forte dei Marmi and Viareggio. Their celebrated fish restaurants are as much of an attraction as the sandy beaches. Spannocchie *are large clawed crustaceans caught on the rocks off the coast. As they are impossible to find elsewhere, you can use large headless shrimp in their place.*

juice of 1 lemon
5 tablespoons (2½ fl oz/80 ml) extra virgin olive oil
salt and freshly ground black pepper
2 lb (900 g) peeled headless shrimp (prawns)
2 garlic cloves
1 tablespoon chopped fresh flat-leaf (Italian) parsley

❧ Stir the lemon juice into the olive oil and season to taste with salt and pepper. Brush the shrimp with this mixture and marinate at room temperature for 30 minutes.
❧ Pour off the marinade into a roasting pan and warm over moderate heat with the garlic. Add the prawns to the pan and sauté them until opaque and curled, not more than 5 minutes. Season to taste with salt and pepper and discard the garlic.
❧ Arrange the shellfish on a platter and sprinkle with the parsley. Serve hot.

SERVES 6

Livorno

Tonno con Piselli

Fresh Tuna with Peas

In Tuscany fish is often prepared with vegetables. The flavors marry well as long as the vegetables have a mild taste.

6 tuna steaks, about 8 oz (240 g) each
3 tablespoons extra virgin olive oil
5 cups (1¼ lb/600 g) shelled green peas
1 tablespoon chopped fresh flat-leaf (Italian) parsley
½ cup (4 fl oz/120 ml) dry white wine
salt and freshly ground black pepper

In a skillet large enough to contain the tuna steaks in a single layer, warm the olive oil over moderate heat. Add the fish and cook on both sides for 5 minutes. Add the peas, parsley and wine; cook for another 5 minutes. Season to taste with salt and pepper.

Arrange the tuna and peas on a platter and serve immediately.

SERVES 6

Pork Escalopes with Mushrooms

Lucca

Scaloppine alla Boscaiola

Pork Escalopes with Mushrooms

The people of Lucchesia prefer white meat to beef. These escalopes are traditionally cut from uncured ham and then cooked in a mushroom sauce. They are called alla boscaiola, *or "woodcutter style," because of the great quantity of mushrooms in the woods.*

10 oz (300 g) fresh *porcini, shiitake* or button mushrooms
⅓ cup (3 fl oz/90 ml) extra virgin olive oil
2 lb (900 g) lean pork, thinly sliced
3 garlic cloves
⅓ cup (3 fl oz/90 ml) dry white wine
1 tablespoon fresh thyme leaves
salt and freshly ground black pepper

Clean the mushrooms by rubbing them with a dampened cloth; do not wash them. Trim the mushroom stems, then slice the mushrooms fairly thinly; set aside.

In a heavy ovenproof pot over moderate heat, warm the olive oil. Add the pork slices and cook, turning once, until golden on both sides, about 2 minutes per side. Add the mushrooms and garlic and sauté for 2 more minutes. Pour in the wine and sprinkle with the thyme. Cook, scraping the browned bits from the bottom of the pan, until the wine evaporates, about 2 minutes. Season to taste with salt and pepper and remove and discard the garlic.

Arrange the pork and mushrooms on a platter and serve.

SERVES 6

Livorno

Zuppa di Muscoli

Mussel Soup

This hearty mussel soup makes an excellent luncheon dish served with a green salad, and is just as interesting made with clams.

6 lb (3 kg) large mussels in the shell
⅓ cup (3 fl oz/90 ml) extra virgin olive oil
2 garlic cloves, chopped
1 lb (450 g) plum (egg) tomatoes, peeled and puréed
1 cup (8 fl oz/240 ml) dry white wine
2 cups (16 fl oz/480 ml) water
salt and freshly ground black pepper
6 slices coarse country bread
2 tablespoons chopped fresh flat-leaf (Italian) parsley

Scrub and debeard the mussels. Put the mussels in a shallow saucepan, cover and place over moderate heat until the shells open, about 5 minutes. Remove from the heat and discard any mussels that did not open; set the mussels aside in their shells. Strain the liquid that the mussels released into the saucepan and set aside.

Preheat an oven to 350°F (180°C).

In a heavy ovenproof pot over low heat, warm the olive oil. Add the garlic and fry gently until translucent, about 5 minutes. Add the tomatoes, wine, liquid from the mussels and the water. Cook over low heat for 30 minutes. Add the mussels and allow the flavors to blend for another 2 minutes. Season to taste with salt and pepper.

Meanwhile, toast the bread slices in the oven until golden, about 10 minutes. Place the slices in individual soup dishes. Ladle the soup over the toast, sprinkle with the parsley and serve immediately.

SERVES 6

Fresh Tuna with Peas (left) and Mussel Soup (right)

Baked Swordfish with Potatoes (left) and Stockfish and Potatoes (right)

Livorno

STOCCAFISSO CON PATATE

Stockfish and Potatoes

Stockfish is unsalted dried cod. Because drying fish without salt is a more difficult process, stockfish is harder to find and more expensive than salt cod.

2½ lb (1.2 kg) stockfish
⅓ cup (3 fl oz/90 ml) extra virgin olive oil
1 small yellow onion, chopped
2 garlic cloves, chopped
¾ cup (6 fl oz/180 ml) dry white wine
2½ lb (1.2 kg) potatoes, peeled and diced
1 tablespoon chopped fresh rosemary
salt and freshly ground black pepper

In a large bowl, soak the stockfish in cold water to cover in the refrigerator for 24 hours, changing the water 3 or 4 times. Drain the fish and remove and discard the bones and skin. Dry with absorbent paper towels. Cut the fish into fairly large pieces.

In a heavy saucepan over moderate heat, warm the olive oil. Add the onion and garlic and fry gently until translucent, about 5 minutes. Add the stockfish and cook, turning the fish, until golden on all sides, about 5 minutes. Pour in the wine, cover and lower the heat. Cook for 10 minutes.

Add the potatoes and rosemary and season to taste with salt and pepper. Cover and cook, stirring occasionally, until the potatoes are tender, about 20 minutes. Add a little water if the pan becomes too dry, and turn the fish and potatoes very gently so that they do not break.

Arrange the stockfish and potatoes on a warm platter and serve hot.

SERVES 6

Grosseto

PESCE SPADA CON PATATE

Baked Swordfish with Potatoes

Although swordfish is generally fished in southern Italy, it is also popular on the coast near Grosseto. There the locals prepare it in the same way as the eels that are bred at Orbetello, a village situated on a beautiful lagoon. Orbetello is also the capital of Monte Argentario, a famous resort area.

1¼ lb (600 g) boiling potatoes
6 tablespoons (3 fl oz/90 ml) extra virgin olive oil
6 pieces filleted swordfish, about 6 oz (180 g) each
2 tablespoons chopped fresh rosemary
3 tablespoons fine dry bread crumbs
3 ripe tomatoes, peeled and sliced
salt and freshly ground black pepper
1 cup (8 fl oz/240 ml) dry white wine

In a saucepan, boil the potatoes in salted water to cover until tender, about 30 minutes. Drain the potatoes, then peel and slice them.

Preheat an oven to 350°F (180°C). Pour 3 tablespoons of the olive oil into an ovenproof earthenware dish. Arrange the potato slices in overlapping concentric circles in the bottom of the dish. Lay the fish on top of the potatoes and sprinkle with the rosemary and bread crumbs. Place the tomato slices on the fish and season to taste with salt and pepper. Drizzle the remaining 3 tablespoons olive oil over the top and pour in the wine. Bake for 20 minutes.

Serve hot directly from the dish.

SERVES 6

Arezzo

Arista al Ramerino

Roast Pork Loin with Rosemary

Roast pork loin is a traditional Sunday lunch in Arezzo. In spring it is served with peas and artichokes; in the winter, cubed, peeled potatoes are added to the roasting pan with the pork during the last half hour of cooking.

4 lb (1.8 kg) pork loin on the bone
2 tablespoons chopped fresh rosemary, plus 4 fresh rosemary sprigs
3 garlic cloves, chopped
salt and freshly ground black pepper
¼ cup (2 fl oz/60 ml) extra virgin olive oil

❧ Preheat an oven to 350°F (180°C).
❧ Using a sharp knife, cut the meat from the bone in a single piece, working very carefully, or ask your butcher to do it. Reserve the rack of bones.
❧ In a small bowl, mix together the chopped rosemary, garlic and salt and pepper to taste. Using a larding needle or something similar, make a hole in the center of the meat through its entire length. Fill this cavity with the rosemary mixture.
❧ Lay the meat back on the bone, place the rosemary sprigs along the top and tie the meat and sprigs to the bone with kitchen string.
❧ Pour the olive oil into a roasting pan and place the meat in it, fat side up. Place in the oven and roast for about 1½ hours, turning occasionally to brown on all sides.
❧ Remove the roast from the oven and snip off the string. Lift the meat from the bone and carve it. Arrange the pork on a platter and serve.

SERVES 6

Arezzo

Braciole col Cavolo

Braised Pork with Cabbage

This particularly hearty dish is prepared after the first frosts, when the black cabbage is at its tastiest. Savoy cabbage may be used as a substitute.

6 slices lean pork, about 6 oz (180 g) each
2 lb (900 g) black cabbage or Savoy cabbage
2 tablespoons extra virgin olive oil
2 garlic cloves
¼ cup (2 fl oz/60 ml) dry white wine
salt and freshly ground black pepper

❧ With a meat mallet, gently flatten the pork slices to about ⅛ in (3 mm) thick.
❧ Remove and discard the hard stalks from the cabbage and slice the leaves thinly.
❧ In a large skillet over moderate heat, warm the olive oil. Add the pork and garlic and cook until the pork is lightly browned on both sides, about 5 minutes' total cooking time. Pour the wine over the meat and add the cabbage. Lower the heat, cover the skillet and cook for another 30 minutes, adding a little water if necessary to keep the meat moist.
❧ Season to taste with salt and pepper. Transfer to a platter and serve immediately.

SERVES 6

Roast Pork Loin with Rosemary (top) and Braised Pork with Cabbage (bottom)

Siena

SPIEDINI ALLA CHIANTIGIANA

Skewered Pork with Sausage

Every butcher in Chianti has his own version of mixed skewered meats, to which some add tomatoes and slices of sweet pepper (capsicum). The classic version, however, sandwiches pieces of bread between the fattier meats. The bread turns crisp and tasty during the cooking.

6 oz (180 g) sweet Italian sausages
6 oz (180 g) *pancetta*
6 oz (180 g) pork tenderloin (fillet)
6 oz (180 g) pork liver
10 oz (300 g) coarse country bread
salt and freshly ground black pepper
¼ cup (2 fl oz/60 ml) extra virgin olive oil

❧ Preheat an oven to 350°F (180°C).
❧ Cut the sausages, *pancetta,* pork tenderloin, pork liver and bread into pieces about 1½ in (4 cm) long and ¼ in (6 mm) thick. Thread the meats onto 6 metal skewers, alternating the various types and always putting a piece of bread between pieces of bacon and sausage. Sprinkle with salt and pepper.
❧ Select a shallow baking dish slightly narrower than the length of the skewers. Balance the skewers on the rim, with the points resting securely on either side so that the cooking juices will fall into the dish. Brush the meats with the olive oil. Place in the oven and cook for about 30 minutes, turning the skewers and brushing them frequently with the juices.
❧ Arrange the skewers on a platter and serve hot.

SERVES 6

Siena

COSTOLECCIO ALLA GRIGLIA

Grilled Spareribs

In Sienese farmhouses, spareribs are often cooked over an open fire. They absorb the flavor of the wood and are juicy and tender. They may also be grilled under a broiler.

4 lb (1.8 kg) pork spareribs
salt and freshly ground black pepper
3 tablespoons extra virgin olive oil

❧ Divide the spareribs into 6 equal pieces and place in a shallow plate. Season to taste with salt and pepper and brush with the oil. Marinate at room temperature for 30 minutes.
❧ Meanwhile, prepare a fire in a charcoal grill. Remove the ribs from the plate, reserving the olive oil. Place the ribs on the grill rack over a hot fire and cook, turning a few times and brushing with the reserved oil until done, about 15 minutes.
❧ Arrange the ribs on a serving platter and serve very hot.

SERVES 6

Lucca

AGNELLO COI CARCIOFI

Lamb with Artichokes

The best cut for this recipe is a leg with a few chops. In Italy we slaughter lamb when it is still quite young and weighs no more than 20 to 25 lb (10 to 12 kg). If you cannot find such young lamb, you can use just the leg. For the artichokes, choose small ones that have been trimmed but left whole.

6 tablespoons (3 fl oz/90 ml) extra virgin olive oil
1 garlic clove
5 lb (2.5 kg) leg of lamb, boned and cut into serving pieces
juice of 1 lemon
6 globe artichokes
1 cup (8 fl oz/240 ml) dry white wine
salt and freshly ground black pepper
1 tablespoon chopped fresh flat-leaf (Italian) parsley

Skewered Pork with Sausage (left) and Grilled Spareribs (right)

❧ In a heavy pan over moderate heat, warm the olive oil and garlic. Add the lamb and cook, turning the lamb so that it browns on all sides, about 10 minutes.

❧ Meanwhile, fill a large bowl with water and add the lemon juice. Cut the stalks off the artichokes. Remove the tough outer leaves and cut away any sharp leaf points. Cut the artichokes into quarters and remove and discard the furry chokes. Immediately drop them into the bowl of water to prevent discoloration. When all of the artichokes have been cut, drain them and dry with absorbent paper towels.

❧ Add the artichoke to the lamb and cook for 10 minutes. Add the wine to the pan and cook for another 10 minutes, adding a little water if the juices become too dry. Season to taste with salt and pepper.

❧ Arrange the lamb and artichokes on a platter, sprinkle with the parsley and serve.

SERVES 6 *Photograph pages 384–85*

Lucca

ROGNONI COL BATTUTO

Kidneys with Chopped Vegetables and Pancetta

Unless kidneys are cooked very quickly they become tough. In Lucca they are sautéed with chopped vegetables and pancetta. *Liver is excellent cooked in the same way.*

2 lb (900 g) veal kidneys
3 oz (90 g) *pancetta,* chopped
1 tablespoon finely chopped carrot
1 tablespoon finely chopped fresh flat-leaf (Italian) parsley
1 tablespoon finely chopped yellow onion
3 tablespoons extra virgin olive oil
⅓ cup (3 fl oz/90 ml) dry white wine
salt and freshly ground black pepper

❧ Cut the kidneys in half lengthwise; remove the fat and hard white core and the thin membrane covering the lobes. Cut into slices about ¼ in (6 mm) thick; set aside.
❧ In a small skillet over moderate heat, warm the *pancetta.* Add the carrot, parsley and onion and fry gently until the *pancetta* and vegetables are slightly golden, about 3 minutes. Keep warm.
❧ In a large skillet over moderate heat, warm the olive oil. Add the kidney slices and sauté until golden on one side, about 2 minutes. Turn over gently and sauté the other side until golden. Add the wine, scrape the browned bits from the bottom of the skillet and cook over high heat until the wine evaporates, about 1 minute. Season to taste with salt and pepper. Add the vegetables and *pancetta* and stir to blend the flavors.
❧ Transfer to a platter and serve immediately.

SERVES 6

Grosseto

SCOTTIGLIA DI CINGHIALE

Mixed Wild Boar Stew

The hunting season for wild boar is from November to the end of January, and as there is an abundance of wild boar in the Maremma, there are many different ways of cooking it. In this recipe the less choice cuts are traditionally used, so they must be cooked for a fairly long time.

4 lb (1.8 kg) mixed wild boar cuts, such as leg or loin chops, including bone
¼ cup (2 fl oz/60 ml) extra virgin olive oil
2 garlic cloves, chopped
salt and freshly ground black pepper
1 carrot, peeled and chopped
1 celery stalk, trimmed and chopped
1 tablespoon chopped fresh flat-leaf (Italian) parsley
1 tablespoon chopped fresh thyme
small piece of dried chili
1 cup (8 fl oz/240 ml) dry red wine
1¼ lb cup (600 g) plum (egg) tomatoes, peeled and chopped
1 cup (8 fl oz/240 ml) light meat stock (recipe on page 325)

❧ Cut the meat into bite-sized pieces. In a roasting pan over moderate heat, warm the olive oil. Add the garlic and fry gently for a few minutes. Add the wild boar and brown on all sides, about 10 minutes. Season to taste with salt and pepper.
❧ Add the carrot, celery, parsley, thyme and chili. Stir well and pour in the wine. Lower the heat and cook until the wine evaporates, about 10 minutes. Add the tomatoes and cook for 2 hours, gradually adding the stock when the pan becomes too dry.
❧ Ladle the meat and sauce onto a platter and serve.

SERVES 6

Kidneys with Chopped Vegetables and Pancetta (left) and Pork Liver with Fennel (right)

Mixed Wild Boar Stew

Siena

FEGATELLI DI MAIALE AL FINOCCHIO

Pork Liver with Fennel

Pork liver is cooked in a variety of ways around Siena, sometimes with pieces of bread and occasionally with sausage or other types of meat.

2 tablespoons fennel seed
salt and freshly ground black pepper
2 lb (900 g) pork liver
1 piece caul fat, about 20 in (50 cm) long
3 tablespoons extra virgin olive oil

❧ In a small dish, mix together the fennel seed with salt and pepper to taste. Cut the pork liver into 18 pieces and sprinkle it with the fennel mixture.

❧ Cut the caul fat into 18 pieces and wrap a piece of the fat around each piece of pork liver, fastening it in place with a wooden toothpick.

❧ In a large skillet over moderate heat, warm the olive oil. Add the pork liver and cook, gently turning the meat from time to time so that it browns all over, until tender but still pink, about 10 minutes.

❧ Transfer the liver pieces to a platter and serve very hot.

SERVES 6

Drowned Veal Escalopes

Arezzo

BRACIOLINE AFFOGATE

Drowned Veal Escalopes

This dish is cooked very slowly over low heat so that the sauce is thick and the full flavor of the mushrooms comes through.

6 slices dried *porcini* mushrooms
6 boneless veal escalopes, about 6 oz (180 g) each
2 tablespoons extra virgin olive oil
2 garlic cloves, chopped
1 tablespoon fresh thyme
1 lb (450 g) plum (egg) tomatoes, peeled and chopped
salt and freshly ground black pepper

❧ In a small bowl, soak the mushrooms in warm water to cover for 30 minutes. Drain the mushrooms, reserving the liquid, and squeeze out any excess moisture. Chop the mushrooms and set aside. Strain and reserve the liquid.

❧ With a meat mallet, gently flatten the escalopes until they are about ¼ in (3 mm) thick. In a large skillet over high heat, warm the olive oil and garlic. Add the escalopes and cook, turning, until they begin to brown, about 5 minutes. Add the mushrooms, thyme and tomatoes. Cover the skillet, lower the heat and simmer very gently until the sauce is thick, about 1 hour, adding a few tablespoons of the mushroom liquid if the pan becomes too dry.

❧ Season to taste with salt and pepper. Arrange on a platter and serve.

SERVES 6

Livorno

Maiale Ubriaco

Drunken Pork

In Livorno in summertime, pork chops are generally grilled over an open fire and sprinkled with a little garlic and rosemary. On winter days, when the weather is cool and rosemary is more difficult to find, these chops are popular served with mashed potatoes.

6 pork chops, about 8 oz (240 g) each
1 tablespoon extra virgin olive oil
½ teaspoon fennel seed
2 bay leaves
½ cup (4 fl oz/120 ml) dry red wine
salt and freshly ground black pepper

❧ In a skillet large enough to hold all 6 chops in a single layer, warm the olive oil over moderate heat. Add the pork chops; sprinkle them with the fennel seed and top with the bay leaves. Cook for 3 minutes, turn the chops and cook for another 3 minutes on the second side.

❧ Pour in the wine and continue cooking until it evaporates, about 2 minutes. Season to taste with salt and pepper.

❧ Arrange the chops on a platter and serve.

SERVES 6

Siena

Costolette di Maiale al Dragoncello

Fried Pork Chops with Tarragon

Here pork chops are fried quickly and seasoned with fresh tarragon, the most commonly used herb in Siena. This popularity is probably due to the fact that tarragon grows well in the area and has a strong aroma, which may be the result of the quality of the soil.

6 pork chops, about 8 oz (240 g) each
3 tablespoons extra virgin olive oil
½ cup (4 fl oz/120 ml) dry white wine
salt and freshly ground black pepper
3 tablespoons fresh tarragon leaves

❧ In a skillet large enough to hold all the chops in one layer, warm the olive oil over moderate heat. Cook the chops until they begin to turn golden, about 5 minutes on each side.

❧ Add the wine, season to taste with salt and pepper, and sprinkle with the tarragon. Cook a few minutes, turning once, to allow the chops to absorb the flavors and the wine to evaporate a little.

❧ Transfer the chops to a platter and serve hot.

SERVES 6

Photograph pages 384–85

Drunken Pork

VENEZIA
SEZ MAGEN

LIVORNO

LIVORNO

A few years ago the Italian and foreign press devoted a great deal of space to a story that divided the most authoritative art experts. Two stone heads had been fished out of a canal in Livorno and the vast majority of experts pronounced them to be the work of Modigliani, the great Livornese artist. Only after this attribution had been officially accepted did three young men appear on the scene to declare that they had created the heads with the help of an electric drill. To prove their point, they sculpted two more heads live on television. With the exception of several highly embarrassed art experts, the whole of Italy laughed. And those who did not already know the people of Livorno discovered that this is the most ironical and anarchic city in Italy.

This spirit is reproduced in Livorno's most famous recipe, *cacciucco alla livornese,* a soup of mixed fish of the cheaper kinds that deservedly has made Livorno known to cooks the world over. But before going into details about *cacciucco,* it should be explained why the Livornese are like their soup—a great mixture of people who have lived together in harmony for centuries.

In the fourteenth century, when Livorno was just a small village in the middle of the marshes, the Pisans decided to build a port there because their own was silting up. Later Pisa was conquered by Genoa and, in 1451, the Genoese sold the port of Livorno to the Florentines. Cosimo I, a Medici, fortified it, and a village almost abandoned because of malaria was quickly

Left: Weekend sunworshippers and water-lovers flock to the Piazzale Mascagni, the seaside terrace of Livorno. Previous pages: The finish line of Livorno's annual Palio Marinaro boat race. Held every summer, the race takes place between local teams of rowers in traditional boats.

transformed into the second most important city in Tuscany. Later Ferdinand I decided to build a new city close to the original one. He also constructed a new port, which to this day is called the Medici Port and is one of the most important in the Mediterranean.

In order to attract immigrants to the town, the Medicis granted freedom of residence, and Livorno became an open zone for both people and merchandise. It attracted Jews escaping from Spanish persecution, Greeks, Armenians, Englishmen and Dutchmen, as well as outlaws who were safe from arrest there. In other words, Livorno was a haven for all those seeking refuge or an open market. The population rose rapidly, and by the end of 1600 there were twenty thousand inhabitants, of whom five thousand were Jews. There were also many Turks. It was out of this great melting pot that the Livornese, a very particular type of Tuscan, emerged.

It is perhaps not surprising that the Italian Communist Party was established here in 1921. Nor that the most bawdy and irreverent satirical magazine in Italy, *Il Vernacoliere,* is published in Livorno and that only Tuscans can understand what it means.

Sadly, the old town was almost completely destroyed by bombs during the last war. The Livornese spirit survived, however, as did the beauty of its women, who seem to have been blessed with the best of this racial mélange. The most frequently heard interjection is still "deh," said to be a mispronunciation of the English "the."

And now back to *cacciucco,* the culinary equivalent of this great mixture. As with all historic recipes, several different theories about its origin have been handed down. The name seems to come from the Turkish word *kucuk,* which means "small." Legend has it that Homer's heroes dined on *cacciucco* and that the Phoenicians took it from Asia Minor to Greece, and from there to Provence in France, where it became bouillabaisse. Even Cicero and Caesar are said to have been addicted to it. In Livorno it was undoubtedly improved by the guardians of the watchtowers, whose only pastime was fishing. When their catch was small, bread was added. With the discovery of the Americas came tomatoes and chilies, and so we arrive at the modern *cacciucco.* It was born unpretentious and so it has remained.

Livorno is an important fishing center, on any scale. The day's catch may be used to make cacciucco, *the renowned fish soup from Livorno that is said to have inspired similar creations in other countries.*

There are, of course, many other excellent recipes from Livorno, both those based on fish and those that draw upon the produce of the rich hinterland. But the sea certainly dominates, especially as some of the most beautiful islands in all of Italy lie off the Livorno coast. Napoleon was held prisoner on the isle of Elba, where there is still very limited production of the ancient Aleatico and Moscato wines. Then there is Giglio, greenest of islands, with its rare Ansonica vines, and Capraia, heady with the scent of myrtle and mastic. The well-protected island of Montecristo was made famous by Dumas, while Gorgona and Pianosa are private paradises.

The fish recipes range from *gianchetti* (baby sardines and anchovies) and *cee* (baby eels) to *triglie alla livornese* (red rock mullet in tomato sauce) and from *favolli* (a soup made with large crabs) to the classic *spaghetti alle vongole* (spaghetti tossed with clam sauce). Delicious cooked octopus continue to be hawked by fishermen in the streets of Piombino and on Elba in Portoferraio. And on Elba, it is still maintained that cuttlefish with artichokes was one of Napoleon's favorite dishes.

Bordatino, a Livornese soup, was invented on the old sailing ships but contains no fish. Nowadays it is enriched with fresh vegetables, but originally it was simply a cornmeal mush diluted with red bean soup—ingredients that could easily be stored on ships. There are two explanations for the name. The first is that it was so-called because it was made on board. The other comes from a rough, red-striped cotton cloth of the same name that is used for making aprons. When the bean soup is stirred into the cornmeal, it forms a pattern of red streaks that recalls the cloth. Another Livornese soup, *minestra con la palla,* is made with cauliflower, which is much used here, both raw and cooked as well as pickled in vinegar.

The famous artichokes from Antignano are so big they are called *mazzeferrate,* or "cudgels." They are sometimes cut open nearly to the bottom, stuffed with chopped meat, bread crumbs and egg, dipped in flour and egg, and then fried.

Interestingly enough, couscous was once very common in Livorno, where it is called *cuscussa.* It was originally brought back by sailors who visited North African ports, although today there are no official recipes for it. It is seldom made now and is served with anything the cook chooses, including fish, but semolina from the best durum wheat is always used.

The queen of poultry is the famous leghorn hen. In the nineteenth century these native fowl were taken from Livorno to England for crossbreeding and they came back greatly improved. Although their name is foreign, leghorns are the most celebrated chickens in Tuscany. Black or white with yellow feet, they are prized for their tender meat and are usually cooked either *alla diavola* (flattened and grilled) or with cheese, a recipe from Elba said to have been left by Napoleon's court.

It is above all in the realm of cakes and other desserts that the strong Jewish culinary influence is evident in the Livornese kitchen. *Bollo,* a sweet dough enriched with sugar and egg and flavored with aniseed liqueur, is one example. Another is *orecchie di Amman,* which are much

Livorno, often called Leghorn in English, is a major Mediterranean seaport. The town was developed by the Medici family in the late sixteeth century as a free port, bringing goods from around the world to the Grand Duchy of Tuscany.

like the *cenci* (fried biscuits) found in the rest of Tuscany. They take their name from Haman, a favorite of King Ahasuerus of Persia in the biblical book of Esther. Haman advised the king to destroy the Jews, but he failed in his terrible intent and was himself killed. The vendetta continues and "Haman's ears" are still regularly eaten. Then there is Mount Sinai, a typical flourless Passover cake made of almonds. Preserved rosehips, another typical sweet, are, however, of Greek origin.

No visit to Livorno is complete without tasting the famous *ponce alla livornese,* a mispronunciation of punch. The Bar Civili in Livorno is frequented by everyone from bejeweled ladies to stevedores because, although it is far from elegant, the traditional punch is served there. It is prepared in a thick, wide glass that is first half-filled with excellent coffee. Then a spoonful of sugar dissolved under the steam from the coffee machine is added, followed by rum and a slice of lemon peel. Fine Caribbean rum is not used, but rather the dark rum specially made for punch.

The Livornese have two nicknames for their punch—a torpedo and a bomb. Sailors have long found it a very useful drink in winter, when they come ashore shivering from the cold of the sea. At one time anyone with a hoarse voice was described as having a rum-punch voice. That was when the drink was laced with *caramellato,* a mixture of sugar and pure alcohol. Using it was against the law, but all the barkeeps kept it hidden and secretly poured it into the rum. After all, was this pleasant coastal town a haven for outlaws or wasn't it?

LE VERDURE

Tuscan cooks have always found inventive uses for the simplest ingredients.

Le Verdure

Although nutritionists insist that vegetables are vital to our health, fewer and fewer vegetables seem to appear on Italy's restaurant tables these days. It is often hard to find anything more than the ubiquitous—and harmful—fried potato, a few leaves of salad, and vegetables that have been boiled without much enthusiasm.

In Tuscany, however, vegetables have always been important. They are a principal ingredient of molds, omelets and loaves (see Piatti di Mezzo chapter), soups and sauces, as well as some meat and fish recipes.

The region's traditional vegetable dishes are not available everywhere, of course, but in small trattorias it is not unusual to rediscover familiar flavors and fragrances. A good example of this in Lucchesia is *frissoglia,* a subtle combination of zucchini and their flowers, tomatoes and green beans. One of the specialties of Elba is *gurguglione,* a mixture of bell peppers, eggplants and zucchini reminiscent of *ratatouille.* Lunigiana boasts a very special vegetable loaf made of potatoes, onions and eggs.

Admittedly these are distinctly local dishes, but the average Tuscan restaurant offers a far greater variety of vegetables than its equivalent in northern Italy. There are usually zucchini, green beans, asparagus and artichokes prepared in various ways, as well as Swiss chard, spinach and cabbage in many guises.

Above all, the Tuscan bean is never missing from a menu. It may be cooked with sausage or with pork fat, in a flask with just a little garlic and sage, or *all'uccelletto,* with tomatoes. When beans taste truly excellent, they most likely were cooked in a terra-cotta pot over very low heat. Sometimes they are done in the traditional *fagioliera,* an earthenware jar with a narrow mouth and a wide base. The more esoteric *fagioli al fiasco* is prepared in an old wine flask *(fiasco)* buried in the ashes and embers of a dying fire. If you want to experiment with this method, make quite sure you have an old-fashioned

Beans play an important role in the peasant-influenced cucina *of Tuscany. The most popular are white* cannellini *beans.*

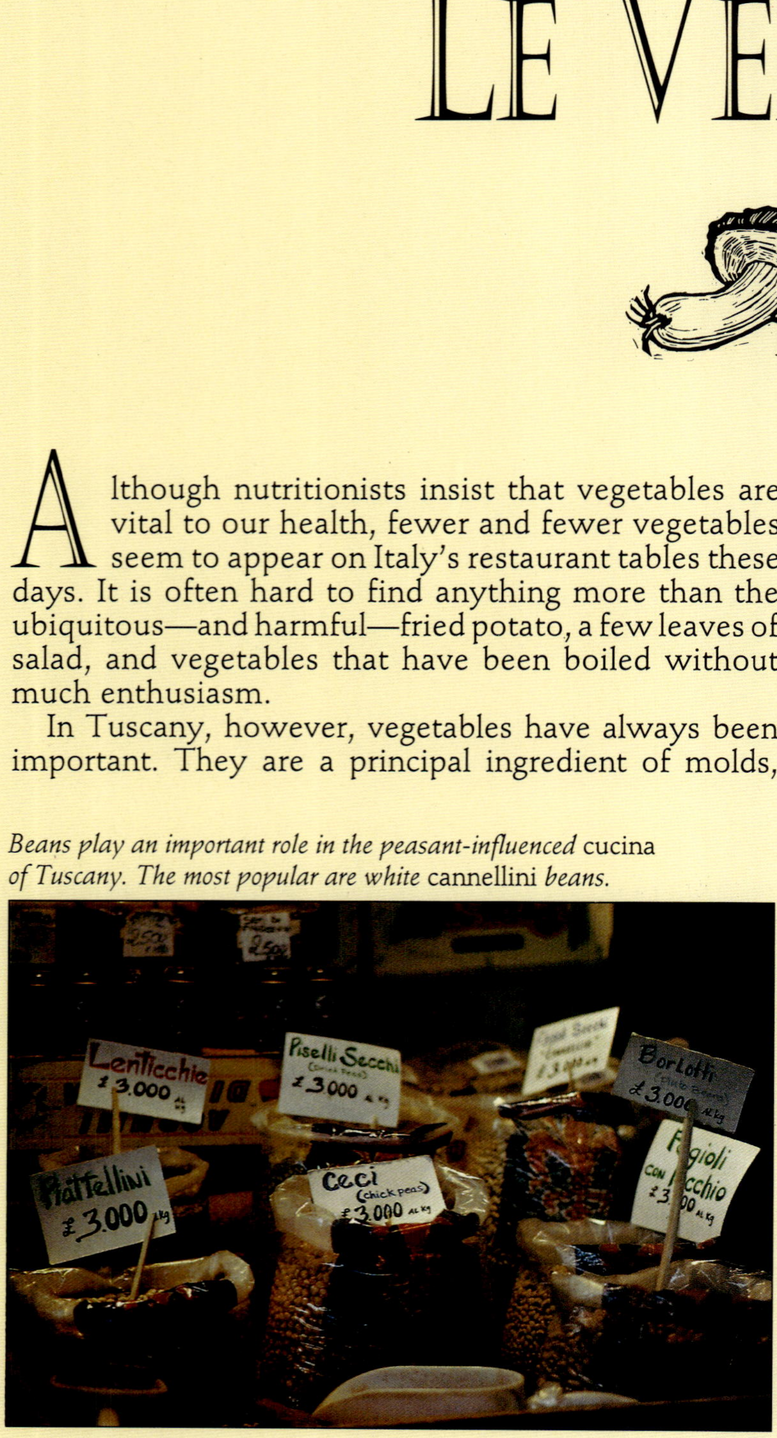

Previous pages: Potatoes Braised in White Wine (page 448), Braised Onions (page 440), Beans and Tomato (rear, page 444).

Shoppers in Tuscany visit the market frequently and choose only the freshest ingredients, planning their meals around what looks best that day.

hand-blown *fiasco,* because the industrially produced flasks sometimes explode in the heat and you might find yourself with a real fiasco. It is probably safer to stick with a *fagioliera* or any other deep earthenware pot.

Broad (fava) beans, or *baccelli* as they are called in Tuscany, are a part of the venerable bean tradition. Dried broad beans are reported to have been found in Egyptian tombs, as well as in prehistoric archaeological sites. Until recently they were considered rather plebeian and left to the farmers, but now they are enjoyed by everyone. When they have just come into season in May, the young, tender beans are presented raw with sheep's milk cheese as an antipasto. The larger ones are stewed with tomatoes and onion and served as a side dish.

Although not botanically a vegetable, mushrooms are treated like one and have always been very popular in Tuscany, where, in some parts, they are found in abundance. The most sought-after mushrooms are *porcini,* meaning "little pigs," so-called because of their shape. They are eaten either fresh or are dried for the winter. Mushrooms, like chestnuts, were once part of the local economy, but recently imports from eastern European countries, particularly Yugoslavia, have come onto the market.

Mushrooms are grilled or fried, served on polenta and pasta, baked with potatoes and parsley, or fried with a little tomato. Although *porcini* are the most highly prized, many other field mushrooms are gathered on the Tuscan hills. Mushroom addicts from every walk of life are prepared to rise at dawn to hunt for them in hidden places that they would not divulge to their closest friends. There is an old saying that only on his deathbed does a Tuscan farmer reveal to his favorite son the exact location of his mushroom ground.

Arezzo

CAROTE IN STUFATO

Braised Carrots

These carrots are so nutritious that woodchoppers often carry them into the forests and have them for lunch on toasted bread. They are more commonly served, however, with lamb or rabbit.

⅓ cup (3 fl oz/90 ml) extra virgin olive oil
4 oz (120 g) *pancetta,* cut into small pieces
1 yellow onion, chopped
1 garlic clove, chopped
2 lb (900 g) carrots, peeled and sliced ⅛ in (2 mm) thick
1 tablespoon chopped fresh flat-leaf (Italian) parsley
⅓ cup (3 fl oz/90 ml) light meat stock (recipe on page 325)
salt and freshly ground black pepper

❧ In a skillet over low heat, warm the olive oil. Add the *pancetta,* onion and garlic and fry gently, stirring frequently, until the onions are translucent, about 5 minutes. Add the carrots and parsley and stir well.

❧ Cook gently for 20 minutes, adding just enough of the stock to keep the carrots moist.

❧ Season to taste with salt and pepper. Spoon the carrots into a serving dish and serve hot.

SERVES 6

Siena

CIPOLLATA

Braised Onions

Generally this dish is prepared with sweet purple or red onions, which can be stored all winter without sprouting. If unavailable, ordinary yellow onions may be used.

2 lb (900 g) purple onions
⅓ cup (3 fl oz/90 ml) extra virgin olive oil
1 cup (8 fl oz/240 ml) dry white wine
½ tablespoon granulated sugar
1 tablespoon fennel seed
salt and freshly ground black pepper

❧ Slice the onions. If you are using very strong-flavored onions, soak the slices in cold water to cover for about 1 hour. Drain and dry with absorbent paper towels.

❧ In a heavy pot over moderate heat, warm the olive oil. Add the onions and cook, stirring carefully, until they begin to change color, about 5 minutes. Add the wine and sprinkle with the sugar and fennel seed. Season to taste with salt and pepper, cover and cook over very low heat until all the liquid evaporates, about 10 minutes.

❧ Spoon the onions onto a serving dish and serve hot.

SERVES 6 *Photograph pages 436–37*

Braised Carrots

Puréed Chick-peas

Grosseto

PASSATO DI CECI

Puréed Chick-peas

Around Grosseto, unlike the rest of Tuscany, chick-peas are just as popular as cannellini *beans, and, when dressed with abundant olive oil, are equally delicious.*

2⅛ cups (14 oz/420 g) dried chick-peas (garbanzos)
1 garlic clove
6 tablespoons (3 fl oz/90 ml) extra virgin olive oil
3 plum (egg) tomatoes, peeled and puréed
salt and freshly ground black pepper

❧ Soak the chick-peas in water to cover for 12 hours.
❧ Drain the chick-peas and place them in a heavy pot. Add the garlic and water to cover and bring slowly to a boil over low heat. Simmer gently until the chick-peas are tender, about 1½ hours.
❧ Drain the chick-peas and put them through the fine disc of a food mill; set aside.
❧ In a heavy pot over low heat, warm 3 tablespoons of the olive oil. Add the puréed chick-peas and the tomato and season to taste with salt and pepper. Cook over low heat, stirring constantly, until the purée is rid of excess moisture.
❧ Arrange the purée in little mounds on a serving platter and make a small hollow in the center of each mound. Pour a little of the remaining 3 tablespoons olive oil into each hollow and sprinkle to taste with salt and pepper. Serve immediately.

SERVES 6

Grosseto

Cipolle alla Grossetana

Baked Stuffed Onions, Grosseto Style

Spices rather than herbs are used for seasoning these baked onions, which identifies this as a fairly old recipe. The spices give the onions a deep, complex taste that goes well with the local wild boar.

6 large purple or yellow onions in their skins
3 oz (90 g) beef, finely chopped
3 oz (90 g) sweet Italian sausage, skinned and crumbled
1 egg
pinch of freshly grated nutmeg
1 whole clove, crushed
pinch of ground cinnamon
salt and freshly ground black pepper
1 tablespoon extra virgin olive oil

Left to right: Cabbage Braised in White Wine, St. Anna Beans and Baked Stuffed Onions

¼ cup (2 fl oz/60 ml) dry white wine
½ cup (4 fl oz/120 ml) water

❧ Preheat an oven to 350°F (180°C).
❧ Bring a large saucepan of water to a boil. Add the unpeeled onions and boil for about 10 minutes. Drain and, when cool enough to handle, peel the onions and cut them in half horizontally.
❧ Dig out about half of the center of each onion half; set the hollowed-out halves aside. Finely chop the onion centers you have removed.
❧ In a bowl, combine the chopped onion, beef, sausage, egg, nutmeg, clove and cinnamon. Season to taste with salt and pepper. Fill the cavities in the onion halves with this mixture.
❧ In a baking dish in which the stuffed onions will fit without crowding, pour in the olive oil, wine and water. Arrange the onions in the dish. Bake until the onions are tender when pierced with a fork, about 20 minutes.
❧ Arrange the onions on a platter and serve hot.

SERVES 6

Grosseto

Cavolo Strascicato

Cabbage Braised in White Wine

The assertive flavor of cabbage goes well with the red meat eaten in this area. Wild fennel is used for seasoning, but if it is not available, fennel seed may be substituted.

2½ lb (1.2 kg) Savoy cabbage
3 tablespoons extra virgin olive oil
2 oz (60 g) *pancetta,* chopped
salt and freshly ground black pepper
3 sprigs wild fennel or 1 teaspoon fennel seed
½ cup (4 fl oz/120 ml) dry white wine

❧ Remove and discard the hard stalks from the cabbage and slice the leaves into narrow strips.
❧ In a heavy pot over moderate heat, warm the olive oil. Add the *pancetta* and fry gently until transparent, about 5 minutes. Add the cabbage, stir well and cook gently for a few minutes to blend the flavors.
❧ Season to taste with salt and pepper. Sprinkle with the fennel and pour in the wine. Cover and cook over low heat until the cabbage is very tender, about 20 minutes. Check from time to time and add a couple of tablespoons of water if the pan becomes too dry.
❧ Arrange the cabbage on a platter and serve hot.

SERVES 6

Arezzo

Fagiolini di Sant'Anna

St. Anna Beans

Although in Italy these beans are grown only in Tuscany, they are quite popular in California, which goes to show that Tuscany and California share more than wine. St. Anna beans, which are sometimes called Chinese long beans or snake beans, are very narrow green beans that measure about 16 in (40 cm) in length.

3 tablespoons extra virgin olive oil
3 garlic cloves, chopped
2 lb (900 g) St. Anna beans or runner beans, trimmed
10 oz (300 g) plum (egg) tomatoes, peeled and chopped
salt and freshly ground black pepper

❧ In a large skillet over low heat, warm the olive oil. Add the garlic and fry gently until translucent, about 3 minutes. Add the beans and tomatoes and season to taste with salt and pepper. Lower the heat and cook until the beans are tender, about 15 minutes.
❧ Transfer the beans to a serving dish and serve hot.

SERVES 6

Siena

FAGIOLI ALL'UCCELLETTO

Beans and Tomato

Fagioli all'uccelletto *is undoubtedly the most popular vegetable dish in Siena and is enjoyed all over Tuscany. In Siena this dish is always served with pork liver (recipe on page 427).*

2⅛ cups (14 oz/420 g) dried *cannellini* beans
6 tablespoons (3 fl oz/80 ml) extra virgin olive oil
3 garlic cloves
1 large handful of fresh sage leaves
1 lb (480 g) plum (egg) tomatoes, peeled and chopped
salt and freshly ground black pepper

❧ In a bowl, soak the beans in water to cover for 12 hours.

❧ Drain the beans and transfer them to a heavy saucepan. Add 2 tablespoons of the olive oil and water just to cover. Bring slowly to a boil over low heat. Simmer gently for 1½ hours, by which time the water should be absorbed and the beans will be almost the consistency of porridge.

❧ Meanwhile, in a saucepan over low heat, warm the remaining 4 tablespoons (2 fl oz/60 ml) olive oil. Add the garlic and sage and fry gently until they start to change color, about 3 minutes. Add the tomatoes and cook over gentle heat until some of the liquid evaporates, about 10 minutes.

❧ Transfer the beans to the saucepan containing the tomatoes and season to taste with salt and pepper. Stir and then cook over low heat for about 10 minutes to allow the flavors to blend. The final result should be rather thin. Pour into a bowl and serve very hot.

SERVES 6 *Photograph pages 436–37*

Cardoons in Sausage Sauce

Grosseto

GOBBI TRIPPATI

Cardoons in Sausage Sauce

This rich, intensely flavored dish is relished by the local people because wild boar sausages are used for the sauce. The identity of cardoons is strong enough not to be smothered by the sauce.

juice of 1 lemon
4 lb (1.8 kg) cardoons
3 tablespoons extra virgin olive oil
1 carrot, peeled and chopped
1 small yellow onion, chopped
1 celery stalk, trimmed and chopped
1 tablespoon chopped fresh flat-leaf (Italian) parsley
10 oz (300 g) wild boar sausages or sweet Italian sausages, skinned and crumbled
10 oz (300 g) plum (egg) tomatoes, peeled and chopped
¼ cup (2 fl oz/60 ml) light meat stock (recipe on page 325)
salt and freshly ground black pepper

❧ Fill a large bowl with water and add the lemon juice. Remove and discard the base from each cardoon and discard any tough stalks. Trim and discard the leaves and spurs from the tender stalks and then scrape the stalks with a small knife to remove all strings and fibers. Cut each stalk crosswise into pieces 2 in (5 cm) long and immediately drop them into the water to prevent discoloration.

❧ In a heavy pot over low heat, warm the olive oil. Add the carrot, onion, celery, parsley and sausage and fry gently until the carrot is cooked, about 10 minutes.

❧ Drain the cardoon pieces and add to the pot along with the tomatoes. Stir well and add the stock. Cook until the cardoons are very tender and the sauce has thickened, about 20 minutes.

❧ Season to taste with salt and pepper. Transfer to a serving dish and serve hot.

SERVES 6

Livorno

GURGUGLIONE

Sautéed Mixed Vegetables

This savory vegetable medley resembles certain southern European dishes, probably due to Livorno's sea trade with the Middle East and with Spain.

3 tablespoons extra virgin olive oil
3 garlic cloves, chopped
1 small yellow onion, chopped
2 Asian (slender) eggplants (aubergines), trimmed and cut into ¾-in (2-cm) cubes
3 zucchini (courgettes), trimmed and sliced ¼ in (6 mm) thick
3 yellow or red bell peppers (capsicums), seeded, deveined and cut into long, narrow strips
10 oz (300 g) ripe plum (egg) tomatoes, peeled and chopped
salt and freshly ground black pepper

❧ In a heavy pot over low heat, warm the olive oil. Add the garlic and onion and fry gently until translucent, about 5 minutes.

❧ Add the eggplants, zucchini and peppers and cook, stirring frequently, for 3 minutes.

❧ Add the tomatoes and season to taste with salt and pepper. Cover and cook over gentle heat until the flavors are well blended, about 40 minutes. If necessary, add a little water to keep the vegetables moist.

❧ Spoon into a serving dish and serve hot.

SERVES 6

Sautéed Mixed Vegetables

Roast Diced Potatoes (left) and Artichoke Fritters (right)

Arezzo

FRITTURA DI CARCIOFI

Artichoke Fritters

Traditionally these fried artichokes are served with baby lamb at Easter. They also go well with roast chicken, or they make a satisfying supper when served with a simple omelet.

juice of 1 lemon
2½ lb (1.2 kg) globe artichokes
2 eggs
salt and freshly ground black pepper
⅔ cup (3 oz/90 g) all-purpose (plain) flour
5 cups (40 fl oz/1.2 l) extra virgin olive oil

❧ Fill a large bowl with water and add the lemon juice. Cut the stalks off the artichokes. Remove the tough outer leaves and cut away any sharp leaf points from the tops. Cut the artichokes lengthwise into eighths and remove and discard the fuzzy chokes. As each artichoke is ready, drop it into the water to prevent discoloration. When all of the artichokes have been trimmed, drain them and pat dry with absorbent paper towels.

❧ In a bowl, beat the eggs with a little salt and pepper. Dredge the artichokes in the flour and shake off any excess, then dip them in the beaten egg.

❧ Meanwhile, in a deep, heavy skillet, heat the olive oil to 350°F (180°C).

❧ A few at a time, slip the artichoke slices into the hot oil without crowding the pan. Fry until golden, about 3 minutes. With a slotted spoon, remove to absorbent paper towels to drain. Continue frying the remaining artichokes in the same manner. Serve piping hot.

SERVES 6

Siena

RAPINI IN PADELLA

Pan-Tossed Broccoli Raab

Broccoli raab is usually picked after the first frosts, when it is tender. It is dressed in various ways and often served with roast pork. At room temperature, splashed with olive oil and lemon, it is excellent.

2 lb (900 g) broccoli raab, trimmed
⅓ cup (3 fl oz/90 ml) extra virgin olive oil
3 garlic cloves
salt and freshly ground black pepper

❧ Bring a large saucepan of slightly salted water to a boil. Add the broccoli raab to the boiling water and cook for just a few minutes. Drain and immediately transfer to a bowl of iced water so that the leaves remain green. Drain and squeeze out any excess water.
❧ In a skillet over low heat, warm the olive oil. Add the garlic and fry until just golden, about 5 minutes. Add the drained greens and season to taste with salt and pepper. Fry gently over low heat, stirring occasionally, until tender, about 5 minutes. Remove and discard the garlic.
❧ Arrange the greens on a serving dish and serve hot.

SERVES 6

Arezzo

PATATE ARROSTO

Roast Diced Potatoes

Arezzo cooks believe that it is practically obligatory to present roast potatoes alongside their celebrated roast pork. The potatoes are seasoned with rosemary and garlic and are generally cooked in the pork drippings. They can, however, also be cooked in olive oil.

1 cup (8 fl oz/240 ml) extra virgin olive oil
2 lb (900 g) baking potatoes, peeled and cut into ¾-in (2-cm) dice
3 garlic cloves
2 tablespoons fresh rosemary leaves

❧ Preheat the oven to 350°F (180°C). Meanwhile, in a roasting pan, on the stovetop, warm the olive oil over moderate heat. Add the potatoes, garlic and rosemary and stir to coat all the ingredients with the oil. Transfer the pan to the oven and roast the potatoes, stirring frequently, until golden, about 40 minutes.
❧ Remove the potatoes from the oven. With a slotted spoon, transfer them to absorbent paper towels to drain. Arrange on a warm serving dish and serve immediately.

SERVES 6

Siena

FAGIOLI CON LE COTENNE

Pork and Beans

Cotenne is scalded pork rind with a lot of fat on it and is customarily cooked with dried beans. This dish is usually prepared during the grape harvest when the beans are fresh and everyone is very hungry.

2⅛ cups (14 oz/420 g) dried *cannellini* beans
1 handful of fresh sage leaves
10 oz (300 g) pork rind or *pancetta,* in one piece
3 garlic cloves
salt and freshly ground black pepper

❧ In a bowl, soak the beans in cold water to cover for 12 hours.
❧ Drain the beans and transfer them to a heavy saucepan. Add the sage and water just to cover. Bring slowly to a boil over low heat.
❧ Simmer gently for 1½ hours, by which time the water should be absorbed and the beans will be almost the consistency of porridge.
❧ Meanwhile, in a saucepan, combine the pork rind (or *pancetta*) with water to cover. Bring to a boil and boil until the pork rind is tender, about 50 minutes. Drain and cut into short, narrow strips.
❧ In a large skillet over low heat, cook the pork strips and garlic until just golden, about 5 minutes. Add the cooked beans and season to taste with salt and pepper. Stir and then cook over low heat for a few minutes to allow the flavors to blend.
❧ Pour into a serving bowl and serve hot.

SERVES 6

Pan-Tossed Broccoli Raab (left) and Pork and Beans (right)

Grosseto

TEGAMATA DI PEPERONI

Red and Yellow Peppers with Tomato and Basil

The Grosseto plains are now covered with acres of tomato and pepper plants. The peppers ripen well here and are sweet and tangy.

6 large yellow and red bell peppers (capsicums), in any combination
3 tablespoons extra virgin olive oil
2 oz (60 g) *pancetta,* chopped
3 garlic cloves, chopped
10 oz (300 g) ripe plum (egg) tomatoes, peeled and chopped
salt and freshly ground black pepper
10 fresh basil leaves

Preheat an oven to 350°F (180°C). Arrange the peppers in a shallow pan and bake for 10 minutes.

Remove the peppers and wrap them in aluminum foil. Let stand for 10 minutes. (This step will make them easy to peel.) Peel the peppers, remove the seeds and veins and cut into narrow strips.

In a skillet over moderate heat, warm the olive oil. Add the *pancetta* and fry gently until transparent, about 5 minutes. Lower the heat, add the garlic and pepper strips and cook, stirring, for 2 minutes.

Add the tomatoes, stir well and season to taste with salt and pepper. Cook over low heat until the peppers have practically disintegrated and the liquid has evaporated, about 20 minutes.

Uncover and sprinkle with the basil. Transfer to a serving platter and serve hot.

SERVES 6

Lucca

BIETOLE CON PINOLI

Swiss Chard and Pine Nuts

All along the coast from Viareggio to Pisa stand great woods of umbrella pines. These trees produce so many pine nuts that the nuts are exported all over Europe.

2 lb (900 g) Swiss chard (silverbeet)
3 tablespoons extra virgin olive oil
salt
1 handful of pine nuts

Bring a large saucepan of lightly salted water to a boil. Meanwhile, trim off the white stalks from the green Swiss chard leaves.

Add the stalks to the boiling water and boil for about 5 minutes. Add the leaves and boil for 2 minutes longer. Drain and immediately transfer to a bowl of iced water so that the leaves remain green. Drain and squeeze out any excess water.

In a skillet over moderate heat, warm the olive oil. Add the chard and fry gently, stirring occasionally, for 2 or 3 minutes to allow the flavors to blend. Season to taste with salt and pepper.

Arrange the chard on a platter and sprinkle with the pine nuts. Serve hot.

SERVES 6

Siena

PATATE ALL'UMIDO

Potatoes Braised in White Wine

These potatoes are braised in white wine and seasoned with rosemary. In some kitchens, a little tomato paste is added. They are an excellent accompaniment to meat loaf or stew.

1 tablespoon tomato paste
¼ cup (2 fl oz/60 ml) light meat stock (recipe on page 325)
3 tablespoons extra virgin olive oil
3 garlic cloves
1 fresh rosemary sprig
2 lb (900 g) boiling potatoes, peeled and sliced about ⅛ in (3 mm) thick
1 cup (8 fl oz/240 ml) dry white wine
salt and freshly ground black pepper

Dissolve the tomato paste in the stock and set aside.

In a heavy saucepan over moderate heat, warm the olive oil. Add the garlic, rosemary and potatoes and cook until the garlic is just golden, about 5 minutes.

Pour in the wine, lower the heat and continue cooking gently. As the liquid evaporates, gradually add the stock to keep the contents moist.

After about 20 minutes, the potatoes should be tender. Season to taste with salt and pepper.

Remove and discard the garlic and rosemary. Serve very hot.

SERVES 6 *Photograph pages 436–37*

Lucca

FRISSOGLIA

Green Beans and Zucchini with Flowers

In Lucchesia zucchini are picked when very young. Their flowers are considered a great delicacy. Here the zucchini are cooked with green beans and tomato and flavored with fresh basil.

10 oz (300 g) unopened zucchini (courgette) flowers
⅓ cup (3 fl oz/90 ml) extra virgin olive oil
1 garlic clove, chopped
10 oz (300 g) small zucchini (courgettes), trimmed and sliced ⅛ in (3 mm) thick
10 oz (300 g) plum (egg) tomatoes, peeled and chopped
10 oz (300 g) green beans, trimmed
1 tablespoon fresh basil leaves
salt and freshly ground black pepper

With a small, sharp knife, make a small incision in the side of each flower and remove the pistil. Cut off the stalk and set aside.

In a skillet over moderate heat, warm the olive oil. Add the garlic and zucchini and fry gently, turning the zucchini occasionally, until lightly golden, about 10 minutes. Remove the zucchini from the skillet and set aside.

Add the tomatoes, green beans and zucchini flowers to the skillet and stir well. Lower the heat and cook until nearly all the liquid evaporates, about 10 minutes.

Return the zucchini to the skillet and add the basil. Stir and then cook over low heat for 2 minutes to allow the flavors to blend. Season to taste with salt and pepper.

Transfer to a serving bowl and serve hot.

SERVES 6

Red and Yellow Peppers with Tomato and Basil, Swiss Chard and Pine Nuts, and Green Beans and Zucchini with Flowers (rear)

Siena

Fiori di Zucca

Stuffed Zucchini Flowers

Throughout spring and summer small bunches of zucchini flowers are available in all the markets of Tuscany. They are fried or stuffed. Anchovy makes a good contrast to the bloom's delicate flavor. Be sure to buy flowers that are still closed.

3 tablespoons extra virgin olive oil
36 unopened zucchini (courgette) flowers
5 oz (150 g) canned flat anchovy fillets in olive oil, drained
½ cup (2 oz/60 g) fine dry bread crumbs
freshly ground black pepper

❧ Preheat an oven to 350°F (180°C). Brush a 20-by-12-in (50-by-30-cm) baking dish with half of the olive oil.

❧ With a small, sharp knife, make a small incision in the side of each flower and remove the pistil. Cut off the stalk.

❧ In a small bowl, combine the anchovies, bread crumbs and a touch of pepper and mash together to blend well. Carefully open the incision in each flower and insert a little of the anchovy mixture. Squeeze the opening closed.

❧ Arrange the zucchini flowers in one layer in the prepared baking dish and sprinkle with the remaining olive oil. Cover the dish with aluminum foil and bake until the flowers and their stuffing are sizzling hot, about 15 minutes.

❧ Arrange the flowers on a warm serving dish. Serve very hot.

SERVES 6

Left to right: Bean Purée, Stuffed Zucchini Flowers, Green Peas with Pancetta, and Grilled Mushrooms

Firenze

PISELLI ALL'OLIO

Green Peas with Pancetta

The tiny, tender and sweet peas of Tuscany are cooked with a little sugar for quite a long time in this recipe. This permits the peas to absorb the flavor of the oil and pancetta. *They lose a little color but acquire an intense bouquet.*

2 oz (60 g) *pancetta,* chopped
7 cups (2 lb/900 g) shelled peas
3 tablespoons extra virgin olive oil
1 teaspoon granulated sugar
2 thin slices yellow onion
6 tablespoons (3 fl oz/90 ml) water
salt and freshly ground black pepper

❧ In a saucepan over low heat, cook the *pancetta* until the fat is rendered. Add the peas, olive oil, sugar, onion and the water and stir well. Season to taste with salt and pepper.
❧ Bring the peas to a gentle boil over low heat and cook until the water evaporates, about 20 minutes.
❧ Transfer to a serving dish and serve hot.

SERVES 6

Siena

FUNGHI IN GRATELLA

Grilled Mushrooms

This is the simplest and tastiest way to prepare truly fresh mushrooms. If the stalks are not perfect, cook only the caps.

2 lb (900 g) fresh *porcini* mushrooms or *shiitake* mushrooms
2 garlic cloves, chopped
3 tablespoons extra virgin olive oil
1 tablespoon fresh calamint or thyme
salt and freshly ground black pepper

❧ Prepare a fire in a charcoal grill or preheat a broiler (grill).
❧ Trim off the ends of the mushroom stems. Clean the mushrooms by wiping them with a damp cloth; do not wash them. Cut the mushrooms into slices about ¼ in (6 mm) thick.
❧ In a cup, combine the garlic, olive oil, calamint and salt and pepper to taste. Stir well. Brush the mushrooms with this mixture.
❧ Arrange the mushrooms on the grill or on a broiler pan (grill tray) and position them so that they are not too close to the source of heat. Grill for 3 minutes. Turn the mushrooms over and grill for another 3 minutes. Serve very hot.

SERVES 6

Firenze

PASSATO DI FAGIOLI

Bean Purée

In Florence puréed beans are served with a variety of meat dishes, in much the same way mashed potatoes are in other regions of Italy. In less traditional kitchens, the same purée is often used for stuffing ravioli or, diluted with stock and a little melted butter, as an excellent sauce on tagliatelle *or vegetables.*

2⅓ cups (14 oz/420 g) dried *cannellini* beans
1 handful of fresh sage leaves
6 tablespoons (3 fl oz/90 ml) extra virgin olive oil
salt and freshly ground black pepper

❧ In a bowl, soak the beans in water to cover for 12 hours.
❧ Drain the beans and place them in a saucepan. Add the sage and water to cover. Cover the pan and bring to a very gentle boil over low heat. Allow to simmer very slowly, until tender, about 1½ hours.
❧ Remove the beans from the pan and put them through a food mill fitted with a fine disc. Pour 3 tablespoons of the olive oil into a skillet, add the bean purée and place over low heat. Cook, stirring constantly, for a few minutes to allow the moisture to evaporate. Season to taste with salt and pepper.
❧ Transfer the purée to a serving dish, sprinkle with the remaining 3 tablespoons olive oil and serve hot.

SERVES 6

Livorno

CAVOLO ALL'ACCIUGATA

Braised Cabbage with Anchovies

Part of the large anchovy catch in this area is preserved in salt and used to season numerous dishes. Raw anchovies soaked in lemon juice are also popular.

2½ lb (1.2 kg) black cabbage or Savoy cabbage
3 tablespoons extra virgin olive oil
3 garlic cloves
1 cup (8 fl oz/240 ml) water
6 anchovies in salt
salt and freshly ground black pepper

❧ Remove and discard the hard stalks from the cabbage leaves and slice the leaves into strips about ¾ in (2 cm) wide.
❧ Bring a large saucepan of water to a boil. Add the cabbage and boil for 2 minutes. Drain and immediately transfer to a bowl of iced water so that the leaves remain green. Drain and set aside.
❧ In a heavy pot over low heat, warm the olive oil. Add the garlic and fry gently until translucent, about 5 minutes. Add the cabbage and the 1 cup of water. Cook over low heat until the water evaporates, about 30 minutes.
❧ Meanwhile, remove the heads from the anchovies. Rinse the salt off the anchovies under cold running water. Slit the bodies lengthwise along the belly and remove and discard the bones. Divide the anchovies into fillets. Add the anchovy fillets to the cabbage during the last 10 minutes of cooking.
❧ Season the cabbage lightly with salt and pepper. Arrange on a platter and serve hot.

SERVES 6

Firenze

PINZIMONIO

Vegetables Dipped in Oil

Pinzimonio *is the name given to the custom of eating raw vegetables dipped in oil. A variety of vegetables such as carrots, cauliflower, artichokes and radishes may be served, or simply the fennel and Belgian endive suggested here.*

1 fennel bulb
2 carrots
2 Belgian endives (witloof/chicory)
1 cup (8 fl oz/240 ml) extra virgin olive oil
salt and freshly ground black pepper

❧ Trim the base of the fennel bulb and cut the bulb into 6 wedges. Peel the carrots and cut them into slender sticks. Trim the Belgian endive and separate the leaves.
❧ Arrange the vegetables on a serving dish. Divide the oil among 6 little bowls. Season each portion with a touch of salt and pepper.
❧ Place the dish of vegetables in the center of the table and pass around the bowls of oil.

SERVES 6

Braised Cabbage with Anchovies

Vegetables Dipped in Oil

Parslied Potatoes (top), Fried Green Tomatoes and Braised Mushrooms (bottom)

Lucca

POMODORI FRITTI

Fried Green Tomatoes

Slightly sour, hard green tomatoes with very little juice are used in this dish. The golden fried slices are excellent served with boiled meats.

6 large unripe, green tomatoes
salt
⅔ cup (3 oz/90 g) all-purpose (plain) flour
5 cups (40 fl oz/1.2 l) extra virgin olive oil for frying

❧ Cut the tomatoes into slices about ¾ in (2 cm) thick. Sprinkle the slices with salt and arrange them on a wire rack. Let drain for 2 hours.

❧ Pat the tomato slices dry with absorbent paper towels. Pour the flour into a shallow bowl.

❧ In a deep, heavy skillet, heat the olive oil to 350°F (180°C). Dip the tomato slices in the flour, coating well on both sides. A few at a time, slip the slices into the hot oil without crowding the pan. Fry until golden, about 5 minutes. With a slotted spoon, remove the slices to absorbent paper towels to drain briefly. Continue frying the remaining slices in the same manner.

❧ Transfer the tomato slices to a serving plate and sprinkle with salt. Serve very hot.

SERVES 6

Lucca

PATATE AL PREZZEMOLO

Parslied Potatoes

This dish offers a good way to enjoy the extraordinary flavor of the olive oil produced near Lucca. The potatoes go well with an omelet or cold meats in the summer.

2 lb (900 g) boiling potatoes
salt and freshly ground black pepper
½ tablespoon white wine vinegar
1 garlic clove, chopped
⅓ cup (3 fl oz/90 ml) extra virgin olive oil
1 tablespoon chopped fresh flat-leaf (Italian) parsley

In a saucepan, boil the unpeeled potatoes in salted water to cover until tender, about 30 minutes. Drain the potatoes and peel them. Let cool to room temperature.

Cut the potatoes crosswise into slices ¼ in (5 mm) thick. Transfer the slices to a salad bowl.

In a small bowl, dissolve salt and pepper to taste in the vinegar and mix in the garlic. Sprinkle the vinegar mixture over the potatoes. Drizzle the olive oil over the potatoes and stir gently to mix well; be careful not to break up the potatoes.

Sprinkle the parsley over the top and serve at room temperature.

SERVES 6

Lucca

CARCIOFI IN TEGAME

Pan-Roasted Artichokes

For this recipe, the artichokes are always prepared in an earthenware pan, which cooks them gently at a low temperature. If you use an ordinary skillet, they should be transferred to a warm dish for serving. In Lucchesia the artichokes are fairly large but quite tender.

juice of 1 lemon
6 globe artichokes
3 tablespoons extra virgin olive oil
3 oz (90 g) *pancetta,* chopped
6 garlic cloves
1 tablespoon chopped fresh flat-leaf (Italian) parsley
salt and freshly ground black pepper

Fill a large bowl with water and add the lemon juice. Cut the stalks off the artichokes. Remove the tough outer leaves and cut away the sharp leaf points from the tops. Pull the leaves apart gently and, with a spoon, scoop out and discard the prickly choke. Thinly slice the artichokes lengthwise, dropping them as you do into the water to prevent discoloration.

In a flameproof earthenware casserole over moderate heat, warm the olive oil. Add the *pancetta* and garlic and fry gently, stirring occasionally, until just golden, about 5 minutes.

Meanwhile, drain the artichoke slices and pat them dry with absorbent paper towels. Add them to the casserole, sprinkle with the parsley and season to taste with salt and pepper. Cover, lower the heat and cook gently until tender, about 15 minutes, adding a little water to keep the artichokes moist.

Remove and discard the garlic and serve immediately from the casserole.

SERVES 6

Lucca

FUNGHI IN UMIDO

Braised Mushrooms

At the end of the summer, after the first rains, women carrying baskets of mushrooms walk along the beaches of the Versilia coast and call out, "Bei funghi, funghi morecci"*—"beautiful mushrooms,* morecci *mushrooms." Morecci are the finest* porcini, *with dark caps and firm white stalks.*

2 lb (900 g) fresh *porcini* mushrooms or *shiitake* mushrooms
⅓ cup (3 fl oz/90 ml) extra virgin olive oil
2 garlic cloves
1 tablespoon fresh calamint or chopped fresh flat-leaf (Italian) parsley
⅓ cup (3 fl oz/90 ml) dry white wine
salt and freshly ground black pepper
1 tablespoon tomato paste

Trim off and discard the ends of the mushroom stems and then cut off the stems and set aside. Clean the mushrooms by wiping them with a dampened cloth; do not wash them. Cut the mushroom caps vertically into slices about ⅛ in (3 mm) thick; cut the stalks horizontally into slices about ⅛ in (3 mm) thick.

In a skillet over moderate heat, warm the olive oil. Add the garlic and fry gently until translucent, about 3 minutes. Add the mushrooms and the calamint and cook, stirring occasionally, for 5 minutes. Add the wine and season to taste with salt and pepper. Stir in the tomato paste, lower the heat and cook for a few more minutes.

Remove and discard the garlic. Transfer the mushrooms to a serving dish and serve at once.

SERVES 6

Pan-Roasted Artichokes

Livorno

Ceci di Magro

Chick-peas with Salt Cod

Traditionally this dish is served on Fridays, which for hundreds of years was a meatless day in Catholic countries. It is substantial enough to be offered as a main course.

10 oz (300 g) salt cod
1½ cups (10 oz/300 g) dried chick-peas (garbanzos)
1 fresh rosemary sprig
⅓ cup (3 fl oz/90 ml) extra virgin olive oil
1 garlic clove
10 oz (300 g) plum (egg) tomatoes, peeled and chopped
freshly ground black pepper

Soak the salt cod in water to cover in the refrigerator for 24 hours, changing the water 3 or 4 times.

Meanwhile, soak the chick-peas in water to cover for 12 hours.

Drain the chick-peas and place them in a heavy pot. Add the rosemary and water to cover and bring slowly to a boil over low heat. Simmer gently until the chick-peas are tender, about 1½ hours. Drain and set aside.

Drain the salt cod and remove and discard the skin and bones. Slice into fairly large pieces and set aside.

In a heavy pot over moderate heat, warm the olive oil. Add the garlic and salt cod and fry gently, turning once, until the cod is golden on both sides, about 5 minutes. Add the chick-peas and tomatoes and season to taste with pepper only, as the fish is salty. Lower the heat and cook until the liquid from the tomatoes evaporates, about 20 minutes.

Arrange on a serving platter and serve hot.

SERVES 6

Chick-peas with Salt Cod

Livorno

Fagioli con la Bottarga

Beans with Fish Roe

Bottarga, *a great delicacy, is salted fish roe, usually tuna, pressed and left to mature for at least six months. It is always sliced very finely and is sometimes dressed with oil and lemon and served on canapés.* Bottarga *is also served with pasta. If unavailable, black lumpfish roe is a good substitute.*

2⅛ cups (14 oz/420 g) dried *cannellini* beans
salt and freshly ground black pepper
¼ cup (2 fl oz/60 ml) extra virgin olive oil
3 oz (90 g) *bottarga,* sliced paper thin, or lumpfish roe
juice of ½ lemon

❧ In a bowl, soak the beans in water to cover for 12 hours.
❧ Drain the beans and transfer them to a heavy pot. Add water to cover by ⅓ in (1 cm) and bring slowly to a boil over low heat. Simmer gently for 1½ hours, by which time the water should be absorbed and the beans will be almost the consistency of porridge.
❧ Season the beans to taste with salt and pepper. Transfer to a serving platter and add the olive oil and *bottarga* (or lumpfish roe). Mix gently. Sprinkle with the lemon juice and serve.

SERVES 6

Livorno

Patate al Ramerino

Baked Potatoes with Rosemary

Strongly scented rosemary grows wild all along the Livorno coast and shows up in many local dishes.

12 small baking potatoes
12 small fresh rosemary sprigs
salt and freshly ground black pepper
2 tablespoons extra virgin olive oil

❧ Preheat an oven to 350°F (180°C).
❧ Cut each unpeeled potato lengthwise, about three quarters of the way through the center. Insert a sprig of rosemary into each incision. Sprinkle the potatoes with salt and pepper to taste.
❧ Pour the olive oil into a baking dish in which the potatoes will fit without crowding. Add the potatoes and roll them in the oil to coat all sides. Bake until the potatoes are tender, about 1 hour. Serve immediately.

SERVES 6

Livorno

Frittura di Zucchine

Deep-Fried Zucchini

Deep-fried vegetables are superb in Livorno because they are always fried in the best available extra virgin olive oil. Fried zucchini and baby squid are a traditional Livornese combination.

2 lb (900 g) small zucchini (courgettes)
⅔ cup (3 oz/90 g) all-purpose (plain) flour
5 cups (40 fl oz/1.2 l) extra virgin olive oil
salt

Baked Potatoes with Rosemary, Deep-Fried Zucchini, and Beans with Fish Roe

❧ Trim the ends off the zucchini and cut in half lengthwise. Scoop out and discard the seeds if large. Cut the zucchini into strips 2⅜ in (6 cm) long and ⅓ in (1 cm) thick. Place in a bowl and add iced water to cover. Let stand for 1 hour in the refrigerator. Drain and dry on absorbent paper towels. (This procedure keeps the zucchini strips crisp.)
❧ Sprinkle the zucchini strips with the flour and shake off any excess. Meanwhile, in a deep, heavy skillet, heat the olive oil to 350°F (180°C). A few at a time, slip the zucchini strips into the hot oil without crowding the pan. Fry until golden, about 3 minutes. With a slotted spoon, remove the strips to absorbent paper towels to drain. Continue frying the remaining strips in the same manner.
❧ Arrange the zucchini strips on a serving plate and sprinkle with salt. Serve hot.

SERVES 6

Firenze

Carciofi Ritti

Upright Artichokes

These artichokes are so-called because they are stuffed and cooked standing up, side by side. The stuffing varies and may be made with sweetbreads, sausage, anchovies, chopped meat or whatever is on hand.

1 slice crustless coarse country bread
1 cup (8 fl oz/240 ml) milk
juice of ½ lemon
6 globe artichokes
2 tablespoons chopped fresh flat-leaf (Italian) parsley
1 tablespoon chopped fresh calamint or mint
1 garlic clove, finely chopped
2 oz (60 g) *pancetta,* chopped
salt and freshly ground black pepper
2 tablespoons extra virgin olive oil
2 tablespoons water

❧ In a bowl, soak the bread in the milk for 10 minutes. Drain and squeeze out the excess milk.

❧ Fill a large bowl with water and add the lemon juice. Cut the stalks off the artichokes. Peel the stalks so that only the tender inner part remains, then slice them finely and drop them into the water to prevent discoloration. Remove the tough outer leaves and cut away the sharp leaf points from the tops of the artichokes. Pull the leaves apart gently and, with a spoon, scoop out and discard the prickly choke. Drop

Left to right: Upright Artichokes, Broad Beans with Ham, and Beans with Sausage

the artichokes into the water.
❧ Finely chop the bread and sliced artichoke stalks. In a small bowl, combine the bread, artichoke stalks, parsley, calamint, garlic and *pancetta.* Mix well and season to taste with salt and pepper.
❧ Push the artichoke leaves slightly apart and stuff the bread mixture in between the rows of leaves.
❧ Pour the oil into a shallow pan large enough to hold the artichokes upright in a single layer. Arrange the artichokes side by side, stem end down. Add the water and cover the pan. Cook over low heat, occasionally adding a little water to keep the contents moist, until the artichokes are tender, about 20 minutes.
❧ Arrange them on a serving platter and serve hot.

SERVES 6

Siena

Fagioli con Salsicce

Beans with Sausage

The marriage of two of Siena's finest ingredients makes for a superb dish. Sienese sausages are fairly lean because a little veal is added to the pork.

1½ cups (10 oz/300 g) dried *cannellini* beans
1 garlic clove
1 handful of fresh sage leaves
3 tablespoons extra virgin olive oil
1¼ lb (600 g) sweet Italian sausages
1 tablespoon red wine vinegar
salt and freshly ground black pepper

❧ In a bowl, soak the beans in water to cover for 12 hours.
❧ Drain the beans and transfer them to a heavy pot. Add the garlic, sage, 1 tablespoon of the olive oil and water just to cover. Bring slowly to a boil over low heat. Simmer gently for about 1½ hours, by which time the water should be absorbed and the beans will be almost the consistency of porridge.
❧ In a heavy pot over moderate heat, warm the remaining 2 tablespoons olive oil. Add the sausages and cook until browned on all sides, about 10 minutes.
❧ Add the vinegar and cook until it evaporates, about 2 minutes.
❧ Skim the excess fat from the sausages. Add the beans and lower the heat. Cover and cook for about 5 minutes to allow the flavors to blend. Season to taste with salt and pepper.
❧ Transfer the beans and sausages to a warm platter and serve hot.

SERVES 6

Firenze

Baccelli al Prosciutto

Broad Beans with Ham

Tuscan broad (fava) beans are more tender than most other broad beans, so they are shelled and cooked without removing the bean's thin outer skin, which is very sweet. If the outer skins of the beans are tough they should be removed, in which case you will need an additional 1 lb (480 g) for this recipe. Broad beans are often eaten raw with pecorino *cheese at the end of a meal or cooked and served as an accompaniment to white meats like chicken or turkey.*

3 tablespoons extra virgin olive oil
1 small yellow onion, sliced
3 oz (90 g) *prosciutto,* diced
3½ cups (2 lb/900 g) shelled broad (fava) beans or 4¼ lb (2.1 kg) unshelled
3 plum (egg) tomatoes, peeled and chopped
¼ cup (2 fl oz/60 ml) dry white wine
salt and freshly ground black pepper

❧ In a saucepan over low heat, warm the olive oil. Add the onion and fry gently, stirring, until translucent, about 5 minutes. Add the *prosciutto* and cook, stirring, for 2 minutes. Add the beans, tomatoes and wine and season to taste with salt and pepper. Cook over low heat until the beans are tender and most of the liquid evaporates, about 10 minutes.
❧ Transfer the beans to a platter and serve hot.

SERVES 6

Firenze

Fagioli al Forno

Baked Beans

Beans taste best when they are cooked very, very slowly. Traditionally they are put into old wine flasks from which the straw covering has been removed and nestled overnight in hot embers. By morning the beans are perfectly cooked. They can, however, also be baked successfully.

2⅛ cups (14 oz/420 g) dried *cannellini* beans
1 handful of fresh sage leaves
1 tablespoon extra virgin olive oil
salt and freshly ground black pepper

❧ In a bowl, soak the beans in water to cover for 12 hours.
❧ Preheat an oven to 250°F (120°C).
❧ Drain the beans and place them in an ovenproof pot, preferably of earthenware. Mix in the sage and sprinkle with the olive oil. Pour in water to cover the beans by about ½ in (12 mm). Cover, place in the oven and slowly bring to a boil.
❧ When the beans begin to boil, reduce the heat to 225°F (100°C) and simmer very gently until they are tender and have absorbed nearly all the water, about 3 hours.
❧ The beans should still be slightly soupy when they are done. Season to taste with salt and pepper. Serve hot.

SERVES 6

Firenze

Sedani al Sugo di Carne

Celery with Meat Sauce

This is another of those dishes that, during the winter, when celery is at its best, the farmers take to the fields for their lunch and eat with a chunk of hearty salt-free Tuscan bread.

2½ lb (1.2 kg) white celery
3 tablespoons extra virgin olive oil
1 garlic clove, finely chopped
1 tablespoon finely chopped yellow onion
2 oz (60 g) *pancetta,* coarsely chopped
3 oz (90 g) sweet Italian sausages, skinned and crumbled
3 oz (90 g) beef, coarsely chopped
3 oz (90 g) pork, coarsely chopped
1 tablespoon finely chopped fresh flat-leaf (Italian) parsley
1 cup (8 fl oz/240 ml) dry white wine
1 large plum (egg) tomato, peeled and coarsely chopped
salt and freshly ground black pepper

❧ Break off the celery stalks. With a small knife, remove the strings and cut off and discard the leaves. Cut the stalks into 2-in (5-cm) lengths; set aside.
❧ In a heavy saucepan over moderate heat, warm the olive oil. Add the garlic, onion, *pancetta,* sausage, beef and pork and fry, stirring frequently, for 5 minutes. Add the parsley and wine and cook until the liquid evaporates, about 10 minutes.
❧ Add the tomato and celery. Season to taste with salt and pepper, cover and cook over low heat until the celery is tender, about 20 minutes, adding a little water if the pan becomes too dry.
❧ Arrange on a platter and serve hot.

SERVES 6

Baked Beans (left) and Celery with Meat Sauce (right)

Sautéed Green Beans (top) and Swiss Chard with Lemon Dressing (bottom)

Arezzo

Biete all'Agro di Limone

Swiss Chard with Lemon Dressing

This is an excellent preparation for other green vegetables as well, especially spinach and young broccoli raab.

2 lb (900 g) Swiss chard (silverbeet)
salt and freshly ground black pepper
2 tablespoons fresh lemon juice
½ cup (4 fl oz/120 ml) extra virgin olive oil

♣ Bring a large saucepan of lightly salted water to a boil. Meanwhile, trim off the white stalks from the green Swiss chard leaves. Cut the stalks into pieces 2 in (5 cm) long, removing any strings.
♣ Add the stalks to the boiling water and boil for about 5 minutes. Add the leaves and cook for 2 minutes longer. Drain and immediately transfer to a bowl of iced water so that the leaves remain green. Drain and pat dry with absorbent paper towels.
♣ Arrange the Swiss chard in a serving dish. In a small bowl, dissolve salt and pepper to taste in the lemon juice. Sprinkle the lemon juice mixture over the Swiss chard. Drizzle the olive oil over the Swiss chard and stir well. Serve warm or at room temperature.

SERVES 6

Arezzo

GOBBI IN GRATELLA

Grilled Cardoons

Tuscans call cardoons gobbi, *or "hunchbacks," because they are curved. They flourish here as they need little water. In one of his best-known poems, Tuscan-born Giosue Carducci, who won the Nobel Prize in 1906, describes a gray donkey munching cardoons.*

juice of 1 lemon
4 lb (1.8 kg) cardoons
1 tablespoon all-purpose (plain) flour
3 tablespoons extra virgin olive oil
salt and freshly ground black pepper

❧ Preheat a broiler (grill).

❧ Fill a large bowl with water and add the lemon juice. Remove and discard the base from each cardoon and discard any tough stalks. Trim and discard the leaves and spurs from the tender stalks and then scrape the stalks with a small knife to remove all strings and fibers. Cut each stalk crosswise into pieces 2 in (5 cm) long and immediately drop them into the water to prevent discoloration.

❧ Bring a large saucepan of lightly salted water to a boil. Drain the cardoons and drop them into the boiling water. Sprinkle the surface of the water with the flour to keep the cardoons from darkening. Boil the cardoons for 5 minutes. Drain well and dry with absorbent paper towels.

❧ In a small bowl, mix together the olive oil and salt and pepper to taste.

❧ Arrange the cardoons on a broiler pan (grill tray) and brush them with some of the oil mixture. Slip the cardoons under the broiler and grill, turning to cook evenly and brushing them with more of the oil mixture, until tender, about 10 minutes.

❧ Arrange the cardoons on a serving plate. Serve hot.

SERVES 6

Grosseto

FAGIOLINI RIPASSATI IN PADELLA

Sautéed Green Beans

Because green beans take so long to string, cooks often prepare a large quantity at a time for more than one meal. The beans are boiled and then seasoned with fresh olive oil for the first day, and the following day the leftover cooked beans are sautéed with tomatoes.

3 tablespoons extra virgin olive oil
3 garlic cloves, chopped
2 lb (900 g) green beans, blanched 2 minutes and drained
1 lb (480 g) plum (egg) tomatoes, peeled and chopped
1 tablespoon fresh marjoram leaves
salt and freshly ground black pepper

❧ In a heavy pot over low heat, warm the olive oil. Add the garlic and fry gently until translucent, about 5 minutes. Add the beans, tomatoes, marjoram and salt and pepper to taste. Cook over low heat until the liquid evaporates, about 20 minutes.

❧ Transfer the green beans to a platter and serve hot.

SERVES 6

Grilled Cardoons

GROSSETO

RISTORANTE
F-12

GROSSETO

Grosseto is the largest city in the region of western Tuscany known as the Maremma. *"Sia maledetta Maremma . . . Maremma amara,"* an old Tuscan folk song goes. "Maremma be damned . . . Maremma the bitter." The coast of the Maremma was, in fact, until the early 1900s, a malarial and bandit-ridden swamp. Throughout the eighteenth and nineteenth centuries, travelers forced to cross it in order to get to Rome hastened through as fast as their horses would carry them. Nevertheless, since Etruscan times this stretch of indescribably beautiful untamed land lying between the sea and the mountains has been rich in towns, villages and culture.

When the Medicis ruled Tuscany, they reclaimed some of the land with highly advanced drainage systems. Then, at the beginning of this century, all the swamps were drained and a dangerous mosquito-infested coast was transformed into a rich and fertile plain. Since then, the Maremma coast has become one of the most exclusive in Italy. Sadly, some of the coastline was spoiled by overdevelopment, but other parts were spared and are still intact.

Now recognized as a wetland of international value, the Maremma is still enchanting. Orbetello, where there is a lagoon protected by two narrow strips of land, is a fascinating place. The early Romans installed a system of nets there for catching eels, which are even now a specialty of the region. And in 1544, a chronicler reported

Left: A familiar dot on the landscape, the olive trees of Tuscany produce the finest oil in Italy. The Romans introduced olives to Italy; before then olive oil was imported from Greece. Previous pages: Some of Italy's most luxurious pleasure craft are moored at Porto Ercole, an exclusive resort on the south of the Argentario peninsula.

that the area was "swarming with very good mullet, eels and a variety of other fish."

The Argentario, some 2100 feet of granite cliffs rising straight out of the sea, is just as intriguing. So, too, is the pristine interior at Roselle, Saturnia, Pitigliano and Sovana—sites of the most complete Etruscan remains found to date. At the beautiful national park of Uccellina, visitors are allowed to enter at dawn if accompanied by a warden, but must leave by dusk. The park is where the *butteri*—Italian cowboys—oversee on horseback the famous herds of cattle and the last wild horses roaming free. Everywhere the Mediterranean brush is heady with the scent of tamarisk, broom and rosemary. Wild boar, stags, fallow deer and porcupines thrive undisturbed in the woods.

The Maremma cuisine, with its perfect blend of foods from the sea and the land, is equally appealing. Its fragrances and flavors are wisely mixed. This is most apparent around Grosseto, where one still senses the splendor of the past and finds its many traces, first of Etruscan and Roman influences and then those of the Middle Ages. Crossbows are no longer used for hunting and the rudimentary fishing techniques have been abandoned, but game and fish are brought to table with exactly the same enthusiasm. Around here even the simplest trattoria is nearly always a pleasant surprise. Local cooking at its very best, however, is to be found in restaurants like Leonardo Cappelli in Follonica, Buca di San Lorenzo in Grosseto, and La Bussala at Punta Ala

A fisherman at Porto Santo Stefano unloads his catch at the end of the day. The local waters yield an abundance of mullet, sea bass, sardines, squid, cuttlefish and shellfish.

The antipasti range from the classic cured meats to the celebrated *anguille sfumate,* smoked eel from the lagoon at Orbetello. They are called *sfumate* because they are first rubbed with ash, then threaded onto skewers between bay leaves. They are smoked in special rooms filled with smoldering scented herbs and are sprinkled with oil and vinegar. Eels are also found in many other local dishes. *Scaveccio dei bovari,* or "cowboys' halters," are fairly large eels fried with garlic, chili and rosemary and liberally sprinkled with red vinegar.

Nearly all the eels served in Italy come from the breeding grounds in the lagoon at Orbetello, including *capitone,* which is served as the traditional Christmas Eve dinner all over central Italy. A *capitone* is a large female eel just ready to enter the sea. Although eels are generally considered fresh-water fish, they are born, breed and die in the open sea. In this area, an eel soup made with tomatoes and broccoli was once the traditional Christmas lunch.

A variety of crustaceans are found around Orbetello. The most popular are called *femminelle* and are caught in the nets cast to catch eels. *Femminelle* are small crabs that make an excellent soup, and their roe is used to flavor a celebrated risotto.

The local recipe for turtle soup is fortunately no longer used. At one time a great number of turtles were found in the sea, but they are now a protected species. It is interesting to discover that there was once an everyday Tuscan turtle soup, for it is considered very exotic fare by most Italians.

Along the Argentario a typical fish soup called *caldaro* is prepared. It has a unique flavor from the limpets that are prized off the rocks and put straight into the soup with seaweed still attached to their shells, giving the concoction a strong taste of the sea.

The area also offers an excellent bean soup called Lombard soup, although it is completely unknown in Lombardy. Apparently it was first made in the eighteenth century by men from that region who came to work on reclaiming the land.

The best known soup of the Maremma, however, is *acquacotta,* or "cooked water," which, despite its name, is much more than a simple soup. It is the symbol of generations of poverty, when *acquacotta* was just bread, water and herbs. That was when the cowherds, charcoalburners and shepherds had to fill a pot with a little water, bread and whatever the season presented—garlic, an onion, or some tomato. Today there are a hundred different kinds of *acquacotta,* some with mushrooms or asparagus, others with peppers or egg. Every village, indeed every household has its own version, a firmly established family tradition so that no members ever forget the long period when their ancestors lived and died hungry.

Grosseto also enjoys rich and tasty first and second courses, such as *tortelli maremmani al sugo,* stuffed pasta with meat sauce; *pasta alla buttera condita con pancetta,* pasta with bacon sauce; *tagliolini con i fagioli o con i ceci,* fresh pasta with beans or chick-peas; and *zuppa con i funghi,* a soup made with mushrooms gathered on the mountainside. *Ciaffagnoni* is a delicate dish that comes as rather a surprise in these parts. A specialty of Manciano, the dish consists of thin pancakes filled with mushrooms and folded in half. They are as good as their better-known French cousins, crêpes.

Nevertheless, Maremma cooking is at its best with game, and above all wild boar, which have been hunted here for millennia. They grow to an enormous size, some weighing as much as 770 pounds and reaching six and a half feet in length. Wild boar is the ancestor of all domestic pigs and, at least in this area, none of it goes to waste. The cowboys even use the skins for making their saddles. It is a much sought-after hunting trophy and is cooked in many different ways between Grosseto and Rome. It can be roasted with vegetables or herbs, slightly salted, or prepared in the Renaissance manner, *dolceforte,* with a sweet and sharp sauce. In a few country stores it is still possible to find *coppiette di cinghiale,* or "wild boar pairs." They are strips of meat about six inches long that are salted, sprinkled with chili, tied together at both ends, then hung in front of the fire and smoked.

Another Maremma delicacy are *granelli,* testicles of wild boar, sheep, veal or beef. They are deep-fried, sautéed in oil and rosemary, or grilled. On wild boar hunts, the testicles are given to the huntsman who first spotted the prey. According to popular belief the wild boar testicles have a positive effect on the man who is lucky enough to eat them.

But wild boar is not the only game available in the Maremma. At one time there was an unlimited supply of pheasant and woodcock. Nowadays there are far fewer of these birds, but they are still bagged with quail, wild goose, deer and hare. Porcupine is an animal now very seldom eaten because it is protected. For centuries they were hunted because of the excellent flavor of their flesh, usually prepared in a stew, but now they are only cooked if accidentally run over by a car.

Lamb is served in many different ways all over the Maremma, whereas kid is confined to the rockier parts. A typical dish from Capalbio is *buglione d'agnello,* in which wild boar is added to chunks of lamb and stewed in tomato and white wine flavored with garlic and rosemary. At one time, kid was widely available along the rocky Argentario coast, but now fewer goats are raised.

Another Maremma dish that is just as good as its more celebrated French counterpart is *chiocciole alla maremmana,* snails sautéed with celery, onion and carrot and sprinkled with calamint or thyme.

Because there are so many vegetable soups, there is not a great tradition of other vegetable dishes. The Maremma is, however, famous for *cipolle alla grossetana,* onions prepared in the style of Grosseto. They are a work of art and not very easy to prepare. Onions are boiled in their skins and half emptied. The pulp is chopped and sautéed with sausage meat and chopped beef seasoned with nutmeg and cinnamon. The mixture is then bound with egg and grated sheep's milk cheese and used to stuff the onions, which are then baked. Needless to say, they are excellent.

A shepherd with his flock near Pitigliano. Pecorino *(sheep's milk cheese) is still made on small farms and vineyards throughout Tuscany.*

The town of Sorano clings to its hillside. The Etruscans built their cities atop hills to protect themselves from invaders. Later, Roman and medieval additions grew on the original Etruscan sites.

This being a land where there never was much to spare, Grosseto and the Maremma do not have many traditional desserts. Those few that can be regarded as typical are extremely simple, such as *sfratti* (round biscuits made with honey and walnuts), *frittelle di San Giuseppe* (St. Joseph's pancakes) or candied figs. These last are usually prepared in a wood-burning oven after bread has been baked. The figs are put into a baking pan, sprinkled with sugar and honey, and moistened with a little lemon juice. Half an hour in the oven, half a glass of Vin Santo allowed to evaporate, and then, when the figs are cold, the discovery that absolute simplicity can give great delight even to the most discriminating palate.

Proof of man's triumph over a hostile countryside is provided by some excellent wines that are now produced in this area. Two names can speak for all: Pitigliano, a white wine that although of ancient origin has only made a name for itself since the 1950s, and Morellino from Scansano.

I Dolci

Panforte, *a spicy cake from Siena traditionally enjoyed at Christmastime.*

I DOLCI

There are not many Tuscan cakes and other desserts, and nearly all of them are linked to some religious celebration, such as the special biscuits served at Carnival and Easter and the traditional cakes for Halloween and Christmas. They are all very simple, their few ingredients occasionally enriched with candied citrus peel and flavored with spices.

Cenci, the traditional Carnival fritters, are direct descendants of *cincius,* which were eaten by the ancient Romans during the Saturnalia, the long orgiastic feast held every year in honor of Saturn. Made with flour and water, *cenci* have changed little in the last two thousand years. Then there are *brigidini* from Lamporecchio, large wafers so celebrated that for centuries almost every Tuscan writer has mentioned them in poetry and prose. *Brigidini* are so much a part of Tuscan life that going to a market or fair inevitably involves buying a bag of them and gobbling them one by one until they are all gone, just like popcorn.

But the real cake and sweet boom comes at Easter, when the forty days of Lent, traditionally spent doing penance and fasting, end in great gastronomic transgressions. Hence the ring cakes, sweet flat breads, rice and semolina puddings, and the sweet rosemary bread from Florence.

Sienese *pan pepato, panforte* and *ricciarelli* were all originally Christmas sweetmeats, and the *sfratti* from Sorano are said to have originated in Etruscan times. On Twelfth Night, when legend says that a witch brings presents to good children and coal to naughty ones, *befanini,* or "little witches" (large biscuits decorated with hundreds and thousands of colored pralines), are seen in abundance in Versilia and Lucchesia.

A match made in heaven: the celebrated almond biscuits from Prato are dipped in Vin Santo before eating.

Previous pages: Candied Figs (left, page 498) and Honey Cake (right, page 482).

Local cakes and biscuits are found in various parts of Tuscany. The famous biscuits of Prato, called *cantucci,* are made with almonds and are so hard that they are always dipped in a glass of Vin Santo before being eaten. In Lunigiana *spongata* is filled with honey or fig jam and sometimes with candied peel or nuts and raisins. The once-large Jewish population of Livorno introduced several traditional cakes that even now are recognized as familiar by travelers who have tasted them in various guises all over the world. *Bucellato,* Lucca's most famous cake, is flavored with aniseed. Lucca is also known for its *torta co' becchi,* pastry filled with chocolate or sweetened Swiss chard flavored with spices. In Pisa they make *torta co' bischeri,* pastry with a rice filling. At Massa and Carrara, where the country's premier marble is quarried, the locals prepare a magnificent rice cake, rich with eggs. On the feast of St. Peter the citizens of Castelnuovo di Garfagnana honor their patron saint by serving a delicious almond cake.

Since the Middle Ages many Tuscan cakes have been seasoned with aniseed because it was thought not only to give flavor, but also to ward off evil spells. In Florence cakes are often made with *alchermes,* a sweet red liqueur that the monks of Santa Maria Novella have been producing since the Medici ruled the city.

There are also innumerable Tuscan cakes and desserts made with chestnuts or chestnut flour. These go back to the days when the people living in the mountains were so poor that their staple diet was chestnuts. *Castagnaccio* is the most traditional and originally came from Lucca, although it is now made all over Tuscany. According to the *Commentario* for 1500, a certain Pilade of Lucca was the first person to make *castagnazzi,* as it was then called. Rather dry, this flat bread is at its best served with fresh ricotta. In Lucchesia roasted chestnuts sprinkled with grappa, rum or Vin Santo often end an autumn dinner.

A shepherd from Pietrasanta weighs a round of pecorino *cheese. Many Tuscan meals end with a platter of cheese and fruit.*

Fresh fruit plays a starring role in local desserts. These peaches may be baked into cakes, or perhaps stuffed with meringue.

Sweet Carnival Pizza

Coffee on a Fork

Firenze

STIACCIATA ALLA FIORENTINA

Sweet Carnival Pizza

Like most Italian cakes, this sweet Florentine pizza is linked to a religious feast: Carnival. At one time lard was used instead of butter, which added to the flavor.

¾ cup (6 fl oz/180 ml) lukewarm water (105° to 115°F/42° to 46°C)
1 oz (30 g) fresh cake yeast or 2 packages (1 scant tablespoon each) active dry yeast
2¾ cups (11 oz/330 g) all-purpose (plain) flour
pinch of salt
⅓ cup (3 oz/90 g) unsalted butter, plus extra for cake pan
⅓ cup (3 oz/90 g) granulated sugar
grated zest of 1 lemon
2 eggs
1 tablespoon confectioners' (icing) sugar

Place the lukewarm water in a small bowl. Sprinkle the yeast on top of the water and let stand until dissolved and foamy, about 10 minutes.

Heap the flour on a work surface and make a well in the center. Pour the dissolved yeast into the well and add the salt. With a fork, gradually work in the flour until all of it is absorbed. On a lightly floured surface, knead the dough until it is smooth and elastic, about 5 minutes. Shape the dough into a ball. Transfer the dough ball to a lightly floured bowl and cover with plastic wrap. Let rise at room temperature until doubled in bulk, about 2 hours.

Turn the dough out onto a floured work surface. Punch down the dough and gradually work in the ⅓ cup (3 oz/90 g) butter, granulated sugar, lemon zest and the eggs, one at a time. Lift the now-soft dough and slam it down on a hard surface several times. Using the heel of your hand, knead until the dough is no longer sticky.

Butter a 9-in (23-cm) round cake pan. Shape the dough in the bottom of the prepared pan. Let rise at room temperature until doubled in size, about 1 hour. Meanwhile, preheat an oven to 400°F (200°C).

Bake the cake until just golden, about 30 minutes. Remove from the pan and immediately transfer to a wire rack. Sprinkle with the confectioners' sugar. Cool to room temperature before serving.

SERVES 6

Lucca

CAFFÈ IN FORCHETTA

Coffee on a Fork

This pudding is called "coffee on a fork" because it is a coffee-flavored baked custard that is eaten with a fork.

1 tablespoon almond oil
4 eggs
⅓ cup (3 oz/90 g) granulated sugar
1¾ cups (14 fl oz/420 ml) milk
¼ cup (2 fl oz/60 ml) strong brewed coffee

Preheat an oven to 350°F (180°C). Brush a 9-in (23-cm) square cake pan with the almond oil.

In a bowl, whisk together the eggs and sugar until well blended and thick. Gradually whisk in the milk and coffee.

Pour the egg mixture into the prepared pan. Place the pan in a baking dish. Pour the water into the dish to a depth of 1 in (2.5 cm). Bake the pudding for 20 minutes. Cover the pan with aluminum foil and continue baking until the custard is set, about 40 minutes longer.

Remove from the oven and let cool slightly on a wire rack. Run a thin, sharp knife blade around the pan edges and invert the custard onto a platter. Serve warm.

SERVES 6

Siena

BUDINONE DI RISO

Cinnamon Rice Pudding

The Sienese have several versions of rice pudding. It is sometimes made with a little candied fruit, but the classic addition is cinnamon.

4 cups (32 fl oz/1 l) milk
1½ cups (10 oz/300 g) Arborio rice
1 tablespoon ground cinnamon
⅓ cup (3 oz/100 g) granulated sugar
6 tablespoons (3 oz/90 g) unsalted butter
3 eggs, separated

❧ In a fairly large saucepan over moderate heat, bring the milk to a boil. Add the rice and stir well. Boil gently until all the milk is absorbed, about 30 minutes. Remove the pan from the heat and stir in the cinnamon, sugar and 5 tablespoons (2½ oz/75 g) of the butter. Let cool to room temperature. Meanwhile, preheat an oven to 350°F (180°C).

❧ Add the egg yolks to the cold rice mixture, mixing in well. In a bowl, beat the egg whites until stiff peaks form. Fold them gently into the rice mixture.

❧ Brush a 9-in (23-cm) round mold with the remaining 1 tablespoon butter. Press the rice mixture into the mold and smooth the top. Bake the pudding until set and lightly brown on top, about 1 hour.

❧ Remove the pudding from the oven and let cool slightly on a wire rack. Slip a knife around the edges and invert onto a serving plate. Serve while still warm.

SERVES 6

Siena

FRITTELLE DI CREMA

Custard Fritters

At Carnival time in Siena these fritters are served hot in the cafés. They are also a popular year-round Sunday dessert.

4 eggs, separated
⅓ cup (3 oz/90 g) granulated sugar
1¼ cups (5 oz/150 g) all-purpose (plain) flour
2 cups (16 fl oz/480 ml) milk
grated zest of 1 lemon
⅔ cup (3 oz/90 g) fine dry bread crumbs
5 cups (40 fl oz/1.2 l) extra virgin olive oil for frying
1 tablespoon confectioners' (icing) sugar

❧ Place the egg yolks in a mixing bowl. Add the granulated sugar and beat in well. Gradually add the flour, milk and lemon zest, mixing until thoroughly blended. Transfer the mixture to a shallow, heavy saucepan.

❧ Lightly oil a large plate about 12 in (30 cm) in diameter. Place the saucepan over low heat and cook, stirring constantly, until the custard mixture begins to boil and coats a spoon. Remove the custard from the heat and pour it onto the prepared plate. It should form a layer about ⅓ in (1 cm) high. Let cool completely. When the custard is cold, slice it into 1¼-by-2-in (3-by-5-cm) rectangles. Dredge the rectangles in the bread crumbs to coat evenly on all sides.

❧ In a deep, heavy skillet, heat the olive oil to 350°F (180°C). A few at a time, slip the rectangles into the hot oil without crowding the pan. Fry until golden, about 3 minutes. With a slotted spoon, remove to absorbent paper towels to drain briefly. Continue frying the remaining rectangles in the same manner.

❧ Arrange the fritters on a serving dish. Sprinkle with the confectioners' sugar and serve very hot.

MAKES 20–30 FRITTERS

Custard Fritters (left) and Cinnamon Rice Pudding (right)

Sweet Bread with Fresh Grapes

Siena

Panello con l'Uva

Sweet Bread with Fresh Grapes

Until very recently this recipe was made only during the grape harvest, when just-picked tiny wine grapes were available. Now, because imported grapes are in the market throughout the year, the tradition has been lost. This sweet flat bread is much tastier, however, when made with small grapes.

1 cup (8 fl oz/240 ml) lukewarm water (105° to 115°F/42° to 46°C)
1 oz (30 g) fresh cake yeast or 2 packages (1 scant tablespoon each) active dry yeast
3 cups (12 oz/360 g) all-purpose (plain) flour
¼ cup (2 oz/60 g) granulated sugar
pinch of salt
¼ cup (2 fl oz/60 ml) extra virgin olive oil
1 cup (3 oz/90 g) walnuts, chopped
10 oz (300 g) black grapes, stemmed

❧ Place the lukewarm water in a small bowl. Sprinkle the yeast on top of the water and let stand until dissolved and foamy, about 10 minutes.

❧ Heap the flour on a work surface and make a well in the center. Pour the dissolved yeast into the well and add the sugar and salt. With a fork, gradually work in the flour until all of it is absorbed. On a lightly floured surface, knead the dough until it is smooth and elastic, about 5 minutes. Shape the dough into a ball. Transfer the dough ball to a lightly oiled bowl, cover with plastic wrap and let rise at room temperature until doubled in bulk, about 2 hours.

❧ Meanwhile, in a small skillet over very low heat, warm the olive oil. Add the nuts and fry gently until toasted, about 2 minutes. Remove from the heat and let the oil and nuts cool completely.

❧ Turn the dough out onto a floured work surface. Punch down the dough and knead in the cold nuts and oil. When well mixed, shape the dough in the bottom of a round 9-in (23-cm) springform pan. Arrange the grapes on top, lightly pressing them into the dough. Let rise at room temperature until doubled in size, about 30 minutes. Meanwhile, preheat an oven to 400°F (200°C).

❧ Bake the bread until just golden, about 30 minutes. Remove the bread from the oven and remove the pan sides. Transfer the bread to a serving plate and serve while still slightly warm.

SERVES 6

Grosseto

Pane Toscano

Tuscan White Loaf

Because Tuscan bread is saltless and keeps well, until very recently it was baked in a wood-fired oven only once a week. This is the ideal bread to use in all recipes calling for coarse country bread. It may also be seasoned with rosemary or olives and baked in a flat circle about 12 in (30 cm) in diameter. In that case, it will bake in about 20 minutes.

1 cup (8 fl oz/240 ml) lukewarm water (105° to 115°F/42° to 46°C)
1 oz (30 g) fresh cake yeast or 2 packages (1 scant tablespoon each) active dry yeast
2⅔ cups (12 oz/360 g) bread flour

❧ Place the lukewarm water in a small bowl. Sprinkle the yeast on top of the water and let stand until dissolved and foamy, about 10 minutes.

❧ Heap the flour on a work surface and make a well in the center. Pour the dissolved yeast into the well and, with a fork, gradually work in the flour until all of it is absorbed. On a lightly floured board, knead the dough until it is smooth and soft, about 5 minutes. Shape the dough into a ball. Place the dough ball in a lightly floured bowl and cover with plastic wrap. Let rise at room temperature until doubled in bulk, about 2 hours.

❧ Turn the dough out onto a floured work surface. Punch down the dough and divide it in half. Shape each half into an oval loaf about 8 in (20 cm) long.

❧ Lightly dust a baking sheet with flour and place the loaves on it. Let rise at room temperature until doubled in size, about 30 minutes. Meanwhile, preheat an oven to 400°F (200°C).

❧ Bake the bread until golden brown, about 30 minutes. Remove from the oven and let cool completely on a wire rack before slicing.

SERVES 6

Livorno

Bolli

Sweet Buns

The orange flower water and cinnamon in these buns are examples of the Middle Eastern influence present in Livorno.

1 cup (8 fl oz/240 ml) lukewarm water (105° to 115°F/42° to 46°C)
1 oz (30 g) fresh cake yeast or 2 packages (1 scant tablespoon each) active dry yeast
3 cups (12 oz/360 g) all-purpose (plain) flour
4 egg yolks
1 cup (8 oz/240 g) granulated sugar
3 tablespoons extra virgin olive oil
2 tablespoons anisette liqueur
1 tablespoon aniseed
1 teaspoon ground cinnamon
1 tablespoon orange flower water or freshly grated orange zest
1 tablespoon unsalted butter

❧ Place the lukewarm water in a medium-sized bowl. Sprinkle the yeast on top of the water and let stand until dissolved and foamy, about 10 minutes.

❧ Gradually add ⅔ cup (3 oz/90 g) of the flour to the yeast mixture, stirring constantly to prevent lumps from forming. Cover the bowl with plastic wrap and let rise at room temperature until doubled in bulk, about 1 hour.

❧ Heap the remaining flour on a work surface. Make a well in the center and add the yeast and flour mixture to it. With a fork, work together the yeast mixture and flour until the flour is absorbed. On a lightly floured surface, knead the dough until soft and smooth, about 5 minutes. Shape the dough into a ball. Transfer it to a lightly floured bowl. Cover with plastic wrap and let rise at room temperature until doubled in bulk, about 30 minutes.

❧ Turn the dough out onto a lightly floured work surface. Punch down the dough and add the egg yolks, one at a time. Add the sugar, the oil, anisette, aniseed, cinnamon and orange flower water (or orange zest). Knead until the dough is smooth and very soft, about 5 minutes.

❧ Grease a baking sheet with the butter and then lightly flour it. Divide the dough into pieces, each about the size of an egg, and flatten them slightly. Arrange the buns on the prepared baking sheet and let them rise at room temperature until doubled in size, about 30 minutes. Meanwhile, preheat an oven to 350°F (180°C).

❧ Bake the buns until golden, about 30 minutes. Remove to a wire rack to cool completely.

MAKES 20–30 BUNS

Tuscan White Loaf (left) and Sweet Buns (right)

Lucca

Dolce di Farro

Spelt Pudding

As spelt is so popular in Lucchesia, the locals prepare several different puddings with it. This particular recipe comes from the mountainous region and is especially good on cold winter evenings.

1¾ cups (10 oz/300 g) spelt
4 cups (32 fl oz/900 ml) milk
⅓ cup (3 oz/90 g) granulated sugar
4 tablespoons (2 oz/60 g) unsalted butter, plus extra for ring mold
3 eggs
¾ cup (6 oz/180 g) ricotta

❧ In a small bowl, soak the spelt in water to cover for at least 12 hours.

Drunken Chestnuts (left), Spelt Pudding (right) and Baked Custard (rear)

❧ Drain the spelt and place it in a heavy pot with the milk. Bring to a boil, lower the heat and simmer until all the milk has been absorbed, about 30 minutes.
❧ Remove the pot from the heat and stir in the sugar and the 4 tablespoons (2 oz/60 g) butter. Let cool completely.
❧ Preheat an oven to 350°F (180°C). Butter a 9-in (23-cm) ring mold.
❧ In a bowl, whisk the eggs until well blended. Add the eggs and ricotta to the cooled spelt mixture. Blend in thoroughly.
❧ Pour the mixture into the prepared mold and smooth the top. Place the mold in a baking dish. Pour water into the dish to a depth of 1 in (2.5 cm). Bake the pudding until golden brown and firm to the touch, about 60 minutes.
❧ Remove from the oven and let cool slightly. Serve while still warm.

SERVES 6

Arezzo

Castagne Ubriache

Drunken Chestnuts

At one time chestnuts were widely ignored because gathering them and removing the spiky husks takes so much time. But now they are quite a luxury in the cities. They are often roasted over the fire and prepared in the following manner. This dessert is delicious served with Vin Santo or another dessert wine.

2½ lb (1.2 kg) chestnuts
1 cup (8 fl oz/240 ml) dry red wine
¼ cup (2 oz/60 g) granulated sugar

❧ Preheat an oven to 350°F (180°C).
❧ With a sharp knife, make a slit on the rounded side of each chestnut. Arrange the chestnuts in a single layer in a baking pan. Place in the oven and bake for 30 minutes. Remove the chestnuts from the oven.
❧ While they are still warm, remove the hard outer shells and the furry inner skins.
❧ In a saucepan over low heat, combine the wine and sugar. Heat, stirring to dissolve the sugar. Add the chestnuts and cook until the wine is reduced to a thick syrup, about 30 minutes.
❧ Transfer the chestnuts to a serving dish and serve hot.

SERVES 6

Arezzo

Lattaiolo

Baked Custard

This very simple dessert is probably the forerunner of the French crème caramel. In his book on Aretine cooking, Guido Gianni points out that originally it was made with whey rather than with milk.

few drops of almond oil
4 eggs
⅓ cup (3 oz/90 g) granulated sugar
pinch of vanilla powder or a few drops of vanilla extract (essence)
2 cups (16 fl oz/480 ml) milk

❧ Preheat an oven to 350°F (180°C). Brush a 9-in (23-cm) ring mold with the almond oil.
❧ In a mixing bowl, beat together the eggs, sugar and vanilla until well blended and thick. Gradually beat in the milk.
❧ Pour the egg mixture into the prepared pan. Place the mold in a baking dish. Pour water into the dish to a depth of 1 in (2.5 cm). Bake the custard for 20 minutes. Cover the mold with aluminum foil and bake until the custard is set, about 40 minutes longer.
❧ Remove from the oven and let cool slightly. Run a knife blade around the pan edges to loosen the custard, then invert onto a serving plate and let cool completely. Serve cold.

SERVES 6

Arezzo

TORTA DI RISO

Rice Cake

This cake—flatter, richer and crisper than rice pudding—may be served with a simple fruit sauce.

⅓ cup (2 oz/60 g) raisins
4 cups (32 fl oz/1 l) milk
1½ cups (10 oz/300 g) Arborio rice
pinch of salt
⅓ cup (3 oz/90 g) granulated sugar
3 oz (90 g) unsalted butter
1 tablespoon candied lemon peel, chopped
1 tablespoon candied orange peel, chopped
1 cup (3 oz/90 g) walnuts, chopped
½ cup (2 oz/60 g) fine dry bread crumbs
3 eggs, beaten

❧ In a small bowl, soak the raisins in water to cover for 30 minutes.

❧ Meanwhile, in a saucepan over moderate heat, bring the milk to a boil. Add the rice and simmer until the milk is absorbed and the rice is fairly dry, about 30 minutes.

❧ Remove from the heat and add the salt, sugar and butter, saving a little to butter the cake pan. Drain the raisins and add them to the rice mixture along with the lemon and orange peels and the chopped nuts. Stir well and let cool to room temperature.

❧ Meanwhile, preheat an oven to 350°F (180°C). Grease a 9-in (23-cm) springform pan with the remaining butter and then coat it with the bread crumbs.

❧ When the rice mixture is completely cold, stir in the eggs. Pour the rice mixture into the prepared pan and smooth the top. Bake the cake until golden and a knife inserted in the center comes out dry, about 45 minutes.

❧ Remove from the oven and let cool slightly. Unclip the pan sides and transfer the cake to a platter. Serve warm.

SERVES 6

Arezzo

MIGLIACCIO AL MIELE

Honey Cake

In Arezzo the wheat flour in this very simple cake is sometimes replaced by cornmeal or chestnut flour.

2 tablespoons extra virgin olive oil
2½ cups (10 oz/300 g) all-purpose (plain) flour
¾ cup (6 fl oz/180 ml) milk
2 eggs, beaten
pinch of salt
½ cup (5 oz/155 g) honey, preferably chestnut

❧ Preheat an oven to 350°F (180°C). Brush a 9-in (23-cm) square baking pan with the olive oil.

❧ Pour the flour into a bowl. Gradually add the milk, whisking continuously to prevent lumps from forming. Stir in the eggs and salt. Pour the milk mixture into the prepared pan. Bake the cake until golden, about 40 minutes.

❧ Remove from the oven and let cool slightly on a wire rack. Run a knife blade around the pan edges to loosen the cake, then invert onto a platter. Pour the honey on top. Serve warm.

SERVES 6

Photograph pages 470–71

Rice Cake

Ring Cake

Lucca

BUCCELLATO

Ring Cake

Here is Lucca's classic cake, which may be flavored with either aniseed or raisins. Traditionally, godparents would give a buccellato *to their godchildren on confirmation day. This recipe is from Ristorante La Mora in Ponte a Moriano.*

6 tablespoons (3 fl oz/90 ml) lukewarm water (105° to 115°F/42° to 46°C)
1 oz (30 g) fresh cake yeast or 2 packages (1 scant tablespoon each) active dry yeast
3 cups (12 oz/360 g) all-purpose (plain) flour
unsalted butter for ring mold, plus 3 tablespoons (1½ oz/45 g), softened
pinch of salt
⅔ cup (5 fl oz/150 ml) milk
2 whole eggs, plus 1 egg white
1 teaspoon aniseed
½ cup (4 oz/120 g) granulated sugar

❧ Place the lukewarm water in a medium-sized bowl. Sprinkle the yeast on top of the water and let stand until dissolved and foamy, about 10 minutes.

❧ Gradually add ½ cup (2 oz/60 g) of the flour to the yeast mixture, stirring constantly to prevent lumps from forming. Cover the bowl with plastic wrap and let rise at room temperature until doubled in bulk, about 2 hours.

❧ Preheat an oven to 350°F (180°C). Butter a 9-in (23-cm) ring mold.

❧ Add the salt to the remaining flour and heap it on a work surface. Make a well in the center and pour in the milk, the 2 whole eggs, aniseed, softened butter, sugar and the raised dough. With a fork, gradually work in the flour until all of it is absorbed. On a lightly floured work surface, knead the dough until it is soft and smooth, about 5 minutes.

❧ Shape the dough in the prepared ring mold and brush the top with the egg white. Bake the cake until well risen and golden, about 45 minutes.

❧ Remove from the oven and let cool completely on a wire rack. Remove from the pan and place on a serving plate. Serve at room temperature.

SERVES 6

Firenze

CANTUCCINI

Almond Cookies of Prato

Cantuccini *are a specialty of Prato, a city near Florence famous for its textiles and its cookies. Commercially produced cookies from Prato are now exported all over the world, but the homemade variety is infinitely superior. They should be dunked in a glass of sweet, amber Vin Santo before being nibbled.*

unsalted butter for baking sheet
2½ cups (10 oz/300 g) all-purpose (plain) flour
¾ cup (6 oz/180 g) sugar
1½ teaspoons baking powder
2 whole eggs, plus 2 egg yolks
pinch of salt
¾ cup (4 oz/120 g) almonds, coarsely chopped
1 tablespoon milk

❧ Preheat an oven to 350°F (180°C). Butter and lightly flour a baking sheet.
❧ In a mixing bowl, combine the flour, sugar, baking powder, whole eggs, 1 of the egg yolks and the salt. Stir until a soft dough forms. Add the almonds and mix until they are evenly distributed. Divide the dough into equal portions and place them on a lightly floured work surface. Using the palms of your hands, roll each dough portion into a sausage shape about 1 in (2.5 cm) in diameter and 12 in (30 cm) long.
❧ In a small bowl, mix together the milk and the remaining egg yolk. Brush the dough rolls with the milk mixture.
❧ Arrange the dough rolls on the prepared baking sheet and bake until golden, about 20 minutes.
❧ Remove the baking sheet from the oven and, while the rolls are still soft, cut them on the diagonal into slices about ½ in (12 mm) wide. Separate the slices so they are not touching, return the baking sheet to the oven and bake until dry, 5 minutes longer.
❧ Remove to a wire rack to cool. Store in an airtight container.

MAKES 20–30 COOKIES

Grosseto

DOLCINI ALLE MANDORLE

Almond Biscuits

Children take these biscuits to school for the morning break. As they keep well in an airtight tin, it is worthwhile making a fairly large batch.

1 tablespoon unsalted butter
1⅞ cups (10 oz/300 g) blanched almonds, chopped
1 cup (5 oz/150 g) confectioners' (icing) sugar
5 egg whites
¼ cup (2 oz/60 g) granulated sugar

❧ Preheat an oven to 350°F (180°C). Line a baking sheet with parchment paper and grease it with the butter.
❧ In a bowl, mix together the almonds and confectioners' sugar. In a large mixing bowl, beat the egg whites until stiff, moist peaks form. Gently fold the granulated sugar and the almond mixture into the egg whites.
❧ Drop the mixture by spoonfuls onto the prepared baking sheet, spacing them about 1 in (2.5 cm) apart. Bake until golden, about 20 minutes.
❧ Lift the biscuits off the parchment and let cool completely on a wire rack. Serve at room temperature.

MAKES 20–30 BISCUITS

Siena

CAVALLUCCI

Spice Cookies

These well-known cookies, like all Sienese confectionery, are highly seasoned. They will keep well in an airtight container for several days.

⅞ cup (7 oz/210 g) granulated sugar
¾ cup (6 fl oz/180 ml) water
1¾ cups (7 oz/210 g) all-purpose (plain) flour
1 cup (4 oz/120 g) chopped walnuts
⅓ cup (2 oz/60 g) candied orange peel
pinch of ground aniseed
pinch of ground cinnamon
1 tablespoon unsalted butter

❧ Preheat an oven to 220°F (100°C).
❧ In a saucepan over low heat, combine the sugar and water. Stir until the sugar dissolves, then increase the heat to moderate and cook until mixture registers 225°F (115°C) on a candy (sugar) thermometer, or until a little of it dropped into a bowl of ice water forms long threads.
❧ Remove from the heat and gradually stir in the flour, nuts, orange peel, aniseed and cinnamon.
❧ Grease a baking sheet well with the butter, then sprinkle it lightly with flour. Drop the batter by spoonfuls onto the baking sheet, spacing the mounds about 1 in (2.5 cm) apart. Press lightly on the top of each mound to flatten it slightly.
❧ Bake the cookies until they are dry in the center but have not changed color, about 1 hour or longer. Remove to a wire rack to cool.

MAKES 20–30 COOKIES

Siena

PAN COI SANTI

Bread with Saints

This sweet bread is called "bread with saints" because it is traditionally made on the first day of November, the Feast of All Saints. Its peppery flavor is quite unusual and, when the bread becomes hard, the Sienese dunk it in red wine before taking a bite.

1 cup (8 fl oz/240 ml) lukewarm water (105° to 115°F/42° to 46°C)
1 oz (30 g) fresh cake yeast or 2 packages (1 scant tablespoon each) active dry yeast
¼ cup (2 fl oz/60 ml) extra virgin olive oil
1 cup (3 oz/90 g) walnuts, chopped
3 cups (12 oz/ 360 g) all-purpose (plain) flour
⅓ cup (3 oz/90 g) granulated sugar
1 tablespoon freshly ground black pepper
pinch of salt

❧ Place the lukewarm water in a small bowl. Sprinkle the yeast on top of the water and let stand until dissolved and foamy, about 10 minutes.
❧ Meanwhile, in a small skillet over very low heat, warm the olive oil. Add the nuts and fry gently until toasted, about 2 minutes. Remove from the heat and let the oil and nuts cool completely.
❧ Combine the flour, sugar, pepper and salt. Heap this mixture on a work surface and make a well in the center. Pour the dissolved yeast into the well along with the cooled nuts and oil. With a fork, gradually work in the flour mixture until all of it is absorbed. On a lightly floured work surface, knead the dough until it is elastic, about 10 minutes. Shape the dough into a ball. Transfer the dough ball to a lightly oiled bowl,

Almond Cookies of Prato (front), Spice Cookies (left), Almond Biscuits (right) and Bread with Saints (rear)

cover with plastic wrap and let rise at room temperature until doubled in bulk, about 2 hours.

❧ Turn the dough out onto a floured work surface. Punch down the dough and form it into a flat oval loaf about 1 in (2.5 cm) thick at the center and ½ in (12 mm) thick at the edges. Lightly oil a baking sheet and place the loaf on it. Let rise at room temperature until doubled in size, about 30 minutes. Meanwhile, preheat an oven to 400°F (200°C).

❧ Bake the bread for about 30 minutes, or until a wooden toothpick inserted into the center of the loaf comes out dry. Remove the bread from the oven and let cool completely on a wire rack. Place on a serving plate and serve.

SERVES 6

Apple Cake (left) and Almond Cookies (right)

Arezzo

TORTA DI MELE

Apple Cake

Like so many Tuscan dishes, this cake is made with leftover bread. It is very simple and children love it as an afternoon snack.

6 oz (180 g) coarse country bread
2 cups (16 fl oz/480 ml) milk
1 tablespoon unsalted butter
3 eggs
⅓ cup (3 oz/90 g) granulated sugar
3 tablespoons all-purpose (plain) flour
grated zest of 1 lemon
4 Golden Delicious apples or other sweet apples

Soak the bread in 1 cup (8 fl oz/240 ml) of the milk for about 30 minutes. Drain and squeeze out any excess moisture; set aside.

Preheat an oven to 350°F (180°C). Grease a 9-in (23-cm) cake pan with the butter.

In a mixing bowl, beat together the eggs, sugar and flour. Add the remaining milk and the lemon zest and mix well.

Peel and core the apples. Cut them into fairly thick slices.

Place the soaked bread in a layer on the bottom of the prepared pan. Arrange the apples in concentric circles on top of the bread. Pour the egg mixture over the apples. Bake until the top is golden and a knife inserted in the center comes out dry, about 50 minutes.

Remove from the oven and let cool a little. Run a knife around the pan edges to loosen the cake and transfer to a platter. Serve warm.

SERVES 6

Siena

RICCIARELLI

Almond Cookies

Like most Italian almond sweetmeats, ricciarelli *were probably introduced to Siena by crusaders returning from the Middle East. They are now produced commercially, but when homemade they are softer at the center, the secret of a good* ricciarello. *The wafers mentioned in the recipe, which are made from rice flour, look like communion hosts. If they are not available, rice paper may be used or the cookies may simply be baked on parchment paper.*

2 cups (10 oz/300 g) blanched almonds
1¼ cups (10 oz/300 g) granulated sugar
1¼ cups (7 oz/210 g) confectioners' (icing) sugar
1 teaspoon vanilla powder or 1 teaspoon vanilla extract (essence)
2 egg whites
36 thin wafers (see note above), about 2 in (5 cm) in diameter

Preheat an oven to 250°F (120°C). Spread the almonds in a single layer in a shallow pan and place them in the oven to dry for 10 minutes; do not allow them to darken.

Transfer the almonds to a blender container and add the granulated sugar. Blend until evenly pulverized. Add 1 cup (5 oz/150 g) of the confectioners' sugar, the vanilla and egg whites. Blend briefly.

Sprinkle each wafer with a little of the remaining confectioners' sugar, reserving some sugar for sprinkling on later. Place a spoonful of the almond mixture on each wafer. Flatten the mounds to about ⅓ in (9 mm) and, using a sharp knife, cut each of them into diamond shapes. Arrange the diamonds on a baking sheet and let stand in a cool place for at least 12 hours.

Preheat an oven to 250°F (120°C). Place the cookies in the oven and turn off the heat immediately. Leave the cookies in the oven until dry but still soft in the center, about 3 hours. Remove from the oven and cool on a wire rack.

When completely cold, sprinkle them with the remaining confectioners' sugar and serve. Store in an airtight container.

MAKES 36 COOKIES

Livorno

PANNA COTTA AL CARAMELLO

Cooked Cream with Caramel

Cooked cream, an old Tuscan dish, has recently been discovered by the rest of Italy and is now very much in vogue. In Livorno it is flavored with cinnamon. The cream can be kept in the refrigerator for 24 hours, in which case the caramel will dissolve by itself and the cream will be easily inverted onto the platter.

2 tablespoons unflavored powdered gelatin
6 tablespoons (3 fl oz/90 ml) water
2 cups (16 fl oz/480 ml) heavy (double) cream
⅞ cup (7 oz/210 g) granulated sugar
1 teaspoon ground cinnamon

❧ In a small bowl, sprinkle the gelatin over 4 tablespoons of the water and let soften for about 3 minutes without stirring.

❧ In a heavy saucepan over low heat, warm half of the cream with half of the sugar and the cinnamon, stirring to dissolve the sugar. Heat the mixture to just below the boiling point; do not allow it to boil.

❧ Remove from the heat and stir in the gelatin. Let cool to room temperature.

❧ Whip the rest of the cream until stiff peaks form. When the cream-sugar mixture is at room temperature, gently fold in the whipped cream.

❧ In a small, heavy saucepan over low heat, melt the remaining sugar in the remaining 2 tablespoons water, stirring to dissolve the sugar completely. Increase the heat and cook without stirring until the sugar caramelizes and is a rich brown, about 3 minutes.

❧ Remove the caramelized sugar from the heat and immediately pour it into a 9-in (23-cm) ring mold. Tilt the mold so that the caramelized sugar coats the bottom and sides. When the caramel is completely cold, pour in the cream mixture. Cover and refrigerate for at least 3 hours.

❧ Just before serving, briefly dip the bottom of the cake pan in hot water to soften the caramel. Then invert onto a plate and serve.

SERVES 6

Cooked Cream with Caramel

Bomboloni

Lucca

BOMBOLONI

Doughnuts

These particular doughnuts are one of the specialties of Forte dei Marmi, a fashionable beach resort near Lucca. Every morning and late afternoon, men dressed in white walk along the beach, carrying baskets of hot doughnuts for the hungry bathers.

1 cup (8 fl oz/240 ml) lukewarm water (105° to 115°F/42° to 46°C)
1 oz (30 g) fresh cake yeast or 2 packages (1 scant tablespoon each) active dry yeast
3 cups (12 oz/360 g) all-purpose (plain) flour
⅓ cup (3 oz/90 g) granulated sugar
¼ cup (2 oz/60 g) unsalted butter, softened
grated zest of 1 lemon
salt
5 cups (40 fl oz/1.2 l) extra virgin olive oil for frying

Place the lukewarm water in a small bowl. Sprinkle the yeast on top of the water and let stand until dissolved and foamy, about 10 minutes.

Heap the flour on a work surface and make a well in the center. Pour the dissolved yeast into the well along with ¼ cup (2 oz/60 g) of the sugar, the softened butter, lemon zest and salt. With a fork, gradually work in the flour until all of it is absorbed. On a lightly floured work surface, knead the dough with energy until it is very elastic and smooth, about 10 minutes. Shape the dough into a ball.

Transfer the dough to a lightly floured bowl, cover with plastic wrap and let rise at room temperature until doubled in bulk, about 2 hours.

Lightly flour a baking sheet. On a lightly floured work surface, punch down the dough and divide it into about 18 ovals about the size of an egg. Flatten them until they are ½ in (12 mm) thick. Arrange the doughnuts on the baking sheet and let rise at room temperature until doubled in size, about 30 minutes.

In a deep, heavy skillet, heat the olive oil to 350°F (180°C). A few at a time, slip the doughnuts into the hot oil and fry until golden on both sides, about 3 minutes. With a slotted spoon, remove to absorbent paper towels to drain. Continue frying the remaining doughnuts in the same manner.

Arrange on a serving plate and sprinkle with the remaining 2 tablespoons sugar. Serve hot.

MAKES 20–30 DOUGHNUTS

Apple and Rice Pudding

Livorno

Pasticcio di Riso e Mele

Apple and Rice Pudding

All the fine restaurants on the island of Elba serve this delicious pudding at Christmastime.

⅓ cup (2 oz/60 g) raisins
1 cup (8 fl oz/240 ml) Vin Santo or other white dessert wine
4 cups (32 fl oz/900 ml) milk
pinch of salt
1½ cups (10 oz/300 g) Arborio rice
pinch of freshly grated nutmeg
1 teaspoon ground cinnamon
6 tablespoons (3 oz/90 g) granulated sugar
1 tablespoon unsalted butter
3 eggs, beaten
2 Golden Delicious apples or other sweet apples

In a small bowl, soak the raisins in the Vin Santo for 6 hours.

In a heavy saucepan over moderate heat, bring the milk to a boil with the salt. Add the rice, lower the heat and simmer until all the milk has been absorbed and the rice is fairly dry, about 30 minutes. Remove the pan from the heat and stir in the nutmeg, cinnamon and 4 tablespoons (2 oz/60 g) of the sugar. Drain the raisins and mix them in as well. Let cool completely.

Meanwhile, preheat an oven to 350°F (180°C). Butter a 9-in (23-cm) springform pan.

When the rice mixture is cold, stir in the eggs, then pour the batter into the prepared pan. Peel and core the apples, then thinly slice them. Arrange the apple slices in concentric circles on top of the batter and sprinkle them with the remaining 2 tablespoons sugar. Bake the pudding until set, about 1 hour.

Remove from the oven and let cool slightly on a wire rack. Remove the pan sides and transfer the pudding to a plate. Serve warm.

SERVES 6

Firenze

CASTAGNACCIO

Chestnut Flour Cake

This is one of the most traditional Florentine cakes and it should be made with very fresh chestnut flour. If the flour is stale, it gives the cake a slightly bitter flavor. Seasoned with rosemary and pine nuts, castagnaccio *is sold in Florence during the autumn.*

2½ cups (10 oz/300 g) chestnut flour
6 tablespoons (3 fl oz/90 ml) extra virgin olive oil
1½ cups (12 fl oz/350 ml) water
pinch of salt
½ cup (2 oz/60 g) pine nuts
2 tablespoons fresh rosemary leaves

Preheat an oven to 350°F (180°C).

Pour the flour into a mixing bowl. Stir in 2 tablespoons of the olive oil. Gradually add the water, whisking constantly to prevent lumps from forming. Season with the salt.

Pour the remaining 4 tablespoons (2 fl oz/60 ml) olive oil into an 11-in (28-cm) square cake pan, tipping the pan to coat the bottom and sides evenly. Pour the batter into the pan and sprinkle the surface with the pine nuts and rosemary. Do not be concerned if there seems to be too much oil; it is required for the cake to cook properly.

Bake the cake until the surface starts to crack, about 20 minutes. Remove from the oven and pour off any excess oil.

Loosen the cake with a knife, and with the help of a large spatula, transfer the cake to a serving dish. Serve while still warm.

SERVES 6

Chesnut Flour Cake

Livorno

CROCCANTINI DI FRUTTA CANDITA

Candied Fruit Macaroons

When the Medici family made Livorno a free port at the end of the sixteenth century, many immigrants were attracted to it. Among them were Spanish and Portuguese Jews who greatly influenced Livornese cooking, as this Jewish recipe illustrates.

2 egg whites
¾ cup (3 oz/90 g) slivered blanched almonds
1 tablespoon all-purpose (plain) flour
¼ cup (2 oz/60 g) granulated sugar
1 tablespoon honey
1 tablespoon candied (glacé) cherries, chopped
1 tablespoon candied (glacé) orange peel, chopped
1 tablespoon candied (glacé) lemon peel, chopped
unsalted butter for baking sheet
3 oz (90 g) bittersweet (dark) chocolate

Preheat an oven to 350°F (180°C).

In a mixing bowl, whisk the egg whites with a fork until only just frothy. Add the almonds, flour, sugar, honey, cherries and orange and lemon peels.

Brush a baking sheet with the butter. Drop the batter by spoonfuls onto the baking sheet, spacing them about 1 in (2.5 cm) apart. Flatten the tops with a wet teaspoon.

Bake the cookies until golden and set, about 10 minutes. Remove from the oven and transfer to a flat surface. Let cool completely.

Place the chocolate in a small saucepan or dish. Set the vessel inside a large pan of barely simmering water atop the stove. The water should reach about halfway up the sides of the vessel holding the chocolate. As soon as the chocolate melts, brush some onto the surface of each cookie. Let the chocolate cool and set, then arrange the cookies on a plate and serve.

MAKES ABOUT 18 MACAROONS

Candied Fruit Macaroons

Livorno

OSSA DI MORTO

Munchy Bones

These cookies originated on the island of Elba, where they are served with Aleatico, a dessert wine produced on the island. They will keep well in an airtight tin for several days.

2⅛ cups (12 oz/360 g) blanched almonds
4 egg whites
⅞ cup (7 oz/210 g) granulated sugar
1⅝ cups (7 oz/210 g) all-purpose (plain) flour
grated zest of 1 lemon
grated zest of 1 orange
1 tablespoon unsalted butter

Preheat an oven to 350°F (180°C).

Place the almonds in a blender container and blend just until evenly pulverized.

In a mixing bowl, whisk the egg whites with a fork until only just frothy. Add the almonds, sugar, flour and lemon and orange zests. Stir until the mixture is smooth but not too stiff. Divide the mixture into sticks about 2 in (5 cm) long and ¼ in (6 mm) wide.

Grease a baking sheet with the butter and dust lightly with flour. Arrange the sticks on the baking sheet and press each slightly in the middle to form a bone shape.

Bake the cookies until golden, about 20 minutes. Remove to a wire rack to cool completely.

MAKES 20–30 COOKIES

Lucca

BRIGIDINI

Aniseed Wafers

Although these thin wafers originated in Lucchesia, they are now sold in markets throughout Tuscany. They are cooked between two hot, round flatirons called stiacce *that are about 4 in (10 cm) in diameter. They may also be baked in an oven.*

1½ cups (6 oz/180 g) all-purpose (plain) flour
½ cup (4 oz/120 g) granulated sugar
2 eggs
1 tablespoon aniseed

In a food processor, combine the flour, sugar, eggs and aniseed. Process the ingredients until you have a soft, elastic dough similar to pasta dough. Alternatively, combine all the ingredients in a bowl and beat with a wooden spoon.

Preheat the two flatirons on top of the stove over high heat. Divide the dough into balls the size of walnuts. Flatten them slightly, then, one at a time, press them between the hot irons. Hold the irons together until the wafer is crisp, about 2 minutes. Reheat the irons before cooking the next wafer.

Alternatively, preheat an oven to 350°F (180°C). On a lightly floured surface, roll out each dough ball into a very thin round about 4 in (10 cm) in diameter. Arrange the dough rounds on a baking sheet. Bake the cookies until crisp, about 3 minutes. Remove to a wire rack and let cool completely.

Arrange on a platter to serve. These wafers keep well in an airtight container.

MAKES 20–30 WAFERS

Left to right: Selection of Nut Brittles, Munchy Bones and Aniseed Wafers

Lucca

CROCCANTE

Walnut Brittle

This brittle is sold on the beaches in Versilia, as well as at village festivals.

1 tablespoon almond oil
1⅓ cups (10 oz/300 g) granulated sugar
½ cup (4 fl oz/120 ml) water
juice of 1 lemon
2¼ cups (7 oz/210 g) walnuts

❧ Brush a board with the almond oil.
❧ In a deep, heavy saucepan over low heat, melt the sugar in the water, stirring to dissolve the sugar. Increase the heat and cook the sugar without stirring until it caramelizes and turns a deep, rich brown, about 10 minutes.
❧ Remove from the heat and gradually add the lemon juice and nuts, taking care not to burn yourself as the hot sugar syrup may splatter when the cold lemon juice is added.
❧ Pour the syrup mixture onto the oiled board, forming a layer about ¼ in (6 mm) thick. Let the brittle cool completely.
❧ Lift the brittle with a spatula and break it into pieces. Arrange on a platter to serve. Store any leftovers in an airtight container.

SERVES 6

Lucca

MANDORLATA

Almond Brittle

In the Garfagnana the bees produce particularly delicious honey. In the past, this honey-rich brittle was always made there for the feast of Santa Lucia on December 13. Nowadays it is available year-round.

1⅔ cups (1¼ lb/600 g) honey
1 tablespoon almond oil
1¾ cups (10 oz/300 g) blanched almonds, chopped

❧ In a heavy saucepan over low heat, warm the honey until a drop poured into a cup of cold water forms a firm ball when rolled between your fingers, about 5 minutes.
❧ Lightly brush a board with the almond oil and pour the honey on it. Let the honey stand until it is cool enough to knead by hand, then knead until it is pale yellow, about 3 minutes. Add the nuts and knead them in well to mix evenly. If the mixture becomes too hard to work with, return it to a saucepan and reheat it until it softens and is just pliable enough to spread into a thin sheet.
❧ Smooth the mixture into an even sheet about ¼ in (6 mm) thick. Cut into 1¼-in (3-cm) squares and transfer to parchment paper. Cool to room temperature before serving.

SERVES 6

Arezzo

RICOTTA ALL'UVETTA

Ricotta with Raisins

The Aretines are very fussy about ricotta and only eat it raw on the day it is made. The next day it is used in tortelli *or* gnocchi.

⅓ cup (2 oz/60 g) raisins
1 cup (8 fl oz/250 ml) Vin Santo or other white dessert wine
2½ cups (1¼ lb/600 g) fresh ricotta
3 tablespoons granulated sugar
1 teaspoon ground cinnamon

❧ In a small bowl, soak the raisins in the Vin Santo for about 6 hours. Drain them.
❧ Position a sieve over a mixing bowl. Press the ricotta through the sieve to remove any lumps. Add the sugar and raisins and stir gently.
❧ Shape the ricotta mixture into a mound on a serving plate. Put the cinnamon in a fine sieve and sprinkle it over the ricotta. Serve at room temperature.

SERVES 6

Grosseto

TORTA AL FINOCCHIO

Fennel Cake

Rosemary, thyme and fennel are used to season cakes and breads in Tuscany. The fennel accent makes this simple cake particularly interesting.

1 tablespoon unsalted butter
1 cup (4 oz/120 g) all-purpose (plain) flour
1 cup (4 oz/120 g) ground almonds
1 cup (8 oz/240 g) granulated sugar
1 teaspoon baking powder
1 cup (8 fl oz/240 ml) milk
1 tablespoon fennel seed

❧ Preheat an oven to 350°F (180°C). Grease a 9-in (23-cm) springform pan with the butter.
❧ In a mixing bowl, combine the flour, almonds, sugar and baking powder. Mix well. Gradually stir in the milk and then mix in the fennel seed.
❧ Pour the batter into the prepared pan. Bake the cake until golden and a wooden toothpick inserted in the center comes out dry, about 1 hour.
❧ Remove from the oven and let cool completely on a wire rack. Unclip the pan sides and transfer the cake to a serving platter. Serve at room temperature.

SERVES 6

Grosseto

CROSTATA DI RICOTTA

Ricotta Tart

The Grosseto area produces a great deal of pecorino, *sheep's milk cheese. As the sheep graze close to the sea, the* pecorino *is saltier than most. Ricotta made from the whey is a local specialty.*

PASTRY

1¾ cups (7 oz/210 g) all-purpose (plain) flour
⅓ cup (3 oz/90 g) granulated sugar
grated zest of ½ lemon
⅓ cup (3 oz/90 g) butter, softened
1 egg

FILLING

1¼ cups (10 oz/300 g) ricotta
3 eggs, separated
¼ cup (2 oz/60 g) granulated sugar

½ tablespoon unsalted butter

❧ To prepare the pastry: combine the flour, sugar, lemon zest, butter and egg in the bowl of a food processor. Process with brief pulses until the dough begins to come together in a ball.

Left to right: Ricotta Tart, Ricotta with Raisins, and Fennel Cake

Alternatively, combine the ingredients in a mixing bowl and beat together with a wooden spoon until the dough begins to come together in a ball. Gather the dough into a ball, wrap in aluminum foil and refrigerate for about 1 hour.

❧ Meanwhile, to prepare the filling: combine the ricotta, egg yolks and sugar in a large mixing bowl and blend well. In a separate bowl, beat the egg whites until stiff, moist peaks form. Gently fold the egg whites into the ricotta mixture.

❧ Preheat an oven to 350°F (180°C). Select a 9-in (23-cm) tart pan (flan tin) with a removable bottom and grease the bottom with the butter. On a lightly floured work surface, roll out the dough into a round about 10½ in (26.5 cm) in diameter. Carefully transfer it to the prepared pan and press gently against the bottom and sides. Trim the dough even with the rim of the tart pan. Spoon the filling into the pastry shell and smooth the surface. Bake the tart until just golden, about 45 minutes.

❧ Remove from the oven and let cool completely on a wire rack. Transfer the tart to a platter and serve at room temperature.

SERVES 6

Stuffed Peaches (front), Flat Fruit Cake (left) and Strawberries and Ricotta (right)

Siena

PANFORTE

Flat Fruit Cake

Panforte, *literally "strong bread," is the most famous Sienese cake and is now exported all over the world. Originally it was a Christmas treat. Historian Giovanni Righi Parenti tells us that it was first written about in 1205. To make true* panforte *at home is not easy, because the dough is very sticky and you would need dozens of different spices. This version is much simpler but quite good.*

1¼ cups (6 oz/180 g) toasted almonds, chopped
1¼ cups (6 oz/180 g) mixed candied peel, cubed
1½ cups (6 oz/180 g) all-purpose (plain) flour
1 teaspoon ground cinnamon
1 tablespoon mixed ground spices (coriander, nutmeg, cloves, aniseed)
unsalted butter for cake pan
⅔ cup (9 oz/270 g) honey
½ teaspoon ground cinnamon mixed with 1 tablespoon all-purpose (plain) flour

❧ In a large bowl, combine the almonds, candied peel, flour, cinnamon and mixed spices. Mix well.

❧ Preheat an oven to 350°F (180°C). Line an 11-in (28-cm) cake pan with parchment paper and butter the paper well.

❧ In a saucepan over low heat, heat the honey and cook, stirring continuously, for about 2 minutes. Stir the hot honey into the flour mixture, blending well. Taking care not to burn your fingers, shape the mixture into a ball.

❧ Flatten the ball of dough evenly in the prepared pan. Pour the cinnamon-flour mixture into a sieve and shake it over the top of the cake. Bake the cake until golden brown, about 40 minutes.

❧ Remove the cake from the pan and let cool on a wire rack. When cool, peel off the parchment and place the cake on a platter. Any leftover cake can be stored in an airtight container.

SERVES 6

Firenze

RICOTTA CON LE FRAGOLE

Strawberries and Ricotta

Small, strongly flavored wild strawberries are commonly used to prepare this dessert. Larger strawberries should be sliced.

10 oz (300 g) wild strawberries, hulled
1 cup (8 fl oz/240 ml) Vin Santo or other sweet white wine
⅓ cup (3 oz/90 g) granulated sugar
2 cups (1 lb/480 g) ricotta
2 egg whites

❧ Combine the strawberries, wine and half of the sugar in a bowl. Toss to mix and let stand for 2 hours. Drain the strawberries and set aside a few for decorating the dessert.
❧ Position a sieve over a medium-sized bowl. Press the ricotta through the sieve to remove any lumps. Gradually stir in the strawberries and the remaining sugar.
❧ In a separate bowl, beat the egg whites until stiff, moist peaks form. Fold the egg whites into the ricotta-strawberry mixture.
❧ Arrange the mixture in a dome shape in the middle of a serving plate. Decorate with the reserved strawberries and serve immediately.

SERVES 6

Grosseto

PESCHE RIPIENE

Stuffed Peaches

Make sure that the peaches are not too ripe or they will disintegrate while cooking. When a more substantial dessert is required, the peaches are served on a slice of sponge cake sprinkled with alchermes, *a sweet red liqueur.*

3 underripe peaches
1 cup (8 fl oz/240 ml) dry red wine
⅓ cup (3 oz/90 g) granulated sugar
2 tablespoons blanched almonds, chopped
2 egg whites
⅓ cup (2 oz/60 g) confectioners' (icing) sugar
2 cups (16 fl oz/480 ml) milk

❧ Cut the peaches in half and carefully remove and discard the pits. Place the peaches in a shallow saucepan with the wine and granulated sugar. Cook over low heat until the peaches are soft, about 10 minutes.
❧ Meanwhile, preheat an oven to 350°F (180°C). Place the almonds in a small pan and toast them until golden brown, about 10 minutes. Remove from the oven and set aside.
❧ With a slotted spoon, remove the peaches to a plate. Cook the wine over moderate heat until the sauce reduces and coats a spoon, about 5 minutes. Remove from the heat and let cool completely.
❧ In a bowl, beat the egg whites until soft peaks form. Add the confectioners' sugar, a spoonful at a time, and continue beating until stiff, moist peaks form.
❧ In a shallow saucepan, bring the milk to a simmer. Using 2 large spoons, shape the egg whites into oval meringues by scooping up the egg white with one spoon and gently covering it with the other. You should have 6 meringues in all. Slip the meringues into the milk without crowding the pan and poach on both sides until just firm, 1–2 minutes per side. With a slotted spoon, remove the meringues to a plate and let cool. Continue poaching the remaining egg whites in the same manner.
❧ Arrange the peach halves flat side up on a serving dish. Place a meringue on each peach and sprinkle with the almonds. Pour the cold wine sauce over them. Serve at room temperature.

SERVES 6

Grosseto

PAN DI MIELE

Honey Bread

In Grosseto this bread is made with honey from hives placed near strawberry plants. Try to use a honey that has a strong flavor and is slightly bitter.

1 cup (8 fl oz/240 ml) milk, heated to lukewarm (105° to 115°F/42° to 46°C)
1 oz (30 g) fresh cake yeast or 2 packages (1 scant tablespoon each) active dry yeast
2⅔ cups (12 oz/360 g) all-purpose (plain) flour
1 tablespoon granulated sugar
2 tablespoons honey (not too sweet)
salt

❧ Place the lukewarm milk in a small bowl. Sprinkle the yeast on top of the milk and let stand until dissolved and foamy, about 10 minutes.
❧ Heap the flour on a work surface and make a well in the center. Pour the dissolved yeast into the well along with the sugar, honey and salt. With a fork, gradually work in the flour until all of it is absorbed. On a lightly floured surface, knead the dough until it is smooth and soft, about 5 minutes. Shape the dough into a ball.
❧ Transfer the dough ball to a lightly floured bowl and cover with plastic wrap. Let rise at room temperature until doubled in bulk, about 2 hours.
❧ Turn the dough out onto a floured surface. Punch down the dough and shape it into an oval loaf about 12 in (30 cm) long. Lightly dust a baking sheet and place the loaf on it. Let rise at room temperature until doubled in size, about 30 minutes.
❧ Meanwhile, preheat an oven to 400°F (200°C). Bake the bread until golden, about 30 minutes. Remove from the oven and let cool completely on a wire rack before slicing.

SERVES 6

Honey Bread

Firenze

Torta Soffice di Mele

Light Apple Cake

This family cake is particularly tasty in autumn, when the apples have just been picked and are still strongly scented and hard. Granny Smith and Golden Delicious apples are suitable for this recipe.

2½ cups (10 oz/300 g) all-purpose (plain) flour
⅔ cup (5 oz/150 g) granulated sugar
3 eggs
⅔ cup (5 oz/150 g) unsalted butter, melted, plus extra for pan
grated zest of 1 lemon
pinch of freshly grated nutmeg
1 teaspoon baking powder
⅓ cup (3 fl oz/90 ml) milk
3 apples

❧ Preheat an oven to 350°F (180°C).
❧ In a food processor, combine all the ingredients except the apples. Process until a smooth batter is formed. Or combine all the ingredients in a bowl and beat with an electric mixer at medium speed until a smooth batter is formed.
❧ Butter and flour a 9-in (23-cm) springform pan. Pour in the batter.
❧ Peel and core the apples, then slice them thinly. Arrange the slices in concentric circles on top of the batter; they will sink in a little.
❧ Bake the cake until a wooden toothpick inserted into the center of the cake comes out dry, about 1 hour. Remove from the oven and let cool slightly on a wire rack. Remove the pan sides and slip the cake onto a serving plate. Serve at room temperature.

SERVES 6

Grosseto

Fichi Canditi

Candied Figs

This is another ancient recipe that Giovanni Righi Parenti mentions in his book, La grande cucina toscana, *published in 1972. Presoaked prunes may be used in place of the figs.*

⅓ cup (3 oz/90 g) granulated sugar
18 fresh figs, peeled
grated zest of 1 lemon
2 tablespoons honey
few drops of almond oil

❧ Preheat an oven to 350°F (180°C).
❧ Sprinkle half of the sugar in the bottom of a baking pan and arrange the figs in the pan side by side. Sprinkle the figs with the remaining sugar and the lemon zest. Drizzle with the honey.
❧ Bake the figs until the sugar caramelizes and is pale gold, about 30 minutes. Remove the pan from the oven.
❧ Brush a serving dish with the almond oil. With a spatula remove the figs to the dish. Serve cold.

SERVES 6 *Photograph pages 470–71*

Light Apple Cake

Africans

Siena

AFRICANI

Africans

At one time there were several Tuscan convents where the nuns prepared these cookies, but nowadays they are hard to come by. You can still find them in Greve in Chianti on Saturdays, when the weekly market is held and the local cake shop has them for sale.

6 egg yolks
¾ cup (6 oz/180 g) granulated sugar

❧ Using a fork, combine the egg yolks and sugar in a mixing bowl. Beat together until the sugar completely dissolves and you have a white, creamy mixture, about 1 hour. (Do not use an egg beater for this step; it makes the mixture too light and dry.) Preheat an oven to 250°F (120°C).

❧ Place small, pleated paper cups on a baking sheet and fill them with the mixture. Place the cookies in the oven and turn off the heat immediately. Leave the cookies in the oven until they have risen but are still creamy at the center, about 1 hour.

❧ If the oven gets too cold toward the end of the cooking time, it may be reheated to 185°F (90°C). Remove the cookies to a wire rack to cool completely, then arrange on a platter and serve.

MAKES 20–30 COOKIES

Firenze

FRAGOLE AL VINO ROSSO

Strawberries in Red Wine

Here is the simplest and most traditional way Italians serve small wild strawberries; large cultivated ones can also be used. Florentines always use a well-aged Chianti Classico for the red wine. This makes an excellent dessert for a summer luncheon.

1¼ lb (600 g) wild strawberries, hulled
⅓ cup (3 oz/90 g) granulated sugar
1 cup (8 fl oz/240 ml) Chianti Classico Riserva
small strip of lemon peel

❧ Place the strawberries in a large bowl. Sprinkle with the sugar and pour in the wine. Cover and refrigerate for at least 12 hours.
❧ Drain the strawberries, reserving the marinade, and set the strawberries aside in a serving bowl. Pour the marinade into a small saucepan. Add the lemon peel and heat gently, stirring occasionally, until the wine becomes syrupy and coats a spoon.
❧ Remove the pan from the heat. Remove and discard the lemon peel. Let the wine cool completely.
❧ Put the strawberries in a serving bowl, pour the cold wine syrup over them and serve.

SERVES 6

Firenze

FRITTELLE DI TONDONE

Pancake Fritters

A tondone *is a type of hard pancake that is crumbled, mixed with egg and made into little fritters. This recipe has been used in Florentine kitchens for centuries.*

½ cup (3 oz/90 g) raisins
⅔ cup (5 fl oz/150 ml) water
2½ cups (10 oz/300 g) all-purpose (plain) flour
pinch of salt
1 tablespoon extra virgin olive oil, plus 5 cups (40 fl oz/1.2 l) for frying
6 eggs
grated zest of 1 lemon
1 tablespoon confectioners' (icing) sugar

❧ In a small bowl, soak the raisins in warm water to cover for about 1 hour.
❧ Pour the water into a bowl and gradually add the flour, whisking constantly to prevent lumps from forming. Stir the salt into the batter.
❧ In a nonstick skillet, heat the 1 tablespoon olive oil. Add the batter and cook over low heat until the pancake sets, about 15 minutes or until a toothpick inserted in the center comes out dry.
❧ Turn out onto a plate, browned side up. Slide the pancake back into the skillet and cook the other side for about 2 minutes. The pancake should be well cooked but not golden. Turn the pancake out onto a plate and let cool to room temperature.
❧ Crumble the pancake into a blender container. Add 2 of the eggs. Separate the remaining 4 eggs and add the yolks to the blender; set the whites aside in a medium-sized bowl. Drain the raisins and add to the blender along with the lemon zest. Whirl to blend well. Pour into a large bowl.
❧ Beat the egg whites until stiff, moist peaks form. Fold them delicately into the batter.
❧ In a deep, heavy skillet, heat the olive oil for frying to 350°F (180°C). Drop the batter by spoonfuls into the hot oil without crowding the pan. Fry a few at a time until just golden, about 3 minutes. With a slotted spoon, remove the fritters to absorbent paper towels to drain. Continue frying the remaining batter in the same manner.
❧ Arrange the fritters on a platter, sprinkle with the confectioners' sugar and serve piping hot.

MAKES 20–30 FRITTERS

Firenze

FRITTELLE DI RISO

Rice Fritters

Florentines love sweet fritters, especially these tasty rice-studded ones. During Carnival they also prepare them with apples, semolina or just with a simple egg-and-flour batter.

4 cups (30 fl oz/900 ml) milk
6 tablespoons (3 oz/90 g) granulated sugar
2 tablespoons unsalted butter
grated zest of 1 lemon
1½ cups (10 oz/300 g) Arborio rice
2 eggs, separated
5 cups (40 fl oz/1.2 l) extra virgin olive oil for frying

❧ In a heavy saucepan, combine the milk with half of the sugar, the butter and the lemon zest. Bring to a boil, stirring to dissolve the sugar, and add the rice. Lower the heat and simmer until the liquid is absorbed and the rice is fairly dry, about 30 minutes. Remove from the heat and let cool to room temperature.
❧ When the rice mixture is completely cold, add the egg yolks, mixing in well. Whip the egg whites until stiff peaks form and then fold them gently into the rice mixture.
❧ In a deep, heavy skillet, heat the olive oil to 350°F (180°C). Drop the batter by spoonfuls into the hot oil without crowding the pan. Fry a few at a time until golden, about 3 minutes. With a slotted spoon, remove the fritters to absorbent paper towels to drain. Continue frying the remaining batter in the same manner.
❧ Arrange the fritters on a platter, sprinkle with the remaining sugar and serve very hot.

MAKES 20–30 FRITTERS

Pancake Fritters (left), Rice Fritters (right) and Strawberries in Red Wine (rear)

Glossary

ACQUACOTTA is a popular Tuscan bread soup. Originally a very simple dish, it is now enriched with a variety of vegetables poured over bread.

AFFOGATO means "drowned"; in culinary terms, drowned in seasoned wine or tomato sauce.

ALLA DIAVOLA is a method of cooking chicken. The chicken is split open, flattened and grilled while being basted with olive oil. When ready it is crisp outside and soft within.

ALL'UCCELLETTO means "like a bird." Describes dishes prepared with olive oil, garlic and sage, the classic treatment for small game birds. A little tomato is added to the celebrated Tuscan beans *all'uccelletto*.

ALMOND OIL, a fragrant oil expressed from almonds, is commonly found in the kitchens of Italy, France, Spain and Portugal. Almond oil produced elsewhere is generally milder in flavor. Look for almond oil in shops specializing in southern European foods and in some health food stores. Refrigerate this oil to preserve its delicate flavor.

ANCHOVIES are preserved in oil in cans or jars, or in salt, usually in cans. Oil-packed anchovies come already filleted; if working with salt-packed anchovies, brush off all visible salt and then bone the fish before using. Anchovies in oil (preferably olive oil) can be found in supermarkets; anchovies in salt are available at well-stocked Italian shops.

ARBORIO RICE is a variety of short-grain rice grown in the Po Valley of northern Italy. Its stubby kernels absorb a remarkable amount of liquid as they cook, resulting in round, plump grains that, because of their high starch content, become quite creamy when tender. Arborio rice can be found in Italian shops and well-stocked supermarkets. If unavailable, short-grain rice may be substituted.

ARROSTO MORTO is a pot roast, cooked fairly slowly in a little wine flavored with vegetables.

ARTICHOKE, native to the Mediterranean, is grown for its flower, which is picked before it blooms. The flower, or head, is globelike, with thick, firm, thorn-topped leaves surrounding a tender heart and a prickly, inedible choke. The more mature the artichoke, the more developed the choke. Artichokes range in size from tiny buds of no more than 2 oz (60 g), which can be eaten whole after light trimming, to large globes up to 5 in (13 cm) in diameter. In this book, the larger artichokes are called globe artichokes, after the most common variety, Green Globe, to distinguish them from the tiny buds, which are referred to as small artichokes.

BACCALÀ see *salted cod.*

BATTUTO is the Tuscan term for *soffritto* (q.v.), but in Tuscany *pancetta* (q.v.) or lard is sometimes added to the chopped vegetables.

BEANS form the basis of many of Tuscany's best-known dishes. *Cannellini* are the classic Tuscan white beans. These relatively long, thin-skinned, kidney-shaped beans are at their best at the end of summer, when they are eaten fresh. *Cannellini* beans can be found in Italian shops dried or in cans. White kidney beans, Great Northern beans (which are slightly smaller and rounder) or white haricot beans (which are slightly larger and rounder) may be substituted. *Borlotti* beans, also known as cranberry beans, are pale beige, oval beans with reddish mottling. They, too, are eaten fresh at summer's end, as well as dried. Dried *borlotti* are easily found in many supermarkets. Fava beans, also known as broad beans, are encased in flat green pods that range from about 4 in (10 cm) up to 1 foot (30 cm) or so in length. Only the very youngest fava beans may be eaten pod and all; larger pods must be discarded. Each moist, flat green bean is covered with a sturdy skin that should be removed by splitting the skin and slipping it off. Fresh fava beans can be found in the markets from spring to early summer. Fava beans are also available dried.

BIANCHETTI are tiny anchovies and sardines less than an inch (2.5 cm) long and as narrow as toothpicks. Their flavor is more delicate and they are less oily than baby eels.

BIROLDO see *sanguinaccio.*

BLACK CABBAGE, or *cavolo nero,* has long, narrow, very deep green leaves with a bumpy surface. Although in Italy cultivated only in Tuscany, black cabbage is now in demand all over the country. Its strong, slightly bitter flavor, which is most fully developed after the first frosts, is excellent in hearty Tuscan soups. Savoy cabbage may be substituted.

BLACK TRUFFLE is a roundish, highly aromatic, extremely costly fungus, usually about the size of a small mandarin orange, that grows underground and must be hunted with a dog or pig whose job it is to sniff it out. It has a rough surface, dense interior and earthy flavor. Southwest France and Umbria, which abuts Tuscany, are the sources of Europe's finest black truffles, which are exported fresh in the autumn to specialty food stores. They can also be purchased in jars or cans. If unavailable (or too expensive), omit truffles from the recipes.

BORAGE is a flowering plant native to the Mediterranean basin. When young, its bristly leaves, which taste faintly of cucumber, are used whole or chopped in salads or as a seasoning in beverages and other preparations; more mature leaves are cooked (which causes the bristles to disappear) and served in the same manner as other greens. Borage is not widely cultivated and is therefore found only in specialty vegetable markets (from late spring to early autumn) and in home gardens. Other greens such as spinach may be substituted. The lovely blue flowers, which are slightly sweet, are also edible.

BORLOTTI see *beans.*

BORRAGGINE, the wild varieties of borage (q.v.) and comfrey, grow well in Lucchesia, where they are used to flavor meats, frittatas and ravioli stuffings.

BRACIOLE are large, fairly thin slices of boneless beef, veal or pork. They may be grilled, fried or braised with tomatoes.

BROCCOLI RAAB, also known in Italian as *rapini, rape* and *cima di rape,* is a variety of foliage turnip that does not produce an enlarged base, hence its other common English name, turnip tops. It has dark green leaves on sturdy stalks topped with small flower clusters. This cool-weather vegetable is sautéed in oil with garlic or boiled and dressed with olive oil and lemon. It may also be served in tomato sauce.

BRODO means "broth" or "stock." In Italy it is made by simply putting a large piece of boneless beef or a chicken in a deep pot with a carrot, onion, celery, parsley and a pinch of salt. The meat and vegetables are abundantly covered with water and left to simmer for a couple of hours. Unlike the French method, no roasted bones or marrow bones are added. The stock is light, not fatty, and has a very fresh flavor. Herbs such as thyme and tarragon may be added.

CACCIUCCO is a famous Livornese fish soup. In Tuscany, however, the term is also used to describe a method of cooking in which fish, meat or vegetables are gently fried in chopped onion, celery, carrot and parsley before being cooked in a tomato sauce.

CALAMINT, or *nepitella,* is a perennial herb found in the Mediterranean basin and Asia. It has small grayish-green leaves and pale blue blossoms that recall those of thyme. Calamint is a member of the mint family. In Italy, where it is used to season soups and sauces, it is always tucked into the bundle when you buy fresh *porcini* (q.v.). Peppermint or a similar mint may be substituted.

CANNELLINI see *beans.*

CAPERS are the unopened flower buds of a bush native to the Mediterranean. The buds, which range in size from very tiny to about the size of a pea, are preserved in vinegar in jars or packed in salt in wooden boxes. Capers in vinegar are readily found on supermarket shelves; capers in salt are available in Italian shops. If working with the latter, rinse them briefly in cold water before using.

CARDOON, called *gobbi* in Tuscan dialect, is related to the artichoke and looks somewhat like an overgrown celery plant. The tenderest cardoons are those that have been wrapped in paper as they grow, to produce white stalks. Green cardoons are tougher and their flavor is less delicate. Cardoons can be found in better-stocked supermarkets.

CASTAGNE are chestnuts. Fortunately, chestnut woods in Tuscany survived the terrible blight that struck at the turn of the century. Chestnuts, also called *ballotte,* are used for stuffing poultry, puréed for serving with game, and are made into desserts. During the grape harvest they are at their peak. Toasted on an open fire in a special perforated pan, they are eaten hot with a glass of red wine.

CAUL FAT is the fat-ribbed transparent membrane that holds the organs of the abdominal cavity of mammals in place. It is used as a wrapping for meats to keep them moist as they cook. Caul fat can sometimes be purchased fresh, but more often frozen, in better meat markets and butcher shops.

CAVOLO NERO see *black cabbage.*

CHESTNUT FLOUR is milled from dried chestnuts and is high in both starch and sugar. The flour is used for making pasta, polenta, bread and desserts and can be purchased in shops specializing in Italian or French foods.

CHIANTI is the name of an area that lies between Siena and Florence and of the wine produced there. Chianti Classico, one of the finest wines in Italy, is a DOCG wine, meaning that it complies with strict regulations set by the government concerning grape variety, geographic origin, aging requirements and so on. It is produced in the heartland of the Chianti region and is aged not less than 18 months. In contrast, Chianti Riserva may originate anywhere in the Chianti region but must be aged for over 3 years. Chianti Classico Riserva is a higher-quality Chianti Classico and must be aged not less than 3 years. Chianti wine is principally made from the Sangiovese grape, usually with the addition of Canaiolo, Trebbiano or other grapes. The exact proportions of the grape varieties depend upon the type of Chianti being bottled. Any good-quality, full-bodied, dry red wine may be substituted.

CHICK-PEA FLOUR (garbanzo flour) is a fine flour milled from dried chick-peas, known as *ceci* in Italy. The flour can be found in shops specializing in Italian, Middle Eastern, Pakistani or Indian foods. In the latter it will be labeled *besan.*

COARSE-GRAINED CORNMEAL is most commonly eaten in Italy in the form of polenta, a thick, hot porridge that can also be cooled, sliced and fried or grilled. (Polenta is also made from other ingredients, including barley and chestnuts.) Look for coarse-grained yellow cornmeal marketed under the name polenta in Italian food stores and well-stocked supermarkets, or use any coarsely ground yellow cornmeal.

COPATE are honey biscuits enclosed in very fine wafers that for centuries were made by nuns. Each convent had its own jealously guarded recipe. They are now hard to find, but are worth looking for.

CORNMEAL see *coarse-grained cornmeal.*

COSTATA is a large T-bone steak. Cut from young beef, it is a famous Florentine specialty. Everywhere except in Tuscany it is called *bistecca alla fiorentina.*

CROCCHETTE, unlike *polpette* (q.v.), are meatballs made with cooked meat. The finely chopped meat is combined with egg, mashed potatoes and herbs. The meatballs are rolled in flour or bread crumbs before being fried in olive oil until crisp.

CROSTINI are a popular Tuscan antipasto. They are slices of bread that have been toasted, fried or quickly dipped in broth and then spread with a topping. The two most widely used toppings are made of chicken livers and spleen.

CUTTLEFISH is a marine mollusk that looks very much like a squid but with a broader, thicker oval body. It has prominent eyes on a wide head, ten tentacles and an ink sac. Cleaned and cooked in much the same way as squid, cuttlefish are enjoyed in Italy, Spain, Greece and many Asian countries. Look for cuttlefish in fish markets that cater to Asian or southern European communities.

DOLCEFORTE is an ancient, sweet and pungent sauce still used with wild boar. A little vinegar, sugar and garlic are added to the pot at the last minute. For a richer sauce, raisins, candied lemon peel and pine nuts are used.

DRAGONCELLO see *tarragon.*

ELDER FLOWERS are harvested from the elder, a large shrub that also produces an edible purple berry. The delicate white blossoms are used to flavor preserves, wines, breads and cakes.

EXTRA VIRGIN OLIVE OIL, or *olio extravergine d'oliva,* is something no Tuscan cook could live without. Butter is very seldom used and was unknown in Tuscany until quite recently. To be called extra virgin, olive oil must contain less than 1 percent acid. True extra virgin oil is quite expensive because it is cold pressed and the olives must be picked by hand to avoid bruising them, which raises the acid content. Always purchase the best-quality olive oil that you can afford.

FARRO see *spelt.*

FEGATELLI are pieces of pork liver. They are generally wrapped in a piece of caul fat (q.v.) before being sautéed with pepper and fennel seed. They are also put on skewers with sausage and chunks of bread, which absorb the fat while they are grilling.

FENNEL, or *finocchio,* grows wild all over Tuscany. Its umbels of yellow flowers are very decorative. In autumn the seeds are collected for seasoning many well-known Tuscan dishes. Fennel bulbs come from a cultivated variety of this plant.

FIASCO is a large, round-bottomed bottle wrapped in straw. Although very picturesque, these bottles usually contain inferior wine.

FINOCCHIO see *fennel.*

FRANTOIO is a mill where olives are pressed as soon as possible after picking. To get extra virgin olive oil, the olives are pressed between two huge granite grindstones. The oil flows into a special bath and is passed through a paper filter to rid it of any impurities that might cause the oil to go rancid.

FRITTURA can be deep-fried vegetables, meat, fish or sweet things, all of which are very popular in Tuscany, where extra virgin olive oil is always used for frying. Extra virgin olive oil has no bad odor when heated and even when very hot does not release toxins. Frying oil should be used only once.

GAETA OLIVES are small, salt-cured olives with wrinkled black skins. Small, black Greek or Spanish olives may be substituted.

GALLO NERO, or "black rooster," is the symbol of Chianti Classico, the wine produced in a specific area between Florence and Siena.

GARMUGIA is a celebrated soup from Lucchesia made with very young green vegetables and wild herbs; occasionally a little meat is added as well.

GNOCCHI is a generic term for small dumplings served as a first course. They are made of potatoes, ricotta and spinach, cornmeal or semolina. Potato gnocchi are generally turned against the prongs of a fork to give them their characteristic ridges.

GOBBI see *cardoon.*

GRATELLA is the Tuscan word for a grill used to cook over an open fire. It is an essential part of every Tuscan household because it is used not only for grilling meat and vegetables, but also for toasting bread that is later rubbed with garlic and sprinkled with oil.

JUNIPER BERRIES are the fruit of the evergreen shrub of the same name. The pungent, small, hard berries, which are a deep blue black, are used to make gin and to flavor game and other meat dishes. They can be found bottled in the spice section of most supermarkets.

MARSALA WINE is a rich amber wine produced in the Sicilian provinces of Trapani, Agrigento and Palermo. It is a prized dessert wine and is used in desserts as well. Any well-stocked wine shop will carry a selection of Sicilian Marsalas.

MEZZALUNA is a large two-handled knife with a semi-circular blade. It is efficient and easy to use because it is simply rolled from side to side to chop herbs, meats and vegetables. It usually has a single blade, but double-bladed knives of this type are available.

MINESTRA is a light stock enriched with pasta, egg, diced vegetables or small pieces of meat.

MINESTRONE is a very thick soup made of coarsely chopped mixed vegetables to which a little rice or pasta is added.

MORTADELLA is among the most popular of all Italian sausages, in Italy as well as abroad. Its distinctive pattern comes from the mixing of finely ground (minced) pork with coarsely diced pork fat. The slowly cooked sausage, which usually measures about 6 in (15 cm) in diameter, is a popular sandwich meat and is sold at most delicatessens.

OLIO EXTRAVERGINE D'OLIVA see *extra virgin olive oil.*

OVOLI are the most highly prized wild mushrooms in Italy. They are now very rare and extremely expensive. They have orange caps and white stalks and are generally gathered very young when they are still egg shaped. They are excellent sliced raw and dressed with olive oil, lemon and thin shavings of Parmesan cheese. Although they are not nearly as special as *ovoli,* button (cultivated) mushrooms can be used in their place.

PANCETTA is Italian bacon, usually a tightly rolled slab that is sliced crosswise to form spirals of meat and fat. In its most common form, *pancetta* is salt-cured pork belly, although a *pancetta affumicata* (smoked *pancetta*) is also made. *Pancetta* can be purchased in Italian shops and in most markets specializing in European foods. The recipes in this book call for unsmoked *pancetta;* if unavailable, unsmoked bacon may be substituted.

PANPEPATO is a Sienese fruit cake flavored with pepper. It is much like *pan coi santi,* for which the recipe is included in the Dolci chapter.

PANS travel under different names in the international kitchen. In this book, a "heavy pot" is any thick-walled, fairly deep, heavy pan equipped with a lid. It should be made of a material that retains heat well, such as enameled cast iron. The British call this type of pot a flameproof casserole; American cooks may use their Dutch ovens. A heavy saucepan would also work well. What is termed a skillet in these pages is the same utensil as a frying pan, while cake pans, which are round unless otherwise indicated, are the same as cake tins.

PANZANELLA is a salad originally invented to use up stale bread. In the classic version, the dampened bread is mixed with tomatoes and onion and dressed with olive oil and a little vinegar. Occasionally tuna fish, capers and cucumbers are added. In some places it is called *panmolle,* or "wet bread."

PAPPARDELLE is a homemade Tuscan pasta (q.v.). The egg-and-flour dough is rolled very thinly and cut into broad ribbons about 1¼ in (3 cm) wide and 4 in (10 cm) long. It is usually served with a hare or game sauce.

PARMESAN CHEESE, which is made from cow's milk, is a hard cheese with a granular texture and a pleasantly sharp flavor. It is used in cooking and as a condiment, especially on pastas. True Italian Parmesan is produced between April 1 and November 11 in a region that stretches from Parma Province to Mantua Province on one side and Bologna on the other. The best is *parmigiano reggiano,* marked clearly on the crust. A great deal of Parmesan is also made in the United States, Argentina, Australia and other countries with large populations of Italian descent. Italian Parmesan is quite expensive and other good-quality, aged Parmesan cheese can be substituted. Never purchase pre-grated Parmesan cheese and do not grate the cheese until you are ready to use it, as the flavor of the cheese is at its peak immediately upon grating.

PARSLEY is available in two basic varieties, curly leaf and flat leaf. Although the former is more easily found in markets outside of Italy, the latter, which has a more pungent flavor, is preferred for the recipes in this book.

PASTA. Fresh pasta is most easily made with a hand-cranked pasta machine that rolls out the dough into very thin sheets for cutting into noodles of any width or for forming stuffed pastas. (Electric machines work well, too, but are expensive; manual ones, in contrast, are quite reasonably priced.) You will need to feed the dough, a small piece at a time, through the machine's rollers, beginning with the rollers set at their widest opening and gradually adjusting the rollers to narrower settings until the desired thickness is achieved. At each degree of thickness, the dough should be put through the rollers until it is smooth and elastic, dusting it lightly with flour whenever it becomes sticky. Once you have a thin sheet of pasta, the machine blades may be adjusted to the noodle width desired. *Taglierini,* for example, would probably require the narrowest setting, while *tagliatelle* would call for a setting of slightly less than ¼ in (6 mm) wide. Rolling out pasta dough by hand is difficult for all but the most experienced cooks, as it is a challenge to produce a very thin, very even sheet of dough. If, however, no pasta machine is available, the dough can be rolled out on a lightly floured work surface. Divide the dough into 3 or 4 portions to make the rolling more manageable. Flatten the dough into a disc and roll from the center outward, using no more strokes than are necessary. To cut the dough into noodles, let it rest for a few minutes, then roll it up into a cylinder, flatten the top slightly and cut crosswise into the width desired.

PECORINO is sheep's milk cheese made in several parts of Italy, but the Tuscan variety is considered the best. Fresh *pecorino* is called *marzolino* because it is made in the spring when the ewes have just lambed and have abundant milk. The cheese is put into oval terra-cotta molds. Mature *pecorino,* which is sometimes aged under ashes, has a much stronger flavor but is never very sharp.

PEPOLINO is a small-leaved wild thyme used to flavor many soups, including the famed *ribollita,* a hearty soup of vegetables and bread. It has a much stronger aroma than cultivated thyme.

PLUM TOMATOES, also known as egg, Roma and pear tomatoes, are oval in shape and particularly suitable for making sauces because of their meaty flesh. If fresh, flavorful plum tomatoes are unavailable, canned ones may be substituted; drain before using. Look for cans that contain whole, peeled plum tomatoes imported from Italy, as the Italian tomatoes have the finest, fullest flavor.

POLENTA see *coarse-grained cornmeal.*

POLPETTE are meatballs made of raw ground (minced) meat seasoned with herbs and cooked in tomato sauce. *Polpettone* is a meat loaf, and in Italy the center is generally filled with hard-cooked eggs, slices of ham or thin omelet strips.

PORCINI is the common name of *boletus edulis,* the most sought-after wild mushrooms. Called *cèpes* by the French, they come up in early autumn after the first rain, when, as the local farmers say, "the earth boils." The stalks are broad and pale and the cap thick and dark. The darker the cap, the better the mushroom, and when buying them you should make sure the stalks are firm. In autumn they are thinly sliced and dried for use when out of season. Good-quality dried slices usually measure about 2 in (5 cm) long.

PROSCIUTTO is raw, salt-cured ham that has been aged to produce moist, lightly veined, intense pink meat with an edge of fat. Imported Italian *prosciutto* is quite costly (the best is from Parma), but many domestic products are of good quality and can be used. Avoid *prosciutti* that taste too salty, and buy only what is needed, as cut *prosciutto* dries out rapidly. *Prosciutto* can be found in Italian shops, delicatessens and many supermarkets. If unavailable, substitute another raw, salt-cured ham, such as French Bayonne or German Westphalian; do not use a smoked ham.

RAPINI see *broccoli raab.*

RICOTTA in Tuscany is made from sheep's milk whey left after making *pecorino* cheese. The whey is reboiled, hence its name, and strained. Once it has thickened, ricotta is eaten fresh. There is also a blander cow's milk ricotta on the Italian market. Elsewhere cow's milk ricotta is often the only type available.

RISOTTO is made with Arborio (q.v.) or Vialone Nano rice. The plump grains contain a large amount of starch that is released during cooking and gives the risotto a creamy quality. Liquid is gradually added to the rice so that the kernels are always just covered but never floating in it.

ROSEMARY, a hearty shrub that belongs to the mint family, has needlelike leaves, blue flowers and a strong, woodsy scent. Italian cooks regularly use it with roasted meats such as pork, lamb and chicken. It can be found dried in bottles on supermarket spice shelves or fresh in many vegetable sections. It is also easily grown in the home garden.

SAGE, called *salvia* in Italian, has gray-green leaves and a potent flavor. Tuscans like to add the coarse-textured, oval leaves to bean dishes and meats. Better supermarkets stock fresh sage year-round; dried sage in various forms is carried on the spice shelves.

SALTED COD is cod that has been preserved by first salting and then drying. It is available both boneless and with bones and is most commonly found in Portuguese, Italian, French, Spanish, Greek and Caribbean markets. Sometimes salted cod is sold packed in small wooden boxes that hold about 1 lb (500 g); other times large pieces are stacked in a heap and you select the one you want. Before cooking salted cod, it should be soaked in cold water to cover in the refrigerator for 24 hours, changing the water 3 or 4 times, to soften it and rid it of excess salt. (In Italy it is often sold presoaked.)

SALVIA see *sage.*

SANGUINACCIO, a highly spiced sausage made with pig's blood, is sometimes called *biroldo.* There is a sweet version, flavored with raisins and pine nuts. Traditionally the sausage is made in autumn when local farmers kill pigs to make ham, salamis and sausages.

SCHIACCIATA is a flat bread, about half an inch (12 mm) thick, sprinkled with olive oil and salt. It is sometimes flavored with sage or rosemary. An even flatter variety is called *ciaccino.*

SCOTTIGLIA is a mixture of meats cooked in a tomato sauce; the greater the variety the tastier the dish. In some parts of Tuscany, however, this dish is made with only chicken, rabbit and lamb.

SOFFRITTO is chopped onion, celery, carrot and parsley gently fried in a little olive oil over low heat before the main ingredient is added to the pan. This method is used all over Italy.

SOPPRESSATA is a headcheese (brawn) made from rendered meat from a pig's head, forehock and skin, as well as the aspic from the reduced cooking liquid. It is seasoned with herbs and spices and left to set in a special mold.

SPELT, called *farro* in Italian, is an ancient variety of wheat with small, reddish brown grains. The early Romans made a dish called *puls,* which was something like a polenta, made of ground spelt. Spelt is still popular in Lazio and Umbria but above all in the Garfagnana, an area of Lucchesia. Spelt is sold in well-stocked Italian shops and some health food stores.

SPIEDINI, which are similar to kabobs, are made from pieces of meat, sausage, bread, tomatoes or peppers (capsicums) and sometimes onion. They are nearly always cooked over the embers of a wood fire. Butchers in Italy sell them ready prepared—especially in autumn and winter when fires are lit in the open hearths.

STOCCAFISSO is cod dried in the sun without salting.

STRASCICATO literally means "dragged." You will hear this word mentioned with pasta in Tuscan trattorias, where cooked pasta is often tossed into the skillet with the sauce and dragged around the pan.

SUGO DI CARNE is meat sauce, of which there are several varieties in Tuscany. Pieces of pork and beef are gently braised with a chicken liver, a little bacon, tomato and herbs. The meat is not chopped until after it is cooked.

SUGO FINTO is tomato sauce, called "fake sauce" because to Tuscans the only real sauce is made of meat.

SWEET ITALIAN SAUSAGE in northern Italy is a fresh link sausage made from pork seasoned with black pepper. In the south of Italy, they are seasoned with fennel and garlic, and a hot version includes red chili pepper in the mixture. Italian sausage is available in Italian shops and some supermarkets.

TARRAGON, called *dragoncello* in Italian, is the most popular herb in Siena, although it is used nowhere else in Tuscany or Italy. It appears in soups and sauces, and from spring to autumn every Sienese trattoria has at least one tarragon-flavored dish.

TEGAME is a wide, shallow pan that until recently was always earthenware. It is generally used for gentle cooking in wine or tomato sauce.

TOPINI, or "little mice," are oval gnocchi (q.v.) in Tuscany.

TORTELLI, TORDELLI and TORTELLONI are various names for fresh pasta (q.v.) generally stuffed with spinach and ricotta in Tuscany. The name varies according to the size; Tuscan *tortelli* are, for example, smaller than *tortelloni.*

TORTINO is another name for frittata, but with the difference that *tortini* are sometimes cooked in the oven or, if over direct heat, on one side only until the eggs are almost set but still very moist on top.

TRIPPATA means "cooked like tripe," i.e., first sautéed in a *soffritto* (q.v.), then cooked in tomato sauce.

TUSCAN COUNTRY BREAD is a coarse-textured, dense, chewy, unsalted loaf with a pleasantly tough crust (see recipe on page 227). Any bread of the same type, including a lightly salted one, may be substituted.

UMIDO is the Tuscan way of describing meat or vegetables cooked and served in a small amount of liquid that could be wine, water, stock or tomato sauce.

VIN SANTO is a Tuscan dessert wine produced from Trebbiano and Malvasia grapes. Pleasantly sweet and smooth, this brilliant amber wine is traditionally served with *cantucci* (almond cookies) for dipping. It can be found in better wine shops.

WHITEBAIT are small fish, at their best when no more than 2 to 3 in (5 to 7.5 cm) in length. They are most often fried crisp and eaten whole, bones and all. The name is given to both very young herring and smelt. Look for whitebait in better fish markets.

WHITE CELERY owes its pale color to the fact that it is blanched, or covered, as it grows. This treatment produces particularly tender stalks and a delicate heart. Young, very fresh green celery may be substituted.

WILD BOAR have long been pursued by hunters in Italy, France and Germany. These fierce, menacingly tusked descendants of domestic pigs are best when eaten fairly young; as they age their meat toughens. A number of different species can be found in Europe, Asia and the Americas. Laws restrict the sale of wild animals in many countries, but farm-raised boar is available at some supermarkets, butcher shops and game specialty suppliers. If unavailable, similar cuts of pork may be substituted.

WOODCOCK is a small game bird with a long, slender, pointed beak and dark meat. Native to Europe and North America, woodcocks are considered particularly fine eating birds and farm-raised ones can be purchased from game specialty suppliers.

ZUPPA is a soup that is poured over slices of bread. The bread is first either browned in the oven or fried in olive oil.

ACKNOWLEDGMENTS

Weldon Owen would like to thank the following people and organizations for their assistance in the preparation of this book:
Jacki Passmore, Norma MacMillan, Helen Cooney, Amy Morton, Stephanie Baartz, Ruth Jacobson, Ken DellaPenta, Italian Government Travel Office of San Francisco, Richard VanOosterhout, Fee-Ling Tan, Lesley Schwartz, Pete Friedrich, Rapid Lasergraphics (San Francisco).

Peter Johnson and Janice Baker wish to thank the following: Jennifer Grillo, for her generous hospitality and invaluable assistance on location in Tuscany; Elizabeth McLeod and Cara Hobday for assisting with food preparation and styling; Robert White for helping with the photography.

Michael Freeman thanks Romano Cagnoni, Patricia Franceschetti and Pasquale Brogini for their assistance.

Props used in this book are from the following sources in Sydney, Australia: Appley Hoare Antiques, Woollahra; The Bay Tree, Woollahra; Country Floors, Woollahra; Country Road Australia Ltd; Accoutrement, Mosman; Parterre Garden, Woollahra; Corso di Fiori, Chatswood; Ventura for Alessi; The Art of Food and Wine, Woollahra; Jacobus, Woollahra; Sentimental Journey at Mosman Antiques, Mosman; Hale Imports for Pillivuyt; Villeroy and Boch, Brookvale; The Country Trader, Woollahra; Porters Original Limewash, Sydney; The Fragrant Garden, Erina; The Lacquer Chest, London. In addition, Susan Whitter, Karen Byak, Inger Marchant, Elizabeth McLeod, Janice Baker and Peter Johnson kindly lent privately owned items for propping.

INDEX